Solutions Manual fc

Physics

An Incremental Development

JOHN H. SAXON, JR.

SAXON PUBLISHERS, INC.

This manual contains solutions to every problem in the *Physics* textbook by John Saxon. Early solutions of a problem of a particular type contain every step. Later solutions omit steps considered unnecessary.

Printed in the United States of America

ISBN: 978-1-56-577007-2

Manufacturing Code: 16 2266 19

4500764893

PROBLEM SET 1

1. 0.0000652
We place the decimal point just to the right of the first nonzero digit and note that it really should be five places to the left. We do this and get $\mathbf{6.52 \times 10^{-5}}$.

2. 476.32
We place the decimal point just to the right of the first nonzero digit and note that it really should be two places to the right. We do this and get $\mathbf{4.7632 \times 10^{2}}$.

3. 475,000,000
We place the decimal point just to the right of the first nonzero digit and note that it really should be eight places to the right. We do this and get $\mathbf{4.75 \times 10^{8}}$.

4. 0.000376
We place the decimal point just to the right of the first nonzero digit and note that it really should be four places to the left. We do this and get $\mathbf{3.76 \times 10^{-4}}$.

5. Five hundred ten millionths
We begin by writing this number in standard form and get 0.000510. We place the decimal point just to the right of the first nonzero digit and note that it really should be four places to the left. We do this and get $\mathbf{5.10 \times 10^{-4}}$.

6. Seven hundred forty-two hundred-millionths
We begin by writing this number in standard form and get 0.00000742. We place the decimal point just to the right of the first nonzero digit and note that it really should be six places to the left. We do this and get $\mathbf{7.42 \times 10^{-6}}$.

7. 26.2300 cm has **6** significant digits because of rules 1 and 3.

8. 56,001 m^2 has **5** significant digits because of rules 1 and 2.

9. 3600 mi has **2** significant digits because of rule 1.

10. 9000.02 $in.^3$ has **6** significant digits because of rules 1 and 2.

11. $26,\bar{0}00$ km has **4** significant digits because $26,\bar{0}00$ has a range of uncertainty of ±10.

12. 0.000416 gallon has **3** significant digits because of rules 1 and 4.

13. $(5.1 \times 10^7) + (2.3 \times 10^6)$
To add these numbers, line up the decimal points.

$$\begin{array}{r} 51{,}000{,}000. \\ +\ 2{,}300{,}000. \\ \hline \mathbf{53{,}300{,}000} \end{array} = \mathbf{5.33 \times 10^7}$$

14. $(4.506 \times 10^{-4}) + (2.022 \times 10^{-2})$
To add these numbers, line up the decimal points.

$$\begin{array}{r} 0.04506 \times 10^{-2} \\ +\ 2.022 \quad \times 10^{-2} \\ \hline \mathbf{2.06706 \times 10^{-2}} \end{array}$$

15. $$\frac{(0.00077 \times 10^{-3})(40 \times 10^{6})}{(0.00011 \times 10^{5})(140{,}000)} = \frac{(7.7 \times 10^{-7})(4 \times 10^{7})}{(1.1 \times 10^{1})(1.4 \times 10^{5})}$$
$$= \left(\frac{7.7 \times 4}{1.1 \times 1.4}\right)\left(\frac{10^{-7} \times 10^{7}}{10^{1} \times 10^{5}}\right) = 20 \times 10^{-7+7-1-5}$$
$$= 20 \times 10^{-6} = \mathbf{2 \times 10^{-5}}$$

16. $$\frac{(3000 \times 10^{-14})(0.00008)}{(0.0002 \times 10^{5})(200{,}000)} = \frac{(3 \times 10^{-11})(8 \times 10^{-5})}{(2 \times 10^{1})(2 \times 10^{5})}$$
$$= 6 \times 10^{-11-5-1-5} = \mathbf{6 \times 10^{-22}}$$

17. $$\frac{(0.0006 \times 10^{-42})(2000 \times 10^{-4})}{0.004 \times 10^{-13}} = \frac{(6 \times 10^{-46})(2 \times 10^{-1})}{4 \times 10^{-16}}$$
$$= 3 \times 10^{-46-1+16} = \mathbf{3 \times 10^{-31}}$$

18. $$\frac{(0.0035 \times 10^{15})(0.002 \times 10^{17})}{7000 \times 10^{33}} = \frac{(3.5 \times 10^{12})(2 \times 10^{14})}{7 \times 10^{36}}$$
$$= 1 \times 10^{12+14-36} = \mathbf{1 \times 10^{-10}}$$

19. $$\frac{(0.0007 \times 10^{-23})(4000 \times 10^{6})}{(0.00004)(7{,}000{,}000)} = \frac{(7 \times 10^{-27})(4 \times 10^{9})}{(4 \times 10^{-5})(7 \times 10^{6})}$$
$$= 1 \times 10^{-27+9+5-6} = \mathbf{1 \times 10^{-19}}$$

20. $$\frac{(0.00056 \times 10^{4})(7 \times 10^{3})}{(0.00049 \times 10^{16})(0.00002 \times 10^{-5})} = \frac{(5.6 \times 10^{0})(7 \times 10^{3})}{(4.9 \times 10^{12})(2 \times 10^{-10})}$$
$$= 4 \times 10^{0+3-12+10} = 4 \times 10^{1} = \mathbf{40}$$

Problem Set 2

1. (24)(5280)(5280)(5280)(12)(12)(12)

$\approx (2 \times 10^1)(5 \times 10^3)(5 \times 10^3)(5 \times 10^3)(1 \times 10^1)(1 \times 10^1)(1 \times 10^1)$

$= (2)(5)(5)(5) \times 10^{13} = 250 \times 10^{13} \xrightarrow{SD} \mathbf{3 \times 10^{15}}$

2. $\dfrac{(4353)(933{,}216 \times 10^{-11})}{(319{,}214)(0.01603 \times 10^{-31})} \approx \dfrac{(4 \times 10^3)(9 \times 10^{-6})}{(3 \times 10^5)(2 \times 10^{-33})} = \mathbf{6 \times 10^{25}}$

3. $\dfrac{(2472)(570{,}185 \times 10^{-12})}{(243{,}195)(0.0003128 \times 10^{-6})} \approx \dfrac{(2 \times 10^3)(6 \times 10^{-7})}{(2 \times 10^5)(3 \times 10^{-10})} = 2 \times 10^1 = \mathbf{20}$

4. $\dfrac{(0.013926 \times 10^{-12})(27{,}153 \times 10^{21})}{6354 \times 10^{-31}} \approx \dfrac{(1 \times 10^{-14})(3 \times 10^{25})}{6 \times 10^{-28}}$

$= 0.5 \times 10^{39} = \mathbf{5 \times 10^{38}}$

5. $\dfrac{(0.0319743 \times 10^{-15})(61{,}853 \times 10^{37})}{6934 \times 10^{-29}} \approx \dfrac{(3 \times 10^{-17})(6 \times 10^{41})}{7 \times 10^{-26}}$

$= 2.57 \times 10^{50} \xrightarrow{SD} \mathbf{3 \times 10^{50}}$

6. $0.063\ \text{km}^2 \times \dfrac{1000\ \text{m}}{1\ \text{km}} \times \dfrac{1000\ \text{m}}{1\ \text{km}} \times \dfrac{100\ \text{cm}}{1\ \text{m}} \times \dfrac{100\ \text{cm}}{1\ \text{m}} \times \dfrac{1\ \text{in.}}{2.54\ \text{cm}}$

$\times \dfrac{1\ \text{in.}}{2.54\ \text{cm}} \times \dfrac{1\ \text{ft}}{12\ \text{in.}} \times \dfrac{1\ \text{ft}}{12\ \text{in.}} \times \dfrac{1\ \text{mi}}{5280\ \text{ft}} \times \dfrac{1\ \text{mi}}{5280\ \text{ft}}$

$= 2.4324 \times 10^{-2}\ \text{mi}^2 \xrightarrow{SD} \mathbf{2.4 \times 10^{-2}\ mi^2}$

7. $10\bar{0}\ \text{ft}^2 \times \dfrac{12\ \text{in.}}{1\ \text{ft}} \times \dfrac{12\ \text{in.}}{1\ \text{ft}} \times \dfrac{2.54\ \text{cm}}{1\ \text{in.}} \times \dfrac{2.54\ \text{cm}}{1\ \text{in.}}$

$= 9.290304 \times 10^4\ \text{cm}^2 \xrightarrow{SD} \mathbf{9.29 \times 10^4\ cm^2}$

8. $32\ \text{m} \times \dfrac{100\ \text{cm}}{1\ \text{m}} \times \dfrac{1\ \text{in.}}{2.54\ \text{cm}} \times \dfrac{1\ \text{ft}}{12\ \text{in.}} \times \dfrac{1\ \text{yd}}{3\ \text{ft}} = 34.996\ \text{yd} \xrightarrow{SD} \mathbf{35\ yd}$

9. $6\bar{0}\ \dfrac{\text{mi}}{\text{hr}} \times \dfrac{5280\ \text{ft}}{1\ \text{mi}} \times \dfrac{12\ \text{in.}}{1\ \text{ft}} \times \dfrac{2.54\ \text{cm}}{1\ \text{in.}} \times \dfrac{1\ \text{m}}{100\ \text{cm}} \times \dfrac{1\ \text{km}}{1000\ \text{m}} \times \dfrac{1\ \text{hr}}{60\ \text{min}}$

$\times \dfrac{1\ \text{min}}{60\ \text{s}} = 2.68224 \times 10^{-2}\ \dfrac{\text{km}}{\text{s}} \xrightarrow{SD} \mathbf{2.7 \times 10^{-2}\ \dfrac{km}{s}}$

10. $4\ \text{yd}^3 \times \dfrac{3\ \text{ft}}{1\ \text{yd}} \times \dfrac{3\ \text{ft}}{1\ \text{yd}} \times \dfrac{3\ \text{ft}}{1\ \text{yd}} \times \dfrac{12\ \text{in.}}{1\ \text{ft}} \times \dfrac{12\ \text{in.}}{1\ \text{ft}} \times \dfrac{12\ \text{in.}}{1\ \text{ft}} \times \dfrac{2.54\ \text{cm}}{1\ \text{in.}}$

$\times \dfrac{2.54\ \text{cm}}{1\ \text{in.}} \times \dfrac{2.54\ \text{cm}}{1\ \text{in.}} \times \dfrac{1\ \text{m}}{100\ \text{cm}} \times \dfrac{1\ \text{m}}{100\ \text{cm}} \times \dfrac{1\ \text{m}}{100\ \text{cm}}$

$= 3.06\ \text{m}^3 \xrightarrow{SD} \mathbf{3\ m^3}$

11. $(46.32 \times 10^5) + (0.3484 \times 10^6)$

To add these numbers, line up the decimal points.

$$\begin{array}{r} 4.632\ \times 10^6 \\ +\ 0.3484 \times 10^6 \\ \hline \mathbf{4.9804 \times 10^6} \end{array}$$

12. $(0.0065 \times 10^7) + (0.032 \times 10^9)$

To add these numbers, line up the decimal points.

$$\begin{array}{l} 0.0065 \times 10^7 \\ +\ 3.2\ \times 10^7 \\ \hline \mathbf{3.2065 \times 10^7} \end{array}$$

13. $(6.302 \times 10^2) + (9.468 \times 10^5)$

To add these numbers, line up the decimal points.

$$\begin{array}{l} 0.006302 \times 10^5 \\ +\ 9.468\ \times 10^5 \\ \hline \mathbf{9.474302 \times 10^5} \end{array}$$

14. $(6.816 \times 10^1) + (3.32 \times 10^{-1})$

To add these numbers, line up the decimal points.

$$\begin{array}{r} 68.16 \\ +\ 0.332 \\ \hline 68.492 \end{array} = \mathbf{6.8492 \times 10^1}$$

15. $(3.14 \times 10^{-2})(1.621 \times 10^3) = (3.14 \times 1.621)(10^{-2} \times 10^3)$

$= 5.08994 \times 10^1 \xrightarrow{SD} \mathbf{50.9}$

16. To add these numbers, line up the decimal points.

$$\begin{array}{r} 4.123 \\ +\ 2.6 \\ \hline 6.723 \end{array} \xrightarrow{SD} \mathbf{6.7}$$

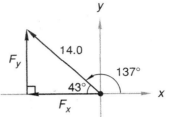

17. $\dfrac{6.02 \times 10^4}{5.1 \times 10^6} = \left(\dfrac{6.02}{5.1}\right)\left(\dfrac{10^4}{10^6}\right) = 1.18039 \times 10^{-2} \xrightarrow{\text{SD}}$ $\mathbf{1.2 \times 10^{-2}}$

18. To subtract these numbers, line up the decimal points.

$$\begin{array}{r} 12.01 \\ -\ 4.362 \\ \hline 7.648 \end{array} \xrightarrow{\text{SD}} \mathbf{7.65}$$

19. $$\begin{array}{r} 12.2 \\ \times\ 3.4 \\ \hline 41.48 \end{array} \xrightarrow{\text{SD}} \mathbf{41}$$

20. To add these numbers, line up the decimal points.

$$\begin{array}{r} 0.023 \\ +\ 2.36 \\ \hline 2.383 \end{array} \xrightarrow{\text{SD}} \mathbf{2.38}$$

Problem Set 3

1.

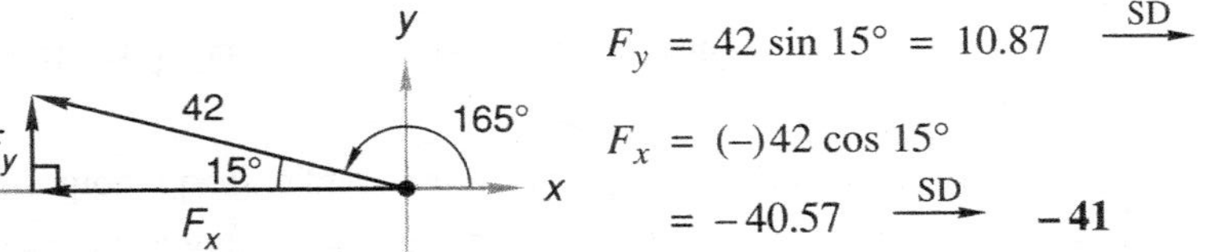

$F_y = 42 \sin 15° = 10.87 \xrightarrow{\text{SD}}$ **11**

$F_x = (-)42 \cos 15°$

$= -40.57 \xrightarrow{\text{SD}}$ **−41**

2.

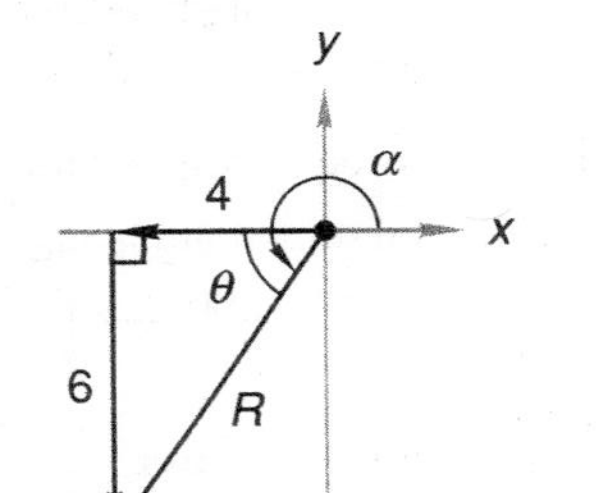

$R = \sqrt{(4)^2 + (6)^2} = 7.21$

$\theta = \tan^{-1} \dfrac{6}{4} = 56.31°$

$\alpha = 180° + 56.31° = 236.31°$

$\vec{R} = 7.21\underline{/236.31°} \xrightarrow{\text{SD}}$ $\mathbf{7\underline{/236.31°}}$

3.

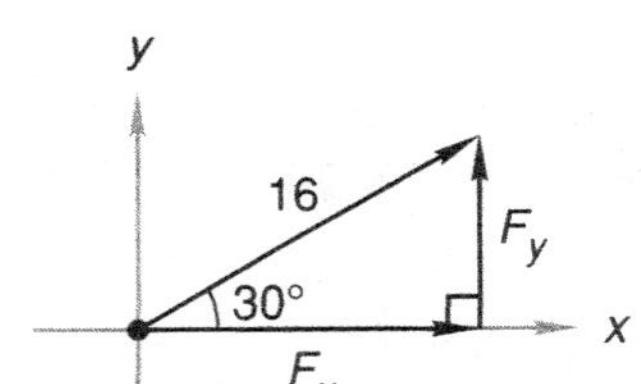

$F_x = 16 \cos 30° = 13.86$

$F_y = 16 \sin 30° = 8.00$

$\vec{F} = 13.86i + 8.00j \xrightarrow{\text{SD}}$ $\mathbf{14i + 8.0j}$

4. $$\begin{array}{r} 12i - 4.0j \\ +\ 7.0i + 6.0j \\ \hline \mathbf{19i + 2.0j} \end{array}$$

5.

$F_x = (-)14.0 \cos 43° = -10.24$

$F_y = 14.0 \sin 43° = 9.55$

$P_x = (-)25 \cos 13° = -24.36$

$P_y = (-)25 \sin 13° = -5.62$

$R_x = F_x + P_x = -10.24 - 24.36 = -34.60$

$R_y = F_y + P_y = 9.55 - 5.62 = 3.93$

$\vec{R} = -34.60i + 3.93j \xrightarrow{\text{SD}}$ $\mathbf{-35i + 3.9j}$

6. $\dfrac{(32.145)(18.003 \times 10^{-2})}{(0.01234 \times 10^5)} \approx \dfrac{(3 \times 10^1)(2 \times 10^{-1})}{(1 \times 10^3)} = \mathbf{6 \times 10^{-3}}$

7. $\dfrac{(1000 \times 10^{-3})(3251 \times 10^4)}{(0.003251 \times 10^{10})} \approx \dfrac{(1 \times 10^0)(3 \times 10^7)}{(3 \times 10^7)} = \mathbf{1}$

8. $\dfrac{(20\bar{0})(0.0036 \times 10^3)}{(5.45 \times 10^{-3})(9.73 \times 10^{-5})} \approx \dfrac{(2 \times 10^2)(4 \times 10^0)}{(5 \times 10^{-3})(1 \times 10^{-4})}$

$= 1.6 \times 10^9 \xrightarrow{\text{SD}}$ $\mathbf{2 \times 10^9}$

9. $\dfrac{(4.2 \times 10^6)(6.4 \times 10^{-2})}{(2.1 \times 10^3)(2.0 \times 10^1)} \approx \dfrac{(4 \times 10^6)(6 \times 10^{-2})}{(2 \times 10^3)(2 \times 10^1)} = \mathbf{6}$

10. $125\ \text{cm}^3 \times \dfrac{1\ \text{in.}^3}{(2.54)^3\ \text{cm}^3} \times \dfrac{1\ \text{ft}^3}{(12)^3\ \text{in.}^3} \times \dfrac{1\ \text{mi}^3}{(5280)^3\ \text{ft}^3}$

$= 2.999 \times 10^{-14}\ \text{mi}^3 \xrightarrow{\text{SD}}$ $\mathbf{3.00 \times 10^{-14}\ mi^3}$

11. $45.77\ \cancel{\text{in.}^3} \times \dfrac{(2.54)^3\ \text{cm}^3}{1\ \cancel{\text{in.}^3}} = 750.036\ \text{cm}^3 \xrightarrow{\text{SD}}$ **750.0 cm³**

12. $5.08\ \dfrac{\cancel{\text{m}}}{\text{s}} \times \dfrac{100\ \cancel{\text{cm}}}{1\ \cancel{\text{m}}} \times \dfrac{1\ \text{in.}}{2.54\ \cancel{\text{cm}}} = \mathbf{20\bar{0}\ \dfrac{in.}{s}}$

13. $128\ \dfrac{\cancel{\text{in.}}}{\cancel{\text{min}}} \times \dfrac{1\ \text{ft}}{12\ \cancel{\text{in.}}} \times \dfrac{1\ \cancel{\text{min}}}{60\ \text{s}} = 0.1778\ \dfrac{\text{ft}}{\text{s}} \xrightarrow{\text{SD}} \mathbf{0.178\ \dfrac{ft}{s}}$

14. 93,570,000
Place the decimal point just to the right of the first nonzero digit and note that it really should be seven places to the right. Do this and get $\mathbf{9.357 \times 10^7}$.

15. 0.00004310
Place the decimal point just to the right of the first nonzero digit and note that it really should be five places to the left. Do this and get $\mathbf{4.310 \times 10^{-5}}$.

16. 1760 ft has **3** significant digits because of rule 1.

17. 4046.87 m^2 has **6** significant digits because of rules 1 and 2.

18. $(3.002 \times 10^2) + (3.0 \times 10^{-1})$
To add these numbers, line up the decimal points.

$$\begin{array}{r} 3.002 \times 10^2 \\ +\ 0.0030 \times 10^2 \\ \hline \mathbf{3.005 \times 10^2} \end{array}$$

19. $\dfrac{(0.123 \times 10^6)(34.7 \times 10^{-3})}{(2.42 \times 10^{-18})(3.00 \times 10^8)(6.243)}$

$= \dfrac{(1.23 \times 10^5)(3.47 \times 10^{-2})}{(2.42 \times 10^{-18})(3.00 \times 10^8)(6.243 \times 10^0)}$

$= 9.4168 \times 10^{11} \xrightarrow{\text{SD}} \mathbf{9.42 \times 10^{11}}$

20. $\dfrac{(0.056)(4.2 \times 10^{-3})(3\bar{0})}{(0.021)(2.006 \times 10^4)(2.8 \times 10^{-4})} + 16.4938$

$= \dfrac{(5.6 \times 10^{-2})(4.2 \times 10^{-3})(3.0 \times 10^1)}{(2.1 \times 10^{-2})(2.006 \times 10^4)(2.8 \times 10^{-4})} + 16.4938$

$= 0.060 + 16.4938 = 16.5538 \xrightarrow{\text{SD}} \mathbf{16.554}$

PROBLEM SET 4

1. Begin by drawing a diagram and recording the data.

$D_W = 2\bar{0}$ km
$T_W = 1.0$ hr
$D_N = 6\bar{0}$ km
$T_N = 3.0$ hr

(a) $D_T = D_N + D_W$
$= 60\ \text{km} + 20\ \text{km}$
$= \mathbf{8\bar{0}\ km}$

(b) $v = \dfrac{D_T}{T_T}$
$= \dfrac{80\ \text{km}}{4.0\ \text{hr}} = \mathbf{2\bar{0}\ \dfrac{km}{hr}}$

(c) $D = \sqrt{(60)^2 + (20)^2} = 63.2\ \text{km}$

$\theta = \tan^{-1} \dfrac{20}{60} = 18.43°$

$\alpha = 90° + 18.43° = 108.43°$

$\vec{D} = 63.2\underline{/108.43°}\ \text{km} \xrightarrow{\text{SD}}$ **63/108.43° km**

(d) $\vec{v} = \dfrac{\vec{D}}{T_T} = \dfrac{63.2\underline{/108.43°}\ \text{km}}{4.0\ \text{hr}}$

$= 15.8\underline{/108.43°}\ \dfrac{\text{km}}{\text{hr}} \xrightarrow{\text{SD}} \mathbf{16\underline{/108.43°}\ \dfrac{km}{hr}}$

2. Begin by drawing a diagram and recording the data.

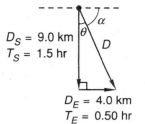

$D_S = 9.0$ km
$T_S = 1.5$ hr

$D_E = 4.0$ km
$T_E = 0.50$ hr

(a) $D_T = D_S + D_E = 9.0\text{ km} + 4.0\text{ km} = \mathbf{13\ km}$

(b) $D = \sqrt{(9.0)^2 + (4.0)^2} = 9.849\text{ km}$

$\theta = \tan^{-1}\dfrac{4.0}{9.0} = 23.96°$

$\alpha = -90° + 23.96° = -66.04°$

$\vec{D} = 9.849\angle{-66.04°}\text{ km} \xrightarrow{SD} \mathbf{9.8\angle{-66.04°}\ km}$

(c) $v = \dfrac{D_T}{T_T} = \dfrac{13\text{ km}}{2.0\text{ hr}} = \mathbf{6.5\ \dfrac{km}{hr}}$

(d) $\vec{v} = \dfrac{\vec{D}}{T_T} = \dfrac{9.849\angle{-66.04°}\text{ km}}{2.0\text{ hr}}$

$= 4.92\angle{-66.04°}\ \dfrac{\text{km}}{\text{hr}} \xrightarrow{SD} \mathbf{4.9\angle{-66.04°}\ \dfrac{km}{hr}}$

3. $w = mg = 462\text{ kg} \times 9.81\ \dfrac{\text{N}}{\text{kg}} = 4532\text{ N} \xrightarrow{SD} \mathbf{4530\ N}$

4. $w = mg$

$9840\text{ N} = m \times 9.81\ \dfrac{\text{N}}{\text{kg}}$

$m = 1003\text{ kg} \xrightarrow{SD} \mathbf{10\bar{0}0\ kg}$

5. $w = mg$

$105\text{ N} = m \times 9.81\ \dfrac{\text{N}}{\text{kg}}$

$m = 10.70\text{ kg} \xrightarrow{SD} \mathbf{10.7\ kg}$

6. Begin by finding the mass of the block.

$w = mg$

$107\text{ N} = m \times 9.81\ \dfrac{\text{N}}{\text{kg}}$

$m = 10.91\text{ kg}$

Calculate the volume.

$\rho = \dfrac{m}{V}$

$10{,}500\ \dfrac{\text{kg}}{\text{m}^3} = \dfrac{10.91\text{ kg}}{V}$

$V = 1.039 \times 10^{-3}\text{ m}^3 \xrightarrow{SD} \mathbf{1.04 \times 10^{-3}\ m^3}$

7. $\rho = \dfrac{m}{V}$

$0.178\ \dfrac{\text{kg}}{\text{m}^3} = \dfrac{m}{0.25\text{ m}^3}$

$m = 4.45 \times 10^{-2}\text{ kg} \xrightarrow{SD} \mathbf{4.5 \times 10^{-2}\ kg}$

8. $\rho = \dfrac{m}{V}$

$= \dfrac{3.0\text{ kg}}{0.045\text{ m}^3}$

$= 66.67\ \dfrac{\text{kg}}{\text{m}^3} \xrightarrow{SD} \mathbf{67\ \dfrac{kg}{m^3}}$

Yes, this density is less than the density of water.

9.

y
F_x
6°
21
F_y
96°
x

$F_y = 21\cos 6° = 20.88 \xrightarrow{SD} \mathbf{21}$

$F_x = (-)21\sin 6° = -2.20 \xrightarrow{SD} \mathbf{-2.2}$

10.

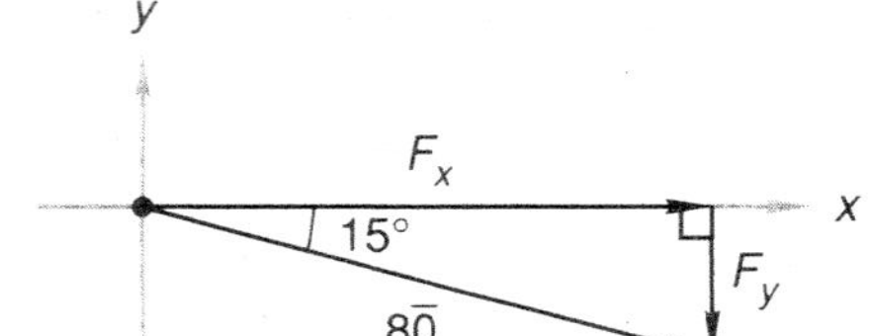

$$F_y = (-)80 \sin 15^\circ$$
$$= -20.71 \xrightarrow{\text{SD}} \mathbf{-21}$$
$$F_x = 80 \cos 15^\circ$$
$$= 77.27 \xrightarrow{\text{SD}} \mathbf{77}$$

11.

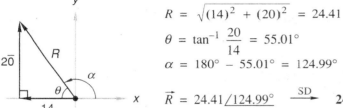

y
R
20
14
θ
α
x

$$R = \sqrt{(14)^2 + (20)^2} = 24.41$$
$$\theta = \tan^{-1}\frac{20}{14} = 55.01^\circ$$
$$\alpha = 180^\circ - 55.01^\circ = 124.99^\circ$$
$$\vec{R} = 24.41\underline{/124.99^\circ} \xrightarrow{\text{SD}} \mathbf{24\underline{/124.99^\circ}}$$

12. Add these vectors to find the resultant in rectangular form.

$$\vec{F}_1 = 46i + 23j$$
$$\vec{F}_2 = -10i + 7j$$
$$\vec{F}_R = 36i + 30j$$

Convert the resultant to polar form and get:

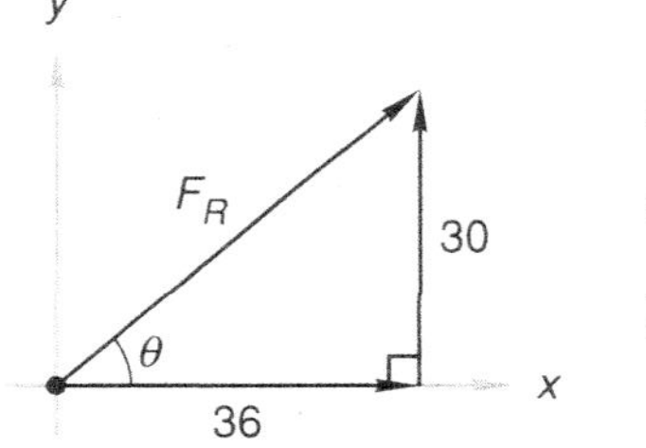

$$F_R = \sqrt{(36)^2 + (30)^2} = 46.86$$
$$\theta = \tan^{-1}\frac{30}{36} = 39.81^\circ$$
$$\vec{F}_R = 46.86\underline{/39.81^\circ} \xrightarrow{\text{SD}} \mathbf{50\underline{/39.81^\circ}}$$

13.

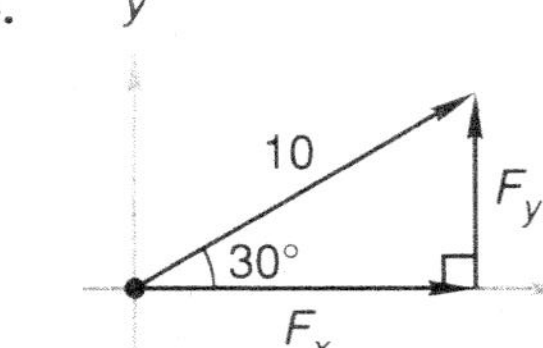

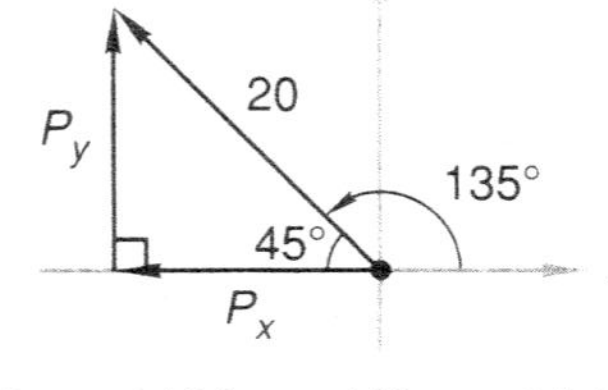

$$F_x = 10 \cos 30^\circ = 8.66 \qquad P_x = (-)20 \cos 45^\circ = -14.14$$
$$F_y = 10 \sin 30^\circ = 5.00 \qquad P_y = 20 \sin 45^\circ = 14.14$$

$$R_x = F_x + P_x = 8.66 - 14.14 = -5.48$$
$$R_y = F_y + P_y = 5.00 + 14.14 = 19.14$$

$$\vec{R} = -5.48i + 19.14j \xrightarrow{\text{SD}} \mathbf{-5i + 20j}$$

14.
$$\frac{(0.0321)(21\bar{0} \times 10^{-4})(2.14 \times 10^3)}{(0.931)(41\bar{0}0 \times 10^{-5})}$$
$$\approx \frac{(3 \times 10^{-2})(2 \times 10^{-2})(2 \times 10^3)}{(9 \times 10^{-1})(4 \times 10^{-2})}$$
$$= 33 \xrightarrow{\text{SD}} \mathbf{30}$$

15.
$$\frac{(3.12 \times 10^{-3})(0.0071 \times 10^7)}{(4.6 \times 10^{-20})(36.7)}$$
$$\approx \frac{(3 \times 10^{-3})(7 \times 10^4)}{(5 \times 10^{-20})(4 \times 10^1)}$$
$$= 1.05 \times 10^{20} \xrightarrow{\text{SD}} \mathbf{1 \times 10^{20}}$$

16.
$$\frac{(2.4 \times 10^2)(7.5 \times 10^{-3})}{(2.002 \times 10^{-6})(30.5)(0.00412)}$$
$$\approx \frac{(2 \times 10^2)(8 \times 10^{-3})}{(2 \times 10^{-6})(3 \times 10^1)(4 \times 10^{-3})}$$
$$= 6.7 \times 10^6 \xrightarrow{\text{SD}} \mathbf{7 \times 10^6}$$

17. $4.63 \frac{\text{mi}}{\text{hr}} \times \frac{5280 \text{ ft}}{1 \text{ mi}} \times \frac{12 \text{ in.}}{1 \text{ ft}} \times \frac{2.54 \text{ cm}}{1 \text{ in.}} \times \frac{1 \text{ m}}{100 \text{ cm}} \times \frac{1 \text{ km}}{1000 \text{ m}}$

$= 7.451 \frac{\text{km}}{\text{hr}} \xrightarrow{\text{SD}} \mathbf{7.45 \frac{km}{hr}}$

18. $145 \frac{\text{cm}}{\text{s}} \times \frac{60 \text{ s}}{1 \text{ min}} = \mathbf{87\bar{0}0 \frac{cm}{min}}$

19. $4047 \text{ m}^2 \times \frac{100 \text{ cm}}{1 \text{ m}} \times \frac{100 \text{ cm}}{1 \text{ m}} \times \frac{1 \text{ in.}}{2.54 \text{ cm}} \times \frac{1 \text{ in.}}{2.54 \text{ cm}} \times \frac{1 \text{ ft}}{12 \text{ in.}} \times \frac{1 \text{ ft}}{12 \text{ in.}}$

$= 43{,}562 \text{ ft}^2 \xrightarrow{\text{SD}} \mathbf{43{,}560 \ ft^2}$

20. $(3.002 \times 10^{38}) + (3.3 \times 10^{36})$

To add these numbers, line up the decimal points.

$$\begin{array}{r} 3.002 \times 10^{38} \\ +\ 0.033 \times 10^{38} \\ \hline \mathbf{3.035 \times 10^{38}} \end{array}$$

21. $\frac{(162 \text{ m}^2)(0.53 \times 10^2 \text{ m}^2)}{31.2 \text{ m}^3} = \frac{8.586 \times 10^3 \text{ m}^4}{31.2 \text{ m}^3} = 275 \text{ m}$

Convert to centimeters and get:

$275 \text{ m} \times \frac{100 \text{ cm}}{1 \text{ m}} = 27{,}500 \text{ cm} \xrightarrow{\text{SD}} \mathbf{28{,}000 \ cm}$

22. $\frac{(124 \text{ in.}^2)(36 \text{ ft})}{1448 \text{ in.}^2} = 3.083 \text{ ft}$

Convert to centimeters and get:

$3.083 \text{ ft} \times \frac{12 \text{ in.}}{1 \text{ ft}} \times \frac{2.54 \text{ cm}}{1 \text{ in.}} = 93.97 \text{ cm} \xrightarrow{\text{SD}} \mathbf{94 \ cm}$

Problem Set 5

1. (a) $0.764T_1 - 0.181T_2 = 4.62$
(b) $-0.316T_1 + 0.540T_2 = 2.13$

Solve (b) for T_2 and get:

(b′) $T_2 = \frac{2.13}{0.540} + \frac{0.316}{0.540}T_1$

Substitute (b′) into (a) and get:

(a) $0.764T_1 - 0.181\left(\frac{2.13}{0.540} + \frac{0.316}{0.540}T_1\right) = 4.62$

$0.764T_1 - 0.7139 - 0.1059T_1 = 4.62$

$0.6581T_1 = 5.334$

$T_1 = 8.105 \xrightarrow{\text{SD}} \mathbf{8.11}$

Substitute T_1 into (b′) and get:

(b′) $T_2 = \frac{2.13}{0.540} + \frac{0.316}{0.540}(8.105) = 8.687 \xrightarrow{\text{SD}} \mathbf{8.69}$

2.

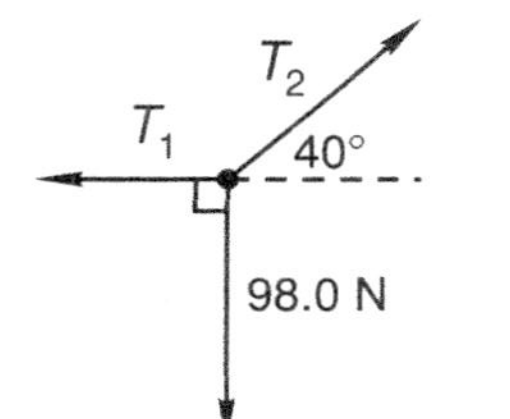

(a) $\sum F_x = 0;\ T_2 \cos 40° - T_1 = 0$
(b) $\sum F_y = 0;\ T_2 \sin 40° - 98.0 \text{ N} = 0$

Solve (b) for T_2 and get:
(b) $T_2 \sin 40° = 98.0 \text{ N}$

$T_2 = 152.46 \text{ N} \xrightarrow{\text{SD}} \mathbf{152 \ N}$

Substitute T_2 into (a) and get:
(a) $T_1 = T_2 \cos 40°$
$= (152.46 \text{ N}) \cos 40°$
$= 116.79 \text{ N} \xrightarrow{\text{SD}} \mathbf{117 \ N}$

3.

(a) $\Sigma F_x = 0;\ T_2 \cos 43° - T_1 \cos 27° = 0$
(b) $\Sigma F_y = 0;\ T_1 \sin 27° + T_2 \sin 43° - 296\text{ N} = 0$

Solve (a) for T_2 and get:

(a) $T_2 \cos 43° = T_1 \cos 27°$

$T_2 = 1.218T_1$ (a′)

Substitute (a′) into (b) and get:

(b) $T_1 \sin 27° + (1.218T_1) \sin 43° = 296\text{ N}$

$1.285T_1 = 296\text{ N}$

$T_1 = 230.35\text{ N} \xrightarrow{SD} \mathbf{23\bar{0}\ N}$

Substitute T_1 into (a′) and get:

(a′) $T_2 = 1.218(230.35\text{ N})$

$= 280.57\text{ N} \xrightarrow{SD} \mathbf{281\ N}$

4. Begin by drawing a diagram and recording the data.

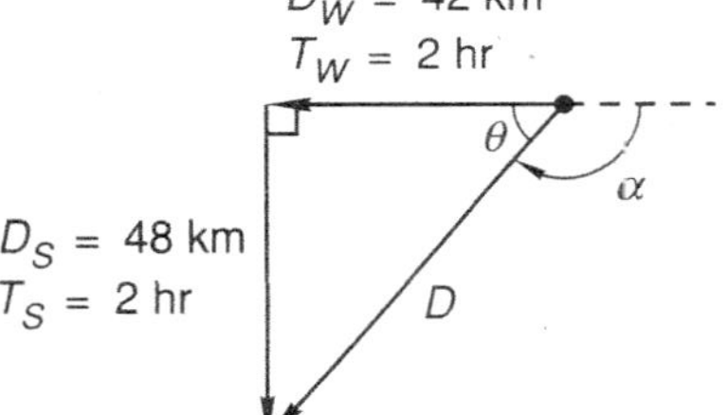

(a) $D_T = D_W + D_S = 42\text{ km} + 48\text{ km} = \mathbf{90\ km}$

(b) $D = \sqrt{(42)^2 + (48)^2} = 63.8\text{ km}$

$\theta = \tan^{-1} \dfrac{48}{42} = 48.81°$

$\alpha = -180° + 48.81° = -131.19°$

$\vec{D} = 63.8\underline{/-131.19°}\text{ km} \xrightarrow{SD} \mathbf{60\underline{/-131.19°}\ km}$

(c) $v = \dfrac{D_T}{T_T} = \dfrac{90\text{ km}}{4\text{ hr}} = 22.5\ \dfrac{\text{km}}{\text{hr}} \xrightarrow{SD} \mathbf{20\ \dfrac{km}{hr}}$

(d) $\vec{v} = \dfrac{\vec{D}}{T_T} = \dfrac{63.8\underline{/-131.19°}\text{ km}}{4\text{ hr}}$

$= 15.95\underline{/-131.19°}\ \dfrac{\text{km}}{\text{hr}} \xrightarrow{SD} \mathbf{20\underline{/-131.19°}\ \dfrac{km}{hr}}$

5. Begin by drawing a diagram and recording the data.

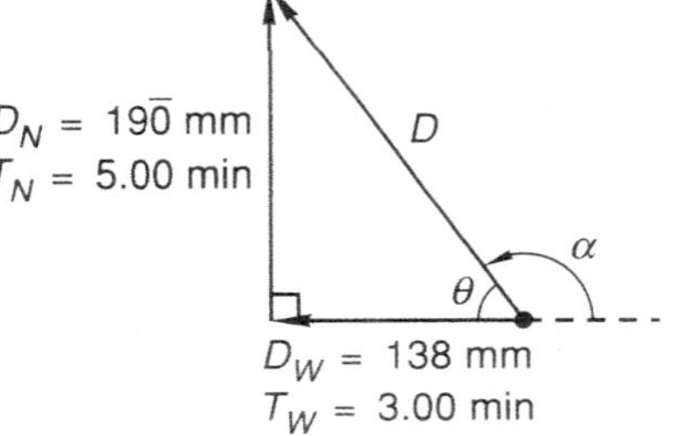

(a) $D_T = D_W + D_N = 138\text{ mm} + 190\text{ mm} = \mathbf{328\ mm}$

(b) $D = \sqrt{(138)^2 + (190)^2} = 234.83\text{ mm}$

$\theta = \tan^{-1} \dfrac{190}{138} = 54.01°$

$\alpha = 180° - 54.01° = 125.99°$

$\vec{D} = 234.83\underline{/125.99°}\text{ mm} \xrightarrow{SD} \mathbf{235\underline{/125.99°}\ mm}$

(c) $v = \dfrac{D_T}{T_T} = \dfrac{328\text{ mm}}{8.00\text{ min}} = \mathbf{41.0\ \dfrac{mm}{min}}$

(d) $\vec{v} = \dfrac{\vec{D}}{T_T} = \dfrac{234.83\underline{/125.99°}\text{ mm}}{8.00\text{ min}}$

$= 29.35\underline{/125.99°}\ \dfrac{\text{mm}}{\text{min}} \xrightarrow{SD} \mathbf{29.4\underline{/125.99°}\ \dfrac{mm}{min}}$

6. (a) $\rho = \dfrac{m}{V}$

$13{,}600\ \dfrac{\text{kg}}{\text{m}^3} = \dfrac{m}{0.0600\text{ m}^3}$

$m = \mathbf{816\ kg}$

(b) $w = mg = 816\,\cancel{\text{kg}} \times 9.81\ \dfrac{\text{N}}{\cancel{\text{kg}}} = 8004.96\text{ N} \xrightarrow{SD} \mathbf{80\bar{0}0\ N}$

7. Begin by finding the mass of the box.

$$w = mg$$

$$5000 \text{ N} = m \times 9.81 \frac{\text{N}}{\text{kg}}$$

$$m = 509.7 \text{ kg}$$

Calculate the density.

$$\rho = \frac{m}{V} = \frac{509.7 \text{ kg}}{0.45 \text{ m}^3} = 1132.7 \frac{\text{kg}}{\text{m}^3} \xrightarrow{\text{SD}} \mathbf{1000 \frac{kg}{m^3}}$$

No, the box will not float in a liquid whose density is $60\bar{0}$ kg·m^{-3}.

8. $w = mg = 117 \cancel{\text{kg}} \times 9.81 \frac{\text{N}}{\cancel{\text{kg}}} = 1147.77 \text{ N} \xrightarrow{\text{SD}}$ **1150 N**

9.

$$w = mg$$

$$612 \text{ N} = m \times 9.81 \frac{\text{N}}{\text{kg}}$$

$$m = 62.39 \text{ kg} \xrightarrow{\text{SD}} \mathbf{62.4 \ kg}$$

10. Begin by adding the weights.

$w_T = 485 \text{ N} + 983 \text{ N} = 1468 \text{ N}$

Calculate the mass.

$$w = mg$$

$$1468 \text{ N} = m \times 9.81 \frac{\text{N}}{\text{kg}}$$

$$m = 149.6 \text{ kg} \xrightarrow{\text{SD}} \mathbf{15\bar{0} \ kg}$$

11.

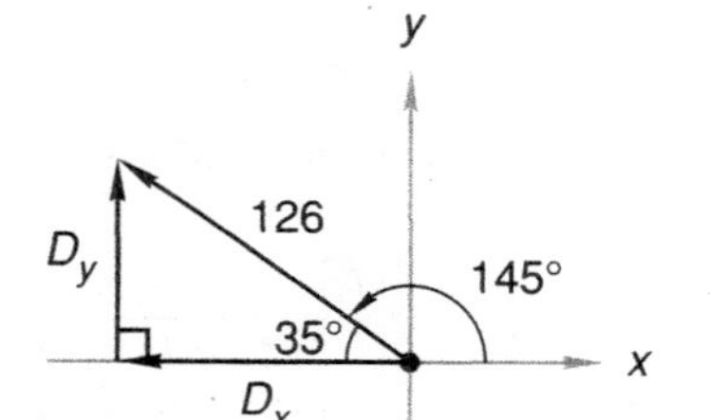

$$D_x = (-)126 \cos 35°$$

$$= -103.2 \xrightarrow{\text{SD}} \mathbf{-103}$$

$$D_y = 126 \sin 35°$$

$$= 72.27 \xrightarrow{\text{SD}} \mathbf{72.3}$$

12.

$$E_x = 26 \cos 30° = 22.5 \xrightarrow{\text{SD}} \mathbf{23}$$

$$E_y = 26 \sin 30° = 13.0 \xrightarrow{\text{SD}} \mathbf{13}$$

13.

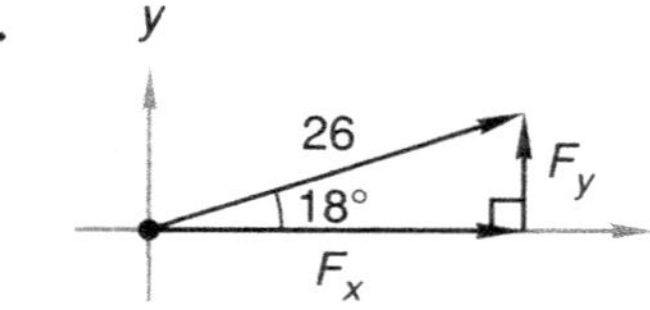

$$R = \sqrt{(12)^2 + (7.6)^2} = 14.2$$

$$\theta = \tan^{-1} \frac{7.6}{12} = 32.35°$$

$$\alpha = 180° - 32.35° = 147.65°$$

$$\vec{R} = 14.2\underline{/147.65°} \xrightarrow{\text{SD}} \mathbf{14\underline{/147.65°}}$$

14.

$$F_x = 26 \cos 18° = 24.73$$

$$F_y = 26 \sin 18° = 8.03$$

$$P_x = 108 \cos 39° = 83.93$$

$$P_y = 108 \sin 39° = 67.97$$

$$R_x = F_x - P_x = 24.73 - 83.93 = -59.20$$

$$R_y = F_y - P_y = 8.03 - 67.97 = -59.94$$

$$\vec{R} = -59.20i - 59.94j \xrightarrow{\text{SD}} \mathbf{-59i - 6\bar{0}j}$$

15. Begin by adding the vectors in rectangular form.

$$\begin{array}{r} 26.0i + 31.0j \\ + \; 312i - 26.0j \\ \hline 338i + 5.00j \end{array}$$

Convert the resultant to polar form and get:

$$R = \sqrt{(338)^2 + (5.00)^2} = 338.04$$

$$\theta = \tan^{-1}\frac{5.00}{338} = 0.85°$$

$$\vec{R} = 338.04\angle 0.85° \xrightarrow{SD} \mathbf{338\angle 0.85°}$$

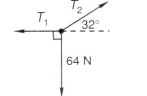

16. $$\frac{(0.00398 \times 10^{21})(6.291 \times 10^{-5})}{18.98 \times 10^{15}} \approx \frac{(4 \times 10^{18})(6 \times 10^{-5})}{2 \times 10^{16}}$$

$$= 1.2 \times 10^{-2} \xrightarrow{SD} \mathbf{1 \times 10^{-2}}$$

17. $$\frac{(7.20 \times 10^4)(3.06 \times 10^{-4})}{(-6.193)(0.0903)} + (3 \times 10^1)$$

$$\approx \frac{(7 \times 10^4)(3 \times 10^{-4})}{(-6 \times 10^0)(9 \times 10^{-2})} + (3 \times 10^1) = -39 + 30 = \mathbf{-9}$$

18. $$0.0040 \text{ mi} \times \frac{5280 \text{ ft}}{1 \text{ mi}} \times \frac{12 \text{ in.}}{1 \text{ ft}} \times \frac{2.54 \text{ cm}}{1 \text{ in.}} = 643.7 \text{ cm} \xrightarrow{SD} \mathbf{640 \text{ cm}}$$

19. $$\frac{(4.0 \times 10^2 \text{ kg})\left(-0.04 \frac{\text{km}}{\text{hr}}\right)}{1.6 \times 10^{-3} \text{ kg}} = -1 \times 10^4 \frac{\text{km}}{\text{hr}}$$

Convert to meters per second and get:

$$-1 \times 10^4 \frac{\text{km}}{\text{hr}} \times \frac{1000 \text{ m}}{1 \text{ km}} \times \frac{1 \text{ hr}}{60 \text{ min}} \times \frac{1 \text{ min}}{60 \text{ s}}$$

$$= -2778 \frac{\text{m}}{\text{s}} \xrightarrow{SD} \mathbf{-3000 \frac{m}{s}}$$

20. $$\frac{7.83 \times 10^{-6} \text{ cm}}{2.4 \times 10^{-8} \text{ s}} = 326.25 \frac{\text{cm}}{\text{s}}$$

Convert to meters per second and get:

$$326.25 \frac{\text{cm}}{\text{s}} \times \frac{1 \text{ m}}{100 \text{ cm}} = 3.2625 \frac{\text{m}}{\text{s}} \xrightarrow{SD} \mathbf{3.3 \frac{m}{s}}$$

Problem Set 6

1. First, we determine the number of degrees above or below the freezing temperature of water.

$$-40° - 32 = -72°$$

Thus, we are 72 Fahrenheit degrees below freezing. Since the ratio of the increments is

$$\text{Ratio} = \frac{°\text{C}}{°\text{F}} = \frac{100}{180} = \frac{5}{9}$$

it takes fewer Celsius degrees to measure an interval, so we multiply by 5 over 9.

$$-72° \times \frac{5}{9} = \mathbf{-40°C}$$

2. $$T_K = T_C + 273$$
$$400 = T_C + 273$$
$$T_C = \mathbf{127°C}$$

3. $$T_K = T_C + 273$$
$$= 100 + 273$$
$$= \mathbf{373 \text{ K}}$$

4.

(a) $\sum F_x = 0;\ T_2 \cos 32° - T_1 = 0$
(b) $\sum F_y = 0;\ T_2 \sin 32° - 64 \text{ N} = 0$

Solve (b) for T_2 and get:
(b) $T_2 \sin 32° = 64 \text{ N}$

$$T_2 = 120.77 \text{ N} \xrightarrow{SD} \mathbf{120 \text{ N}}$$

Substitute T_2 into (a) and get:
(a) $T_1 = T_2 \cos 32°$

$$= (120.77 \text{ N}) \cos 32° = 102.42 \text{ N} \xrightarrow{SD} \mathbf{1\bar{0}0 \text{ N}}$$

5.

T_1, T_2, 30°, 54°, 86 N

(a) $\Sigma F_x = 0;\ T_2 \cos 54^\circ - T_1 \cos 30^\circ = 0$
(b) $\Sigma F_y = 0;\ T_1 \sin 30^\circ + T_2 \sin 54^\circ - 86\text{ N} = 0$

Solve (a) for T_2 and get:

(a) $T_2 \cos 54^\circ = T_1 \cos 30^\circ$

$$T_2 = 1.473T_1 \qquad \text{(a')}$$

Substitute (a') into (b) and get:

(b) $T_1 \sin 30^\circ + (1.473T_1) \sin 54^\circ = 86\text{ N}$

$$1.692T_1 = 86\text{ N}$$

$$T_1 = 50.83\text{ N} \xrightarrow{\text{SD}} \mathbf{51\ N}$$

Substitute T_1 into (a') and get:

(a') $T_2 = 1.473(50.83\text{ N})$

$$= 74.87\text{ N} \xrightarrow{\text{SD}} \mathbf{75\ N}$$

6. Begin by drawing a diagram and recording the data.

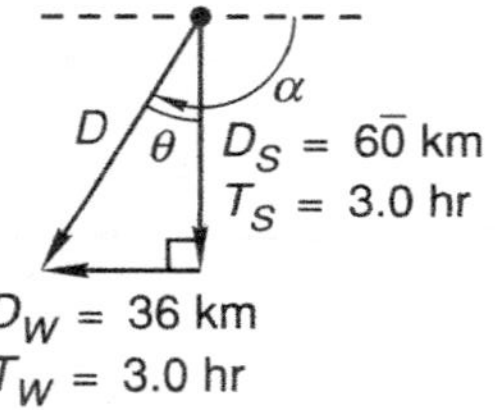

(a) $D_T = D_S + D_W = 60\text{ km} + 36\text{ km} = \mathbf{96\ km}$

(b) $D = \sqrt{(60)^2 + (36)^2} = 69.97\text{ km}$

$$\theta = \tan^{-1}\frac{36}{60} = 30.96^\circ$$

$$\alpha = -90^\circ - 30.96^\circ = -120.96^\circ$$

$$\vec{D} = 69.97\underline{\angle -120.96^\circ}\text{ km} \xrightarrow{\text{SD}} \mathbf{7\bar{0}\underline{\angle -120.96^\circ}\ km}$$

(c) $\vec{v} = \dfrac{\vec{D}}{T_T} = \dfrac{69.97\underline{\angle -120.96^\circ}\text{ km}}{6.0\text{ hr}}$

$$= 11.66\underline{\angle -120.96^\circ}\ \frac{\text{km}}{\text{hr}} \xrightarrow{\text{SD}} \mathbf{12\underline{\angle -120.96^\circ}\ \frac{km}{hr}}$$

(d) $v = \dfrac{D_T}{T_T} = \dfrac{96\text{ km}}{6.0\text{ hr}} = \mathbf{16\ \dfrac{km}{hr}}$

7. Begin by drawing a diagram and recording the data.

D_E = 120 mi
T_E = 2.0 hr
D_N = 160 mi
T_N = 4.0 hr
θ, α

(a) $D_T = D_N + D_E$

$$= 160\text{ mi} + 120\text{ mi}$$

$$= \mathbf{280\ mi}$$

(b) $T_T = T_N + T_E$

$$= 4.0\text{ hr} + 2.0\text{ hr} = \mathbf{6.0\ hr}$$

(c) $D = \sqrt{(160)^2 + (120)^2} = 2\bar{0}0\text{ mi}$

$$\theta = \tan^{-1}\frac{120}{160} = 36.87^\circ$$

$$\alpha = 90^\circ - 36.87^\circ = 53.13^\circ$$

$$\vec{D} = \mathbf{2\bar{0}0\underline{\angle 53.13^\circ}\ mi}$$

(d) $\vec{v} = \dfrac{\vec{D}}{T_T} = \dfrac{2\bar{0}0\underline{\angle 53.13^\circ}\text{ mi}}{6.0\text{ hr}} = 33.3\underline{\angle 53.13^\circ}\ \dfrac{\text{mi}}{\text{hr}} \xrightarrow{\text{SD}} \mathbf{33\underline{\angle 53.13^\circ}\ \dfrac{mi}{hr}}$

$$v = \frac{D_T}{T_T} = \frac{280\text{ mi}}{6.0\text{ hr}} = 46.67\ \frac{\text{mi}}{\text{hr}} \xrightarrow{\text{SD}} \mathbf{47\ \frac{mi}{hr}}$$

8. (a) Begin by converting 14,600 grams to kilograms.

$$14{,}600\,\cancel{g} \times \frac{1\text{ kg}}{1000\,\cancel{g}} = 14.6\text{ kg}$$

Calculate the weight.

$$w = mg = 14.6\,\cancel{\text{kg}} \times 9.81\,\frac{\text{N}}{\cancel{\text{kg}}} = 143.23\text{ N} \xrightarrow{\text{SD}} \mathbf{143\ N}$$

(b)

$$\rho = \frac{m}{V}$$

$$8920\,\frac{\text{kg}}{\text{m}^3} = \frac{14.6\text{ kg}}{V}$$

$$V = 1.637 \times 10^{-3}\text{ m}^3 \xrightarrow{\text{SD}} \mathbf{1.64 \times 10^{-3}\ m^3}$$

9. (a) Begin by converting $5\bar{0}00\text{ cm}^3$ to m^3.

$$5\bar{0}00\,\cancel{\text{cm}^3} \times \frac{1\text{ m}}{100\,\cancel{\text{cm}}} \times \frac{1\text{ m}}{100\,\cancel{\text{cm}}} \times \frac{1\text{ m}}{100\,\cancel{\text{cm}}} = 5.00 \times 10^{-3}\text{ m}^3$$

Calculate the density.

$$\rho = \frac{m}{V} = \frac{2.5\text{ kg}}{5.00 \times 10^{-3}\text{ m}^3} = \mathbf{50\bar{0}\ \frac{kg}{m^3}}$$

(b) **Pine**

10. $w = mg = 7.25\,\cancel{\text{kg}} \times 9.81\,\frac{\text{N}}{\cancel{\text{kg}}} = 71.12\text{ N} \xrightarrow{\text{SD}} \mathbf{71.1\ N}$

11.

$$w = mg$$

$$645\text{ N} = m \times 9.81\,\frac{\text{N}}{\text{kg}}$$

$$m = 65.749\text{ kg} \xrightarrow{\text{SD}} \mathbf{65.7\ kg}$$

12.

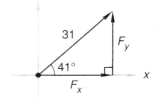

$$F_x = 31 \cos 41° = 23.40 \xrightarrow{\text{SD}} \mathbf{23}$$

$$F_y = 31 \sin 41° = 20.34 \xrightarrow{\text{SD}} \mathbf{2\bar{0}}$$

13.

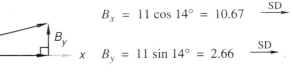

$$B_x = 11 \cos 14° = 10.67 \xrightarrow{\text{SD}} \mathbf{11}$$

$$B_y = 11 \sin 14° = 2.66 \xrightarrow{\text{SD}} \mathbf{2.7}$$

14.

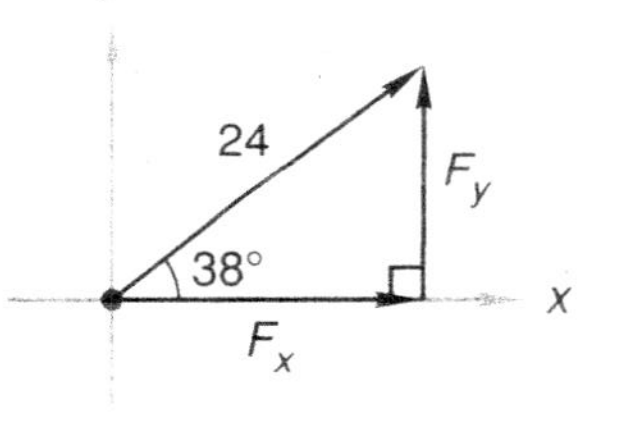

$$F_x = 24 \cos 38° = 18.912$$
$$F_y = 24 \sin 38° = 14.776$$

$$P_x = (-)4.0 \sin 5° = -0.349$$
$$P_y = (-)4.0 \cos 5° = -3.985$$

$$R_x = F_x + P_x = 18.912 - 0.349 = 18.563$$
$$R_y = F_y + P_y = 14.776 - 3.985 = 10.791$$

$$\vec{R} = 18.563i + 10.791j \xrightarrow{\text{SD}} \mathbf{19}\boldsymbol{i} + \mathbf{11}\boldsymbol{j}$$

Convert this to polar form and get:

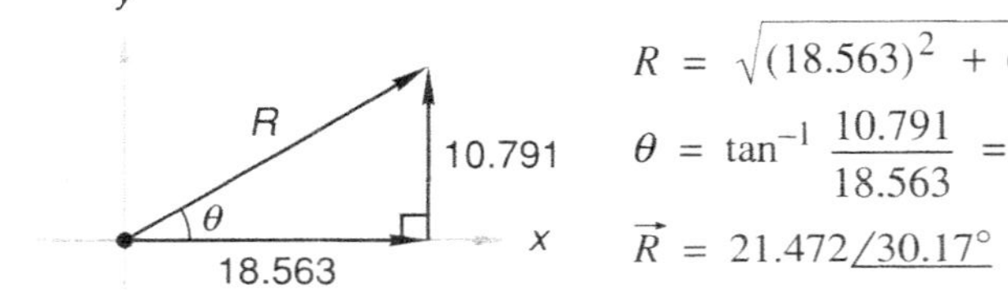

$$R = \sqrt{(18.563)^2 + (10.791)^2} = 21.472$$

$$\theta = \tan^{-1}\frac{10.791}{18.563} = 30.17°$$

$$\vec{R} = 21.472\angle 30.17° \xrightarrow{\text{SD}} \mathbf{21\angle 30.17°}$$

15. Begin by adding the vectors in rectangular form.

$$\begin{array}{r} 12i - 14j \\ -4.3i + 48j \\ \hline \mathbf{7.7i + 34j} \end{array}$$

Convert the resultant to polar form and get:

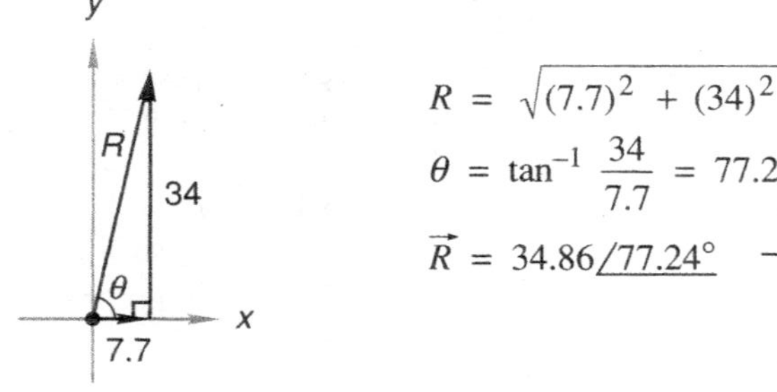

$$R = \sqrt{(7.7)^2 + (34)^2} = 34.86$$

$$\theta = \tan^{-1}\frac{34}{7.7} = 77.24°$$

$$\vec{R} = 34.86\underline{/77.24°} \xrightarrow{SD} \mathbf{35\underline{/77.24°}}$$

16. $$\frac{(1.036 \times 10^4)(640)}{(0.00032)(2.5 \times 10^{-1})} \approx \frac{(1 \times 10^4)(6 \times 10^2)}{(3 \times 10^{-4})(3 \times 10^{-1})}$$

$$= 6.7 \times 10^{10} \xrightarrow{SD} \mathbf{7 \times 10^{10}}$$

17. $$\frac{(6.93 \times 10^{14})(-5.06 \times 10^3)}{(3.51 \times 10^{-6})(2.2 \times 10^3)} \approx \frac{(7 \times 10^{14})(-5 \times 10^3)}{(4 \times 10^{-6})(2 \times 10^3)}$$

$$= -4.375 \times 10^{20} \xrightarrow{SD} \mathbf{-4 \times 10^{20}}$$

18. $$1500\overline{0}\ \text{mi}^3 \times \frac{(5280)^3\ \text{ft}^3}{1\ \text{mi}^3} \times \frac{(12)^3\ \text{in.}^3}{1\ \text{ft}^3} \times \frac{(2.54)^3\ \text{cm}^3}{1\ \text{in.}^3} \times \frac{1\ \text{m}^3}{(100)^3\ \text{cm}^3}$$

$$= 6.25227 \times 10^{12}\ \text{m}^3 \xrightarrow{SD} \mathbf{6.252 \times 10^{12}\ m^3}$$

19. $$\frac{\left(7.89\ \frac{\text{g}}{\text{cm}^3}\right)\left(6.022 \times 10^{23}\ \frac{\text{molecules}}{\text{mol}}\right)}{14.8\ \frac{\text{g}}{\text{mol}}}$$

$$= 3.2104 \times 10^{23}\ \frac{\text{molecules}}{\text{cm}^3} \xrightarrow{SD} \mathbf{3.21 \times 10^{23}\ \frac{molecules}{cm^3}}$$

20. $$\frac{(214 \times 10^{-3})(0.034 \times 10^{13})(91.4)}{(3.14 \times 10^4)(7.36 \times 10^{-5})}$$

$$= \frac{(2.14 \times 10^{-1})(3.4 \times 10^{11})(9.14 \times 10^1)}{(3.14 \times 10^4)(7.36 \times 10^{-5})}$$

$$= 2.878 \times 10^{12} \xrightarrow{SD} \mathbf{2.9 \times 10^{12}}$$

PROBLEM SET 7

1. $$v_{av} = \frac{x_2 - x_1}{t_2 - t_1} = \frac{24{,}367 - (-1200.0)}{40 - 11.00}\ \frac{\text{m}}{\text{s}} = +881.6\ \frac{\text{m}}{\text{s}} \xrightarrow{SD} \mathbf{+900\ \frac{m}{s}}$$

2. $$a_{av} = \frac{v_2 - v_1}{t_2 - t_1} = \frac{58 - 2\overline{0}}{3.0 - 0}\ \frac{\text{m/s}}{\text{s}} = +12.7\ \frac{\text{m}}{\text{s}^2} \xrightarrow{SD} \mathbf{+13\ \frac{m}{s^2}}$$

$$a_{av} = \frac{v_2 - v_1}{t_2 - t_1} = \frac{12 - 58}{8.0 - 0}\ \frac{\text{m/s}}{\text{s}} = -5.75\ \frac{\text{m}}{\text{s}^2} \xrightarrow{SD} \mathbf{-5.8\ \frac{m}{s^2}}$$

3. $$v = \frac{\Delta x}{\Delta t} = \frac{15\ \text{mi}}{18\ \text{min}} = 0.833\ \frac{\text{mi}}{\text{min}}$$

Convert to mi/hr and get:

$$0.833\ \frac{\text{mi}}{\text{min}} \times \frac{60\ \text{min}}{1\ \text{hr}} = 49.98\ \frac{\text{mi}}{\text{hr}} \xrightarrow{SD} \mathbf{5\overline{0}\ \frac{mi}{hr}}$$

4. Since the ratio of the increments is

$$\text{Ratio} = \frac{°\text{F}}{°\text{C}} = \frac{180}{100} = \frac{9}{5}$$

it takes more Fahrenheit degrees in an interval than there are Celsius degrees, so we multiply by 9 over 5.

$$-20° \times \frac{9}{5} = -36°$$

Thus, we are 36 Fahrenheit degrees below freezing. Water freezes at 32 degrees Fahrenheit, and we are 36° below that temperature.

$$-36° + 32 = \mathbf{-4°F}$$

5. $T_K = T_C + 273$

$295 = T_C + 273$

$T_C = \mathbf{22.0°C}$

6. (a) $3.0F_1 + 5.0F_2 = 16$

(b) $5.1F_1 - 1.5F_2 = 4.2$

Solve (b) for F_2 and get:

(b′) $F_2 = 3.4F_1 - 2.8$

Substitute (b′) into (a) and get:

(a) $3.0F_1 + 5.0(3.4F_1 - 2.8) = 16$

$3.0F_1 + 17F_1 - 14 = 16$

$20F_1 = 30$

$F_1 = \mathbf{1.5}$

Substitute F_1 into (b′) and get:

(b′) $F_2 = 3.4(1.5) - 2.8 = \mathbf{2.3}$

7.

T_2, T_1, 15°, 30°, 416 N

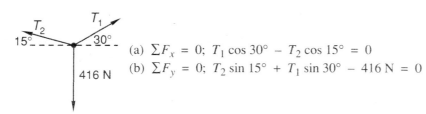

(a) $\Sigma F_x = 0;\ T_1 \cos 30° - T_2 \cos 15° = 0$

(b) $\Sigma F_y = 0;\ T_2 \sin 15° + T_1 \sin 30° - 416\text{ N} = 0$

Solve (a) for T_2 and get:

(a) $T_2 \cos 15° = T_1 \cos 30°$

$T_2 = 0.8966T_1$ (a′)

Substitute (a′) into (b) and get:

(b) $(0.8966T_1) \sin 15° + T_1 \sin 30° = 416\text{ N}$

$0.7321T_1 = 416\text{ N}$

$T_1 = 568.23\text{ N} \xrightarrow{SD} \mathbf{568\ N}$

Substitute T_1 into (a′) and get:

(a′) $T_2 = 0.8966(568.23\text{ N}) = 509.48\text{ N} \xrightarrow{SD} \mathbf{509\ N}$

8. Begin by drawing a diagram and recording the data.

$D_S = 2\bar{0}$ km, $T_S = 2.0$ hr, α, θ, D

$D_E = 8.0$ km, $T_E = 4.0$ hr

(a) $D_T = D_S + D_E = 20\text{ km} + 8.0\text{ km} = \mathbf{28\ km}$

(b) $D = \sqrt{(20)^2 + (8.0)^2} = 21.54\text{ km}$

$\theta = \tan^{-1} \dfrac{8.0}{20} = 21.80°$

$\alpha = -90° + 21.80° = -68.20°$

$\vec{D} = 21.54\angle{-68.20°}\text{ km} \xrightarrow{SD} \mathbf{22\angle{-68.20°}\ km}$

(c) $\vec{v} = \dfrac{\vec{D}}{T_T} = \dfrac{21.54\angle{-68.20°}\text{ km}}{6.0\text{ hr}} = \mathbf{3.6\angle{-68.20°}\ \dfrac{km}{hr}}$

(d) $v = \dfrac{D_T}{T_T} = \dfrac{28\text{ km}}{6.0\text{ hr}} = 4.67\ \dfrac{\text{km}}{\text{hr}} \xrightarrow{SD} \mathbf{4.7\ \dfrac{km}{hr}}$

9. Begin by finding the mass of the ethyl alcohol.

$\rho = \dfrac{m}{V}$

$806\ \dfrac{\text{kg}}{\text{m}^3} = \dfrac{m}{648\text{ m}^3}$

$m = 522{,}288\text{ kg}$

Calculate the weight.

$w = mg = 522{,}288\ \cancel{\text{kg}} \times 9.81\ \dfrac{\text{N}}{\cancel{\text{kg}}} = 5.124 \times 10^6\text{ N} \xrightarrow{SD} \mathbf{5.12 \times 10^6\ N}$

10. Begin by converting 1800 cm^3 to m^3.

$1800\ \cancel{\text{cm}^3} \times \dfrac{1\text{ m}^3}{(100)^3\ \cancel{\text{cm}^3}} = 1.8 \times 10^{-3}\text{ m}^3$

Calculate the density.

$\rho = \dfrac{m}{V} = \dfrac{3.8\text{ kg}}{1.8 \times 10^{-3}\text{ m}^3} = 2111\ \dfrac{\text{kg}}{\text{m}^3} \xrightarrow{SD} \mathbf{2100\ \dfrac{kg}{m^3}}$

11. $w = mg$

$800 \text{ N} = m \times 9.81 \frac{\text{N}}{\text{kg}}$

$m = 81.549 \text{ kg} \xrightarrow{\text{SD}}$ **81.5 kg**

12. $w = mg$

$= 999 \cancel{\text{kg}} \times 9.81 \frac{\text{N}}{\cancel{\text{kg}}} = 9800.19 \text{ N} \xrightarrow{\text{SD}}$ **$98\bar{0}0$ N**

13.

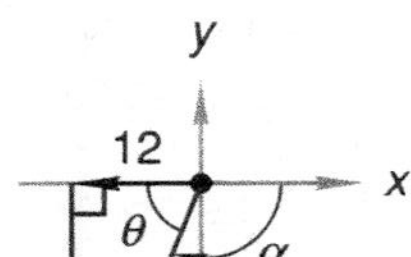

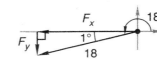

$R = \sqrt{(12)^2 + (31)^2} = 33.24$

$\theta = \tan^{-1} \frac{31}{12} = 68.84°$

$\alpha = -180° + 68.84° = -111.16°$

$\vec{R} = 33.24\underline{/-111.16°} \xrightarrow{\text{SD}}$ **$33\underline{/-111.16°}$**

14.

$R = \sqrt{(42)^2 + (64)^2} = 76.55$

$\theta = \tan^{-1} \frac{64}{42} = 56.73°$

Since θ is a 4th-quadrant angle: $\theta = -56.73°$

$\vec{R} = 76.55\underline{/-56.73°} \xrightarrow{\text{SD}}$ **$77\underline{/-56.73°}$**

15.

$F_x = 16 \cos 34° = 13.26$
$F_y = 16 \sin 34° = 8.95$

$P_x = 16 \cos 34° = 13.26$
$P_y = (-)16 \sin 34° = -8.95$

$R_x = F_x + P_x = 13.26 + 13.26 = 26.52$
$R_y = F_y + P_y = 8.95 - 8.95 = 0$

$\vec{R} = 26.52i + 0j$

Convert this to polar form and get:

$R = 26.52$
$\theta = 0°$

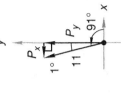

$\vec{R} = 26.52\underline{/0°} \xrightarrow{\text{SD}}$ **$27\underline{/0°}$**

16.

$F_x = (-)18 \cos 1° = -17.997$
$F_y = (-)18 \sin 1° = -0.314$

$P_x = (-)11 \sin 1° = -0.192$
$P_y = 11 \cos 1° = 10.998$

$R_x = F_x + P_x = -17.997 - 0.192 = -18.189$
$R_y = F_y + P_y = -0.314 + 10.998 = 10.684$

$\vec{R} = -18.189i + 10.684j$

Convert this to polar form and get:

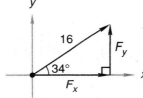

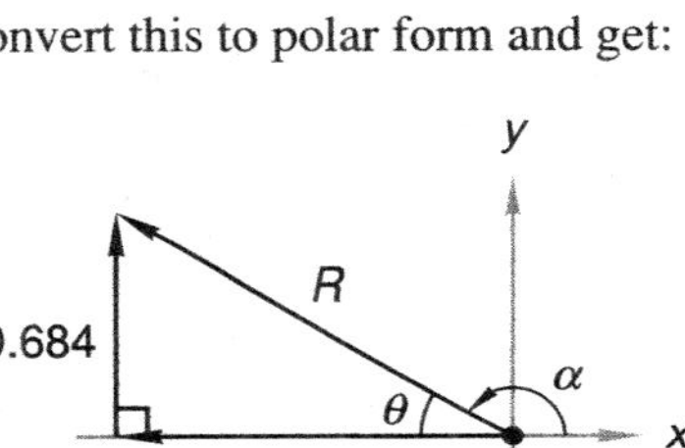

$R = \sqrt{(18.189)^2 + (10.684)^2} = 21$

$\theta = \tan^{-1} \frac{10.684}{18.189} = 30.43°$

$\alpha = 180° - 30.43° = 149.57°$

$\vec{R} =$ **$21\underline{/149.57°}$**

17. $\frac{(125)(1.03 \times 10^{-6})(8.36)}{(5.13 \times 10^{4})(-0.052 \times 10^{3})} \approx \frac{(1 \times 10^{2})(1 \times 10^{-6})(8 \times 10^{0})}{(5 \times 10^{4})(-5 \times 10^{1})}$

$= -3.2 \times 10^{-10} \xrightarrow{\text{SD}}$ **-3×10^{-10}**

18. $\dfrac{(1.206 \times 10^{86})(3.42 \times 10^{-6})}{(1024)(2.048 \times 10^{8})(9.52 \times 10^{2})} \approx \dfrac{(1 \times 10^{86})(3 \times 10^{-6})}{(1 \times 10^{3})(2 \times 10^{8})(1 \times 10^{3})}$

$= 1.5 \times 10^{66} \xrightarrow{SD} \mathbf{2 \times 10^{66}}$

19. $1500 \dfrac{\cancel{yd}}{\cancel{g}} \times \dfrac{3\ \cancel{ft}}{1\ \cancel{yd}} \times \dfrac{12\ \cancel{in.}}{1\ \cancel{ft}} \times \dfrac{2.54\ \cancel{cm}}{1\ \cancel{in.}} \times \dfrac{1\text{ m}}{100\ \cancel{cm}} \times \dfrac{1000\ \cancel{g}}{1\text{ kg}}$

$= 1.37 \times 10^{6}\ \dfrac{\text{m}}{\text{kg}} \xrightarrow{SD} \mathbf{1.4 \times 10^{6}\ \dfrac{m}{kg}}$

20. $\dfrac{\left(3.45 \times 10^{3}\ \dfrac{\text{in.}}{\text{s}}\right)(4.06 \times 10^{-6}\text{ s})\left(\dfrac{2.54\text{ cm}}{1\text{ in.}}\right)}{(1.02 \times 10^{-4})(3.1416)} = 1.1103 \times 10^{2}\text{ cm}$

Convert to meters and get:

$1.1103 \times 10^{2}\ \cancel{cm} \times \dfrac{1\text{ m}}{100\ \cancel{cm}} = 1.1103\text{ m} \xrightarrow{SD} \mathbf{1.11\ m}$

Problem Set 8

1. $F = F_s = \mu_s F_N$

$640\text{ N} = \mu_s(942\text{ N})$

$\mu_s = 0.6794 \xrightarrow{SD} \mathbf{0.679}$

2. $F = F_s = \mu_s F_N$

$= 0.62(9.0\ \cancel{kg})\left(9.81\ \dfrac{\text{N}}{\cancel{kg}}\right)$

$= 54.74\text{ N} \xrightarrow{SD} \mathbf{55\ N}$

3. $F = F_k = \mu_k F_N$

$39\text{ N} = \mu_k(96\text{ N})$

$\mu_k = 0.4063 \xrightarrow{SD} \mathbf{0.41}$

4. $F = F_s = \mu_s F_N$

$= 0.84(10.0\ \cancel{kg})\left(9.81\ \dfrac{\text{N}}{\cancel{kg}}\right)$

$= 82.404\text{ N}$

Since the applied force is greater than the force of friction, **the block will move.**

5. $v_{av} = \dfrac{x_2 - x_1}{t_2 - t_1} = \dfrac{14 - 38}{10 - 6}\ \dfrac{\text{m}}{\text{s}} = \mathbf{-6\ \dfrac{m}{s}}$

6. $a_{av} = \dfrac{v_2 - v_1}{t_2 - t_1} = \dfrac{184 - 131}{8.00 - 0}\ \dfrac{\text{km/hr}}{\text{s}} = +6.625\ \dfrac{\text{km/hr}}{\text{s}}$

Convert to m·s^{-2} and get:

$+6.625\ \dfrac{\cancel{km}}{\cancel{hr}\cdot\text{s}} \times \dfrac{1000\text{ m}}{1\ \cancel{km}} \times \dfrac{1\ \cancel{hr}}{60\ \cancel{min}} \times \dfrac{1\ \cancel{min}}{60\text{ s}}$

$= +1.8403\ \dfrac{\text{m}}{\text{s}^2} \xrightarrow{SD} \mathbf{+1.84\ \dfrac{m}{s^2}}$

7. $v_{av} = \dfrac{x_2 - x_1}{t_2 - t_1} = \dfrac{14 - 12}{32.0 - 2.0}\ \dfrac{\text{cm}}{\text{s}} = +6.67 \times 10^{-2}\ \dfrac{\text{cm}}{\text{s}}$

Convert to m·s^{-1} and get:

$+6.67 \times 10^{-2}\ \dfrac{\cancel{cm}}{\text{s}} \times \dfrac{1\text{ m}}{100\ \cancel{cm}}$

$= +6.67 \times 10^{-4}\ \dfrac{\text{m}}{\text{s}} \xrightarrow{SD} \mathbf{+6.7 \times 10^{-4}\ \dfrac{m}{s}}$

8. First, we draw the diagram.

°F	°C	
212°	100°	**Boiling**
180 spaces	100 spaces	
32°	0°	**Freezing**

Then, we determine the number of degrees above or below the freezing temperature of water.

$$68° - 32 = 36°$$

Thus, we are 36 Fahrenheit degrees above freezing. Since the ratio of the increments is

$$\text{Ratio} = \frac{°\text{C}}{°\text{F}} = \frac{100}{180} = \frac{5}{9}$$

it takes fewer Celsius degrees to measure an interval, so we multiply by 5 over 9.

$$36° \times \frac{5}{9} = \mathbf{2\overline{0}°C}$$

9. Convert 1465 K to °C.

$$T_K = T_C + 273$$
$$1465 = T_C + 273$$
$$T_C = 1192°C$$

Convert 1192°C to °F.

$$T_F = \frac{9}{5}T_C + 32$$
$$= \frac{9}{5}(1192°) + 32$$
$$= 2177.6°F \xrightarrow{SD} \mathbf{2178°F}$$

10. (a) $32T_1 + 18T_2 = 14 \rightarrow (1) \rightarrow \quad 32T_1 + 18T_2 = 14$

(b) $8T_1 + 6T_2 = 2 \rightarrow (-3) \rightarrow \quad -24T_1 - 18T_2 = -6$

$$8T_1 = 8$$
$$T_1 = \mathbf{1}$$

Substitute T_1 into (b) and get:

(b) $8(1) + 6T_2 = 2$

$$6T_2 = -6$$
$$T_2 = \mathbf{-1}$$

11.

T_2 T_1 35°   50°   68 N

(a) $\Sigma F_x = 0;\ T_1 \cos 50° - T_2 \cos 35° = 0$

(b) $\Sigma F_y = 0;\ T_2 \sin 35° + T_1 \sin 50° - 68\text{ N} = 0$

Solve (a) for T_2 and get:

(a) $T_2 \cos 35° = T_1 \cos 50°$

$$T_2 = 0.785T_1 \qquad (a')$$

Substitute (a′) into (b) and get:

(b) $(0.785T_1) \sin 35° + T_1 \sin 50° = 68\text{ N}$

$$1.216T_1 = 68\text{ N}$$
$$T_1 = 55.92\text{ N} \xrightarrow{SD} \mathbf{56\ N}$$

Substitute T_1 into (a′) and get:

(a′) $T_2 = 0.785(55.92\text{ N}) = 43.90\text{ N} \xrightarrow{SD} \mathbf{44\ N}$

12. Begin by drawing a diagram and recording the data.

$D_E = 42$ km
$T_E = 6$ hr
$D_S = 16$ km
$T_S = 8$ hr
θ D

Find the average speed.

$$v = \frac{D_T}{T_T} = \frac{42\text{ km} + 16\text{ km}}{6\text{ hr} + 8\text{ hr}} = 4.14\ \frac{\text{km}}{\text{hr}} \xrightarrow{SD} \mathbf{4\ \frac{km}{hr}}$$

Find the average velocity.

$$D = \sqrt{(42)^2 + (16)^2} = 44.94\text{ km}$$

$$\theta = \tan^{-1}\frac{16}{42} = 20.85°$$

Since θ is a 4th-quadrant angle: $\theta = -20.85°$

$$\vec{v} = \frac{D\angle\theta}{T_T} = \frac{44.94\angle{-20.85°}\text{ km}}{14\text{ hr}}$$

$$= 3.21\angle{-20.85°}\ \frac{\text{km}}{\text{hr}} \xrightarrow{SD} \mathbf{3\angle{-20.85°}\ \frac{km}{hr}}$$

13. Begin by finding the mass of the block.

$$\rho = \frac{m}{V}$$

$$19{,}300\ \frac{\text{kg}}{\text{m}^3} = \frac{m}{0.00400\text{ m}^3}$$

$$m = 77.2\text{ kg}$$

Calculate the weight.

$$w = mg = 77.2\ \cancel{\text{kg}} \times 9.81\ \frac{\text{N}}{\cancel{\text{kg}}} = 757.33\text{ N} \xrightarrow{SD} \mathbf{757\ N}$$

To calculate how much the block is worth, use two unit multipliers and get:

$$757.33\ \cancel{\text{N}} \times \frac{3.280\ \cancel{\text{troy oz.}}}{1\ \cancel{\text{N}}} \times \frac{\$300}{1\ \cancel{\text{troy oz.}}} = \$745{,}213 \xrightarrow{SD} \mathbf{\$700{,}000}$$

14. $\rho = \frac{m}{V} = \frac{234\text{ kg}}{0.33\text{ m}^3} = 709.09\ \frac{\text{kg}}{\text{m}^3}$

Since this density is less than the density of water, **the object will float in water.**

15. $w = mg$

$12.5 \text{ N} = m \times 9.81 \frac{\text{N}}{\text{kg}}$

$m = 1.274 \text{ kg} \xrightarrow{\text{SD}}$ **1.27 kg**

16. Add these vectors in rectangular form.

$12i - 48j$
$-4.0i + 16j$
$\mathbf{8.0i - 32j}$

17.

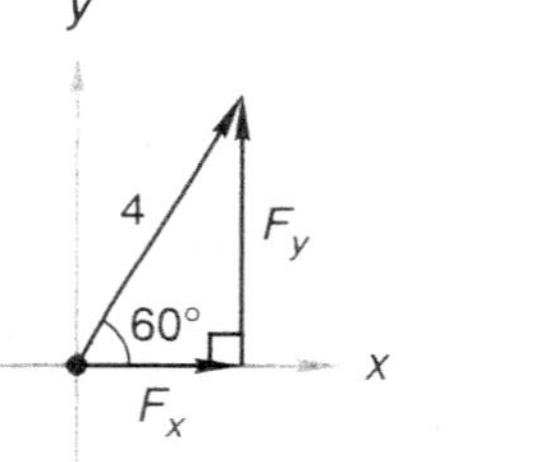

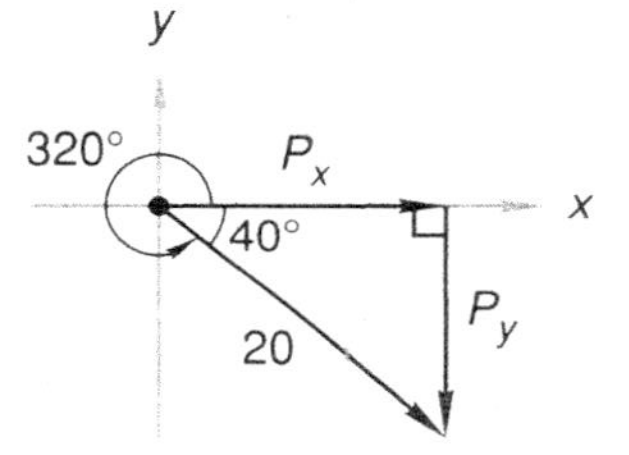

$F_x = 4 \cos 60° = 2.000$
$F_y = 4 \sin 60° = 3.464$

$P_x = 20 \cos 40° = 15.321$
$P_y = (-)20 \sin 40° = -12.856$

$R_x = F_x + P_x = 2.000 + 15.321 = 17.321$
$R_y = F_y + P_y = 3.464 - 12.856 = -9.392$

$\vec{R} = 17.321i - 9.392j$

Convert this to polar form and get:

$R = \sqrt{(17.321)^2 + (9.392)^2} = 19.703$

$\theta = \tan^{-1} \frac{9.392}{17.321} = 28.47°$

Since θ is a 4th-quadrant angle: $\theta = -28.47°$

$\vec{R} = 19.703\angle{-28.47°} \xrightarrow{\text{SD}}$ $\mathbf{20\angle{-28.47°}}$

18. $\frac{(4682 \times 10^{-14})(8.25 \times 10^5)}{(5786 \times 10^{-7})(0.000462 \times 10^5)} \approx \frac{(5 \times 10^{-11})(8 \times 10^5)}{(6 \times 10^{-4})(5 \times 10^1)}$

$= 1.3 \times 10^{-3} \xrightarrow{\text{SD}}$ $\mathbf{1 \times 10^{-3}}$

19. $50\bar{0} \frac{\cancel{\text{m}^2}}{\cancel{\text{L}}} \times \frac{(100)^2 \cancel{\text{cm}^2}}{1 \cancel{\text{m}^2}} \times \frac{1 \cancel{\text{in.}^2}}{(2.54)^2 \cancel{\text{cm}^2}} \times \frac{1 \cancel{\text{ft}^2}}{(12)^2 \cancel{\text{in.}^2}} \times \frac{1 \text{ yd}^2}{(3)^2 \cancel{\text{ft}^2}}$

$\times \frac{3.785 \cancel{\text{L}}}{1 \text{ gal}} = 2263.4 \frac{\text{yd}^2}{\text{gal}} \xrightarrow{\text{SD}}$ $\mathbf{2260 \frac{yd^2}{gal}}$

20. $\frac{\left(0.038 \frac{\text{mi}}{\text{hr}}\right)\left(5.280 \times 10^3 \frac{\text{ft}}{\text{mi}}\right)\left(12.0 \frac{\text{in.}}{\text{ft}}\right)}{\left(0.3937 \frac{\text{in.}}{\text{cm}}\right)\left(1.00 \times 10^2 \frac{\text{cm}}{\text{m}}\right)} = 61.155 \frac{\text{m}}{\text{hr}}$

Convert to meters per second and get:

$61.155 \frac{\text{m}}{\cancel{\text{hr}}} \times \frac{1 \cancel{\text{hr}}}{60 \cancel{\text{min}}} \times \frac{1 \cancel{\text{min}}}{60 \text{ s}} = 1.699 \times 10^{-2} \frac{\text{m}}{\text{s}} \xrightarrow{\text{SD}}$ $\mathbf{1.7 \times 10^{-2} \frac{m}{s}}$

PROBLEM SET 9

1.

$\Sigma M = 0$
$-8 \text{ N}(14 \text{ m}) - 2 \text{ N}(6 \text{ m}) + 6 \text{ N}(4 \text{ m}) + F(5 \text{ m}) = 0$
$-112 \text{ N·m} - 12 \text{ N·m} + 24 \text{ N·m} + F(5 \text{ m}) = 0$
$F(5 \text{ m}) = 100 \text{ N·m}$
$F =$ **20 N**

2. $\Sigma\tau = 30 \text{ N}(9 \text{ cm}) - 40 \text{ N}(6 \text{ cm})$
$= 270 \text{ N·cm} - 240 \text{ N·cm} = 30 \text{ N·cm}$

Convert to N·m and get:

$30 \text{ N·}\cancel{\text{cm}} \times \frac{1 \text{ m}}{100 \cancel{\text{cm}}} = 0.3 \text{ N·m}$

$\tau =$ **0.3 N·m; Positive (clockwise) torque**

3.

$\Sigma M = 0$
$-15{,}455(5) - 8543(1) + F(2.00) + 10{,}000(7.0) = 0$
$-77{,}275 - 8543 + F(2.00) + 70{,}000 = 0$
$F(2.00) = 15{,}818$
$F = 7909 \text{ N} \xrightarrow{\text{SD}}$ **8000 N**

4. $F = F_k = \mu_k F_N$

$312\text{ N} = \mu_k(700\text{ N})$

$\mu_k = 0.4457 \xrightarrow{SD}$ **0.446**

5. $F = F_s = \mu_s F_N$

$= 0.53(76\text{ kg})\left(9.81\ \frac{\text{N}}{\text{kg}}\right)$

$= 395.15\text{ N} \xrightarrow{SD}$ **4$\bar{0}$0 N**

6. The value of F_N equals the weight of the block.

$F = F_k = \mu_k F_N$

$89\text{ N} = 0.43F_N$

$F_N = 206.98\text{ N} \xrightarrow{SD}$ **210 N**

Calculate the mass of the block.

$w = mg$

$206.98\text{ N} = m \times 9.81\ \frac{\text{N}}{\text{kg}}$

$m = 21.10\text{ kg} \xrightarrow{SD}$ **21 kg**

7. $v_{av} = \frac{x_2 - x_1}{t_2 - t_1} = \frac{100 - 50}{5.2 - 0}\frac{\text{yd}}{\text{s}} = +9.615\ \frac{\text{yd}}{\text{s}}$

Convert to $\text{m}\cdot\text{s}^{-1}$ and get:

$+9.615\ \frac{\text{yd}}{\text{s}} \times \frac{3\text{ ft}}{1\text{ yd}} \times \frac{12\text{ in.}}{1\text{ ft}} \times \frac{2.54\text{ cm}}{1\text{ in.}} \times \frac{1\text{ m}}{100\text{ cm}}$

$= +8.79\ \frac{\text{m}}{\text{s}} \xrightarrow{SD}$ **+8.8 $\frac{\text{m}}{\text{s}}$**

8. $v_{av} = \frac{y_2 - y_1}{t_2 - t_1} = \frac{48{,}600 - 26}{560 - 120}\frac{\text{cm}}{\text{s}} = +110.40\ \frac{\text{cm}}{\text{s}} \xrightarrow{SD}$ **+110 $\frac{\text{cm}}{\text{s}}$**

9. First, we draw the diagram.

°F	°C	
212°	100°	**Boiling**
180 spaces	100 spaces	
32°	0°	**Freezing**

Then, we determine the number of degrees above or below the freezing temperature of water.

$$-10° - 32 = -42°$$

Thus, we are 42 Fahrenheit degrees below freezing. Since the ratio of the increments is

$$\text{Ratio} = \frac{°\text{C}}{°\text{F}} = \frac{100}{180} = \frac{5}{9}$$

it takes fewer Celsius degrees to measure an interval, so we multiply by 5 over 9.

$$-42° \times \frac{5}{9} = -23.3°\text{C} \xrightarrow{SD} \mathbf{-23°C}$$

10. Convert 472 K to °C.

$T_K = T_C + 273$

$472 = T_C + 273$

$T_C = 199°\text{C}$

Convert 199°C to °F.

$T_F = \frac{9}{5}T_C + 32$

$= \frac{9}{5}(199°) + 32$

$= 390.2°\text{F} \xrightarrow{SD}$ **39$\bar{0}$°F**

11.

T_2, T_1, 32°, P, 315 N

(a) $\Sigma F_x = 0;\ T_1 \cos 32° - T_2 = 0$

(b) $\Sigma F_y = 0;\ T_1 \sin 32° - 315\text{ N} = 0$

Solve (b) for T_1 and get:

(b) $T_1 \sin 32° = 315\text{ N}$

$T_1 = 594.43\text{ N} \xrightarrow{SD}$ **594 N**

Substitute T_1 into (a) and get:

(a) $T_2 = T_1 \cos 32°$

$= (594.43\text{ N}) \cos 32° = 504.11\text{ N} \xrightarrow{SD}$ **504 N**

12.

(a) $\Sigma F_x = 0;\ 36\text{ N} - T_1 \cos 41° = 0$

(b) $\Sigma F_y = 0;\ T_1 \sin 41° - T_2 = 0$

Solve (a) for T_1 and get:

(a) $T_1 \cos 41° = 36\text{ N}$

$$T_1 = 47.70\text{ N} \xrightarrow{\text{SD}} \mathbf{48\ N}$$

Substitute T_1 into (b) and get:

(b) $T_2 = T_1 \sin 41°$

$$= (47.70\text{ N}) \sin 41° = 31.29\text{ N} \xrightarrow{\text{SD}} \mathbf{31\ N}$$

13. Begin by drawing a diagram and recording the data.

$D_E = 30\bar{0}$ m
$T_E = 30.0$ s
$D_S = 20\bar{0}$ m
$T_S = 20.0$ s
$15\bar{0}$ m
$D_N = 50.0$ m
$T_N = 5.00$ s

(a) $D_T = D_E + D_S + D_N = 300\text{ m} + 200\text{ m} + 50.0\text{ m} = \mathbf{55\bar{0}\ m}$

(b) $v = \dfrac{D_T}{T_T} = \dfrac{550\text{ m}}{55.0\text{ s}} = \mathbf{10.0\ \dfrac{m}{s}}$

(c) $D = \sqrt{(300)^2 + (150)^2} = 335.41\text{ m}$

$\theta = \tan^{-1} \dfrac{150}{300} = 26.57°$

Since θ is a 4th-quadrant angle: $\theta = -26.57°$

$\vec{D} = 335.41\underline{/-26.57°}\text{ m} \xrightarrow{\text{SD}} \mathbf{335\underline{/-26.57°}\ m}$

(d) $\vec{v} = \dfrac{\vec{D}}{T_T} = \dfrac{335.41\underline{/-26.57°}\text{ m}}{55.0\text{ s}}$

$$= 6.098\underline{/-26.57°}\ \frac{\text{m}}{\text{s}} \xrightarrow{\text{SD}} \mathbf{6.10\underline{/-26.57°}\ \frac{m}{s}}$$

14. $w = mg$

$$42\text{ N} = m \times 9.81\ \frac{\text{N}}{\text{kg}}$$

$$m = 4.281\text{ kg} \xrightarrow{\text{SD}} \mathbf{4.3\ kg}$$

15. Begin by converting 2.14 $\text{g}\cdot\text{cm}^{-3}$ to $\text{kg}\cdot\text{m}^{-3}$.

$$2.14\ \frac{\cancel{\text{g}}}{\cancel{\text{cm}^3}} \times \frac{1\text{ kg}}{1000\ \cancel{\text{g}}} \times \frac{(100)^3\ \cancel{\text{cm}^3}}{1\text{ m}^3} = 2140\ \frac{\text{kg}}{\text{m}^3}$$

Calculate the volume.

$$\rho = \frac{m}{V}$$

$$2140\ \frac{\text{kg}}{\text{m}^3} = \frac{28.4\text{ kg}}{V}$$

$$V = 1.327 \times 10^{-2}\text{ m}^3 \xrightarrow{\text{SD}} \mathbf{1.33 \times 10^{-2}\ m^3}$$

16.

$$\rho = \frac{m}{V}$$

$$2700\ \frac{\text{kg}}{\text{m}^3} = \frac{m}{0.53\text{ m}^3}$$

$$m = 1431\text{ kg} \xrightarrow{\text{SD}} \mathbf{1400\ kg}$$

17.

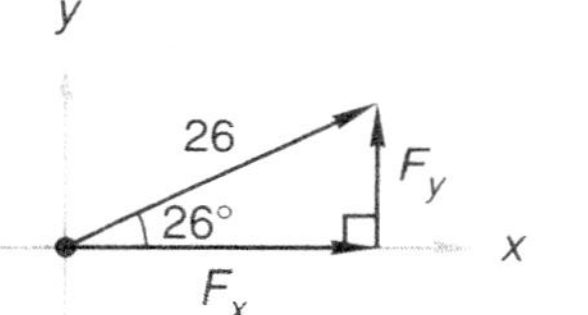

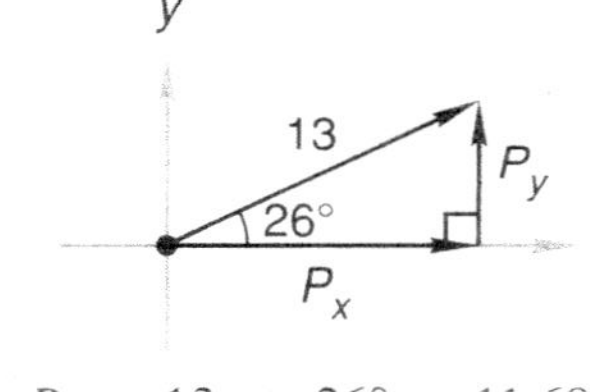

$F_x = 26 \cos 26° = 23.37$

$F_y = 26 \sin 26° = 11.40$

$P_x = 13 \cos 26° = 11.68$

$P_y = 13 \sin 26° = 5.70$

$R_x = F_x - P_x = 23.37 - 11.68 = 11.69$

$R_y = F_y - P_y = 11.40 - 5.70 = 5.70$

$$\vec{R} = 11.69i + 5.70j \xrightarrow{\text{SD}} \mathbf{12i + 5.7j}$$

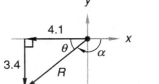

18. $R = \sqrt{(4.1)^2 + (3.4)^2} = 5.33$

$\theta = \tan^{-1}\frac{3.4}{4.1} = 39.67°$

$\alpha = -180° + 39.67° = -140.33°$

$\vec{R} = 5.33\angle{-140.33°} \xrightarrow{SD} \mathbf{5.3\angle{-140.33°}}$

19. $$\frac{\left(0.56\ \frac{cm^3}{g}\right)\left(128\ \frac{g}{mole}\right)}{\left(6.022 \times 10^{23}\ \frac{molecules}{mole}\right)}$$

$= 1.190 \times 10^{-22}\ \frac{cm^3}{molecule} \xrightarrow{SD} \mathbf{1.2 \times 10^{-22}\ \frac{cm^3}{molecule}}$

20. $$\left(\frac{1\ cm^3}{0.97\ g} \cdot \frac{23\ g}{1\ mole} \cdot \frac{1\ mole}{6.022 \times 10^{23}}\right)^{1/3} = (3.937 \times 10^{-23}\ cm^3)^{1/3}$$

$= 3.402 \times 10^{-8}\ cm \xrightarrow{SD} \mathbf{3.4 \times 10^{-8}\ cm}$

Problem Set 10

1. $v_{av} = \frac{x_2 - x_1}{t_2 - t_1} = \frac{90 - 30}{8.0 - 4.0}\frac{m}{s} = \mathbf{+15\ \frac{m}{s}}$

2. Answers to this problem may vary due to differing data points. One possible solution is given here:

$a_{av} = \frac{v_2 - v_1}{t_2 - t_1} = \frac{5 - 25}{5.0 - 2.0}\frac{m/s}{s} = -6.67\ \frac{m}{s^2} \xrightarrow{SD} \mathbf{-6.7\ \frac{m}{s^2}}$

3. Calculate the displacements for the following time intervals:

$\Delta x_{0,2} = -20\ \frac{m}{\cancel{s}} \times 2\cancel{s} = -40\ m \qquad \Delta x_{2,4} = \frac{-20\ \frac{m}{\cancel{s}} \times 2\cancel{s}}{2} = -20\ m$

$\Delta x_{4,8} = \frac{30\ \frac{m}{\cancel{s}} \times 4\cancel{s}}{2} = +60\ m$

Sum these displacements with the initial position and get:
$x_8 = 10\ m - 40\ m - 20\ m + 60\ m = \mathbf{1\bar{0}\ m}$

4. $\Sigma\tau = -50\ N(10\ cm) + 60\ N(7\ cm) = -80\ N\cdot cm$

Convert to N·m and get:

$-80\ N\cdot\cancel{cm} \times \frac{1\ m}{100\ \cancel{cm}} = -0.8\ N\cdot m$

$\tau =$ **0.8 N·m; Negative (counterclockwise) torque**

5.
$$\begin{aligned}\Sigma M &= 0\\ -3\ N(7\ cm) - 7\ N(5\ cm) + F(3\ cm) + 4\ N(5\ cm) &= 0\\ -21\ N\cdot cm - 35\ N\cdot cm + F(3\ cm) + 20\ N\cdot cm &= 0\\ F(3\ cm) &= 36\ N\cdot cm\\ F &= 12\ N \xrightarrow{SD} \mathbf{10\ N}\end{aligned}$$

6.
$$\begin{aligned}\Sigma M &= 0\\ -8\ N(5\ cm) - 12\ N(3\ cm) + F(4\ cm) + 6\ N(7\ cm) &= 0\\ -40\ N\cdot cm - 36\ N\cdot cm + F(4\ cm) + 42\ N\cdot cm &= 0\\ F(4\ cm) &= 34\ N\cdot cm\\ F &= 8.5\ N \xrightarrow{SD} \mathbf{9\ N}\end{aligned}$$

7. Begin by finding the weight of the block.

$w = mg = (42\ \cancel{kg})\left(9.81\ \frac{N}{\cancel{kg}}\right) = 412.02\ N$

Calculate the force.
$F = F_s = \mu_s F_N$
$= 0.62(412.02\ N)$
$= 255.45\ N \xrightarrow{SD} \mathbf{260\ N}$

8. $F = F_k = \mu_k F_N = 0.31(113\ \cancel{kg})\left(9.81\ \frac{N}{\cancel{kg}}\right) = 343.64\ N \xrightarrow{SD} \mathbf{340\ N}$

9. Begin by converting units to feet.

$x_1 = 10\ \cancel{units} \times \frac{2000\ ft}{1\ \cancel{unit}} = 20{,}000\ ft$

$x_2 = 2\ \cancel{units} \times \frac{2000\ ft}{1\ \cancel{unit}} = 4000\ ft$

$v_{av} = \frac{x_2 - x_1}{t_2 - t_1} = \frac{4000 - 20{,}000}{214 - 205}\frac{ft}{s} = -1777.78\ \frac{ft}{s} \xrightarrow{SD} -2000\ \frac{ft}{s}$

Since the distance between the missile and the target decreases over the time interval, the velocity may be written as **2000 ft/s toward the target.**

10. $v_{av} = \frac{y_2 - y_1}{t_2 - t_1} = \frac{80{,}000 - 2000}{30 - 10}\frac{\text{ft}}{\text{s}} = +3900\ \frac{\text{ft}}{\text{s}}$

Convert to $\text{m}\cdot\text{s}^{-1}$ and get:

$+3900\ \frac{\text{ft}}{\text{s}} \times \frac{12\ \text{in.}}{1\ \text{ft}} \times \frac{2.54\ \text{cm}}{1\ \text{in.}} \times \frac{1\ \text{m}}{100\ \text{cm}}$

$= +1188.72\ \frac{\text{m}}{\text{s}} \xrightarrow{\text{SD}} \mathbf{+1000\ \frac{m}{s}}$

11. Convert 26 K to °C.

$T_K = T_C + 273$
$26 = T_C + 273$
$T_C = -247°\text{C}$

Convert –247°C to °F.

$T_F = \frac{9}{5}T_C + 32$
$= \frac{9}{5}(-247°) + 32$
$= -412.6°\text{F} \xrightarrow{\text{SD}} \mathbf{-410°F}$

12.

(a) $\sum F_x = 0;\ T_2 \cos 41° - T_1 \cos 27° = 0$
(b) $\sum F_y = 0;\ T_1 \sin 27° + T_2 \sin 41° - 37\ \text{N} = 0$

Solve (a) for T_1 and get:
(a) $T_1 \cos 27° = T_2 \cos 41°$
$T_1 = 0.847T_2$ (a′)

Substitute (a′) into (b) and get:
(b) $(0.847T_2) \sin 27° + T_2 \sin 41° = 37\ \text{N}$
$1.041T_2 = 37\ \text{N}$
$T_2 = 35.54\ \text{N} \xrightarrow{\text{SD}} \mathbf{36\ N}$

Substitute T_2 into (a′) and get:
(a′) $T_1 = 0.847(35.54\ \text{N})$
$= 30.10\ \text{N} \xrightarrow{\text{SD}} \mathbf{3\bar{0}\ N}$

13.

(a) $\sum F_x = 0;\ (193\ \text{N}) \cos 36° - T_1 = 0$
(b) $\sum F_y = 0;\ (193\ \text{N}) \sin 36° - T_2 = 0$

Solve (a) for T_1 and get:
(a) $T_1 = (193\ \text{N}) \cos 36°$
$= 156.14\ \text{N} \xrightarrow{\text{SD}} \mathbf{156\ N}$

Solve (b) for T_2 and get:
(b) $T_2 = (193\ \text{N}) \sin 36°$
$= 113.44\ \text{N} \xrightarrow{\text{SD}} \mathbf{113\ N}$

14. Begin by drawing a diagram and recording the data.

$D_E = 115$ km, $T_E = 1.00$ hr
$D_N = 50.0$ km, $T_N = 0.500$ hr
$D_W = 12\bar{0}$ km, $T_W = 1.00$ hr
5.00 km

(a) $D_T = D_W + D_N + D_E = 120\ \text{km} + 50.0\ \text{km} + 115\ \text{km} = \mathbf{285\ km}$

(b) $v = \frac{D_T}{T_T} = \frac{285\ \text{km}}{2.50\ \text{hr}} = \mathbf{114\ \frac{km}{hr}}$

(c) $D = \sqrt{(5.00)^2 + (50.0)^2} = 50.249\ \text{km}$

$\theta = \tan^{-1}\frac{50.0}{5.00} = 84.29°$

$\alpha = 180° - 84.29° = 95.71°$

$\vec{D} = 50.249\underline{/95.71°}\ \text{km} \xrightarrow{\text{SD}} \mathbf{50.2\underline{/95.71°}\ km}$

(d) $\vec{v} = \frac{\vec{D}}{T_T} = \frac{50.249\underline{/95.71°}\ \text{km}}{2.50\ \text{hr}}$

$= 20.10\underline{/95.71°}\ \frac{\text{km}}{\text{hr}} \xrightarrow{\text{SD}} \mathbf{20.1\underline{/95.71°}\ \frac{km}{hr}}$

15. Begin by converting 1630 kg to grams.

$$1630 \text{ kg} \times \frac{1000 \text{ g}}{1 \text{ kg}} = 1.63 \times 10^6 \text{ g}$$

Calculate the density.

$$\rho = \frac{m}{V} = \frac{1.63 \times 10^6 \text{ g}}{5.13 \times 10^5 \text{ cm}^3} = 3.177 \frac{\text{g}}{\text{cm}^3} \xrightarrow{\text{SD}} \mathbf{3.18 \frac{g}{cm^3}}$$

16. Begin by finding the mass of the sculpture.

$$w = mg$$

$$300 \text{ N} = m \times 9.81 \frac{\text{N}}{\text{kg}}$$

$$m = 30.58 \text{ kg}$$

Calculate the volume.

$$\rho = \frac{m}{V}$$

$$265 \frac{\text{kg}}{\text{m}^3} = \frac{30.58 \text{ kg}}{V}$$

$$V = 0.1154 \text{ m}^3 \xrightarrow{\text{SD}} \mathbf{0.115 \ m^3}$$

17. $w = mg = 312 \text{ kg} \times 9.81 \frac{\text{N}}{\text{kg}} = 3060.72 \text{ N} \xrightarrow{\text{SD}} \mathbf{3060 \ N}$

18.

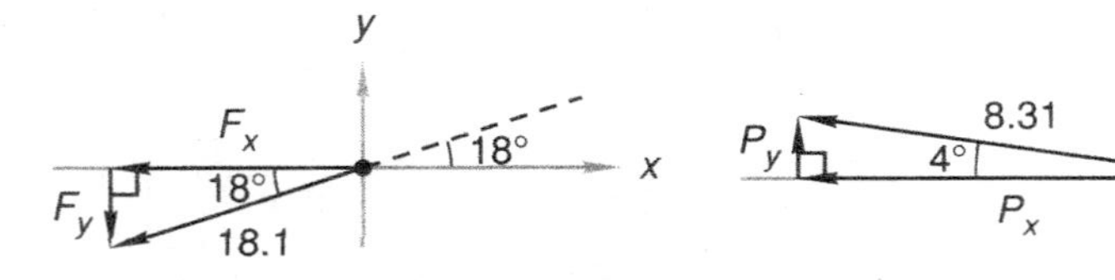

$F_x = (-)18.1 \cos 18° = -17.21$
$F_y = (-)18.1 \sin 18° = -5.59$

$P_x = (-)8.31 \cos 4° = -8.29$
$P_y = 8.31 \sin 4° = 0.580$

$R_x = F_x + P_x = -17.21 - 8.29 = -25.50$
$R_y = F_y + P_y = -5.59 + 0.580 = -5.01$

$$\vec{R} = -25.50i - 5.01j \xrightarrow{\text{SD}} \mathbf{-25.5i - 5.01j}$$

19. $4.80 \times 10^5 \text{ in.}^3 \times \frac{(2.54)^3 \text{ cm}^3}{1 \text{ in.}^3} \times \frac{1 \text{ m}^3}{(100)^3 \text{ cm}^3}$

$$= 7.866 \text{ m}^3 \xrightarrow{\text{SD}} \mathbf{7.87 \ m^3}$$

20. $\frac{(246 \times 10^{-6})(3.45 \times 10^{10})}{(6.3 \times 10^{-3})(8 \times 10^8)} \approx \frac{(2 \times 10^{-4})(3 \times 10^{10})}{(6 \times 10^{-3})(8 \times 10^8)}$

$$= 1.25 \xrightarrow{\text{SD}} \mathbf{1}$$

Problem Set 11

1.
$$\vec{F} = m\vec{a}$$
$$40\angle 20° \text{ N} = (4 \text{ kg})\,\vec{a}$$
$$\vec{a} = \mathbf{10\angle 20° \ m \cdot s^{-2}}$$

2. $\vec{F} = m\vec{a} = 10 \text{ kg}\left(30\angle 312° \frac{\text{m}}{\text{s}^2}\right) = \mathbf{300\angle 312° \ N}$

3. (a) $a_{av} = \frac{v_2 - v_1}{t_2 - t_1} = \frac{0 - 20}{2 - 0} \frac{\text{m/s}}{\text{s}} = \mathbf{-1\bar{0} \ \frac{m}{s^2}}$

(b) Calculate the displacements for the following time intervals:

$$\Delta x_{0,2} = \frac{20 \frac{\text{m}}{\text{s}} \times 2 \text{ s}}{2} = +20 \text{ m} \qquad \Delta x_{2,3} = -10 \frac{\text{m}}{\text{s}} \times 1 \text{ s} = -10 \text{ m}$$

Sum these displacements with the initial position and get:
$x_3 = -10 \text{ m} + 20 \text{ m} - 10 \text{ m} = \mathbf{0 \ m}$

4. (a) The graph shows that $x_0 = \mathbf{1\bar{0}0 \ m}$.

(b) $v_{av} = \frac{0 - 100}{5 - 0} \frac{\text{m}}{\text{s}} = \mathbf{-2\bar{0} \ \frac{m}{s}}$

(c) $v_{av} = \frac{-50 - 100}{15 - 0} \frac{\text{m}}{\text{s}} = \mathbf{-1\bar{0} \ \frac{m}{s}}$

5. $\sum \tau = 100 \text{ N}(4.0 \text{ cm}) - 60 \text{ N}(12 \text{ cm}) = -320 \text{ N} \cdot \text{cm}$

Convert to N·m and get:

$$-320 \text{ N} \cdot \text{cm} \times \frac{1 \text{ m}}{100 \text{ cm}} = -3.2 \text{ N} \cdot \text{m}$$

$\tau =$ **3.2 N·m; Negative (counterclockwise) torque**

6.
$$\Sigma M = 0$$
$$-3 \text{ N}(5 \text{ cm}) - 7 \text{ N}(3 \text{ cm}) + F(4 \text{ cm}) + 6 \text{ N}(6 \text{ cm}) = 0$$
$$-15 \text{ N} \cdot \text{cm} - 21 \text{ N} \cdot \text{cm} + F(4 \text{ cm}) + 36 \text{ N} \cdot \text{cm} = 0$$
$$F(4 \text{ cm}) = 0 \text{ N} \cdot \text{cm}$$
$$F = \mathbf{0 \ N}$$

7. $\sum \tau = 80\text{ N}(10\text{ cm}) - 60\text{ N}(15\text{ cm}) = -100\text{ N}\cdot\text{cm}$

Convert to N·m and get:

$$-100\text{ N}\cdot\cancel{\text{cm}} \times \frac{1\text{ m}}{100\ \cancel{\text{cm}}} = -1\text{ N}\cdot\text{m}$$

τ = **1 N·m; Negative (counterclockwise) torque**

8. $F = F_k = \mu_k F_N$

$$386\text{ N} = \mu_k(48\ \cancel{\text{kg}})\left(9.81\ \frac{\text{N}}{\cancel{\text{kg}}}\right)$$

$$\mu_k = 0.820 \xrightarrow{\text{SD}} \mathbf{0.82}$$

9. $F = F_s = \mu_s F_N$

$$525\text{ N} = \mu_s(201\ \cancel{\text{kg}})\left(9.81\ \frac{\text{N}}{\cancel{\text{kg}}}\right)$$

$$\mu_s = 0.2663 \xrightarrow{\text{SD}} \mathbf{0.266}$$

10. $$a_{av} = \frac{21.0576 - (23.58 \times 10^{-2})}{10 - 0}\ \frac{\text{m/s}}{\text{s}} = +2.08\ \frac{\text{m}}{\text{s}^2} \xrightarrow{\text{SD}} \mathbf{+2\ \frac{m}{s^2}}$$

11. (a) $v = \dfrac{5\text{ mi}}{30\ \cancel{\text{min}}} \times \dfrac{60\ \cancel{\text{min}}}{1\text{ hr}} = \mathbf{10\ \dfrac{mi}{hr}}$

(b) $\vec{v} = \dfrac{D\angle\theta}{T_T} = \dfrac{1\angle 90°\text{ mi}}{0.5\text{ hr}} = \mathbf{2\angle 90°\ \dfrac{mi}{hr}}$

12. Convert 194.5 K to °C.

$$T_K = T_C + 273$$
$$194.5 = T_C + 273$$
$$T_C = -78.50°\text{C}$$

Convert −78.50°C to °F.

$$T_F = \frac{9}{5}T_C + 32$$
$$= \frac{9}{5}(-78.50°) + 32$$
$$= \mathbf{-109.3°F}$$

13.

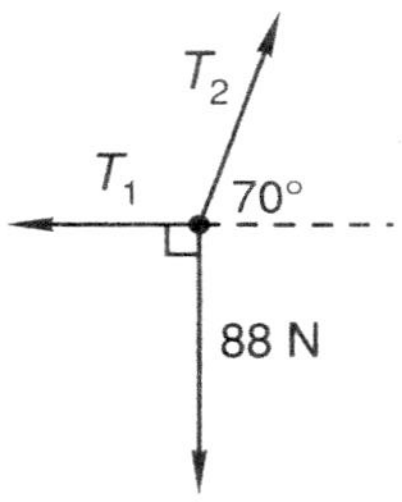

(a) $\sum F_x = 0;\ T_2 \cos 70° - T_1 = 0$
(b) $\sum F_y = 0;\ T_2 \sin 70° - 88\text{ N} = 0$

Solve (b) for T_2 and get:
(b) $T_2 \sin 70° = 88\text{ N}$

$$T_2 = 93.65\text{ N} \xrightarrow{\text{SD}} \mathbf{94\ N}$$

Substitute T_2 into (a) and get:

(a) $T_1 = (93.65\text{ N}) \cos 70° = 32.03\text{ N} \xrightarrow{\text{SD}} \mathbf{32\ N}$

14.

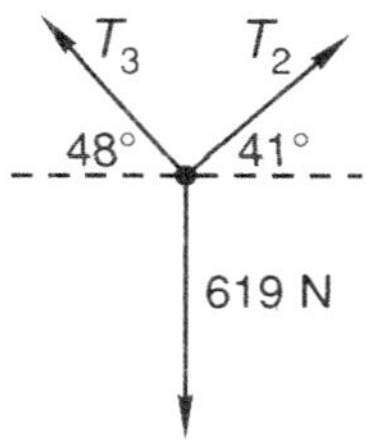

(a) $\sum F_x = 0;\ T_2 \cos 41° - T_3 \cos 48° = 0$
(b) $\sum F_y = 0;\ T_3 \sin 48° + T_2 \sin 41° - 619\text{ N} = 0$

Solve (a) for T_3 and get:
(a) $T_3 \cos 48° = T_2 \cos 41°$

$$T_3 = 1.128T_2 \qquad (a')$$

Substitute (a′) into (b) and get:
(b) $(1.128T_2) \sin 48° + T_2 \sin 41° = 619\text{ N}$

$$1.494T_2 = 619\text{ N}$$
$$T_2 = 414.32\text{ N} \xrightarrow{\text{SD}} \mathbf{414\ N}$$

Substitute T_2 into (a′) and get:

(a′) $T_3 = 1.128(414.32\text{ N}) = 467.35\text{ N} \xrightarrow{\text{SD}} \mathbf{467\ N}$

15. Begin by drawing a diagram and recording the data.

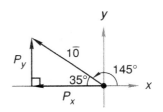

$D_S = 6.0$ ft
$T_S = 5.0$ min

$D_E = 3.0$ ft
$T_E = 2.0$ min

(a) $v = \frac{D_T}{T_T} = \frac{9.0 \text{ ft}}{7.0 \text{ min}} = 1.29 \frac{\text{ft}}{\text{min}} \xrightarrow{\text{SD}} \mathbf{1.3 \frac{ft}{min}}$

(b) $D = \sqrt{(6.0)^2 + (3.0)^2} = 6.71$ ft

$\theta = \tan^{-1}\frac{3.0}{6.0} = 26.57°$

$\alpha = -90° + 26.57° = -63.43°$

$\vec{v} = \frac{D\angle\alpha}{T_T} = \frac{6.71\angle{-63.43°} \text{ ft}}{7.0 \text{ min}}$

$= 0.959\angle{-63.43°} \frac{\text{ft}}{\text{min}} \xrightarrow{\text{SD}} \mathbf{0.96\angle{-63.43°} \frac{ft}{min}}$

16. Begin by finding the mass of the bar.

$w = mg$

$5292 \text{ N} = m \times 9.81 \frac{\text{N}}{\text{kg}}$

$m = 539.45$ kg

Calculate the density.

$\rho = \frac{m}{V} = \frac{539.45 \text{ kg}}{0.20 \text{ m}^3} = 2697.25 \frac{\text{kg}}{\text{m}^3} \xrightarrow{\text{SD}} \mathbf{2700 \frac{kg}{m^3}}$

Aluminum has a density of 2700 kg·m^{-3}.

17. Begin by finding the mass of the silver.

$\rho = \frac{m}{V}$

$10{,}500 \frac{\text{kg}}{\text{m}^3} = \frac{m}{0.086 \text{ m}^3}$

$m = 903$ kg

Now calculate the weight.

$w = mg$

$= 903 \text{ kg} \times 9.81 \frac{\text{N}}{\text{kg}}$

$= 8858.43 \text{ N} \xrightarrow{\text{SD}} \mathbf{8900 \text{ N}}$

To calculate the cost, use two unit multipliers and get:

$8858.43 \text{ N} \times \frac{3.28 \text{ troy oz.}}{1 \text{ N}} \times \frac{\$30}{1 \text{ troy oz.}} = \$871{,}670 \xrightarrow{\text{SD}} \mathbf{\$900{,}000}$

18. $w = mg$

$= 101 \text{ kg} \times 9.81 \frac{\text{N}}{\text{kg}}$

$= 990.81 \text{ N} \xrightarrow{\text{SD}} \mathbf{991 \text{ N}}$

19.

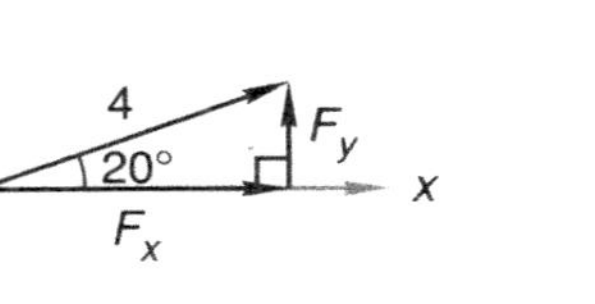

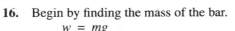

y, 10, P_y, 145°, 35°, x, P_x

$F_x = 4 \cos 20° = 3.76$
$F_y = 4 \sin 20° = 1.37$

$P_x = (-)10 \cos 35° = -8.19$
$P_y = 10 \sin 35° = 5.74$

$R_x = F_x + P_x = 3.76 - 8.19 = -4.43$
$R_y = F_y + P_y = 1.37 + 5.74 = 7.11$

$\vec{R} = -4.43i + 7.11j \xrightarrow{\text{SD}} \mathbf{-4i + 7j}$

20. $\left(\frac{1 \text{ cm}^3}{3.51 \text{ g}} \cdot \frac{12 \text{ g}}{1 \text{ mole}} \cdot \frac{1 \text{ mole}}{6.022 \times 10^{23}}\right)^{1/3} = (5.677 \times 10^{-24} \text{ cm}^3)^{1/3}$

$= 1.78 \times 10^{-8} \text{ cm} \xrightarrow{\text{SD}} \mathbf{1.8 \times 10^{-8} \text{ cm}}$

Problem Set 12

1. $W = F \times D$

$$= 155{,}500\,\cancel{\text{kg}}\left(9.81\,\frac{\text{N}}{\cancel{\text{kg}}}\right) \times (2.43 \times 10^4\text{ m})$$

$$= 3.707 \times 10^{10}\text{ joules} \xrightarrow{\text{SD}} \mathbf{3.71 \times 10^{10}\text{ joules}}$$

$$P_{\text{av}} = \frac{W}{\Delta t} = \frac{3.707 \times 10^{10}\text{ joules}}{9\,\cancel{\text{min}} \times \frac{60\text{ s}}{1\,\cancel{\text{min}}}}$$

$$= \frac{3.707 \times 10^{10}\text{ joules}}{540\text{ s}}$$

$$= 6.865 \times 10^7\text{ watts} \xrightarrow{\text{SD}} \mathbf{7 \times 10^7\text{ watts}}$$

2. $W = F \times D$

$$= (68\text{ N})\cos 30^\circ \times 20\text{ m} = 1177.8\text{ joules} \xrightarrow{\text{SD}} \mathbf{1200\text{ joules}}$$

$$P_{\text{av}} = \frac{W}{\Delta t} = \frac{1177.8\text{ joules}}{4\text{ s}} = 294.5\text{ watts} \xrightarrow{\text{SD}} \mathbf{300\text{ watts}}$$

3. $\vec{F} = m\vec{a} = 10.0\text{ kg}(42\angle 300^\circ\text{ m}\cdot\text{s}^{-2}) = \mathbf{420\angle 300^\circ\text{ N}}$

4. $\vec{F} = m\vec{a} = 26\text{ kg}(13\angle 48^\circ\text{ m}\cdot\text{s}^{-2}) = 338\angle 48^\circ\text{ N} \xrightarrow{\text{SD}} \mathbf{340\angle 48^\circ\text{ N}}$

5. $a_{\text{av}} = \frac{v_2 - v_1}{t_2 - t_1} = \frac{0 - (-40)}{10 - 0}\frac{\text{m/s}}{\text{s}} = \mathbf{+4.0\,\frac{m}{s^2}}$

Calculate the displacements for the following time intervals:

$\Delta x_{0,3} = -40\,\frac{\text{m}}{\cancel{\text{s}}} \times 3\cancel{\text{s}} = -120\text{ m}$ $\Delta x_{3,10} = 20\,\frac{\text{m}}{\cancel{\text{s}}} \times 7\cancel{\text{s}} = +140\text{ m}$

Sum these displacements with the initial position and get:
$x_{10} = 25\text{ m} - 120\text{ m} + 140\text{ m} = \mathbf{45\text{ m}}$

6. $v_{\text{av}} = \frac{x_2 - x_1}{t_2 - t_1} = \frac{-30 - 0}{10 - 0}\frac{\text{m}}{\text{s}} = \mathbf{-3.0\,\frac{m}{s}}$

The position when $t = 10$ seconds was $x = \mathbf{-3\bar{0}\text{ m}}$.

7.

$$\Sigma M = 0$$
$$-35\text{ N}(22\text{ cm}) + 24\text{ N}(11\text{ cm}) + F(19\text{ cm}) = 0$$
$$-770\text{ N}\cdot\text{cm} + 264\text{ N}\cdot\text{cm} + F(19\text{ cm}) = 0$$
$$F(19\text{ cm}) = 506\text{ N}\cdot\text{cm}$$
$$F = 26.63\text{ N} \xrightarrow{\text{SD}} \mathbf{27\text{ N}}$$

8. $\Sigma\tau = 120\text{ N}(12\text{ cm}) - 120\text{ N}(20\text{ cm}) = -960\text{ N}\cdot\text{cm}$

Convert to newton-meters and get:

$$-960\text{ N}\cdot\cancel{\text{cm}} \times \frac{1\text{ m}}{100\,\cancel{\text{cm}}} = -9.6\text{ N}\cdot\text{m}$$

$\tau =$ **9.6 N·m; Negative (counterclockwise) torque**

9. $F = F_s = \mu_s F_N$

$$3038\text{ N} = \mu_s(500\,\cancel{\text{kg}})\left(9.81\,\frac{\text{N}}{\cancel{\text{kg}}}\right)$$

$$\mu_s = 0.6194 \xrightarrow{\text{SD}} \mathbf{0.619}$$

10. $F = F_k = \mu_k F_N$

$$916\text{ N} = \mu_k(212\,\cancel{\text{kg}})\left(9.81\,\frac{\text{N}}{\cancel{\text{kg}}}\right)$$

$$\mu_k = 0.4404 \xrightarrow{\text{SD}} \mathbf{0.440}$$

11. $a_{\text{av}} = \frac{v_2 - v_1}{t_2 - t_1} = \frac{154 - 295}{5.00 - 0}\frac{\text{km/hr}}{\text{s}} = -28.2\,\frac{\text{km/hr}}{\text{s}}$

Convert to $\text{m}\cdot\text{s}^{-2}$ and get:

$$-28.2\,\frac{\cancel{\text{km}}}{\cancel{\text{hr}}\cdot\text{s}} \times \frac{1000\text{ m}}{1\,\cancel{\text{km}}} \times \frac{1\,\cancel{\text{hr}}}{60\,\cancel{\text{min}}} \times \frac{1\,\cancel{\text{min}}}{60\text{ s}} = -7.833\,\frac{\text{m}}{\text{s}^2} \xrightarrow{\text{SD}} \mathbf{-7.83\,\frac{m}{s^2}}$$

12. Begin by converting v_1 and v_2 to meters per second.

$$v_1 = 1.5\,\frac{\cancel{\text{km}}}{\cancel{\text{hr}}} \times \frac{1000\text{ m}}{1\,\cancel{\text{km}}} \times \frac{1\,\cancel{\text{hr}}}{60\,\cancel{\text{min}}} \times \frac{1\,\cancel{\text{min}}}{60\text{ s}} = 0.4167\,\frac{\text{m}}{\text{s}}$$

$$v_2 = 85\,\frac{\cancel{\text{mi}}}{\cancel{\text{hr}}} \times \frac{5280\,\cancel{\text{ft}}}{1\,\cancel{\text{mi}}} \times \frac{12\,\cancel{\text{in.}}}{1\,\cancel{\text{ft}}} \times \frac{2.54\,\cancel{\text{cm}}}{1\,\cancel{\text{in.}}} \times \frac{1\text{ m}}{100\,\cancel{\text{cm}}} \times \frac{1\,\cancel{\text{hr}}}{60\,\cancel{\text{min}}} \times \frac{1\,\cancel{\text{min}}}{60\text{ s}}$$

$$= 38.00\,\frac{\text{m}}{\text{s}}$$

Now find the average acceleration.

$$a_{av} = \frac{v_2 - v_1}{t_2 - t_1}$$

$$= \frac{38.00 - 0.4167}{5010 - 10}\,\frac{\text{m/s}}{\text{s}}$$

$$= +7.517 \times 10^{-3}\,\frac{\text{m}}{\text{s}^2} \xrightarrow{\text{SD}} \mathbf{+7.5 \times 10^{-3}\,\frac{m}{s^2}}$$

13. $T_K = T_C + 273$

$231 = T_C + 273$

$T_C = \mathbf{-42.0°C}$

14.

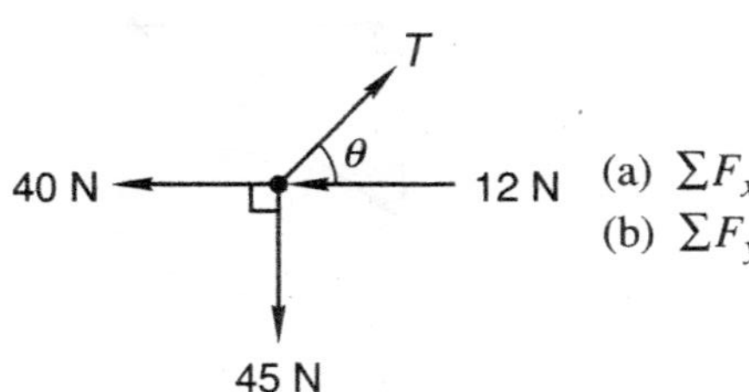

(a) $\Sigma F_x = 0;\ T\cos\theta - 12\text{ N} - 40\text{ N} = 0$

(b) $\Sigma F_y = 0;\ T\sin\theta - 45\text{ N} = 0$

Solve (a) for $T\cos\theta$ and get:

(a′) $T\cos\theta = 52\text{ N}$

Solve (b) for $T\sin\theta$ and get:

(b′) $T\sin\theta = 45\text{ N}$

Divide (b′) by (a′) and get:

$$\frac{T\sin\theta}{T\cos\theta} = \frac{45\text{ N}}{52\text{ N}}$$

$$\tan\theta = \frac{45\text{ N}}{52\text{ N}}$$

$$\theta = 40.87°$$

Substitute θ into (a′) and solve for T.

(a′) $T\cos(40.87°) = 52\text{ N}$

$T = 68.77\text{ N}$

$$\vec{T} = 68.77\underline{/40.87°}\text{ N} \xrightarrow{\text{SD}} \mathbf{70\underline{/40.87°}\ N}$$

15.

80.0 N
F_1
30°
F_2

(a) $\Sigma F_x = 0;\ F_1 - (80.0\text{ N})\cos 30° = 0$

(b) $\Sigma F_y = 0;\ F_2 - (80.0\text{ N})\sin 30° = 0$

Solve (a) for F_1 and get:

(a) $F_1 = (80.0\text{ N})\cos 30°$

$= 69.28\text{ N} \xrightarrow{\text{SD}} \mathbf{69.3\ N}$

Solve (b) for F_2 and get:

(b) $F_2 = (80.0\text{ N})\sin 30°$

$= 40.00\text{ N} \xrightarrow{\text{SD}} \mathbf{40.0\ N}$

16. $$v = \frac{D_T}{T_T} = \frac{25\text{ mi}}{3.0\text{ hr}} = 8.33\,\frac{\text{mi}}{\text{hr}} \xrightarrow{\text{SD}} \mathbf{8.3\,\frac{mi}{hr}}$$

$$\vec{v} = \frac{\vec{D}}{T_T} = \frac{25\underline{/180°}\text{ mi}}{3.0\text{ hr}} = 8.33\underline{/180°}\,\frac{\text{mi}}{\text{hr}} \xrightarrow{\text{SD}} \mathbf{8.3\underline{/180°}\,\frac{mi}{hr}}$$

17. Begin by finding the mass of the sugar in grams.

$$w = mg$$

$$0.0468\text{ N} = m \times 9.81\,\frac{\text{N}}{\text{kg}}$$

$$m = 4.771 \times 10^{-3}\,\cancel{\text{kg}} \times \frac{1000\text{ g}}{1\,\cancel{\text{kg}}} = 4.771\text{ g}$$

Calculate the density.

$$\rho = \frac{m}{V} = \frac{4.771\text{ g}}{3.0\text{ cm}^3} = 1.590\,\frac{\text{g}}{\text{cm}^3} \xrightarrow{\text{SD}} \mathbf{1.6\,\frac{g}{cm^3}}$$

18. Begin by finding the mass of the statue.

$$w = mg$$

$$2450 \text{ N} = m \times 9.81 \frac{\text{N}}{\text{kg}}$$

$$m = 249.75 \text{ kg}$$

Calculate the volume.

$$\rho = \frac{m}{V}$$

$$2720 \frac{\text{kg}}{\text{m}^3} = \frac{249.75 \text{ kg}}{V}$$

$$V = 9.182 \times 10^{-2} \text{ m}^3 \xrightarrow{\text{SD}} \mathbf{9.18 \times 10^{-2}\ m^3}$$

19.

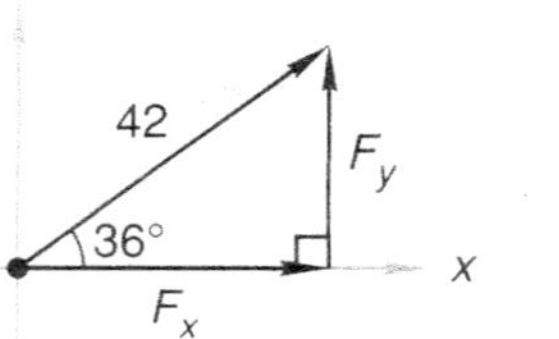

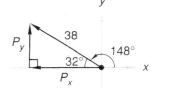

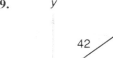

$F_x = 42 \cos 36° = 33.98$
$F_y = 42 \sin 36° = 24.69$

$P_x = (-)38 \cos 32° = -32.23$
$P_y = 38 \sin 32° = 20.14$

$R_x = F_x + P_x = 33.98 - 32.23 = 1.75$
$R_y = F_y + P_y = 24.69 + 20.14 = 44.83$

$$\vec{R} = 1.75i + 44.83j \xrightarrow{\text{SD}} \mathbf{1.8i + 45j}$$

20. $14 \text{ hp} \times \frac{746 \text{ watts}}{1 \text{ hp}} = 10{,}444 \text{ watts} \xrightarrow{\text{SD}} \mathbf{1\bar{0},000\ watts}$

PROBLEM SET 13

1. Answers to this problem may vary due to differing data points. One possible solution is given here. Choose the points (3, 50) and (3.7, 0) and get:

$$v_{inst} = \frac{\Delta x}{\Delta t} = \frac{0 - 50}{3.7 - 3}\frac{\text{m}}{\text{s}} = -71.4 \frac{\text{m}}{\text{s}} \xrightarrow{\text{SD}} \mathbf{-71\ \frac{m}{s}}$$

2. Answers to this problem may vary due to differing data points. One possible solution is given here. Choose the points (2, −40) and (6, −20) and get:

$$a_{inst} = \frac{\Delta v}{\Delta t} = \frac{-20 - (-40)}{6 - 2}\frac{\text{m/s}}{\text{s}} = \mathbf{+5.0\ \frac{m}{s^2}}$$

3. Answers to this problem may vary due to differing data points. One possible solution is given here. Choose the points (2, 5) and (8, −20) and get:

$$a_{av} = \frac{v_2 - v_1}{t_2 - t_1} = \frac{-20 - 5}{8 - 2}\frac{\text{m/s}}{\text{s}} = -4.17 \frac{\text{m}}{\text{s}^2} \xrightarrow{\text{SD}} \mathbf{-4.2\ \frac{m}{s^2}}$$

4. Answers to this problem may vary due to differing data points. One possible solution is given here. Choose the points (6, 20) and (15, 10) and get:

$$a_{av} = \frac{v_2 - v_1}{t_2 - t_1} = \frac{10 - 20}{15 - 6}\frac{\text{m/s}}{\text{s}} = -1.11 \frac{\text{m}}{\text{s}^2} \xrightarrow{\text{SD}} \mathbf{-1.1\ \frac{m}{s^2}}$$

5. $W = F \times D$

$$= 86 \cancel{\text{kg}}\left(9.81 \frac{\text{N}}{\cancel{\text{kg}}}\right) \times 14 \text{ m} = 11{,}811 \text{ joules} \xrightarrow{\text{SD}} \mathbf{12{,}000\ joules}$$

$$P_{av} = \frac{W}{\Delta t} = \frac{11{,}811 \text{ joules}}{2.0 \cancel{\text{min}} \times \frac{60 \text{ s}}{1 \cancel{\text{min}}}} = 98.43 \text{ watts} \xrightarrow{\text{SD}} \mathbf{98\ watts}$$

6. $W = F \times D$

$$= 20{,}000 \cancel{\text{kg}}\left(9.81 \frac{\text{N}}{\cancel{\text{kg}}}\right) \times 54 \text{ m}$$

$$= 1.059 \times 10^7 \text{ joules} \xrightarrow{\text{SD}} \mathbf{1 \times 10^7\ joules}$$

$$P_{av} = \frac{W}{\Delta t} = \frac{1.059 \times 10^7 \text{ joules}}{130 \text{ s}}$$

$$= 8.146 \times 10^4 \text{ watts} \xrightarrow{\text{SD}} \mathbf{8 \times 10^4\ watts}$$

7. $\vec{F} = m\vec{a}$

$$= 40.0 \text{ kg}\left(426\angle 140° \frac{\text{m}}{\text{s}^2}\right) = 17{,}040\angle 140° \text{ N} \xrightarrow{\text{SD}} \mathbf{17{,}\bar{0}00\angle 140°\ N}$$

8. $F = ma = 10 \text{ kg}(2 \text{ m}\cdot\text{s}^{-2}) = \mathbf{20\ N}$

9. $\tau = F \times x$

$61.5 \text{ N}\cdot\text{m} = 85 \text{ N} \times x$

$x = 0.724 \text{ m} \xrightarrow{\text{SD}}$ **0.72 m**

10. $\Sigma\tau = -10 \text{ N}(20 \text{ cm}) - 15 \text{ N}(15 \text{ cm}) = -425 \text{ N}\cdot\text{cm} \xrightarrow{\text{SD}}$ **−400 N·cm**

11. $F = F_k = \mu_k F_N$

$960 \text{ N} = \mu_k(162 \text{ kg})\left(9.81 \frac{\text{N}}{\text{kg}}\right)$

$\mu_k = 0.6041 \xrightarrow{\text{SD}}$ **0.60**

12. $F = F_s = \mu_s F_N$

$= 0.87(10 \text{ kg})\left(9.81 \frac{\text{N}}{\text{kg}}\right)$

$= 85.35 \text{ N} \xrightarrow{\text{SD}}$ **85 N**

13. $v_{av} = \frac{x_2 - x_1}{t_2 - t_1} = \frac{190 - 1.2}{28 - 1.5} \frac{\text{m}}{\text{s}} = +7.125 \frac{\text{m}}{\text{s}} \xrightarrow{\text{SD}}$ **+7.1 m/s**

14. First, we draw the diagram.

°F °C
212° 100° Boiling
180 spaces 100 spaces
32° 0° Freezing

Since the ratio of the increments is

$$\text{Ratio} = \frac{°\text{F}}{°\text{C}} = \frac{180}{100} = \frac{9}{5}$$

it takes more Fahrenheit degrees in an interval than there are Celsius degrees, so we multiply by 9 over 5.

$$2067° \times \frac{9}{5} = 3720.6°$$

Thus, we are 3720.6 Fahrenheit degrees above freezing. Water freezes at 32 degrees Fahrenheit, and we are 3720.6° above that temperature.

$3720.6° + 32 = 3752.6°\text{F} \xrightarrow{\text{SD}}$ **3753°F**

15.

T_2 T_1 50° 25° 36 N

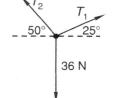

(a) $\Sigma F_x = 0;\ T_1 \cos 25° - T_2 \cos 50° = 0$

(b) $\Sigma F_y = 0;\ T_2 \sin 50° + T_1 \sin 25° - 36 \text{ N} = 0$

Solve (a) for T_2 and get:

(a) $T_2 \cos 50° = T_1 \cos 25°$

$T_2 = 1.410T_1$ (a′)

Substitute (a′) into (b) and get:

(b) $(1.410T_1) \sin 50° + T_1 \sin 25° = 36 \text{ N}$

$1.503T_1 = 36 \text{ N}$

$T_1 = 23.95 \text{ N} \xrightarrow{\text{SD}}$ **24 N**

Substitute T_1 into (a′) and get:

(a′) $T_2 = 1.410(23.95 \text{ N})$

$= 33.77 \text{ N} \xrightarrow{\text{SD}}$ **34 N**

16.

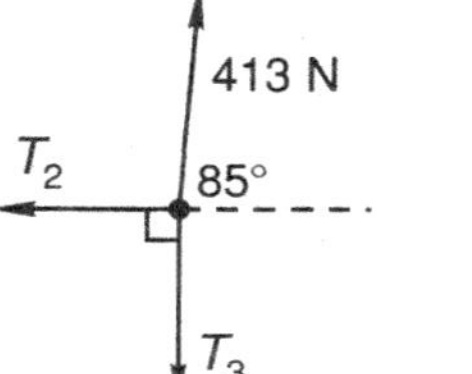

(a) $\Sigma F_x = 0;\ (413 \text{ N}) \cos 85° - T_2 = 0$

(b) $\Sigma F_y = 0;\ (413 \text{ N}) \sin 85° - T_3 = 0$

Solve (a) for T_2 and get:

(a) $T_2 = (413 \text{ N}) \cos 85°$

$= 36.00 \text{ N} \xrightarrow{\text{SD}}$ **36.0 N**

Solve (b) for T_3 and get:

(b) $T_3 = (413 \text{ N}) \sin 85°$

$= 411.43 \text{ N} \xrightarrow{\text{SD}}$ **411 N**

17. Begin by converting 50 minutes to hours.

$$50\ \cancel{\text{min}} \times \frac{1\ \text{hr}}{60\ \cancel{\text{min}}} = 0.833\ \text{hr}$$

Calculate the average speed and velocity.

$$v = \frac{D_T}{T_T} = \frac{63.54\ \text{mi}}{0.833\ \text{hr}} = 76.28\ \frac{\text{mi}}{\text{hr}} \xrightarrow{\text{SD}} \mathbf{80\ \frac{mi}{hr}}$$

$$\vec{v} = \frac{D\angle\theta}{T_T} = \frac{50.75\angle 90°\ \text{mi}}{0.833\ \text{hr}} = 60.92\angle 90°\ \frac{\text{mi}}{\text{hr}} \xrightarrow{\text{SD}} \mathbf{60\angle 90°\ \frac{mi}{hr}}$$

Yes, Kathy was speeding because her average speed was 80 mi/hr and the speed limit was only 65.0 mi/hr.

18. Begin by finding the mass of the object.

$$w = mg$$
$$0.89\ \text{N} = m \times 9.81\ \frac{\text{N}}{\text{kg}}$$
$$m = 0.0907\ \text{kg}$$

Calculate the density.

$$\rho = \frac{m}{V} = \frac{0.0907\ \text{kg}}{4.0\ \text{m}^3} = 2.268 \times 10^{-2}\ \frac{\text{kg}}{\text{m}^3} \xrightarrow{\text{SD}} \mathbf{2.3 \times 10^{-2}\ \frac{kg}{m^3}}$$

19. Begin by finding the mass of the block.

$$\rho = \frac{m}{V}$$
$$261\ \frac{\text{kg}}{\text{m}^3} = \frac{m}{2.6\ \text{m}^3}$$
$$m = 678.6\ \text{kg}$$

Calculate the weight.

$$w = mg = 678.6\ \cancel{\text{kg}} \times 9.81\ \frac{\text{N}}{\cancel{\text{kg}}} = 6657\ \text{N} \xrightarrow{\text{SD}} \mathbf{6700\ N}$$

20. $$76.0\ \frac{\cancel{\text{gal}}}{\cancel{\text{in.}}} \times \frac{3.785\ \text{L}}{1\ \cancel{\text{gal}}} \times \frac{1\ \cancel{\text{in.}}}{2.54\ \text{cm}} = 113.25\ \frac{\text{L}}{\text{cm}} \xrightarrow{\text{SD}} \mathbf{113\ \frac{L}{cm}}$$

Problem Set 14

1.

$$\Sigma F_y = ma_y$$
$$T - mg = ma_y$$
$$480\ \text{N} - 40\ \cancel{\text{kg}}\left(9.81\ \frac{\text{N}}{\cancel{\text{kg}}}\right) = (40\ \text{kg})a_y$$
$$87.6\ \text{N} = (40\ \text{kg})a_y$$
$$a_y = 2.19\ \frac{\text{m}}{\text{s}^2} \xrightarrow{\text{SD}} \mathbf{2.2\ \frac{m}{s^2}}$$

2.

$$\Sigma F_y = ma_y$$
$$F_N - mg = ma_y$$
$$F_N - 78\ \cancel{\text{kg}}\left(9.81\ \frac{\text{N}}{\cancel{\text{kg}}}\right) = 78\ \text{kg}\left(1.8\ \frac{\text{m}}{\text{s}^2}\right)$$
$$F_N = 905.58\ \text{N} \xrightarrow{\text{SD}} \mathbf{910\ N}$$

3.

$$\Sigma F_y = ma_y$$
$$F_N - mg = ma_y$$
$$F_N - 70\ \cancel{\text{kg}}\left(9.81\ \frac{\text{N}}{\cancel{\text{kg}}}\right) = 70\ \text{kg}\left(-0.80\ \frac{\text{m}}{\text{s}^2}\right)$$
$$F_N = 630.7\ \text{N} \xrightarrow{\text{SD}} \mathbf{630\ N}$$

4. Answers to this problem may vary due to differing data points. One possible solution is given here. Choose the points (6, 0) and (10, 20) and get:

$$v_{\text{inst}} = \frac{\Delta x}{\Delta t} = \frac{20 - 0}{10 - 6}\ \frac{\text{m}}{\text{s}} = \mathbf{+5.0\ \frac{m}{s}}$$

5. $$v_{\text{av}} = \frac{x_2 - x_1}{t_2 - t_1} = \frac{20 - (-60)}{10 - 0}\ \frac{\text{m}}{\text{s}} = \mathbf{+8.0\ \frac{m}{s}}$$

6. Answers to this problem may vary due to differing data points. One possible solution is given here. Choose the points (0, 17) and (45, 30) and get:

$$a_{\text{inst}} = \frac{\Delta v}{\Delta t} = \frac{30 - 17}{45 - 0}\ \frac{\text{km/min}}{\text{min}} = +0.289\ \frac{\text{km}}{\text{min}^2} \xrightarrow{\text{SD}} \mathbf{+0.29\ \frac{km}{min^2}}$$

7. $$a_{\text{av}} = \frac{v_2 - v_1}{t_2 - t_1} = \frac{40 - 10}{90 - 30}\ \frac{\text{km/min}}{\text{min}} = \mathbf{+0.50\ \frac{km}{min^2}}$$

8. $W = F \times D$

$= 962\text{ kg}\left(9.81\ \frac{\text{N}}{\text{kg}}\right) \times 62\text{ m} = 585{,}108\text{ joules} \xrightarrow{\text{SD}}$ **590,000 joules**

$P_{av} = \frac{W}{\Delta t} = \frac{585{,}108\text{ joules}}{3\text{ min} \times \frac{60\text{ s}}{1\text{ min}}} = 3250.6\text{ watts} \xrightarrow{\text{SD}}$ **3000 watts**

9. $P_{av} = \frac{W}{\Delta t} = \frac{F \times D}{\Delta t} = \frac{36{,}000\text{ N} \times 1600\text{ m}}{4.0\text{ min} \times \frac{60\text{ s}}{1\text{ min}}} = \mathbf{2.4 \times 10^5\ watts}$

10. $\vec{F} = m\vec{a}$

$= 62.0\text{ kg}(402\underline{/64°}\text{ m}\cdot\text{s}^{-2}) = 24{,}924\underline{/64°}\text{ N} \xrightarrow{\text{SD}}$ **24,900/64° N**

11. $\vec{F} = m\vec{a}$

$= 219\text{ kg}(26\underline{/180°}\text{ m}\cdot\text{s}^{-2}) = 5694\underline{/180°}\text{ N} \xrightarrow{\text{SD}}$ **5700/180° N**

12. $\Sigma\tau = 12\text{ N}(30\text{ cm}) - 6.0\text{ N}(40\text{ cm}) = \mathbf{+120\ N\cdot cm}$

13.

$$\begin{aligned} \Sigma M &= 0 \\ -6.0\text{ N}(20\text{ cm}) - 18\text{ N}(20\text{ cm}) + F(30\text{ cm}) &= 0 \\ -120\text{ N}\cdot\text{cm} - 360\text{ N}\cdot\text{cm} + F(30\text{ cm}) &= 0 \\ F(30\text{ cm}) &= 480\text{ N}\cdot\text{cm} \\ F &= \mathbf{16\ N} \end{aligned}$$

14. $F = F_s = \mu_s F_N$

$= 0.62(96\text{ kg})\left(9.81\ \frac{\text{N}}{\text{kg}}\right)$

$= 583.89\text{ N} \xrightarrow{\text{SD}}$ **580 N**

15. (a) $F_k = \mu_k F_N$

$= 0.20(1400\text{ N})$

$= \mathbf{280\ N}$

(b) Since the force of friction is opposite to the direction of motion, it is a negative force.

$W = F \times D = -280\text{ N} \times 10\text{ m} = -2800\text{ joules} \xrightarrow{\text{SD}}$ **−3000 joules**

16. Convert 180°F to °C.

$T_C = \frac{5}{9}(T_F - 32)$

$= \frac{5}{9}(180° - 32)$

$= 82.22°\text{C}$

Convert 82.22°C to kelvins.

$T_K = T_C + 273$

$= 82.22 + 273$

$= 355.22\text{ K} \xrightarrow{\text{SD}}$ **355 K**

17.

T_1, T_2, 80°, 169 N

(a) $\Sigma F_x = 0;\ T_1 \cos 80° - T_2 = 0$

(b) $\Sigma F_y = 0;\ T_1 \sin 80° - 169\text{ N} = 0$

Solve (b) for T_1 and get:

(b) $T_1 \sin 80° = 169\text{ N}$

$T_1 = 171.61\text{ N} \xrightarrow{\text{SD}}$ **172 N**

Substitute T_1 into (a) and get:

(a) $T_2 = (171.61\text{ N}) \cos 80° = 29.80\text{ N} \xrightarrow{\text{SD}}$ **29.8 N**

18.

T_2, T_3, 71°, 36°, 991 N

(a) $\Sigma F_x = 0;\ T_3 \cos 36° - T_2 \cos 71° = 0$

(b) $\Sigma F_y = 0;\ T_2 \sin 71° + T_3 \sin 36° - 991\text{ N} = 0$

Solve (a) for T_3 and get:

(a) $T_3 \cos 36° = T_2 \cos 71°$

$T_3 = 0.402T_2$ (a′)

Substitute (a′) into (b) and get:

(b) $T_2 \sin 71° + (0.402T_2) \sin 36° = 991\text{ N}$

$1.182T_2 = 991\text{ N}$

$T_2 = 838.41\text{ N} \xrightarrow{\text{SD}}$ **838 N**

Substitute T_2 into (a′) and get:

(a′) $T_3 = 0.402(838.41\text{ N}) = 337.04\text{ N} \xrightarrow{\text{SD}}$ **337 N**

19. Begin by finding the mass of the unspecified object.

$$w = mg$$

$$1.77 \times 10^8 \text{ N} = m \times 9.81 \frac{\text{N}}{\text{kg}}$$

$$m = 1.804 \times 10^7 \text{ kg}$$

Calculate the density.

$$\rho = \frac{m}{V} = \frac{1.804 \times 10^7 \text{ kg}}{36{,}000 \text{ m}^3} = 501.11 \frac{\text{kg}}{\text{m}^3} \xrightarrow{\text{SD}} \mathbf{501 \frac{kg}{m^3}}$$

Pine, with a density of 500 kg/m^3, is a substance of which this object could be composed.

20. $$42 \frac{\cancel{\text{in.}^3}}{\cancel{\text{s}}} \times \frac{(2.54)^3 \cancel{\text{cm}^3}}{1 \cancel{\text{in.}^3}} \times \frac{1 \text{ m}^3}{(100)^3 \cancel{\text{cm}^3}} \times \frac{60 \cancel{\text{s}}}{1 \text{ min}}$$

$$= 4.130 \times 10^{-2} \frac{\text{m}^3}{\text{min}} \xrightarrow{\text{SD}} \mathbf{4.1 \times 10^{-2} \frac{m^3}{min}}$$

PROBLEM SET 15

1.
$$\Sigma M_B = 0$$
$$F_A(10.0 \text{ cm}) - 40 \text{ N}(6.0 \text{ cm}) = 0$$
$$F_A(10.0 \text{ cm}) = 240 \text{ N}\cdot\text{cm}$$
$$F_A = \mathbf{24 \text{ N}}$$

$$\Sigma F_y = 0$$
$$F_A + F_B - 40 \text{ N} = 0$$
$$(24 \text{ N}) + F_B - 40 \text{ N} = 0$$
$$F_B = \mathbf{16 \text{ N}}$$

2.
$$\Sigma M_B = 0$$
$$F_A(14.0 \text{ cm}) - 25.0 \text{ N}(11.0 \text{ cm}) = 0$$
$$F_A(14.0 \text{ cm}) = 275 \text{ N}\cdot\text{cm}$$
$$F_A = 19.64 \text{ N} \xrightarrow{\text{SD}} \mathbf{19.6 \text{ N}}$$

$$\Sigma F_y = 0$$
$$F_A + F_B - 25.0 \text{ N} = 0$$
$$(19.64 \text{ N}) + F_B - 25.0 \text{ N} = 0$$
$$F_B = \mathbf{5.36 \text{ N}}$$

3.
$$\Sigma F_y = ma_y$$
$$T - mg = ma_y$$
$$86 \text{ N} - 10 \cancel{\text{kg}} \left(9.81 \frac{\text{N}}{\cancel{\text{kg}}}\right) = (10 \text{ kg})a_y$$
$$a_y = -1.21 \frac{\text{m}}{\text{s}^2} \xrightarrow{\text{SD}} -1.2 \frac{\text{m}}{\text{s}^2}$$

The magnitude of the acceleration is $\mathbf{1.2 \frac{m}{s^2}}$.

4.
$$\Sigma F_y = ma_y$$
$$F_N - mg = ma_y$$
$$F_N - 113.398 \cancel{\text{kg}} \left(9.81 \frac{\text{N}}{\cancel{\text{kg}}}\right) = 113.398 \text{ kg}(-6 \text{ m}\cdot\text{s}^{-2})$$
$$F_N = 432.05 \text{ N} \xrightarrow{\text{SD}} \mathbf{400 \text{ N}}$$

5. Answers to this problem may vary due to differing data points. One possible solution is given here. Choose the points (0, –32) and (30, –20) and get:

$$a_{inst} = \frac{\Delta v}{\Delta t} = \frac{-20 - (-32)}{30 - 0} \frac{\text{m/s}}{\text{s}} = \mathbf{+0.40 \frac{m}{s^2}}$$

6. $$a_{av} = \frac{v_2 - v_1}{t_2 - t_1} = \frac{20 - (-40)}{30 - 0} \frac{\text{m/s}}{\text{s}} = \mathbf{+2.0 \frac{m}{s^2}}$$

7. (a) Answers to this problem may vary due to differing data points. One possible solution is given here. Choose the points (0, –10) and (40, 10) and get:

$$v_{inst} = \frac{\Delta x}{\Delta t} = \frac{10 - (-10)}{40 - 0} \frac{\text{m}}{\text{s}} = \mathbf{+0.50 \frac{m}{s}}$$

(b) $$v_{av} = \frac{x_2 - x_1}{t_2 - t_1} = \frac{15 - 0}{80 - 20} \frac{\text{m}}{\text{s}} = \mathbf{+0.25 \frac{m}{s}}$$

8. Calculate the displacements for the following time intervals:

$$\Delta x_{0,10} = \frac{-10 \frac{\text{m}}{\cancel{\text{s}}} \times 10 \cancel{\text{s}}}{2} = -50 \text{ m} \qquad \Delta x_{10,30} = \frac{20 \frac{\text{m}}{\cancel{\text{s}}} \times 20 \cancel{\text{s}}}{2} = +200 \text{ m}$$

Sum these displacements with the initial position and get:

$$x_{30} = -20 \text{ m} - 50 \text{ m} + 200 \text{ m} = \mathbf{130 \text{ m}}$$

9. $W = F \times D$

$$= 60\,\cancel{kg}\left(9.81\,\frac{N}{\cancel{kg}}\right) \times 64\text{ m} = 37{,}670\text{ joules} \xrightarrow{SD} \textbf{38,000 joules}$$

$$P_{av} = \frac{W}{\Delta t} = \frac{37{,}670\text{ joules}}{3600\text{ s}} = 10.46\text{ watts} \xrightarrow{SD} \textbf{10 watts}$$

10. $W = F \times D$

$$= 45\,\cancel{kg}\left(9.81\,\frac{N}{\cancel{kg}}\right) \times 35\text{ m} = 15{,}451\text{ joules} \xrightarrow{SD} \textbf{15,000 joules}$$

$$P_{av} = \frac{W}{\Delta t} = \frac{15{,}451\text{ joules}}{30\,\cancel{min} \times \frac{60\text{ s}}{1\,\cancel{min}}} = 8.584\text{ watts} \xrightarrow{SD} \textbf{8.6 watts}$$

11. $\vec{F} = m\vec{a} = 720\text{ kg}(42\underline{/30^\circ}\text{ m}\cdot\text{s}^{-2}) = 30{,}240\underline{/30^\circ}\text{ N} \xrightarrow{SD} \mathbf{3\bar{0},000\underline{/30^\circ}\text{ N}}$

12.

$$\vec{F} = m\vec{a}$$

$$25\underline{/20^\circ}\text{ N} = m(3.1\underline{/20^\circ}\text{ m}\cdot\text{s}^{-2})$$

$$m = 8.06\text{ kg} \xrightarrow{SD} \textbf{8.1 kg}$$

13.

$$\tau = F \times x$$

$$150\text{ N}\cdot\text{m} = 250\text{ N} \times x$$

$$x = \mathbf{0.60\text{ m}}$$

14. $F = F_k = \mu_k F_N$

$$900\text{ N} = \mu_k(1700\,\cancel{kg})\left(9.81\,\frac{N}{\cancel{kg}}\right)$$

$$\mu_k = 0.0540 \xrightarrow{SD} \mathbf{0.054}$$

15. $F = F_s = \mu_s F_N$

$$250\text{ N} = \mu_s(35\,\cancel{kg})\left(9.81\,\frac{N}{\cancel{kg}}\right)$$

$$\mu_s = 0.728 \xrightarrow{SD} \mathbf{0.73}$$

16. First, we draw the diagram.

°F	°C	
212°	100°	**Boiling**
180 spaces	100 spaces	
32°	0°	**Freezing**

Since the ratio of the increments is

$$\text{Ratio} = \frac{°\text{F}}{°\text{C}} = \frac{180}{100} = \frac{9}{5}$$

it takes more Fahrenheit degrees in an interval than there are Celsius degrees, so we multiply by 9 over 5.

$$809° \times \frac{9}{5} = 1456.2°$$

Thus, we are 1456.2 Fahrenheit degrees above freezing. Water freezes at 32 degrees Fahrenheit, and we are 1456.2° above that temperature.

$$1456.2° + 32 = 1488.2°\text{F} \xrightarrow{SD} \mathbf{1490°F}$$

17.

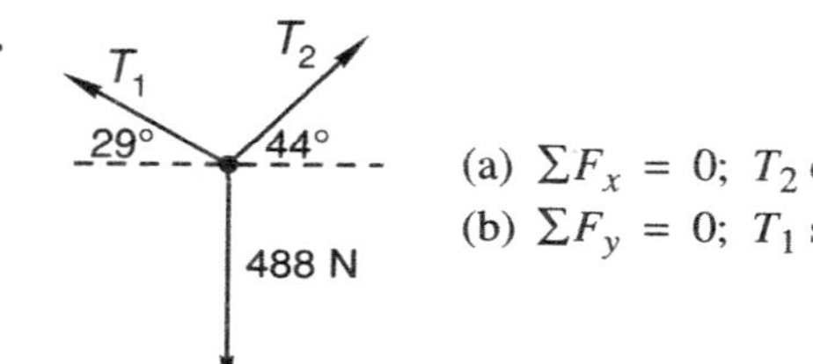

(a) $\Sigma F_x = 0;\ T_2 \cos 44° - T_1 \cos 29° = 0$

(b) $\Sigma F_y = 0;\ T_1 \sin 29° + T_2 \sin 44° - 488\text{ N} = 0$

Solve (a) for T_2 and get:

(a) $T_2 \cos 44° = T_1 \cos 29°$

$$T_2 = 1.216T_1 \qquad (a')$$

Substitute (a′) into (b) and get:

(b) $T_1 \sin 29° + (1.216T_1) \sin 44° = 488\text{ N}$

$$1.330T_1 = 488\text{ N}$$

$$T_1 = 366.92\text{ N} \xrightarrow{SD} \mathbf{367\text{ N}}$$

Substitute T_1 into (a′) and get:

(a′) $T_2 = 1.216(366.92\text{ N}) = 446.17\text{ N} \xrightarrow{SD} \mathbf{446\text{ N}}$

18.

(a) $\Sigma F_x = 0;\ T_2 \cos 35° - T_1 \cos 75° - 12\text{ N} = 0$
(b) $\Sigma F_y = 0;\ T_1 \sin 75° + T_2 \sin 35° - 78\text{ N} = 0$

Solve (a) for T_2 and get:

(a) $T_2 \cos 35° = T_1 \cos 75° + 12\text{ N}$

$T_2 = 0.316T_1 + 14.649\text{ N}$ (a′)

Substitute (a′) into (b) and get:

(b) $T_1 \sin 75° + (0.316T_1 + 14.649\text{ N}) \sin 35° = 78\text{ N}$

$1.147T_1 + 8.402\text{ N} = 78\text{ N}$

$1.147T_1 = 69.598\text{ N}$

$T_1 = 60.678\text{ N} \xrightarrow{SD}$ **61 N**

Substitute T_1 into (a′) and get:

(a′) $T_2 = 0.316(60.678\text{ N}) + 14.649\text{ N} = 33.823\text{ N} \xrightarrow{SD}$ **34 N**

19. Begin by converting km^3 to m^3.

$$1083 \times 10^9 \text{ km}^3 \times \frac{(1000)^3 \text{ m}^3}{1 \text{ km}^3} = 1.083 \times 10^{21} \text{ m}^3$$

Calculate the mass.

$$\rho = \frac{m}{V}$$

$$5517 \frac{\text{kg}}{\text{m}^3} = \frac{m}{1.083 \times 10^{21} \text{ m}^3}$$

$$m = 5.9749 \times 10^{24} \text{ kg} \xrightarrow{SD} \mathbf{5.975 \times 10^{24}\ kg}$$

20. $1127 \frac{\text{ft}}{\text{s}} \times \frac{1 \text{ mi}}{5280 \text{ ft}} \times \frac{60 \text{ s}}{1 \text{ min}} \times \frac{60 \text{ min}}{1 \text{ hr}} = 768.41 \frac{\text{mi}}{\text{hr}} \xrightarrow{SD} \mathbf{768.4\ \frac{mi}{hr}}$

Problem Set 16

1. Begin by finding the weight of the block.

$$w = mg = 300 \text{ kg} \times 9.81 \frac{\text{N}}{\text{kg}} = 2943 \text{ N}$$

(a) There are two upward forces acting on the weight, so

$$F = \frac{2943 \text{ N}}{2} = 1471.5 \text{ N} \xrightarrow{SD} \mathbf{1470\ N}$$

(b) The weight of the block is 2943 N and it takes a force of 1471.5 N to lift it at a constant velocity, so the mechanical advantage is **2.00**.

(c) Work done by girl = work done on weight

$1471.5\text{ N} \times x = 2943\text{ N} \times 2.00\text{ m}$

$x =$ **4.00 m**

(d) $W = F \times D = 1471.5\text{ N} \times 4.00\text{ m} = 5886\text{ J} \xrightarrow{SD}$ **5890 J**

(e) $W = F \times D = 2943\text{ N} \times 2.00\text{ m} = 5886\text{ J} \xrightarrow{SD}$ **5890 J**

2. $W_1 = 468\text{ J} \times 0.800 = 374.4\text{ J}$

$W_2 = 374.4\text{ J} \times 0.400 = 149.76\text{ J} \xrightarrow{SD}$ **15$\bar{0}$ J**

3. (a)

$\Sigma M = 0$

$-F(3.00\text{ m}) + 1620\text{ N}(1.00\text{ m}) = 0$

$F(3.00\text{ m}) = 1620\text{ N}\cdot\text{m}$

$F =$ **54$\bar{0}$ N**

(b) $F_u = 540\text{ N} + 1620\text{ N} =$ **2160 N**

4. (a)

$\Sigma M_A = 0$

$76\text{ N}(3.0\text{ m}) - F_B(13\text{ m}) = 0$

$F_B(13\text{ m}) = 228\text{ N}\cdot\text{m}$

$F_B = 17.54\text{ N} \xrightarrow{SD}$ **18 N**

(b)

$\Sigma F_y = 0$

$F_A + F_B - 76\text{ N} = 0$

$F_A + (17.54\text{ N}) - 76\text{ N} = 0$

$F_A = 58.46\text{ N} \xrightarrow{SD}$ **58 N**

5. (a)
$$\Sigma M_A = 0$$
$$290\text{ N}(4.00\text{ m}) - F_B(7.00\text{ m}) = 0$$
$$F_B(7.00\text{ m}) = 1160\text{ N}\cdot\text{m}$$
$$F_B = 165.71\text{ N} \xrightarrow{\text{SD}} \mathbf{166\ N}$$

(b)
$$\Sigma F_y = 0$$
$$F_A + F_B - 290\text{ N} = 0$$
$$F_A + (165.71\text{ N}) - 290\text{ N} = 0$$
$$F_A = 124.29\text{ N} \xrightarrow{\text{SD}} \mathbf{124\ N}$$

6.
$$\Sigma F_y = ma_y$$
$$F_N - mg = ma_y$$
$$F_N - 100\,\cancel{\text{kg}}\left(9.81\,\frac{\text{N}}{\cancel{\text{kg}}}\right) = 100\text{ kg}(8.00\text{ m}\cdot\text{s}^{-2})$$
$$F_N = 1781\text{ N} \xrightarrow{\text{SD}} \mathbf{1780\ N}$$

7.
$$\Sigma F_y = ma_y$$
$$F_N - mg = ma_y$$
$$F_N - 120\,\cancel{\text{kg}}\left(9.81\,\frac{\text{N}}{\cancel{\text{kg}}}\right) = 120\text{ kg}(40.0\text{ m}\cdot\text{s}^{-2})$$
$$F_N = 5977.2\text{ N} \xrightarrow{\text{SD}} \mathbf{5980\ N}$$

8. (a) Answers to this problem may vary due to differing data points. One possible solution is given here. Choose the points (2.5, –80) and (4, –40) and get:
$$v_{\text{inst}} = \frac{\Delta x}{\Delta t} = \frac{-40 - (-80)}{4 - 2.5}\,\frac{\text{m}}{\text{s}} = +26.7\,\frac{\text{m}}{\text{s}} \xrightarrow{\text{SD}} \mathbf{+27\,\frac{m}{s}}$$

(b)
$$v_{\text{av}} = \frac{x_2 - x_1}{t_2 - t_1} = \frac{-120 - 20}{4 - 1}\,\frac{\text{m}}{\text{s}} = -46.7\,\frac{\text{m}}{\text{s}} \xrightarrow{\text{SD}} \mathbf{-47\,\frac{m}{s}}$$

9. Calculate the displacements for the following time intervals:
$$\Delta x_{0,1.5} = -5\,\frac{\text{m}}{\cancel{\text{s}}} \times 1.5\,\cancel{\text{s}} = -7.5\text{ m} \qquad \Delta x_{1.5,3} = \frac{10\,\frac{\text{m}}{\cancel{\text{s}}} \times 1.5\,\cancel{\text{s}}}{2} = +7.5\text{ m}$$
$$\Delta x_{3,4} = 10\,\frac{\text{m}}{\cancel{\text{s}}} \times 1\,\cancel{\text{s}} = +10\text{ m}$$

Sum these displacements with the initial position and get:
$x_4 = 10\text{ m} - 7.5\text{ m} + 7.5\text{ m} + 10\text{ m} = \mathbf{\overline{2}0\ m}$

10. $W = F \times D = 124{,}000\text{ N} \times 420.0\text{ m} = \mathbf{52{,}080{,}000\ J}$

11. $\vec{F} = m\vec{a} = 9.0\text{ kg}(2.0\angle 37^\circ\text{ cm}\cdot\text{s}^{-2}) = \mathbf{18\angle 37^\circ\,\frac{kg\cdot cm}{s^2}}$

12.
$$\vec{F} = m\vec{a}$$
$$210\angle 90^\circ\text{ N} = m(2.00\angle 90^\circ\text{ m}\cdot\text{s}^{-2})$$
$$m = \mathbf{105\ kg}$$

13. (a)
$$\Sigma M = 0$$
$$F(2.0\text{ m}) - 60\text{ N}(4.0\text{ m}) + 105\text{ N}(2.0\text{ m}) = 0$$
$$F(2.0\text{ m}) - 240\text{ N}\cdot\text{m} + 210\text{ N}\cdot\text{m} = 0$$
$$F(2.0\text{ m}) = 30\text{ N}\cdot\text{m}$$
$$F = \mathbf{15\ N}$$

(b)
$$\Sigma F_y = 0$$
$$F_u + F - 60\text{ N} - 105\text{ N} = 0$$
$$F_u + (15\text{ N}) - 60\text{ N} - 105\text{ N} = 0$$
$$F_u = \mathbf{150\ N}$$

14.
$$F = F_s = \mu_s F_N$$
$$= 0.86(460\,\cancel{\text{kg}})\left(9.81\,\frac{\text{N}}{\cancel{\text{kg}}}\right)$$
$$= 3881\text{ N} \xrightarrow{\text{SD}} \mathbf{3900\ N}$$

15.
$$\Sigma F_x = 13{,}622\text{ N} - 9625\text{ N} - \mu_k F_N$$
$$= 13{,}622\text{ N} - 9625\text{ N} - 0.6(240.799\,\cancel{\text{kg}})\left(9.81\,\frac{\text{N}}{\cancel{\text{kg}}}\right)$$
$$= 2579.66\text{ N}$$

$$F = ma$$
$$2579.66\text{ N} = (240.799\text{ kg})a$$
$$a = 10.71\,\frac{\text{m}}{\text{s}^2} \xrightarrow{\text{SD}} \mathbf{10\,\frac{m}{s^2}}$$

16. Convert 316°F to °C.
$$T_C = \frac{5}{9}(T_F - 32)$$
$$= \frac{5}{9}(316^\circ - 32)$$
$$= 157.8^\circ\text{C}$$

Convert 157.8°C to kelvins.
$$T_K = T_C + 273$$
$$= 157.8 + 273$$
$$= 430.8\text{ K} \xrightarrow{\text{SD}} \mathbf{431\ K}$$

17.

640̄ N, T_1, 40°, T_2

(a) $\Sigma F_x = 0;\ T_1 \cos 40° - 640\text{ N} = 0$
(b) $\Sigma F_y = 0;\ T_1 \sin 40° - T_2 = 0$

Solve (a) for T_1 and get:
(a) $T_1 \cos 40° = 640\text{ N}$

$$T_1 = 835.46\text{ N} \xrightarrow{\text{SD}} \mathbf{835\ N}$$

Substitute T_1 into (b) and get:

(b) $T_2 = (835.46\text{ N}) \sin 40° = 537.02\text{ N} \xrightarrow{\text{SD}} \mathbf{537\ N}$

18. Begin by converting 27.0 cm^3 to m^3.

$$27.0\ \cancel{\text{cm}^3} \times \frac{1\text{ m}^3}{(100)^3\ \cancel{\text{cm}^3}} = 2.70 \times 10^{-5}\text{ m}^3$$

Calculate the density.

$$\rho = \frac{m}{V}$$
$$= \frac{291\text{ kg}}{2.70 \times 10^{-5}\text{ m}^3}$$
$$= 1.078 \times 10^7\ \frac{\text{kg}}{\text{m}^3} \xrightarrow{\text{SD}} \mathbf{1.08 \times 10^7\ \frac{kg}{m^3}}$$

19. $$42\ \frac{\cancel{\text{mi}}}{\cancel{\text{hr}}} \times \frac{5280\ \cancel{\text{ft}}}{1\ \cancel{\text{mi}}} \times \frac{12\ \cancel{\text{in.}}}{1\ \cancel{\text{ft}}} \times \frac{2.54\text{ cm}}{1\ \cancel{\text{in.}}} \times \frac{1\ \cancel{\text{hr}}}{60\ \cancel{\text{min}}} \times \frac{1\ \cancel{\text{min}}}{60\text{ s}}$$
$$= 1877.6\ \frac{\text{cm}}{\text{s}} \xrightarrow{\text{SD}} \mathbf{1900\ \frac{cm}{s}}$$

20. $w = mg = 100\ \cancel{\text{kg}} \times 8.86\ \frac{\text{N}}{\cancel{\text{kg}}} = \mathbf{886\ N}$

Problem Set 17

1. (a) $\Sigma F_x = 0;\ (40\text{ N}) \cos 20° - \mu_k F_N = 0$
(b) $\Sigma F_y = 0;\ (40\text{ N}) \sin 20° + F_N - w = 0$

Solve (a) for F_N and get:

$$\text{(a)}\quad \mu_k F_N = (40\text{ N}) \cos 20°$$
$$(0.60)F_N = (40\text{ N}) \cos 20°$$
$$F_N = 62.646\text{ N}$$

Substitute F_N into (b) and get:

(b) $w = (40\text{ N}) \sin 20° + (62.646\text{ N}) = 76.327\text{ N} \xrightarrow{\text{SD}} \mathbf{76\ N}$

2. (a) $\Sigma F_x = 0;\ (40\text{ N}) \cos 20° - \mu_k F_N = 0$
(b) $\Sigma F_y = 0;\ F_N - w - (40\text{ N}) \sin 20° = 0$

Solve (a) for F_N and get:

$$\text{(a)}\quad \mu_k F_N = (40\text{ N}) \cos 20°$$
$$(0.60)F_N = (40\text{ N}) \cos 20°$$
$$F_N = 62.646\text{ N}$$

Substitute F_N into (b) and get:

(b) $w = (62.646\text{ N}) - (40\text{ N}) \sin 20° = 48.965\text{ N} \xrightarrow{\text{SD}} \mathbf{49\ N}$

3. (a) $\Sigma F_x = 0;\ (60.0\text{ N}) \cos 40° - \mu_k F_N = 0$
(b) $\Sigma F_y = 0;\ F_N + (60.0\text{ N}) \sin 40° - w = 0$

Solve (b) for F_N and get:

(b) $F_N = w - (60.0\text{ N}) \sin 40°$
$= 98\text{ N} - (60.0\text{ N}) \sin 40° = 59.433\text{ N}$

Substitute F_N into (a) and get:

$$\text{(a)}\quad \mu_k F_N = (60.0\text{ N}) \cos 40°$$
$$\mu_k (59.433\text{ N}) = (60.0\text{ N}) \cos 40°$$
$$\mu_k = 0.773 \xrightarrow{\text{SD}} \mathbf{0.77}$$

4.
$$R_1F_w = R_2F_A$$
$$(10 \text{ cm})F_w = (18 \text{ cm})(20 \text{ N})$$
$$F_w = \mathbf{36\ N}$$

$$\text{Mechanical advantage} = \frac{\text{force out}}{\text{force in}} = \frac{36 \text{ N}}{20 \text{ N}} = \mathbf{1.8}$$

5. Begin by finding the weight of the block.

$$w = mg = 468 \not{\text{kg}} \times 9.81 \frac{\text{N}}{\not{\text{kg}}} = 4591.08 \text{ N}$$

(a) There are three upward forces acting on the weight, so

$$T = \frac{4591.08 \text{ N}}{3} = 1530.36 \text{ N} \xrightarrow{\text{SD}} \mathbf{1530\ N}$$

(b) The weight of the block is 4591.08 N and it takes a force of 1530.36 N to lift it at a constant velocity, so the mechanical advantage is **3.00**.

6.
$$P_1 = 50{,}000 \frac{\text{J}}{\text{hr}} \times 0.400 = 20{,}000 \frac{\text{J}}{\text{hr}}$$
$$P_2 = 20{,}000 \frac{\text{J}}{\text{hr}} \times 0.600 = \mathbf{12{,}000 \frac{J}{hr}}$$

Convert 12,000 J/hr to watts and get:

$$12{,}000 \frac{\text{J}}{\not{\text{hr}}} \times \frac{1 \not{\text{hr}}}{60 \not{\text{min}}} \times \frac{1 \not{\text{min}}}{60 \text{ s}} = 3.33 \text{ watts} \xrightarrow{\text{SD}} \mathbf{3.3\ watts}$$

7. (a)
$$\Sigma M_B = 0$$
$$F_A(9.00 \text{ m}) - 166 \text{ N}(6.00 \text{ m}) = 0$$
$$F_A(9.00 \text{ m}) = 996 \text{ N}\cdot\text{m}$$
$$F_A = 110.67 \text{ N} \xrightarrow{\text{SD}} \mathbf{111\ N}$$

(b)
$$\Sigma F_y = 0$$
$$F_A + F_B - 166 \text{ N} = 0$$
$$(110.67 \text{ N}) + F_B - 166 \text{ N} = 0$$
$$F_B = 55.33 \text{ N} \xrightarrow{\text{SD}} \mathbf{55.3\ N}$$

8. (a)
$$\Sigma M_B = 0$$
$$65.4982(2.000) - 488.6310(4.0000) + F_A(5) = 0$$
$$F_A(5) = 1823.53$$
$$F_A = 365 \text{ N} \xrightarrow{\text{SD}} \mathbf{400\ N}$$

(b)
$$\Sigma F_y = 0$$
$$F_A + F_B - 488.6310 - 65.4982 = 0$$
$$(365) + F_B - 488.6310 - 65.4982 = 0$$
$$F_B = 189 \text{ N} \xrightarrow{\text{SD}} \mathbf{200\ N}$$

9.
$$\Sigma F_y = ma_y$$
$$F_N - mg = ma_y$$
$$F_N - 72 \not{\text{kg}}\left(9.81 \frac{\text{N}}{\not{\text{kg}}}\right) = 72 \text{ kg}(8.0 \text{ m}\cdot\text{s}^{-2})$$
$$F_N = 1282.32 \text{ N} \xrightarrow{\text{SD}} \mathbf{1300\ N}$$

10. (a)
$$\Sigma F_y = ma_y$$
$$F_N = ma_y$$
$$F_N = 70 \text{ kg}(4.9 \text{ m}\cdot\text{s}^{-2}) = 343 \text{ N} \xrightarrow{\text{SD}} \mathbf{340\ N}$$

(b)
$$4.9 \not{\text{m}\cdot\text{s}^{-2}} \times \frac{1g}{9.81 \not{\text{m}\cdot\text{s}^{-2}}} = 0.499g \xrightarrow{\text{SD}} \mathbf{0.50}g$$

11. (a)
$$a_{\text{inst}} = \frac{\Delta v}{\Delta t} = \frac{0 - (-30)}{3 - 1} \frac{\text{m/s}}{\text{s}} = \mathbf{+15 \frac{m}{s^2}}$$

(b)
$$a_{\text{av}} = \frac{v_2 - v_1}{t_2 - t_1} = \frac{-10 - 20}{4.0 - 0} \frac{\text{m/s}}{\text{s}} = \mathbf{-7.5 \frac{m}{s^2}}$$

12. Calculate the displacements for the following time intervals:

$$\Delta x_{0,2} = 20 \frac{\text{m}}{\not{\text{s}}} \times 2 \not{\text{s}} = +40 \text{ m}$$
$$\Delta x_{2,3.5} = \frac{-20 \frac{\text{m}}{\not{\text{s}}} \times 1.5 \not{\text{s}}}{2} = -15 \text{ m}$$
$$\Delta x_{3.5,4} = 0 \text{ m}$$

Sum these displacements with the initial position and g

$$x_{4.0} = 20 \text{ m} + 40 \text{ m} - 15 \text{ m} + 0 \text{ m} = \mathbf{45\ m}$$

13. (a) $W = \dfrac{2\text{ N} \times 0.20\text{ m}}{2} = \mathbf{0.20\ J}$

(b) $P_{av} = \dfrac{W}{\Delta t} = \dfrac{0.20\text{ J}}{1.2\text{ s}} = 0.167\text{ watt} \xrightarrow{SD} \mathbf{0.17\ watt}$

14. Begin by calculating the resultant force.

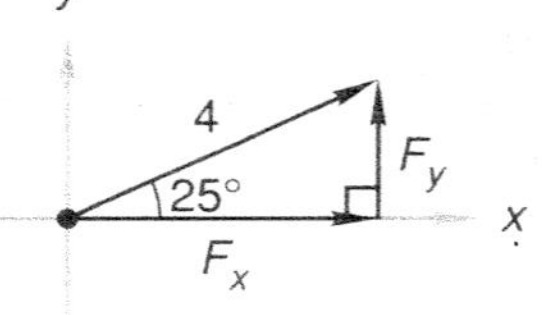

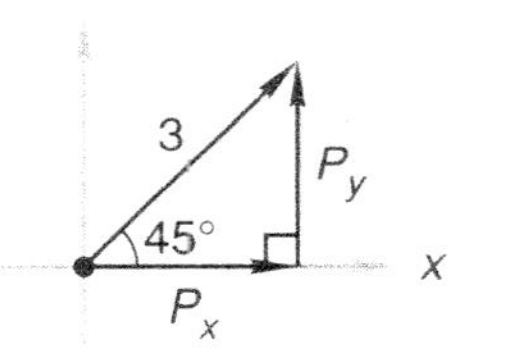

$F_x = 4\cos 25° = 3.6252$
$F_y = 4\sin 25° = 1.6905$

$P_x = 3\cos 45° = 2.1213$
$P_y = 3\sin 45° = 2.1213$

$R_x = F_x + P_x = 3.6252 + 2.1213 = 5.7465\text{ N}$
$R_y = F_y + P_y = 1.6905 + 2.1213 = 3.8118\text{ N}$
$\vec{R} = (5.7465i + 3.8118j)\text{ N}$

Convert this to polar form and get:

$R = \sqrt{(5.7465)^2 + (3.8118)^2} = 6.8958\text{ N}$

$\theta = \tan^{-1}\dfrac{3.8118}{5.7465} = 33.56°$

$\vec{R} = 6.8958\underline{/33.56°}\text{ N}$

Use this resultant force to calculate the acceleration.

$\vec{F} = m\vec{a}$

$6.8958\underline{/33.56°}\text{ N} = (4\text{ kg})\vec{a}$

$\vec{a} = 1.7240\underline{/33.56°}\ \dfrac{\text{m}}{\text{s}^2} \xrightarrow{SD} \mathbf{2\underline{/33.56°}\ \dfrac{m}{s^2}}$

15. (a)

$\Sigma M = 0$
$F(1.4\text{ m}) - 28.4\text{ N}(0.40\text{ m}) + 10.1\text{ N}(0.83\text{ m}) = 0$
$F(1.4\text{ m}) = 2.977\text{ N·m}$
$F = 2.126\text{ N} \xrightarrow{SD} \mathbf{2.1\ N}$

(b)

$\Sigma F_y = 0$
$F + F_u - 28.4\text{ N} - 10.1\text{ N} = 0$
$(2.126\text{ N}) + F_u - 28.4\text{ N} - 10.1\text{ N} = 0$
$F_u = 36.374\text{ N} \xrightarrow{SD} \mathbf{36\ N}$

16. Begin by finding the force of static friction, F_s.

$F_s = \mu_s F_N$
$= 0.8(86\text{ kg})\left(9.81\ \dfrac{\text{N}}{\text{kg}}\right)$
$= 674.93\text{ N}$

Yes, an 820-newton force will cause the mass to move because this force is greater than the force of static friction.

17.

(a) $\Sigma F_x = 0;\ T_2\cos 50° - T_1\cos 30° = 0$
(b) $\Sigma F_y = 0;\ T_1\sin 30° + T_2\sin 50° - 688\text{ N} = 0$

Solve (a) for T_2 and get:

(a) $T_2\cos 50° = T_1\cos 30°$
$T_2 = 1.347T_1$ (a′)

Substitute (a′) into (b) and get:

(b) $T_1\sin 30° + (1.347T_1)\sin 50° = 688\text{ N}$
$1.532T_1 = 688\text{ N}$
$T_1 = 449.09\text{ N} \xrightarrow{SD} \mathbf{449\ N}$

Substitute T_1 into (a′) and get:

(a′) $T_2 = 1.347(449.09\text{ N}) = 604.92\text{ N} \xrightarrow{SD} \mathbf{605\ N}$

18. Begin by finding the mass of the object.

$w = mg$

$2446\text{ N} = m \times 9.81\ \dfrac{\text{N}}{\text{kg}}$

$m = 249.34\text{ kg}$

Calculate the density.

$\rho = \dfrac{m}{V} = \dfrac{249.34\text{ kg}}{0.830\text{ m}^3} = 300.41\ \dfrac{\text{kg}}{\text{m}^3} \xrightarrow{SD} \mathbf{30\bar{0}\ \dfrac{kg}{m^3}}$

19. Begin by drawing a diagram and recording the data.

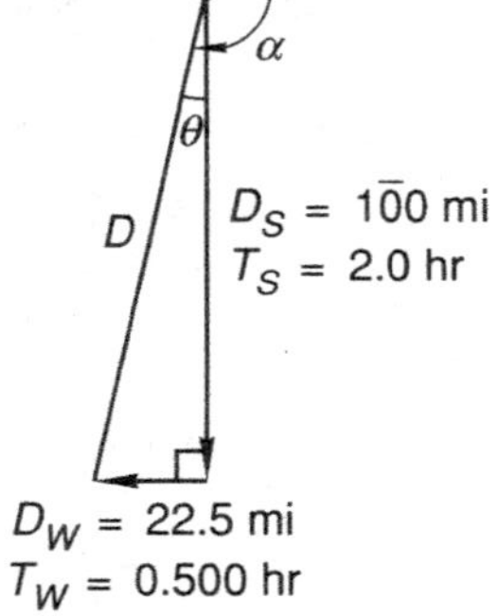

(a) $D_T = 100 \text{ mi} + 22.5 \text{ mi}$

$= 122.5 \text{ mi} \xrightarrow{\text{SD}}$ **120 mi**

(b) $v = \dfrac{D_T}{T_T}$

$= \dfrac{122.5 \text{ mi}}{2.5 \text{ hr}}$

$= \mathbf{49 \dfrac{mi}{hr}}$

(c) $D = \sqrt{(100)^2 + (22.5)^2} = 102.5 \text{ mi}$

$\theta = \tan^{-1} \dfrac{22.5}{100} = 12.68°$

$\alpha = -90° - 12.68° = -102.68°$

$\vec{D} = 102.5\underline{/-102.68°} \text{ mi} \xrightarrow{\text{SD}} \mathbf{1\bar{0}0\underline{/-102.68°} \text{ mi}}$

(d) $\vec{v} = \dfrac{\vec{D}}{T_T} = \dfrac{102.5\underline{/-102.68°} \text{ mi}}{2.5 \text{ hr}} = \mathbf{41\underline{/-102.68°} \dfrac{mi}{hr}}$

20. $4x^2 - 3x - 30 = 0 \longrightarrow a = 4, b = -3, c = -30$

Place these values in the quadratic formula and solve.

$$x = \frac{-b \pm \sqrt{b^2 - 4ac}}{2a} = \frac{-(-3) \pm \sqrt{(-3)^2 - 4(4)(-30)}}{2(4)}$$

$$= \frac{3}{8} \pm \frac{\sqrt{489}}{8} \approx \mathbf{+3.14} \text{ and } \mathbf{-2.39}$$

Problem Set 18

1. Begin by finding the weight of the mass and drawing a free-body diagram of the forces acting on the junction of the ropes.

$w = mg$

$= 694 \text{ kg} \times 9.81 \dfrac{\text{N}}{\text{kg}}$

$= 6808.14 \text{ N}$

Now sum the horizontal and vertical forces to zero.

(a) $\Sigma F_x = 0;\ T_2 - T_1 \cos 40° = 0$

(b) $\Sigma F_y = 0;\ T_1 \sin 40° - 6808.14 \text{ N} = 0$

Solve (b) for T_1 and get:

(b) $T_1 \sin 40° = 6808.14 \text{ N}$

$T_1 = 10{,}592 \text{ N} \xrightarrow{\text{SD}}$ **10,600 N**

Substitute T_1 into (a) and get:

(a) $T_2 = (10{,}592 \text{ N}) \cos 40° = 8114 \text{ N} \xrightarrow{\text{SD}}$ **8110 N**

2. Begin by finding the weight of the mass and drawing a free-body diagram of the forces acting on the junction of the ropes.

$w = mg$

$= 694 \text{ kg} \times 9.81 \dfrac{\text{N}}{\text{kg}}$

$= 6808.14 \text{ N}$

Now sum the horizontal and vertical forces to zero.

(a) $\Sigma F_x = 0;\ T_1 \cos 40° - T_2 \sin 55° = 0$

(b) $\Sigma F_y = 0;\ T_1 \sin 40° - T_2 \cos 55° - 6808.14 \text{ N} = 0$

Solve (a) for T_2 and get:

(a) $T_2 \sin 55° = T_1 \cos 40°$

$T_2 = 0.9352 T_1$ (a′)

Substitute (a′) into (b) and get:

(b) $T_1 \sin 40° - (0.9352 T_1) \cos 55° = 6808.14 \text{ N}$

$0.1064 T_1 = 6808.14 \text{ N}$

$T_1 = 63{,}986 \text{ N} \xrightarrow{\text{SD}}$ **64,$\bar{0}$00 N**

Substitute T_1 into (a′) and get:

(a′) $T_2 = 0.9352(63{,}986 \text{ N}) = 59{,}840 \text{ N} \xrightarrow{\text{SD}}$ **59,800 N**

3. (a) $\Sigma F_x = 0;\ (66\text{ N})\cos 27° - \mu_k F_N = 0$
(b) $\Sigma F_y = 0;\ F_N - (66\text{ N})\sin 27° - w = 0$

Solve (a) for F_N and get:

(a) $\mu_k F_N = (66\text{ N})\cos 27°$

$(0.58)F_N = (66\text{ N})\cos 27°$

$F_N = 101.39\text{ N}$

Substitute F_N into (b) and get:

(b) $101.39\text{ N} - (66\text{ N})\sin 27° - w = 0$

$w = 71.43\text{ N} \xrightarrow{\text{SD}}$ **71 N**

Calculate the mass of the block.

$w = mg$

$71.43\text{ N} = m \times 9.81\ \frac{\text{N}}{\text{kg}}$

$m = 7.28\text{ kg} \xrightarrow{\text{SD}}$ **7.3 kg**

4. (a) $\Sigma F_x = 0;\ (62\text{ N})\cos 37° - \mu_k F_N = 0$
(b) $\Sigma F_y = 0;\ F_N + (62\text{ N})\sin 37° - w = 0$

Solve (b) for F_N and get:

(b) $F_N = w - (62\text{ N})\sin 37°$

$= 144\text{ N} - (62\text{ N})\sin 37° = 106.69\text{ N}$

Substitute F_N into (a) and get:

(a) $\mu_k F_N = (62\text{ N})\cos 37°$

$\mu_k(106.69\text{ N}) = (62\text{ N})\cos 37°$

$\mu_k = 0.464 \xrightarrow{\text{SD}}$ **0.46**

5. Begin by finding the weight of the mass.

$w = mg = 40\,\cancel{\text{kg}} \times 9.81\ \frac{\text{N}}{\cancel{\text{kg}}} = 392.4\text{ N}$

Now set the torques equal to each other and find F.

$F(18.61520\text{ cm}) = 392.4\text{ N}(12.0318\text{ cm})$

$F = 253.62\text{ N} \xrightarrow{\text{SD}}$ **300 N**

$$\text{Mechanical advantage} = \frac{\text{force out}}{\text{force in}} = \frac{392.4\text{ N}}{253.62\text{ N}} = 1.55 \xrightarrow{\text{SD}} 2$$

6. (a) There are two upward forces acting on the weight, so

$F = \frac{500\text{ N}}{2} = \mathbf{250\text{ N}}$

(b) The weight of the block is 500 N and it takes a force of 250 N to balance the weight, so the mechanical advantage is **2.0**.

7. $W_1 = 96{,}000\text{ J} \times 0.400 = 38{,}400\text{ J}$

$W_2 = 38{,}400\text{ J} \times 0.900 = 34{,}560\text{ J} \xrightarrow{\text{SD}}$ **34,600 J**

8. (a) $\Sigma M_B = 0$

$F_A(17.0\text{ m}) - 284\text{ N}(14.0\text{ m}) = 0$

$F_A(17.0\text{ m}) = 3976\text{ N}\cdot\text{m}$

$F_A = 233.9\text{ N} \xrightarrow{\text{SD}}$ **234 N**

(b) $\Sigma F_y = 0$

$F_A + F_B - 284\text{ N} = 0$

$(233.9\text{ N}) + F_B - 284\text{ N} = 0$

$F_B =$ **50.1 N**

9. (a) $\Sigma M_B = 0$

$F_A(9.00\text{ m}) - 316\text{ N}(5.00\text{ m}) = 0$

$F_A(9.00\text{ m}) = 1580\text{ N}\cdot\text{m}$

$F_A = 175.56\text{ N} \xrightarrow{\text{SD}}$ **176 N**

(b) $\Sigma F_y = 0$

$F_A + F_B - 316\text{ N} = 0$

$(175.56\text{ N}) + F_B - 316\text{ N} = 0$

$F_B = 140.44\text{ N} \xrightarrow{\text{SD}}$ **14$\bar{0}$ N**

10. $\Sigma F_y = ma_y$

$F_N - mg = ma_y$

$F_N - 290\,\cancel{\text{kg}}\left(9.81\ \frac{\text{N}}{\cancel{\text{kg}}}\right) = 290\text{ kg}(40\text{ m}\cdot\text{s}^{-2})$

$F_N = 14{,}444.9\text{ N} \xrightarrow{\text{SD}}$ **14,000 N**

11.
$$\Sigma F_y = ma_y$$
$$F_N - mg = ma_y$$
$$F_N - 118\,\cancel{kg}\left(9.81\,\frac{N}{\cancel{kg}}\right) = 118\text{ kg}(-2.0\text{ m}\cdot\text{s}^{-2})$$
$$F_N = 921.58\text{ N} \xrightarrow{SD} \mathbf{920\ N}$$

12. (a) Answers to this problem may vary due to differing data points. One possible solution is given here. Choose the points (2, 2) and (4, 12) and get:

$$v_{inst} = \frac{\Delta x}{\Delta t} = \frac{12 - 2}{4 - 2}\,\frac{\text{m}}{\text{s}} = \mathbf{+5.0\ \frac{m}{s}}$$

(b) $$v_{av} = \frac{x_2 - x_1}{t_2 - t_1} = \frac{8 - 0}{4 - 0}\,\frac{\text{m}}{\text{s}} = \mathbf{+2.0\ \frac{m}{s}}$$

13. Calculate the displacements for the following time intervals:

$$\Delta x_{0,1} = \frac{-40\,\frac{\text{m}}{\cancel{s}} \times 1\cancel{s}}{2} = -20\text{ m}$$

$$\Delta x_{1,4} = 20\,\frac{\text{m}}{\cancel{s}} \times 3\cancel{s} = +60\text{ m}$$

Sum these displacements with the initial position and get:
$x_4 = -40\text{ m} - 20\text{ m} + 60\text{ m} = \mathbf{0\ m}$

14. (a) $W = F \times D$

$$= 4000\,\cancel{kg}\left(9.81\,\frac{N}{\cancel{kg}}\right) \times 2\text{ m} = 78{,}480\text{ J} \xrightarrow{SD} \mathbf{80{,}000\ J}$$

(b) $$P_{av} = \frac{78{,}480\text{ J}}{20\text{ s}} = 3924\text{ watts} \xrightarrow{SD} \mathbf{4000\ watts}$$

15. $\vec{F} = m\vec{a} = 150\text{ kg}(500\underline{/110°}\text{ m}\cdot\text{s}^{-2}) = \mathbf{75{,}000\underline{/110°}\ N}$

16. (a) $\Sigma F_x = 25\text{ N} - 25\text{ N} = \mathbf{0\ N}$
(b) $\Sigma F_y = 25\text{ N} - 25\text{ N} = \mathbf{0\ N}$
(c) $\Sigma\tau = -25\text{ N}(4.0\text{ cm}) - 25\text{ N}(4.0\text{ cm}) - 25\text{ N}(4.0\text{ cm}) - 25\text{ N}(4.0\text{ cm})$
$= \mathbf{-4\bar{0}0\ N\cdot cm}$

17. $F = F_s = \mu_s F_N$

$$= 0.68(4.2\,\cancel{kg})\left(9.81\,\frac{N}{\cancel{kg}}\right)$$
$$= 28.02\text{ N} \xrightarrow{SD} \mathbf{28\ N}$$

18. $2x^2 + 2x - 35 = 0 \longrightarrow a = 2, b = 2, c = -35$
Place these values in the quadratic formula and solve.

$$x = \frac{-b \pm \sqrt{b^2 - 4ac}}{2a} = \frac{-2 \pm \sqrt{2^2 - 4(2)(-35)}}{2(2)} = -\frac{1}{2} \pm \frac{\sqrt{71}}{2}$$
$$\approx \mathbf{+3.71\ and\ -4.71}$$

19. $$9.81\,\frac{\cancel{N}}{\cancel{kg}} \times \frac{\cancel{kg}\cdot\text{m}}{\cancel{N}\cdot\text{s}^2} = \mathbf{9.81\ \frac{m}{s^2}}$$

20. $$v_{av} = \frac{x_2 - x_1}{t_2 - t_1} = \frac{310 - 200}{200 - 0}\,\frac{\text{m}}{\text{s}} = \mathbf{+0.55\ \frac{m}{s}}$$

Problem Set 19

1. (a) $v(t) = v_0 + at$

$$v(6.0) = 1.0\,\frac{\text{m}}{\text{s}} + 0.25\,\frac{\text{m}}{\text{s}^2}(6.0\text{ s}) = \mathbf{+2.5\ \frac{m}{s}}$$

(b) $x(t) = x_0 + v_0 t + \frac{1}{2}at^2$

$$\Delta x = 1.0\,\frac{\text{m}}{\text{s}}(6.0\text{ s}) + \frac{1}{2}\left(0.25\,\frac{\text{m}}{\text{s}^2}\right)(6.0\text{ s})^2$$
$$= 10.5\text{ m} \xrightarrow{SD} \mathbf{11\ m}$$

2. (a) $$a = \frac{v_2 - v_1}{t_2 - t_1} = \frac{2.0 - 63}{8.0 - 0}\,\frac{\text{m/s}}{\text{s}} = -7.625\,\frac{\text{m}}{\text{s}^2} \xrightarrow{SD} \mathbf{-7.6\ \frac{m}{s^2}}$$

(b) $x(t) = x_0 + v_0 t + \frac{1}{2}at^2$

$$\Delta x = 63\,\frac{\text{m}}{\text{s}}(8.0\text{ s}) + \frac{1}{2}\left(-7.625\,\frac{\text{m}}{\text{s}^2}\right)(8.0\text{ s})^2 = \mathbf{260\ m}$$

3. (a)

$$x(t) = x_0 + v_0t + \frac{1}{2}at^2$$

$$63 = 0 + 0.20t + \frac{1}{2}(2.2)t^2$$

$$1.1t^2 + 0.20t - 63 = 0$$

Use the quadratic formula to solve this equation for t.

$$t = \frac{-0.20 \pm \sqrt{(0.20)^2 - 4(1.1)(-63)}}{2(1.1)} = 7.478 \text{ s} \xrightarrow{\text{SD}} \mathbf{7.5 \text{ s}}$$

(b)

$$v(t) = v_0 + at$$

$$v(7.478) = 0.20 + 2.2(7.478)$$

$$= +16.65 \frac{\text{m}}{\text{s}} \xrightarrow{\text{SD}} \mathbf{+17 \frac{m}{s}}$$

4. Begin by finding the weight of the mass and drawing a free-body diagram of the forces acting on the junction of the ropes.

$$w = mg$$

$$= 968 \text{ kg} \times 9.81 \frac{\text{N}}{\text{kg}}$$

$$= 9496.08 \text{ N}$$

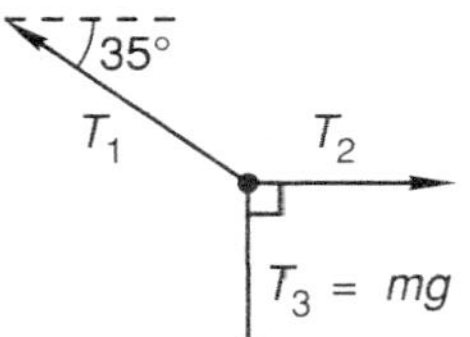

Now note that T_3 equals the weight of the mass.

$$T_3 = mg = 9496.08 \text{ N} \xrightarrow{\text{SD}} \mathbf{95\bar{0}0 \text{ N}}$$

Next, sum the horizontal and vertical forces to zero.

(a) $\Sigma F_x = 0;\ T_2 - T_1 \cos 35° = 0$

(b) $\Sigma F_y = 0;\ T_1 \sin 35° - mg = 0$

Solve (b) for T_1 and get:

(b) $T_1 \sin 35° = 9496.08 \text{ N}$

$$T_1 = 16{,}555.9 \text{ N} \xrightarrow{\text{SD}} \mathbf{16{,}600 \text{ N}}$$

Substitute T_1 into (a) and get:

(a) $T_2 = (16{,}555.9 \text{ N}) \cos 35° = 13{,}561.8 \text{ N} \xrightarrow{\text{SD}} \mathbf{13{,}600 \text{ N}}$

5. Begin by finding the weight of the mass and drawing a free-body diagram of the forces acting on the junction of the ropes.

$$w = mg$$

$$= 968 \text{ kg} \times 9.81 \frac{\text{N}}{\text{kg}}$$

$$= 9496.08 \text{ N}$$

Now sum the horizontal and vertical forces to zero.

(a) $\Sigma F_x = 0;\ T_2 \cos 50° - T_1 \sin 60° = 0$

(b) $\Sigma F_y = 0;\ T_2 \sin 50° - T_1 \cos 60° - 9496.08 \text{ N} = 0$

Solve (a) for T_2 and get:

(a) $T_2 \cos 50° = T_1 \sin 60°$

$$T_2 = 1.347T_1 \qquad (a')$$

Substitute (a′) into (b) and get:

(b) $(1.347T_1) \sin 50° - T_1 \cos 60° = 9496.08 \text{ N}$

$$0.532T_1 = 9496.08 \text{ N}$$

$$T_1 = 17{,}849.8 \text{ N} \xrightarrow{\text{SD}} \mathbf{17{,}800 \text{ N}}$$

Substitute T_1 into (a′) and get:

(a′) $T_2 = 1.347(17{,}849.8 \text{ N})$

$$= 24{,}043.7 \text{ N} \xrightarrow{\text{SD}} \mathbf{24{,}\bar{0}00 \text{ N}}$$

6. (a) $\Sigma F_x = 0;\ (3814 \text{ N}) \cos 20° - \mu_k F_N = 0$

(b) $\Sigma F_y = 0;\ F_N - (3814 \text{ N}) \sin 20° - mg = 0$

Solve (b) for F_N and get:

(b) $F_N = (3814 \text{ N}) \sin 20° + 462 \text{ kg}\left(9.81 \frac{\text{N}}{\text{kg}}\right) = 5836.68 \text{ N}$

Substitute F_N into (a) and get:

(a) $\mu_k F_N = (3814 \text{ N}) \cos 20°$

$$\mu_k(5836.68 \text{ N}) = (3814 \text{ N}) \cos 20°$$

$$\mu_k = 0.6140 \xrightarrow{\text{SD}} \mathbf{0.614}$$

7. (a) $\Sigma F_x = 0;\ (680\text{ N})\cos 32° - \mu_k F_N = 0$

(b) $\Sigma F_y = 0;\ F_N + (680\text{ N})\sin 32° - mg = 0$

Solve (a) for F_N and get:

(a)
$$\mu_k F_N = (680\text{ N})\cos 32°$$
$$(0.62)F_N = (680\text{ N})\cos 32°$$
$$F_N = 930.12\text{ N}$$

Substitute F_N into (b) and get:

(b)
$$mg = F_N + (680\text{ N})\sin 32°$$
$$m\left(9.81\ \frac{\text{N}}{\text{kg}}\right) = 930.12\text{ N} + (680\text{ N})\sin 32°$$
$$m = 131.55\text{ kg} \xrightarrow{\text{SD}} \mathbf{130\ kg}$$

8. (a) Begin by finding the weight of the mass.

$$w = mg = 12\,\cancel{\text{kg}} \times 9.81\ \frac{\text{N}}{\cancel{\text{kg}}} = 117.72\text{ N}$$

Now set the torques equal to each other and find F.

$F(22\text{ cm}) = 117.72\text{ N}(6.0\text{ cm})$

$$F = 32.11\text{ N} \xrightarrow{\text{SD}} \mathbf{32\ N}$$

(b) Mechanical advantage $= \dfrac{\text{force out}}{\text{force in}} = \dfrac{117.72\text{ N}}{32.11\text{ N}} = 3.67 \xrightarrow{\text{SD}} \mathbf{3.7}$

9. (a) $F = \dfrac{62{,}488\text{ N}}{5} = 12{,}497.6\text{ N} \xrightarrow{\text{SD}} \mathbf{10{,}000\ N}$

(b) Find the work Cindy does on the object.

$$W = F \times D = 62{,}488\text{ N} \times 0.1000\text{ m} = 6248.8\text{ J} \xrightarrow{\text{SD}} \mathbf{6249\ J}$$

10. $W_1 = 468\text{ J} \times 0.41 = 191.88\text{ J}$

Percent eff. $= \dfrac{W_{out}}{W_{in}} \times 100\% = \dfrac{150\text{ J}}{191.88\text{ J}} \times 100\% = 78.2\% \xrightarrow{\text{SD}} \mathbf{78\%}$

11.
$$\Sigma M_B = 0$$
$$680\text{ N}(14\text{ m}) - F(10\text{ m}) = 0$$
$$F(10\text{ m}) = 9520\text{ N}\cdot\text{m}$$
$$F = 952\text{ N} \xrightarrow{\text{SD}} \mathbf{950\ N}$$

$$\Sigma F_y = 0$$
$$680\text{ N} + F_B - F = 0$$
$$680\text{ N} + F_B - (952\text{ N}) = 0$$
$$F_B = 272\text{ N} \xrightarrow{\text{SD}} \mathbf{270\ N}$$

12.
$$\Sigma M_B = 0$$
$$200\text{ N}(4.0\text{ m}) - 600\text{ N}(5.0\text{ m}) + F_A(17\text{ m}) = 0$$
$$F_A(17\text{ m}) = 2200\text{ N}\cdot\text{m}$$
$$F_A = 129.4\text{ N} \xrightarrow{\text{SD}} \mathbf{130\ N}$$

$$\Sigma F_y = 0$$
$$F_A + 200\text{ N} + F_B - 600\text{ N} = 0$$
$$(129.4\text{ N}) + 200\text{ N} + F_B - 600\text{ N} = 0$$
$$F_B = 270.6\text{ N} \xrightarrow{\text{SD}} \mathbf{270\ N}$$

13.
$$\Sigma F_y = ma_y$$
$$T - mg = ma_y$$
$$T - 20\,\cancel{\text{kg}}\left(9.81\ \frac{\text{N}}{\cancel{\text{kg}}}\right) = 20\text{ kg}(4.0\text{ m}\cdot\text{s}^{-2})$$
$$T = 276.2\text{ N} \xrightarrow{\text{SD}} \mathbf{280\ N}$$

14. (a) Answers to this problem may vary due to differing data points. One possible solution is given here. Choose the points (3.4, 12) and (6.9, 3.8) and get:

$$a_{inst} = \frac{\Delta v}{\Delta t} = \frac{3.8 - 12}{6.9 - 3.4}\ \frac{\text{knots}}{\text{min}} = -2.34\ \frac{\text{knots}}{\text{min}} \xrightarrow{\text{SD}} \mathbf{-2.3\ \frac{knots}{min}}$$

(b) $a_{av} = \dfrac{v_2 - v_1}{t_2 - t_1} = \dfrac{10 - 4}{4.0 - 1.0}\ \dfrac{\text{knots}}{\text{min}} = \mathbf{+2.0\ \dfrac{knots}{min}}$

15. Calculate the displacements for the following time intervals:

$$\Delta x_{0,4} = \frac{-40\,\frac{\text{m}}{\cancel{\text{min}}} \times 4\,\cancel{\text{min}}}{2} = -80\text{ m}$$

$$\Delta x_{4,6} = 80\,\frac{\text{m}}{\cancel{\text{min}}} \times 2\,\cancel{\text{min}} = +160\text{ m}$$

Sum these displacements with the initial position and get:

$x_{6.0} = -200\text{ m} - 80\text{ m} + 160\text{ m} = \mathbf{-120\ m}$

16. Begin by calculating the resultant force.

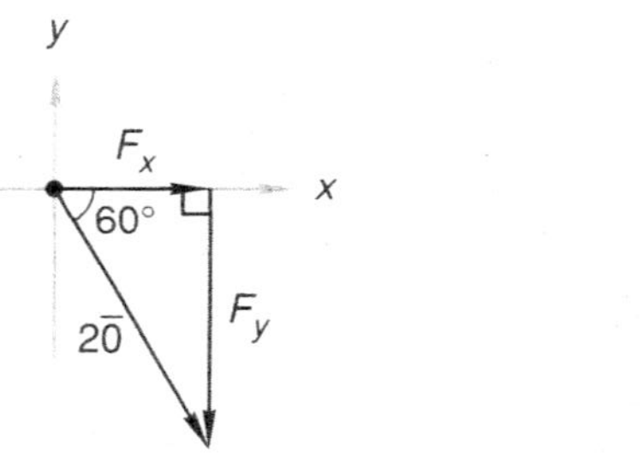

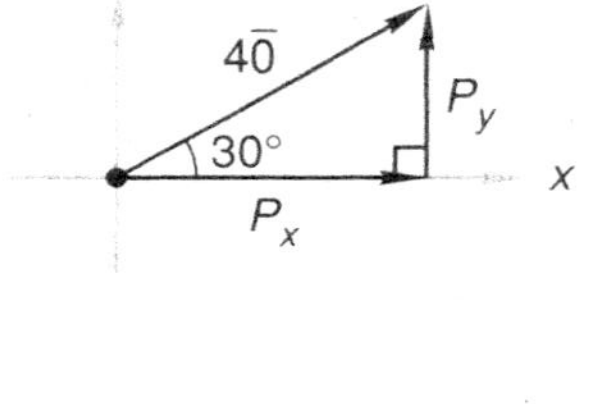

$F_x = 20\cos 60° = 10.000$
$F_y = (-)20\sin 60° = -17.321$

$P_x = 40\cos 30° = 34.641$
$P_y = 40\sin 30° = 20.000$

$R_x = F_x + P_x = 10.000 + 34.641 = 44.641\text{ N}$
$R_y = F_y + P_y = -17.321 + 20.000 = 2.679\text{ N}$
$\vec{R} = (44.641i + 2.679j)\text{ N}$

Convert this to polar form and get:

$R = \sqrt{(44.641)^2 + (2.679)^2} = 44.72\text{ N}$

$\theta = \tan^{-1}\frac{2.679}{44.641} = 3.43°$

$\vec{R} = 44.72\angle 3.43°\text{ N}$

Use this resultant to calculate the acceleration.

$\vec{F} = m\vec{a}$
$44.72\angle 3.43°\text{ N} = (2.0\text{ kg})\vec{a}$
$\vec{a} = 22.36\angle 3.43°\ \frac{\text{m}}{\text{s}^2} \xrightarrow{\text{SD}} \mathbf{22\angle 3.43°\ \frac{m}{s^2}}$

17.

$\Sigma F_y = 0$
$64\text{ N} - 42\text{ N} - F = 0$
$F = \mathbf{22\ N}$

$\Sigma M = 0$
$F(8.0\text{ m} + x) - 64\text{ N}(8.0\text{ m}) = 0$
$22\text{ N}(8.0\text{ m}) + (22\text{ N})x - 512\text{ N}\cdot\text{m} = 0$
$(22\text{ N})x = 336\text{ N}\cdot\text{m}$
$x = 15.27\text{ m} \xrightarrow{\text{SD}} \mathbf{15\ m}$

18. $F = F_s = \mu_s F_N$

$= 0.24(0.80\,\cancel{\text{kg}})\left(9.81\,\frac{\text{N}}{\cancel{\text{kg}}}\right)$

$= 1.88\text{ N} \xrightarrow{\text{SD}} \mathbf{1.9\ N}$

19.

$\rho = \frac{m}{V}$

$98.6\,\frac{\text{kg}}{\text{m}^3} = \frac{16\text{ kg}}{V}$

$V = 0.162\text{ m}^3 \xrightarrow{\text{SD}} \mathbf{0.16\ m^3}$

20. First, we draw the diagram.

°F	°C	
212°	100°	**Boiling**
180 spaces	100 spaces	
32°	0°	**Freezing**

Then we determine the number of degrees above or below the freezing temperature of water.

$291° - 32 = 259°$

Thus, we are 259 Fahrenheit degrees above freezing. Since the ratio of the increments is

$$\text{Ratio} = \frac{°\text{C}}{°\text{F}} = \frac{100}{180} = \frac{5}{9}$$

it takes fewer Celsius degrees to measure an interval, so we multiply by 5 over 9.

$$259° \times \frac{5}{9} = 143.9°\text{C} \xrightarrow{\text{SD}} \mathbf{144°C}$$

Problem Set 20

1. Begin by finding the energy expended during 100 lifts.
   50 joules × 100 = 5000 joules

   Now convert joules to food calories.

   $$5000\ \cancel{\text{joules}} \times \frac{1\ \text{food calorie}}{4186\ \cancel{\text{joules}}}$$

   $$= 1.19\ \text{food calories} \xrightarrow{\text{SD}} \mathbf{1\ food\ calorie}$$

2. $$Q = mc\Delta T$$

   $$= 4.0\ \cancel{\text{kg}}\left(899\ \frac{\text{J}}{\cancel{\text{kg}}\cdot\cancel{\text{C}^\circ}}\right)(27\ \cancel{\text{C}^\circ})$$

   $$= 9.7092 \times 10^4\ \text{J} \xrightarrow{\text{SD}} \mathbf{9.7 \times 10^4\ J}$$

3. Motion equation: $\boldsymbol{v(t) = v_0 + at}$

   Position equation: $\boldsymbol{x(t) = x_0 + v_0 t + \frac{1}{2}at^2}$

   $$v(6.0) = 40\ \frac{\text{m}}{\text{s}} + \left(-4.0\ \frac{\text{m}}{\text{s}^2}\right)(6.0\ \text{s})$$

   $$= \mathbf{+16\ \frac{m}{s}}$$

4. $$x(6.0) = 0\ \text{m} + 40\ \frac{\text{m}}{\text{s}}(6.0\ \text{s}) + \frac{1}{2}\left(-4.0\ \frac{\text{m}}{\text{s}^2}\right)(6.0\ \text{s})^2$$

   $$= 168\ \text{m} \xrightarrow{\text{SD}} \mathbf{170\ m}$$

5. Begin by finding the weight of the mass and drawing a free-body diagram of the forces acting on the junction of the ropes.

   $$w = mg$$

   $$= 136\ \cancel{\text{kg}} \times 9.81\ \frac{\text{N}}{\cancel{\text{kg}}}$$

   $$= 1334.16\ \text{N}$$

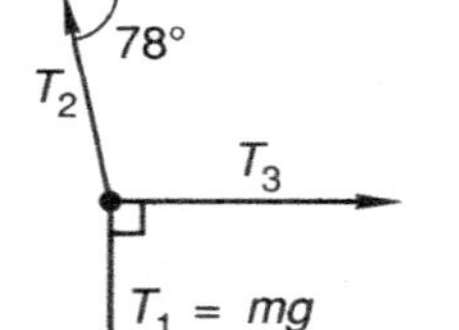

   Now note that T_1 equals the weight of the mass.

   $$T_1 = mg = 1334.16\ \text{N} \xrightarrow{\text{SD}} \mathbf{1330\ N}$$

   Next, sum the horizontal and vertical forces to zero.
   (a) $\Sigma F_x = 0;\ T_3 - T_2 \cos 78° = 0$
   (b) $\Sigma F_y = 0;\ T_2 \sin 78° - mg = 0$

   Solve (b) for T_2 and get:
   (b) $T_2 \sin 78° = 1334.16\ \text{N}$

   $$T_2 = 1363.97\ \text{N} \xrightarrow{\text{SD}} \mathbf{1360\ N}$$

   Substitute T_2 into (a) and get:

   (a) $T_3 = (1363.97\ \text{N}) \cos 78° = 283.59\ \text{N} \xrightarrow{\text{SD}} \mathbf{284\ N}$

6. Begin by finding the weight of the mass and drawing a free-body diagram of the forces acting on the junction of the ropes.

   $$w = mg$$

   $$= 42\ \cancel{\text{kg}} \times 9.81\ \frac{\text{N}}{\cancel{\text{kg}}}$$

   $$= 412.02\ \text{N}$$

   Now sum the horizontal and vertical forces to zero.
   (a) $\Sigma F_x = 0;\ T_2 \cos 30° - T_1 \cos 60° = 0$
   (b) $\Sigma F_y = 0;\ T_1 \sin 60° + T_2 \sin 30° - 412.02\ \text{N} = 0$

   Solve (a) for T_2 and get:
   (a) $T_2 \cos 30° = T_1 \cos 60°$

   $$T_2 = 0.577T_1 \qquad (\text{a}')$$

   Substitute (a′) into (b) and get:
   (b) $T_1 \sin 60° + (0.577T_1) \sin 30° = 412.02\ \text{N}$

   $$1.155T_1 = 412.02\ \text{N}$$

   $$T_1 = 356.73\ \text{N} \xrightarrow{\text{SD}} \mathbf{360\ N}$$

   Substitute T_1 into (a′) and get:

   (a′) $T_2 = 0.577(356.73\ \text{N}) = 205.83\ \text{N} \xrightarrow{\text{SD}} \mathbf{210\ N}$

7. (a) $F_N = mg + (2500\text{ N})\sin 20°$

$$= 120\text{ kg}\left(9.81\ \frac{\text{N}}{\text{kg}}\right) + (2500\text{ N})\sin 20°$$

$$= 2.032 \times 10^3\text{ N} \xrightarrow{\text{SD}} \mathbf{2.0 \times 10^3\ N}$$

(b) $F_k = \mu_k F_N = 0.35(2.032 \times 10^3\text{ N}) = 711.2\text{ N} \xrightarrow{\text{SD}} \mathbf{710\ N}$

(c)

$$\Sigma F_x = ma_x$$

$$(2500\text{ N})\cos 20° - F_k = ma_x$$

$$(2500\text{ N})\cos 20° - 711.2\text{ N} = (120\text{ kg})a_x$$

$$a_x = 13.65\ \frac{\text{m}}{\text{s}^2} \xrightarrow{\text{SD}} \mathbf{14\ \frac{m}{s^2}\ to\ the\ right}$$

8. (a) $\Sigma F_x = 0;\ F\cos 20° - \mu_k F_N = 0$

(b) $\Sigma F_y = 0;\ F_N - F\sin 20° - mg = 0$

Solve (a) and (b) for F_N and get:

(a)

$$\mu_k F_N = F\cos 20°$$

$$(0.23)F_N = F\cos 20°$$

$$F_N = 4.086F \qquad \text{(a')}$$

(b) $F_N = F\sin 20° + 0.40\text{ kg}\left(9.81\ \frac{\text{N}}{\text{kg}}\right)$

$$= F\sin 20° + 3.924\text{ N} \qquad \text{(b')}$$

Now equate (a') and (b') and get:

$4.086F = F\sin 20° + 3.924\text{ N}$

$3.744F = 3.924\text{ N}$

$$F = 1.048\text{ N} \xrightarrow{\text{SD}} \mathbf{1.0\ N}$$

9. Begin by equating the torques. Remember F equals force in and w equals force out.

$F(1.5\text{ m}) = w(1.1\text{ m})$

$$\text{Mechanical advantage} = \frac{\text{force out}}{\text{force in}} = \frac{w}{F} = \frac{1.5\text{ m}}{1.1\text{ m}} = 1.36 \xrightarrow{\text{SD}} \mathbf{1.4}$$

10. (a) Begin by finding the weight of the mass.

$$w = mg$$

$$= 1000\text{ kg} \times 9.81\ \frac{\text{N}}{\text{kg}}$$

$$= 9810\text{ N}$$

There are five upward forces acting on the weight, so

$$T = \frac{9810\text{ N}}{5} = 1962\text{ N} \xrightarrow{\text{SD}} \mathbf{2000\ N}$$

(b) The weight of the mass is 9810 N and the tension is 1962 N, so the mechanical advantage is **5**.

11.

$$\text{Percent eff.} = \frac{6996\text{ J}}{12{,}286\text{ J}} \times 100\%$$

$$= 56.943\% \xrightarrow{\text{SD}} \mathbf{56.94\%}$$

12.

$$\Sigma M_B = 0$$

$$F_A(6.0\text{ m}) + 10\text{ N}(5.0\text{ m}) - 20\text{ N}(4.0\text{ m}) - 60\text{ N}(2.0\text{ m}) = 0$$

$$F_A(6.0\text{ m}) = 150\text{ N}\cdot\text{m}$$

$$F_A = \mathbf{25\ N}$$

$$\Sigma F_y = 0$$

$$F_A + 10\text{ N} + F_B - 20\text{ N} - 60\text{ N} = 0$$

$$(25\text{ N}) + 10\text{ N} + F_B - 20\text{ N} - 60\text{ N} = 0$$

$$F_B = \mathbf{45\ N}$$

13.

$$\Sigma F_y = ma_y$$

$$F_N - mg = ma_y$$

$$F_N - 100\text{ kg}\left(9.81\ \frac{\text{N}}{\text{kg}}\right) = 100\text{ kg}(-5\text{ m}\cdot\text{s}^{-2})$$

$$F_N = 481\text{ N} \xrightarrow{\text{SD}} \mathbf{500\ N}$$

14. (a) Answers to this problem may vary due to differing data points. One possible solution is given here. Choose the points (1.2, 2) and (2, 4) and get:

$$v_{\text{inst}} = \frac{\Delta x}{\Delta t} = \frac{4 - 2}{2 - 1.2}\,\frac{\text{mi}}{\text{hr}} = \mathbf{+2.5\ \frac{mi}{hr}}$$

(b) $$v_{\text{av}} = \frac{x_2 - x_1}{t_2 - t_1} = \frac{14 - 4}{5.0 - 2.0}\,\frac{\text{mi}}{\text{hr}} = +3.33\ \frac{\text{mi}}{\text{hr}} \xrightarrow{\text{SD}} \mathbf{+3.3\ \frac{mi}{hr}}$$

15. (a) The acceleration is positive on intervals where the slope of the graph is positive. Thus, $a > 0$ on the interval $\mathbf{0 < t < 2}$.

$$a = \frac{6 - 4}{2 - 0}\,\frac{\text{m/s}}{\text{s}} = +1.0\ \frac{\text{m}}{\text{s}^2}$$

(b) The acceleration is negative on intervals where the slope of the graph is negative. Thus, $a < 0$ on the interval $\mathbf{4 < t < 6}$.

$$a = \frac{4 - 6}{6 - 4}\,\frac{\text{m/s}}{\text{s}} = -1.0\ \frac{\text{m}}{\text{s}^2}$$

(c) The acceleration is zero on intervals where the slope of the graph is zero. Thus, $a = 0$ on the interval $\mathbf{2 < t < 4}$.

$$a = \frac{6 - 6}{4 - 2}\,\frac{\text{m/s}}{\text{s}} = 0\ \frac{\text{m}}{\text{s}^2}$$

(d)

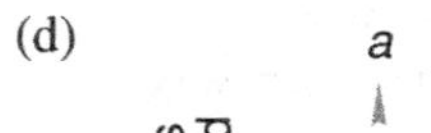

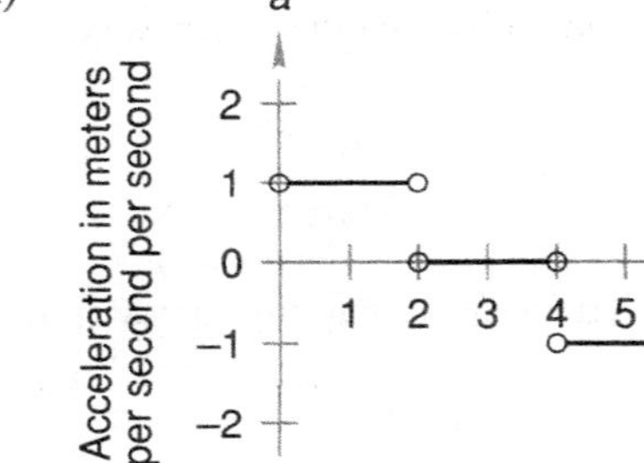

16.

$$\vec{F} = m\vec{a}$$
$$60\angle 20°\ \text{N} = (20\ \text{kg})\vec{a}$$
$$\vec{a} = \mathbf{3\angle 20°\ \frac{m}{s^2}}$$

17. (a)

$$\Sigma M = 0$$
$$210{,}842\ \text{N}(10\ \text{m}) - T_y(6.000\ \text{m}) = 0$$
$$T_y = 351{,}403\ \text{N} \xrightarrow{\text{SD}} \mathbf{400{,}000\ N}$$

(b) Now use T_y to find T. Then find T_x.

$$T \sin 32° = T_y$$
$$T \sin 32° = 351{,}403\ \text{N}$$
$$T = 663{,}126\ \text{N} \xrightarrow{\text{SD}} \mathbf{700{,}000\ N}$$

$$T \cos 32° = T_x$$
$$T_x = (663{,}126\ \text{N}) \cos 32°$$
$$= 562{,}363\ \text{N} \xrightarrow{\text{SD}} \mathbf{600{,}000\ N}$$

(c) Sum the vertical forces to zero to find F_y.

$$F_y + T_y - 210{,}842\ \text{N} = 0$$
$$F_y = -351{,}403\ \text{N} + 210{,}842\ \text{N}$$
$$= -140{,}561\ \text{N} \xrightarrow{\text{SD}} \mathbf{-100{,}000\ N}$$

(d) Sum the horizontal forces to zero to find F_x.

$$F_x - T_x = 0$$
$$F_x = T_x = 562{,}363\ \text{N} \xrightarrow{\text{SD}} \mathbf{600{,}000\ N}$$

18.

$$F = F_s = \mu_s F_N$$
$$= 0.86(2.4\ \cancel{\text{kg}})\left(9.81\ \frac{\text{N}}{\cancel{\text{kg}}}\right)$$
$$= 20.25\ \text{N} \xrightarrow{\text{SD}} \mathbf{2\bar{0}\ N}$$

19. (a) Begin by converting 42 cm^3 to m^3.

$$42\ \cancel{\text{cm}^3} \times \frac{1\ \text{m}^3}{(100)^3\ \cancel{\text{cm}^3}} = 4.2 \times 10^{-5}\ \text{m}^3$$

Calculate the mass of the seawater.

$$\rho = \frac{m}{V}$$
$$1025\ \frac{\text{kg}}{\text{m}^3} = \frac{m}{4.2 \times 10^{-5}\ \text{m}^3}$$
$$m = 4.305 \times 10^{-2}\ \text{kg} \xrightarrow{\text{SD}} \mathbf{4.3 \times 10^{-2}\ kg}$$

(b) $$w = mg = 4.305 \times 10^{-2}\ \cancel{\text{kg}}\left(9.81\ \frac{\text{N}}{\cancel{\text{kg}}}\right) = 0.4223\ \text{N} \xrightarrow{\text{SD}} \mathbf{0.42\ N}$$

20. $$689\ \cancel{\text{km}^2} \times \frac{(1000)^2\ \cancel{\text{m}^2}}{1\ \cancel{\text{km}^2}} \times \frac{(100)^2\ \text{cm}^2}{1\ \cancel{\text{m}^2}} = \mathbf{6.89 \times 10^{12}\ cm^2}$$

PROBLEM SET 21

1. (a)
$$F\Delta t = \Delta(mv)$$
$$4.0\text{ N}(1.5\text{ s}) = \Delta(mv)$$
$$\Delta(mv) = 6.0\text{ N}\cdot\text{s} = \mathbf{6.0\ \frac{kg\cdot m}{s}}$$

(b)
$$F\Delta t = \Delta(mv)$$
$$4.0\text{ N}(1.5\text{ s}) = 0.50\text{ kg}\left(v_2 - 0\ \frac{\text{m}}{\text{s}}\right)$$
$$12\ \frac{\text{m}}{\text{s}} = v_2 - 0\ \frac{\text{m}}{\text{s}}$$
$$v_2 = \mathbf{12\ \frac{m}{s}}$$

(c) Begin by finding the acceleration of the timer.
$$F = ma$$
$$4.0\text{ N} = (0.50\text{ kg})a$$
$$a = 8.0\ \frac{\text{m}}{\text{s}^2}$$

Now use the motion equation to find the speed when $t = 1.5$ s.
$$v(t) = v_0 + at$$
$$v(1.5) = 0\ \frac{\text{m}}{\text{s}} + 8.0\ \frac{\text{m}}{\text{s}^2}(1.5\text{ s}) = \mathbf{12\ \frac{m}{s}}$$

2. (a)
$$\Delta(mv) = m(v_2 - v_1)$$
$$= 0.25\text{ kg}\left(+32i\ \frac{\text{m}}{\text{s}} - \left(-25i\ \frac{\text{m}}{\text{s}}\right)\right)$$
$$= +14.25i\ \frac{\text{kg}\cdot\text{m}}{\text{s}} \xrightarrow{\text{SD}} \mathbf{+14}\boldsymbol{i}\ \mathbf{\frac{kg\cdot m}{s}}$$

(b)
$$F\Delta t = \Delta(mv)$$
$$F(0.092\text{ s}) = +14.25i\ \frac{\text{kg}\cdot\text{m}}{\text{s}}$$
$$F = +154.89i\text{ N} \xrightarrow{\text{SD}} \mathbf{+150}\boldsymbol{i}\ \mathbf{N}$$

3. Begin by finding the energy expended during $\overline{20}$ lifts.
$70.04918\text{ J} \times 20 = 1400.9836\text{ J}$
Now convert joules to food calories.
$$1400.9836\,\cancel{\text{J}} \times \frac{1\text{ food calorie}}{4186\,\cancel{\text{J}}}$$
$$= 0.3347\text{ food calorie} \xrightarrow{\text{SD}} \mathbf{0.33\ food\ calorie}$$

4.
$$Q = mc\Delta T$$
$$= 4.54\,\cancel{\text{kg}}\left(447\ \frac{\text{J}}{\cancel{\text{kg}}\cdot\cancel{\text{C}^\circ}}\right)(14.0\,\cancel{\text{C}^\circ})$$
$$= 2.8411 \times 10^4\text{ J} \xrightarrow{\text{SD}} \mathbf{2.84 \times 10^4\ J}$$

5.
$$v(t) = v_0 + at$$
$$= 880\ \frac{\text{m}}{\text{s}} + \left(-22.0\ \frac{\text{m}}{\text{s}^2}\right)(3\text{ s})$$
$$= +814\ \frac{\text{m}}{\text{s}} \xrightarrow{\text{SD}} \mathbf{+800\ \frac{m}{s}}$$

6.
$$x(t) = x_0 + v_0t + \frac{1}{2}at^2$$
$$x(3) = 0\text{ m} + 880\ \frac{\text{m}}{\text{s}}(3\text{ s}) + \frac{1}{2}\left(-22.0\ \frac{\text{m}}{\text{s}^2}\right)(3\text{ s})^2$$
$$= 2541\text{ m} \xrightarrow{\text{SD}} \mathbf{3000\ m}$$

7. Begin by finding the weight of the mass and drawing a free-body diagram of the forces acting on the junction of the ropes.
$$w = mg$$
$$= 786\,\cancel{\text{kg}} \times 9.81\ \frac{\text{N}}{\cancel{\text{kg}}}$$
$$= 7710.66\text{ N}$$

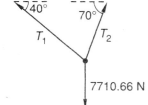

40°
70°
T_1
T_2
7710.66 N

Now sum the horizontal and vertical forces to zero.
(a) $\sum F_x = 0;\ T_2 \cos 70° - T_1 \cos 40° = 0$
(b) $\sum F_y = 0;\ T_1 \sin 40° + T_2 \sin 70° - 7710.66\text{ N} = 0$

Solve (a) for T_2 and get:

(a) $T_2 \cos 70° = T_1 \cos 40°$

$T_2 = 2.240T_1$ (a′)

Substitute (a′) into (b) and get:

(b) $T_1 \sin 40° + (2.240T_1) \sin 70° = 7710.66 \text{ N}$

$2.748T_1 = 7710.66 \text{ N}$

$T_1 = 2805.92 \text{ N} \xrightarrow{SD}$ **2810 N**

Substitute T_1 into (a′) and get:

(a′) $T_2 = 2.240(2805.92 \text{ N})$

$= 6285.26 \text{ N} \xrightarrow{SD}$ **6290 N**

8. Begin by finding the weight of the mass and drawing a free-body diagram of the forces acting on the junction of the ropes.

$w = mg$

$= 412 \text{ kg} \times 9.81 \frac{\text{N}}{\text{kg}}$

$= 4041.72 \text{ N}$

48° 30° T_1 T_2 4041.72 N

Now sum the horizontal and vertical forces to zero.

(a) $\Sigma F_x = 0;\ T_2 \cos 30° - T_1 \cos 48° = 0$

(b) $\Sigma F_y = 0;\ T_1 \sin 48° + T_2 \sin 30° - 4041.72 \text{ N} = 0$

Solve (a) for T_2 and get:

(a) $T_2 \cos 30° = T_1 \cos 48°$

$T_2 = 0.773T_1$ (a′)

Substitute (a′) into (b) and get:

(b) $T_1 \sin 48° + (0.773T_1) \sin 30° = 4041.72 \text{ N}$

$1.130T_1 = 4041.72 \text{ N}$

$T_1 = 3576.7 \text{ N} \xrightarrow{SD}$ **3580 N**

Substitute T_1 into (a′) and get:

(a′) $T_2 = 0.773(3576.7 \text{ N})$

$= 2764.8 \text{ N} \xrightarrow{SD}$ **2760 N**

9. $\Sigma F_x = ma_x$

$F - \mu_k F_N = ma_x$

$F - 0.340(51.0 \text{ kg})\left(9.81 \frac{\text{N}}{\text{kg}}\right) = 51.0 \text{ kg}\left(2.00 \frac{\text{m}}{\text{s}^2}\right)$

$F = 272.11 \text{ N} \xrightarrow{SD}$ **272 N**

10. Begin by writing a $\Sigma F_x = ma_x$ equation for the forces in the x direction and summing the forces in the y direction to zero.

(a) $\Sigma F_x = ma_x;\ (259 \text{ N}) \cos 36° - \mu_k F_N = ma_x$

(b) $\Sigma F_y = 0;\ F_N - (259 \text{ N}) \sin 36° - mg = 0$

Solve (b) for F_N and get:

(b) $F_N = (259 \text{ N}) \sin 36° + mg$

$= (259 \text{ N}) \sin 36° + 20 \text{ kg}\left(9.81 \frac{\text{N}}{\text{kg}}\right) = 348.44 \text{ N}$

Substitute F_N into (a) and solve for a_x.

(a) $(259 \text{ N}) \cos 36° - 0.28(348.44 \text{ N}) = (20 \text{ kg})a_x$

$a_x = 5.599 \frac{\text{m}}{\text{s}^2} \xrightarrow{SD}$ **5.6 $\frac{\text{m}}{\text{s}^2}$**

11. (a) Begin by finding the weight of the object.

$w = mg$

$= 19 \text{ kg} \times 9.81 \frac{\text{N}}{\text{kg}}$

$= 186.39 \text{ N}$

Now set the torques equal to each other and find F.

$F(36 \text{ cm}) = 186.39 \text{ N}(12 \text{ cm})$

$F = 62.13 \text{ N} \xrightarrow{SD}$ **62 N**

(b) Mechanical advantage $= \frac{\text{force out}}{\text{force in}} = \frac{186.39 \text{ N}}{62.13 \text{ N}} =$ **3.0**

12. Percent eff. $= \frac{3444 \text{ J}}{6313 \text{ J}} \times 100\%$

$= 54.554\% \xrightarrow{SD}$ **54.55%**

13.

$$\Sigma M_B = 0$$
$$301.0\text{ N}(25.00\text{ m}) - F(7.000\text{ m}) = 0$$
$$F(7.000\text{ m}) = 7525\text{ N}\cdot\text{m}$$
$$F = \mathbf{1075\text{ N}}$$

$$\Sigma F_y = 0$$
$$301.0\text{ N} + F_B - F = 0$$
$$301.0\text{ N} + F_B - (1075\text{ N}) = 0$$
$$F_B = \mathbf{774.0\text{ N}}$$

14.

$$\Sigma F_y = ma_y$$
$$F_N - mg = ma_y$$
$$F_N - 55\cancel{\text{kg}}\left(9.81\frac{\text{N}}{\cancel{\text{kg}}}\right) = 55\text{ kg}(2.0\text{ m}\cdot\text{s}^{-2})$$
$$F_N = 649.55\text{ N} \xrightarrow{\text{SD}} \mathbf{650\text{ N}}$$

15. Begin by finding the mass of the astronaut.

$$w = mg$$
$$686\text{ N} = m \times 9.81\frac{\text{N}}{\text{kg}}$$
$$m = 69.93\text{ kg}$$

Now write a $\Sigma F_y = ma_y$ equation for the forces in the y direction.

$$\Sigma F_y = ma_y$$
$$F_N - w = ma_y$$
$$F_N - 686\text{ N} = 69.93\text{ kg}(32.0\text{ m}\cdot\text{s}^{-2})$$
$$F_N = 2923.76\text{ N} \xrightarrow{\text{SD}} \mathbf{2920\text{ N}}$$

16. (a) Answers to this problem may vary due to differing data points. One possible solution is given here. Choose the points (1, 100) and (3, 200) and get:

$$a_{\text{inst}} = \frac{\Delta v}{\Delta t} = \frac{200 - 100}{3 - 1}\frac{\text{mi/hr}}{\text{hr}} = \mathbf{+5\bar{0}\ \frac{mi}{hr^2}}$$

(b) $$a_{\text{av}} = \frac{v_2 - v_1}{t_2 - t_1} = \frac{400 - 150}{6.0 - 2.0}\frac{\text{mi/hr}}{\text{hr}} = +62.5\frac{\text{mi}}{\text{hr}^2} \xrightarrow{\text{SD}} \mathbf{+63\ \frac{mi}{hr^2}}$$

17.

$$\vec{F} = m\vec{a}$$
$$212\underline{/21^\circ}\text{ N} = m(3\underline{/21^\circ}\text{ m}\cdot\text{s}^{-2})$$
$$m = 70.67\text{ kg} \xrightarrow{\text{SD}} \mathbf{70\text{ kg}}$$

18. (a)

$$\Sigma M = 0$$
$$36\text{ N}(12\text{ m}) - T_y(18\text{ m}) = 0$$
$$T_y(18\text{ m}) = 432\text{ N}\cdot\text{m}$$
$$T_y = \mathbf{24\text{ N}}$$

Now use T_y to find T. Then find T_x.

$$T\sin 22^\circ = T_y$$
$$T\sin 22^\circ = 24\text{ N}$$
$$T = 64.1\text{ N} \xrightarrow{\text{SD}} \mathbf{64\text{ N}}$$

$$T\cos 22^\circ = T_x$$
$$(64.1\text{ N})\cos 22^\circ = T_x$$
$$T_x = 59.4\text{ N} \xrightarrow{\text{SD}} \mathbf{59\text{ N}}$$

(b) Sum the vertical forces to zero to find F_y.

$$F_y + T_y - 36\text{ N} = 0$$
$$F_y + (24\text{ N}) - 36\text{ N} = 0$$
$$F_y = \mathbf{12\text{ N}}$$

Sum the horizontal forces to zero to find F_x.

$$F_x - T_x = 0$$
$$F_x = T_x = 59.4\text{ N} \xrightarrow{\text{SD}} \mathbf{59\text{ N}}$$

19. Begin by drawing a diagram and recording the data.

$D_E = 9.0$ mi
$T_E = 2.0$ hr
$D_N = 18$ mi
$T_N = 2.0$ hr
D
θ
α

(a) $D_T = 18\text{ mi} + 9.0\text{ mi} = \mathbf{27\text{ mi}}$

(b) $$v = \frac{D_T}{T_T} = \frac{27\text{ mi}}{4.0\text{ hr}} = 6.75\frac{\text{mi}}{\text{hr}} \xrightarrow{\text{SD}} \mathbf{6.8\ \frac{mi}{hr}}$$

(c) $D = \sqrt{(18)^2 + (9.0)^2} = 20.12\text{ mi}$

$\theta = \tan^{-1}\frac{9.0}{18} = 26.57°$

$\alpha = 90° - 26.57° = 63.43°$

$\vec{D} = 20.12\underline{/63.43°}\text{ mi} \xrightarrow{SD} \mathbf{2\bar{0}\underline{/63.43°}\ mi}$

(d) $\vec{v} = \frac{\vec{D}}{T_T} = \frac{20.12\underline{/63.43°}\text{ mi}}{4.0\text{ hr}}$

$= 5.03\underline{/63.43°}\ \frac{\text{mi}}{\text{hr}} \xrightarrow{SD} \mathbf{5.0\underline{/63.43°}\ \frac{mi}{hr}}$

20. (a) Begin by finding the mass of the solution.

$\rho = \frac{m}{V}$

$892\ \frac{\text{kg}}{\text{m}^3} = \frac{m}{10.0\text{ m}^3}$

$m = \mathbf{8920\ kg}$

(b) Now find the weight.

$w = mg$

$= 8920\,\cancel{\text{kg}} \times 9.81\ \frac{\text{N}}{\cancel{\text{kg}}}$

$= 8.75052 \times 10^4\text{ N} \xrightarrow{SD} \mathbf{8.75 \times 10^4\ N}$

Problem Set 22

1. (a) Answers to this problem may vary due to differing data points. One possible solution is given here. Choose the points (2.3, 0) and (4, 15) and get:

$v_{inst} = \frac{15 - 0}{4 - 2.3}\ \frac{\text{m}}{\text{s}} = +8.82\ \frac{\text{m}}{\text{s}} \xrightarrow{SD} \mathbf{+8.8\ \frac{m}{s}}$

(b) $x(t) = t^3 - 3t^2 + 6$ — function

$\frac{dx}{dt} = 3t^2 - 6t + 0$ — velocity

$\left.\frac{dx}{dt}\right|_{3.0} = 3(3.0)^2 - 6(3.0) = \mathbf{+9.0\ \frac{m}{s}}$ — solved

2. (a) $v(t) = -2t^2 + 3t + 20$ — function

$\frac{dv}{dt} = -4t + 3 + 0$ — acceleration

$\left.\frac{dv}{dt}\right|_{3.0} = -4(3.0) + 3 = \mathbf{-9.0\ \frac{m}{s^2}}$ — solved

(b) Distance $= \int_{1.0}^{4.0}\left(-2t^2 + 3t + 20\right)dt$

$= \left[-\frac{2t^3}{3} + \frac{3t^2}{2} + 20t\right]_{1.0}^{4.0}$

$= \left[-\frac{2(4.0)^3}{3} + \frac{3(4.0)^2}{2} + 20(4.0)\right]$

$- \left[-\frac{2(1.0)^3}{3} + \frac{3(1.0)^2}{2} + 20(1.0)\right]$

$= 40.5\text{ m} \xrightarrow{SD} \mathbf{41\ m}$

3. (a) $v(t) = t^2 - 2t + 5$ — function

$\frac{dv}{dt} = 2t - 2 + 0$ — acceleration

$\left.\frac{dv}{dt}\right|_{2.0} = 2(2.0) - 2 = \mathbf{+2.0\ \frac{m}{s^2}}$ — solved

(b) Distance $= \int_{0}^{5.0}\left(t^2 - 2t + 5\right)dt$

$= \left[\frac{t^3}{3} - t^2 + 5t\right]_{0}^{5.0}$

$= \left[\frac{(5.0)^3}{3} - (5.0)^2 + 5(5.0)\right] - \left[\frac{(0)^3}{3} - (0)^2 + 5(0)\right]$

$= 41.7\text{ m} \xrightarrow{SD} \mathbf{42\ m}$

4. (a) $\Delta(mv) = m(v_2 - v_1)$

$$= 1.5\text{ kg}\left(-29i\,\frac{\text{m}}{\text{s}} - 18i\,\frac{\text{m}}{\text{s}}\right)$$

$$= -70.5i\,\frac{\text{kg}\cdot\text{m}}{\text{s}} \xrightarrow{\text{SD}} \mathbf{-71}\boldsymbol{i}\,\frac{\textbf{kg}\cdot\textbf{m}}{\textbf{s}}$$

(b) $F\Delta t = \Delta(mv)$

$$F(0.052\text{ s}) = -70.5i\,\frac{\text{kg}\cdot\text{m}}{\text{s}}$$

$$F = -1355.8i\text{ N} \xrightarrow{\text{SD}} \mathbf{-1400}\boldsymbol{i}\,\textbf{N}$$

5. (a) $F\Delta t = \Delta(mv)$

$$-7190i\text{ N}(0.112\text{ s}) = \Delta(mv)$$

$$\Delta(mv) = -805.28i\,\frac{\text{kg}\cdot\text{m}}{\text{s}} \xrightarrow{\text{SD}} \mathbf{-805}\boldsymbol{i}\,\frac{\textbf{kg}\cdot\textbf{m}}{\textbf{s}}$$

(b) $F\Delta t = \Delta(mv)$

$$-805.28i\,\frac{\text{kg}\cdot\text{m}}{\text{s}} = 95.2\text{ kg}\left(v_2 - 7.2i\,\frac{\text{m}}{\text{s}}\right)$$

$$-8.459i\,\frac{\text{m}}{\text{s}} = v_2 - 7.2i\,\frac{\text{m}}{\text{s}}$$

$$v_2 = -1.259i\,\frac{\text{m}}{\text{s}} \xrightarrow{\text{SD}} \mathbf{-1.3}\boldsymbol{i}\,\frac{\textbf{m}}{\textbf{s}}$$

6. $W = F \times D$

$$= 226\,\cancel{\text{kg}}\left(9.81\,\frac{\text{N}}{\cancel{\text{kg}}}\right) \times 2.10\text{ m} = 4.656 \times 10^3\text{ J} \xrightarrow{\text{SD}} \mathbf{4.66 \times 10^3\text{ J}}$$

Convert joules to food calories and get:

$$(4.656 \times 10^3\,\cancel{\text{J}}) \times \frac{1\text{ food calorie}}{4186\,\cancel{\text{J}}}$$

$$= 1.1123\text{ food calories} \xrightarrow{\text{SD}} \textbf{1.11 food calories}$$

7. $Q = mc\Delta T$

$$= 5.2054\text{ kg}\left(322\,\frac{\text{J}}{\text{kg}\cdot\text{C}^\circ}\right)(52.43^\circ\text{C} - 22^\circ\text{C})$$

$$= 5.10 \times 10^4\text{ J} \xrightarrow{\text{SD}} \mathbf{5.1 \times 10^4\text{ J}}$$

8. $x(t) = x_0 + v_0t + \frac{1}{2}at^2$

$$x(7.0) = 15\text{ m} + \left(-5.0\,\frac{\text{m}}{\text{s}}\right)(7.0\text{ s}) + \frac{1}{2}\left(27\,\frac{\text{m}}{\text{s}^2}\right)(7.0\text{ s})^2$$

$$= 641.5\text{ m} \xrightarrow{\text{SD}} \textbf{640 m}$$

9. $v(t) = v_0 + at$

$$v(12) = -25\,\frac{\text{m}}{\text{s}} + 2.2\,\frac{\text{m}}{\text{s}^2}(12\text{ s}) = \mathbf{+1.4}\,\frac{\textbf{m}}{\textbf{s}}$$

10. Begin by finding the weight of the mass and drawing a free-body diagram of the forces acting on the junction of the ropes.

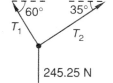

$w = mg$

$$= 25.0\,\cancel{\text{kg}} \times 9.81\,\frac{\text{N}}{\cancel{\text{kg}}}$$

$$= 245.25\text{ N}$$

Now sum the horizontal and vertical forces to zero.

(a) $\sum F_x = 0;\ T_2 \cos 35^\circ - T_1 \cos 60^\circ = 0$

(b) $\sum F_y = 0;\ T_1 \sin 60^\circ + T_2 \sin 35^\circ - 245.25\text{ N} = 0$

Solve (a) for T_2 and get:

(a) $T_2 \cos 35^\circ = T_1 \cos 60^\circ$

$T_2 = 0.610T_1$ (a′)

Substitute (a′) into (b) and get:

(b) $T_1 \sin 60^\circ + (0.610T_1) \sin 35^\circ = 245.25\text{ N}$

$$1.216T_1 = 245.25\text{ N}$$

$$T_1 = 201.69\text{ N} \xrightarrow{\text{SD}} \textbf{202 N}$$

Substitute T_1 into (a′) and get:

(a′) $T_2 = 0.610(201.69\text{ N}) = 123.03\text{ N} \xrightarrow{\text{SD}} \textbf{123 N}$

11. Begin by drawing a free-body diagram of the forces acting on the junction of the ropes. Then sum the horizontal and vertical forces to zero.

625 N, T_2, 80°, T_3, 25°

(a) $\Sigma F_x = 0;\ T_2 \sin 80° + T_3 \sin 25° - 625\text{ N} = 0$
(b) $\Sigma F_y = 0;\ T_2 \cos 80° - T_3 \cos 25° = 0$

Solve (b) for T_3 and get:
(b) $T_3 \cos 25° = T_2 \cos 80°$

$T_3 = 0.1916T_2$ (b′)

Substitute (b′) into (a) and get:
(a) $T_2 \sin 80° + (0.1916T_2) \sin 25° = 625\text{ N}$

$1.066T_2 = 625\text{ N}$

$T_2 = 586.3\text{ N} \xrightarrow{SD}$ **586 N**

Substitute T_2 into (b′) and get:
(b′) $T_3 = 0.1916(586.3\text{ N})$

$= 112.3\text{ N} \xrightarrow{SD}$ **112 N**

12. (a) $F_N = mg + (475\text{ N}) \sin 25°$

$= 45.2\text{ kg}\left(9.81\ \frac{\text{N}}{\text{kg}}\right) + (475\text{ N}) \sin 25°$

$= 644.16\text{ N} \xrightarrow{SD}$ **644 N**

(b) $F_k = \mu_k F_N$

$= 0.270(644.16\text{ N})$

$= 173.92\text{ N} \xrightarrow{SD}$ **174 N**

(c) $\Sigma F_x = ma_x$

$(475\text{ N}) \cos 25° - F_k = ma_x$

$(475\text{ N}) \cos 25° - 173.92\text{ N} = (45.2\text{ kg})a_x$

$a_x = 5.676\ \frac{\text{m}}{\text{s}^2} \xrightarrow{SD}$ **5.68 $\frac{\text{m}}{\text{s}^2}$ to the right**

13. (a) $F_N = mg - (1750\text{ N}) \sin 15°$

$= 250\text{ kg}\left(9.81\ \frac{\text{N}}{\text{kg}}\right) - (1750\text{ N}) \sin 15°$

$= 1999.6\text{ N} \xrightarrow{SD}$ **$20\bar{0}0$ N**

(b) $F_k = \mu_k F_N$

$= 0.253(1999.6\text{ N})$

$= 505.9\text{ N} \xrightarrow{SD}$ **506 N**

(c) $\Sigma F_x = ma_x$

$(1750\text{ N}) \cos 15° - F_k = ma_x$

$(1750\text{ N}) \cos 15° - 505.9\text{ N} = (250\text{ kg})a_x$

$a_x = 4.738\ \frac{\text{m}}{\text{s}^2} \xrightarrow{SD}$ **4.74 $\frac{\text{m}}{\text{s}^2}$ to the left**

14. Begin by finding the weight of the log.
$w = mg$

$= 126\text{ kg} \times 9.81\ \frac{\text{N}}{\text{kg}}$

$= 1236.06\text{ N}$

Now set the torques equal to each other and find T_2.
$T_2(1.20\text{ m}) = 1236.06\text{ N}(0.0500\text{ m})$

$T_2 = 51.50\text{ N} \xrightarrow{SD}$ **51.5 N**

$F_1d_1 = F_2d_2$

$1236.06\text{ N}(1.00\text{ m}) = (51.50\text{ N})d_2$

$d_2 = 24.00\text{ m} \xrightarrow{SD}$ **24.0 m**

Mechanical advantage $= \frac{\text{force out}}{\text{force in}} = \frac{1236.06\text{ N}}{51.50\text{ N}} = 24.00 \xrightarrow{SD}$ **24.0**

15. (a) $P_E = 1700\text{ W} \times 0.460 =$ **782 W**

(b) $P_T = 782\text{ W} \times 0.810 = 633.42\text{ W} \xrightarrow{SD}$ **633 W**

(c) Percent eff. $= \frac{633.42\text{ W}}{1700\text{ W}} \times 100\% = 37.26\% \xrightarrow{SD}$ **37.3%**

16.

$$\Sigma M_A = 0$$
$$75(3.0) + 120(5.5) - 25(6.5) - F_B(8.0) = 0$$
$$F_B(8.0) = 722.5$$
$$F_B = 90.3 \text{ N} \xrightarrow{\text{SD}} \mathbf{9\bar{0}\ N}$$

$$\Sigma F_y = 0$$
$$F_A + 25 + F_B - 75 - 120 = 0$$
$$F_A + 25 + (90.3) - 75 - 120 = 0$$
$$F_A = 79.7 \text{ N} \xrightarrow{\text{SD}} \mathbf{8\bar{0}\ N}$$

17.

$$\Sigma F_y = ma_y$$
$$F_N - mg = ma_y$$
$$F_N - 45\,\cancel{\text{kg}}\left(9.81\,\frac{\text{N}}{\cancel{\text{kg}}}\right) = 45\text{ kg}\left(2.3\,\frac{\text{m}}{\text{s}^2}\right)$$
$$F_N = 544.95 \text{ N} \xrightarrow{\text{SD}} \mathbf{540\ N}$$

18.

$$F = ma$$
$$146 \text{ N} = m(3.81 \text{ m}\cdot\text{s}^{-2})$$
$$m = 38.32 \text{ kg} \xrightarrow{\text{SD}} \mathbf{38.3\ kg}$$

19. $\tau = FL\sin\theta = (125\text{ N})(12.0\text{ cm})\sin 65° = 1359.46\text{ N}\cdot\text{cm}$

Convert to N·m and get:

$$1359.46\text{ N}\cdot\cancel{\text{cm}} \times \frac{1\text{ m}}{100\,\cancel{\text{cm}}} = 13.5946\text{ N}\cdot\text{m} \xrightarrow{\text{SD}} 13.6\text{ N}\cdot\text{m}$$

τ = **13.6 N·m; Negative torque**

20. $F = F_k = \mu_k F_N$

$$5.6\text{ N} = 0.19(m)\left(9.81\,\frac{\text{N}}{\text{kg}}\right)$$
$$m = 3.004\text{ kg} \xrightarrow{\text{SD}} \mathbf{3.0\ kg}$$

Problem Set 23

1. Choose the lower left-hand corner of the tin sheet as the origin.

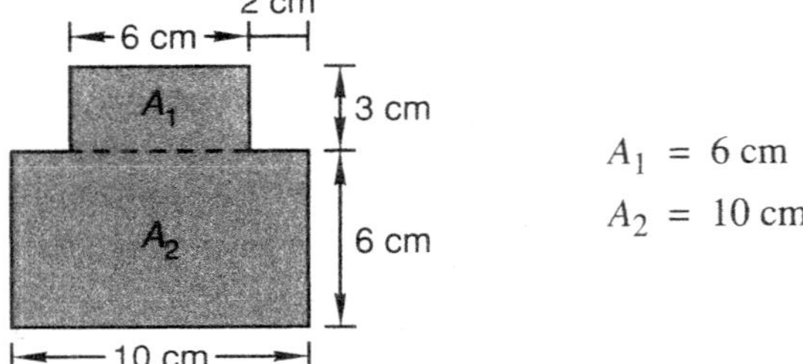

$$A_1 = 6\text{ cm} \times 3\text{ cm} = 18\text{ cm}^2$$
$$A_2 = 10\text{ cm} \times 6\text{ cm} = 60\text{ cm}^2$$

There is a vertical line of symmetry at $x = 5$ cm, so the x distance to the center of mass is 5 cm. To find the y distance to the center of mass, note that the y distance to the center of the 18-cm² rectangle is 7.5 cm and to the center of the 60-cm² rectangle is 3 cm. Arbitrarily assign a weight of 1 N to each square centimeter of area. Then sum the moments and get:
18 N(7.5 cm) + 60 N(3 cm) = 315 N·cm

This is the same moment that would be produced by all 78 N placed at a distance y to the center of mass.
(78 N)y = 315 N·cm

$$y = 4.04\text{ cm} \xrightarrow{\text{SD}} 4\text{ cm}$$

Center of mass is at x = 5 cm and y = 4 cm.

2.

$$\Sigma M = 0$$
$$400\text{ N}(1.5\text{ m}) - 1200\text{ N}(x) + 800\text{ N}(4.5\text{ m}) = 0$$
$$1200\text{ N}(x) = 4200\text{ N}\cdot\text{m}$$
$$x = \mathbf{3.5\ m}$$

3.

$x(t) = 2t^3 + 3t^2 + 5$	function
$\frac{dx}{dt} = 6t^2 + 6t + 0$	velocity
$\frac{dv}{dt} = 12t + 6$	acceleration
$\left.\frac{dv}{dt}\right\rvert_{7.00} = 12(7.00) + 6 = \mathbf{+90\ \frac{m}{s^2}}$	solved

4. (a) $v(t) = -t^2 + 6t$ function

$\frac{dv}{dt} = -2t + 6$ acceleration

$\left.\frac{dv}{dt}\right|_{4.0} = -2(4.0) + 6 = \mathbf{-2.0\ \frac{m}{s^2}}$ solved

(b) $\text{Distance} = \int_{2.0}^{6.0} \left(-t^2 + 6t\right) dt$

$= \left[-\frac{t^3}{3} + \frac{6t^2}{2}\right]_{2.0}^{6.0}$

$= \left[-\frac{(6.0)^3}{3} + \frac{6(6.0)^2}{2}\right] - \left[-\frac{(2.0)^3}{3} + \frac{6(2.0)^2}{2}\right]$

$= 26.7 \text{ m} \xrightarrow{SD}$ **27 m**

5. Begin by finding the ball's initial momentum.

$mv_i = 0.15 \text{ kg}(18i + 3.2j)\ \frac{\text{m}}{\text{s}}$

$= \mathbf{(2.7i + 0.48j)\ \frac{kg \cdot m}{s}}$

The wall only changes the ball's horizontal velocity, so write an impulse-momentum equation to solve for v_{xf}.

$F\Delta t = m(v_{xf} - v_{xi})$

$-88.0i \text{ N}(0.060 \text{ s}) = 0.15 \text{ kg}\left(v_{xf} - 18i\ \frac{\text{m}}{\text{s}}\right)$

$-35.2i\ \frac{\text{m}}{\text{s}} = v_{xf} - 18i\ \frac{\text{m}}{\text{s}}$

$v_{xf} = -17.2i\ \frac{\text{m}}{\text{s}}$

Use v_{xf} to find the ball's final momentum.

$mv_f = 0.15 \text{ kg}(-17.2i + 3.2j)\ \frac{\text{m}}{\text{s}}$

$= (-2.58i + 0.48j)\ \frac{\text{kg} \cdot \text{m}}{\text{s}} \xrightarrow{SD} \mathbf{(-2.6i + 0.48j)\ \frac{kg \cdot m}{s}}$

6. (a) Begin by converting v_1 and v_2 to rectangular form.

$v_1 = 15.0\angle 0°\ \frac{\text{m}}{\text{s}} = (15.0i + 0j)\ \frac{\text{m}}{\text{s}}$

$v_2 = 21.5\angle 90°\ \frac{\text{m}}{\text{s}} = (0i + 21.5j)\ \frac{\text{m}}{\text{s}}$

Now find the change in momentum.

$\Delta(mv) = m(v_2 - v_1)$

$= 850 \text{ kg}((0i + 21.5j) - (15.0i + 0j))\ \frac{\text{m}}{\text{s}}$

$= 850 \text{ kg}(-15.0i + 21.5j)\ \frac{\text{m}}{\text{s}}$

$= (-12{,}750i + 18{,}275j) \xrightarrow{SD} \mathbf{(-13{,}000i + 18{,}000j)\ \frac{kg \cdot m}{s}}$

Convert this change in momentum to polar form and get:

18,275
M
θ
α
12,750

$M = \sqrt{(12{,}750)^2 + (18{,}275)^2}$

$= 22{,}283\ \frac{\text{kg} \cdot \text{m}}{\text{s}}$

$\theta = \tan^{-1} \frac{18{,}275}{12{,}750} = 55.10°$

$\alpha = 180° - 55.10° = 124.90°$

$\vec{M} = 22{,}283\angle 124.90°\ \frac{\text{kg} \cdot \text{m}}{\text{s}} \xrightarrow{SD} \mathbf{22{,}000\angle 124.90°\ \frac{kg \cdot m}{s}}$

(b) $F\Delta t = \Delta(mv)$

$F(0.26 \text{ s}) = 22{,}283\angle 124.90°\ \frac{\text{kg} \cdot \text{m}}{\text{s}}$

$F = 85{,}704\angle 124.90° \text{ N} \xrightarrow{SD} \mathbf{86{,}000\angle 124.90°\ N}$

7. $W = F \times D = 512 \text{ N} \times 25.0 \text{ m} = \mathbf{1.28 \times 10^4\ J}$

Now find the energy expended if this is done 10.0 times.

$(1.28 \times 10^4 \text{ J}) \times 10.0 = \mathbf{1.28 \times 10^5\ J}$

Convert joules to food calories and get:

$(1.28 \times 10^5 \text{ J}) \times \frac{1 \text{ food calorie}}{4186 \text{ J}}$

$= 30.578 \text{ food calories} \xrightarrow{SD}$ **30.6 food calories**

8. $Q = mc\Delta T$

$$= 9.5\,\cancel{\text{kg}}\left(703\,\frac{\text{J}}{\cancel{\text{kg}}\cdot\cancel{\text{C}^\circ}}\right)(12\,\cancel{\text{C}^\circ})$$

$$= 8.014 \times 10^4\text{ J} \xrightarrow{\text{SD}} \mathbf{8.0 \times 10^4\ J}$$

9. $v(t) = v_0 + at$

$$v(4.0) = 45\,\frac{\text{m}}{\text{s}} + 4.1\,\frac{\text{m}}{\text{s}^2}(4.0\text{ s})$$

$$= +61.4\,\frac{\text{m}}{\text{s}} \xrightarrow{\text{SD}} \mathbf{+61\,\frac{m}{s}}$$

10. $x(t) = x_0 + v_0t + \frac{1}{2}at^2$

$$x(4.0) = 0\text{ m} + 45\,\frac{\text{m}}{\text{s}}(4.0\text{ s}) + \frac{1}{2}\left(4.1\,\frac{\text{m}}{\text{s}^2}\right)(4.0\text{ s})^2$$

$$= 212.8\text{ m} \xrightarrow{\text{SD}} \mathbf{210\ m}$$

11. Begin by finding the weight of the mass and drawing a free-body diagram of the forces acting on the junction of the ropes.

$w = mg$

$$= 341\,\cancel{\text{kg}} \times 9.81\,\frac{\text{N}}{\cancel{\text{kg}}}$$

$$= 3345.21\text{ N}$$

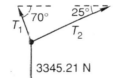

70° 25° T_1 T_2 3345.21 N

Now sum the horizontal and vertical forces to zero.

(a) $\Sigma F_x = 0;\ T_2 \cos 25° - T_1 \cos 70° = 0$

(b) $\Sigma F_y = 0;\ T_1 \sin 70° + T_2 \sin 25° - 3345.21\text{ N} = 0$

Solve (a) for T_2 and get:

(a) $T_2 \cos 25° = T_1 \cos 70°$

$T_2 = 0.377T_1$ (a′)

Substitute (a′) into (b) and get:

(b) $T_1 \sin 70° + (0.377T_1)\sin 25° = 3345.21\text{ N}$

$1.099T_1 = 3345.21\text{ N}$

$T_1 = 3043.9\text{ N} \xrightarrow{\text{SD}} \mathbf{3040\ N}$

Substitute T_1 into (a′) and get:

(a′) $T_2 = 0.377(3043.9\text{ N}) = 1147.6\text{ N} \xrightarrow{\text{SD}} \mathbf{1150\ N}$

12. (a) $\Sigma F_x = ma_x;\ (1500\text{ N})\cos 38° - \mu_k F_N = ma_x$

(b) $\Sigma F_y = 0;\ F_N - (1500\text{ N})\sin 38° - mg = 0$

Solve (b) for F_N and get:

(b) $F_N = (1500\text{ N})\sin 38° + mg$

$$= (1500\text{ N})\sin 38° + 210\,\cancel{\text{kg}}\left(9.81\,\frac{\text{N}}{\cancel{\text{kg}}}\right) = 2983.6\text{ N}$$

Substitute F_N into (a) and solve for a_x.

(a) $(1500\text{ N})\cos 38° - 0.260(2983.6\text{ N}) = (210\text{ kg})a_x$

$$a_x = 1.9347\,\frac{\text{m}}{\text{s}^2} \xrightarrow{\text{SD}} \mathbf{1.93\,\frac{m}{s^2}}$$

13. (a) Begin by finding the weight of the mass.

$$w = mg = 350\,\cancel{\text{kg}} \times 9.81\,\frac{\text{N}}{\cancel{\text{kg}}} = 3433.5\text{ N}$$

There are two upward forces acting on the weight, so

$$T = \frac{3433.5\text{ N}}{2} = 1716.75\text{ N} \xrightarrow{\text{SD}} \mathbf{1700\ N}$$

(b) The weight of the block is 3433.5 N and the tension in the rope is 1716.75 N, so the mechanical advantage is **2.0**.

14. Begin by finding the power output of the machine.

$P = 4560\text{ W} \times 0.78 = 3556.8\text{ W}$

Now find the amount of work in joules the machine did in $2\overline{0}$ minutes.

$$W = P \times t = 3556.8\text{ W} \times \left(20\,\cancel{\text{min}} \times \frac{60\text{ s}}{1\,\cancel{\text{min}}}\right)$$

$$= 4.268 \times 10^6\text{ J} \xrightarrow{\text{SD}} \mathbf{4.3 \times 10^6\ J}$$

15. (a) $\Sigma M_A = 0$

$-25(1.0) + 16(2.0) - F_B(6.0) + 34(9.0) = 0$

$F_B(6.0) = 313$

$F_B = 52.17\text{ N} \xrightarrow{\text{SD}} \mathbf{52\ N}$

(b) $\Sigma F_y = 0$

$F_A + F_B - 25\text{ N} - 16\text{ N} - 34\text{ N} = 0$

$F_A + (52.17\text{ N}) - 25\text{ N} - 16\text{ N} - 34\text{ N} = 0$

$F_A = 22.83\text{ N} \xrightarrow{\text{SD}} \mathbf{23\ N}$

16.

$$\Sigma F_y = ma_y$$
$$F_N - mg = ma_y$$
$$F_N - 50.0\,\cancel{kg}\left(9.81\,\frac{N}{\cancel{kg}}\right) = 50.0\text{ kg}\left(-3.50\,\frac{m}{s^2}\right)$$
$$F_N = 315.5\text{ N} \xrightarrow{SD} \mathbf{316\ N}$$

17. (a)

$$\Sigma M = 0$$
$$196.2(6.00) - T_y(8.00) + 98.1(12.00) = 0$$
$$T_y(8.00) = 2354.4$$
$$T_y = 294.3\text{ N} \xrightarrow{SD} \mathbf{294\ N}$$

Now use T_y to find T. Then find T_x.

$$T\sin 30° = T_y$$
$$T\sin 30° = 294.3\text{ N}$$
$$T = 588.6\text{ N} \xrightarrow{SD} \mathbf{589\ N}$$

$$T\cos 30° = T_x$$
$$(588.6\text{ N})\cos 30° = T_x$$
$$T_x = 509.7\text{ N} \xrightarrow{SD} \mathbf{51\bar{0}\ N}$$

(b) Sum the vertical forces to zero to find F_y.

$$F_y + T_y - 196.2\text{ N} - 98.1\text{ N} = 0$$
$$F_y + (294.3\text{ N}) - 196.2\text{ N} - 98.1\text{ N} = 0$$
$$F_y = \mathbf{0\ N}$$

Sum the horizontal forces to zero to find F_x.

$$F_x - T_x = 0$$
$$F_x = T_x = 509.7\text{ N} \xrightarrow{SD} \mathbf{51\bar{0}\ N}$$

18. $\tau = FL\sin\theta = (92\text{ N})(10\text{ cm})\sin 40° = 591.36\text{ N}\cdot\text{cm}$

Convert 591.36 N·cm to N·m and get:

$$591.36\text{ N}\cdot\cancel{cm} \times \frac{1\text{ m}}{100\,\cancel{cm}} = 5.9136\text{ N}\cdot\text{m} \xrightarrow{SD} 5.9\text{ N}\cdot\text{m}$$

$\tau =$ **5.9 N·m; Negative torque**

19. (a)

$$\rho = \frac{m}{V}$$
$$312\,\frac{kg}{m^3} = \frac{m}{2.43\text{ m}^3}$$
$$m = 758.16\text{ kg} \xrightarrow{SD} \mathbf{758\ kg}$$

(b) $w = mg = 758.16\,\cancel{kg} \times 9.81\,\frac{N}{\cancel{kg}} = 7437.5\text{ N} \xrightarrow{SD} \mathbf{7440\ N}$

20. $a_{av} = \frac{v_2 - v_1}{t_2 - t_1} = \frac{3690 - 400}{53.819 - 39.478}\,\frac{m/s}{s} = +229.4\,\frac{m}{s^2} \xrightarrow{SD} \mathbf{+230\,\frac{m}{s^2}}$

PROBLEM SET 24

1. Use the displacement equation to find the time.

$$\Delta y = v_0 t + \frac{1}{2}at^2$$
$$0 = 50.0t + \frac{1}{2}(-9.81)t^2$$
$$4.905t^2 = 50.0t$$
$$t = 10.19\text{ s} \xrightarrow{SD} \mathbf{10.2\ s}$$

Use the motion equation to find the velocity.

$$v(t) = v_0 + at$$
$$v(10.19) = 50.0 + (-9.81)(10.19) = -49.96\,\frac{m}{s} \xrightarrow{SD} \mathbf{-50.0\,\frac{m}{s}}$$

2. Use the displacement equation to find the time.

$$\Delta y = v_0 t + \frac{1}{2}at^2$$
$$-800 = (0)t + \frac{1}{2}(-9.81)t^2$$
$$4.905t^2 = 800$$
$$t = 12.77\text{ s} \xrightarrow{SD} \mathbf{12.8\ s}$$

Use the motion equation to find the velocity.

$$v(t) = v_0 + at$$
$$v(12.77) = (0) + (-9.81)(12.77) = -125.27\,\frac{m}{s} \xrightarrow{SD} \mathbf{-125\,\frac{m}{s}}$$

3. The line of action of the suspending force for a sphere from any point on the sphere will pass through the center of the sphere. Therefore, the center of gravity of the sphere is at the **center of the sphere**.

4. $v(t) = 2t^2 - 3t + 5$ function

$\frac{dv}{dt} = 4t - 3 + 0$ acceleration

$\left.\frac{dv}{dt}\right|_3 = 4(3) - 3 = \mathbf{+9\ \frac{m}{s^2}}$ solved

5. $$\text{Distance} = \int_0^{5.0} \left(6t^2 - 2t\right) dt = \left[2t^3 - t^2\right]_0^{5.0} = \left[2(5.0)^3 - (5.0)^2\right] - \left[2(0)^3 - (0)^2\right] = 225 \text{ m}$$

Add this distance to the initial position of the object and get:
225 m + 25 m = **250 m**

6. (a) $\Delta(mv) = m(v_2 - v_1) = 0.050 \text{ kg}\left(42 \frac{\text{m}}{\text{s}} - 0 \frac{\text{m}}{\text{s}}\right) = \mathbf{2.1\ \frac{kg \cdot m}{s}}$

(b) $F\Delta t = \Delta(mv)$

$F(0.0015 \text{ s}) = 2.1 \frac{\text{kg} \cdot \text{m}}{\text{s}}$

$F = \mathbf{1400\ N}$

7. (a) Impulse $= F\Delta t = 62 \text{ N} \times 23 \text{ s} = 1426 \text{ N} \cdot \text{s} \xrightarrow{\text{SD}}$ **1400 N·s**

(b) $F\Delta t = m(v_2 - v_1)$

$1426 \text{ N} \cdot \text{s} = 4.2 \text{ kg}\left(v_2 - 0 \frac{\text{m}}{\text{s}}\right)$

$v_2 = 339.52 \frac{\text{m}}{\text{s}} \xrightarrow{\text{SD}} \mathbf{340\ \frac{m}{s}}$

8. $W = F \times D = 46 \text{ N} \times 10.0 \text{ m} = \mathbf{460\ J}$

Convert 460 J to food calories and get:

$460 \cancel{\text{J}} \times \frac{1 \text{ food calorie}}{4186 \cancel{\text{J}}} = 0.1099 \text{ food calorie} \xrightarrow{\text{SD}}$ **0.11 food calorie**

9. $Q = mc\Delta T$

$3266 \text{ cal} = 3.00 \text{ kg}(c)(25.0°\text{C} - 20.0°\text{C})$

$c = 217.73 \frac{\text{cal}}{\text{kg} \cdot \text{C}°} \xrightarrow{\text{SD}} \mathbf{218\ \frac{cal}{kg \cdot C°}}$

10. $v(t) = v_0 + at$

$v(5) = 400 \frac{\text{m}}{\text{s}} + \left(-20 \frac{\text{m}}{\text{s}^2}\right)(5 \text{ s}) = \mathbf{+300\ \frac{m}{s}}$

11. $x(t) = x_0 + v_0 t + \frac{1}{2}at^2$

$x(6.0) = 30 \text{ m} + 10 \frac{\text{m}}{\text{s}}(6.0 \text{ s}) + \frac{1}{2}\left(-20 \frac{\text{m}}{\text{s}^2}\right)(6.0 \text{ s})^2 = \mathbf{-270\ m}$

12. Begin by finding the weight of the mass and drawing a free-body diagram of the forces acting on the junction of the ropes.

$w = mg$

$= 10 \cancel{\text{kg}} \times 9.81 \frac{\text{N}}{\cancel{\text{kg}}}$

$= 98.1 \text{ N}$

T_1 T_2 45° T_3 30°

Now sum the horizontal and vertical forces to zero. Note that T_1 equals 98.1 N.

(a) $\Sigma F_x = 0;\ T_2 \sin 45° + T_3 \sin 30° - 98.1 \text{ N} = 0$

(b) $\Sigma F_y = 0;\ T_2 \cos 45° - T_3 \cos 30° = 0$

Solve (b) for T_3 and get:

(b) $T_3 \cos 30° = T_2 \cos 45°$

$T_3 = 0.816T_2$ (b′)

Substitute (b′) into (a) and get:

(a) $T_2 \sin 45° + (0.816T_2) \sin 30° = 98.1 \text{ N}$

$1.115T_2 = 98.1 \text{ N}$

$T_2 = 87.98 \text{ N} \xrightarrow{\text{SD}}$ **88 N**

Substitute T_2 into (b′) and get:

(b′) $T_3 = 0.816(87.98 \text{ N}) = 71.79 \text{ N} \xrightarrow{\text{SD}}$ **72 N**

13. (a) $\Sigma F_x = ma_x$; $(134 \text{ N}) \cos 30° - \mu_k F_N = ma_x$
(b) $\Sigma F_y = 0$; $F_N - mg - (134 \text{ N}) \sin 30° = 0$

Solve (b) for F_N and get:

(b) $F_N = 25 \text{ kg}\left(9.81 \frac{\text{N}}{\text{kg}}\right) + (134 \text{ N}) \sin 30°$
$= 312.25 \text{ N}$

Substitute F_N into (a) and find a_x.
(a) $(134 \text{ N}) \cos 30° - 0.32(312.25 \text{ N}) = (25 \text{ kg})a_x$

$$a_x = 0.645 \frac{\text{m}}{\text{s}^2} \xrightarrow{\text{SD}} \mathbf{0.65 \frac{m}{s^2}}$$

14. (a) Begin by finding the weight of the mass.

$$w = mg = 1000 \text{ kg} \times 9.81 \frac{\text{N}}{\text{kg}} = 9810 \text{ N}$$

There are two upward forces acting on the weight, so

$$T = \frac{9810 \text{ N}}{2} = 4905 \text{ N} \xrightarrow{\text{SD}} \mathbf{4900 \text{ N}}$$

(b) The weight of the mass is 9810 N, and the tension in the rope is 4905 N, so the mechanical advantage is **2.0**.

15. Begin by finding the power output of the grinder.
$P = 22{,}486.1 \text{ W} \times 0.008 = 179.89 \text{ W}$

Now find the work done by the machine in 185 seconds.

$$W = P \times t = 179.89 \text{ W} \times 185 \text{ s} = 33{,}280 \text{ J} \xrightarrow{\text{SD}} \mathbf{30{,}000 \text{ J}}$$

16. (a)

$$\Sigma M_B = 0$$
$$42 \text{ N}(6.0 \text{ m}) - F(4.0 \text{ m}) - 20 \text{ N}(2.0 \text{ m}) = 0$$
$$F(4.0 \text{ m}) = 212 \text{ N}\cdot\text{m}$$
$$F = \mathbf{53 \text{ N}}$$

(b)

$$\Sigma F_y = 0$$
$$42 \text{ N} + F_B - F - 20 \text{ N} = 0$$
$$42 \text{ N} + F_B - (53 \text{ N}) - 20 \text{ N} = 0$$
$$F_B = \mathbf{31 \text{ N}}$$

17.

$$\Sigma F_y = ma_y$$
$$-F_N - mg = ma_y$$
$$-F_N - 82 \text{ kg}\left(9.81 \frac{\text{N}}{\text{kg}}\right) = 82 \text{ kg}(-20 \text{ m}\cdot\text{s}^{-2})$$
$$F_N = 835.58 \text{ N} \xrightarrow{\text{SD}} \mathbf{840 \text{ N}}$$

18. In each figure, there is a 15-N force acting at a distance of 10 cm perpendicular from the line of action of the force to the point of rotation. Thus, the torques produced in (a), (b), and (c) are equal. One calculation is given below.
$\tau = F \times D = +(15 \text{ N} \times 10 \text{ cm}) = \mathbf{+150 \text{ N}\cdot\text{cm}}$

19. $F = F_k = \mu_k F_N$

$$3.2 \text{ N} = 0.16(m)\left(9.81 \frac{\text{N}}{\text{kg}}\right)$$
$$m = 2.0387 \text{ kg} \xrightarrow{\text{SD}} \mathbf{2.0 \text{ kg}}$$

20. $2.998 \times 10^8 \frac{\text{m}}{\text{s}} \times \frac{100 \text{ cm}}{1 \text{ m}} \times \frac{1 \text{ in.}}{2.54 \text{ cm}} \times \frac{1 \text{ ft}}{12 \text{ in.}} \times \frac{1 \text{ mi}}{5280 \text{ ft}} \times \frac{60 \text{ s}}{1 \text{ min}}$
$\times \frac{60 \text{ min}}{1 \text{ hr}} = 6.706335 \times 10^8 \frac{\text{mi}}{\text{hr}} \xrightarrow{\text{SD}} \mathbf{6.706 \times 10^8 \frac{mi}{hr}}$

Problem Set 25

1. (a) $10 \frac{\text{rev}}{\text{min}} \times \frac{2\pi \text{ rad}}{1 \text{ rev}} \times \frac{1 \text{ min}}{60 \text{ s}} = 1.047 \frac{\text{rad}}{\text{s}} \xrightarrow{\text{SD}} \mathbf{1.0 \frac{rad}{s}}$
(b) $v = r\omega$

$$= (2.0 \text{ m})\left(1.047 \frac{\text{rad}}{\text{s}}\right)$$
$$= 2.094 \frac{\text{m}}{\text{s}} \xrightarrow{\text{SD}} \mathbf{2.1 \frac{m}{s}}$$

2.

$$v = r\omega$$
$$12 \frac{\text{m}}{\text{s}} = 0.50 \text{ m} \times \omega$$
$$\omega = \mathbf{24 \frac{rad}{s}}$$

3. (a) Use the displacement equation to find the time.

$$\Delta y = v_0 t + \frac{1}{2}at^2$$

$$-50 = -2.0t + \frac{1}{2}(-9.81)t^2$$

$$0 = 4.905t^2 + 2.0t - 50$$

Use the quadratic formula to solve this equation for t.

$$t = \frac{-2.0 \pm \sqrt{(2.0)^2 - 4(4.905)(-50)}}{2(4.905)} = 2.995 \text{ s} \xrightarrow{\text{SD}} \mathbf{3.0\ s}$$

(b) Use the motion equation to find the velocity.

$$v(t) = v_0 + at$$

$$v(2.995) = -2.0 + (-9.81)(2.995)$$

$$= -31.38 \frac{\text{m}}{\text{s}} \xrightarrow{\text{SD}} \mathbf{-31 \frac{m}{s}}$$

4. (a)

$$v(t) = v_0 + at$$

$$0 = 4.00 + (-9.81)t$$

$$9.81t = 4.00$$

$$t = 0.4077 \text{ s} \xrightarrow{\text{SD}} \mathbf{0.408\ s}$$

(b)

$$y(t) = y_0 + v_0 t + \frac{1}{2}at^2$$

$$y(0.4077) = 36.0 + 4.00(0.4077) + \frac{1}{2}(-9.81)(0.4077)^2$$

$$= 36.82 \text{ m} \xrightarrow{\text{SD}} \mathbf{36.8\ m}$$

5. The lines of symmetry for each shape is shown below.

(a) 3 m, 7 m, CM (b) CM, 5 m, 3 m (c) 4 m, 60°, 60°, CM

6. (a) Answers to this problem may vary due to differing data points. One possible solution is given here. Choose the points (2, 5) and (3, 3) and get:

$$v_{\text{inst}} = \frac{\Delta x}{\Delta t} = \frac{3 - 5}{3 - 2} \frac{\text{m}}{\text{s}} = \mathbf{-2.0 \frac{m}{s}}$$

(b)

$$x(t) = -t^2 + 4t \quad \text{function}$$

$$\frac{dx}{dt} = -2t + 4 \quad \text{velocity}$$

$$\left.\frac{dx}{dt}\right|_{3.0} = -2(3.0) + 4 = \mathbf{-2.0 \frac{m}{s}} \quad \text{solved}$$

7. (a)

$$\Delta(mv) = m(v_2 - v_1)$$

$$= 0.10 \text{ kg}((-11i - 1.4j) - (12i - 1.4j)) \frac{\text{m}}{\text{s}}$$

$$= 0.10 \text{ kg}\left(-23i \frac{\text{m}}{\text{s}}\right) = \mathbf{-2.3}\boldsymbol{i} \mathbf{\frac{kg \cdot m}{s}}$$

(b)

$$F\Delta t = \Delta(mv)$$

$$(-185i \text{ N})\Delta t = -2.3i \frac{\text{kg} \cdot \text{m}}{\text{s}}$$

$$\Delta t = 0.0124 \text{ s} \xrightarrow{\text{SD}} \mathbf{0.012\ s}$$

8. (a) Sum the horizontal forces to find the net force.

$$\Sigma F_x = -425i \text{ N} + 53.0i \text{ N} = \mathbf{-372}\boldsymbol{i}\mathbf{\ N}$$

(b)

$$F\Delta t = m(v_2 - v_1)$$

$$-372i \text{ N}(6.00 \text{ s}) = 15 \text{ kg}\left(v_2 - 0 \frac{\text{m}}{\text{s}}\right)$$

$$-2232i \text{ N} \cdot \text{s} = 15 \text{ kg}(v_2)$$

$$v_2 = -148.8i \frac{\text{m}}{\text{s}} \xrightarrow{\text{SD}} \mathbf{-150}\boldsymbol{i} \mathbf{\frac{m}{s}}$$

9.

$$W = F \times D = 136 \text{ N} \times 4.30 \text{ m} = 584.8 \text{ J} \xrightarrow{\text{SD}} \mathbf{585\ J}$$

Convert 584.8 J to food calories and get:

$$584.8 \cancel{\text{J}} \times \frac{1 \text{ food calorie}}{4186 \cancel{\text{J}}} = 0.1397 \text{ food calorie} \xrightarrow{\text{SD}} \mathbf{0.140\ food\ calorie}$$

10. $Q = mc\Delta T = 1.5\text{ kg}\left(64.0\,\frac{\text{cal}}{\text{kg}\cdot\text{C}^\circ}\right)(41^\circ\text{C} - 27^\circ\text{C}) = 1344\text{ calories}$

Convert 1344 calories to joules and get:

$1344\text{ calories} \times \frac{4.186\text{ J}}{1\text{ calorie}} = 5625.98\text{ J} \xrightarrow{\text{SD}}$ **5600 J**

11. Use the position equation to find the time.

$$x(t) = x_0 + v_0t + \frac{1}{2}at^2$$
$$120.0 = 10.0 + 0(t) + \frac{1}{2}(4.0)t^2$$
$$2.0t^2 = 110.0$$
$$t = 7.416\text{ s} \xrightarrow{\text{SD}} \mathbf{7.4\text{ s}}$$

12. Use the displacement equation to find the distance.

$$\Delta x = v_0t + \frac{1}{2}at^2$$
$$= 15.0(25.0) + \frac{1}{2}(5.00)(25.0)^2 = 1937.5\text{ m} \xrightarrow{\text{SD}} \mathbf{1940\text{ m}}$$

13. Begin by finding the weight of the mass and drawing a free-body diagram of the forces acting on the junction of the ropes.

$$w = mg$$
$$= 40\text{ kg} \times 9.81\,\frac{\text{N}}{\text{kg}}$$
$$= 392.4\text{ N}$$

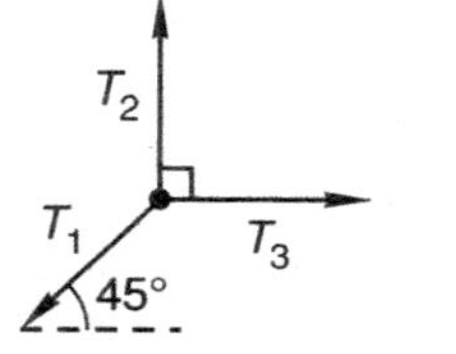

Now sum the horizontal and vertical forces to zero. Note that T_1 equals 392.4 N.

(a) $\Sigma F_x = 0;\; T_3 - (392.4\text{ N})\cos 45^\circ = 0$

(b) $\Sigma F_y = 0;\; T_2 - (392.4\text{ N})\sin 45^\circ = 0$

Solve (a) for T_3 and (b) for T_2 and get:

(a) $T_3 = (392.4\text{ N})\cos 45^\circ = 277.47\text{ N} \xrightarrow{\text{SD}}$ **280 N**

(b) $T_2 = (392.4\text{ N})\sin 45^\circ = 277.47\text{ N} \xrightarrow{\text{SD}}$ **280 N**

14.

$$\Sigma F_x = ma_x$$
$$F - \mu_k F_N = ma_x$$
$$F - 0.39(49\text{ kg})\left(9.81\,\frac{\text{N}}{\text{kg}}\right) = 49\text{ kg}(2.3\angle 0^\circ\text{ m}\cdot\text{s}^{-2})$$
$$F = 300.17\angle 0^\circ\text{ N} \xrightarrow{\text{SD}} \mathbf{3\bar{0}0\angle 0^\circ\text{ N}}$$

15. (a) Begin by finding the weight of the mass.

$$w = mg$$
$$= 1500\text{ kg} \times 9.81\,\frac{\text{N}}{\text{kg}}$$
$$= 14{,}715\text{ N}$$

There are three upward forces acting on the weight, so

$$T = \frac{14{,}715\text{ N}}{3} = 4905\text{ N} \xrightarrow{\text{SD}} \mathbf{4900\text{ N}}$$

(b) The weight of the mass is 14,715 N and the tension in the rope is 4905 N, so the mechanical advantage is **3.0**.

16. (a) $P_1 = 1000\text{ W} \times 0.98 =$ **980 W**

(b) $P_2 = 980\text{ W} \times 0.76 = 744.8\text{ W} \xrightarrow{\text{SD}}$ **740 W**

(c) $\text{Percent eff.} = \frac{744.8\text{ W}}{1000\text{ W}} \times 100\%$

$= 74.48\% \xrightarrow{\text{SD}}$ **74%**

17. (a)

$$\Sigma M_B = 0$$
$$F_A(16.59) - 32.59(17.59) - 14.187(4.55) = 0$$
$$F_A(16.59) = 637.81$$
$$F_A = 38.45\text{ N} \xrightarrow{\text{SD}} \mathbf{40\text{ N}}$$

(b)

$$\Sigma F_y = 0$$
$$F_A + F_B - 32.59\text{ N} - 14.187\text{ N} = 0$$
$$(38.45\text{ N}) + F_B - 32.59\text{ N} - 14.187\text{ N} = 0$$
$$F_B = 8.33\text{ N} \xrightarrow{\text{SD}} \mathbf{8\text{ N}}$$

18. (a) Calculate the displacements for the following time intervals:

$$\Delta x_{0,1} = 20\ \frac{\text{m}}{\cancel{\text{s}}} \times 1\cancel{\text{s}} = +20\text{ m}$$

$$\Delta x_{1,3} = \left(20\ \frac{\text{m}}{\cancel{\text{s}}} \times 2\cancel{\text{s}}\right) + \left(\frac{20\ \frac{\text{m}}{\cancel{\text{s}}} \times 2\cancel{\text{s}}}{2}\right) = +60\text{ m}$$

$$\Delta x_{3,5} = 40\ \frac{\text{m}}{\cancel{\text{s}}} \times 2\cancel{\text{s}} = +80\text{ m}$$

Sum these displacements with the initial position and get:
$x_{5.0} = 10.0\text{ m} + 20\text{ m} + 60\text{ m} + 80\text{ m} = \mathbf{170\ m}$

(b) $a_{av} = \dfrac{v_2 - v_1}{t_2 - t_1} = \dfrac{40 - 20}{5.0 - 0}\ \dfrac{\text{m/s}}{\text{s}} = \mathbf{+4.0\ \dfrac{m}{s^2}}$

19. Begin by finding the volume of the right rectangular solid.
Volume $= l \times w \times h$
$= 18\text{ cm} \times 12\text{ cm} \times 6.0\text{ cm} = 1296\text{ cm}^3$

Now use this volume and the density to find the mass.

$$\rho = \frac{m}{V}$$

$$2.34\ \frac{\text{g}}{\text{cm}^3} = \frac{m}{1296\text{ cm}^3}$$

$$m = 3.033 \times 10^3\text{ g} \xrightarrow{\text{SD}} \mathbf{3.0 \times 10^3\ g}$$

20. Begin by finding the weight of the beam and the weight of the mass. Then draw a diagram of the forces acting on the beam.

$$w_b = m_b g = 50.0\ \cancel{\text{kg}} \times 9.81\ \frac{\text{N}}{\cancel{\text{kg}}} = 490.5\text{ N}$$

$$w_m = m_m g = 40.0\ \cancel{\text{kg}} \times 9.81\ \frac{\text{N}}{\cancel{\text{kg}}} = 392.4\text{ N}$$

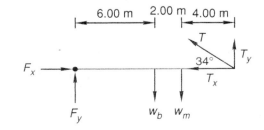

Now sum the moments about the left end of the beam to zero.

$$\Sigma M = 0$$
$$w_b(6.00\text{ m}) + w_m(8.00\text{ m}) - T_y(12.00\text{ m}) = 0$$
$$490.5\text{ N}(6.00\text{ m}) + 392.4\text{ N}(8.00\text{ m}) - T_y(12.00\text{ m}) = 0$$
$$T_y(12.00\text{ m}) = 6082.2\text{ N}\cdot\text{m}$$
$$T_y = 506.85\text{ N}$$

Now use T_y to find T.
$T \sin 34° = T_y$
$T \sin 34° = 506.85\text{ N}$
$T = 906.40\text{ N} \xrightarrow{\text{SD}} \mathbf{906\ N}$

Sum the horizontal forces to zero to find F_x.
$F_x - T_x = 0$
$F_x = T_x$
$F_x = T\cos 34° = (906.40\text{ N})\cos 34° = 751.44\text{ N} \xrightarrow{\text{SD}} \mathbf{751\ N}$

Sum the vertical forces to zero to find F_y.
$$F_y + T_y - w_b - w_m = 0$$
$$F_y + (506.85\text{ N}) - 490.5\text{ N} - 392.4\text{ N} = 0$$
$$F_y = 376.05\text{ N} \xrightarrow{\text{SD}} \mathbf{376\ N}$$

Problem Set 26

1. Begin by finding the pressure produced by the gasoline.

$$P_G = 680\ \frac{\cancel{\text{kg}}}{\text{m}^{\cancel{3}2}} \times 25\ \cancel{\text{m}} \times 9.81\ \frac{\text{N}}{\cancel{\text{kg}}} = 166{,}770\text{ Pa}$$

Now sum this pressure with the atmospheric pressure and find P.

$$P = 166{,}770\text{ Pa} + 101{,}300\text{ Pa} = 2.6807 \times 10^5\text{ Pa} \xrightarrow{\text{SD}} \mathbf{2.7 \times 10^5\ Pa}$$

2.
$$\frac{F_1}{A_1} = \frac{F_2}{A_2}$$
$$\frac{60\text{ N}}{0.010\text{ m}^2} = \frac{F_2}{0.25\text{ m}^2}$$
$$F_2 = \mathbf{1500\ N}$$

3. Begin by converting 1.56 g/cm³ to kg/m³.

$$1.56\ \frac{\cancel{g}}{\cancel{cm^3}} \times \frac{1\text{ kg}}{1000\ \cancel{g}} \times \frac{(100)^3\ \cancel{cm^3}}{1\text{ m}^3} = 1560\ \frac{\text{kg}}{\text{m}^3}$$

Now find the pressure produced by the liquid.

$$P_L = 1560\ \frac{\cancel{kg}}{\text{m}^{\cancel{3}2}} \times 9.81\ \frac{\text{N}}{\cancel{kg}} \times 12\ \cancel{m} = 1.8364 \times 10^5\text{ Pa}$$

Now sum this pressure with the atmospheric pressure and find P.

$$P = 1.8364 \times 10^5\text{ Pa} + 1.013 \times 10^5\text{ Pa}$$

$$= 2.8494 \times 10^5\text{ Pa} \xrightarrow{SD} \mathbf{2.8 \times 10^5\ Pa}$$

4.

$$v = r\omega$$

$$20\ \frac{\text{m}}{\text{s}} = (0.25\text{ m})\omega$$

$$\omega = \mathbf{8\bar{0}\ \frac{rad}{s}}$$

Convert $8\bar{0}$ rad/s to revolutions per minute.

$$80\ \frac{\cancel{rad}}{\cancel{s}} \times \frac{1\text{ rev}}{2\pi\ \cancel{rad}} \times \frac{60\ \cancel{s}}{1\text{ min}} = 763.9\ \frac{\text{rev}}{\text{min}} \xrightarrow{SD} \mathbf{760\ \frac{rev}{min}}$$

5. (a) The radius is half the diameter, or 6.00 in.. Convert to meters and get:

$$6.00\ \cancel{in.} \times \frac{2.54\ \cancel{cm}}{1\ \cancel{in.}} \times \frac{1\text{ m}}{100\ \cancel{cm}} = 0.1524\text{ m} \xrightarrow{SD} \mathbf{0.152\ m}$$

(b) $$33.3\ \frac{\cancel{rev}}{\cancel{min}} \times \frac{2\pi\text{ rad}}{1\ \cancel{rev}} \times \frac{1\ \cancel{min}}{60\text{ s}} = 3.487\ \frac{\text{rad}}{\text{s}} \xrightarrow{SD} \mathbf{3.49\ \frac{rad}{s}}$$

(c) $$v = r\omega = 0.1524\text{ m} \times 3.487\ \frac{\text{rad}}{\text{s}} = 0.5314\ \frac{\text{m}}{\text{s}} \xrightarrow{SD} \mathbf{0.531\ \frac{m}{s}}$$

6. (a) Use the displacement equation to find the time.

$$\Delta y = v_0 t + \frac{1}{2}at^2$$

$$-126 = -22t + \frac{1}{2}(-9.81)t^2$$

$$0 = 4.905t^2 + 22t - 126$$

Use the quadratic formula to solve this equation for t.

$$t = \frac{-22 \pm \sqrt{(22)^2 - 4(4.905)(-126)}}{2(4.905)} = 3.300\text{ s} \xrightarrow{SD} \mathbf{3.3\ s}$$

(b) Use the motion equation to find the velocity.

$$v(t) = v_0 + at$$

$$v(3.300) = -22 + (-9.81)(3.300)$$

$$= -54.37\ \frac{\text{m}}{\text{s}} \xrightarrow{SD} \mathbf{-54\ \frac{m}{s}}$$

7. (a)

$$v(t) = v_0 + at$$

$$0 = 30 + (-9.81)t$$

$$9.81t = 30$$

$$t = 3.058\text{ s} \xrightarrow{SD} \mathbf{3.1\ s}$$

(b) $$\Delta y = v_0 t + \frac{1}{2}at^2$$

$$= 30(3.058) + \frac{1}{2}(-9.81)(3.058)^2$$

$$= 45.87\text{ m} \xrightarrow{SD} \mathbf{46\ m}$$

8. (a) To find the weight, sum the vertical forces to zero and solve for w.

$$\Sigma F_y = 0$$

$$560\text{ N} + 320\text{ N} + 80\text{ N} - w = 0$$

$$w = \mathbf{960\ N}$$

(b)

$$\Sigma M = 0$$

$$w(x) - 320\text{ N}(7.0\text{ m}) - 80\text{ N}(8.0\text{ m}) = 0$$

$$(960\text{ N})(x) - 2240\text{ N}\cdot\text{m} - 640\text{ N}\cdot\text{m} = 0$$

$$960\text{ N}(x) = 2880\text{ N}\cdot\text{m}$$

$$x = \mathbf{3.0\ m}$$

9. (a)

$$x(t) = t^3 + 3t^2 + 5t + 6 \quad \text{function}$$

$$\frac{dx}{dt} = 3t^2 + 6t + 5 + 0 \quad \text{velocity}$$

$$\left.\frac{dx}{dt}\right|_{2.0} = 3(2.0)^2 + 6(2.0) + 5 = \mathbf{+29\ \frac{m}{s}} \quad \text{solved}$$

(b)

$$v(t) = 3t^2 + 6t + 5 \quad \text{velocity}$$

$$\frac{dv}{dt} = 6t + 6 + 0 \quad \text{acceleration}$$

$$\left.\frac{dv}{dt}\right|_{2.0} = 6(2.0) + 6 = \mathbf{+18\ \frac{m}{s^2}} \quad \text{solved}$$

10. (a) Impulse $= F\Delta t = 280\text{ N} \times 13\text{ s}$

$$= 3.64 \times 10^3\text{ N}\cdot\text{s} \xrightarrow{\text{SD}} \mathbf{3.6 \times 10^3\ N\cdot s}$$

(b) $F\Delta t = m(v_2 - v_1)$

$$3.64 \times 10^3\text{ N}\cdot\text{s} = 2\text{ kg}\left(v_2 - 0\,\frac{\text{m}}{\text{s}}\right)$$

$$v_2 = 1.82 \times 10^3\,\frac{\text{m}}{\text{s}} \xrightarrow{\text{SD}} \mathbf{2 \times 10^3\,\frac{m}{s}}$$

11. (a) To find the net force, sum the horizontal forces.

$$\Sigma F_x = 111{,}563\text{ N} - 400\text{ N} = 111{,}163\text{ N} \xrightarrow{\text{SD}} \mathbf{100{,}000\ N}$$

(b) $F\Delta t = m(v_2 - v_1)$

$$111{,}163\text{ N}(4.1743\text{ s}) = 20.418\text{ kg}\left(v_2 - 0\,\frac{\text{m}}{\text{s}}\right)$$

$$v_2 = 22{,}726\,\frac{\text{m}}{\text{s}} \xrightarrow{\text{SD}} \mathbf{20{,}000\,\frac{m}{s}\ \text{to the right}}$$

12. $W = F \times D = 420\text{ N} \times 68\text{ m} = 2.856 \times 10^4\text{ J} \xrightarrow{\text{SD}} \mathbf{2.9 \times 10^4\ J}$

Convert to food calories and get:

$$2.856 \times 10^4\,\cancel{\text{J}} \times \frac{1\text{ food calorie}}{4186\,\cancel{\text{J}}}$$

$$= 6.823\text{ food calories} \xrightarrow{\text{SD}} \textbf{6.8 food calories}$$

13. $Q = mc\Delta T$

$$= 24\,\cancel{\text{kg}} \times 899\,\frac{\text{J}}{\cancel{\text{kg}}\cdot\cancel{\text{C}^\circ}} \times 210\,\cancel{\text{C}^\circ}$$

$$= 4.531 \times 10^6\text{ J} \xrightarrow{\text{SD}} \mathbf{4.5 \times 10^6\ J}$$

14. Use the displacement equation to find the distance.

$$\Delta x = v_0 t + \frac{1}{2}at^2$$

$$= 35.0(60.0) + \frac{1}{2}(4.00)(60.0)^2$$

$$= \mathbf{93\bar{0}0\ m}$$

15. Begin by finding the weight of the mass and drawing a free-body diagram of the forces acting on the junction of the ropes.

$$w = mg$$

$$= 16\,\cancel{\text{kg}} \times 9.81\,\frac{\text{N}}{\cancel{\text{kg}}}$$

$$= 156.96\text{ N}$$

T_4 30° T_3 40° T_5

Now sum the horizontal and vertical forces to zero. Note that T_3 is equal to 156.96 N.

(a) $\Sigma F_x = 0;\ T_4 \sin 30° + T_5 \sin 40° - 156.96\text{ N} = 0$

(b) $\Sigma F_y = 0;\ T_4 \cos 30° - T_5 \cos 40° = 0$

Solve (b) for T_5 and get:

(b) $T_5 \cos 40° = T_4 \cos 30°$

$T_5 = 1.13T_4$ (b′)

Substitute (b′) into (a) and get:

(a) $T_4 \sin 30° + (1.13T_4) \sin 40° = 156.96\text{ N}$

$1.23T_4 = 156.96\text{ N}$

$T_4 = 127.61\text{ N} \xrightarrow{\text{SD}} \mathbf{130\ N}$

Substitute T_4 into (b′) and get:

(b′) $T_5 = 1.13(127.61\text{ N}) = 144.20\text{ N} \xrightarrow{\text{SD}} \mathbf{140\ N}$

16. (a) $\Sigma F_x = ma_x;\ (138\text{ N}) \cos 4° - \mu_k F_N = ma_x$

(b) $\Sigma F_y = 0;\ F_N - (138\text{ N}) \sin 4° - mg = 0$

Solve (b) for F_N and get:

(b) $F_N = (138\text{ N}) \sin 4° + mg$

$$= (138\text{ N}) \sin 4° + 28\,\cancel{\text{kg}}\left(9.81\,\frac{\text{N}}{\cancel{\text{kg}}}\right) = 284.31\text{ N}$$

Substitute F_N into (a) and solve for a_x.

(a) $(138\text{ N}) \cos 4° - 0.23(284.31\text{ N}) = (28\text{ kg})a_x$

$$a_x = 2.581\,\frac{\text{m}}{\text{s}^2} \xrightarrow{\text{SD}} \mathbf{2.6\,\frac{m}{s^2}}$$

17. (a) Begin by finding the weight of the mass.

$$w = mg = 25\,\text{kg} \times 9.81\,\frac{\text{N}}{\text{kg}} = 245.25\text{ N}$$

There are four upward forces acting on the weight, so

$$T = \frac{245.25\text{ N}}{4} = 61.3125\text{ N} \xrightarrow{\text{SD}} \mathbf{61\ N}$$

(b) The weight of the mass is 245.25 N and the tension in the rope is 61.3125 N, so the mechanical advantage is **4.0**.

18. (a) $P_1 = 1350\text{ W} \times 0.620 = \mathbf{837\ W}$

(b) $P_2 = 837\text{ W} \times 0.710 = 594.27\text{ W} \xrightarrow{\text{SD}} \mathbf{594\ W}$

(c) $\text{Percent eff.} = \dfrac{594.27\text{ W}}{1350\text{ W}} \times 100\% = 44.02\% \xrightarrow{\text{SD}} \mathbf{44.0\%}$

19. In each figure, there is a 31-N force acting at a distance of 11 m perpendicular from the line of action of the force to the point of rotation. Thus, the torques produced in (a), (b), and (c) are equal. One calculation is given below.

$$\tau = F \times D$$
$$= -(31\text{ N} \times 11\text{ m})$$
$$= -341\text{ N}\cdot\text{m} \xrightarrow{\text{SD}} \mathbf{-340\ N\cdot m}$$

20. Begin by drawing a diagram of the path of the particle. The directions are not important; they need only be at right angles.

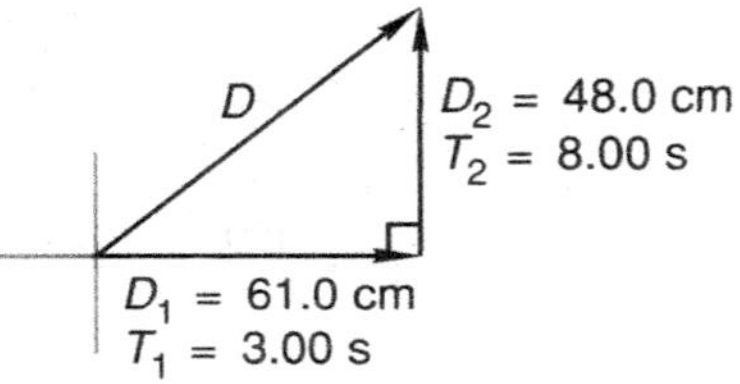

(a) $D_T = 61.0\text{ cm} + 48.0\text{ cm} = \mathbf{109\ cm}$

(b) $v = \dfrac{D_T}{T_T} = \dfrac{109\text{ cm}}{11.00\text{ s}} = 9.909\,\dfrac{\text{cm}}{\text{s}} \xrightarrow{\text{SD}} \mathbf{9.91\,\dfrac{cm}{s}}$

(c) $D = \sqrt{(61.0)^2 + (48.0)^2} = 77.62\text{ cm} \xrightarrow{\text{SD}} \mathbf{77.6\ cm}$

(d) $v = \dfrac{D}{T_T} = \dfrac{77.62\text{ cm}}{11.00\text{ s}} = 7.056\,\dfrac{\text{cm}}{\text{s}} \xrightarrow{\text{SD}} \mathbf{7.06\,\dfrac{cm}{s}}$

Problem Set 27

1. Begin by finding the weight of the block and the component of the weight parallel to the plane.

$$w = mg = 26\,\text{kg} \times 9.81\,\frac{\text{N}}{\text{kg}} = 255.06\text{ N}$$
$$w_x = (255.06\text{ N})\sin 20° = 87.24\text{ N}$$

Now sum the forces parallel to the plane and get:

$$\Sigma F_x = ma_x$$
$$-87.24\text{ N} = (26\text{ kg})a_x$$
$$a_x = -3.355\,\frac{\text{m}}{\text{s}^2} \xrightarrow{\text{SD}} \mathbf{3.4\,\frac{m}{s^2}\ down\ the\ plane}$$

2. (a) Begin by finding the weight of the block. Then find w_x.

$$w = mg = 85.0\,\text{kg} \times 9.81\,\frac{\text{N}}{\text{kg}} = 833.85\text{ N}$$
$$w_x = (833.85\text{ N})\sin 30° = 416.93\text{ N} \xrightarrow{\text{SD}} \mathbf{417\ N}$$

(b) $w_y = (833.85\text{ N})\cos 30° = 722.14\text{ N} \xrightarrow{\text{SD}} \mathbf{722\ N}$

$$F_s = \mu_s F_N = 0.300(722.14\text{ N}) = 216.64\text{ N} \xrightarrow{\text{SD}} \mathbf{217\ N}$$

(c) Now sum the forces parallel to the plane. Note that since μ_k equals μ_s, F_k equals 216.64 N.

$$\Sigma F_x = ma_x$$
$$F_k - w_x = ma_x$$
$$216.64\text{ N} - 416.93\text{ N} = (85.0\text{ kg})a_x$$
$$a_x = -2.356\,\frac{\text{m}}{\text{s}^2} \xrightarrow{\text{SD}} \mathbf{2.36\,\frac{m}{s^2}\ down\ the\ plane}$$

3. Begin by finding the pressure produced by the fluid.

$$P_F = 850\,\frac{\text{kg}}{\text{m}^{3}} \times 9.81\,\frac{\text{N}}{\text{kg}} \times 0.21\text{ m} = 1.7511 \times 10^3\text{ Pa}$$

Now sum this pressure with the atmospheric pressure and find P.

$$P = 1.7511 \times 10^3\text{ Pa} + 1.013 \times 10^5\text{ Pa}$$
$$= 1.0305 \times 10^5\text{ Pa} \xrightarrow{\text{SD}} \mathbf{1.0 \times 10^5\ Pa}$$

4.
$$\frac{F_1}{A_1} = \frac{F_2}{A_2}$$
$$\frac{45\text{ N}}{10\text{ m}^2} = \frac{F_2}{100\text{ m}^2}$$
$$F_2 = \mathbf{450\ N}$$

5.
$$v = r\omega$$
$$314\ \frac{\text{m}}{\text{s}} = 0.50\text{ m} \times \omega$$
$$\omega = 628\ \frac{\text{rad}}{\text{s}} \xrightarrow{\text{SD}} \mathbf{630\ \frac{rad}{s}}$$

Now convert to rev/min.

$$628\ \frac{\cancel{\text{rad}}}{\cancel{\text{s}}} \times \frac{1\text{ rev}}{2\pi\ \cancel{\text{rad}}} \times \frac{60\ \cancel{\text{s}}}{1\text{ min}} = 5.997 \times 10^3\ \frac{\text{rev}}{\text{min}} \xrightarrow{\text{SD}} \mathbf{6.0 \times 10^3\ \frac{rev}{min}}$$

6. (a) The radius is half the diameter, or 1.75 in.. Convert to meters and get:
$$1.75\ \cancel{\text{in.}} \times \frac{2.54\ \cancel{\text{cm}}}{1\ \cancel{\text{in.}}} \times \frac{1\text{ m}}{100\ \cancel{\text{cm}}} = 0.04445\text{ m} \xrightarrow{\text{SD}} \mathbf{0.044\ m}$$

(b) $$600\ \frac{\cancel{\text{rev}}}{\cancel{\text{min}}} \times \frac{2\pi\text{ rad}}{1\ \cancel{\text{rev}}} \times \frac{1\ \cancel{\text{min}}}{60\text{ s}} = 62.83\ \frac{\text{rad}}{\text{s}} \xrightarrow{\text{SD}} \mathbf{62.8\ \frac{rad}{s}}$$

(c) $$v = r\omega = 0.04445\text{ m} \times 62.83\ \frac{\text{rad}}{\text{s}} = 2.793\ \frac{\text{m}}{\text{s}} \xrightarrow{\text{SD}} \mathbf{2.8\ \frac{m}{s}}$$

7. (a) Use the displacement equation to find the time.
$$\Delta y = v_0 t + \frac{1}{2}at^2$$
$$-75.0 = -2.0t + \frac{1}{2}(-9.81)t^2$$
$$0 = 4.905t^2 + 2.0t - 75.0$$

Use the quadratic formula to solve this equation for t.
$$t = \frac{-2.0 \pm \sqrt{(2.0)^2 - 4(4.905)(-75.0)}}{2(4.905)} = 3.71\text{ s} \xrightarrow{\text{SD}} \mathbf{3.7\ s}$$

(b) Use the motion equation to find the velocity.
$$v(t) = v_0 + at$$
$$v(3.71) = -2.0 + (-9.81)(3.71)$$
$$= -38.40\ \frac{\text{m}}{\text{s}} \xrightarrow{\text{SD}} \mathbf{-38\ \frac{m}{s}}$$

8. (a)
$$v(t) = v_0 + at$$
$$0 = 2.0 + (-9.81)t$$
$$9.81t = 2.0$$
$$t = 0.204\text{ s} \xrightarrow{\text{SD}} \mathbf{0.20\ s}$$

(b)
$$y(t) = y_0 + v_0 t + \frac{1}{2}at^2$$
$$y(0.204) = 0 + 2.0(0.204) + \frac{1}{2}(-9.81)(0.204)^2$$
$$= 0.204\text{ m} \xrightarrow{\text{SD}} \mathbf{0.20\ m}$$

9. (a) $\Sigma F_y = 0;\ F_A + 1\bar{0}\text{ N} - F_B - 2\bar{0}\text{ N} - 3\bar{0}\text{ N} = 0$
(b) $\Sigma M_B = 0;\ -F_A(1.0\text{ m}) - 1\bar{0}\text{ N}(9.0\text{ m}) + 2\bar{0}\text{ N}(4.0\text{ m}) + 3\bar{0}\text{ N}(7.0\text{ m}) = 0$

Solve (b) for F_A and get:
(b) $-F_A(1.0\text{ m}) - 90\text{ N}\cdot\text{m} + 80\text{ N}\cdot\text{m} + 210\text{ N}\cdot\text{m} = 0$
$$-F_A(1.0\text{ m}) = -200\text{ N}\cdot\text{m}$$
$$F_A = \mathbf{2\bar{0}0\ N}$$

Substitute F_A into (a) to find F_B.
(a) $(200\text{ N}) + 10\text{ N} - F_B - 20\text{ N} - 30\text{ N} = 0$
$$F_B = \mathbf{160\ N}$$

10.
$$\text{Distance} = \int_0^{4.0} (5t^3 + 3t^2 + 5)\,dt$$
$$= \left[\frac{5t^4}{4} + t^3 + 5t\right]_0^{4.0}$$
$$= \left[\frac{5(4.0)^4}{4} + (4.0)^3 + 5(4.0)\right] - \left[\frac{5(0)^4}{4} + (0)^3 + 5(0)\right]$$
$$= 404\text{ m}$$
Add this distance to the initial position of the object and get:
$404\text{ m} + 16\text{ m} = \mathbf{420\ m}$

11. (a) Impulse $= F\Delta t = 126\text{ N} \times 5.0\text{ s} = \mathbf{630\ N\cdot s}$

(b)
$$F\Delta t = m(v_2 - v_1)$$
$$630\text{ N}\cdot\text{s} = 34\text{ kg}\left(v_2 - 0\ \frac{\text{m}}{\text{s}}\right)$$
$$v_2 = 18.53\ \frac{\text{m}}{\text{s}} \xrightarrow{\text{SD}} \mathbf{19\ \frac{m}{s}}$$

12. (a) Begin by finding the weight of the block.

$$w = mg$$
$$= 15\,\cancel{kg} \times 9.81\,\frac{N}{\cancel{kg}}$$
$$= 147.15\text{ N}$$

Now find the kinetic friction force, F_k.

$$F_k = \mu_k mg$$
$$= 0.38(147.15\text{ N})$$
$$= 55.92\text{ N} \xrightarrow{SD} \mathbf{56\ N}$$

(b) Sum the horizontal forces to find the net force.

$$\Sigma F_x = 310\text{ N} - 55.92\text{ N} = 254.08\text{ N}$$

Now use the impulse-momentum equation to find v_2.

$$F\Delta t = m(v_2 - v_1)$$
$$254.08\text{ N}(3.0\text{ s}) = 15\text{ kg}\left(v_2 - 0\,\frac{m}{s}\right)$$
$$(15\text{ kg})v_2 = 762.24\text{ N}\cdot\text{s}$$
$$v_2 = 50.82\,\frac{m}{s} \xrightarrow{SD} \mathbf{51\,\frac{m}{s}\ to\ the\ right}$$

13.
$$Q = mc\Delta T$$
$$3430\text{ J} = 1.5\text{ kg} \times c \times 18\text{ C}^\circ$$
$$c = 127.04\,\frac{J}{kg\cdot C^\circ} \xrightarrow{SD} \mathbf{130\,\frac{J}{kg\cdot C^\circ}}$$

14. Begin by converting 58.0 km/hr to m/s.

$$58.0\,\frac{\cancel{km}}{\cancel{hr}} \times \frac{1000\text{ m}}{1\,\cancel{km}} \times \frac{1\,\cancel{hr}}{60\,\cancel{min}} \times \frac{1\,\cancel{min}}{60\text{ s}} = 16.11\,\frac{m}{s}$$

Now use the displacement equation to find the distance Roy traveled.

$$\Delta x = v_0t + \frac{1}{2}at^2$$
$$= 16.11(5) + \frac{1}{2}(456.18)(5)^2$$
$$= 5782.8\text{ m} \xrightarrow{SD} \mathbf{6000\ m}$$

15. Begin by finding the weight of the mass and drawing a free-body diagram of the forces acting on the junction of the ropes.

$$w = mg$$
$$= 35\,\cancel{kg} \times 9.81\,\frac{N}{\cancel{kg}}$$
$$= 343.35\text{ N}$$

Now sum the horizontal and vertical forces to zero. Note that T_3 equals 343.35 N.

(a) $\Sigma F_x = 0;\ 343.35\text{ N} - T_4 \sin 30° - T_5 \sin 40° = 0$
(b) $\Sigma F_y = 0;\ T_4 \cos 30° - T_5 \cos 40° = 0$

Solve (b) for T_5 and get:

(b) $T_5 \cos 40° = T_4 \cos 30°$
$T_5 = 1.13T_4$ (b′)

Substitute (b′) into (a) and get:

(a) $T_4 \sin 30° + (1.13T_4) \sin 40° = 343.35\text{ N}$
$1.23T_4 = 343.35\text{ N}$
$T_4 = 279.15\text{ N} \xrightarrow{SD} \mathbf{280\ N}$

Substitute T_4 into (b′) and get:

(b′) $T_5 = 1.13(279.15\text{ N}) = 315.44\text{ N} \xrightarrow{SD} \mathbf{320\ N}$

16. (a) $\Sigma F_x = ma_x;\ (351\text{ N})\cos 20° - F_k = ma_x$
(b) $\Sigma F_y = 0;\ F_N - (351\text{ N})\sin 20° - mg = 0$

Solve (a) for F_k and get:

(a) $F_k = (351\text{ N})\cos 20° - 112\text{ kg}(2.30\text{ m}\cdot\text{s}^{-2})$
$= 72.23\text{ N} \xrightarrow{SD} \mathbf{72.2\ N}$

Solve (b) for F_N and get:

(b) $F_N = (351\text{ N})\sin 20° + 112\,\cancel{kg}\left(9.81\,\frac{N}{\cancel{kg}}\right) = 1218.8\text{ N}$

Now find the coefficient of kinetic friction.

$$F_k = \mu_k F_N$$
$$72.23\text{ N} = \mu_k(1218.8\text{ N})$$
$$\mu_k = 0.05926 \xrightarrow{SD} \mathbf{0.0593}$$

17. Begin by finding the weight of the mass.

$$w = mg = 78\,\cancel{\text{kg}} \times 9.81\,\frac{\text{N}}{\cancel{\text{kg}}} = 765.18\text{ N}$$

Now set the torques equal to each other and find F.

$$F(5.0\text{ m}) = 765.18\text{ N}(0.50\text{ m})$$

$$F = 76.518\text{ N} \xrightarrow{\text{SD}} \mathbf{77\ N}$$

$$\text{Mechanical advantage} = \frac{\text{force out}}{\text{force in}} = \frac{765.18\text{ N}}{76.518\text{ N}} = \mathbf{1\bar{0}}$$

18. (a) $P_1 = 2350\text{ W} \times 0.530 = 1245.5\text{ W} \xrightarrow{\text{SD}} \mathbf{1250\ W}$

(b) $P_2 = 1245.5\text{ W} \times 0.860 = 1071.13\text{ W} \xrightarrow{\text{SD}} \mathbf{1070\ W}$

(c) $\text{Percent eff.} = \dfrac{1071.13\text{ W}}{2350\text{ W}} \times 100\% = 45.58\% \xrightarrow{\text{SD}} \mathbf{45.6\%}$

19.

$$\Sigma F_y = ma_y$$

$$-F_N - mg = ma_y$$

$$-F_N - 80.0\,\cancel{\text{kg}}\left(9.81\,\frac{\text{N}}{\cancel{\text{kg}}}\right) = 80.0\text{ kg}(-22.0\text{ m}\cdot\text{s}^{-2})$$

$$F_N = 975.2\text{ N} \xrightarrow{\text{SD}} \mathbf{975\ N}$$

20. Convert 36 K to °C.

$$T_K = T_C + 273$$

$$36 = T_C + 273$$

$$T_C = -237°\text{C}$$

Convert −237°C to °F.

$$T_F = \frac{9}{5}T_C + 32$$

$$= \frac{9}{5}(-237°) + 32$$

$$= -394.6°\text{F} \xrightarrow{\text{SD}} \mathbf{-390°F}$$

PROBLEM SET 28

1.

$$F = \frac{Gm_em_a}{r^2}$$

$$= \frac{(6.67 \times 10^{-11})(5.98 \times 10^{24})(462.588)}{(2 \times 10^7)^2}$$

$$= 461.3\text{ N} \xrightarrow{\text{SD}} \mathbf{500\ N}$$

2. Begin by finding the weight of the block and the component of the weight parallel to the plane.

$$w = mg = 80\,\cancel{\text{kg}} \times 9.81\,\frac{\text{N}}{\cancel{\text{kg}}} = 784.8\text{ N}$$

$$w_x = (784.8\text{ N}) \sin 30° = 392.4\text{ N}$$

Now sum the forces parallel to the plane and get:

$$\Sigma F_x = ma_x$$

$$-392.4\text{ N} = (80\text{ kg})a_x$$

$$a_x = -4.905\,\frac{\text{m}}{\text{s}^2} \xrightarrow{\text{SD}} \mathbf{4.9\ \frac{m}{s^2}\ down\ the\ plane}$$

3. (a) Begin by finding the weight of the block. Then find w_x.

$$w = mg = 36\,\cancel{\text{kg}} \times 9.81\,\frac{\text{N}}{\cancel{\text{kg}}} = 353.16\text{ N}$$

$$w_x = (353.16\text{ N}) \sin 20° = 120.79\text{ N} \xrightarrow{\text{SD}} \mathbf{120\ N}$$

(b) $w_y = (353.16\text{ N}) \cos 20° = 331.86\text{ N} \xrightarrow{\text{SD}} \mathbf{330\ N}$

(c) $F_s = \mu_s F_N = 0.29(331.86\text{ N}) = 96.24\text{ N} \xrightarrow{\text{SD}} \mathbf{96\ N}$

(d) $F_k = \mu_k F_N = 0.18(331.86\text{ N}) = 59.73\text{ N}$

Now sum the forces parallel to the plane and get:

$$-w_x + F_k = ma_x$$

$$-120.79\text{ N} + 59.73\text{ N} = (36\text{ kg})a_x$$

$$a_x = -1.696\,\frac{\text{m}}{\text{s}^2} \xrightarrow{\text{SD}} \mathbf{1.7\ \frac{m}{s^2}\ down\ the\ plane}$$

4. Begin by finding the pressure produced by the fluid.

$$P_F = 200\,\frac{\cancel{\text{kg}}}{\text{m}^{\cancel{3}2}} \times 9.81\,\frac{\text{N}}{\cancel{\text{kg}}} \times 0.5\,\cancel{\text{m}} = 981\text{ Pa}$$

Now sum this pressure with the atmospheric pressure and find P.

$$P = 981\text{ Pa} + 101{,}300\text{ Pa} = 1.0228 \times 10^5\text{ Pa} \xrightarrow{\text{SD}} \mathbf{1 \times 10^5\ Pa}$$

5.

$$\frac{F_1}{A_1} = \frac{F_2}{A_2}$$

$$\frac{200\text{ N}}{15\text{ cm}^2} = \frac{F_2}{35\text{ cm}^2}$$

$$F_2 = 466.7\text{ N} \xrightarrow{\text{SD}} \mathbf{470\ N}$$

6. (a)

$$v = r\omega$$

$$27\ \frac{\text{m}}{\text{s}} = 0.23\text{ m} \times \omega$$

$$\omega = 117.39\ \frac{\text{rad}}{\text{s}} \xrightarrow{\text{SD}} \mathbf{120\ \frac{rad}{s}}$$

(b)

$$117.39\ \frac{\text{rad}}{\text{s}} \times \frac{1\text{ rev}}{2\pi\text{ rad}} \times \frac{60\text{ s}}{1\text{ min}}$$

$$= 1.12 \times 10^3\ \frac{\text{rev}}{\text{min}} \xrightarrow{\text{SD}} \mathbf{1.1 \times 10^3\ \frac{rev}{min}}$$

7. (a)

$$22{,}000\ \frac{\text{rev}}{\text{min}} \times \frac{2\pi\text{ rad}}{1\text{ rev}} \times \frac{1\text{ min}}{60\text{ s}} = 2304\ \frac{\text{rad}}{\text{s}} \xrightarrow{\text{SD}} \mathbf{23\bar{0}0\ \frac{rad}{s}}$$

(b) The diameter of the disk is 0.220 m, so the radius is 0.110 m.

$$v = r\omega = 0.110\text{ m} \times 2304\ \frac{\text{rad}}{\text{s}} = 253.44\ \frac{\text{m}}{\text{s}} \xrightarrow{\text{SD}} \mathbf{253\ \frac{m}{s}}$$

8. (a) Use the displacement equation to find the time.

$$\Delta y = v_0 t + \frac{1}{2}at^2$$

$$-18 = -2.5t + \frac{1}{2}(-9.81)t^2$$

$$0 = 4.905t^2 + 2.5t - 18$$

Use the quadratic formula to solve this equation for t.

$$t = \frac{-2.5 \pm \sqrt{(2.5)^2 - 4(4.905)(-18)}}{2(4.905)} = 1.68\text{ s} \xrightarrow{\text{SD}} \mathbf{1.7\ s}$$

(b) Use the motion equation to find the velocity.

$$v(t) = v_0 + at$$

$$v(1.68) = -2.5 + (-9.81)(1.68) = -18.98\ \frac{\text{m}}{\text{s}} \xrightarrow{\text{SD}} \mathbf{-19\ \frac{m}{s}}$$

9. (a)

$$v(t) = v_0 + at$$

$$0 = 3 + (-9.81)t$$

$$9.81t = 3$$

$$t = 0.306\text{ s} \xrightarrow{\text{SD}} \mathbf{0.3\ s}$$

(b)

$$y(t) = y_0 + v_0 t + \frac{1}{2}at^2$$

$$y(0.306) = 0 + 3(0.306) + \frac{1}{2}(-9.81)(0.306)^2$$

$$= 0.459\text{ m} \xrightarrow{\text{SD}} \mathbf{0.5\ m}$$

10. Choose the lower left-hand corner of the iron plate as the origin.

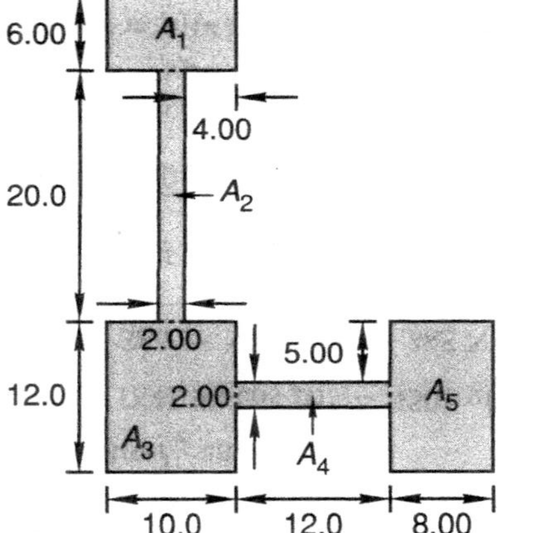

$$A_1 = 6.00 \times 10.0 = 60.0\text{ m}^2$$
$$A_2 = 20.0 \times 2.00 = 40.0\text{ m}^2$$
$$A_3 = 12.0 \times 10.0 = 120.0\text{ m}^2$$
$$A_4 = 2.00 \times 12.0 = 24.0\text{ m}^2$$
$$A_5 = 12.0 \times 8.00 = 96.0\text{ m}^2$$

There is both a horizontal and vertical distance to the center of mass. To find the x distance to the center of mass, note that the x distance to the centers of A_1, A_2, and A_3 is 5.00 m, to the center of A_4 is 16.0 m, and to the center of A_5 is 26.0 m. Arbitrarily assign a weight of 1 N to each square meter of area and sum the moments.

$$(60.0 + 40.0 + 120.0)(5.00) + 24.0(16.0) + 96.0(26.0) = 3980\text{ N}\cdot\text{m}$$

This is the same moment that would be produced by all 340 N placed at a distance x to the center of mass.

$$(340\text{ N})x = 3980\text{ N}\cdot\text{m}$$

$$x = 11.71\text{ m} \xrightarrow{\text{SD}} 11.7\text{ m}$$

Follow the same procedure to find the y distance to the center of mass.

$$(120.0 + 24.0 + 96.0)(6.00) + 40.0(22.0) + 60.0(35.0) = 4420\text{ N}\cdot\text{m}$$

This is the same moment that would be produced by all 340 N placed at a distance y to the center of mass.

$$(340\text{ N})y = 4420\text{ N}\cdot\text{m}$$

$$y = 13.0\text{ m}$$

Center of mass is at x = 11.7 m and y = 13.0 m.

11.
$$x(t) = 2t^4 + 2t^3 - 5t \quad \text{function}$$
$$\frac{dx}{dt} = 8t^3 + 6t^2 - 5 \quad \text{velocity}$$
$$\frac{dv}{dt} = 24t^2 + 12t - 0 \quad \text{acceleration}$$
$$\left.\frac{dv}{dt}\right|_{3.00} = 24(3.00)^2 + 12(3.00) = \mathbf{+252\ \frac{m}{s^2}} \quad \text{solved}$$

12. (a) Impulse $= F\Delta t = 300\text{ N} \times 2\text{ s} =$ **600 N·s**
(b)
$$F\Delta t = m(v_2 - v_1)$$
$$600\text{ N}\cdot\text{s} = 150\text{ kg}\left(v_2 - 0\,\frac{\text{m}}{\text{s}}\right)$$
$$v_2 = \mathbf{4\ \frac{m}{s}}$$

13. (a) Begin by finding the weight of the crate.
$$w = mg = 412\text{ kg} \times 9.81\,\frac{\text{N}}{\text{kg}} = 4041.72\text{ N}$$

Now find the kinetic friction force.
$$F_k = \mu_k mg = 0.25(4041.72\text{ N}) = 1010.43\text{ N} \xrightarrow{\text{SD}} \mathbf{1\bar{0}00\ N}$$

(b) Sum the horizontal forces to find the net force.
$\sum F_x = 1630\text{ N} - 1010.43\text{ N} = 619.57\text{ N}$
Now use the impulse-momentum equation to find v_2.
$$F\Delta t = m(v_2 - v_1)$$
$$619.57\text{ N}(3.5\text{ s}) = 412\text{ kg}\left(v_2 - 0\,\frac{\text{m}}{\text{s}}\right)$$
$$v_2 = 5.263\,\frac{\text{m}}{\text{s}} \xrightarrow{\text{SD}} \mathbf{5.3\ \frac{m}{s}\ \text{to the left}}$$

14.
$$Q = mc\Delta T$$
$$8.06 \times 10^6\text{ J} = 200\text{ kg} \times c \times 45.0\text{ C}^\circ$$
$$c = 895.56\,\frac{\text{J}}{\text{kg}\cdot\text{C}^\circ} \xrightarrow{\text{SD}} \mathbf{896\ \frac{J}{kg\cdot C^\circ}}$$

Convert 8.06×10^6 J to food calories.
$$8.06 \times 10^6\,\cancel{\text{J}} \times \frac{1\text{ food calorie}}{4186\,\cancel{\text{J}}}$$
$$= 1.925 \times 10^3\text{ food calories} \xrightarrow{\text{SD}} \mathbf{1.93 \times 10^3\ food\ calories}$$

15. Use the displacement equation to find the distance. Note that 1.0 minute is equal to 60 seconds.
$$\Delta x = v_0 t + \frac{1}{2}at^2$$
$$= 38(60) + \frac{1}{2}(4.5)(60)^2 = 1.038 \times 10^4\text{ m} \xrightarrow{\text{SD}} \mathbf{1.0 \times 10^4\ m}$$

16. (a) $\sum M = 0;\ mg\,\frac{L}{2}\cos\theta - F_w L\sin\theta = 0$

(b)
$$mg\,\frac{L}{2}\cos\theta - F_s L\sin\theta = 0$$
$$mg\,\frac{L}{2}\cos\theta - \mu_s F_N L\sin\theta = 0$$
$$mg\,\frac{L}{2}\cos\theta - \mu_s mgL\sin\theta = 0$$

(c)
$$\mu_s mgL\sin\theta = mg\,\frac{L}{2}\cos\theta$$
$$\sin\theta = \frac{\cos\theta}{2\mu_s}$$

(d)
$$\frac{\sin\theta}{\cos\theta} = \frac{\cos\theta}{2\mu_s\cos\theta}$$
$$\mathbf{\tan\theta = \frac{1}{2\mu_s}}$$

17. (a) $\sum F_x = ma_x;\ (841\text{ N})\cos 20^\circ - F_k = ma_x$
(b) $\sum F_y = 0;\ F_N + (841\text{ N})\sin 20^\circ - mg = 0$

Solve (a) for F_k and get:

(a) $F_k = (841\text{ N})\cos 20^\circ - 450\text{ kg}(0.900\text{ m}\cdot\text{s}^{-2})$
$$= 385.28\text{ N} \xrightarrow{\text{SD}} \mathbf{385\ N}$$

Solve (b) for F_N and get:

(b) $F_N = 450\,\cancel{\text{kg}}\left(9.81\,\frac{\text{N}}{\cancel{\text{kg}}}\right) - (841\text{ N})\sin 20^\circ = 4126.86\text{ N}$

Now find the coefficient of kinetic friction.
$$F_k = \mu_k F_N$$
$$385.28\text{ N} = \mu_k(4126.86\text{ N})$$
$$\mu_k = 0.09336 \xrightarrow{\text{SD}} \mathbf{0.0934}$$

18. Begin by finding the weight of the vacuum chamber.

$$w = mg = 82.0\text{ kg} \times 9.81\frac{\text{N}}{\text{kg}} = 804.42\text{ N}$$

Now set the torques equal to each other and find T_2.

$$T_2R_2 = T_1R_1$$
$$T_2R_2 = mgR_1$$
$$T_2(0.50\text{ m}) = 804.42\text{ N}(0.020\text{ m})$$
$$T_2 = 32.1768\text{ N} \xrightarrow{\text{SD}} \mathbf{32\ N}$$

$$\text{Mechanical advantage} = \frac{\text{force out}}{\text{force in}} = \frac{804.42\text{ N}}{32.1768\text{ N}} = \mathbf{25}$$

19. $F = ma = 95\text{ kg} \times 12\text{ m}\cdot\text{s}^{-2} = 1140\text{ N} \xrightarrow{\text{SD}} \mathbf{1100\ N}$

20. $v_{av} = \dfrac{x_2 - x_1}{t_2 - t_1} = \dfrac{118 - 26}{42 - 8.0}\dfrac{\text{m}}{\text{s}} = +2.706\dfrac{\text{m}}{\text{s}} \xrightarrow{\text{SD}} \mathbf{+2.7\ \dfrac{m}{s}}$

Problem Set 29

1. (a) $PE = mgh = 0.200\text{ kg} \times 9.81\dfrac{\text{N}}{\text{kg}} \times 10.0\text{ m} = 19.62\text{ J}$

$$KE = \frac{1}{2}mv^2$$
$$19.62\text{ J} = \frac{1}{2}(0.200\text{ kg})v^2$$
$$v = -14.007\frac{\text{m}}{\text{s}} \xrightarrow{\text{SD}} \mathbf{-14.0\ \frac{m}{s}}$$

(b) $PE = mgh = 0.200\text{ kg} \times 9.81\dfrac{\text{N}}{\text{kg}} \times 9.00\text{ m} = 17.658\text{ J}$

$$KE = \frac{1}{2}mv^2$$
$$17.658\text{ J} = \frac{1}{2}(0.200\text{ kg})v^2$$
$$v = +13.288\frac{\text{m}}{\text{s}} \xrightarrow{\text{SD}} \mathbf{+13.3\ \frac{m}{s}}$$

(c) $\Delta KE = 19.62\text{ J} - 17.658\text{ J} = 1.962\text{ J} \xrightarrow{\text{SD}} \mathbf{1.96\ J}$

2. $PE = mgh = 4.00\text{ kg} \times 9.81\dfrac{\text{N}}{\text{kg}} \times 10.0\text{ m} = 392.4\text{ J}$

$$KE = \frac{1}{2}mv^2$$
$$392.4\text{ J} = \frac{1}{2}(4.00\text{ kg})v^2$$
$$v = 14.007\frac{\text{m}}{\text{s}} \xrightarrow{\text{SD}} \mathbf{14.0\ \frac{m}{s}}$$

3. $F = \dfrac{Gm_e m_m}{r^2} = \dfrac{(6.67 \times 10^{-11})(5.98 \times 10^{24})(7.36 \times 10^{22})}{(3.8 \times 10^8)^2}$

$$= 2.03 \times 10^{20}\text{ N} \xrightarrow{\text{SD}} 2.0 \times 10^{20}\text{ N}$$

The force that the earth exerts on the moon is equal to the force that the moon exerts on the earth. This force equals $\mathbf{2.0 \times 10^{20}\ N}$.

4. Begin by finding the weight of the block and the component of the weight parallel to the plane.

$$w = mg = 425\text{ kg} \times 9.81\frac{\text{N}}{\text{kg}} = 4169.25\text{ N}$$
$$w_x = (4169.25\text{ N})\sin 38° = 2566.85\text{ N}$$

Now sum the forces parallel to the plane and get:

$$\Sigma F_x = ma_x$$
$$-2566.85\text{ N} = (425\text{ kg})a_x$$
$$a_x = -6.0396\frac{\text{m}}{\text{s}^2} \xrightarrow{\text{SD}} \mathbf{6.04\ \frac{m}{s^2}\ \text{down the plane}}$$

5. (a) Begin by finding the weight of the block. Then find w_x.

$$w = mg = 24\text{ kg} \times 9.81\frac{\text{N}}{\text{kg}} = 235.44\text{ N}$$
$$w_x = (235.44\text{ N})\sin 25° = 99.50\text{ N} \xrightarrow{\text{SD}} \mathbf{1\bar{0}0\ N}$$

(b) $w_y = (235.44\text{ N})\cos 25° = 213.38\text{ N} \xrightarrow{\text{SD}} \mathbf{210\ N}$

(c) $F_s = \mu_s F_N = 0.65(213.38\text{ N}) = 138.70\text{ N} \xrightarrow{\text{SD}} \mathbf{140\ N}$

The component of the weight of the block parallel to the plane, w_x, is less than the force of static friction, F_s. Thus, **the block will not slide down the plane.**

6. Begin by finding the pressure produced by the seawater.

$$P_S = 1025\ \frac{\text{kg}}{\text{m}^3} \times 9.81\ \frac{\text{N}}{\text{kg}} \times 16\ \text{m} = 1.609 \times 10^5\ \text{Pa}$$

Now sum this pressure with the atmospheric pressure and find P.

$$P = 1.609 \times 10^5\ \text{Pa} + 1.01 \times 10^5\ \text{Pa}$$
$$= 2.619 \times 10^5\ \text{Pa} \xrightarrow{\text{SD}} \mathbf{2.6 \times 10^5\ Pa}$$

7. $$\frac{F_2}{A_2} = \frac{F_1}{A_1}$$
$$\frac{F_2}{8\ \text{m}^2} = \frac{362.19\ \text{N}}{2.01633\ \text{m}^2}$$
$$F_2 = 1437\ \text{N} \xrightarrow{\text{SD}} \mathbf{1000\ N}$$

8. (a) $$44\ \frac{\text{rev}}{\text{min}} \times \frac{2\pi\ \text{rad}}{1\ \text{rev}} \times \frac{1\ \text{min}}{60\ \text{s}} = 4.608\ \frac{\text{rad}}{\text{s}} \xrightarrow{\text{SD}} \mathbf{4.6\ \frac{rad}{s}}$$
(b) The diameter of the disk is 4.0 m, so the radius is 2.0 m.
$$v = r\omega = 2.0\ \text{m} \times 4.608\ \frac{\text{rad}}{\text{s}} = 9.216\ \frac{\text{m}}{\text{s}} \xrightarrow{\text{SD}} \mathbf{9.2\ \frac{m}{s}}$$

9. (a) $$33\ \frac{\text{rev}}{\text{min}} \times \frac{2\pi\ \text{rad}}{1\ \text{rev}} \times \frac{1\ \text{min}}{60\ \text{s}} = 3.456\ \frac{\text{rad}}{\text{s}} \xrightarrow{\text{SD}} \mathbf{3.5\ \frac{rad}{s}}$$
(b) $$v = r\omega$$
$$20.7\ \frac{\text{m}}{\text{s}} = r \times 3.456\ \frac{\text{rad}}{\text{s}}$$
$$r = 5.990\ \text{m} \xrightarrow{\text{SD}} \mathbf{6.0\ m}$$

10. (a) Use the displacement equation to find the time.
$$\Delta y = v_0 t + \frac{1}{2}at^2$$
$$-200 = -10.0t + \frac{1}{2}(-9.81)t^2$$
$$0 = 4.905t^2 + 10.0t - 200$$

Use the quadratic formula to solve this equation for t.
$$t = \frac{-10.0 \pm \sqrt{(10.0)^2 - 4(4.905)(-200)}}{2(4.905)} = 5.447\ \text{s} \xrightarrow{\text{SD}} \mathbf{5.45\ s}$$

(b) Use the motion equation to find the velocity.
$$v(t) = v_0 + at$$
$$v(5.447) = -10.0 + (-9.81)(5.447)$$
$$= -63.44\ \frac{\text{m}}{\text{s}} \xrightarrow{\text{SD}} \mathbf{-63.4\ \frac{m}{s}}$$

11. (a) $$v(t) = v_0 + at$$
$$0 = 250 + (-9.81)t$$
$$9.81t = 250$$
$$t = 25.48\ \text{s} \xrightarrow{\text{SD}} \mathbf{25.5\ s}$$
(b) Use the position equation to find the maximum height.
$$y(t) = y_0 + v_0 t + \frac{1}{2}at^2$$
$$y(25.48) = 0 + 250(25.48) + \frac{1}{2}(-9.81)(25.48)^2$$
$$= 3185.5\ \text{m} \xrightarrow{\text{SD}} \mathbf{3190\ m}$$

12. (a) $\Sigma F_y = 0;\ F_B + 60\ \text{N} - F_A = 0$
(b) $\Sigma M_B = 0;\ 60\ \text{N}(6.0\ \text{m}) - F_A(2.0\ \text{m}) = 0$

Solve (b) for F_A and get:
(b) $F_A(2.0\ \text{m}) = 60\ \text{N}(6.0\ \text{m})$
$$F_A = \mathbf{180\ N}$$

Substitute F_A into (a) to find F_B.
(a) $F_B + 60\ \text{N} - (180\ \text{N}) = 0$
$$F_B = \mathbf{120\ N}$$

13. (a)

$$v(t) = -2t^2 + 4t + 40 \qquad \text{function}$$
$$\frac{dv}{dt} = -4t + 4 + 0 \qquad \text{acceleration}$$
$$\left.\frac{dv}{dt}\right|_{5.0} = -4(5.0) + 4 = \mathbf{-16\ \frac{m}{s^2}} \qquad \text{solved}$$

(b) $$\text{Distance} = \int_0^{5.0} (-2t^2 + 4t + 40)\,dt$$

$$= \left[-\frac{2t^3}{3} + 2t^2 + 40t \right]_0^{5.0}$$

$$= \left[-\frac{2(5.0)^3}{3} + 2(5.0)^2 + 40(5.0) \right]$$

$$= 166.67 \text{ m} \xrightarrow{\text{SD}} \mathbf{170 \text{ m}}$$

14. (a) $\text{Impulse} = F\Delta t = 140 \text{ N} \times 3.0 \text{ s} = \mathbf{420 \text{ N}\cdot\text{s}}$

(b) $$F\Delta t = m(v_2 - v_1)$$

$$420 \text{ N}\cdot\text{s} = 65 \text{ kg}\left(v_2 - 0 \frac{\text{m}}{\text{s}}\right)$$

$$v_2 = 6.4615 \frac{\text{m}}{\text{s}} \xrightarrow{\text{SD}} \mathbf{6.5 \frac{m}{s}}$$

15. (a) $F_k = \mu_k F_N$

$$= 0.41(210 \cancel{\text{kg}})\left(9.81 \frac{\text{N}}{\cancel{\text{kg}}}\right) = 844.64 \text{ N} \xrightarrow{\text{SD}} \mathbf{840 \text{ N}}$$

(b) Sum the horizontal forces to find the net force.
$\Sigma F_x = 1300 \text{ N} - 844.64 \text{ N} = 455.36 \text{ N}$

Now use the impulse-momentum equation to find v_2.

$$F\Delta t = m(v_2 - v_1)$$

$$455.36 \text{ N}(8.0 \text{ s}) = 210 \text{ kg}\left(v_2 - 0 \frac{\text{m}}{\text{s}}\right)$$

$$v_2 = 17.347 \frac{\text{m}}{\text{s}} \xrightarrow{\text{SD}} \mathbf{17 \frac{m}{s} \text{ to the right}}$$

16. $Q = mc\Delta T = 0.500 \cancel{\text{kg}} \times 300 \frac{\text{J}}{\cancel{\text{kg}}\cdot\cancel{\text{C}^\circ}} \times 15.0 \cancel{\text{C}^\circ} = 2250 \text{ J}$

Now convert 2250 J to calories.

$$2250 \cancel{\text{J}} \times \frac{1 \text{ calorie}}{4.186 \cancel{\text{J}}} = 537.51 \text{ calories} \xrightarrow{\text{SD}} \mathbf{538 \text{ calories}}$$

17. Begin by converting units so the answer is solved in meters.

$$v_0 = 447 \frac{\cancel{\text{cm}}}{\text{s}} \times \frac{1 \text{ m}}{100 \cancel{\text{cm}}} = 4.47 \frac{\text{m}}{\text{s}}$$

$$a = 10.0 \frac{\cancel{\text{cm}}}{\text{s}^2} \times \frac{1 \text{ m}}{100 \cancel{\text{cm}}} = 0.100 \frac{\text{m}}{\text{s}^2}$$

$$t = 2.00 \cancel{\text{min}} \times \frac{60 \text{ s}}{1 \cancel{\text{min}}} = 120 \text{ s}$$

Now use the displacement equation to find the distance.

$$\Delta x = v_0 t + \frac{1}{2}at^2$$

$$= 4.47(120) + \frac{1}{2}(0.100)(120)^2$$

$$= 1256.4 \text{ m} \xrightarrow{\text{SD}} \mathbf{1260 \text{ m}}$$

18.

$$\Sigma M = 0$$

$$mg \frac{L}{2} \cos\theta - F_w L \sin\theta = 0$$

$$mg \frac{L}{2} \cos\theta - F_s L \sin\theta = 0$$

$$mg \frac{L}{2} \cos\theta - \mu_s F_N L \sin\theta = 0$$

$$mg \frac{L}{2} \cos\theta - \mu_s mgL \sin\theta = 0$$

$$\mu_s mgL \sin\theta = mg \frac{L}{2} \cos\theta$$

$$\sin\theta = \frac{\cos\theta}{2\mu_s}$$

Divide both sides of the equation by $\cos\theta$ and get:

$$\frac{\sin\theta}{\cos\theta} = \frac{\cos\theta}{2\mu_s \cos\theta}$$

$$\tan\theta = \frac{1}{2\mu_s}$$

$$\mu_s = \frac{1}{2 \tan 48^\circ}$$

$$= 0.4502 \xrightarrow{\text{SD}} \mathbf{0.45}$$

19. (a) $\sum F_x = ma_x$; $(531\text{ N})\cos 40° - F_k = ma_x$
(b) $\sum F_y = 0$; $F_N - (531\text{ N})\sin 40° - mg = 0$

Solve (a) for F_k and get:

(a) $F_k = (531\text{ N})\cos 40° - 160\text{ kg}(1.31\text{ m}\cdot\text{s}^{-2})$
$= 197.17\text{ N} \xrightarrow{\text{SD}} \mathbf{197\ N}$

Solve (b) for F_N and get:

(b) $F_N = 160\,\cancel{\text{kg}}\left(9.81\,\frac{\text{N}}{\cancel{\text{kg}}}\right) + (531\text{ N})\sin 40° = 1910.9\text{ N}$

Now find the coefficient of kinetic friction.

$F_k = \mu_k F_N$
$197.17\text{ N} = \mu_k(1910.9\text{ N})$
$\mu_k = 0.10318 \xrightarrow{\text{SD}} \mathbf{0.103}$

20. $319\bar{0}\,\cancel{\text{cm}^3} \times \frac{1\,\cancel{\text{m}^3}}{(100)^3\,\cancel{\text{cm}^3}} \times \frac{1\text{ km}^3}{(1000)^3\,\cancel{\text{m}^3}} = \mathbf{3.190 \times 10^{-12}\ km^3}$

PROBLEM SET 30

1. Begin by writing a momentum equation.

$$m_1v_1 + m_2v_2 = (m_1 + m_2)v_3$$
$$2.00(10.0\underline{/30°}) + 15.0(20.0\underline{/80°}) = (2.00 + 15.0)v_3$$
$$20.0\underline{/30°} + 300\underline{/80°} = (17.0)v_3 \qquad \text{(a)}$$

Now find the sum of the x and y components of the initial momenta.

$\sum mv_x = 20.0\cos 30° + 300\cos 80° = 69.41\text{ kg}\cdot\text{m}\cdot\text{s}^{-1}$

$\sum mv_y = 20.0\sin 30° + 300\sin 80° = 305.44\text{ kg}\cdot\text{m}\cdot\text{s}^{-1}$

$\sum mv_R = (69.41i + 305.44j)\text{ kg}\cdot\text{m}\cdot\text{s}^{-1}$

Convert this resultant to polar form and get:

$\sum mv_R = \sqrt{(69.41)^2 + (305.44)^2} = 313.23\text{ kg}\cdot\text{m}\cdot\text{s}^{-1}$

$\theta = \tan^{-1}\frac{305.44}{69.41} = 77.20°$

$\sum mv_R = 313.23\underline{/77.20°}\text{ kg}\cdot\text{m}\cdot\text{s}^{-1}$

Use this momentum in (a) to find v_3.

(a) $313.23\underline{/77.20°} = (17.0)v_3$

$$v_3 = 18.43\underline{/77.20°}\ \frac{\text{m}}{\text{s}} \xrightarrow{\text{SD}} \mathbf{18.4\underline{/77.20°}\ \frac{m}{s}}$$

2. Begin by writing a momentum equation. Note that the sum of the momenta must equal zero.

$$\sum mv = 0$$
$$m_pv_p + m_cv_c = 0$$
$$m_cv_c = -m_pv_p$$
$$(50)v_c = -0.020(400)$$
$$v_c = \mathbf{-0.16\ \frac{m}{s}}$$

3. (a) $PE = mgh = 0.1\,\cancel{\text{kg}} \times 9.81\,\frac{\text{N}}{\cancel{\text{kg}}} \times 15.5005\text{ m} = 15.21\text{ J}$

$$KE = \frac{1}{2}mv^2$$
$$15.21\text{ J} = \frac{1}{2}(0.1\text{ kg})v^2$$
$$v = -17.44\ \frac{\text{m}}{\text{s}} \xrightarrow{\text{SD}} \mathbf{-20\ \frac{m}{s}}$$

(b) $PE = mgh = 0.1\,\cancel{\text{kg}} \times 9.81\,\frac{\text{N}}{\cancel{\text{kg}}} \times 13.680\text{ m} = 13.42\text{ J}$

$$KE = \frac{1}{2}mv^2$$
$$13.42\text{ J} = \frac{1}{2}(0.1\text{ kg})v^2$$
$$v = +16.38\ \frac{\text{m}}{\text{s}} \xrightarrow{\text{SD}} \mathbf{+20\ \frac{m}{s}}$$

(c) $\Delta KE = 15.21\text{ J} - 13.42\text{ J} = 1.79\text{ J} \xrightarrow{\text{SD}} \mathbf{2\ J}$

4. $PE = mgh = 12\,\cancel{\text{kg}} \times 9.81\,\frac{\text{N}}{\cancel{\text{kg}}} \times 30\text{ m} = 3531.6\text{ J}$

$$KE = \frac{1}{2}mv^2$$
$$3531.6\text{ J} = \frac{1}{2}(12\text{ kg})v^2$$
$$v = 24.26\ \frac{\text{m}}{\text{s}} \xrightarrow{\text{SD}} \mathbf{24\ \frac{m}{s}}$$

5. $F = \frac{Gm_1m_2}{r^2} = \frac{(6.67 \times 10^{-11})(5.6 \times 10^7)(5.6 \times 10^7)}{(85)^2}$

$= 28.95 \text{ N} \xrightarrow{SD} \mathbf{29\ N}$

6. Begin by finding the weight of the block and the component of the weight parallel to the plane.

$w = mg = 850 \text{ kg} \times 9.81 \frac{\text{N}}{\text{kg}} = 8338.5 \text{ N}$

$w_x = (8338.5 \text{ N}) \sin 20° = 2851.93 \text{ N}$

Now sum the forces parallel to the plane and get:

$\Sigma F_x = ma_x$

$-2851.93 \text{ N} = (850 \text{ kg})a_x$

$a_x = -3.355 \frac{\text{m}}{\text{s}^2} \xrightarrow{SD} \mathbf{3.4\ \frac{m}{s^2}}$ **down the plane**

7. (a) Begin by finding the weight of the block. Then find w_x.

$w = mg = 33.0 \text{ kg} \times 9.81 \frac{\text{N}}{\text{kg}} = 323.73 \text{ N}$

$w_x = (323.73 \text{ N}) \sin 45° = 228.91 \text{ N} \xrightarrow{SD} \mathbf{229\ N}$

(b) $w_y = (323.73 \text{ N}) \cos 45° = 228.91 \text{ N} \xrightarrow{SD} \mathbf{229\ N}$

(c) $F_s = \mu_s F_N = 0.32(228.91 \text{ N}) = 73.25 \text{ N} \xrightarrow{SD} \mathbf{73\ N}$

The component of the weight of the block parallel to the plane, w_x, is greater than the force of static friction, F_s. Thus, **the block will slide down the plane**.

8. Begin by finding the pressure produced by the fluid.

$P_F = 283 \frac{\text{kg}}{\text{m}^{3}} \times 9.81 \frac{\text{N}}{\text{kg}} \times 2.000 \text{ m} = 5552.46 \text{ Pa}$

Now sum this pressure with the atmospheric pressure and find P.

$P = 5552.46 \text{ Pa} + 101{,}300 \text{ Pa} = 1.0685 \times 10^5 \text{ Pa} \xrightarrow{SD} \mathbf{1.07 \times 10^5\ Pa}$

9. $\frac{F_2}{A_2} = \frac{F_1}{A_1}$

$\frac{F_2}{251 \text{ cm}^2} = \frac{75 \text{ N}}{105 \text{ cm}^2}$

$F_2 = 179.29 \text{ N} \xrightarrow{SD} \mathbf{180\ N}$

10. (a) $312 \frac{\text{rev}}{\text{min}} \times \frac{2\pi \text{ rad}}{1 \text{ rev}} \times \frac{1 \text{ min}}{60 \text{ s}} = 32.67 \frac{\text{rad}}{\text{s}} \xrightarrow{SD} \mathbf{32.7\ \frac{rad}{s}}$

(b) The diameter of the disk is 3.3 meters, so the radius is 1.65 meters.

$v = r\omega$

$= 1.65 \text{ m} \times 32.67 \frac{\text{rad}}{\text{s}}$

$= 53.91 \frac{\text{m}}{\text{s}} \xrightarrow{SD} \mathbf{54\ \frac{m}{s}}$

11. (a) $36{,}\bar{5}00 \frac{\text{rev}}{\text{min}} \times \frac{2\pi \text{ rad}}{1 \text{ rev}} \times \frac{1 \text{ min}}{60 \text{ s}} = 3822.27 \frac{\text{rad}}{\text{s}} \xrightarrow{SD} \mathbf{3822\ \frac{rad}{s}}$

(b) $v = r\omega$

$95.0 \frac{\text{m}}{\text{s}} = r \times 3822.27 \frac{\text{rad}}{\text{s}}$

$r = 0.02485 \text{ m}$

The diameter is twice the radius, so

$d = 2r$

$= 2(0.02485 \text{ m})$

$= \mathbf{0.0497\ m}$

12. (a) Use the displacement equation to find the time.

$\Delta y = v_0 t + \frac{1}{2}at^2$

$-150 = -6.0t + \frac{1}{2}(-9.81)t^2$

$0 = 4.905t^2 + 6.0t - 150$

Use the quadratic formula to solve this equation for t.

$t = \frac{-6.0 \pm \sqrt{(6.0)^2 - 4(4.905)(-150)}}{2(4.905)} = 4.95 \text{ s} \xrightarrow{SD} \mathbf{5.0\ s}$

(b) Use the motion equation to find the velocity.

$v(t) = v_0 + at$

$v(4.95) = -6.0 + (-9.81)(4.95)$

$= -54.56 \frac{\text{m}}{\text{s}} \xrightarrow{SD} \mathbf{-55\ \frac{m}{s}}$

13. (a)
$$v(t) = v_0 + at$$
$$0 = 17.8 + (-9.81)t$$
$$9.81t = 17.8$$
$$t = 1.814 \text{ s} \xrightarrow{SD} \mathbf{1.81 \text{ s}}$$

(b)
$$y(t) = y_0 + v_0t + \frac{1}{2}at^2$$
$$y(1.814) = 0 + 17.8(1.814) + \frac{1}{2}(-9.81)(1.814)^2$$
$$= 16.149 \text{ m} \xrightarrow{SD} \mathbf{16.1 \text{ m}}$$

14. Choose the lower left-hand corner of the object as the origin.

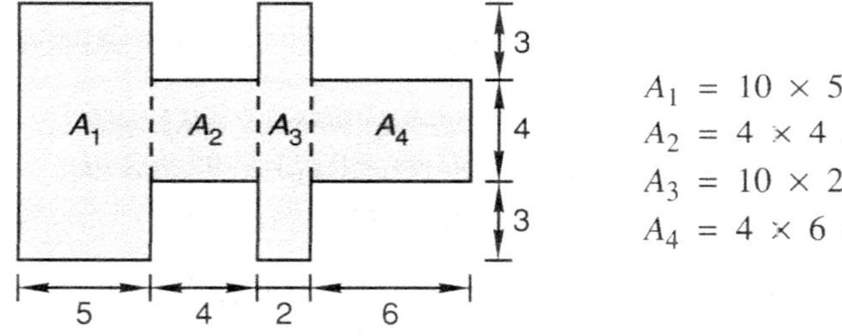

$A_1 = 10 \times 5 = 50$ sq. units
$A_2 = 4 \times 4 = 16$ sq. units
$A_3 = 10 \times 2 = 20$ sq. units
$A_4 = 4 \times 6 = 24$ sq. units

There is both a vertical and a horizontal distance to the center of mass. Since there is a horizontal axis of symmetry at $y = 5$ units, the y distance to the center of mass is 5 units. To find the x distance to the center of mass, arbitrarily assign a weight of 1 N to each square unit of area and sum the moments.

$$50(2.5) + 16(7) + 20(10) + 24(14) = 773 \text{ N}\cdot\text{units}$$

This is the same moment that would be produced by all 110 N placed at a distance x to the center of mass.

$$(110 \text{ N})x = 773 \text{ N}\cdot\text{units}$$
$$x = 7.027 \text{ units} \xrightarrow{SD} 7 \text{ units}$$

Center of mass is at x = 7 units and y = 5 units.

15. (a) Impulse $= F\Delta t = 216 \text{ N} \times 7.0 \text{ s} = 1512 \text{ N}\cdot\text{s} \xrightarrow{SD} \mathbf{1500 \text{ N}\cdot\text{s}}$

(b)
$$F\Delta t = m(v_2 - v_1)$$
$$1512 \text{ N}\cdot\text{s} = 19 \text{ kg}\left(v_2 - 0\frac{\text{m}}{\text{s}}\right)$$
$$v_2 = 79.58 \frac{\text{m}}{\text{s}} \xrightarrow{SD} \mathbf{8\bar{0} \frac{m}{s}}$$

16. (a) $F_k = \mu_k F_N = 0.34(93 \cancel{\text{kg}})\left(9.81 \frac{\text{N}}{\cancel{\text{kg}}}\right) = 310.19 \text{ N} \xrightarrow{SD} \mathbf{310 \text{ N}}$

(b) Sum the horizontal forces to find the net force.
$\Sigma F_x = 435 \text{ N} - 310.19 \text{ N} = 124.81 \text{ N}$

Now use the impulse-momentum equation to find v_2.
$$F\Delta t = m(v_2 - v_1)$$
$$124.81 \text{ N}(6 \text{ s}) = 93 \text{ kg}\left(v_2 - 0\frac{\text{m}}{\text{s}}\right)$$
$$v_2 = 8.052 \frac{\text{m}}{\text{s}} \xrightarrow{SD} \mathbf{8 \frac{m}{s} \text{ to the right}}$$

17. $Q = mc\Delta T = 43.0 \cancel{\text{kg}} \times 5000 \frac{\text{J}}{\cancel{\text{kg}}\cdot\cancel{\text{C}°}} \times 30.0 \cancel{\text{C}°} = 6{,}450{,}000 \text{ J}$

Now convert 6,450,000 J to food calories.

$$6{,}450{,}000 \cancel{\text{J}} \times \frac{1 \text{ food calorie}}{4186 \cancel{\text{J}}}$$
$$= 1540.85 \text{ food calories} \xrightarrow{SD} \mathbf{1540 \text{ food calories}}$$

18. Begin by drawing a free-body diagram of the forces acting on the junction of the ropes.

45° 30° T_1 T_2 46 N

(a) $\Sigma F_x = 0;\ T_2 \cos 30° - T_1 \cos 45° = 0$
(b) $\Sigma F_y = 0;\ T_1 \sin 45° + T_2 \sin 30° - 46 \text{ N} = 0$

Solve (a) for T_2 and get:
(a) $T_2 \cos 30° = T_1 \cos 45°$
$T_2 = 0.816T_1$ (a′)

Substitute (a′) into (b) and get:
(b) $T_1 \sin 45° + (0.816T_1) \sin 30° = 46 \text{ N}$
$1.115T_1 = 46 \text{ N}$
$T_1 = 41.256 \text{ N} \xrightarrow{SD} \mathbf{41 \text{ N}}$

Substitute T_1 into (a′) and get:

(a′) $T_2 = 0.816(41.256 \text{ N}) = 33.665 \text{ N} \xrightarrow{SD} \mathbf{34 \text{ N}}$

19.

$$\Sigma F_y = ma_y$$
$$F_N - mg = ma_y$$
$$F_N - 41\,\cancel{\text{kg}}\left(9.81\,\frac{\text{N}}{\cancel{\text{kg}}}\right) = 41\text{ kg}(2.1\text{ m}\cdot\text{s}^{-2})$$
$$F_N = 488.31\text{ N} \xrightarrow{\text{SD}} \mathbf{490\ N}$$

20.

$$\Sigma M = 0$$
$$ws\cos\theta - F_w L\sin\theta = 0$$
$$ws\cos\theta - F_s L\sin\theta = 0$$
$$ws\cos\theta - w\mu_s L\sin\theta = 0$$
$$ws\cos\theta = w\mu_s L\sin\theta$$
$$s\cos\theta = \mu_s L\sin\theta$$
$$s = \boldsymbol{\mu_s L\tan\theta}$$

Problem Set 31

1. $n = \frac{c}{v} = \frac{c}{0.5c} = \mathbf{2}$

2.

$$n_1\sin\theta_1 = n_2\sin\theta_2$$
$$(1)\sin 45^\circ = (1.3330)\sin\theta_2$$
$$\theta_2 = \mathbf{32.04^\circ}$$

3. (a)

$$m_1v_1 + m_2v_2 = (m_1 + m_2)v_3$$
$$(0.005)(500.00) + (2.002)(0) = (2.007)v_3$$
$$v_3 = +1.246\,\frac{\text{m}}{\text{s}} \xrightarrow{\text{SD}} \mathbf{+1\,\frac{m}{s}}$$

(b)

$$KE = \frac{1}{2}mv_3^2$$
$$= \frac{1}{2}(2.007)(1.246)^2$$
$$= 1.558\text{ J} \xrightarrow{\text{SD}} \mathbf{2\ J}$$

(c)

$$PE = mgh$$
$$1.558 = 2.007(9.81)h$$
$$h = 0.079\text{ m} \xrightarrow{\text{SD}} \mathbf{0.08\ m}$$

4. Begin by writing a momentum equation.

$$m_1v_1 + m_2v_2 = (m_1 + m_2)v_3$$
$$4.00(200\underline{/30^\circ}) + 10.0(40.0\underline{/150^\circ}) = (4.00 + 10.0)v_3$$
$$800\underline{/30^\circ} + 400\underline{/150^\circ} = (14.0)v_3 \qquad \text{(a)}$$

Now find the sum of the x and y components of the initial momenta.

$$\Sigma mv_x = 800\cos 30^\circ + 400\cos 150^\circ = 346.41\text{ kg}\cdot\text{m}\cdot\text{s}^{-1}$$
$$\Sigma mv_y = 800\sin 30^\circ + 400\sin 150^\circ = 600.00\text{ kg}\cdot\text{m}\cdot\text{s}^{-1}$$
$$\Sigma mv_R = (346.41i + 600.00j)\text{ kg}\cdot\text{m}\cdot\text{s}^{-1}$$

Convert this resultant to polar form and get:

$$\Sigma mv_R = \sqrt{(346.41)^2 + (600.00)^2} = 692.82\text{ kg}\cdot\text{m}\cdot\text{s}^{-1}$$
$$\theta = \tan^{-1}\frac{600.00}{346.41} = 60.00^\circ$$
$$\Sigma mv_R = 692.82\underline{/60.00^\circ}\text{ kg}\cdot\text{m}\cdot\text{s}^{-1}$$

Use this momentum in (a) to find v_3.

(a) $692.82\underline{/60.00^\circ} = (14.0)v_3$

$$v_3 = 49.487\underline{/60.00^\circ}\,\frac{\text{m}}{\text{s}} \xrightarrow{\text{SD}} \mathbf{49.5\underline{/60.00^\circ}\,\frac{m}{s}}$$

5. (a)

$$PE = mgh = 2.00\,\cancel{\text{kg}} \times 9.81\,\frac{\text{N}}{\cancel{\text{kg}}} \times 20.0\text{ m} = 392.4\text{ J}$$
$$KE = \frac{1}{2}mv^2$$
$$392.4\text{ J} = \frac{1}{2}(2.00\text{ kg})v^2$$
$$v = -19.809\,\frac{\text{m}}{\text{s}} \xrightarrow{\text{SD}} \mathbf{-19.8\,\frac{m}{s}}$$

(b)

$$PE = mgh = 2.00\,\cancel{\text{kg}} \times 9.81\,\frac{\text{N}}{\cancel{\text{kg}}} \times 16.0\text{ m} = 313.92\text{ J}$$
$$KE = \frac{1}{2}mv^2$$
$$313.92\text{ J} = \frac{1}{2}(2.00\text{ kg})v^2$$
$$v = +17.718\,\frac{\text{m}}{\text{s}} \xrightarrow{\text{SD}} \mathbf{+17.7\,\frac{m}{s}}$$

(c)

$$\Delta KE = 392.4\text{ J} - 313.92\text{ J} = 78.48\text{ J} \xrightarrow{\text{SD}} \mathbf{78.5\ J}$$

6. $PE = mgh = 28\ \cancel{kg} \times 9.81\ \frac{N}{\cancel{kg}} \times 16\ m = 4394.88\ J$

$$KE = \frac{1}{2}mv^2$$

$$4394.88\ J = \frac{1}{2}(28\ kg)v^2$$

$$v = 17.718\ \frac{m}{s} \xrightarrow{SD} \mathbf{18\ \frac{m}{s}}$$

7. $F = \frac{Gm_n m_a}{r^2} = \frac{(6.67 \times 10^{-11})(9.99 \times 10^{25})(93)}{(2.48 \times 10^7)^2}$

$$= 1.008 \times 10^3\ N \xrightarrow{SD} \mathbf{1.0 \times 10^3\ N}$$

8. Begin by finding the weight of the block and the component of the weight parallel to the plane.

$$w = mg = 312\ \cancel{kg} \times 9.81\ \frac{N}{\cancel{kg}} = 3060.72\ N$$

$$w_x = (3060.72\ N) \sin 35° = 1755.56\ N$$

Now sum the forces parallel to the plane and get:

$$\Sigma F_x = ma_x$$

$$-1755.56\ N = (312\ kg)a_x$$

$$a_x = -5.627\ \frac{m}{s^2} \xrightarrow{SD} \mathbf{5.63\ \frac{m}{s^2}\ down\ the\ plane}$$

9. (a) Begin by finding the weight of the block. Then find w_x.

$$w = mg = 48\ \cancel{kg} \times 9.81\ \frac{N}{\cancel{kg}} = 470.88\ N$$

$$w_x = (470.88\ N) \sin 50° = 360.72\ N \xrightarrow{SD} \mathbf{360\ N}$$

(b) $w_y = (470.88\ N) \cos 50° = 302.68\ N \xrightarrow{SD} \mathbf{3\bar{0}0\ N}$

(c) $F_k = \mu_k F_N = 0.43(302.68\ N) = 130.15\ N$

Now sum the forces parallel to the plane and get:

$$-w_x + F_k = ma_x$$

$$-360.72\ N + 130.15\ N = (48\ kg)a_x$$

$$a_x = -4.804\ \frac{m}{s^2} \xrightarrow{SD} \mathbf{4.8\ \frac{m}{s^2}\ down\ the\ plane}$$

10. Begin by finding the pressure produced by the water.

$$P_W = 1025\ \frac{\cancel{kg}}{m^{\cancel{3}2}} \times 9.81\ \frac{N}{\cancel{kg}} \times 16\ \cancel{m} = 1.609 \times 10^5\ Pa$$

Now sum this pressure with the atmospheric pressure and find P.

$$P = 1.609 \times 10^5\ Pa + 1.012 \times 10^5\ Pa$$

$$= 2.621 \times 10^5\ Pa \xrightarrow{SD} \mathbf{2.6 \times 10^5\ Pa}$$

11. $\frac{F_1}{A_1} = \frac{F_2}{A_2}$

$$\frac{890\ N}{20\ m^2} = \frac{F_2}{45\ m^2}$$

$$F_2 = 2002.5\ N \xrightarrow{SD} \mathbf{2000\ N}$$

12. (a) $78\ \frac{\cancel{rev}}{\cancel{min}} \times \frac{2\pi\ rad}{1\ \cancel{rev}} \times \frac{1\ \cancel{min}}{60\ s} = 8.168\ \frac{rad}{s} \xrightarrow{SD} \mathbf{8.2\ \frac{rad}{s}}$

(b) The diameter of the record is 25.4 cm or 0.254 m, so the radius is 0.127 m.

$$v = r\omega = 0.127\ m \times 8.168\ \frac{rad}{s} = 1.037\ \frac{m}{s} \xrightarrow{SD} \mathbf{1.0\ \frac{m}{s}}$$

13. (a) Use the displacement equation to find the time.

$$\Delta y = v_0 t + \frac{1}{2}at^2$$

$$-150 = 12t + \frac{1}{2}(-9.81)t^2$$

$$0 = 4.905t^2 - 12t - 150$$

Use the quadratic formula to solve this equation for t.

$$t = \frac{-(-12) \pm \sqrt{(-12)^2 - 4(4.905)(-150)}}{2(4.905)} = 6.89\ s \xrightarrow{SD} \mathbf{6.9\ s}$$

(b) Use the motion equation to find the velocity.

$$v(t) = v_0 + at$$

$$v(6.89) = 12 + (-9.81)(6.89)$$

$$= -55.59\ \frac{m}{s} \xrightarrow{SD} \mathbf{-56\ \frac{m}{s}}$$

14. Use the displacement equation to find the time.

$$\Delta y = v_0 t + \frac{1}{2}at^2$$

$$0 = 14.6t + \frac{1}{2}(-9.81)t^2$$

$$4.905t = 14.6$$

$$t = 2.977 \text{ s} \xrightarrow{SD} \mathbf{2.98\ s}$$

15. (a) $\Delta(mv) = m(v_2 - v_1)$

$= 1.05 \text{ kg}((-27i + 4.2j) - (28i + 5.6j)) \text{ m/s}$

$= 1.05 \text{ kg}(-55i - 1.4j) \text{ m/s}$

$= (-57.75i - 1.47j) \text{ kg}\cdot\text{m}\cdot\text{s}^{-1} \xrightarrow{SD} \mathbf{(-58i - 1.5j)\ kg\cdot m\cdot s^{-1}}$

(b) Convert this change in momentum to polar form.

$$\Delta(mv) = \sqrt{(-57.75)^2 + (-1.47)^2} = 57.77 \text{ kg}\cdot\text{m}\cdot\text{s}^{-1}$$

$$\theta = \tan^{-1}\frac{-1.47}{-57.75} = 1.46°$$

Since θ is a 3rd-quadrant angle: $\theta = -180° + 1.46° = -178.54°$

$\Delta(mv) = 57.77\angle{-178.54°} \text{ kg}\cdot\text{m}\cdot\text{s}^{-1}$

Use this in the impulse-momentum equation and get:

$$F\Delta t = \Delta(mv)$$

$$F(0.024 \text{ s}) = 57.77\angle{-178.54°} \text{ kg}\cdot\text{m}\cdot\text{s}^{-1}$$

$$F = 2407\angle{-178.54°} \text{ N} \xrightarrow{SD} \mathbf{2400\angle{-178.54°}\ N}$$

16. (a) $F_k = \mu_k F_N = 0.41(229 \text{ kg})\left(9.81 \frac{\text{N}}{\text{kg}}\right) = 921.06 \text{ N} \xrightarrow{SD} \mathbf{920\ N}$

(b) Sum the horizontal forces to find the net force.

$\Sigma F_x = 963 \text{ N} - 921.06 \text{ N} = 41.94 \text{ N}$

Now use the impulse-momentum equation to find v_2.

$$F\Delta t = \Delta(mv)$$

$$41.94 \text{ N}(4.0 \text{ s}) = 229 \text{ kg}\left(v_2 - 0\frac{\text{m}}{\text{s}}\right)$$

$$v_2 = 0.733 \frac{\text{m}}{\text{s}} \xrightarrow{SD} \mathbf{0.73\ \frac{m}{s}}\ \textbf{to the left}$$

17. $Q = mc\Delta T = (22.0)(733)(60.0) = 967{,}560 \text{ J}$

Convert 967,560 J to food calories and get:

$$967{,}560 \text{ J} \times \frac{1 \text{ food calorie}}{4186 \text{ J}} = \mathbf{231\ food\ calories}$$

18. Begin by finding the weight of m_1 and drawing a free-body diagram of the forces acting on the left junction.

$w = m_1 g$

$= 12.0 \text{ kg} \times 9.81 \frac{\text{N}}{\text{kg}}$

$= 117.72 \text{ N}$

70°
T_1
T_2
117.72 N

Now sum the horizontal and vertical forces to zero.

(a) $\Sigma F_x = 0;\ T_2 - T_1 \cos 70° = 0$

(b) $\Sigma F_y = 0;\ T_1 \sin 70° - 117.72 \text{ N} = 0$

Solve (b) for T_1 and get:

(b) $T_1 \sin 70° = 117.72 \text{ N}$

$$T_1 = 125.28 \text{ N} \xrightarrow{SD} \mathbf{125\ N}$$

Substitute T_1 into (a) and find T_2.

(a) $T_2 = (125.28 \text{ N}) \cos 70° = 42.848 \text{ N} \xrightarrow{SD} \mathbf{42.8\ N}$

Now draw a free-body diagram of the forces acting on the right junction. Note that T_2 equals 42.848 N. Then sum the horizontal and vertical forces to zero.

T_3
T_2
30°
T_4

(c) $\Sigma F_x = 0;\ T_3 \sin 30° - 42.848 \text{ N} = 0$

(d) $\Sigma F_y = 0;\ T_3 \cos 30° - T_4 = 0$

Solve (c) for T_3 and get:

(c) $T_3 \sin 30° = 42.848 \text{ N}$

$$T_3 = 85.696 \text{ N} \xrightarrow{SD} \mathbf{85.7\ N}$$

Substitute T_3 into (d) and find T_4.

(d) $T_4 = (85.696 \text{ N}) \cos 30° = 74.21 \text{ N} \xrightarrow{SD} \mathbf{74.2\ N}$

The weight of m_2 is equal to T_4. Solve for m_2 and get:

$$T_4 = m_2 g$$

$$74.21 \text{ N} = m_2 \times 9.81 \text{ N/kg}$$

$$m_2 = 7.5647 \text{ kg} \xrightarrow{SD} \mathbf{7.56\ kg}$$

19. (a) $\Sigma F_y = 0;\ F_A + F_B - 1200\text{ N} = 0$
(b) $\Sigma M_A = 0;\ 1200\text{ N}(3\text{ m}) - F_B(12\text{ m}) = 0$

Solve (b) for F_B and get:
(b) $F_B(12\text{ m}) = 1200\text{ N}(3\text{ m})$
$F_B = \mathbf{300\ N}$

Substitute F_B into (a) to find F_A.
(a) $F_A + (300\text{ N}) - 1200\text{ N} = 0$
$F_A = \mathbf{900\ N}$

20. Calculate the displacements for the following time intervals:

$\Delta x_{0,1.5} = 20\frac{\text{m}}{\cancel{\text{s}}} \times 1.5\cancel{\text{s}} = +30\text{ m}$ $\quad \Delta x_{1.5,4} = -20\frac{\text{m}}{\cancel{\text{s}}} \times 2.5\cancel{\text{s}} = -50\text{ m}$

$\Delta x_{4,5} = \dfrac{-20\frac{\text{m}}{\cancel{\text{s}}} \times 1\cancel{\text{s}}}{2} = -10\text{ m}$ $\quad \Delta x_{5,7} = \dfrac{20\frac{\text{m}}{\cancel{\text{s}}} \times 2\cancel{\text{s}}}{2} = +20\text{ m}$

Sum the displacements from $t = 0$ s to $t = 4$ s with the initial position and get:
$x_4 = 0\text{ m} + 30\text{ m} - 50\text{ m} = \mathbf{-2\bar{0}\ m}$
Sum the displacements from $t = 4$ s to $t = 7$ s with x_4 and get:
$x_7 = -20\text{ m} - 10\text{ m} + 20\text{ m} = \mathbf{-1\bar{0}\ m}$

Problem Set 32

1. Begin by converting 86°F to kelvins.

$T_C = \frac{5}{9}(T_F - 32)$
$= \frac{5}{9}(86° - 32)$
$= 30°\text{C}$

$T_K = T_C + 273$
$= 30 + 273$
$= 303\text{ K}$

Now use the ideal gas law and get:

$$\frac{V_1}{T_1} = \frac{V_2}{T_2}$$

$$\frac{4.2\text{ L}}{303\text{ K}} = \frac{6.4\text{ L}}{T_2}$$

$$T_2 = 461.71\text{ K} \xrightarrow{\text{SD}} \mathbf{460\ K}$$

2. Begin by converting the temperatures to kelvins.
$T_1 = 95 + 273 = 368\text{ K}$
$T_2 = 5.0 + 273 = 278\text{ K}$

Now use the ideal gas law and get:

$$\frac{P_1}{T_1} = \frac{P_2}{T_2}$$

$$\frac{1.013 \times 10^5\text{ N/m}^2}{368\text{ K}} = \frac{P_2}{278\text{ K}}$$

$$P_2 = 7.653 \times 10^4\ \frac{\text{N}}{\text{m}^2} \xrightarrow{\text{SD}} \mathbf{7.7 \times 10^4\ \frac{N}{m^2}}$$

3.
$$\frac{\sin\theta_1}{v_1} = \frac{\sin\theta_2}{v_2}$$

$$\frac{\sin 58°}{0.73c} = \frac{\sin\theta_2}{0.84c}$$

$$\theta_2 = \mathbf{77.38°}$$

4.
$n_1 \sin\theta_1 = n_2 \sin\theta_2$
$(1.0)\sin 40° = (1.52)\sin\theta_2$
$\theta_2 = \mathbf{25.02°}$

5. (a)
$m_1v_1 + m_2v_2 = (m_1 + m_2)v_3$
$(0.0020)(1000) + (0.80)(0) = (0.802)v_3$
$v_3 = +2.494\ \frac{\text{m}}{\text{s}} \xrightarrow{\text{SD}} \mathbf{+2.5\ \frac{m}{s}}$

(b) $KE = \frac{1}{2}mv_3^2$
$= \frac{1}{2}(0.802)(2.494)^2$
$= 2.494\text{ J} \xrightarrow{\text{SD}} \mathbf{2.5\ J}$

(c) $PE = mgh$
$2.494 = (0.802)(9.81)h$
$h = 0.317\text{ m} \xrightarrow{\text{SD}} \mathbf{0.32\ m}$

6. Begin by writing a momentum equation. Note that the sum of the momenta must equal zero.

$$\Sigma mv = 0$$
$$m_{2.0}v_{2.0} + m_{8.0}v_{8.0} = 0$$
$$m_{2.0}v_{2.0} = -(m_{8.0}v_{8.0})$$
$$(2.0)v_{2.0} = -(8.0)(-1.0)$$
$$v_{2.0} = +4.0\ \frac{m}{s} \xrightarrow{SD} \mathbf{4.0\ \frac{m}{s}\ to\ the\ right}$$

7. $PE = mgh = 0.60\ \cancel{kg} \times 9.81\ \frac{N}{\cancel{kg}} \times 14\ m = 82.404\ J$

$$KE = \frac{1}{2}mv_d^{\,2}$$
$$82.404\ J = \frac{1}{2}(0.60\ kg)v_d^{\,2}$$
$$v_d = -16.57\ \frac{m}{s} \xrightarrow{SD} \mathbf{-17\ \frac{m}{s}}$$

$PE = mgh = 0.60\ \cancel{kg} \times 9.81\ \frac{N}{\cancel{kg}} \times 10\ m = 58.86\ J$

$$KE = \frac{1}{2}mv_u^{\,2}$$
$$58.86\ J = \frac{1}{2}(0.60\ kg)v_u^{\,2}$$
$$v_u = +14.01\ \frac{m}{s} \xrightarrow{SD} \mathbf{+14\ \frac{m}{s}}$$

$\Delta KE = 82.404\ J - 58.86\ J = 23.544\ J \xrightarrow{SD} \mathbf{24\ J}$

8. $PE = mgh = 18\ \cancel{kg} \times 9.81\ \frac{N}{\cancel{kg}} \times 8.0\ m = 1412.64\ J$

$$KE = \frac{1}{2}mv^2$$
$$1412.64\ J = \frac{1}{2}(18\ kg)v^2$$
$$v = 12.53\ \frac{m}{s} \xrightarrow{SD} \mathbf{13\ \frac{m}{s}}$$

9. $F = \frac{Gm_v m_o}{r^2} \longrightarrow m_v = \frac{Fr^2}{Gm_o}$

$$= \frac{(807)(6.31 \times 10^6)^2}{(6.67 \times 10^{-11})(100)}$$
$$= 4.817 \times 10^{24}\ kg \xrightarrow{SD} \mathbf{4.82 \times 10^{24}\ kg}$$

10. Begin by finding the weight of the block and the component of the weight parallel to the plane.

$$w = mg = 927\ \cancel{kg} \times 9.81\ \frac{N}{\cancel{kg}} = 9093.87\ N$$
$$w_x = (9093.87\ N)\sin 42° = 6084.99\ N$$

Now sum the forces parallel to the plane and get:

$$\Sigma F_x = ma_x$$
$$-6084.99\ N = (927\ kg)a_x$$
$$a_x = -6.564\ \frac{m}{s^2} \xrightarrow{SD} \mathbf{6.56\ \frac{m}{s^2}\ down\ the\ plane}$$

11. (a) Begin by finding the weight of the block. Then find w_x.

$$w = mg = 134\ \cancel{kg} \times 9.81\ \frac{N}{\cancel{kg}} = 1314.54\ N$$
$$w_x = (1314.54\ N)\sin 33° = 715.95\ N \xrightarrow{SD} \mathbf{716\ N}$$

(b) $w_y = (1314.54\ N)\cos 33° = 1102.5\ N \xrightarrow{SD} \mathbf{11\bar{0}0\ N}$

(c) $F_s = \mu_s F_N = 0.63(1102.5\ N) = 694.58\ N \xrightarrow{SD} \mathbf{690\ N}$

The component of the weight of the block parallel to the plane, w_x, is greater than the force of static friction, F_s. Thus, **the block will slide down the plane**.

12. Begin by finding the pressure produced by the fluid.

$$P_F = 621\ \frac{\cancel{kg}}{m^{\cancel{3}2}} \times 9.81\ \frac{N}{\cancel{kg}} \times 2.00\ \cancel{m} = 1.218 \times 10^4\ Pa$$

Now sum this pressure with the atmospheric pressure and find P.

$$P = 1.218 \times 10^4\ Pa + 1.013 \times 10^5\ Pa$$
$$= 1.1348 \times 10^5\ Pa \xrightarrow{SD} \mathbf{1.13 \times 10^5\ Pa}$$

13. $\frac{F_1}{A_1} = \frac{F_2}{A_2}$

$\frac{134 \text{ N}}{2.4 \text{ m}^2} = \frac{638 \text{ N}}{A_2}$

$A_2 = 11.43 \text{ m}^2 \xrightarrow{\text{SD}}$ **11 m²**

14. The diameter of the tire is 46.0 cm or 0.460 m, so the radius is 0.230 m.

$v = r\omega$

$25 \frac{\text{m}}{\text{s}} = 0.230 \text{ m} \times \omega$

$\omega = 108.70 \frac{\text{rad}}{\text{s}}$

Now convert 108.70 rad/s to rev/min.

$108.70 \frac{\cancel{\text{rad}}}{\cancel{\text{s}}} \times \frac{1 \text{ rev}}{2\pi \cancel{\text{rad}}} \times \frac{60 \cancel{\text{s}}}{1 \text{ min}}$

$= 1038 \frac{\text{rev}}{\text{min}} \xrightarrow{\text{SD}} \mathbf{1\bar{0}00 \frac{rev}{min}}$

15. (a) Use the displacement equation to find the time.

$\Delta y = v_0 t + \frac{1}{2}at^2$

$-62 = 22t + \frac{1}{2}(-9.81)t^2$

$0 = 4.905t^2 - 22t - 62$

Use the quadratic formula to solve this equation for t.

$t = \frac{-(-22) \pm \sqrt{(-22)^2 - 4(4.905)(-62)}}{2(4.905)} = 6.446 \text{ s} \xrightarrow{\text{SD}}$ **6.4 s**

(b) Use the motion equation to find the velocity.

$v(t) = v_0 + at$

$v(6.446) = 22 + (-9.81)(6.446)$

$= -41.24 \frac{\text{m}}{\text{s}} \xrightarrow{\text{SD}} \mathbf{-41 \frac{m}{s}}$

16. (a) $F_k = \mu_k F_N = 0.13(83 \cancel{\text{kg}})\left(9.81 \frac{\text{N}}{\cancel{\text{kg}}}\right) = 105.85 \text{ N} \xrightarrow{\text{SD}}$ **110 N**

(b) Sum the horizontal forces to find the net force.

$\Sigma F_x = 416 \text{ N} - 105.85 \text{ N} = 310.15 \text{ N}$

Now use the impulse-momentum equation to find v_2.

$F\Delta t = m(v_2 - v_1)$

$310.15 \text{ N}(5.0 \text{ s}) = 83 \text{ kg}\left(v_2 - 0 \frac{\text{m}}{\text{s}}\right)$

$v_2 = 18.68 \frac{\text{m}}{\text{s}} \xrightarrow{\text{SD}} \mathbf{19 \frac{m}{s}}$ **to the left**

17. $Q = mc\Delta T = 415.677 \cancel{\text{kg}} \times 26 \frac{\text{J}}{\cancel{\text{kg}} \cdot \cancel{\text{C}^\circ}} \times 413.069 \cancel{\text{C}^\circ} = 4.4643 \times 10^6 \text{ J}$

Now convert 4.4643×10^6 J to calories.

$(4.4643 \times 10^6 \cancel{\text{J}}) \times \frac{1 \text{ calorie}}{4.186 \cancel{\text{J}}} = 1.0665 \times 10^6 \text{ cal} \xrightarrow{\text{SD}}$ $\mathbf{1.1 \times 10^6}$ **cal**

18. (a) $\Sigma F_y = 0;\ 1110 \text{ N} + 530 \text{ N} - w = 0$

(b) $\Sigma M = 0;\ -1110 \text{ N}(1.0 \text{ m}) + w(x) - 530 \text{ N}(3.0 \text{ m}) = 0$

Solve (a) for w and get:

(a) $w = 1110 \text{ N} + 530 \text{ N} = 1640 \text{ N}$

Substitute w into (b) to find x.

(b) $-1110 \text{ N}(1.0 \text{ m}) + 1640 \text{ N}(x) - 530 \text{ N}(3.0 \text{ m}) = 0$

$1640 \text{ N}(x) = 2700 \text{ N}\cdot\text{m}$

$x =$ **1.6 m**

19. $Q = mc\Delta T$

$= 5.6 \cancel{\text{kg}} \times 712 \frac{\text{J}}{\cancel{\text{kg}} \cdot \cancel{\text{C}^\circ}} \times 50 \cancel{\text{C}^\circ}$

$= 1.99 \times 10^5 \text{ J} \xrightarrow{\text{SD}}$ $\mathbf{2.0 \times 10^5}$ **J**

20. Begin by drawing a diagram and recording the data.

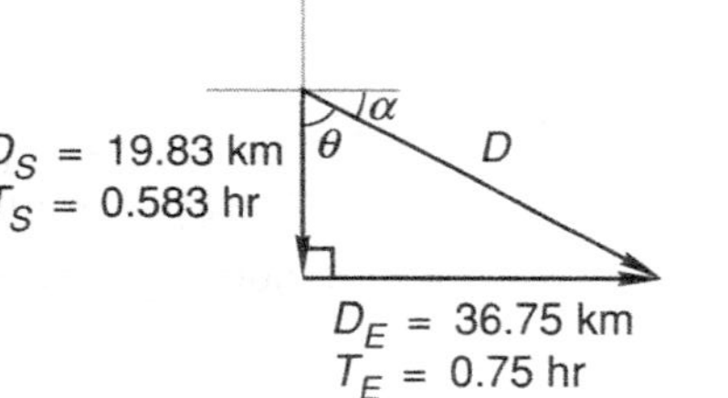

(a) $D_T = 19.83 \text{ km} + 36.75 \text{ km}$

$= 56.58 \text{ km} \xrightarrow{SD} \mathbf{57 \text{ km}}$

(b) $v = \frac{D_T}{T_T} = \frac{56.58 \text{ km}}{1.333 \text{ hr}} = 42.45 \text{ kph} \xrightarrow{SD} \mathbf{42 \text{ kph}}$

(c) $D = \sqrt{(19.83)^2 + (36.75)^2} = 41.76 \text{ km}$

$\theta = \tan^{-1} \frac{36.75}{19.83} = 61.65°$

$\alpha = -90° + 61.65° = -28.35°$

$\vec{D} = 41.76\underline{/-28.35°} \text{ km} \xrightarrow{SD} \mathbf{42\underline{/-28.35°} \text{ km}}$

(d) $\vec{v} = \frac{\vec{D}}{T_T} = \frac{41.76\underline{/-28.35°} \text{ km}}{1.333 \text{ hr}}$

$= 31.33\underline{/-28.35°} \text{ kph} \xrightarrow{SD} \mathbf{31\underline{/-28.35°} \text{ kph}}$

PROBLEM SET 33

1. Begin by writing a $\sum F_x = ma_x$ equation for the 12-kg block. Choose to the right as the positive direction for motion.

$\sum F_x = ma_x$

$T = ma$

$T = 12a \quad \text{(a)}$

Next, write a $\sum F_y = ma_y$ equation for the 3.0-kg block.

$\sum F_y = ma_y$

$mg - T = ma$

$(3.0)(9.81) - T = 3.0a$

$T = 29.43 - 3.0a \quad \text{(b)}$

Substitute (b) into (a) to find the acceleration.

(a) $(29.43 - 3.0a) = 12a$

$29.43 = 15a$

$a = 1.962 \frac{\text{m}}{\text{s}^2} \xrightarrow{SD} \mathbf{2.0 \frac{m}{s^2} \text{ to the right}}$

Substitute the acceleration into (a) to find T.

(a) $T = 12(1.962)$

$= 23.544 \text{ N} \xrightarrow{SD} \mathbf{24 \text{ N}}$

2. Begin by finding the component of the weight of the 8.0-kg block that is parallel to the plane.

$F_x = mg \sin 30°$

$= (8.0)(9.81) \sin 30°$

$= 39.24 \text{ N}$

Next, write a $\sum F_x = ma_x$ equation for the 8.0-kg block. Choose up the plane as the positive direction for motion.

$\sum F_x = ma_x$

$T - F_x = ma$

$T - 39.24 = 8.0a$

$T = 39.24 + 8.0a \quad \text{(a)}$

Now, write a $\sum F_y = ma_y$ equation for the 6.0-kg block.

$\sum F_y = ma_y$

$mg - T = ma$

$(6.0)(9.81) - T = 6.0a$

$T = 58.86 - 6.0a \quad \text{(b)}$

Substitute (b) into (a) to find the acceleration.

(a) $(58.86 - 6.0a) = 39.24 + 8.0a$

$19.62 = 14a$

$a = 1.401 \frac{\text{m}}{\text{s}^2} \xrightarrow{SD} \mathbf{1.4 \frac{m}{s^2} \text{ up the plane}}$

Substitute the acceleration into (a) to find T.

(a) $T = 39.24 + 8.0(1.401)$

$= 50.45 \text{ N} \xrightarrow{SD} \mathbf{5\bar{0} \text{ N}}$

3. Begin by converting – 60°F to kelvins.

$$T_C = \frac{5}{9}(T_F - 32) = \frac{5}{9}(-60° - 32) = -51.11°\text{C}$$

$$T_K = T_C + 273 = -51.11 + 273 = 221.89 \text{ K}$$

Now use the ideal gas law and get:

$$\frac{V_1}{T_1} = \frac{V_2}{T_2}$$

$$\frac{2.00 \text{ m}^3}{221.89 \text{ K}} = \frac{0.0200 \text{ m}^3}{T_2}$$

$$T_2 = 2.22 \text{ K} \xrightarrow{\text{SD}} \mathbf{2.2\ K}$$

4.

$$P_1V_1 = P_2V_2$$

$$P_1(0.5004 \text{ m}^3) = (2 \text{ atm})(255.87 \text{ m}^3)$$

$$P_1 = 1022.7 \text{ atm} \xrightarrow{\text{SD}} \mathbf{1000\ atm}$$

5.

$$\frac{\sin\theta_1}{v_1} = \frac{\sin\theta_2}{v_2}$$

$$\frac{\sin 30°}{0.95c} = \frac{\sin\theta_2}{c}$$

$$\theta_2 = \mathbf{31.76°}$$

6.

$$n_1 \sin\theta_1 = n_2 \sin\theta_2$$

$$(1.333) \sin 20° = (1) \sin\theta_r$$

$$\theta_r = \mathbf{27.12°}$$

7. Begin by writing a momentum equation.

$$(m_{6.0} + m_{4.0})v_{10} = m_{6.0}v_{6.0} + m_{4.0}v_{4.0}$$

$$(6.0 + 4.0)(4.0) = (6.0)(-4.0) + (4.0)v_{4.0}$$

$$64 = (4.0)v_{4.0}$$

$$v_{4.0} = \mathbf{16\ \frac{m}{s}\ to\ the\ right}$$

8. Begin by writing a momentum equation.

$$m_1v_1 + m_2v_2 = (m_1 + m_2)v_3$$

$$5.0(256\angle\underline{80°}) + 15(14\angle\underline{335°}) = (5.0 + 15)v_3$$

$$1280\angle\underline{80°} + 210\angle\underline{335°} = (20)v_3 \qquad \text{(a)}$$

Now find the sum of the x and y components of the initial momenta.

$$\Sigma mv_x = 1280 \cos 80° + 210 \cos 335° = 412.59 \text{ kg·m·s}^{-1}$$

$$\Sigma mv_y = 1280 \sin 80° + 210 \sin 335° = 1171.80 \text{ kg·m·s}^{-1}$$

$$\Sigma mv_R = (412.59i + 1171.80j) \text{ kg·m·s}^{-1}$$

Convert this resultant to polar form and get:

$$\Sigma mv_R = \sqrt{(412.59)^2 + (1171.80)^2} = 1242.31 \text{ kg·m·s}^{-1}$$

$$\theta = \tan^{-1}\frac{1171.80}{412.59} = 70.60°$$

$$\Sigma mv_R = 1242.31\angle\underline{70.60°} \text{ kg·m·s}^{-1}$$

Use this momentum in (a) to find v_3.

(a) $1242.31\angle\underline{70.60°} = (20)v_3$

$$v_3 = 62.12\angle\underline{70.60°}\ \frac{\text{m}}{\text{s}} \xrightarrow{\text{SD}} \mathbf{62\angle\underline{70.60°}\ \frac{m}{s}}$$

9. (a) $PE = mgh = 0.36 \text{ kg} \times 9.81 \frac{\text{N}}{\text{kg}} \times 15 \text{ m} = 52.97 \text{ J}$

$$KE = \frac{1}{2}mv_d^2$$

$$52.97 \text{ J} = \frac{1}{2}(0.36 \text{ kg})v_d^2$$

$$v_d = -17.15\ \frac{\text{m}}{\text{s}} \xrightarrow{\text{SD}} \mathbf{17\ \frac{m}{s}\ downward}$$

$$PE = mgh = 0.36 \text{ kg} \times 9.81 \frac{\text{N}}{\text{kg}} \times 13.5 \text{ m} = 47.68 \text{ J}$$

$$KE = \frac{1}{2}mv_u^2$$

$$47.68 \text{ J} = \frac{1}{2}(0.36 \text{ kg})v_u^2$$

$$v_u = +16.28\ \frac{\text{m}}{\text{s}} \xrightarrow{\text{SD}} \mathbf{16\ \frac{m}{s}\ upward}$$

(b) $\Delta KE = 52.97 \text{ J} - 47.68 \text{ J} = 5.29 \text{ J} \xrightarrow{\text{SD}} \mathbf{5.3\ J}$

10. $PE = mgh = 22\,\cancel{kg} \times 9.81\,\frac{N}{\cancel{kg}} \times 12\text{ m} = 2589.84\text{ J}$

$$KE = \frac{1}{2}mv^2$$

$$2589.84\text{ J} = \frac{1}{2}(22\text{ kg})v^2$$

$$v = 15.34\,\frac{\text{m}}{\text{s}} \xrightarrow{\text{SD}} \mathbf{15\,\frac{m}{s}}$$

11. $F = \frac{Gm_n m_o}{r^2} \rightarrow m_n = \frac{Fr^2}{Gm_o}$

$$= \frac{(13{,}001)(2.475 \times 10^7)^2}{(6.67 \times 10^{-11})(1100)}$$

$$= 1.085 \times 10^{26}\text{ kg} \xrightarrow{\text{SD}} \mathbf{1.09 \times 10^{26}\ kg}$$

12. Begin by finding the weight of the block and the component of the weight parallel to the plane.

$$w = mg = 342\,\cancel{kg} \times 9.81\,\frac{N}{\cancel{kg}} = 3355.02\text{ N}$$

$$w_x = (3355.02\text{ N}) \sin 32° = 1777.89\text{ N}$$

Now sum the forces parallel to the plane and get:

$$\Sigma F_x = ma_x$$

$$-1777.89\text{ N} = (342\text{ kg})a_x$$

$$a_x = -5.199\,\frac{\text{m}}{\text{s}^2} \xrightarrow{\text{SD}} \mathbf{5.20\,\frac{m}{s^2}}\ \textbf{down the plane}$$

13. (a) Begin by finding the weight of the block. Then find w_x.

$$w = mg = 23.2\,\cancel{kg} \times 9.81\,\frac{N}{\cancel{kg}} = 227.59\text{ N}$$

$$w_x = (227.59\text{ N}) \sin 43° = 155.22\text{ N} \xrightarrow{\text{SD}} \mathbf{155\ N}$$

(b) $w_y = (227.59\text{ N}) \cos 43° = 166.45\text{ N} \xrightarrow{\text{SD}} \mathbf{166\ N}$

(c) $F_k = \mu_k F_N = 0.255(166.45\text{ N}) = 42.44\text{ N}$

Now sum the forces parallel to the plane and get:

$$-w_x + F_k = ma_x$$

$$-155.22\text{ N} + 42.44\text{ N} = (23.2\text{ kg})a_x$$

$$a_x = -4.861\,\frac{\text{m}}{\text{s}^2} \xrightarrow{\text{SD}} \mathbf{4.86\,\frac{m}{s^2}}\ \textbf{down the plane}$$

14. $\frac{F_1}{A_1} = \frac{F_2}{A_2}$

$$\frac{25\text{ N}}{1.3\text{ m}^2} = \frac{124\text{ N}}{A_2}$$

$$A_2 = 6.448\text{ m}^2 \xrightarrow{\text{SD}} \mathbf{6.4\ m^2}$$

15. The diameter of the wheel is 52.0 cm or 0.520 m, so the radius is 0.260 m.

$$v = r\omega$$

$$20.0\,\frac{\text{m}}{\text{s}} = 0.260\text{ m} \times \omega$$

$$\omega = 76.92\,\frac{\text{rad}}{\text{s}}$$

Now convert 76.92 rad/s to rev/min.

$$76.92\,\frac{\cancel{rad}}{\cancel{s}} \times \frac{1\text{ rev}}{2\pi\,\cancel{rad}} \times \frac{60\,\cancel{s}}{1\text{ min}} = 734.53\,\frac{\text{rev}}{\text{min}} \xrightarrow{\text{SD}} \mathbf{735\,\frac{rev}{min}}$$

16. (a) Use the displacement equation to find the time.

$$\Delta y = v_0 t + \frac{1}{2}at^2$$

$$-32.0 = 43.0t + \frac{1}{2}(-9.81)t^2$$

$$0 = 4.905t^2 - 43.0t - 32.0$$

Use the quadratic formula to solve this equation for t.

$$t = \frac{-(-43.0) \pm \sqrt{(-43.0)^2 - 4(4.905)(-32.0)}}{2(4.905)}$$

$$= 9.456\text{ s} \xrightarrow{\text{SD}} \mathbf{9.46\ s}$$

(b) Use the motion equation to find the velocity.

$$v(t) = v_0 + at$$

$$v(9.456) = 43.0 + (-9.81)(9.456)$$

$$= -49.76\,\frac{\text{m}}{\text{s}} \xrightarrow{\text{SD}} \mathbf{-49.8\,\frac{m}{s}}$$

17. (a) $F_k = \mu_k F_N = 0.221(123\ \text{kg})\left(9.81\ \frac{\text{N}}{\text{kg}}\right) = 266.67\ \text{N} \xrightarrow{\text{SD}}$ **267 N**

(b) Sum the horizontal forces to find the net force.
$\Sigma F_x = 512\ \text{N} - 266.67\ \text{N} = 245.33\ \text{N}$

Now use the impulse-momentum equation to find v_2.

$$F\Delta t = m(v_2 - v_1)$$

$$245.33\ \text{N}(3.50\ \text{s}) = 123\ \text{kg}\left(v_2 - 0\ \frac{\text{m}}{\text{s}}\right)$$

$$v_2 = 6.981\ \frac{\text{m}}{\text{s}} \xrightarrow{\text{SD}} \mathbf{6.98\ \frac{m}{s}\ \text{to the left}}$$

18. Begin by finding the weight of each block and drawing a free-body diagram of the forces acting on the junction of the ropes.

$$w = mg = 90.0\ \text{kg} \times 9.81\ \frac{\text{N}}{\text{kg}} = 882.9\ \text{N}$$

$$w = mg = 150\ \text{kg} \times 9.81\ \frac{\text{N}}{\text{kg}} = 1471.5\ \text{N}$$

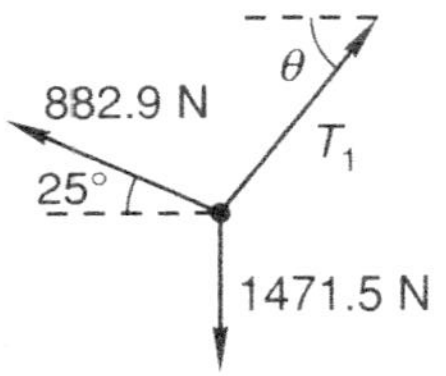

Now sum the horizontal and vertical forces to zero.
(a) $\Sigma F_x = 0;\ T_1 \cos\theta - (882.9\ \text{N}) \cos 25° = 0$
(b) $\Sigma F_y = 0;\ (882.9\ \text{N}) \sin 25° + T_1 \sin\theta - 1471.5\ \text{N} = 0$

Solve (a) for $T_1 \cos\theta$ and get:
(a) $T_1 \cos\theta = (882.9\ \text{N}) \cos 25°$
$T_1 \cos\theta = 800.18\ \text{N}$ (a′)

Solve (b) for $T_1 \sin\theta$ and get:
(b) $T_1 \sin\theta = 1471.5\ \text{N} - (882.9\ \text{N}) \sin 25°$
$T_1 \sin\theta = 1098.37\ \text{N}$ (b′)

Divide (b′) by (a′) and get:

$$\frac{(b')}{(a')} = \frac{T_1 \sin\theta}{T_1 \cos\theta} = \frac{1098.37\ \text{N}}{800.18\ \text{N}} \rightarrow \tan\theta = 1.37265$$

$$\theta = 53.93°$$

Substitute θ into (a′) to find T_1.
(a′) $T_1 \cos(53.93°) = 800.18\ \text{N}$
$T_1 = 1359.06\ \text{N}$

$$\vec{T}_1 = 1359.06\underline{/53.93°}\ \text{N} \xrightarrow{\text{SD}} \mathbf{1360\underline{/53.93°}\ N}$$

19. $W = F \times D = 180\ \text{kg}\left(9.81\ \frac{\text{N}}{\text{kg}}\right) \times 1.7\ \text{m} = 3001.86\ \text{J} \xrightarrow{\text{SD}}$ $\mathbf{3\bar{0}00\ J}$

$$P_{av} = \frac{W}{\Delta t} = \frac{3001.86\ \text{J}}{7.0\ \text{s}} = 428.84\ \text{W} \xrightarrow{\text{SD}} \mathbf{430\ W}$$

20. $v_{av} = \frac{y_2 - y_1}{t_2 - t_1} = \frac{1650 - 340}{4.5 - 3.0}\ \frac{\text{m}}{\text{min}} = +873.33\ \frac{\text{m}}{\text{min}}$

Convert +873.33 m/min to m/s and get:

$$+873.33\ \frac{\text{m}}{\text{min}} \times \frac{1\ \text{min}}{60\ \text{s}} = +14.56\ \frac{\text{m}}{\text{s}} \xrightarrow{\text{SD}} \mathbf{+15\ \frac{m}{s}}$$

PROBLEM SET 34

1. (a) $n = \frac{c}{v}$

$$1.333 = \frac{3.00 \times 10^8\ \text{m/s}}{v}$$

$$v = 2.251 \times 10^8\ \frac{\text{m}}{\text{s}} \xrightarrow{\text{SD}} \mathbf{2.25 \times 10^8\ \frac{m}{s}}$$

(b) $v = f\lambda$

$$2.251 \times 10^8\ \frac{\text{m}}{\text{s}} = (3.10 \times 10^{14}\ \text{Hz})\lambda$$

$$\lambda = 7.261 \times 10^{-7}\ \text{m} \xrightarrow{\text{SD}} \mathbf{7.26 \times 10^{-7}\ m}$$

2. (a) $f = \frac{1}{T} = \frac{1}{6.80 \times 10^{-12}\text{ s}}$

$= 1.4706 \times 10^{11}\text{ Hz} \xrightarrow{\text{SD}} \mathbf{1.47 \times 10^{11}\ Hz}$

(b) $v = f\lambda = (1.4706 \times 10^{11}\text{ Hz})(1.40 \times 10^{-3}\text{ m})$

$= 2.059 \times 10^{8}\ \frac{\text{m}}{\text{s}} \xrightarrow{\text{SD}} \mathbf{2.06 \times 10^{8}\ \frac{m}{s}}$

(c) **No**

3.

$$v = f\lambda$$

$$3.00 \times 10^{8}\ \frac{\text{m}}{\text{s}} = f(1.00\text{ m})$$

$$f = \mathbf{3.00 \times 10^{8}\ Hz}$$

4. Begin by finding the component of the weight of the 7.0-kg block that is parallel to the plane.
$F_x = mg \sin 40° = (7.0)(9.81) \sin 40° = 44.14\text{ N}$

Next, write a $\Sigma F_x = ma_x$ equation for the 7.0-kg block. Choose up the plane as the positive direction for motion.

$$\Sigma F_x = ma_x$$
$$T - F_x = ma$$
$$T - 44.14 = 7.0a$$
$$T = 44.14 + 7.0a \qquad \text{(a)}$$

Now, write a $\Sigma F_y = ma_y$ equation for the 8.0-kg block.

$$\Sigma F_y = ma_y$$
$$mg - T = ma$$
$$(8.0)(9.81) - T = 8.0a$$
$$T = 78.48 - 8.0a \qquad \text{(b)}$$

Substitute (b) into (a) to find the acceleration.
(a) $(78.48 - 8.0a) = 44.14 + 7.0a$
$34.34 = 15.0a$

$$a = 2.289\ \frac{\text{m}}{\text{s}^2} \xrightarrow{\text{SD}} \mathbf{2.3\ \frac{m}{s^2}\ up\ the\ plane}$$

Substitute the acceleration into (a) to find T.
(a) $T = 44.14 + 7.0(2.289) = 60.16\text{ N} \xrightarrow{\text{SD}} \mathbf{6\bar{0}\ N}$

5. Begin by writing a $\Sigma F_x = ma_x$ equation for the 4.0-kg block. Choose to the right as the positive direction for motion.

$$\Sigma F_x = ma_x$$
$$T = ma$$
$$T = 4.0a \qquad \text{(a)}$$

Next, write a $\Sigma F_y = ma_y$ equation for the 6.0-kg block.

$$\Sigma F_y = ma_y$$
$$mg - T = ma$$
$$(6.0)(9.81) - T = 6.0a$$
$$T = 58.86 - 6.0a \qquad \text{(b)}$$

Substitute (b) into (a) to find the acceleration.
(a) $(58.86 - 6.0a) = 4.0a$
$58.86 = 10.0a$

$$a = 5.886\ \frac{\text{m}}{\text{s}^2} \xrightarrow{\text{SD}} \mathbf{5.9\ \frac{m}{s^2}\ to\ the\ right}$$

Substitute the acceleration into (a) to find T.
(a) $T = 4.0(5.886) = 23.54\text{ N} \xrightarrow{\text{SD}} \mathbf{24\ N}$

6. (a) $T_1 = -80.0 + 273 = \mathbf{193\ K}$
$T_2 = 510 + 273 = \mathbf{783\ K}$

(b) $\frac{P_1}{T_1} = \frac{P_2}{T_2}$

$$\frac{2 \times 10^3\text{ Pa}}{193\text{ K}} = \frac{P_2}{783\text{ K}}$$

$$P_2 = 8.114 \times 10^3\text{ Pa} \xrightarrow{\text{SD}} \mathbf{8 \times 10^3\ Pa}$$

7. (a) $T = 50.0 + 273 = \mathbf{323\ K}$

(b) $\frac{V_1}{T_1} = \frac{V_2}{T_2}$

$$\frac{10\text{ m}^3}{323\text{ K}} = \frac{0.50\text{ m}^3}{T_2}$$

$$T_2 = 16.15\text{ K} \xrightarrow{\text{SD}} \mathbf{16\ K}$$

8. $\frac{\sin\theta_1}{v_1} = \frac{\sin\theta_2}{v_2}$

$\frac{\sin 52^\circ}{0.89c} = \frac{\sin\theta_2}{c}$

$\theta_2 = \mathbf{62.30^\circ}$

9. $n_1 \sin\theta_1 = n_2 \sin\theta_2$

$(1.317)\sin 44^\circ = (1)\sin\theta_r$

$\theta_r = \mathbf{66.19^\circ}$

10. (a) $m_1v_1 + m_2v_2 = (m_1 + m_2)v_3$

$(0.0028)(180) + (1.3)(0) = (1.3028)v_3$

$v_3 = +0.38686\ \frac{\text{m}}{\text{s}} \xrightarrow{\text{SD}} \mathbf{+0.39\ \frac{m}{s}}$

(b) $KE = \frac{1}{2}mv_3^2$

$= \frac{1}{2}(1.3028)(0.38686)^2$

$= 9.749 \times 10^{-2}\text{ J} \xrightarrow{\text{SD}} \mathbf{9.7 \times 10^{-2}\ J}$

(c) $PE = mgh$

$9.749 \times 10^{-2}\text{ J} = 1.3028(9.81)h$

$h = 7.628 \times 10^{-3}\text{ m} \xrightarrow{\text{SD}} \mathbf{7.6 \times 10^{-3}\ m}$

11. Begin by writing a momentum equation.

$m_1v_1 + m_2v_2 = (m_1 + m_2)v_3$

$3.50(34.4\underline{/210^\circ}) + 2.40(12.0\underline{/130^\circ}) = (3.50 + 2.40)v_3$

$120.4\underline{/210^\circ} + 28.8\underline{/130^\circ} = (5.90)v_3 \qquad \text{(a)}$

Now find the sum of the x and y components of the initial momenta.

$\sum mv_x = 120.4\cos 210^\circ + 28.8\cos 130^\circ = -122.78\text{ kg}\cdot\text{m}\cdot\text{s}^{-1}$

$\sum mv_y = 120.4\sin 210^\circ + 28.8\sin 130^\circ = -38.14\text{ kg}\cdot\text{m}\cdot\text{s}^{-1}$

$\sum mv_R = (-122.78i - 38.14j)\text{ kg}\cdot\text{m}\cdot\text{s}^{-1}$

Convert this resultant to polar form and get:

$\sum mv_R = \sqrt{(-122.78)^2 + (-38.14)^2} = 128.57\text{ kg}\cdot\text{m}\cdot\text{s}^{-1}$

$\theta = \tan^{-1}\frac{-38.14}{-122.78} = 17.26^\circ$

Since θ is a 3rd-quadrant angle: $\theta = -180^\circ + 17.26^\circ = -162.74^\circ$

$\sum mv_R = 128.57\underline{/-162.74^\circ}\text{ kg}\cdot\text{m}\cdot\text{s}^{-1}$

Use this momentum in (a) to find v_3.

(a) $128.57\underline{/-162.74^\circ} = (5.90)v_3$

$v_3 = 21.79\underline{/-162.74^\circ}\ \frac{\text{m}}{\text{s}} \xrightarrow{\text{SD}} \mathbf{21.8\underline{/-162.74^\circ}\ \frac{m}{s}}$

12. (a) $PE = mgh = 1.45\text{ kg} \times 9.81\ \frac{\text{N}}{\text{kg}} \times 42\text{ m} = 597.43\text{ J}$

$KE = \frac{1}{2}mv_d^2$

$597.43\text{ J} = \frac{1}{2}(1.45\text{ kg})v_d^2$

$v_d = -28.71\ \frac{\text{m}}{\text{s}} \xrightarrow{\text{SD}} \mathbf{-29\ \frac{m}{s}}$

$PE = mgh = 1.45\text{ kg} \times 9.81\ \frac{\text{N}}{\text{kg}} \times 36\text{ m} = 512.08\text{ J}$

$KE = \frac{1}{2}mv_u^2$

$512.08\text{ J} = \frac{1}{2}(1.45\text{ kg})v_u^2$

$v_u = +26.58\ \frac{\text{m}}{\text{s}} \xrightarrow{\text{SD}} \mathbf{+27\ \frac{m}{s}}$

(b) $\Delta KE = 597.43\text{ J} - 512.08\text{ J}$

$= 85.35\text{ J} \xrightarrow{\text{SD}} \mathbf{85\ J}$

13. $PE = mgh = 48\text{ kg} \times 9.81\ \frac{\text{N}}{\text{kg}} \times 18\text{ m} = 8475.84\text{ J}$

$KE = \frac{1}{2}mv^2$

$8475.84\text{ J} = \frac{1}{2}(48\text{ kg})v^2$

$v = 18.79\ \frac{\text{m}}{\text{s}} \xrightarrow{\text{SD}} \mathbf{19\ \frac{m}{s}}$

14. (a) Begin by finding the weight of the block. Then find w_x.

$$w = mg = 89\,\cancel{kg} \times 9.81\,\frac{N}{\cancel{kg}} = 873.09\text{ N}$$

$$w_x = (873.09\text{ N})\sin 37° = 525.44\text{ N} \xrightarrow{SD} \mathbf{530\ N}$$

(b) $$w_y = (873.09\text{ N})\cos 37° = 697.28\text{ N} \xrightarrow{SD} \mathbf{7\bar{0}0\ N}$$

(c) $$F_s = \mu_s F_N = 0.76(697.28\text{ N}) = 529.93\text{ N} \xrightarrow{SD} \mathbf{530\ N}$$

The component of the weight of the block parallel to the plane, w_x, is less than the force of static friction, F_s. Thus, **the block will not slide down the plane.**

15. (a) $\Sigma F_y = 0;\ F_A + 30\text{ N} - 30\text{ N} - F_B = 0$

(b) $\Sigma M_A = 0;\ 30\text{ N}(3\text{ m}) + F_B(9\text{ m}) - 30\text{ N}(6\text{ m}) = 0$

Solve (b) for F_B and get:

(b) $$90\text{ N}\cdot\text{m} + F_B(9\text{ m}) - 180\text{ N}\cdot\text{m} = 0$$

$$F_B(9\text{ m}) = 90\text{ N}\cdot\text{m}$$

$$F_B = \mathbf{10\ N}$$

Substitute F_B into (a) to find F_A.

(a) $$F_A + 30\text{ N} - 30\text{ N} - (10\text{ N}) = 0$$

$$F_A = \mathbf{10\ N}$$

16. (a) Use the displacement equation to find the time.

$$\Delta y = v_0 t + \frac{1}{2}at^2$$

$$0 = 21.0t + \frac{1}{2}(-9.81)t^2$$

$$4.905t = 21.0$$

$$t = 4.281\text{ s} \xrightarrow{SD} \mathbf{4.28\ s}$$

(b) The maximum height the rock reaches occurs at the midpoint of its path, which occurs when the time equals half the value found in (a). Use this time in the position equation to find the height.

$$t = \frac{4.281\text{ s}}{2} = 2.1405\text{ s}$$

$$y(t) = y_0 + v_0 t + \frac{1}{2}at^2$$

$$y(2.1405) = 0 + 21.0(2.1405) + \frac{1}{2}(-9.81)(2.1405)^2$$

$$= 22.477\text{ m} \xrightarrow{SD} \mathbf{22.5\ m}$$

17. (a) $$F_k = \mu_k F_N = 0.366(512\,\cancel{kg})\left(9.81\,\frac{N}{\cancel{kg}}\right) = 1838.32\text{ N} \xrightarrow{SD} \mathbf{1840\ N}$$

(b) Sum the horizontal forces to find the net force.

$$\Sigma F_x = 1896\text{ N} - 1838.32\text{ N} = 57.68\text{ N}$$

Now use the impulse-momentum equation to find v_2.

$$F\Delta t = m(v_2 - v_1)$$

$$57.68\text{ N}(4.00\text{ s}) = 512\text{ kg}\left(v_2 - 0\,\frac{m}{s}\right)$$

$$v_2 = 0.4506\,\frac{m}{s} \xrightarrow{SD} \mathbf{0.451\ \frac{m}{s}\ to\ the\ right}$$

18. $$Q = mc\Delta T = 21\,\cancel{kg} \times 896\,\frac{J}{\cancel{kg}\cdot\cancel{C°}} \times 86\,\cancel{C°} = 1.6182 \times 10^6\text{ J}$$

Now convert 1.6182×10^6 J to calories.

$$1.6182 \times 10^6\,\cancel{J} \times \frac{1\text{ calorie}}{4.186\,\cancel{J}}$$

$$= 3.866 \times 10^5\text{ calories} \xrightarrow{SD} \mathbf{3.9 \times 10^5\ calories}$$

19. Begin by finding the weight of the mass.

$$w = mg = 60\,\cancel{kg} \times 9.81\,\frac{N}{\cancel{kg}} = 588.6\text{ N}$$

Now set the torques equal to each other and find F.

$$FR_2 = mgR_1$$

$$F(1200.00\text{ cm}) = 588.6\text{ N}(518.950\text{ cm})$$

$$F = 254.54\text{ N} \xrightarrow{SD} \mathbf{300\ N}$$

$$\text{Mechanical advantage} = \frac{\text{force out}}{\text{force in}} = \frac{588.6\text{ N}}{254.54\text{ N}} = 2.31 \xrightarrow{SD} \mathbf{2}$$

20. The torque is equal to the component of the 200-N force which is perpendicular to the lever arm times the length of the lever arm.

$$\tau = FL\sin\theta$$

$$= (200\text{ N})(8.50\text{ cm})\sin 43°$$

$$= +1159.4\text{ N}\cdot\text{cm} \xrightarrow{SD} \mathbf{+1160\ N\cdot cm}$$

Problem Set 35

1. (a)

$$a = r\alpha$$

$$2.0\ \frac{\text{m}}{\text{s}^2} = 0.25\ \text{m} \times \alpha$$

$$\alpha = \mathbf{8.0\ \frac{rad}{s^2}}$$

(b)

$$\Delta\theta = \omega_0 t + \frac{1}{2}\alpha t^2$$

$$= (0)(10) + \frac{1}{2}(8.0)(10)^2 = \mathbf{400\ rad}$$

Convert 400 radians to revolutions.

$$400\ \cancel{\text{rad}} \times \frac{1\ \text{rev}}{2\pi\ \cancel{\text{rad}}} = 63.66\ \text{revolutions} \xrightarrow{\text{SD}} \mathbf{60\ revolutions}$$

2. (a)

$$a = r\alpha$$

$$3.0\ \frac{\text{m}}{\text{s}^2} = 0.30\ \text{m} \times \alpha$$

$$\alpha = \mathbf{1\bar{0}\ \frac{rad}{s^2}}$$

(b)

$$\omega(t) = \omega_0 + \alpha t$$

$$\omega(5.0) = 2.2 + 10(5.0)$$

$$= 52.2\ \frac{\text{rad}}{\text{s}} \xrightarrow{\text{SD}} \mathbf{52\ \frac{rad}{s}}$$

3. (a)

$$n = \frac{c}{v}$$

$$1.647 = \frac{3.00 \times 10^8\ \text{m/s}}{v}$$

$$v = 1.8215 \times 10^8\ \frac{\text{m}}{\text{s}} \xrightarrow{\text{SD}} \mathbf{1.82 \times 10^8\ \frac{m}{s}}$$

(b)

$$v = f\lambda$$

$$1.8215 \times 10^8\ \frac{\text{m}}{\text{s}} = f(6.25 \times 10^{-7}\ \text{m})$$

$$f = 2.914 \times 10^{14}\ \text{Hz} \xrightarrow{\text{SD}} \mathbf{2.91 \times 10^{14}\ Hz}$$

4. (a)

$$f = \frac{1}{T} = \frac{1}{4.0 \times 10^{-15}\ \text{s}} = \mathbf{2.5 \times 10^{14}\ Hz}$$

(b)

$$v = f\lambda$$

$$3.00 \times 10^8\ \frac{\text{m}}{\text{s}} = (2.5 \times 10^{14}\ \text{Hz})\lambda$$

$$\lambda = \mathbf{1.2 \times 10^{-6}\ m}$$

5. Begin by writing a $\sum F_x = ma_x$ equation for the 250-kg mass. Choose to the right as the positive direction for motion.

$$\sum F_x = ma_x$$

$$T = ma$$

$$T = 250a \quad \text{(a)}$$

Next, write a $\sum F_y = ma_y$ equation for the 0.25-kg mass.

$$\sum F_y = ma_y$$

$$mg - T = ma$$

$$(0.25)(9.81) - T = 0.25a$$

$$T = 2.453 - 0.25a \quad \text{(b)}$$

Substitute (b) into (a) to find the acceleration.

$$\text{(a)}\quad (2.453 - 0.25a) = 250a$$

$$2.453 = 250.25a$$

$$a = 9.802 \times 10^{-3}\ \frac{\text{m}}{\text{s}^2}$$

$$\xrightarrow{\text{SD}} \mathbf{9.8 \times 10^{-3}\ \frac{m}{s^2}\ to\ the\ right}$$

Substitute the acceleration into (a) to find T.

$$\text{(a)}\quad T = 250(9.802 \times 10^{-3}) = 2.451\ \text{N} \xrightarrow{\text{SD}} \mathbf{2.5\ N}$$

6. Begin by finding the component of the weight of the 12-kg block that is parallel to the plane.

$$F_x = mg \sin 50° = (12)(9.81) \sin 50° = 90.18\ \text{N}$$

Next, write a $\sum F_x = ma_x$ equation for the 12-kg block. Choose up the plane as the positive direction for motion.

$$\sum F_x = ma_x$$

$$T - F_x = ma$$

$$T - 90.18 = 12a$$

$$T = 90.18 + 12a \quad \text{(a)}$$

Now, write a $\sum F_y = ma_y$ equation for the 4.0-kg block.

$$\sum F_y = ma_y$$
$$mg - T = ma$$
$$(4.0)(9.81) - T = 4.0a$$
$$T = 39.24 - 4.0a \qquad \text{(b)}$$

Substitute (b) into (a) to find the acceleration.

(a) $(39.24 - 4.0a) = 90.18 + 12a$

$-50.94 = 16a$

$a = -3.184 \, \frac{\text{m}}{\text{s}^2} \xrightarrow{\text{SD}}$ **3.2 $\frac{\text{m}}{\text{s}^2}$ down the plane**

Substitute the acceleration into (a) to find T.

(a) $T = 90.18 + 12(-3.184) = 51.97 \text{ N} \xrightarrow{\text{SD}}$ **52 N**

7. (a) $T_1 = -35.0 + 273 =$ **238 K**

$T_2 = 300 + 273 =$ **573 K**

(b) $\frac{P_1}{T_1} = \frac{P_2}{T_2}$

$$\frac{4.8 \times 10^3 \text{ Pa}}{238 \text{ K}} = \frac{P_2}{573 \text{ K}}$$

$P_2 = 1.16 \times 10^4 \text{ Pa} \xrightarrow{\text{SD}}$ **1.2 × 10⁴ Pa**

8. (a) $T_1 = 300 + 273 = 573 \text{ K} \xrightarrow{\text{SD}}$ **600 K**

(b) $\frac{V_1}{T_1} = \frac{V_2}{T_2}$

$$\frac{14.543 \text{ m}^3}{573 \text{ K}} = \frac{2.36859 \text{ m}^3}{T_2}$$

$T_2 = 93.32 \text{ K} \xrightarrow{\text{SD}}$ **90 K**

9. $\frac{\sin\theta_1}{v_1} = \frac{\sin\theta_2}{v_2}$

$$\frac{\sin 31^\circ}{0.67c} = \frac{\sin\theta_2}{c}$$

$\theta_2 =$ **50.24°**

10. $n_1 \sin\theta_1 = n_2 \sin\theta_2$

$(1)\sin 35^\circ = (1.333)\sin\theta_r$

$\theta_r =$ **25.49°**

11. (a) $m_1v_1 + m_2v_2 = (m_1 + m_2)v_3$

$(0.00580)(680) + (2.30)(0) = (2.3058)v_3$

$v_3 = +1.710 \, \frac{\text{m}}{\text{s}} \xrightarrow{\text{SD}}$ **+1.71 $\frac{\text{m}}{\text{s}}$**

(b) $KE = \frac{1}{2}mv_3^2 = \frac{1}{2}(2.3058)(1.710)^2 = 3.371 \text{ J} \xrightarrow{\text{SD}}$ **3.37 J**

(c) $PE = mgh$

$3.371 = (2.3058)(9.81)h$

$h = 0.1490 \text{ m} \xrightarrow{\text{SD}}$ **0.149 m**

12. Begin by writing a momentum equation.

$$m_1v_1 + m_2v_2 = (m_1 + m_2)v_3$$
$$5.02(14.0\underline{/36^\circ}) + 1.69(25.4\underline{/341^\circ}) = (5.02 + 1.69)v_3$$
$$70.28\underline{/36^\circ} + 42.93\underline{/341^\circ} = (6.71)v_3 \qquad \text{(a)}$$

Now find the sum of the x and y components of the initial momenta.

$\sum mv_x = 70.28 \cos 36^\circ + 42.93 \cos 341^\circ = 97.45 \text{ kg}\cdot\text{m}\cdot\text{s}^{-1}$

$\sum mv_y = 70.28 \sin 36^\circ + 42.93 \sin 341^\circ = 27.33 \text{ kg}\cdot\text{m}\cdot\text{s}^{-1}$

$\sum mv_R = (97.45i + 27.33j) \text{ kg}\cdot\text{m}\cdot\text{s}^{-1}$

Convert this resultant to polar form and get:

$\sum mv_R = \sqrt{(97.45)^2 + (27.33)^2} = 101.21 \text{ kg}\cdot\text{m}\cdot\text{s}^{-1}$

$\theta = \tan^{-1}\frac{27.33}{97.45} = 15.67^\circ$

$\sum mv_R = 101.21\underline{/15.67^\circ} \text{ kg}\cdot\text{m}\cdot\text{s}^{-1}$

Use this momentum in (a) to find v_3.

(a) $101.21\underline{/15.67^\circ} = (6.71)v_3$

$v_3 = 15.08\underline{/15.67^\circ} \, \frac{\text{m}}{\text{s}} \xrightarrow{\text{SD}}$ **15.1/15.67° $\frac{\text{m}}{\text{s}}$**

13. (a) $PE = mgh = 0.7\,\cancel{kg} \times 9.81\,\frac{N}{\cancel{kg}} \times 258.4\text{ m} = 1774.43\text{ J}$

$$KE = \frac{1}{2}mv_d^{\,2}$$

$$1774.43\text{ J} = \frac{1}{2}(0.7\text{ kg})v_d^{\,2}$$

$$v_d = -71.20\,\frac{m}{s} \xrightarrow{SD} \mathbf{-70\,\frac{m}{s}}$$

$$PE = mgh = 0.7\,\cancel{kg} \times 9.81\,\frac{N}{\cancel{kg}} \times 180.0\text{ m} = 1236.06\text{ J}$$

$$KE = \frac{1}{2}mv_u^{\,2}$$

$$1236.06\text{ J} = \frac{1}{2}(0.7\text{ kg})v_u^{\,2}$$

$$v_u = +59.43\,\frac{m}{s} \xrightarrow{SD} \mathbf{+60\,\frac{m}{s}}$$

(b) $\Delta KE = 1774.43\text{ J} - 1236.06\text{ J} = 538.37\text{ J} \xrightarrow{SD} \mathbf{500\text{ J}}$

14. $PE = mgh = 159\,\cancel{kg} \times 9.81\,\frac{N}{\cancel{kg}} \times 35.0\text{ m} = 54{,}592.65\text{ J}$

$$KE = \frac{1}{2}mv^2$$

$$54{,}592.65\text{ J} = \frac{1}{2}(159\text{ kg})v^2$$

$$v = 26.20\,\frac{m}{s} \xrightarrow{SD} \mathbf{26.2\,\frac{m}{s}}$$

15. $$\frac{F_1}{A_1} = \frac{F_2}{A_2}$$

$$\frac{F_1}{1.29\text{ m}^2} = \frac{146\text{ N}}{4.21\text{ m}^2}$$

$$F_1 = 44.74\text{ N} \xrightarrow{SD} \mathbf{44.7\text{ N}}$$

16. Use the displacement equation to find the time.

$$\Delta y = v_0t + \frac{1}{2}at^2$$

$$-25 = 17t + \frac{1}{2}(-9.81)t^2$$

$$0 = 4.905t^2 - 17t - 25$$

Use the quadratic formula to solve this equation for t.

$$t = \frac{-(-17) \pm \sqrt{(-17)^2 - 4(4.905)(-25)}}{2(4.905)} = 4.579\text{ s} \xrightarrow{SD} \mathbf{4.6\text{ s}}$$

17. (a) Impulse $= F\Delta t = 628\text{ N}(3.00\text{ s}) = 1884\text{ N}\cdot\text{s} \xrightarrow{SD} \mathbf{1880\text{ N}\cdot\text{s}}$

(b) $F\Delta t = m(v_2 - v_1)$

$$1884\text{ N}\cdot\text{s} = 268\text{ kg}\left(v_2 - 0\,\frac{m}{s}\right)$$

$$v_2 = 7.0299\,\frac{m}{s} \xrightarrow{SD} \mathbf{7.03\,\frac{m}{s}}$$

18. Begin by summing the moments about the end of the ladder on the floor to zero.

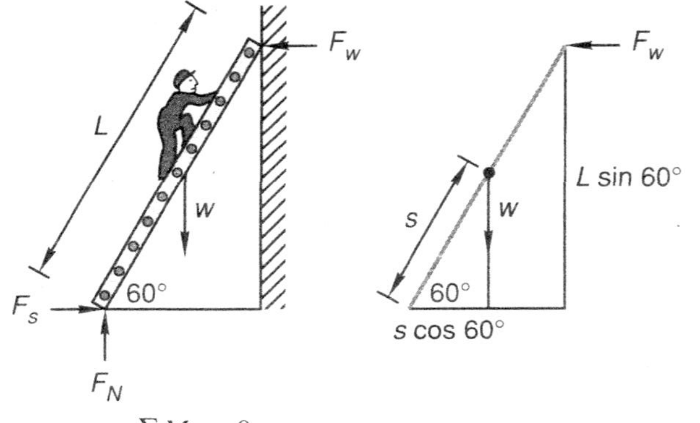

$$\sum M = 0$$

$$ws\cos 60° - F_wL\sin 60° = 0$$

$$ws\cos 60° - F_sL\sin 60° = 0$$

$$ws\cos 60° - w\mu_sL\sin 60° = 0$$

$$s\cos 60° = \mu_sL\sin 60°$$

$$s = \mu_sL\tan 60°$$

$$s = 0.42(10\text{ m})\tan 60° = 7.2746\text{ m} \xrightarrow{SD} \mathbf{7.3\text{ m}}$$

19. (a) $F = ma = 75\text{ kg} \times 5.3\ \frac{\text{m}}{\text{s}^2} = 397.5\text{ N} \xrightarrow{\text{SD}} \mathbf{4\bar{0}0\ N}$

(b) $\Sigma F_x = 530\text{ N} - 397.5\text{ N} = 132.5\text{ N} \xrightarrow{\text{SD}} \mathbf{130\ N}$

20. Answers to this problem may vary due to differing data points. One possible solution is given here. To find v_{10}, choose the points (5, 85) and (10, 250) and get:

$$v_{10} = \frac{\Delta x}{\Delta t} = \frac{250 - 85}{10 - 5}\ \frac{\text{mi}}{\text{hr}} = \mathbf{+33\ \frac{mi}{hr}}$$

To find v_{25}, choose the points (25, 350) and (30, 300) and get:

$$v_{25} = \frac{\Delta x}{\Delta t} = \frac{300 - 350}{30 - 25}\ \frac{\text{mi}}{\text{hr}} = \mathbf{-1\bar{0}\ \frac{mi}{hr}}$$

Problem Set 36

1. (a) $m_w = 1000\ \frac{\text{kg}}{\cancel{\text{m}^3}} \times 0.10\ \cancel{\text{m}^3} = \mathbf{1\bar{0}0\ kg}$

(b) $F_B = 100\ \cancel{\text{kg}} \times 9.81\ \frac{\text{N}}{\cancel{\text{kg}}} = 981\text{ N} \xrightarrow{\text{SD}} \mathbf{980\ N}$

(c) $F = mg - F_B = 200\ \cancel{\text{kg}}\left(9.81\ \frac{\text{N}}{\cancel{\text{kg}}}\right) - 981\text{ N} = 981\text{ N} \xrightarrow{\text{SD}} \mathbf{980\ N}$

2. (a) Begin by finding the volume of the model that is submerged.
$V_s = 0.25\text{ m}^3 \times 0.60 = 0.15\text{ m}^3$

Now find the mass of the water displaced.

$m_w = 1000\ \frac{\text{kg}}{\cancel{\text{m}^3}} \times 0.15\ \cancel{\text{m}^3} = \mathbf{150\ kg}$

(b) $F_B = 150\ \cancel{\text{kg}} \times 9.81\ \frac{\text{N}}{\cancel{\text{kg}}} = 1471.5\text{ N} \xrightarrow{\text{SD}} \mathbf{1500\ N}$

(c) The weight of the ship equals the buoyancy force of the water, and the mass of the ship equals the mass of the water displaced.
$w_s = F_B = \mathbf{1500\ N}$
$m_s = m_w = \mathbf{150\ kg}$

3. (a) $\omega(t) = \omega_0 + \alpha t$

$\omega(20.0) = 2.00 + 5.00(20.0) = \mathbf{102\ \frac{rad}{s}}$

(b) $\Delta\theta = \omega_0 t + \frac{1}{2}\alpha t^2$

$= 2.00(20.0) + \frac{1}{2}(5.00)(20.0)^2 = \mathbf{1040\ rad}$

4. $\alpha = \frac{\Delta\omega}{\Delta t} = \frac{85.0 - 1.0}{12 - 0}\ \frac{\text{rad/s}}{\text{s}} = \mathbf{7.0\ \frac{rad}{s^2}}$

$\Delta\theta = \omega_0 t + \frac{1}{2}\alpha t^2$

$= (1.0)(12) + \frac{1}{2}(7.0)(12)^2 = 516\text{ rad} \xrightarrow{\text{SD}} \mathbf{520\ rad}$

5. (a) $n = \frac{c}{v}$

$1.333 = \frac{3.00 \times 10^8\text{ m/s}}{v}$

$v = 2.251 \times 10^8\ \frac{\text{m}}{\text{s}} \xrightarrow{\text{SD}} \mathbf{2.25 \times 10^8\ \frac{m}{s}}$

(b) $v = f\lambda$

$2.251 \times 10^8\ \frac{\text{m}}{\text{s}} = (1.2 \times 10^{12}\text{ Hz})\lambda$

$\lambda = 1.876 \times 10^{-4}\text{ m} \xrightarrow{\text{SD}} \mathbf{1.9 \times 10^{-4}\ m}$

6. (a) $n = \frac{c}{v}$

$1.554 = \frac{3.00 \times 10^8\text{ m/s}}{v}$

$v = 1.931 \times 10^8\ \frac{\text{m}}{\text{s}} \xrightarrow{\text{SD}} \mathbf{1.93 \times 10^8\ \frac{m}{s}}$

(b) $v = f\lambda$

$1.931 \times 10^8\ \frac{\text{m}}{\text{s}} = (1.5 \times 10^{12}\text{ Hz})\lambda$

$\lambda = 1.287 \times 10^{-4}\text{ m} \xrightarrow{\text{SD}} \mathbf{1.3 \times 10^{-4}\ m}$

7. Begin by writing a $\Sigma F_x = ma_x$ equation for the 34-kg block. Choose to the right as the positive direction for motion.

$$\Sigma F_x = ma_x$$
$$T = ma$$
$$T = 34a \qquad \text{(a)}$$

Next, write a $\Sigma F_y = ma_y$ equation for the 16-kg block.

$$\Sigma F_y = ma_y$$
$$mg - T = ma$$
$$(16)(9.81) - T = 16a$$
$$T = 156.96 - 16a \qquad \text{(b)}$$

Substitute (b) into (a) to find the acceleration.

(a) $(156.96 - 16a) = 34a$

$$156.96 = 50a$$
$$a = 3.139\ \frac{\text{m}}{\text{s}^2} \xrightarrow{\text{SD}} \mathbf{3.1\ \frac{m}{s^2}\ to\ the\ right}$$

Substitute the acceleration into (a) to find T.

(a) $T = 34(3.139) = 106.73\text{ N} \xrightarrow{\text{SD}}$ **110 N**

8. Begin by finding the component of the weight of the 67-kg block that is parallel to the plane.

$F_x = mg \sin 48° = 67(9.81) \sin 48° = 488.45\text{ N}$

Next, write a $\Sigma F_x = ma_x$ equation for the 67-kg block. Choose up the plane as the positive direction for motion.

$$\Sigma F_x = ma_x$$
$$T - F_x = ma$$
$$T - 488.45 = 67a$$
$$T = 488.45 + 67a \qquad \text{(a)}$$

Now, write a $\Sigma F_y = ma_y$ equation for the 45-kg block.

$$\Sigma F_y = ma_y$$
$$mg - T = ma$$
$$(45)(9.81) - T = 45a$$
$$T = 441.45 - 45a \qquad \text{(b)}$$

Substitute (b) into (a) to find the acceleration.

(a) $(441.45 - 45a) = 488.45 + 67a$

$$-47 = 112a$$
$$a = -0.4196\ \frac{\text{m}}{\text{s}^2} \xrightarrow{\text{SD}} \mathbf{0.42\ \frac{m}{s^2}\ down\ the\ plane}$$

Substitute the acceleration into (a) to find T.

(a) $T = 488.45 + 67(-0.4196) = 460.34\text{ N} \xrightarrow{\text{SD}}$ **460 N**

9. (a) $T_1 = -65.0 + 273 =$ **208 K**

$T_2 = 120 + 273 =$ **393 K**

(b)
$$\frac{V_1}{T_1} = \frac{V_2}{T_2}$$
$$\frac{3.5\text{ m}^3}{208\text{ K}} = \frac{V_2}{393\text{ K}}$$
$$V_2 = 6.613\text{ m}^3 \xrightarrow{\text{SD}} \mathbf{6.6\ m^3}$$

10. (a) $T_1 = 25.0 + 273 =$ **298 K**

(b)
$$\frac{V_1}{T_1} = \frac{V_2}{T_2}$$
$$\frac{1.4\text{ m}^3}{298\text{ K}} = \frac{23\text{ m}^3}{T_2}$$
$$T_2 = 4896\text{ K} \xrightarrow{\text{SD}} \mathbf{4900\ K}$$

11. Begin by finding the speed of light in water in terms of c.

$$1.333 = \frac{c}{v_2}$$
$$v_2 = \frac{c}{1.333} = 0.7502c$$

Now use Snell's law to find θ_r.

$$\frac{\sin \theta_1}{v_1} = \frac{\sin \theta_2}{v_2}$$
$$\frac{\sin 54°}{0.69c} = \frac{\sin \theta_r}{0.7502c}$$
$$\theta_r = \mathbf{61.59°}$$

12. $n_1 \sin\theta_1 = n_2 \sin\theta_2$

$(1.553)\sin 15° = (1.333)\sin\theta_r$

$\theta_r = \mathbf{17.55°}$

13. (a) $m_1v_1 + m_2v_2 = (m_1 + m_2)v_3$

$(0.00285)(1230) + (6.81)(0) = (6.81285)v_3$

$v_3 = +0.5145\ \frac{\text{m}}{\text{s}} \xrightarrow{\text{SD}} \mathbf{+0.515\ \frac{m}{s}}$

(b) $KE = \frac{1}{2}mv_3^2 = \frac{1}{2}(6.81285)(0.5145)^2 = 0.9017\text{ J} \xrightarrow{\text{SD}} \mathbf{0.902\ J}$

(c) $PE = mgh$

$0.9017 = (6.81285)(9.81)h$

$h = 1.349 \times 10^{-2}\text{ m} \xrightarrow{\text{SD}} \mathbf{1.35 \times 10^{-2}\ m}$

14. Begin by writing a momentum equation.

$m_1v_1 + m_2v_2 = (m_1 + m_2)v_3$

$6.05(86.0\angle 78°) + 10.7(5.14\angle 279°) = (6.05 + 10.7)v_3$

$520.3\angle 78° + 54.998\angle 279° = (16.75)v_3$ (a)

Now find the sum of the x and y components of the initial momenta.

$\Sigma mv_x = 520.3\cos 78° + 54.998\cos 279° = 116.78\text{ kg·m·s}^{-1}$

$\Sigma mv_y = 520.3\sin 78° + 54.998\sin 279° = 454.61\text{ kg·m·s}^{-1}$

$\Sigma mv_R = (116.78i + 454.61j)\text{ kg·m·s}^{-1}$

Convert this resultant to polar form and get:

$\Sigma mv_R = \sqrt{(116.78)^2 + (454.61)^2} = 469.37\text{ kg·m·s}^{-1}$

$\theta = \tan^{-1}\frac{454.61}{116.78} = 75.59°$

$\Sigma mv_R = 469.37\angle 75.59°\text{ kg·m·s}^{-1}$

Use this momentum in (a) to find v_3.

(a) $469.37\angle 75.59° = (16.75)v_3$

$v_3 = 28.02\angle 75.59°\ \frac{\text{m}}{\text{s}} \xrightarrow{\text{SD}} \mathbf{28.0\angle 75.59°\ \frac{m}{s}}$

15. (a) $PE = mgh = 1.75\text{ kg} \times 9.81\frac{\text{N}}{\text{kg}} \times 134\text{ m} = 2300.4\text{ J}$

$KE = \frac{1}{2}mv_d^2$

$2300.4\text{ J} = \frac{1}{2}(1.75\text{ kg})v_d^2$

$v_d = -51.27\ \frac{\text{m}}{\text{s}} \xrightarrow{\text{SD}} \mathbf{-51.3\ \frac{m}{s}}$

$PE = mgh = 1.75\text{ kg} \times 9.81\frac{\text{N}}{\text{kg}} \times 120\text{ m} = 2060.1\text{ J}$

$KE = \frac{1}{2}mv_u^2$

$2060.1\text{ J} = \frac{1}{2}(1.75\text{ kg})v_u^2$

$v_u = +48.52\ \frac{\text{m}}{\text{s}} \xrightarrow{\text{SD}} \mathbf{+48.5\ \frac{m}{s}}$

(b) $\Delta KE = 2300.4\text{ J} - 2060.1\text{ J} = 240.3\text{ J} \xrightarrow{\text{SD}} \mathbf{24\bar{0}\ J}$

16. (a) $\Sigma F_y = 0;\ F_A + F_B - 80{,}4\bar{0}0\text{ N} - 60{,}568\text{ N} = 0$

(b) $\Sigma M_A = 0;\ 80{,}4\bar{0}0\text{ N}(2\text{ m}) + 60{,}568\text{ N}(4\text{ m}) - F_B(6\text{ m}) = 0$

Solve (b) for F_B and get:

(b) $160{,}800 + 242{,}272 - F_B(6) = 0$

$-F_B(6) = -403{,}072$

$F_B = 67{,}179\text{ N} \xrightarrow{\text{SD}} \mathbf{70{,}000\ N}$

Substitute F_B into (a) to find F_A.

(a) $F_A + (67{,}179) - 80{,}400 - 60{,}568 = 0$

$F_A = 73{,}789\text{ N} \xrightarrow{\text{SD}} \mathbf{70{,}000\ N}$

17. Use the displacement equation to find the time.

$\Delta y = v_0t + \frac{1}{2}at^2$

$-12 = 21t + \frac{1}{2}(-9.81)t^2$

$0 = 4.905t^2 - 21t - 12$

Use the quadratic formula to solve this equation for t.

$t = \frac{-(-21) \pm \sqrt{(-21)^2 - 4(4.905)(-12)}}{2(4.905)} = 4.792\text{ s} \xrightarrow{\text{SD}} \mathbf{4.8\ s}$

18. (a) $v(t) = v_0 + at$

$v(6.0) = 13 + 4.5(6.0) = \mathbf{4\bar{0}\ \frac{m}{s}}$ **to the right**

(b) $x(t) = x_0 + v_0t + \frac{1}{2}at^2$

$x(6.0) = 14 + 13(6.0) + \frac{1}{2}(4.5)(6.0)^2$

$= 173\text{ m} \xrightarrow{SD} \mathbf{170\text{ m}}$

19.

$$\Sigma F_y = ma_y$$
$$T - mg = ma_y$$
$$3550\text{ N} - 321\text{ kg}\left(9.81\ \frac{\text{N}}{\text{kg}}\right) = (321\text{ kg})a_y$$
$$a_y = 1.249\ \frac{\text{m}}{\text{s}^2} \xrightarrow{SD} \mathbf{1.25\ \frac{m}{s^2}\ upward}$$

20. Calculate the displacements for the following time intervals:

$\Delta x_{0,1.5} = -30\ \frac{\text{m}}{\text{s}} \times 1.5\text{ s} = -45\text{ m}$

$\Delta x_{1.5,4} = 15\ \frac{\text{m}}{\text{s}} \times 2.5\text{ s} = +37.5\text{ m}$

$\Delta x_{4,4.5} = 15\ \frac{\text{m}}{\text{s}} \times 0.5\text{ s} = +7.5\text{ m}$

$\Delta x_{4.5,6} = \dfrac{-30\ \frac{\text{m}}{\text{s}} \times 1.5\text{ s}}{2} = -22.5\text{ m}$

Sum the displacements from $t = 0$ s to $t = 4.0$ s with the initial position and get:
$x_{4.0} = 0\text{ m} - 45\text{ m} + 37.5\text{ m} = \mathbf{-7.5\text{ m}}$

Sum the displacements from $t = 4.0$ s to $t = 6.00$ s with $x_{4.0}$ and get:

$x_{6.00} = -7.5\text{ m} + 7.5\text{ m} - 22.5\text{ m} = -22.5\text{ m} \xrightarrow{SD} \mathbf{-23\text{ m}}$

Problem Set 37

1. Begin by finding the cross-sectional area of the beam.
$A = 0.10\text{ m} \times 0.20\text{ m} = 0.020\text{ m}^2$

Now find the electrical resistance.

$$R = \rho\frac{L}{A} = \frac{(10 \times 10^{-8}\ \Omega\cdot\text{m})(5.00\text{ m})}{0.020\text{ m}^2}$$
$$= 2.5 \times 10^{-5}\ \Omega \xrightarrow{SD} \mathbf{3 \times 10^{-5}\ \Omega}$$

2. (a) $I = \frac{V}{R} = \frac{20\text{ V}}{200\ \Omega} = \mathbf{0.1\text{ A}}$

(b) $0.1\ \frac{\text{coulomb}}{\text{s}} \times \frac{1\text{ electron}}{1.60 \times 10^{-19}\text{ coulomb}}$

$= 6.25 \times 10^{17}\text{ electrons} \xrightarrow{SD} \mathbf{6 \times 10^{17}\ electrons}$

3. (a) $m_g = 680\ \frac{\text{kg}}{\text{m}^3} \times 0.085\text{ m}^3 = 57.8\text{ kg} \xrightarrow{SD} \mathbf{58\text{ kg}}$

(b) $F_B = 57.8\text{ kg} \times 9.81\ \frac{\text{N}}{\text{kg}} = 567\text{ N} \xrightarrow{SD} \mathbf{570\text{ N}}$

(c) $T = F_B - mg = 567\text{ N} - 48\text{ kg}\left(9.81\ \frac{\text{N}}{\text{kg}}\right) = 96.12\text{ N} \xrightarrow{SD} \mathbf{96\text{ N}}$

4. (a) $F_B = w_{out} - w_{in} = 688\text{ N} - 248\text{ N} = \mathbf{44\bar{0}\text{ N}}$

(b) $m_w = \frac{F_B}{g} = \frac{440\text{ N}}{9.81\ \frac{\text{N}}{\text{kg}}} = 44.85\text{ kg} \xrightarrow{SD} \mathbf{44.9\text{ kg}}$

(c) $V = \frac{m}{\rho} = \frac{44.85\text{ kg}}{1000\text{ kg/m}^3} = 4.485 \times 10^{-2}\text{ m}^3 \xrightarrow{SD} \mathbf{4.49 \times 10^{-2}\text{ m}^3}$

5. (a) $a = r\alpha$

$3\ \frac{\text{m}}{\text{s}^2} = (0.36150\text{ m})\alpha$

$\alpha = 8.299\ \frac{\text{rad}}{\text{s}^2} \xrightarrow{SD} \mathbf{8\ \frac{rad}{s^2}}$

(b) $\omega(t) = \omega_0 + \alpha t$

$24.005 = 0 + (8.299)t$

$t = 2.893\text{ s} \xrightarrow{SD} \mathbf{3\text{ s}}$

6. (a) $\omega(t) = \omega_0 + \alpha t$

$\omega(4.5) = 23 + 3.4(4.5) = 38.3\ \frac{\text{rad}}{\text{s}} \xrightarrow{\text{SD}}$ **38 $\frac{\text{rad}}{\text{s}}$**

(b) $\Delta\theta = \omega_0 t + \frac{1}{2}\alpha t^2$

$= 23(4.5) + \frac{1}{2}(3.4)(4.5)^2 = 137.9 \text{ rad} \xrightarrow{\text{SD}}$ **140 rad**

7. (a) $n = \frac{c}{v}$

$2.417 = \frac{3.00 \times 10^8 \text{ m/s}}{v}$

$v = 1.241 \times 10^8\ \frac{\text{m}}{\text{s}} \xrightarrow{\text{SD}}$ **1.24 × 10⁸ $\frac{\text{m}}{\text{s}}$**

(b) $v = f\lambda$

$1.241 \times 10^8\ \frac{\text{m}}{\text{s}} = (5.2 \times 10^{14} \text{ s}^{-1})\lambda$

$\lambda = 2.387 \times 10^{-7} \text{ m} \xrightarrow{\text{SD}}$ **2.4×10^{-7} m**

8. (a) $n = \frac{c}{v} = \frac{3.00 \times 10^8 \text{ m/s}}{1.997 \times 10^8 \text{ m/s}} = 1.502 \xrightarrow{\text{SD}}$ **1.50**

(b) $v = f\lambda$

$1.997 \times 10^8\ \frac{\text{m}}{\text{s}} = (4.3 \times 10^{14} \text{ s}^{-1})\lambda$

$\lambda = 4.644 \times 10^{-7} \text{ m} \xrightarrow{\text{SD}}$ **4.6×10^{-7} m**

9. Begin by writing a $\Sigma F_x = ma_x$ equation for the 14.0-kg block. Choose to the right as the positive direction for motion.

$\Sigma F_x = ma_x$

$T = ma$

$T = 14.0a$ (a)

Next, write a $\Sigma F_y = ma_y$ equation for the 5.50-kg block.

$\Sigma F_y = ma_y$

$mg - T = ma$

$(5.50)(9.81) - T = 5.50a$

$T = 53.96 - 5.50a$ (b)

Substitute (b) into (a) to find the acceleration.

(a) $(53.96 - 5.50a) = 14.0a$

$53.96 = 19.5a$

$a = 2.767\ \frac{\text{m}}{\text{s}^2} \xrightarrow{\text{SD}}$ **2.77 $\frac{\text{m}}{\text{s}^2}$ to the right**

Substitute the acceleration into (a) to find T.

(a) $T = 14.0(2.767) = 38.738 \text{ N} \xrightarrow{\text{SD}}$ **38.7 N**

10. Begin by finding the component of the weight of the 267-kg block that is parallel to the plane.

$F_x = mg \sin 30°$

$= (267)(9.81) \sin 30°$

$= 1309.64$ N

Next, write a $\Sigma F_x = ma_x$ equation for the 267-kg block. Choose up the plane as the positive direction for motion.

$\Sigma F_x = ma_x$

$T - F_x = ma$

$T - 1309.64 = 267a$

$T = 1309.64 + 267a$ (a)

Now, write a $\Sigma F_y = ma_y$ equation for the 143-kg block.

$\Sigma F_y = ma_y$

$mg - T = ma$

$(143)(9.81) - T = 143a$

$T = 1402.83 - 143a$ (b)

Substitute (b) into (a) to find the acceleration.

(a) $(1402.83 - 143a) = 1309.64 + 267a$

$93.19 = 410a$

$a = 0.2273\ \frac{\text{m}}{\text{s}^2} \xrightarrow{\text{SD}}$ **0.227 $\frac{\text{m}}{\text{s}^2}$ up the plane**

Substitute the acceleration into (a) to find T.

(a) $T = 1309.64 + 267(0.2273) = 1370.33 \text{ N} \xrightarrow{\text{SD}}$ **1370 N**

11. (a) $T_1 = 365 + 273 = \mathbf{638\ K}$

$T_2 = 10.0 + 273 = \mathbf{283\ K}$

(b) $\frac{V_1}{T_1} = \frac{V_2}{T_2}$

$\frac{5.1\ m^3}{638\ K} = \frac{V_2}{283\ K}$

$V_2 = 2.26\ m^3 \xrightarrow{SD} \mathbf{2.3\ m^3}$

12. (a) $T_1 = -25.0 + 273 = \mathbf{248\ K}$

(b) $\frac{V_1}{T_1} = \frac{V_2}{T_2}$

$\frac{3.6\ m^3}{248\ K} = \frac{6.7\ m^3}{T_2}$

$T_2 = 461.6\ K \xrightarrow{SD} \mathbf{460\ K}$

13. $\frac{\sin\theta_1}{v_1} = \frac{\sin\theta_2}{v_2}$

$\frac{\sin 35°}{0.65c} = \frac{\sin\theta_r}{c}$

$\theta_r = \mathbf{61.94°}$

14. (a) $m_1v_1 + m_2v_2 = (m_1 + m_2)v_3$

$(9.5 \times 10^{-4})(123) + (1.81)(0) = (1.81095)v_3$

$v_3 = +6.452 \times 10^{-2}\ \frac{m}{s} \xrightarrow{SD} \mathbf{+6.5 \times 10^{-2}\ \frac{m}{s}}$

(b) $KE = \frac{1}{2}mv_3^2$

$= \frac{1}{2}(1.81095)(6.452 \times 10^{-2})^2$

$= 3.77 \times 10^{-3}\ J \xrightarrow{SD} \mathbf{3.8 \times 10^{-3}\ J}$

(c) $PE = mgh$

$3.77 \times 10^{-3} = (1.81095)(9.81)h$

$h = 2.12 \times 10^{-4}\ m \xrightarrow{SD} \mathbf{2.1 \times 10^{-4}\ m}$

15. (a) $PE = mgh = 1.50\ \cancel{kg} \times 9.81\ \frac{N}{\cancel{kg}} \times 3.05\ m = 44.88\ J$

$KE = \frac{1}{2}mv_d^2$

$44.88\ J = \frac{1}{2}(1.50\ kg)v_d^2$

$v_d = -7.736\ \frac{m}{s} \xrightarrow{SD} \mathbf{7.74\ \frac{m}{s}\ downward}$

$PE = mgh = 1.50\ \cancel{kg} \times 9.81\ \frac{N}{\cancel{kg}} \times 2.00\ m = 29.43\ J$

$KE = \frac{1}{2}mv_u^2$

$29.43\ J = \frac{1}{2}(1.50\ kg)v_u^2$

$v_u = +6.264\ \frac{m}{s} \xrightarrow{SD} \mathbf{6.26\ \frac{m}{s}\ upward}$

(b) $\Delta KE = 44.88\ J - 29.43\ J = 15.45\ J \xrightarrow{SD} \mathbf{15.5\ J}$

16. $\frac{F_1}{A_1} = \frac{F_2}{A_2}$

$\frac{46\ N}{0.29\ m^2} = \frac{F_2}{2.21\ m^2}$

$F_2 = 350.6\ N \xrightarrow{SD} \mathbf{350\ N}$

17. Use the displacement equation to find the time.

$\Delta y = v_0t + \frac{1}{2}at^2$

$0 = (16)t + \frac{1}{2}(-9.81)t^2$

$4.905t = 16$

$t = 3.262\ s \xrightarrow{SD} \mathbf{3.3\ s}$

18. $Q = mc\Delta T$

$1.98 \times 10^5\ J = 3.7\ kg \times c \times 75\ C°$

$c = 713.5\ \frac{J}{kg \cdot C°} \xrightarrow{SD} \mathbf{710\ \frac{J}{kg \cdot C°}}$

19. Begin by finding the weight of the beam and the weight of the 10.0-kg mass.

$$w_b = m_b g$$
$$= 20.0\,\cancel{\text{kg}} \times 9.81\,\frac{\text{N}}{\cancel{\text{kg}}}$$
$$= 196.2\text{ N}$$
$$w_m = m_m g$$
$$= 10.0\,\cancel{\text{kg}} \times 9.81\,\frac{\text{N}}{\cancel{\text{kg}}}$$
$$= 98.1\text{ N}$$

Next sum the moments about the left end of the beam.

$$\Sigma M = 0$$
$$w_b(2.50) + w_m(5.00) - F_{Ty}(5.00) = 0$$
$$(196.2)(2.50) + (98.1)(5.00) - F_{Ty}(5.00) = 0$$
$$F_{Ty}(5.00) = 981$$
$$F_{Ty} = 196.2\text{ N}$$

Now use F_{Ty} to find F_T.

$$F_T \sin 45° = F_{Ty}$$
$$F_T \sin 45° = 196.2\text{ N}$$
$$F_T = 277.47\text{ N} \xrightarrow{\text{SD}} \mathbf{277\text{ N}}$$

Sum the vertical forces to zero to find F_y.

$$F_y - 196.2\text{ N} - 98.1\text{ N} + 196.2\text{ N} = 0$$
$$F_y = \mathbf{98.1\text{ N}}$$

Sum the horizontal forces to zero to find F_x.

$$F_x - F_T \cos 45° = 0$$
$$F_x = (277.47\text{ N}) \cos 45°$$
$$= 196.2\text{ N} \xrightarrow{\text{SD}} \mathbf{196\text{ N}}$$

20. $826\,\frac{\cancel{\text{J}}}{\cancel{\text{kg}}\cdot\cancel{\text{C°}}} \times \frac{1\text{ calorie}}{4.186\,\cancel{\text{J}}} \times \frac{1\,\cancel{\text{kg}}}{1000\text{ g}} \times \frac{1\,\cancel{\text{C°}}}{1\text{ K}}$

$= 0.1973\,\frac{\text{calorie}}{\text{g}\cdot\text{K}} \xrightarrow{\text{SD}} \mathbf{0.197\,\frac{calorie}{g\cdot K}}$

Problem Set 38

1. $\frac{P_1V_1}{T_1} = \frac{P_2V_2}{T_2} \rightarrow \frac{P_1V_1}{T_1} = \frac{(3P_1)V_2}{\left(\frac{T_1}{2}\right)}$

$$\frac{\cancel{P_1}V_1}{\cancel{T_1}} \times \frac{\cancel{T_1}}{\cancel{P_1}} = \frac{(3\cancel{P_1})V_2}{\left(\frac{\cancel{T_1}}{2}\right)} \times \frac{\cancel{T_1}}{\cancel{P_1}}$$
$$\mathbf{\frac{V_1}{6}} = V_2$$

2. $\frac{P_1V_1}{T_1} = \frac{P_2V_2}{T_2} \rightarrow \frac{P_1V_1}{T_1} = \frac{P_2(2V_1)}{(4T_1)}$

$$\frac{P_1\cancel{V_1}}{\cancel{T_1}} \times \frac{\cancel{T_1}}{\cancel{V_1}} = \frac{P_2(2\cancel{V_1})}{(4\cancel{T_1})} \times \frac{\cancel{T_1}}{\cancel{V_1}}$$
$$\mathbf{2P_1} = P_2$$

3. Begin by finding the cross-sectional area of the rod.

$A = \pi r^2 = \pi(1.55 \times 10^{-2}\text{ m})^2 = 7.548 \times 10^{-4}\text{ m}^2$

Now find the electrical resistance.

$$R = \rho\frac{L}{A} = \frac{(1.7 \times 10^{-8}\ \Omega\cdot\cancel{\text{m}})(2.50684\ \cancel{\text{m}})}{7.548 \times 10^{-4}\ \cancel{\text{m}^2}}$$
$$= 5.646 \times 10^{-5}\ \Omega \xrightarrow{\text{SD}} \mathbf{5.6 \times 10^{-5}\ \Omega}$$

4. (a) $I = \frac{V}{R} = \frac{12\text{ V}}{1500\ \Omega} = \mathbf{8.0 \times 10^{-3}\text{ A}}$

(b) $8.0 \times 10^{-3}\,\frac{\cancel{\text{coulomb}}}{\text{s}} \times \frac{1\text{ electron}}{1.60 \times 10^{-19}\ \cancel{\text{coulomb}}} = \mathbf{5.0 \times 10^{16}\text{ electrons}}$

5. (a) $m_w = 1000\,\frac{\text{kg}}{\cancel{\text{m}^3}} \times 0.300\ \cancel{\text{m}^3} = \mathbf{30\bar{0}\text{ kg}}$

(b) $F_B = 300\,\cancel{\text{kg}} \times 9.81\,\frac{\text{N}}{\cancel{\text{kg}}} = 2943\text{ N} \xrightarrow{\text{SD}} \mathbf{2940\text{ N}}$

(c) $T = F_B - mg = 2943\text{ N} - 22.0\,\cancel{\text{kg}}\left(9.81\,\frac{\text{N}}{\cancel{\text{kg}}}\right)$

$= 2727\text{ N} \xrightarrow{\text{SD}} \mathbf{2730\text{ N}}$

6. (a) Begin by finding the volume of the ice that is submerged.

$V_s = 3.50\text{ m}^3 \times 0.850 = 2.975\text{ m}^3$

Now find the mass of the water displaced.

$$m_w = 1000\,\frac{\text{kg}}{\text{m}^3} \times 2.975\text{ m}^3 = 2975\text{ kg} \xrightarrow{\text{SD}} \mathbf{2980\ kg}$$

(b) $F_B = 2975\text{ kg} \times 9.81\,\frac{\text{N}}{\text{kg}} = 2.918 \times 10^4\text{ N} \xrightarrow{\text{SD}} \mathbf{2.92 \times 10^4\ N}$

(c) The weight of the ice equals the buoyancy force of the water, and the mass of the ice equals the mass of the water displaced.

$w_i = F_B = \mathbf{2.92 \times 10^4\ N}$

$m_i = m_w = \mathbf{2980\ kg}$

7. (a) $\omega(t) = \omega_0 + \alpha t$

$$\omega(3.50) = 8.52 + 1.40(3.50) = 13.42\,\frac{\text{rad}}{\text{s}} \xrightarrow{\text{SD}} \mathbf{13.4\,\frac{rad}{s}}$$

(b) $\Delta\theta = \omega_0 t + \frac{1}{2}\alpha t^2$

$$= 8.52(3.50) + \frac{1}{2}(1.40)(3.50)^2 = 38.395\text{ rad} \xrightarrow{\text{SD}} \mathbf{38.4\ rad}$$

8. (a) $n = \frac{c}{v}$

$$1.461 = \frac{3.00 \times 10^8\text{ m/s}}{v}$$

$$v = 2.053 \times 10^8\,\frac{\text{m}}{\text{s}} \xrightarrow{\text{SD}} \mathbf{2.05 \times 10^8\,\frac{m}{s}}$$

(b) $v = f\lambda$

$$2.053 \times 10^8\,\frac{\text{m}}{\text{s}} = f(3.42 \times 10^{-7}\text{ m})$$

$$f = 6.003 \times 10^{14}\text{ Hz} \xrightarrow{\text{SD}} \mathbf{6.00 \times 10^{14}\ Hz}$$

9. Begin by writing a $\Sigma F_x = ma_x$ equation for the 32-kg block. Choose to the right as the positive direction for motion.

$\Sigma F_x = ma_x$

$T = ma$

$T = 32a$ (a)

Next, write a $\Sigma F_y = ma_y$ equation for the 20-kg block.

$\Sigma F_y = ma_y$

$mg - T = ma$

$(20)(9.81) - T = 20a$

$T = 196.2 - 20a$ (b)

Substitute (b) into (a) to find the acceleration.

(a) $(196.2 - 20a) = 32a$

$196.2 = 52a$

$$a = 3.773\,\frac{\text{m}}{\text{s}^2} \xrightarrow{\text{SD}} \mathbf{3.8\,\frac{m}{s^2}\ to\ the\ right}$$

Substitute the acceleration into (a) to find T.

(a) $T = 32(3.773) = 120.74\text{ N} \xrightarrow{\text{SD}} \mathbf{120\ N}$

10. Begin by finding the component of the weight of the 167-kg block that is parallel to the plane.

$F_x = mg\sin 48° = (167)(9.81)\sin 48° = 1217.47\text{ N}$

Next, write a $\Sigma F_x = ma_x$ equation for the 167-kg block. Choose up the plane as the positive direction for motion.

$\Sigma F_x = ma_x$

$T - F_x = ma$

$T - 1217.47 = 167a$

$T = 1217.47 + 167a$ (a)

Now, write a $\Sigma F_y = ma_y$ equation for the 61-kg block.

$\Sigma F_y = ma_y$

$mg - T = ma$

$(61)(9.81) - T = 61a$

$T = 598.41 - 61a$ (b)

Substitute (b) into (a) to find the acceleration.

(a) $(598.41 - 61a) = 1217.47 + 167a$

$-619.06 = 228a$

$$a = -2.715\,\frac{\text{m}}{\text{s}^2} \xrightarrow{\text{SD}} \mathbf{2.7\,\frac{m}{s^2}\ down\ the\ plane}$$

Substitute the acceleration into (a) to find T.

(a) $T = 1217.47 + 167(-2.715) = 764.07\text{ N} \xrightarrow{\text{SD}} \mathbf{760\ N}$

11. (a) $T_1 = 5.00 + 273 = \mathbf{278\ K}$

$T_2 = 120 + 273 = \mathbf{393\ K}$

(b) $\frac{V_1}{T_1} = \frac{V_2}{T_2}$

$\frac{2.1\ \text{m}^3}{278\ \text{K}} = \frac{V_2}{393\ \text{K}}$

$V_2 = 2.969\ \text{m}^3 \xrightarrow{\text{SD}} \mathbf{3.0\ m^3}$

12. (a) $T_1 = -12.0 + 273 = \mathbf{261\ K}$

(b) $\frac{V_1}{T_1} = \frac{V_2}{T_2}$

$\frac{5.2\ \text{m}^3}{261\ \text{K}} = \frac{16.7\ \text{m}^3}{T_2}$

$T_2 = 838.2\ \text{K} \xrightarrow{\text{SD}} \mathbf{840\ K}$

13. $\frac{\sin\theta_1}{v_1} = \frac{\sin\theta_2}{v_2}$

$\frac{\sin 25°}{0.67c} = \frac{\sin\theta_r}{c}$

$\theta_r = \mathbf{39.11°}$

14. (a) $\Sigma F_y = 0;\ 60.00\ \text{N} + F_A + F_B - 300.0\ \text{N} = 0$

(b) $\Sigma M_B = 0;\ F_A(8.000\ \text{m}) + 60.00\ \text{N}(10.00\ \text{m}) - 300.0\ \text{N}(3.000\ \text{m}) = 0$

Solve (b) for F_A and get:

(b) $F_A(8.000\ \text{m}) + 600.0\ \text{N}\cdot\text{m} - 900.0\ \text{N}\cdot\text{m} = 0$

$F_A(8.000\ \text{m}) = 300\ \text{N}\cdot\text{m}$

$F_A = \mathbf{37.50\ N}$

Substitute F_A into (a) to find F_B.

(a) $60.00\ \text{N} + (37.50\ \text{N}) + F_B - 300.0\ \text{N} = 0$

$F_B = \mathbf{202.5\ N}$

15. (a) $PE = mgh = 0.25\ \text{kg} \times 9.81\ \frac{\text{N}}{\text{kg}} \times 4.3\ \text{m} = 10.55\ \text{J}$

$KE = \frac{1}{2}mv_d^2$

$10.55\ \text{J} = \frac{1}{2}(0.25\ \text{kg})v_d^2$

$v_d = -9.187\ \frac{\text{m}}{\text{s}} \xrightarrow{\text{SD}} \mathbf{-9.2\ \frac{m}{s}}$

$PE = mgh = 0.25\ \text{kg} \times 9.81\ \frac{\text{N}}{\text{kg}} \times 0.63\ \text{m} = 1.55\ \text{J}$

$KE = \frac{1}{2}mv_u^2$

$1.55\ \text{J} = \frac{1}{2}(0.25\ \text{kg})v_u^2$

$v_u = +3.521\ \frac{\text{m}}{\text{s}} \xrightarrow{\text{SD}} \mathbf{+3.5\ \frac{m}{s}}$

(b) $\Delta KE = 10.55\ \text{J} - 1.55\ \text{J} = \mathbf{9.0\ J}$

16. $\frac{F_1}{A_1} = \frac{F_2}{A_2}$

$\frac{F_1}{1.39\ \text{m}^2} = \frac{36\ \text{N}}{6.52\ \text{m}^2}$

$F_1 = 7.67\ \text{N} \xrightarrow{\text{SD}} \mathbf{7.7\ N}$

17. $F = \frac{Gm_1m_2}{r^2} = \frac{(6.67 \times 10^{-11})(3.51 \times 10^{18})(2.63 \times 10^{17})}{(420{,}000)^2}$

$= 3.4905 \times 10^{14}\ \text{N} \xrightarrow{\text{SD}} \mathbf{3.49 \times 10^{14}\ N}$

18. (a) $F_k = \mu_k F_N = 0.398(84.0\ \text{kg})\left(9.81\ \frac{\text{N}}{\text{kg}}\right) = 327.97\ \text{N} \xrightarrow{\text{SD}} \mathbf{328\ N}$

(b) Sum the horizontal forces to find the net force.

$\Sigma F_x = 465\ \text{N} - 327.97\ \text{N} = 137.03\ \text{N}$

Now use the impulse-momentum equation to find v_2.

$F\Delta t = m(v_2 - v_1)$

$137.03\ \text{N}(4.60\ \text{s}) = 84.0\ \text{kg}(v_2 - 0\ \text{m/s})$

$v_2 = 7.504\ \text{m/s} \xrightarrow{\text{SD}}$ **7.50 m/s to the left**

19. Begin by finding the weight of the mass.

$$w = mg = 318\,\text{kg} \times 9.81\,\frac{\text{N}}{\text{kg}} = 3119.58\text{ N}$$

Now set the torques equal to each other and find F.

$$FR_1 = mgR_2$$
$$F(15.0\text{ cm}) = 3119.58\text{ N}(8.00\text{ cm})$$
$$F = 1663.776\text{ N} \xrightarrow{\text{SD}} \mathbf{1660\ N}$$

$$\text{Mechanical advantage} = \frac{\text{force out}}{\text{force in}} = \frac{3119.58\text{ N}}{1663.776\text{ N}} = 1.875 \xrightarrow{\text{SD}} \mathbf{1.88}$$

20. $\rho = \dfrac{m}{V} = \dfrac{36.0\text{ kg}}{0.01\text{ m}^3} = 3600\,\dfrac{\text{kg}}{\text{m}^3}$

Convert 3600 kg/m^3 to g/cm^3 and get:

$$3600\,\frac{\text{kg}}{\text{m}^3} \times \frac{1000\text{ g}}{1\text{ kg}} \times \frac{1\text{ m}^3}{(100)^3\text{ cm}^3} = 3.6\,\frac{\text{g}}{\text{cm}^3} \xrightarrow{\text{SD}} \mathbf{4\,\frac{g}{cm^3}}$$

Problem Set 39

1. (a) $Q = mc\Delta T$

$$= 1.00\,\text{kg} \times 30.8\,\frac{\text{cal}}{\text{kg}\cdot\text{C}^\circ} \times 1038\,\text{C}^\circ$$
$$= 3.197 \times 10^4\text{ calories} \xrightarrow{\text{SD}} \mathbf{3.2 \times 10^4\ calories}$$

(b) $Q = 1.00\,\text{kg} \times 64.5 \times 10^3\,\dfrac{\text{J}}{\text{kg}} = \mathbf{6.45 \times 10^4\ J}$

2.
$$Q_1 = 0.020(2050)(10) = 410\text{ J}$$
$$Q_2 = 0.020(334 \times 10^3) = 6680\text{ J}$$
$$Q_3 = 0.020(4186)(100) = 8372\text{ J}$$
$$Q_4 = 0.020(2256 \times 10^3) = 45{,}120\text{ J}$$
$$Q_5 = 0.020(2009)(10) = 401.8\text{ J}$$
$$Q_T = 6.098 \times 10^4\text{ J} \xrightarrow{\text{SD}} \mathbf{6.1 \times 10^4\ J}$$

3. $\dfrac{P_1V_1}{T_1} = \dfrac{P_2V_2}{T_2} \longrightarrow \dfrac{P_1V_1}{T_1} = \dfrac{(2P_1)V_2}{\left(\dfrac{T_1}{2}\right)}$

$$\frac{P_1V_1}{T_1} \times \frac{T_1}{P_1} = \frac{(2P_1)V_2}{\left(\dfrac{T_1}{2}\right)} \times \frac{T_1}{P_1}$$

$$\mathbf{\frac{V_1}{4}} = V_2$$

4. Begin by finding the cross-sectional area of the rod.

$A = \pi r^2 = \pi(2\text{ m})^2 = 12.57\text{ m}^2$

Now find the electrical resistance.

$$R = \rho\frac{L}{A} = \frac{(5.6 \times 10^{-8}\ \Omega\cdot\text{m})(180\text{ m})}{12.57\text{ m}^2}$$
$$= 8.019 \times 10^{-7}\ \Omega \xrightarrow{\text{SD}} \mathbf{8 \times 10^{-7}\ \Omega}$$

5. (a) $I = \dfrac{V}{R} = \dfrac{3.5\text{ V}}{180\ \Omega} = 1.944 \times 10^{-2}\text{ A} \xrightarrow{\text{SD}} \mathbf{1.9 \times 10^{-2}\ A}$

(b) $1.944 \times 10^{-2}\,\dfrac{\text{coulomb}}{\text{s}} \times \dfrac{1\text{ electron}}{1.60 \times 10^{-19}\text{ coulomb}}$

$$= 1.215 \times 10^{17}\text{ electrons} \xrightarrow{\text{SD}} \mathbf{1.2 \times 10^{17}\ electrons}$$

6. (a) $m_w = 1000\,\dfrac{\text{kg}}{\text{m}^3} \times 0.240\text{ m}^3 = \mathbf{24\bar{0}\ kg}$

(b) $F_B = 240\,\text{kg} \times 9.81\,\dfrac{\text{N}}{\text{kg}} = 2354.4\text{ N} \xrightarrow{\text{SD}} \mathbf{2350\ N}$

(c) $F = mg - F_B = 250\,\text{kg}\left(9.81\,\dfrac{\text{N}}{\text{kg}}\right) - 2354.4\text{ N} = \mathbf{98.1\ N}$

7. (a) Begin by finding the volume of the block that is submerged.

$V_s = 1.5\text{ m}^3 \times 0.62 = 0.93\text{ m}^3$

Now find the mass of the water displaced.

$$m_w = 1000\,\frac{\text{kg}}{\text{m}^3} \times 0.93\text{ m}^3 = \mathbf{930\ kg}$$

(b) $F_B = 930\,\text{kg} \times 9.81\,\dfrac{\text{N}}{\text{kg}} = 9123.3\text{ N} \xrightarrow{\text{SD}} \mathbf{9100\ N}$

(c) The weight of the block equals the buoyancy force of the water, and the mass of the block equals the mass of the water displaced.

$w_b = F_B = \mathbf{9100\ N}$

$m_b = m_w = \mathbf{930\ kg}$

8. (a) $\omega(t) = \omega_0 + \alpha t$

$\omega(5.0) = 16 + 2.3(5.0) = 27.5\ \frac{\text{rad}}{\text{s}} \xrightarrow{\text{SD}} \mathbf{28\ \frac{rad}{s}}$

(b) $\Delta\theta = \omega_0 t + \frac{1}{2}\alpha t^2$

$= 16(5.0) + \frac{1}{2}(2.3)(5.0)^2 = 108.75\text{ rad} \xrightarrow{\text{SD}} \mathbf{110\ rad}$

9. (a) $n = \frac{c}{v}$

$1.473 = \frac{3.00 \times 10^8\ \text{m/s}}{v}$

$v = 2.037 \times 10^8\ \frac{\text{m}}{\text{s}} \xrightarrow{\text{SD}} \mathbf{2.04 \times 10^8\ \frac{m}{s}}$

(b) $v = f\lambda$

$2.037 \times 10^8\ \frac{\text{m}}{\text{s}} = f(5.02 \times 10^{-7}\text{ m})$

$f = 4.058 \times 10^{14}\text{ Hz} \xrightarrow{\text{SD}} \mathbf{4.06 \times 10^{14}\ Hz}$

10. Begin by writing a $\Sigma F_x = ma_x$ equation for the 3.5-kg block. Choose to the right as the positive direction for motion.

$\Sigma F_x = ma_x$

$T = ma$

$T = 3.5a$ (a)

Next, write a $\Sigma F_y = ma_y$ equation for the 2.5-kg object.

$\Sigma F_y = ma_y$

$mg - T = ma$

$(2.5)(9.81) - T = 2.5a$

$T = 24.53 - 2.5a$ (b)

Substitute (b) into (a) to find the acceleration.

(a) $(24.53 - 2.5a) = 3.5a$

$24.53 = 6.0a$

$a = 4.088\ \frac{\text{m}}{\text{s}^2} \xrightarrow{\text{SD}} \mathbf{4.1\ \frac{m}{s^2}}$ **to the right**

Substitute the acceleration into (a) to find T.

(a) $T = 3.5(4.088) = 14.308\text{ N} \xrightarrow{\text{SD}} \mathbf{14\ N}$

11. Begin by finding the component of the weight of the 63-kg block that is parallel to the plane.

$F_x = mg \sin 47°$

$= (63)(9.81) \sin 47°$

$= 452.0\text{ N}$

Next, write a $\Sigma F_x = ma_x$ equation for the 63-kg block. Choose up the plane as the positive direction for motion.

$\Sigma F_x = ma_x$

$T - F_x = ma$

$T - 452.0 = 63a$

$T = 452.0 + 63a$ (a)

Now, write a $\Sigma F_y = ma_y$ equation for the 21-kg object.

$\Sigma F_y = ma_y$

$mg - T = ma$

$(21)(9.81) - T = 21a$

$T = 206.0 - 21a$ (b)

Substitute (b) into (a) to find the acceleration.

(a) $(206.0 - 21a) = 452.0 + 63a$

$-246.0 = 84a$

$a = -2.929\ \frac{\text{m}}{\text{s}^2} \xrightarrow{\text{SD}} \mathbf{2.9\ \frac{m}{s^2}}$ **down the plane**

Substitute the acceleration into (a) to find T.

(a) $T = 452.0 + 63(-2.929) = 267.5\text{ N} \xrightarrow{\text{SD}} \mathbf{270\ N}$

12. Begin by converting the temperature to kelvins.

$T_1 = 25.0 + 273 = 298 \text{ K}$

Now use the ideal gas law and get:

$$\frac{P_1}{T_1} = \frac{P_2}{T_2}$$

$$\frac{1.01 \times 10^5 \text{ Pa}}{298 \text{ K}} = \frac{3.50 \times 10^5 \text{ Pa}}{T_2}$$

$$T_2 = 1033 \text{ K} \xrightarrow{\text{SD}} \mathbf{1030 \text{ K}}$$

Convert the temperature to °C and get: $1033 - 273 = \mathbf{7\bar{6}0°C}$

13. Begin by finding the speed of light in water in terms of c.

$$n = \frac{c}{v}$$

$$1.333 = \frac{c}{v_2}$$

$$v_2 = 0.7502c$$

Now use Snell's law to find θ_r.

$$\frac{\sin \theta_1}{v_1} = \frac{\sin \theta_2}{v_2}$$

$$\frac{\sin 41°}{0.659c} = \frac{\sin \theta_r}{0.7502c}$$

$$\theta_r = \mathbf{48.32°}$$

14. (a)

$$m_1v_1 + m_2v_2 = (m_1 + m_2)v_3$$

$$(6.1 \times 10^{-3})(620) + (1.5)(0) = (1.5061)v_3$$

$$v_3 = +2.511 \frac{\text{m}}{\text{s}} \xrightarrow{\text{SD}} \mathbf{+2.5 \frac{m}{s}}$$

(b)

$$KE = \frac{1}{2}mv_3^2$$

$$= \frac{1}{2}(1.5061)(2.511)^2$$

$$= 4.748 \text{ J} \xrightarrow{\text{SD}} \mathbf{4.7 \text{ J}}$$

(c)

$$PE = mgh$$

$$4.748 = (1.5061)(9.81)h$$

$$h = 0.321 \text{ m} \xrightarrow{\text{SD}} \mathbf{0.32 \text{ m}}$$

15. (a)

$$PE = mgh = 0.75 \text{ kg} \times 9.81 \frac{\text{N}}{\text{kg}} \times 2.5 \text{ m} = 18.394 \text{ J}$$

$$KE = \frac{1}{2}mv_d^2$$

$$18.394 \text{ J} = \frac{1}{2}(0.75 \text{ kg})v_d^2$$

$$v_d = -7.00 \frac{\text{m}}{\text{s}} \xrightarrow{\text{SD}} \mathbf{7.0 \frac{m}{s} \text{ downward}}$$

$$PE = mgh = 0.75 \text{ kg} \times 9.81 \frac{\text{N}}{\text{kg}} \times 2.0 \text{ m} = 14.715 \text{ J}$$

$$KE = \frac{1}{2}mv_u^2$$

$$14.715 \text{ J} = \frac{1}{2}(0.75 \text{ kg})v_u^2$$

$$v_u = +6.26 \frac{\text{m}}{\text{s}} \xrightarrow{\text{SD}} \mathbf{6.3 \frac{m}{s} \text{ upward}}$$

(b)

$$\Delta KE = 18.394 \text{ J} - 14.715 \text{ J} = 3.679 \text{ J} \xrightarrow{\text{SD}} \mathbf{3.7 \text{ J}}$$

16.

$$\frac{F_1}{A_1} = \frac{F_2}{A_2}$$

$$\frac{1000 \text{ N}}{A_1} = \frac{2548.5 \text{ N}}{0.3561 \text{ m}^2}$$

$$A_1 = 0.1397 \text{ m}^2 \xrightarrow{\text{SD}} \mathbf{0.1 \text{ m}^2}$$

17. (a) $\Sigma F_y = 0;\ 200 \text{ N} + 100 \text{ N} - F_A - F_B = 0$

(b) $\Sigma M_B = 0;\ F_A(9 \text{ m}) - 200 \text{ N}(4 \text{ m}) - 100 \text{ N}(10 \text{ m}) = 0$

Solve (b) for F_A and get:

(b) $F_A(9 \text{ m}) - 800 \text{ N}\cdot\text{m} - 1000 \text{ N}\cdot\text{m} = 0$

$$F_A(9 \text{ m}) = 1800 \text{ N}\cdot\text{m}$$

$$F_A = \mathbf{200 \text{ N}}$$

Substitute F_A into (a) to find F_B.

(a) $200 \text{ N} + 100 \text{ N} - (200 \text{ N}) - F_B = 0$

$$F_B = \mathbf{100 \text{ N}}$$

18. $P_T = 6.5 \times 10^5 \text{ J} \times 0.75 = 4.875 \times 10^5 \text{ J}$

$P_G = 4.875 \times 10^5 \text{ J} \times 0.59 = 2.876 \times 10^5 \text{ J} \xrightarrow{\text{SD}}$ **2.9×10^5 J**

19. $F = ma = 38 \text{ kg} \times 19.3 \text{ m}\cdot\text{s}^{-2} = 733.4 \text{ N} \xrightarrow{\text{SD}}$ **730 N**

20. Begin by drawing a diagram and recording the data.

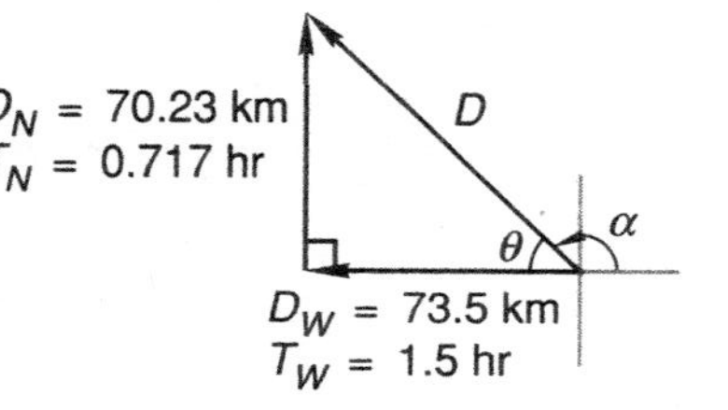

(a) $D_T = 73.5 \text{ km} + 70.23 \text{ km} = 143.7 \text{ km} \xrightarrow{\text{SD}}$ **140 km**

(b) $v = \frac{D_T}{T_T} = \frac{143.7 \text{ km}}{2.217 \text{ hr}} = 64.8 \frac{\text{km}}{\text{hr}} \xrightarrow{\text{SD}}$ **$65 \frac{\text{km}}{\text{hr}}$**

(c) $D = \sqrt{(73.5)^2 + (70.23)^2} = 101.7 \text{ km}$

$\theta = \tan^{-1} \frac{70.23}{73.5} = 43.70°$

$\alpha = 180° - 43.70° = 136.30°$

$\vec{D} = 101.7\angle 136.30° \text{ km} \xrightarrow{\text{SD}}$ **$1\bar{0}0\angle 136.30°$ km**

(d) $\vec{v} = \frac{\vec{D}}{T_T} = \frac{101.7\angle 136.30° \text{ km}}{2.217 \text{ hr}}$

$= 45.87\angle 136.30° \frac{\text{km}}{\text{hr}} \xrightarrow{\text{SD}}$ **$46\angle 136.30° \frac{\text{km}}{\text{hr}}$**

Problem Set 40

1. The distance to the cliff is 200 m, so the total distance to the cliff and back is 400 m.

$D = R \times T$

$400 \text{ m} = 350 \frac{\text{m}}{\text{s}} \times T$

$T = 1.143 \text{ s} \xrightarrow{\text{SD}}$ **1.14 s**

2. $D = R \times T = 325 \frac{\text{m}}{\cancel{\text{s}}} \times 2.50\cancel{\text{s}} = 812.5 \text{ m} \xrightarrow{\text{SD}}$ **813 m**

3. (a) $Q = 1.30 \cancel{\text{kg}} \times 31.0 \frac{\text{cal}}{\cancel{\text{kg}}\cdot\cancel{\text{C}°}} \times 304.3 \cancel{\text{C}°}$

$= 1.226 \times 10^4 \text{ calories} \xrightarrow{\text{SD}}$ **1.23×10^4 calories**

(b) $Q = 1.30 \cancel{\text{kg}} \times 24.5 \times 10^3 \frac{\text{J}}{\cancel{\text{kg}}} = 3.185 \times 10^4 \text{ J} \xrightarrow{\text{SD}}$ **3.19×10^4 J**

4. $Q_1 = 21.5 \cancel{\text{kg}} \times 56.0 \frac{\text{cal}}{\cancel{\text{kg}}\cdot\cancel{\text{C}°}} \times 951 \cancel{\text{C}°} = 1.145 \times 10^6 \text{ cal}$

Convert this to joules and get:

$Q_1 = 1.145 \times 10^6 \cancel{\text{cal}} \times \frac{4.186 \text{ J}}{1 \cancel{\text{cal}}} = 4.793 \times 10^6 \text{ J}$

$Q_2 = 21.5 \cancel{\text{kg}} \times 88.3 \times 10^3 \frac{\text{J}}{\cancel{\text{kg}}} = 1.898 \times 10^6 \text{ J}$

To find the total heat, sum Q_1 and Q_2.

$Q_T = 4.793 \times 10^6 \text{ J} + 1.898 \times 10^6 \text{ J}$

$= 6.691 \times 10^6 \text{ J} \xrightarrow{\text{SD}}$ **6.69×10^6 J**

5. $\frac{P_1V_1}{T_1} = \frac{P_2V_2}{T_2} \rightarrow \frac{P_1V_1}{T_1} = \frac{(3P_1)(2V_1)}{T_2}$

$\frac{\cancel{P_1V_1}}{T_1} \times \frac{1}{\cancel{P_1V_1}} = \frac{(3\cancel{P_1})(2\cancel{V_1})}{T_2} \times \frac{1}{\cancel{P_1V_1}}$

$T_2 = \mathbf{6T_1}$

6. Begin by finding the cross-sectional area of the bar.
$A = 3.0 \text{ m} \times 1.0 \text{ m} = 3.0 \text{ m}^2$

Now find the electrical resistance.

$R = \rho\frac{L}{A} = \frac{(2.82 \times 10^{-8} \ \Omega\cdot\cancel{\text{m}})(25 \cancel{\text{m}})}{3.0 \cancel{\text{m}^2}}$

$= 2.35 \times 10^{-7} \ \Omega \xrightarrow{\text{SD}}$ **2.4×10^{-7} Ω**

7. (a) $25 \times 10^{-3} \frac{\cancel{\text{coulomb}}}{\text{s}} \times \frac{1 \text{ electron}}{1.60 \times 10^{-19} \cancel{\text{coulomb}}}$

$= 1.56 \times 10^{17} \text{ electrons} \xrightarrow{\text{SD}}$ **1.6×10^{17} electrons**

(b) $V = IR = (25 \times 10^{-3} \text{ A})(210 \ \Omega) = 5.25 \text{ V} \xrightarrow{\text{SD}}$ **5.3 V**

8. (a) $m_g = 680\,\frac{\text{kg}}{\cancel{\text{m}^3}} \times 0.64\,\cancel{\text{m}^3} = 435.2\text{ kg} \xrightarrow{\text{SD}} \mathbf{440\ kg}$

(b) $F_B = 435.2\,\cancel{\text{kg}} \times 9.81\,\frac{\text{N}}{\cancel{\text{kg}}} = 4269.3\text{ N} \xrightarrow{\text{SD}} \mathbf{4300\ N}$

(c) $F = mg - F_B = 480.555\,\cancel{\text{kg}}\left(9.81\,\frac{\text{N}}{\cancel{\text{kg}}}\right) - 4269.3\text{ N}$

$= 444.94\text{ N} \xrightarrow{\text{SD}} \mathbf{440\ N}$

9. (a) Begin by finding the volume of the branch that is submerged.

$V_s = 3.8\text{ m}^3 \times 0.76 = 2.888\text{ m}^3$

Now find the mass of the water displaced.

$m_w = 1000\,\frac{\text{kg}}{\cancel{\text{m}^3}} \times 2.888\,\cancel{\text{m}^3} = 2888\text{ kg} \xrightarrow{\text{SD}} \mathbf{2900\ kg}$

(b) $F_B = 2888\,\cancel{\text{kg}} \times 9.81\,\frac{\text{N}}{\cancel{\text{kg}}} = 2.833 \times 10^4\text{ N} \xrightarrow{\text{SD}} \mathbf{2.8 \times 10^4\ N}$

(c) The weight of the branch equals the buoyancy force of the water, and the mass of the branch equals the mass of the water displaced.

$w_b = F_B = \mathbf{2.8 \times 10^4\ N}$

$m_b = m_w = \mathbf{2900\ kg}$

10. (a) $\omega(t) = \omega_0 + \alpha t$

$\omega(7.3) = 262 + (-3.3)(7.3) = 237.91\,\frac{\text{rad}}{\text{s}} \xrightarrow{\text{SD}} \mathbf{240\ \frac{rad}{s}}$

(b) $\Delta\theta = \omega_0 t + \frac{1}{2}\alpha t^2$

$= 262(7.3) + \frac{1}{2}(-3.3)(7.3)^2$

$= 1.825 \times 10^3\text{ rad} \xrightarrow{\text{SD}} \mathbf{1.8 \times 10^3\ rad}$

11. (a) $n = \frac{c}{v} = \frac{3.00 \times 10^8\text{ m/s}}{1.997 \times 10^8\text{ m/s}} = 1.502 \xrightarrow{\text{SD}} \mathbf{1.50}$

(b) $v = f\lambda$

$1.997 \times 10^8\,\frac{\text{m}}{\text{s}} = (5.120 \times 10^{14}\text{ s}^{-1})\lambda$

$\lambda = 3.9004 \times 10^{-7}\text{ m} \xrightarrow{\text{SD}} \mathbf{3.900 \times 10^{-7}\ m}$

12.

$\Sigma M_A = 0$

$500\text{ N}(x) - 400\text{ N}(10\text{ m}) = 0$

$500\text{ N}(x) = 4000\text{ N}\cdot\text{m}$

$x = \mathbf{8\ m}$

$\Sigma F_y = 0$

$F_A + 400\text{ N} - 500\text{ N} = 0$

$F_A = \mathbf{100\ N}$

13. Begin by finding the component of the weight of the 21-kg block that is parallel to the plane.

$F_x = mg\sin 51°$

$= (21)(9.81)\sin 51°$

$= 160.1\text{ N}$

Next, write a $\Sigma F_x = ma_x$ equation for the 21-kg block. Choose up the plane as the positive direction for motion.

$\Sigma F_x = ma_x$

$T - F_x = ma$

$T - 160.1 = 21a$

$T = 160.1 + 21a$ (a)

Now, write a $\Sigma F_y = ma_y$ equation for the 26-kg object.

$\Sigma F_y = ma_y$

$mg - T = ma$

$(26)(9.81) - T = 26a$

$T = 255.06 - 26a$ (b)

Substitute (b) into (a) to find the acceleration.

(a) $(255.06 - 26a) = 160.1 + 21a$

$94.96 = 47a$

$a = 2.020\,\frac{\text{m}}{\text{s}^2} \xrightarrow{\text{SD}} \mathbf{2.0\ \frac{m}{s^2}}$ **up the plane**

Substitute the acceleration into (a) to find T.

(a) $T = 160.1 + 21(2.020) = 202.5\text{ N} \xrightarrow{\text{SD}} \mathbf{2\bar{0}0\ N}$

14. Begin by converting the temperature to kelvins.
$T_1 = 20 + 273 = 293 \text{ K}$

Now use the ideal gas law and get:

$$\frac{V_1}{T_1} = \frac{V_2}{T_2}$$

$$\frac{2.3 \text{ m}^3}{293 \text{ K}} = \frac{5.1 \text{ m}^3}{T_2}$$

$$T_2 = 649.7 \text{ K} \xrightarrow{SD} \mathbf{650\ K}$$

Convert the temperature to °C and get:

$$649.7 - 273 = 376.7°\text{C} \xrightarrow{SD} \mathbf{380°C}$$

15.

$$\frac{\sin \theta_1}{v_1} = \frac{\sin \theta_2}{v_2}$$

$$\frac{\sin 23°}{1.8415 \times 10^8} = \frac{\sin \theta_r}{3.00 \times 10^8}$$

$$\theta_r = \mathbf{39.53°}$$

16. (a)

$$m_1v_1 + m_2v_2 = (m_1 + m_2)v_3$$

$$(3.09 \times 10^{-3})(1700) + (5.52)(0) = (5.52309)v_3$$

$$v_3 = +0.9511 \frac{\text{m}}{\text{s}} \xrightarrow{SD} \mathbf{+0.951 \frac{m}{s}}$$

(b)
$$KE = \frac{1}{2}mv_3^2$$

$$= \frac{1}{2}(5.52309)(0.9511)^2$$

$$= 2.498 \text{ J} \xrightarrow{SD} \mathbf{2.50\ J}$$

(c)
$$PE = mgh$$

$$2.498 = (5.52309)(9.81)h$$

$$h = 4.610 \times 10^{-2} \text{ m} \xrightarrow{SD} \mathbf{4.61 \times 10^{-2}\ m}$$

17. (a) To find the ball's velocity on the way down, use the displacement equation to find t. Then use the motion equation to find $v(t)$. Note that energy conservation cannot be used to solve this part of the problem.

$$\Delta y = v_0t + \frac{1}{2}at^2$$

$$-21 = -8.2t + \frac{1}{2}(-9.81)t^2$$

$$0 = 4.905t^2 + 8.2t - 21$$

Use the quadratic formula to solve this equation for t.

$$t = \frac{-8.2 \pm \sqrt{(8.2)^2 - 4(4.905)(-21)}}{2(4.905)} = 1.396 \text{ s}$$

Use this time in the motion equation to find v_d.

$$v(t) = v_0 + at$$

$$v_d = -8.2 + (-9.81)(1.396)$$

$$v_d = -21.89 \frac{\text{m}}{\text{s}} \xrightarrow{SD} \mathbf{-22 \frac{m}{s}}$$

Use energy conservation to find the maximum velocity on the way up.

$$PE = mgh = 1.5 \cancel{\text{kg}} \times 9.81 \frac{\text{N}}{\cancel{\text{kg}}} \times 13 \text{ m} = 191.30 \text{ J}$$

$$KE = \frac{1}{2}mv_u^2$$

$$191.30 \text{ J} = \frac{1}{2}(1.5 \text{ kg})v_u^2$$

$$v_u = +15.97 \frac{\text{m}}{\text{s}} \xrightarrow{SD} \mathbf{+16 \frac{m}{s}}$$

(b)
$$\Delta KE = KE_d - KE_u$$

$$= \frac{1}{2}(1.5)(-21.89)^2 - 191.30$$

$$= 168.1 \text{ J} \xrightarrow{SD} \mathbf{170\ J}$$

18. (a)
$$\vec{F} = m\vec{a}$$

$$= 513 \text{ kg} \times 52.0 \text{ m}\cdot\text{s}^{-2}$$

$$= 2.668 \times 10^4 \text{ N} \xrightarrow{SD} \mathbf{2.67 \times 10^4\ N\ to\ the\ right}$$

(b) $\Sigma\vec{F}_x = 28{,}340 \text{ N} - 2.668 \times 10^4 \text{ N} = \mathbf{1.66 \times 10^3\ N\ to\ the\ left}$

19. (a) $W = F \times D = 136\,\cancel{kg}\left(9.81\,\frac{N}{\cancel{kg}}\right) \times 1.5\text{ m} = 2001\text{ J} \xrightarrow{SD} \mathbf{2\bar{0}00\ J}$

(b) $P_{av} = \frac{W}{\Delta t} = \frac{2001\text{ J}}{11\text{ s}} = 181.9\text{ W} \xrightarrow{SD} \mathbf{180\ W}$

20. Convert 204°F to °C.

$T_C = \frac{5}{9}(T_F - 32)$

$= \frac{5}{9}(204° - 32)$

$= 95.56°C$

Convert 95.56°C to kelvins.

$T_K = T_C + 273$

$= 95.56 + 273$

$= 368.56\text{ K} \xrightarrow{SD} \mathbf{369\ K}$

PROBLEM SET 41

1. (a) Begin by finding the weight supported by the seat and spring.

$w = 320\text{ N} \times 0.900 = 288\text{ N}$

Now calculate the spring constant.

$F = kx$

$288\text{ N} = k(2.00\text{ cm})$

$k = \mathbf{144\ \frac{N}{cm}}$

Convert to N/m and get:

$144\,\frac{N}{\cancel{cm}} \times \frac{100\,\cancel{cm}}{1\text{ m}} = \mathbf{1.44 \times 10^4\ \frac{N}{m}}$

(b) $W = \frac{1}{2}kx^2 = \frac{1}{2}(1.44 \times 10^4)(2.00 \times 10^{-2})^2 = \mathbf{2.88\ J}$

2. (a) Begin by finding the weight of the mass.

$w = mg = 5.0\,\cancel{kg} \times 9.81\,\frac{N}{\cancel{kg}} = 49.05\text{ N}$

Now calculate the spring constant.

$F = kx$

$49.05\text{ N} = k(5.0\text{ cm})$

$k = 9.81\,\frac{N}{cm} \xrightarrow{SD} \mathbf{9.8\ \frac{N}{cm}}$

Convert to N/m and get:

$9.81\,\frac{N}{\cancel{cm}} \times \frac{100\,\cancel{cm}}{1\text{ m}} = 981\,\frac{N}{m} \xrightarrow{SD} \mathbf{980\ \frac{N}{m}}$

(b) $W = \frac{1}{2}kx^2 = \frac{1}{2}(981)(0.050)^2 = 1.226\text{ J} \xrightarrow{SD} \mathbf{1.2\ J}$

3. $D = R \times T$

$2500\text{ m} = 341\,\frac{m}{s} \times T$

$T = 7.331\text{ s} \xrightarrow{SD} \mathbf{7.3\ s}$

4. $D = R \times T$

$150\text{ m} = R \times 0.430\text{ s}$

$R = 348.84\,\frac{m}{s} \xrightarrow{SD} \mathbf{349\ \frac{m}{s}}$

5. (a) $Q = 0.65\,\cancel{kg} \times 4186\,\frac{J}{\cancel{kg}\cdot\cancel{C°}} \times 27\,\cancel{C°}$

$= 7.346 \times 10^4\text{ J} \xrightarrow{SD} \mathbf{7.3 \times 10^4\ J}$

(b) $Q = 0.65\,\cancel{kg} \times 334 \times 10^3\,\frac{J}{\cancel{kg}} = 2.171 \times 10^5\text{ J} \xrightarrow{SD} \mathbf{2.2 \times 10^5\ J}$

6. $Q_1 = 12.5\,\cancel{kg} \times 93.0\,\frac{cal}{\cancel{kg}\cdot\cancel{C°}} \times 1095\,\cancel{C°} = 1.273 \times 10^6\text{ cal}$

Convert this to joules and get:

$1.273 \times 10^6\,\cancel{cal} \times \frac{4.186\text{ J}}{1\,\cancel{cal}} = 5.329 \times 10^6\text{ J}$

$Q_2 = 12.5\,\cancel{kg} \times 134 \times 10^3\,\frac{J}{\cancel{kg}} = 1.675 \times 10^6\text{ J}$

To find the total heat, sum Q_1 and Q_2.

$Q_T = 5.329 \times 10^6\text{ J} + 1.675 \times 10^6\text{ J}$

$= 7.004 \times 10^6\text{ J} \xrightarrow{SD} \mathbf{7.00 \times 10^6\ J}$

7. $\frac{P_1V_1}{T_1} = \frac{P_2V_2}{T_2} \rightarrow \frac{P_1V_1}{T_1} = \frac{P_2\left(\frac{V_1}{3}\right)}{(3T_1)}$

$\frac{P_1\cancel{V_1}}{\cancel{T_1}} \times \frac{\cancel{T_1}}{\cancel{V_1}} = \frac{P_2\left(\frac{\cancel{V_1}}{3}\right)}{(3\cancel{T_1})} \times \frac{\cancel{T_1}}{\cancel{V_1}}$

$\mathbf{9P_1 = P_2}$

8. Begin by finding the cross-sectional area of the material.
$A = 4.0\text{ m} \times 1.5\text{ m} = 6.0\text{ m}^2$

Now find the resistivity, ρ.

$$R = \rho\frac{L}{A}$$
$$123\ \Omega = \frac{\rho(8.0\text{ m})}{6.0\text{ m}^2}$$
$$\rho = 92.25\ \Omega\cdot\text{m} \xrightarrow{\text{SD}} \mathbf{92\ \Omega\cdot m}$$

9. (a) $0.23\,\frac{\text{coulomb}}{\text{s}} \times \frac{1\text{ electron}}{1.60 \times 10^{-19}\text{ coulomb}}$

$= 1.4375 \times 10^{18}\text{ electrons} \xrightarrow{\text{SD}} \mathbf{1.4 \times 10^{18}\ electrons}$

(b) $V = IR = (0.23\text{ A})(1200\ \Omega) = 276\text{ V} \xrightarrow{\text{SD}} \mathbf{280\ V}$

10. (a) $m_e = 0.81\,\frac{\text{g}}{\text{cm}^3} \times 1.00\text{ cm}^3 = \mathbf{0.81\ g}$

Convert 0.81 g to kg and get:

$0.81\text{ g} \times \frac{1\text{ kg}}{1000\text{ g}} = \mathbf{8.1 \times 10^{-4}\ kg}$

(b) $F_B = 8.1 \times 10^{-4}\text{ kg} \times 9.81\,\frac{\text{N}}{\text{kg}}$

$= 7.946 \times 10^{-3}\text{ N} \xrightarrow{\text{SD}} \mathbf{7.9 \times 10^{-3}\ N}$

(c) $F = mg - F_B = (0.100\text{ kg})\left(9.81\,\frac{\text{N}}{\text{kg}}\right) - 7.946 \times 10^{-3}\text{ N}$

$= 0.973\text{ N} \xrightarrow{\text{SD}} \mathbf{0.97\ N}$

11. (a) Begin by finding the volume of the sailboat that is submerged.
$V_s = 36.0\text{ m}^3 \times 0.650 = 23.4\text{ m}^3$

Now find the mass of the water displaced.

$m_w = 1000\,\frac{\text{kg}}{\text{m}^3} \times 23.4\text{ m}^3 = \mathbf{2.34 \times 10^4\ kg}$

(b) $F_B = 2.34 \times 10^4\text{ kg} \times 9.81\,\frac{\text{N}}{\text{kg}}$

$= 2.2955 \times 10^5\text{ N} \xrightarrow{\text{SD}} \mathbf{2.30 \times 10^5\ N}$

(c) The weight of the boat equals the buoyancy force of the water, and the mass of the boat equals the mass of the water displaced.

$w_b = F_B = \mathbf{2.30 \times 10^5\ N}$

$m_b = m_w = \mathbf{2.34 \times 10^4\ kg}$

12. (a) $\omega(t) = \omega_0 + \alpha t$

$\omega(3.5) = 65 + (-5.1)(3.5) = 47.15\,\frac{\text{rad}}{\text{s}} \xrightarrow{\text{SD}} \mathbf{47\ \frac{rad}{s}}$

(b) $\Delta\theta = \omega_0 t + \frac{1}{2}\alpha t^2$

$= (65)(3.5) + \frac{1}{2}(-5.1)(3.5)^2 = 196.3\text{ rad} \xrightarrow{\text{SD}} \mathbf{2\bar{0}0\ rad}$

13. (a) $n = \frac{c}{v} = \frac{3.00 \times 10^8\text{ m/s}}{1.9426 \times 10^8\text{ m/s}} = 1.544 \xrightarrow{\text{SD}} \mathbf{1.54}$

(b) $v = f\lambda$

$1.9426 \times 10^8\text{ m/s} = (7121.56 \times 10^{11}\text{ s}^{-1})\lambda$

$\lambda = 2.72777 \times 10^{-7}\text{ m} \xrightarrow{\text{SD}} \mathbf{2.7278 \times 10^{-7}\ m}$

14. Begin by writing a $\Sigma F_x = ma_x$ equation for the 12-kg block. Choose to the left as the positive direction for motion.

$\Sigma F_x = ma_x$
$T = ma$
$T = 12a$ (a)

Next, write a $\Sigma F_y = ma_y$ equation for the 14-kg object.

$\Sigma F_y = ma_y$
$mg - T = ma$
$14(9.81) - T = 14a$
$T = 137.34 - 14a$ (b)

Substitute (b) into (a) to find the acceleration.
(a) $(137.34 - 14a) = 12a$
$137.34 = 26a$

$a = 5.282\,\frac{\text{m}}{\text{s}^2} \xrightarrow{\text{SD}} \mathbf{5.3\ \frac{m}{s^2}\ to\ the\ left}$

Substitute the acceleration into (a) to find T.
(a) $T = 12(5.282) = 63.38\text{ N} \xrightarrow{\text{SD}} \mathbf{63\ N}$

15. Begin by finding the component of the weight of the 15-kg block that is parallel to the plane.
$F_x = mg \sin 34° = (15)(9.81) \sin 34° = 82.285 \text{ N}$

Next, write a $\sum F_x = ma_x$ equation for the 15-kg block. Choose up the plane as the positive direction for motion.

$$\sum F_x = ma_x$$
$$T - F_x = ma$$
$$T - 82.285 = 15a$$
$$T = 82.285 + 15a \quad \text{(a)}$$

Now, write a $\sum F_y = ma_y$ equation for the 5.3-kg block.

$$\sum F_y = ma_y$$
$$mg - T = ma$$
$$(5.3)(9.81) - T = 5.3a$$
$$T = 51.99 - 5.3a \quad \text{(b)}$$

Substitute (b) into (a) to find the acceleration.

(a) $(51.99 - 5.3a) = 82.285 + 15a$
$-30.295 = 20.3a$

$$a = -1.492 \frac{\text{m}}{\text{s}^2} \xrightarrow{\text{SD}} \mathbf{1.5 \frac{m}{s^2} \text{ down the plane}}$$

Substitute the acceleration into (a) to find T.

(a) $T = 82.285 + 15(-1.492) = 59.9 \text{ N} \xrightarrow{\text{SD}} \mathbf{6\bar{0} \text{ N}}$

16. Begin by converting the temperatures to kelvins.
$T_1 = 18 + 273 = 291 \text{ K}$
$T_2 = 78 + 273 = 351 \text{ K}$

Now use the ideal gas law and get:

$$\frac{P_1V_1}{T_1} = \frac{P_2V_2}{T_2}$$

$$\frac{(1.02 \times 10^5 \text{ Pa})(5.3 \text{ m}^3)}{291 \text{ K}} = \frac{P_2(1.6 \text{ m}^3)}{351 \text{ K}}$$

$$P_2 = 4.075 \times 10^5 \text{ Pa} \xrightarrow{\text{SD}} \mathbf{4.1 \times 10^5 \text{ Pa}}$$

17. Begin by writing a momentum equation.

$$m_1v_1 + m_2v_2 = (m_1 + m_2)v_3$$
$$2.3(2.7\underline{/31°}) + 2.0(4.5\underline{/105°}) = (2.3 + 2.0)v_3$$
$$6.21\underline{/31°} + 9.0\underline{/105°} = (4.3)v_3 \quad \text{(a)}$$

Now find the sum of the x and y components of the initial momenta.

$\sum mv_x = 6.21 \cos 31° + 9.0 \cos 105° = 2.994 \text{ kg·m·s}^{-1}$

$\sum mv_y = 6.21 \sin 31° + 9.0 \sin 105° = 11.892 \text{ kg·m·s}^{-1}$

$\sum mv_R = (2.994i + 11.892j) \text{ kg·m·s}^{-1}$

Convert this resultant to polar form and get:

$\sum mv_R = \sqrt{(2.994)^2 + (11.892)^2} = 12.263 \text{ kg·m·s}^{-1}$

$\theta = \tan^{-1} \frac{11.892}{2.994} = 75.87°$

$\sum mv_R = 12.263\underline{/75.87°} \text{ kg·m·s}^{-1}$

Use this momentum in (a) to find v_3.

(a) $12.263\underline{/75.87°} = (4.3)v_3$

$$v_3 = 2.85\underline{/75.87°} \frac{\text{m}}{\text{s}} \xrightarrow{\text{SD}} \mathbf{2.9\underline{/75.87°} \frac{m}{s}}$$

18. (a) $\vec{F} = m\vec{a}$

$365 \text{ N} = (15 \text{ kg})\vec{a}$

$$\vec{a} = 24.33 \frac{\text{m}}{\text{s}^2} \xrightarrow{\text{SD}} \mathbf{24 \frac{m}{s^2} \text{ to the left}}$$

(b) Impulse $= F\Delta t$

$= 365 \text{ N} \times 6.0 \text{ s} = 2.190 \times 10^3 \text{ N·s} \xrightarrow{\text{SD}} \mathbf{2.2 \times 10^3 \text{ N·s}}$

(c) $F\Delta t = m(v_2 - v_1)$

$$2.190 \times 10^3 \text{ N·s} = 15 \text{ kg}\left(v_2 - 0 \frac{\text{m}}{\text{s}}\right)$$

$$v_2 = 146 \frac{\text{m}}{\text{s}} \xrightarrow{\text{SD}} \mathbf{150 \frac{m}{s} \text{ to the left}}$$

19. (a) $F = ma = 207 \text{ kg} \times 3.40 \frac{\text{m}}{\text{s}^2} = 703.8 \text{ N} \xrightarrow{\text{SD}} \mathbf{704 \text{ N}}$

(b) $\Sigma F_x = 800 \text{ N} - 703.8 \text{ N} = \mathbf{96.2 \text{ N}}$

20. $a_{\text{av}} = \frac{v_2 - v_1}{t_2 - t_1} = \frac{89 - 16}{61 - 6.0} \frac{\text{km/hr}}{\text{s}} = 1.327 \frac{\text{km}}{\text{hr} \cdot \text{s}}$

Convert this to $\text{m} \cdot \text{s}^{-2}$ and get:

$1.327 \frac{\text{km}}{\text{hr} \cdot \text{s}} \times \frac{1000 \text{ m}}{1 \text{ km}} \times \frac{1 \text{ hr}}{60 \text{ min}} \times \frac{1 \text{ min}}{60 \text{ s}}$

$= +0.369 \frac{\text{m}}{\text{s}^2} \xrightarrow{\text{SD}} \mathbf{+0.37 \frac{m}{s^2}}$

Problem Set 42

1. (a) $I = \frac{V}{R} = \frac{20 \text{ V}}{10 \, \Omega} = \mathbf{2 \text{ A}}$

(b) $P = VI = (20 \text{ V})(2 \text{ A}) = \mathbf{40 \text{ W}}$

(c) $40 \frac{\text{J}}{\text{s}} \times 10 \text{ s} = \mathbf{400 \text{ J}}$

2. (a) $V_R = IR = (2.0 \text{ A})(6.0 \, \Omega) = \mathbf{12 \text{ V}}$

(b) $V_R = IR = (-4.0 \text{ A})(8.0 \, \Omega) = \mathbf{-32 \text{ V}}$

(c) $P = VI = (6.0 \text{ V})(2.0 \text{ A}) = \mathbf{12 \text{ W}}$

(d) $P = VI = (8.0 \text{ V})(-4.0 \text{ A}) = \mathbf{-32 \text{ W}}$

3. (a) Begin by finding the weight of the mass.

$w = mg = 21 \text{ kg} \times 9.81 \frac{\text{N}}{\text{kg}} = 206.01 \text{ N}$

Now calculate the spring constant.

$F = kx$

$206.01 \text{ N} = k(4.0 \text{ cm})$

$k = 51.50 \frac{\text{N}}{\text{cm}} \xrightarrow{\text{SD}} \mathbf{52 \frac{N}{cm}}$

Convert to N/m and get:

$51.50 \frac{\text{N}}{\text{cm}} \times \frac{100 \text{ cm}}{1 \text{ m}} = 5150 \frac{\text{N}}{\text{m}} \xrightarrow{\text{SD}} \mathbf{5200 \frac{N}{m}}$

(b) $W = \frac{1}{2}kx^2 = \frac{1}{2}(5150)(0.040)^2 = 4.12 \text{ J} \xrightarrow{\text{SD}} \mathbf{4.1 \text{ J}}$

4. (a) Begin by finding the weight of the block.

$w = mg = 15 \text{ kg} \times 9.81 \frac{\text{N}}{\text{kg}} = 147.15 \text{ N}$

Now calculate the spring constant.

$F = kx$

$147.15 \text{ N} = k(3.5 \text{ cm})$

$k = 42.04 \frac{\text{N}}{\text{cm}} \xrightarrow{\text{SD}} \mathbf{42 \frac{N}{cm}}$

Convert to N/m and get:

$42.04 \frac{\text{N}}{\text{cm}} \times \frac{100 \text{ cm}}{1 \text{ m}} = 4204 \frac{\text{N}}{\text{m}} \xrightarrow{\text{SD}} \mathbf{4200 \frac{N}{m}}$

(b) $W = \frac{1}{2}kx^2 = \frac{1}{2}(4204)(0.035)^2 = 2.57 \text{ J} \xrightarrow{\text{SD}} \mathbf{2.6 \text{ J}}$

5. $D = R \times T = 339 \frac{\text{m}}{\text{s}} \times 6.2 \text{ s} = 2101.8 \text{ m} \xrightarrow{\text{SD}} \mathbf{2100 \text{ m}}$

6. (a) $Q = 1.5 \text{ kg} \times 4186 \frac{\text{J}}{\text{kg} \cdot \text{C}^\circ} \times 41 \text{ C}^\circ$

$= 2.57 \times 10^5 \text{ J} \xrightarrow{\text{SD}} \mathbf{2.6 \times 10^5 \text{ J}}$

(b) $Q = 1.5 \text{ kg} \times 2256 \times 10^3 \frac{\text{J}}{\text{kg}} = 3.38 \times 10^6 \text{ J} \xrightarrow{\text{SD}} \mathbf{3.4 \times 10^6 \text{ J}}$

7. Begin by finding the heat necessary to melt the mercury.

$Q_1 = 42.7 \text{ kg} \times 11.8 \times 10^3 \frac{\text{J}}{\text{kg}} = 5.039 \times 10^5 \text{ J}$

Next, find the heat necessary to heat the liquid mercury to its boiling point.

$Q_2 = 42.7 \text{ kg} \times 33.0 \frac{\text{cal}}{\text{kg} \cdot \text{C}^\circ} \times 396 \text{ C}^\circ = 5.58 \times 10^5 \text{ cal}$

Convert 5.58×10^5 cal to joules and get:

$Q_2 = 5.58 \times 10^5 \text{ cal} \times \frac{4.186 \text{ J}}{1 \text{ cal}} = 2.336 \times 10^6 \text{ J}$

Now, find the the heat necessary to vaporize the mercury.

$Q_3 = 42.7 \text{ kg} \times 272 \times 10^3 \frac{\text{J}}{\text{kg}} = 1.1614 \times 10^7 \text{ J}$

To find the total heat, sum Q_1, Q_2, and Q_3.

$Q_T = 5.039 \times 10^5 \text{ J} + 2.336 \times 10^6 \text{ J} + 1.1614 \times 10^7 \text{ J}$

$= 1.445 \times 10^7 \text{ J} \xrightarrow{\text{SD}} \mathbf{1.45 \times 10^7 \text{ J}}$

8. $\frac{P_1V_1}{T_1} = \frac{P_2V_2}{T_2} \rightarrow \frac{P_1V_1}{T_1} = \frac{(2P_1)V_2}{(3T_1)}$

$$\frac{\cancel{P_1}V_1}{\cancel{T_1}} \times \frac{\cancel{T_1}}{\cancel{P_1}} = \frac{(2\cancel{P_1})V_2}{(3\cancel{T_1})} \times \frac{\cancel{T_1}}{\cancel{P_1}}$$

$$\mathbf{\frac{3V_1}{2}} = V_2$$

9. Begin by finding the cross-sectional area of the top of the figure.

$A = 10 \text{ m} \times 25 \text{ m} = 250 \text{ m}^2$

Now find the resistivity, ρ.

$$R = \rho\frac{L}{A}$$

$$503\ \Omega = \frac{\rho(50 \text{ m})}{250 \text{ m}^2}$$

$$\rho = 2.515 \times 10^3\ \Omega\cdot\text{m} \xrightarrow{\text{SD}} \mathbf{2.5 \times 10^3\ \Omega\cdot m}$$

10. (a) $m_b = 0.90 \frac{\text{g}}{\cancel{\text{cm}^3}} \times 0.80\ \cancel{\text{cm}^3} = \mathbf{0.72\ g}$

Convert 0.72 g to kg and get:

$$0.72\ \cancel{\text{g}} \times \frac{1 \text{ kg}}{1000\ \cancel{\text{g}}} = \mathbf{7.2 \times 10^{-4}\ kg}$$

(b) $F_B = 7.2 \times 10^{-4}\ \cancel{\text{kg}} \times 9.81 \frac{\text{N}}{\cancel{\text{kg}}}$

$$= 7.06 \times 10^{-3} \text{ N} \xrightarrow{\text{SD}} \mathbf{7.1 \times 10^{-3}\ N}$$

(c) $F = mg - F_B = (0.075)(9.81) - 7.06 \times 10^{-3}$

$$= 0.729 \text{ N} \xrightarrow{\text{SD}} \mathbf{0.73\ N}$$

11. (a) Begin by finding the volume of the buoy that is submerged.

$V_s = 3.50 \text{ m}^3 \times 0.850 = 2.975 \text{ m}^3$

Now find the mass of the water displaced.

$$m_w = 1000 \frac{\text{kg}}{\cancel{\text{m}^3}} \times 2.975\ \cancel{\text{m}^3} = 2975 \text{ kg} \xrightarrow{\text{SD}} \mathbf{2980\ kg}$$

(b) $F_B = 2975\ \cancel{\text{kg}} \times 9.81 \frac{\text{N}}{\cancel{\text{kg}}} = 2.918 \times 10^4 \text{ N} \xrightarrow{\text{SD}} \mathbf{2.92 \times 10^4\ N}$

(c) The weight of the buoy equals the buoyancy force of the water, and the mass of the buoy equals the mass of the water displaced.

$$w_b = F_B = \mathbf{2.92 \times 10^4\ N}$$

$$m_b = m_w = \mathbf{2980\ kg}$$

12. (a) $n = \frac{c}{v}$

$$= \frac{3.00 \times 10^8 \text{ m/s}}{1.559 \times 10^8 \text{ m/s}}$$

$$= 1.924 \xrightarrow{\text{SD}} \mathbf{1.92}$$

(b) $v = f\lambda$

$$1.559 \times 10^8 \text{ m/s} = f(5.886 \times 10^{-7} \text{ m})$$

$$f = 2.6487 \times 10^{14} \text{ Hz} \xrightarrow{\text{SD}} \mathbf{2.649 \times 10^{14}\ Hz}$$

13. Begin by writing a $\sum F_x = ma_x$ equation for the 115-kg block. Choose to the right as the positive direction for motion.

$$\sum F_x = ma_x$$

$$T = ma$$

$$T = 115a \quad \text{(a)}$$

Next, write a $\sum F_y = ma_y$ equation for the 75-kg object.

$$\sum F_y = ma_y$$

$$mg - T = ma$$

$$(75)(9.81) - T = 75a$$

$$T = 735.75 - 75a \quad \text{(b)}$$

Substitute (b) into (a) to find the acceleration.

(a) $(735.75 - 75a) = 115a$

$$735.75 = 190a$$

$$a = 3.872 \frac{\text{m}}{\text{s}^2} \xrightarrow{\text{SD}} \mathbf{3.9 \frac{m}{s^2}\ to\ the\ right}$$

Substitute the acceleration into (a) to find T.

(a) $T = 115(3.872) = 445.28 \text{ N} \xrightarrow{\text{SD}} \mathbf{450\ N}$

14. Begin by converting the temperature to kelvins.
$T_1 = 21.870 + 273 = 294.87\text{ K}$

Now use the ideal gas law and get:

$$\frac{P_1V_1}{T_1} = \frac{P_2V_2}{T_2}$$

$$\frac{(1.028 \times 10^5\text{ Pa})(2.361\text{ m}^3)}{294.87\text{ K}} = \frac{(110.417 \times 10^5\text{ Pa})(5\text{ m}^3)}{T_2}$$

$$T_2 = 6.707 \times 10^4\text{ K} \xrightarrow{\text{SD}} \mathbf{7 \times 10^4\text{ K}}$$

15. Begin by writing a momentum equation.

$$m_1v_1 + m_2v_2 = (m_1 + m_2)v_3$$

$$1.3(6.4\angle\underline{45°}) + 5.7(5.7\angle\underline{180°}) = (1.3 + 5.7)v_3$$

$$8.32\angle\underline{45°} + 32.49\angle\underline{180°} = (7.0)v_3 \qquad \text{(a)}$$

Now find the sum of the x and y components of the initial momenta.

$\Sigma mv_x = 8.32\cos 45° + 32.49\cos 180° = -26.607\text{ kg}\cdot\text{m}\cdot\text{s}^{-1}$

$\Sigma mv_y = 8.32\sin 45° + 32.49\sin 180° = 5.883\text{ kg}\cdot\text{m}\cdot\text{s}^{-1}$

$\Sigma mv_R = (-26.607i + 5.883j)\text{ kg}\cdot\text{m}\cdot\text{s}^{-1}$

Convert this resultant to polar form and get:

$\Sigma mv_R = \sqrt{(-26.607)^2 + (5.883)^2} = 27.250\text{ kg}\cdot\text{m}\cdot\text{s}^{-1}$

$\theta = \tan^{-1}\dfrac{5.883}{-26.607} = -12.47°$

Since θ is a 2nd-quadrant angle: $\theta = 180° - 12.47° = 167.53°$

$\Sigma mv_R = 27.250\angle\underline{167.53°}\text{ kg}\cdot\text{m}\cdot\text{s}^{-1}$

Use this momentum in (a) to find v_3.

(a) $27.250\angle\underline{167.53°} = (7.0)v_3$

$$v_3 = 3.89\angle\underline{167.53°}\ \frac{\text{m}}{\text{s}} \xrightarrow{\text{SD}} \mathbf{3.9\angle\underline{167.53°}\ \frac{m}{s}}$$

16. (a) To find the ball's velocity on the way down, use the displacement equation to find t. Then use the motion equation to find $v(t)$. Note that energy conservation cannot be used to solve this part of the problem.

$$\Delta y = v_0t + \frac{1}{2}at^2$$

$$-45 = -8.6t + \frac{1}{2}(-9.81)t^2$$

$$0 = 4.905t^2 + 8.6t - 45$$

Use the quadratic formula to solve this equation for t.

$$t = \frac{-8.6 \pm \sqrt{(8.6)^2 - 4(4.905)(-45)}}{2(4.905)} = 2.277\text{ s}$$

Use this time in the motion equation to find v_d.

$$v(t) = v_0 + at$$

$$v_d = -8.6 + (-9.81)(2.277)$$

$$= -30.94\ \frac{\text{m}}{\text{s}} \xrightarrow{\text{SD}} \mathbf{-31\ \frac{m}{s}}$$

Use energy conservation to find the maximum velocity on the way up.

$$PE = mgh = 2.3\text{ kg} \times 9.81\ \frac{\text{N}}{\text{kg}} \times 42\text{ m} = 947.65\text{ J}$$

$$KE = \frac{1}{2}mv_u^2$$

$$947.65\text{ J} = \frac{1}{2}(2.3\text{ kg})v_u^2$$

$$v_u = +28.71\ \frac{\text{m}}{\text{s}} \xrightarrow{\text{SD}} \mathbf{+29\ \frac{m}{s}}$$

(b) $\Delta KE = KE_d - KE_u$

$$= \frac{1}{2}(2.3)(-30.94)^2 - 947.65$$

$$= 153.23\text{ J} \xrightarrow{\text{SD}} \mathbf{150\text{ J}}$$

17. Begin by finding the pressure produced by the water.

$$P_W = 1002\ \frac{\text{kg}}{\text{m}^{3}} \times 9.81\ \frac{\text{N}}{\text{kg}} \times 3.000\text{ m} = 2.949 \times 10^4\text{ Pa}$$

Now sum this pressure with the atmospheric pressure and find P.

$$P = 2.949 \times 10^4\text{ Pa} + 1.01 \times 10^5\text{ Pa}$$

$$= 1.3049 \times 10^5\text{ Pa} \xrightarrow{\text{SD}} \mathbf{1.30 \times 10^5\text{ Pa}}$$

18. Begin by converting units in order to get an answer in meters. Then use the displacement equation:

$$v_0 = 5.00\,\frac{\cancel{\text{km}}}{\cancel{\text{hr}}} \times \frac{1000\text{ m}}{1\,\cancel{\text{km}}} \times \frac{1\,\cancel{\text{hr}}}{60\,\cancel{\text{min}}} \times \frac{1\,\cancel{\text{min}}}{60\text{ s}} = 1.389\,\frac{\text{m}}{\text{s}}$$

$$a = 90.0\,\frac{\cancel{\text{cm}}}{\text{s}^2} \times \frac{1\text{ m}}{100\,\cancel{\text{cm}}} = 0.900\,\frac{\text{m}}{\text{s}^2}$$

$$\Delta x = v_0 t + \frac{1}{2}at^2$$

$$= 1.389(45.0) + \frac{1}{2}(0.900)(45.0)^2$$

$$= 973.755\text{ m} \xrightarrow{\text{SD}} \mathbf{974\text{ m}}$$

19.

$$\Sigma F_y = ma_y$$
$$F_N - mg = ma_y$$
$$F_N - 40(9.81) = (40)(11)$$
$$F_N = 832.4\text{ N} \xrightarrow{\text{SD}} \mathbf{830\text{ N}}$$

20.

$$\Sigma M_A = 0$$
$$(300)(x) - (800)(10 - x) = 0$$
$$300x - 8000 + 800x = 0$$
$$1100x = 8000$$
$$x = 7.273\text{ m} \xrightarrow{\text{SD}} \mathbf{7.3\text{ m}}$$

$$\Sigma F_y = 0$$
$$300\text{ N} + 800\text{ N} - F_A = 0$$
$$F_A = \mathbf{11\bar{0}0\text{ N}}$$

Problem Set 43

1. Begin by writing a $\Sigma F_x = ma_x$ equation for the 2.0-kg block. Choose to the right as the positive direction for motion.

$$\Sigma F_x = ma_x$$
$$T - \mu_k mg = ma$$
$$T - (0.20)(2.0)(9.81) = 2.0a$$
$$T = 3.924 + 2.0a \qquad \text{(a)}$$

Next, write a $\Sigma F_y = ma_y$ equation for the 4.0-kg block.

$$\Sigma F_y = ma_y$$
$$mg - T = ma$$
$$(4.0)(9.81) - T = 4.0a$$
$$T = 39.24 - 4.0a \qquad \text{(b)}$$

Substitute (b) into (a) to find the acceleration.

$$\text{(a)}\quad (39.24 - 4.0a) = 3.924 + 2.0a$$
$$35.32 = 6.0a$$
$$a = 5.887\,\frac{\text{m}}{\text{s}^2} \xrightarrow{\text{SD}} \mathbf{5.9\,\frac{m}{s^2}\text{ to the right}}$$

Substitute the acceleration into (a) to find T.

$$\text{(a)}\quad T = 3.924 + 2.0(5.887) = 15.698\text{ N} \xrightarrow{\text{SD}} \mathbf{16\text{ N}}$$

2. Begin by finding the components of the weight of the 3.0-kg block that are parallel and perpendicular to the plane.

$$F_x = mg\sin 40° = (3.0)(9.81)\sin 40° = 18.92\text{ N}$$
$$F_N = mg\cos 40° = (3.0)(9.81)\cos 40° = 22.54\text{ N}$$

Next, compute the weight of the 1.50-kg block.

$$w = mg = (1.50)(9.81) = 14.72\text{ N}$$

Since $F_x > w$, we choose the positive x direction to be down the plane. Now, write a $\Sigma F_x = ma_x$ equation for the 3.0-kg block.

$$\Sigma F_x = ma_x$$
$$F_x - T - \mu_k F_N = ma$$
$$18.92 - T - (0.13)(22.54) = 3.0a$$
$$T = 15.99 - 3.0a \qquad \text{(a)}$$

Now, write a $\Sigma F_y = ma_y$ equation for the 1.50-kg block.

$$\Sigma F_y = ma_y$$
$$T - mg = ma$$
$$T - (14.72) = 1.50a$$
$$T = 14.72 + 1.50a \qquad \text{(b)}$$

Substitute (b) into (a) to find the acceleration.

(a) $(14.72 + 1.50a) = 15.99 - 3.0a$

$1.27 = 4.5a$

$$a = 0.282\ \frac{\text{m}}{\text{s}^2} \xrightarrow{\text{SD}} \mathbf{0.28\ \frac{m}{s^2}}\ \textbf{down the plane}$$

Substitute the acceleration into (a) to find T.

(a) $T = 15.99 - 3.0(0.282) = 15.14\text{ N} \xrightarrow{\text{SD}} \mathbf{15\ N}$

3. (a) $I = \frac{V}{R} = \frac{24\text{ V}}{25\ \Omega} = \mathbf{0.96\ A}$

(b) $P = VI = (24\text{ V})(0.96\text{ A}) = 23.04\text{ W} \xrightarrow{\text{SD}} \mathbf{23\ W}$

(c) $23.04\ \frac{\text{J}}{\cancel{\text{s}}} \times 5.0\cancel{\text{s}} = 115.2\text{ J} \xrightarrow{\text{SD}} \mathbf{120\ J}$

4. (a) $V_R = IR = (12\text{ A})(3.6\ \Omega) = 43.2\text{ V} \xrightarrow{\text{SD}} \mathbf{43\ V}$

(b) $V_R = IR = (-10\text{ A})(2.0\ \Omega) = \mathbf{-20\ V}$

(c) $P = VI = (3.0\text{ V})(8.0\text{ A}) = \mathbf{24\ W}$

(d) $P = VI = (30\text{ V})(-1.5\text{ A}) = \mathbf{-45\ W}$

5. (a) $F = kx$

$130\text{ N} = k(8.0\text{ cm})$

$$k = 16.25\ \frac{\text{N}}{\text{cm}} \xrightarrow{\text{SD}} \mathbf{16\ \frac{N}{cm}}$$

Convert to N/m and get:

$$16.25\ \frac{\text{N}}{\cancel{\text{cm}}} \times \frac{100\ \cancel{\text{cm}}}{1\text{ m}} = 1625\ \frac{\text{N}}{\text{m}} \xrightarrow{\text{SD}} \mathbf{1600\ \frac{N}{m}}$$

(b) $W = \frac{1}{2}kx^2 = \frac{1}{2}(1625)(0.080)^2 = \mathbf{5.2\ J}$

6. (a) Begin by finding the weight of the mass.

$$w = mg = 16\cancel{\text{kg}} \times 9.81\ \frac{\text{N}}{\cancel{\text{kg}}} = 156.96\text{ N}$$

Now calculate the spring constant.

$F = kx$

$156.96\text{ N} = k(4.5\text{ cm})$

$$k = 34.88\ \frac{\text{N}}{\text{cm}} \xrightarrow{\text{SD}} \mathbf{35\ \frac{N}{cm}}$$

Convert to N/m and get:

$$34.88\ \frac{\text{N}}{\cancel{\text{cm}}} \times \frac{100\ \cancel{\text{cm}}}{1\text{ m}} = 3488\ \frac{\text{N}}{\text{m}} \xrightarrow{\text{SD}} \mathbf{3500\ \frac{N}{m}}$$

(b) $W = \frac{1}{2}kx^2 = \frac{1}{2}(3488)(0.045)^2 = 3.53\text{ J} \xrightarrow{\text{SD}} \mathbf{3.5\ J}$

7. $D = R \times T$

$= 355\ \frac{\text{m}}{\cancel{\text{s}}} \times 2.5\cancel{\text{s}}$

$= 887.5\text{ m} \xrightarrow{\text{SD}} \mathbf{890\ m}$

8. (a) $Q = 2.3\cancel{\text{kg}} \times 580\ \frac{\text{cal}}{\cancel{\text{kg}}\cdot\cancel{\text{C}^\circ}} \times 53\ \cancel{\text{C}^\circ}$

$= 7.07 \times 10^4\text{ cal} \xrightarrow{\text{SD}} \mathbf{7.1 \times 10^4\ cal}$

Convert calories to joules and get:

$$7.07 \times 10^4\ \cancel{\text{cal}} \times \frac{4.186\text{ J}}{1\ \cancel{\text{cal}}} = 2.960 \times 10^5\text{ J} \xrightarrow{\text{SD}} \mathbf{3.0 \times 10^5\ J}$$

(b) $Q = 2.3\cancel{\text{kg}} \times 854 \times 10^3\ \frac{\text{J}}{\cancel{\text{kg}}} = 1.964 \times 10^6\text{ J} \xrightarrow{\text{SD}} \mathbf{2.0 \times 10^6\ J}$

9. $Q_1 = 1.5(2050)(23) = 70{,}725\text{ J}$

$Q_2 = 1.5(334 \times 10^3) = 501{,}000\text{ J}$

$Q_3 = 1.5(4186)(100) = 627{,}900\text{ J}$

$Q_4 = 1.5(2256 \times 10^3) = 3{,}384{,}000\text{ J}$

$Q_5 = 1.5(2009)(30) = 90{,}405\text{ J}$

$Q_T = 4.67 \times 10^6\text{ J} \xrightarrow{\text{SD}} \mathbf{4.7 \times 10^6\ J}$

10. $\frac{P_1V_1}{T_1} = \frac{P_2V_2}{T_2} \rightarrow \frac{P_1V_1}{T_1} = \frac{P_2(5V_1)}{\left(\frac{T_1}{2}\right)}$

$$\frac{P_1\cancel{V_1}}{\cancel{T_1}} \times \frac{\cancel{T_1}}{\cancel{V_1}} = \frac{P_2(5\cancel{V_1})}{\left(\frac{\cancel{T_1}}{2}\right)} \times \frac{\cancel{T_1}}{\cancel{V_1}}$$

$$\mathbf{\frac{P_1}{10}} = P_2$$

11. Begin by finding the cross-sectional area of the rod.
$A = \pi r^2 = \pi(0.0075 \text{ m})^2 = 1.767 \times 10^{-4} \text{ m}^2$

Now find the electrical resistance.

$$R = \rho\frac{L}{A} = \frac{(3.5 \times 10^{-5} \ \Omega \cdot \text{m})(0.40 \text{ m})}{1.767 \times 10^{-4} \text{ m}^2} = 0.0792 \ \Omega \xrightarrow{\text{SD}} \mathbf{0.079 \ \Omega}$$

12. (a) $m_w = 1000 \frac{\text{kg}}{\cancel{\text{m}^3}} \times 0.300 \cancel{\text{m}^3} = \mathbf{30\bar{0} \text{ kg}}$

(b) $F_B = 300 \cancel{\text{kg}} \times 9.81 \frac{\text{N}}{\cancel{\text{kg}}} = 2943 \text{ N} \xrightarrow{\text{SD}} \mathbf{2940 \text{ N}}$

(c) $F = mg - F_B = 325(9.81) - 2943 = 245.25 \text{ N} \xrightarrow{\text{SD}} \mathbf{245 \text{ N}}$

13. (a) $n = \frac{c}{v} = \frac{3.00 \times 10^8 \text{ m/s}}{2.052 \times 10^8 \text{ m/s}} = 1.462 \xrightarrow{\text{SD}} \mathbf{1.46}$

(b)
$$v = f\lambda$$
$$2.052 \times 10^8 \text{ m/s} = f(6.216 \times 10^{-7} \text{ m})$$
$$f = 3.3012 \times 10^{14} \text{ Hz} \xrightarrow{\text{SD}} \mathbf{3.301 \times 10^{14} \text{ Hz}}$$

14. Begin by converting the temperatures to kelvins.
$T_1 = 25 + 273 = 298 \text{ K}$
$T_2 = 120 + 273 = 393 \text{ K}$

Now use the ideal gas law and get:

$$\frac{P_1V_1}{T_1} = \frac{P_2V_2}{T_2}$$

$$\frac{(1.23 \times 10^5 \text{ Pa})(3.5 \text{ m}^3)}{298 \text{ K}} = \frac{P_2(1.1 \text{ m}^3)}{393 \text{ K}}$$

$$P_2 = 5.161 \times 10^5 \text{ Pa} \xrightarrow{\text{SD}} \mathbf{5.2 \times 10^5 \text{ Pa}}$$

15. (a)
$$m_1v_1 + m_2v_2 = (m_1 + m_2)v_3$$
$$(8.1 \times 10^{-3})(374) + (2.0)(0) = (2.0081)v_3$$
$$v_3 = +1.5086 \frac{\text{m}}{\text{s}} \xrightarrow{\text{SD}} \mathbf{+1.5 \frac{m}{s}}$$

(b)
$$KE = \frac{1}{2}mv_3^2$$
$$= \frac{1}{2}(2.0081)(1.5086)^2$$
$$= 2.285 \text{ J} \xrightarrow{\text{SD}} \mathbf{2.3 \text{ J}}$$

(c)
$$PE = mgh$$
$$2.285 = (2.0081)(9.81)h$$
$$h = 0.116 \text{ m} \xrightarrow{\text{SD}} \mathbf{0.12 \text{ m}}$$

16.
$$n_1 \sin\theta_1 = n_2 \sin\theta_2$$
$$(1.333) \sin 48° = (1) \sin\theta_r$$
$$\theta_r = \mathbf{82.14°}$$

17.
$$F = \frac{Gm_em_a}{r^2} = \frac{(6.67 \times 10^{-11})(5.98 \times 10^{24})(60)}{(20.568 \times 10^6)^2}$$
$$= 56.57 \text{ N} \xrightarrow{\text{SD}} \mathbf{60 \text{ N}}$$

18. (a) Use the displacement equation to find the time.

$$\Delta y = v_0t + \frac{1}{2}at^2$$
$$-91 = -31t + \frac{1}{2}(-9.81)t^2$$
$$0 = 4.905t^2 + 31t - 91$$

Use the quadratic formula to solve this equation for t.

$$t = \frac{-31 \pm \sqrt{(31)^2 - 4(4.905)(-91)}}{2(4.905)} = 2.182 \text{ s} \xrightarrow{\text{SD}} \mathbf{2.2 \text{ s}}$$

(b) Use this time in the motion equation to find the velocity.

$$v(t) = v_0 + at$$
$$v(2.182) = -31 + (-9.81)(2.182)$$
$$= -52.4 \frac{\text{m}}{\text{s}} \xrightarrow{\text{SD}} \mathbf{-52 \frac{m}{s}}$$

19. Begin by finding the amount of energy expended in 40 lifts.
$600 \text{ J} \times 40 = 24{,}000 \text{ J}$

Now convert joules to food calories.

$$24{,}000 \cancel{\text{J}} \times \frac{1 \text{ food calorie}}{4186 \cancel{\text{J}}}$$

$$= 5.733 \text{ food calories} \xrightarrow{\text{SD}} \textbf{5.7 food calories}$$

20.

$$\Sigma M_B = 0$$
$$F_A(41 \text{ m}) - 68 \text{ N}(44 \text{ m}) - 28 \text{ N}(1.0 \text{ m}) = 0$$
$$F_A(41 \text{ m}) = 3020 \text{ N}\cdot\text{m}$$
$$F_A = 73.7 \text{ N} \xrightarrow{\text{SD}} \textbf{74 N}$$

$$\Sigma F_y = 0$$
$$F_A + F_B - 68 \text{ N} - 28 \text{ N} = 0$$
$$(73.7 \text{ N}) + F_B - 68 \text{ N} - 28 \text{ N} = 0$$
$$F_B = 22.3 \text{ N} \xrightarrow{\text{SD}} \textbf{22 N}$$

Problem Set 44

1. Increase the mass per unit length of the string by a factor of 4.

$$v_1 = \sqrt{\frac{T}{M_L}} \rightarrow v_2 = \sqrt{\frac{T}{4M_L}}$$

Factor the 4 out from under the radical and get:

$$v_2 = \frac{1}{2}\sqrt{\frac{T}{M_L}}$$

Now, note that $\sqrt{\frac{T}{M_L}}$ is equal to v_1. Substitute and get:

$$v_2 = \frac{v_1}{2}$$

2. (a) Begin by finding the tension, mg, and the mass per unit length of the string.

$$T = mg = 10 \cancel{\text{kg}} \times 9.81 \frac{\text{N}}{\cancel{\text{kg}}} = 98.1 \text{ N}$$

$$M_L = \frac{0.010 \text{ kg}}{4.0 \text{ m}} = 2.5 \times 10^{-3} \frac{\text{kg}}{\text{m}}$$

Insert these values into the formula below to find v.

$$v = \sqrt{\frac{T}{M_L}} = \sqrt{\frac{98.1 \text{ N}}{2.5 \times 10^{-3} \frac{\text{kg}}{\text{m}}}} = 198.09 \frac{\text{m}}{\text{s}} \xrightarrow{\text{SD}} \mathbf{2\bar{0}0 \frac{m}{s}}$$

(b)

$$v = f\lambda$$
$$198.09 \frac{\text{m}}{\text{s}} = f(3.0 \text{ m})$$
$$f = 66.03 \text{ Hz} \xrightarrow{\text{SD}} \textbf{66 Hz}$$

3. Begin by writing a $\Sigma F_x = ma_x$ equation for the 18-kg block on the tabletop. Choose to the right as the positive direction for motion.

$$\Sigma F_x = ma_x$$
$$T - \mu_k mg = ma$$
$$T - (0.31)(18)(9.81) = 18a$$
$$T = 54.74 + 18a \qquad \text{(a)}$$

Next, write a $\Sigma F_y = ma_y$ equation for the suspended 18-kg block.

$$\Sigma F_y = ma_y$$
$$mg - T = ma$$
$$(18)(9.81) - T = 18a$$
$$T = 176.58 - 18a \qquad \text{(b)}$$

Substitute (b) into (a) to find the acceleration.

(a) $(176.58 - 18a) = 54.74 + 18a$

$$121.84 = 36a$$

$$a = 3.384 \frac{\text{m}}{\text{s}^2} \xrightarrow{\text{SD}} \mathbf{3.4 \frac{m}{s^2}} \textbf{ to the right}$$

Substitute the acceleration into (a) to find T.

(a) $T = 54.74 + 18(3.384) = 115.65 \text{ N} \xrightarrow{\text{SD}} \textbf{120 N}$

4. Begin by finding the components of the weight of the 43-kg block that are parallel and perpendicular to the plane.

$F_x = mg \sin 36° = (43)(9.81) \sin 36° = 247.95 \text{ N}$

$F_N = mg \cos 36° = (43)(9.81) \cos 36° = 341.27 \text{ N}$

Next, compute the weight of the 20-kg block.

$w = mg = (20)(9.81) = 196.20 \text{ N}$

Since $F_x > w$, we choose the positive x direction to be down the plane. Now, write a $\Sigma F_x = ma_x$ equation for the 43-kg block.

$$\Sigma F_x = ma_x$$
$$F_x - T - \mu_k F_N = ma$$
$$247.95 - T - (0.15)(341.27) = 43a$$
$$T = 196.76 - 43a \qquad \text{(a)}$$

Now, write a $\Sigma F_y = ma_y$ equation for the 20-kg block.

$$\Sigma F_y = ma_y$$
$$T - mg = ma$$
$$T - (196.20) = 20a$$
$$T = 196.20 + 20a \qquad \text{(b)}$$

Substitute (b) into (a) to find the acceleration.

(a) $(196.20 + 20a) = 196.76 - 43a$

$63a = 0.56$

$a = 0.0089 \ \frac{\text{m}}{\text{s}^2} \xrightarrow{\text{SD}}$ **0.009** $\frac{\textbf{m}}{\textbf{s}^2}$ **down the plane**

Substitute the acceleration into (a) to find T.

(a) $T = 196.76 - 43(0.0089) = 196.38 \text{ N} \xrightarrow{\text{SD}}$ **200 N**

5. (a) $I = \frac{V}{R} = \frac{18 \text{ V}}{250\ \Omega} = \mathbf{7.2 \times 10^{-2}\ A}$

(b) $P = I^2R = (7.2 \times 10^{-2} \text{ A})^2(250\ \Omega) = 1.296 \text{ W} \xrightarrow{\text{SD}}$ **1.3 W**

(c) $P = VI = (18 \text{ V})(7.2 \times 10^{-2} \text{ A}) = 1.296 \text{ W} \xrightarrow{\text{SD}}$ **1.3 W**

(d) $1.296 \frac{\text{J}}{\cancel{\text{s}}} \times 12 \cancel{\text{s}} = 15.55 \text{ J} \xrightarrow{\text{SD}}$ **16 J**

6. (a) $V_R = IR = (4.0 \text{ A})(12\ \Omega) = \mathbf{48\ V}$

(b) $V_R = IR = (-3 \text{ A})(10\ \Omega) = \mathbf{-30\ V}$

(c) $P = VI = (3.5 \text{ V})(-2 \text{ A}) = \mathbf{-7\ W}$

(d) $P = VI = (6.0 \text{ V})(4.0 \text{ A}) = \mathbf{24\ W}$

7. (a) Begin by finding Patrick's weight.

$w = mg = 65 \cancel{\text{kg}} \times 9.81 \frac{\text{N}}{\cancel{\text{kg}}} = 637.65 \text{ N}$

Now calculate the spring constant.

$$F = kx$$
$$637.65 \text{ N} = k(0.75 \text{ cm})$$
$$k = 8.502 \times 10^2 \ \frac{\text{N}}{\text{cm}} \xrightarrow{\text{SD}} \mathbf{8.5 \times 10^2\ \frac{N}{cm}}$$

Convert to N/m and get:

$8.502 \times 10^2 \frac{\text{N}}{\cancel{\text{cm}}} \times \frac{100 \cancel{\text{cm}}}{1 \text{ m}} = 8.502 \times 10^4 \ \frac{\text{N}}{\text{m}} \xrightarrow{\text{SD}} \mathbf{8.5 \times 10^4\ \frac{N}{m}}$

(b) $W = \frac{1}{2}kx^2 = \frac{1}{2}(8.502 \times 10^4)(0.0075)^2 = 2.39 \text{ J} \xrightarrow{\text{SD}}$ **2.4 J**

8. (a) Begin by finding the weight of the mass.

$w = mg = 15 \cancel{\text{kg}} \times 9.81 \frac{\text{N}}{\cancel{\text{kg}}} = 147.15 \text{ N}$

Now calculate the distance stretched.

$$F = kx$$
$$147.15 \text{ N} = 2900 \ \frac{\text{N}}{\text{m}}(x)$$
$$x = 5.074 \times 10^{-2} \text{ m} \xrightarrow{\text{SD}} \mathbf{5.1 \times 10^{-2}\ m}$$

(b) $W = \frac{1}{2}kx^2 = \frac{1}{2}(2900)(5.074 \times 10^{-2})^2 = 3.733 \text{ J} \xrightarrow{\text{SD}}$ **3.7 J**

9.

$$D = R \times T$$
$$1500 \text{ m} = R \times 4.4 \text{ s}$$
$$R = 340.91 \ \frac{\text{m}}{\text{s}} \xrightarrow{\text{SD}} \mathbf{340\ \frac{m}{s}}$$

10. (a) $Q = 3.6\text{ kg} \times 580 \frac{\text{cal}}{\text{kg}\cdot\text{C}^\circ} \times 102\text{ C}^\circ$

$= 2.13 \times 10^5 \text{ calories} \xrightarrow{SD}$ **2.1×10^5 calories**

(b) $Q = 3.6\text{ kg} \times 854 \times 10^3 \frac{\text{J}}{\text{kg}} = 3.07 \times 10^6 \text{ J} \xrightarrow{SD}$ **3.1×10^6 J**

11. $Q = 0.85\text{ kg} \times 31 \frac{\text{cal}}{\text{kg}\cdot\text{C}^\circ} \times 650\text{ C}^\circ$

$= 1.71 \times 10^4 \text{ cal} \xrightarrow{SD}$ **1.7×10^4 cal**

Convert to joules and get:

$1.71 \times 10^4 \text{ cal} \times \frac{4.186 \text{ J}}{1 \text{ cal}} = 7.16 \times 10^4 \text{ J} \xrightarrow{SD}$ **7.2×10^4 J**

12. $$\frac{P_1V_1}{T_1} = \frac{P_2V_2}{T_2} \rightarrow \frac{P_1V_1}{T_1} = \frac{\left(\frac{P_1}{2}\right)V_2}{(3T_1)}$$

$$\frac{P_1V_1}{T_1} \times \frac{T_1}{P_1} = \frac{\left(\frac{P_1}{2}\right)V_2}{(3T_1)} \times \frac{T_1}{P_1}$$

$$\mathbf{6V_1 = V_2}$$

13. Begin by finding the cross-sectional area of the bar.
$A = 0.010 \text{ m} \times 0.050 \text{ m} = 5.0 \times 10^{-4} \text{ m}^2$

Now find the electrical resistance.

$$R = \rho\frac{L}{A} = \frac{(22 \times 10^{-8}\ \Omega\cdot\text{m})(0.25 \text{ m})}{5.0 \times 10^{-4} \text{ m}^2} = \mathbf{1.1 \times 10^{-4}\ \Omega}$$

14. (a) $m_g = 680 \frac{\text{kg}}{\text{m}^3} \times 0.0018 \text{ m}^3 = 1.224 \text{ kg} \xrightarrow{SD}$ **1.2 kg**

(b) $F_B = 1.224 \text{ kg} \times 9.81 \frac{\text{N}}{\text{kg}} = 12.01 \text{ N} \xrightarrow{SD}$ **12 N**

(c) $F = mg - F_B = 1.5(9.81) - 12.01 = 2.705 \text{ N} \xrightarrow{SD}$ **2.7 N**

15. Begin by converting the temperatures to kelvins.
$T_1 = 0 + 273 = 273 \text{ K}$
$T_2 = 34 + 273 = 307 \text{ K}$

Now use the ideal gas law and get:

$$\frac{P_1V_1}{T_1} = \frac{P_2V_2}{T_2}$$

$$\frac{(1.01 \times 10^5 \text{ Pa})(1.05 \text{ m}^3)}{273 \text{ K}} = \frac{(2.50 \times 10^5 \text{ Pa})V_2}{307 \text{ K}}$$

$$V_2 = 0.47703 \text{ m}^3 \xrightarrow{SD} \mathbf{0.48 \text{ m}^3}$$

16. (a)

$$m_1v_1 + m_2v_2 = (m_1 + m_2)v_3$$

$$(9.0 \times 10^{-3})(1300) + (6.5)(0) = (6.509)v_3$$

$$v_3 = +1.798 \frac{\text{m}}{\text{s}} \xrightarrow{SD} \mathbf{+1.8 \frac{m}{s}}$$

(b) $KE = \frac{1}{2}mv_3^2$

$= \frac{1}{2}(6.509)(1.798)^2$

$= 10.52 \text{ J} \xrightarrow{SD}$ **11 J**

(c) $PE = mgh$

$10.52 = (6.509)(9.81)h$

$h = 0.1648 \text{ m} \xrightarrow{SD}$ **0.16 m**

17. (a) Begin by converting 4500 rev/min to rad/s.

$$4500 \frac{\text{rev}}{\text{min}} \times \frac{2\pi \text{ rad}}{1 \text{ rev}} \times \frac{1 \text{ min}}{60 \text{ s}} = 471.24 \frac{\text{rad}}{\text{s}}$$

$$\omega(t) = \omega_0 + \alpha t$$

$$\omega(2.50) = 471.24 + 22.0(2.50) = 526.24 \frac{\text{rad}}{\text{s}} \xrightarrow{SD} \mathbf{526 \frac{rad}{s}}$$

(b) $\Delta\theta = \omega_0 t + \frac{1}{2}\alpha t^2$

$= 471.24(2.50) + \frac{1}{2}(22.0)(2.50)^2$

$= 1.2469 \times 10^3 \text{ rad} \xrightarrow{SD}$ **1.25×10^3 rad**

18. (a)
$$\vec{F} = m\vec{a}$$
$$500\text{ N} = (22.223\text{ kg})\vec{a}$$
$$\vec{a} = 22.50\ \frac{\text{m}}{\text{s}^2} \xrightarrow{\text{SD}} \mathbf{20\ \frac{m}{s^2}\ \text{to the right}}$$

(b) Impulse $= F\Delta t$
$$= 500\text{ N} \times 120.500\text{ s} = 6.03 \times 10^4\text{ N·s} \xrightarrow{\text{SD}} \mathbf{6 \times 10^4\ N{\cdot}s}$$

(c)
$$F\Delta t = m(v_2 - v_1)$$
$$6.03 \times 10^4\text{ N·s} = 22.223\text{ kg}\left(v_2 - 0\ \frac{\text{m}}{\text{s}}\right)$$
$$v_2 = 2713\ \frac{\text{m}}{\text{s}} \xrightarrow{\text{SD}} \mathbf{3000\ \frac{m}{s}\ \text{to the right}}$$

19. Percent eff. $= \dfrac{W_{\text{out}}}{W_{\text{in}}} \times 100\% = \dfrac{6128\text{ J}}{11{,}213\text{ J}} \times 100\%$
$$= 54.651\% \xrightarrow{\text{SD}} \mathbf{54.65\%}$$

20. $\tau = FL\sin\theta = -(120\text{ N})(0.100\text{ m})\sin 62°$
$$= -10.595\text{ N·m} \xrightarrow{\text{SD}} \mathbf{-10.6\ N{\cdot}m}$$

PROBLEM SET 45

1. (a) Use the y-displacement equation to find the time.
$$\Delta y = v_{y0}t + \frac{1}{2}a_y t^2$$
$$-2000 = (0) + \frac{1}{2}(-9.81)t^2$$
$$-2000 = -4.905t^2$$
$$t = 20.19\text{ s} \xrightarrow{\text{SD}} \mathbf{20.2\ s}$$

(b) Use this time in the x-position equation to find the distance. Begin by converting 500 mph to m/s.
$$500\ \frac{\text{mi}}{\text{hr}} \times \frac{5280\text{ ft}}{1\text{ mi}} \times \frac{12\text{ in.}}{1\text{ ft}} \times \frac{2.54\text{ cm}}{1\text{ in.}} \times \frac{1\text{ m}}{100\text{ cm}} \times \frac{1\text{ hr}}{3600\text{ s}}$$
$$= 223.52\ \frac{\text{m}}{\text{s}}$$
$$x = x_0 + v_{x0}t + \frac{1}{2}a_x t^2$$
$$= (0) + 223.52(20.19) + (0)$$
$$= 4512.87\text{ m} \xrightarrow{\text{SD}} \mathbf{4510\ m}$$

2. Begin by finding the x and y components of the initial velocity.
$$v_{x0} = 600\cos 25° = 543.78\ \frac{\text{m}}{\text{s}}$$
$$v_{y0} = 600\sin 25° = 253.57\ \frac{\text{m}}{\text{s}}$$
Use the y-displacement equation to find the time.
$$\Delta y = v_{y0}t + \frac{1}{2}a_y t^2$$
$$(0) = 253.57t + \frac{1}{2}(-9.81)t^2$$
$$4.905t^2 = 253.57t$$
$$t = 51.696\text{ s}$$
Use this time in the x-position equation to find the distance.
$$x = x_0 + v_{x0}t + \frac{1}{2}a_x t^2$$
$$= (0) + 543.78(51.696) + (0)$$
$$= 2.811 \times 10^4\text{ m} \xrightarrow{\text{SD}} \mathbf{2.81 \times 10^4\ m}$$

3. Decrease the mass per unit length of the string by a factor of one-half.
$$v_1 = \sqrt{\frac{T}{M_L}} \longrightarrow v_2 = \sqrt{\frac{T}{\frac{M_L}{2}}}$$
Factor the 2 out from under the radical and get:
$$v_2 = \sqrt{2}\sqrt{\frac{T}{M_L}}$$
Now, note that $\sqrt{\dfrac{T}{M_L}}$ is equal to v_1. Substitute and get:
$$v_2 = \mathbf{\sqrt{2}v_1}$$

4. (a) Begin by finding the tension, mg, and the mass per unit length of the string.
$$T = mg = 20.490\text{ kg} \times 9.81\ \frac{\text{N}}{\text{kg}} = 201.01\text{ N}$$
$$M_L = \frac{0.25800\text{ kg}}{4\text{ m}} = 0.0645\ \frac{\text{kg}}{\text{m}}$$
Insert these values into the formula below to find v.
$$v = \sqrt{\frac{T}{M_L}} = \sqrt{\frac{201.01\text{ N}}{0.0645\ \frac{\text{kg}}{\text{m}}}} = 55.83\ \frac{\text{m}}{\text{s}} \xrightarrow{\text{SD}} \mathbf{60\ \frac{m}{s}}$$

(b) $v = f\lambda$

$$55.83\ \frac{\text{m}}{\text{s}} = (85.123\ \text{s}^{-1})\lambda$$

$$\lambda = 0.656\ \text{m} \xrightarrow{\text{SD}} \mathbf{0.7\ m}$$

5. Begin by writing a $\sum F_x = ma_x$ equation for the 23-kg block. Choose to the right as the positive direction for motion.

$$\sum F_x = ma_x$$
$$T - \mu_k mg = ma$$
$$T - (0.19)(23)(9.81) = 23a$$
$$T = 42.87 + 23a \qquad \text{(a)}$$

Next, write a $\sum F_y = ma_y$ equation for the 28-kg object.

$$\sum F_y = ma_y$$
$$mg - T = ma$$
$$(28)(9.81) - T = 28a$$
$$T = 274.68 - 28a \qquad \text{(b)}$$

Substitute (b) into (a) to find the acceleration.

(a) $(274.68 - 28a) = 42.87 + 23a$

$$231.81 = 51a$$

$$a = 4.545\ \frac{\text{m}}{\text{s}^2} \xrightarrow{\text{SD}} \mathbf{4.5\ \frac{m}{s^2}\ to\ the\ right}$$

Substitute the acceleration into (a) to find T.

(a) $T = 42.87 + 23(4.545) = 147.405\ \text{N} \xrightarrow{\text{SD}} \mathbf{150\ N}$

6. Begin by finding the components of the weight of the 16-kg block that are parallel and perpendicular to the plane.

$F_x = mg \sin 21° = (16)(9.81) \sin 21° = 56.25\ \text{N}$

$F_N = mg \cos 21° = (16)(9.81) \cos 21° = 146.53\ \text{N}$

Next, compute the weight of the 18-kg block.

$w = mg = (18)(9.81) = 176.58\ \text{N}$

Since $w > F_x$, we choose the positive x direction to be up the plane. Now, write a $\sum F_x = ma_x$ equation for the 16-kg block.

$$\sum F_x = ma_x$$
$$T - F_x - \mu_k F_N = ma$$
$$T - 56.25 - (0.48)(146.53) = 16a$$
$$T = 126.58 + 16a \qquad \text{(a)}$$

Now, write a $\sum F_y = ma_y$ equation for the 18-kg block.

$$\sum F_y = ma_y$$
$$mg - T = ma$$
$$(176.58) - T = 18a$$
$$T = 176.58 - 18a \qquad \text{(b)}$$

Substitute (b) into (a) to find the acceleration.

(a) $(176.58 - 18a) = 126.58 + 16a$

$$50 = 34a$$

$$a = 1.47\ \frac{\text{m}}{\text{s}^2} \xrightarrow{\text{SD}} \mathbf{1.5\ \frac{m}{s^2}\ up\ the\ plane}$$

Substitute the acceleration into (a) to find T.

(a) $T = 126.58 + 16(1.47) = 150.1\ \text{N} \xrightarrow{\text{SD}} \mathbf{150\ N}$

7. (a) $V = IR = (1.3\ \text{A})(18\ \Omega) = 23.4\ \text{V} \xrightarrow{\text{SD}} \mathbf{23\ V}$

(b) $P = VI = (23.4\ \text{V})(1.3\ \text{A}) = 30.42\ \text{W} \xrightarrow{\text{SD}} \mathbf{3\bar{0}\ W}$

$P = I^2R = (1.3\ \text{A})^2(18\ \Omega) = 30.42\ \text{W} \xrightarrow{\text{SD}} \mathbf{3\bar{0}\ W}$

(c) $30.42\ \frac{\text{J}}{\cancel{\text{s}}} \times 6.0\cancel{\text{s}} = 182.52\ \text{J} \xrightarrow{\text{SD}} \mathbf{180\ J}$

8. (a) $V_R = IR = (0.5\ \text{A})(10\ \Omega) = \mathbf{5\ V}$

(b) $V_R = IR = (-2.0\ \text{A})(8.0\ \Omega) = \mathbf{-16\ V}$

(c) $P = VI = (6.0\ \text{V})(3.0\ \text{A}) = \mathbf{18\ W}$

(d) $P = VI = (12\ \text{V})(-5\ \text{A}) = \mathbf{-60\ W}$

9. (a) $F = kx$

$$160\ \text{N} = k(6.5\ \text{cm})$$

$$k = 24.62\ \frac{\text{N}}{\text{cm}} \xrightarrow{\text{SD}} \mathbf{25\ \frac{N}{cm}}$$

Convert to N/m and get:

$$24.62\ \frac{\text{N}}{\cancel{\text{cm}}} \times \frac{100\ \cancel{\text{cm}}}{\text{m}} = 2.462 \times 10^3\ \frac{\text{N}}{\text{m}} \xrightarrow{\text{SD}} \mathbf{2.5 \times 10^3\ \frac{N}{m}}$$

(b) $W = \frac{1}{2}kx^2 = \frac{1}{2}(2.462 \times 10^3)(0.065)^2 = 5.201\ \text{J} \xrightarrow{\text{SD}} \mathbf{5.2\ J}$

10. (a) Begin by finding the weight of the mass.

$$w = mg = 35\cancel{\text{kg}} \times 9.81\frac{\text{N}}{\cancel{\text{kg}}} = 343.35\text{ N}$$

Now calculate the distance the spring is stretched.

$$F = kx$$

$$343.35\text{ N} = 1900\frac{\text{N}}{\text{m}} \times x$$

$$x = 0.181\text{ m} \xrightarrow{\text{SD}} \mathbf{0.18\ m}$$

(b) $W = \frac{1}{2}kx^2$

$$= \frac{1}{2}(1900)(0.181)^2$$

$$= 31.12\text{ J} \xrightarrow{\text{SD}} \mathbf{31\ J}$$

11. $D = R \times T$

$$= 350\frac{\text{m}}{\cancel{\text{s}}} \times 1.50\cancel{\text{s}}$$

$$= \mathbf{525\ m}$$

12. (a) $Q = 0.500\cancel{\text{kg}} \times 580\frac{\text{cal}}{\cancel{\text{kg}}\cdot\cancel{\text{C}^\circ}} \times 117\cancel{\text{C}^\circ}$

$$= 3.39 \times 10^4\text{ cal} \xrightarrow{\text{SD}} \mathbf{3.4 \times 10^4\ cal}$$

Convert to joules and get:

$$3.39 \times 10^4\cancel{\text{cal}} \times \frac{4.186\text{ J}}{1\cancel{\text{cal}}} = 1.42 \times 10^5\text{ J} \xrightarrow{\text{SD}} \mathbf{1.4 \times 10^5\ J}$$

(b) $Q = 0.500\cancel{\text{kg}} \times 854 \times 10^3\frac{\text{J}}{\cancel{\text{kg}}} = \mathbf{4.27 \times 10^5\ J}$

13. Begin by finding the cross-sectional area of the rod.

$$A = \pi r^2 = \pi(0.0025\text{ m})^2 = 1.96 \times 10^{-5}\text{ m}^2$$

Now find the electrical resistance.

$$R = \rho\frac{L}{A} = \frac{(11 \times 10^{-8}\ \Omega\cdot\text{m})(0.36\text{ m})}{1.96 \times 10^{-5}\text{ m}^2}$$

$$= 2.02 \times 10^{-3}\ \Omega \xrightarrow{\text{SD}} \mathbf{2 \times 10^{-3}\ \Omega}$$

14. Begin by converting the temperatures to kelvins.

$$T_1 = 100 + 273 = 373\text{ K}$$

$$T_2 = 25 + 273 = 298\text{ K}$$

Now use the ideal gas law and get:

$$\frac{P_1V_1}{T_1} = \frac{P_2V_2}{T_2}$$

$$\frac{(3.01 \times 10^5\text{ Pa})(0.55\text{ m}^3)}{373\text{ K}} = \frac{(2.20 \times 10^5\text{ Pa})V_2}{298\text{ K}}$$

$$V_2 = 0.601\text{ m}^3 \xrightarrow{\text{SD}} \mathbf{0.60\ m^3}$$

15. $n_1 \sin\theta_1 = n_2 \sin\theta_2$

$$(1)\sin 35^\circ = (1.434)\sin\theta_r$$

$$\theta_r = \mathbf{23.58^\circ}$$

16. (a)

$$m_1v_1 + m_2v_2 = (m_1 + m_2)v_3$$

$$(6.7 \times 10^{-3})(740) + (4.6)(0) = (4.6067)v_3$$

$$v_3 = +1.076\frac{\text{m}}{\text{s}} \xrightarrow{\text{SD}} \mathbf{+1.1\ \frac{m}{s}}$$

(b) $KE = \frac{1}{2}mv_3^2$

$$= \frac{1}{2}(4.6067)(1.076)^2$$

$$= 2.67\text{ J} \xrightarrow{\text{SD}} \mathbf{2.7\ J}$$

(c) $PE = mgh$

$$2.67 = (4.6067)(9.81)h$$

$$h = 5.908 \times 10^{-2}\text{ m} \xrightarrow{\text{SD}} \mathbf{5.9 \times 10^{-2}\ m}$$

17. (a) $m_g = 680\frac{\text{kg}}{\cancel{\text{m}^3}} \times 0.025\cancel{\text{m}^3} = \mathbf{17\ kg}$

(b) $F_B = 17\cancel{\text{kg}} \times 9.81\frac{\text{N}}{\cancel{\text{kg}}} = 166.77\text{ N} \xrightarrow{\text{SD}} \mathbf{170\ N}$

(c) $F = mg - F_B = 22(9.81) - 166.77 = 49.05\text{ N} \xrightarrow{\text{SD}} \mathbf{49\ N}$

18. Begin by finding the weight of the beam and the weight of the mass.

$w_b = m_b g = (46.0)(9.81) = 451.26\text{ N}$

$w_m = m_m g = (18.0)(9.81) = 176.58\text{ N}$

Next sum the moments about the left end of the beam to zero.

$$\Sigma M = 0$$
$$w_b(6.00\text{ m}) + w_m(12.0\text{ m}) - T_y(9.00\text{ m}) = 0$$
$$451.26\text{ N}(6.00\text{ m}) + 176.58\text{ N}(12.0\text{ m}) - T_y(9.00\text{ m}) = 0$$
$$T_y(9.00\text{ m}) = 4826.52\text{ N·m}$$
$$T_y = 536.28\text{ N}$$

Now use T_y to find T.

$T\sin 37° = T_y$

$T\sin 37° = 536.28\text{ N}$

$T = 891.10\text{ N}$

Sum the horizontal forces to zero to find F_x.

$F_x - T_x = 0$

$F_x = T_x$

$= T\cos 37° = (891.10\text{ N})\cos 37° = 711.66\text{ N} \xrightarrow{\text{SD}}$ **712 N**

Sum the vertical forces to zero to find F_y.

$$F_y + T_y - w_b - w_m = 0$$
$$F_y + (536.28\text{ N}) - 451.26\text{ N} - 176.58\text{ N} = 0$$
$$F_y = 91.56\text{ N} \xrightarrow{\text{SD}} \mathbf{91.6\text{ N}}$$

19. Percent eff. $= \dfrac{W_{out}}{W_{in}} \times 100\% = \dfrac{56\text{ J}}{104\text{ J}} \times 100\% = 53.85\% \xrightarrow{\text{SD}}$ **54%**

20. Calculate the displacements for the following time intervals:

$\Delta x_{0,2} = -15\dfrac{\text{m}}{\text{s}} \times 2\text{ s} = -30\text{ m}$ $\quad\Delta x_{2,3} = 0\text{ m}$ $\quad\Delta x_{3,5} = 0\text{ m}$

$\Delta x_{5,7} = \dfrac{-20\dfrac{\text{m}}{\text{s}} \times 2\text{ s}}{2} = -20\text{ m}$ $\quad\Delta x_{7,8} = -20\dfrac{\text{m}}{\text{s}} \times 1\text{ s} = -20\text{ m}$

Sum the displacements from $t = 0$ s to $t = 3$ s with the initial position:

$x_3 = 0\text{ m} - 30\text{ m} + 0\text{ m} = \mathbf{-3\bar{0}\text{ m}}$

Sum the displacements from $t = 3$ s to $t = 8$ s with x_3:

$x_8 = -30\text{ m} + 0\text{ m} - 20\text{ m} - 20\text{ m} = \mathbf{-7\bar{0}\text{ m}}$

Problem Set 46

1. (a) $a_c = \dfrac{v^2}{r} = \dfrac{(25)^2}{35} = 17.86\dfrac{\text{m}}{\text{s}^2} \xrightarrow{\text{SD}} \mathbf{18\dfrac{m}{s^2}}$

(b) $a_c = \dfrac{v^2}{r} = \dfrac{(25)^2}{50} = 12.5\dfrac{\text{m}}{\text{s}^2} \xrightarrow{\text{SD}} \mathbf{13\dfrac{m}{s^2}}$

2. Begin by finding the centripetal force, F_c, and the weight of the ball.

$F_c = \dfrac{mv^2}{r} = \dfrac{(0.75)(3.50)^2}{0.57} = 16.12\text{ N}$

$w = mg = (0.75)(9.81) = 7.36\text{ N}$

The tension, T, is equal to the vector sum of the horizontal force, F_c, and the vertical force, w.

$T = \sqrt{(16.12)^2 + (7.36)^2} = 17.72\text{ N} \xrightarrow{\text{SD}}$ **18 N**

3. Begin by finding the x and y components of the initial velocity.

$v_{x0} = 190\cos 20° = 178.54\dfrac{\text{m}}{\text{s}}$

$v_{y0} = 190\sin 20° = 64.98\dfrac{\text{m}}{\text{s}}$

(a) Use the y-displacement equation to find the time.

$$\Delta y = v_{y0}t + \frac{1}{2}a_y t^2$$
$$(0) = 64.98t + \frac{1}{2}(-9.81)t^2$$
$$4.905t^2 = 64.98t$$
$$t = 13.248\text{ s} \xrightarrow{\text{SD}} \mathbf{13.2\text{ s}}$$

(b) Use this time in the x-position equation to find the distance.

$$x = x_0 + v_{x0}t + \frac{1}{2}a_x t^2$$
$$= (0) + 178.54(13.248) + (0)$$
$$= 2365.3\text{ m} \xrightarrow{\text{SD}} \mathbf{2370\text{ m}}$$

4. Begin by finding the x and y components of the initial velocity.

$$v_{x0} = 15\cos 40° = 11.49\ \frac{\text{m}}{\text{s}}$$

$$v_{y0} = 15\sin 40° = 9.64\ \frac{\text{m}}{\text{s}}$$

(a) Use the y-displacement equation to find the time.

$$\Delta y = v_{y0}t + \frac{1}{2}a_y t^2$$

$$-21 = 9.64t + \frac{1}{2}(-9.81)t^2$$

$$0 = 4.905t^2 - 9.64t - 21$$

Use the quadratic formula to solve this equation for t.

$$t = \frac{-(-9.64) \pm \sqrt{(-9.64)^2 - 4(4.905)(-21)}}{2(4.905)} = 3.273\text{ s} \xrightarrow{\text{SD}} \mathbf{3.3\ s}$$

(b) Use this time in the x-position equation to find the distance.

$$x = x_0 + v_{x0}t + \frac{1}{2}a_x t^2$$

$$= (0) + 11.49(3.273) + (0)$$

$$= 37.61\text{ m} \xrightarrow{\text{SD}} \mathbf{38\ m}$$

5. Increase the mass per unit length of the string by a factor of three.

$$v_1 = \sqrt{\frac{T}{M_L}} \longrightarrow v_2 = \sqrt{\frac{T}{3M_L}}$$

Factor the 3 out from under the radical and get:

$$v_2 = \frac{1}{\sqrt{3}}\sqrt{\frac{T}{M_L}}$$

Now, note that $\sqrt{\frac{T}{M_L}}$ is equal to v_1. Substitute and get:

$$\mathbf{v_2 = \frac{1}{\sqrt{3}}v_1}$$

6. (a) Begin by finding the tension, mg, and the mass per unit length of the string.

$$T = mg = 36.0\ \cancel{\text{kg}} \times 9.81\ \frac{\text{N}}{\cancel{\text{kg}}} = 353.16\text{ N}$$

$$M_L = \frac{0.535\text{ kg}}{3.50\text{ m}} = 0.1529\ \frac{\text{kg}}{\text{m}}$$

Insert these values into the formula below to find v.

$$v = \sqrt{\frac{T}{M_L}} = \sqrt{\frac{353.16\text{ N}}{0.1529\ \frac{\text{kg}}{\text{m}}}} = 48.06\ \frac{\text{m}}{\text{s}} \xrightarrow{\text{SD}} \mathbf{48.1\ \frac{m}{s}}$$

(b)

$$v = f\lambda$$

$$48.06\ \frac{\text{m}}{\text{s}} = f(1.50\text{ m})$$

$$f = 32.04\text{ Hz} \xrightarrow{\text{SD}} \mathbf{32.0\ Hz}$$

7.

$$\Sigma M_A = 0$$

$$(120)(x) - 80(9.0 - x) = 0$$

$$120x - 720 + 80x = 0$$

$$200x = 720$$

$$x = \mathbf{3.6\ m}$$

$$\Sigma F_y = 0$$

$$120\text{ N} + 80\text{ N} - F_A = 0$$

$$F_A = \mathbf{2\bar{0}0\ N}$$

8. Begin by finding the components of the weight of the 60-kg block that are parallel and perpendicular to the plane.

$F_x = mg\sin 45° = (60)(9.81)\sin 45° = 416.20\text{ N}$

$F_N = mg\cos 45° = (60)(9.81)\cos 45° = 416.20\text{ N}$

Next, compute the weight of the 40-kg block.

$w = mg = (40)(9.81) = 392.4\text{ N}$

Since $F_x > w$, we choose the positive x direction to be down the plane. Now, write a $\Sigma F_x = ma_x$ equation for the 60-kg block.

$$\Sigma F_x = ma_x$$

$$F_x - T - \mu_k F_N = ma$$

$$416.20 - T - (0.05)(416.20) = 60a$$

$$T = 395.39 - 60a \qquad \text{(a)}$$

Now, write a $\Sigma F_y = ma_y$ equation for the 40-kg block.

$$\begin{aligned} \Sigma F_y &= ma_y \\ T - mg &= ma \\ T - (392.4) &= 40a \\ T &= 392.4 + 40a \qquad \text{(b)} \end{aligned}$$

Substitute (b) into (a) to find the acceleration.

(a) $(392.4 + 40a) = 395.39 - 60a$

$100a = 2.99$

$$a = 0.0299\ \frac{\text{m}}{\text{s}^2} \xrightarrow{\text{SD}} \mathbf{0.03\ \frac{m}{s^2}\ down\ the\ plane}$$

Substitute the acceleration into (a) to find T.

(a) $T = 395.39 - 60(0.0299) = 393.60\ \text{N} \xrightarrow{\text{SD}} \mathbf{400\ N}$

9. (a) $V = IR = (0.40\ \text{A})(1500\ \Omega) = \mathbf{6\bar{0}0\ V}$
(b) $P = VI = (600\ \text{V})(0.40\ \text{A}) = \mathbf{240\ W}$

(c) $240\ \frac{\text{J}}{\text{s}} \times 4.5\ \text{s} = 1080\ \text{J} \xrightarrow{\text{SD}} \mathbf{1100\ J}$

10. (a) $V_R = IR = (150\ \text{A})(45{,}000\ \Omega) = 6.75 \times 10^6\ \text{V} \xrightarrow{\text{SD}} \mathbf{6.8 \times 10^6\ V}$
(b) $V_R = IR = (10\ \text{A})(4800\ \Omega) = \mathbf{4.8 \times 10^4\ V}$
(c) $P = VI = (12.0\ \text{V})(5\ \text{A}) = \mathbf{60\ W}$
(d) $P = VI = (18.0\ \text{V})(6.00\ \text{A}) = \mathbf{108\ W}$

11. To find the spring constant, find the slope of the line.

$$k = \text{slope} = \frac{\Delta y}{\Delta x} = \frac{1.0\ \text{N}}{1.5\ \text{m}} = 0.667\ \frac{\text{N}}{\text{m}} \xrightarrow{\text{SD}} \mathbf{0.67\ \frac{N}{m}}$$

12.
$$\begin{aligned} D &= R \times T \\ 740.57\ \text{m} &= R \times 2\ \text{s} \end{aligned}$$

$$R = 370.285\ \frac{\text{m}}{\text{s}} \xrightarrow{\text{SD}} \mathbf{400\ \frac{m}{s}}$$

13. (a) Compute the heat energy for each process.

$$Q_1 = 1.65\ \text{kg} \times 2050\ \frac{\text{J}}{\text{kg}\cdot\text{C}^\circ} \times 39\ \text{C}^\circ = 1.319 \times 10^5\ \text{J}$$

$$Q_2 = 1.65\ \text{kg} \times 334 \times 10^3\ \frac{\text{J}}{\text{kg}} = 5.511 \times 10^5\ \text{J}$$

$$Q_3 = 1.65\ \text{kg} \times 4186\ \frac{\text{J}}{\text{kg}\cdot\text{C}^\circ} \times 100\ \text{C}^\circ = 6.907 \times 10^5\ \text{J}$$

Sum the heat energies and get:

$$Q_T = 1.3737 \times 10^6\ \text{J} \xrightarrow{\text{SD}} \mathbf{1.4 \times 10^6\ J}$$

(b) $Q_4 = 1.65\ \text{kg} \times 2256 \times 10^3\ \frac{\text{J}}{\text{kg}}$

$= 3.722 \times 10^6\ \text{J} \xrightarrow{\text{SD}} \mathbf{3.72 \times 10^6\ J}$

14. Begin by finding the cross-sectional area of the rod.

$A = \pi r^2 = \pi(0.030\ \text{m})^2 = 2.827 \times 10^{-3}\ \text{m}^2$

Now find the electrical resistance.

$$R = \rho\frac{L}{A} = \frac{(1.7 \times 10^{-8}\ \Omega\cdot\text{m})(0.18\ \text{m})}{2.827 \times 10^{-3}\ \text{m}^2}$$

$$= 1.08 \times 10^{-6}\ \Omega \xrightarrow{\text{SD}} \mathbf{1.1 \times 10^{-6}\ \Omega}$$

15. (a) Begin by finding the volume of the boat that is submerged.

$V_s = 6.5 \times 10^{-4}\ \text{m}^3 \times 0.55 = 3.575 \times 10^{-4}\ \text{m}^3$

Now find the mass of the water displaced.

$$m_w = 1000\ \frac{\text{kg}}{\text{m}^3} \times 3.575 \times 10^{-4}\ \text{m}^3 = 0.3575\ \text{kg} \xrightarrow{\text{SD}} \mathbf{0.36\ kg}$$

(b) $F_B = 0.3575\ \text{kg} \times 9.81\ \frac{\text{N}}{\text{kg}} = 3.507\ \text{N} \xrightarrow{\text{SD}} \mathbf{3.5\ N}$

(c) The weight of the boat equals the buoyancy force of the water, and the mass of the boat equals the mass of the water displaced.

$w_b = F_B = \mathbf{3.5\ N}$

$m_b = m_w = \mathbf{0.36\ kg}$

16. Begin by converting the temperatures to kelvins.

$T_1 = 4.0 + 273 = 277\ \text{K}$

$T_2 = 35 + 273 = 308\ \text{K}$

Now use the ideal gas law and get:

$$\frac{V_1}{T_1} = \frac{V_2}{T_2}$$

$$\frac{1.5\ \text{m}^3}{277\ \text{K}} = \frac{V_2}{308\ \text{K}}$$

$$V_2 = 1.668\ \text{m}^3 \xrightarrow{\text{SD}} \mathbf{1.7\ m^3}$$

17. $\frac{P_1V_1}{T_1} = \frac{P_2V_2}{T_2} \longrightarrow \frac{P_1V_1}{T_1} = \frac{(2P_1)V_2}{\left(\frac{T_1}{3}\right)}$

$$\frac{\cancel{P_1}V_1}{\cancel{T_1}} \times \frac{\cancel{T_1}}{\cancel{P_1}} = \frac{(2\cancel{P_1})V_2}{\left(\frac{\cancel{T_1}}{3}\right)} \times \frac{\cancel{T_1}}{\cancel{P_1}}$$

$$\mathbf{\frac{V_1}{6}} = V_2$$

18. (a) Use energy conservation to find x. Note that the potential energy of the ball before it is dropped must equal the kinetic energy of the ball just before it strikes the pavement.

$$PE = KE$$

$$mgx = \frac{1}{2}mv^2$$

$$x = \frac{v^2}{2g}$$

Use this equation to find x. Notice that the mass is not a factor.

$$x = \frac{v^2}{2g} = \frac{(25)^2}{2(9.81)} = 31.86 \text{ m} \xrightarrow{\text{SD}} \mathbf{32\ m}$$

(b) Find the height of the ball after it bounces.

$h = 0.70x = 0.70(31.86) = 22.30 \text{ m}$

Use the height in the equation in part (a) to find v.

$$v^2 = 2gh$$

$$v^2 = 2(9.81)(22.30)$$

$$v = +20.92 \frac{\text{m}}{\text{s}} \xrightarrow{\text{SD}} \mathbf{+21\ \frac{m}{s}}$$

(c) $160 = PE_i - PE_f$

$$160 = mgx - mgh$$

$$160 = m(9.81)(31.86) - m(9.81)(22.30)$$

$$160 = m(93.78)$$

$$m = 1.706 \text{ kg} \xrightarrow{\text{SD}} \mathbf{1.7\ kg}$$

19. (a) Impulse $= F\Delta t = 680 \text{ N} \times 30.0 \text{ s} = \mathbf{2.04 \times 10^4\ N{\cdot}s}$

(b) $F\Delta t = m(v_2 - v_1)$

$$2.04 \times 10^4 \text{ N·s} = 46.0 \text{ kg}\left(v_2 - 0\frac{\text{m}}{\text{s}}\right)$$

$$v_2 = 443.48 \frac{\text{m}}{\text{s}} \xrightarrow{\text{SD}} \mathbf{443\ \frac{m}{s}\ \text{to the right}}$$

20. (a) $\vec{F} = m\vec{a}$

$$= 819 \text{ kg} \times 11 \text{ m·s}^{-2}$$

$$= 9.009 \times 10^3 \text{ N} \xrightarrow{\text{SD}} \mathbf{9.0 \times 10^3\ N\ \text{to the left}}$$

(b) $\Sigma\vec{F}_x = 11{,}260 \text{ N} - 9.009 \times 10^3 \text{ N}$

$$= 2.251 \times 10^3 \text{ N} \xrightarrow{\text{SD}} \mathbf{2.3 \times 10^3\ N\ \text{to the right}}$$

Problem Set 47

1. $I_1 + 3 \text{ A} = 12 \text{ A}$

$$I_1 = \mathbf{9\ A}$$

2. $I_2 = \frac{45.0 \text{ V}}{20.0\ \Omega} = \mathbf{2.25\ A}$

$$I_3 = \frac{45.0 \text{ V}}{60\ \Omega} = \mathbf{0.75\ A}$$

Use Kirchhoff's current law to find I_1.

$I_1 = I_2 + I_3 = 2.25 \text{ A} + 0.75 \text{ A} = \mathbf{3.0\ A}$

3. To find V_{CA}, begin at A and move clockwise to C.

$V_{CA} = -6 \text{ V} + 8 \text{ V} = \mathbf{+2\ V}$

To find V_{BD}, begin at D and move clockwise to B.

$V_{BD} = +9 \text{ V} - 4 \text{ V} - 6 \text{ V} = \mathbf{-1\ V}$

4. Begin at the ground symbol, move clockwise, and sum the voltage changes to zero.

$$-10.0 \text{ V} + 12 \text{ V} - 30.0 \text{ V} + V_2 + 15 \text{ V} = 0$$

$$V_2 = \mathbf{13\ V}$$

5. (a) $F_s = \mu_s F_N = 0.12(5.0 \times 10^{-4}\,\cancel{\text{kg}})\left(9.81\,\frac{\text{N}}{\cancel{\text{kg}}}\right)$

$= 5.886 \times 10^{-4}\text{ N} \xrightarrow{\text{SD}} \mathbf{5.9 \times 10^{-4}\ N}$

(b) Begin by converting 33.3 rev/min to rad/s.

$$33.3\,\frac{\cancel{\text{rev}}}{\cancel{\text{min}}} \times \frac{2\pi\text{ rad}}{1\,\cancel{\text{rev}}} \times \frac{1\,\cancel{\text{min}}}{60\text{ s}} = 3.487\,\frac{\text{rad}}{\text{s}}$$

Now equate the maximum force of friction, part (a), with the centripetal force.

$$F_s = mr\omega^2$$

$$5.886 \times 10^{-4} = (5.0 \times 10^{-4})(r)(3.487)^2$$

$$r = 9.6816 \times 10^{-2}\text{ m} \xrightarrow{\text{SD}} \mathbf{9.7 \times 10^{-2}\ m}$$

6. To find the angular speed, set the tensile strength equal to the centripetal force.

$$T_s = mr\omega^2$$

$$600 = (2.7531)(15.4002)\omega^2$$

$$\omega = 3.762\,\frac{\text{rad}}{\text{s}}$$

Convert 3.762 rad/s to rev/min and get:

$$3.762\,\frac{\cancel{\text{rad}}}{\cancel{\text{s}}} \times \frac{1\text{ rev}}{2\pi\,\cancel{\text{rad}}} \times \frac{60\,\cancel{\text{s}}}{1\text{ min}} = 35.92\,\frac{\text{rev}}{\text{min}} \xrightarrow{\text{SD}} \mathbf{40\,\frac{rev}{min}}$$

7. Begin by finding the x and y components of the initial velocity.

$$v_{x0} = 770\cos 42° = 572.22\,\frac{\text{m}}{\text{s}}$$

$$v_{y0} = 770\sin 42° = 515.23\,\frac{\text{m}}{\text{s}}$$

(a) Use the y-displacement equation to find the time.

$$\Delta y = v_{y0}t + \frac{1}{2}a_y t^2$$

$$(0) = 515.23t + \frac{1}{2}(-9.81)t^2$$

$$4.905t^2 = 515.23t$$

$$t = 105.04\text{ s} \xrightarrow{\text{SD}} \mathbf{105\ s}$$

(b) Use this time in the x-position equation to find the distance.

$$x = x_0 + v_{x0}t + \frac{1}{2}a_x t^2$$

$$= (0) + 572.22(105.04) + (0)$$

$$= 6.011 \times 10^4\text{ m} \xrightarrow{\text{SD}} \mathbf{6.01 \times 10^4\ m}$$

8. Begin by finding the x and y components of the initial velocity.

$$v_{x0} = 19\cos 31° = 16.29\,\frac{\text{m}}{\text{s}}$$

$$v_{y0} = 19\sin 31° = 9.79\,\frac{\text{m}}{\text{s}}$$

(a) Use the y-displacement equation to find the time.

$$\Delta y = v_{y0}t + \frac{1}{2}a_y t^2$$

$$-18 = 9.79t + \frac{1}{2}(-9.81)t^2$$

$$0 = 4.905t^2 - 9.79t - 18$$

Use the quadratic formula to solve this equation for t.

$$t = \frac{-(-9.79) \pm \sqrt{(-9.79)^2 - 4(4.905)(-18)}}{2(4.905)}$$

$$= 3.158\text{ s} \xrightarrow{\text{SD}} \mathbf{3.2\ s}$$

(b) Use this time in the x-position equation to find the distance.

$$x = x_0 + v_{x0}t + \frac{1}{2}a_x t^2$$

$$= (0) + 16.29(3.158) + (0)$$

$$= 51.44\text{ m} \xrightarrow{\text{SD}} \mathbf{51\ m}$$

9. Increasing the mass by a factor of 4 increases the tension in the string by a factor of 4.

$$v_1 = \sqrt{\frac{T}{M_L}} \longrightarrow v_2 = \sqrt{\frac{4T}{M_L}}$$

Factor the 4 out from under the radical and get:

$$v_2 = 2\sqrt{\frac{T}{M_L}}$$

Now, note that $\sqrt{\frac{T}{M_L}}$ is equal to v_1. Substitute and get:

$$v_2 = \mathbf{2v_1}$$

10. (a) Begin by finding the tension, mg, and the mass per unit length of the string.

$$T = mg = 8.90\,\cancel{\text{kg}} \times 9.81\,\frac{\text{N}}{\cancel{\text{kg}}} = 87.31\text{ N}$$

$$M_L = \frac{0.980\text{ kg}}{4.70\text{ m}} = 0.2085\,\frac{\text{kg}}{\text{m}}$$

Insert these values into the formula below to find v.

$$v = \sqrt{\frac{T}{M_L}} = \sqrt{\frac{87.31\text{ N}}{0.2085\,\frac{\text{kg}}{\text{m}}}} = 20.463\,\frac{\text{m}}{\text{s}} \xrightarrow{\text{SD}} \mathbf{20.5\,\frac{m}{s}}$$

(b)

$$v = f\lambda$$

$$20.463\,\frac{\text{m}}{\text{s}} = f(2.07\text{ m})$$

$$f = 9.886\text{ Hz} \xrightarrow{\text{SD}} \mathbf{9.89\text{ Hz}}$$

11. Begin by writing a $\sum F_x = ma_x$ equation for the 25-kg block. Choose to the right as the positive direction for motion.

$$\sum F_x = ma_x$$

$$T - \mu_k mg = ma$$

$$T - (0.37)(25)(9.81) = 25a$$

$$T = 90.74 + 25a \quad \text{(a)}$$

Next, write a $\sum F_y = ma_y$ equation for the 38-kg object.

$$\sum F_y = ma_y$$

$$mg - T = ma$$

$$(38)(9.81) - T = 38a$$

$$T = 372.78 - 38a \quad \text{(b)}$$

Substitute (b) into (a) to find the acceleration.

(a) $(372.78 - 38a) = 90.74 + 25a$

$$282.04 = 63a$$

$$a = 4.48\,\frac{\text{m}}{\text{s}^2} \xrightarrow{\text{SD}} \mathbf{4.5\,\frac{m}{s^2}\text{ to the right}}$$

Substitute the acceleration into (a) to find T.

(a) $T = 90.74 + 25(4.48) = 202.74\text{ N} \xrightarrow{\text{SD}} \mathbf{2\bar{0}0\text{ N}}$

12. Begin by finding the components of the weight of the 13.0-kg block on the plane that are parallel and perpendicular to the plane.

$F_x = mg\sin 15° = (13.0)(9.81)\sin 15° = 33.01\text{ N}$

$F_N = mg\cos 15° = (13.0)(9.81)\cos 15° = 123.18\text{ N}$

Next, compute the weight of the suspended 13.0-kg block.

$w = mg = (13.0)(9.81) = 127.53\text{ N}$

Since $w > F_x$, we choose the positive x direction to be up the plane. Now, write a $\sum F_x = ma_x$ equation for the 13.0-kg block on the plane.

$$\sum F_x = ma_x$$

$$T - F_x - \mu_k F_N = ma$$

$$T - 33.01 - 0.340(123.18) = 13.0a$$

$$T = 74.89 + 13.0a \quad \text{(a)}$$

Now, write a $\sum F_y = ma_y$ equation for the suspended 13.0-kg block.

$$\sum F_y = ma_y$$

$$mg - T = ma$$

$$(127.53) - T = 13.0a$$

$$T = 127.53 - 13.0a \quad \text{(b)}$$

Substitute (b) into (a) to find the acceleration.

(a) $(127.53 - 13.0a) = 74.89 + 13.0a$

$$26.0a = 52.64$$

$$a = 2.0246\,\frac{\text{m}}{\text{s}^2} \xrightarrow{\text{SD}} \mathbf{2.02\,\frac{m}{s^2}\text{ up the plane}}$$

Substitute the acceleration into (a) to find T.

(a) $T = 74.89 + 13.0(2.0246) = 101.21\text{ N} \xrightarrow{\text{SD}} \mathbf{101\text{ N}}$

13. (a) $I = \frac{V}{R} = \frac{12\text{ V}}{100\,\Omega} = \mathbf{0.12\text{ A}}$

(b) $P = VI = (12\text{ V})(0.12\text{ A}) = 1.44\text{ W} \xrightarrow{\text{SD}} \mathbf{1.4\text{ W}}$

$P = I^2R = (0.12\text{ A})^2(100\,\Omega) = 1.44\text{ W} \xrightarrow{\text{SD}} \mathbf{1.4\text{ W}}$

(c) $1.44\,\frac{\text{J}}{\cancel{\text{s}}} \times 7.0\,\cancel{\text{s}} = 10.08\text{ J} \xrightarrow{\text{SD}} \mathbf{1\bar{0}\text{ J}}$

14. (a) $V_R = IR = (3.5\text{ A})(1.5\ \Omega) = 5.25\text{ V} \xrightarrow{\text{SD}}$ **5.3 V**

(b) $V_R = IR = (-1.2\text{ A})(11\ \Omega) = -13.2\text{ V} \xrightarrow{\text{SD}}$ **−13 V**

(c) $P = VI = (8.0\text{ V})(3.0\text{ A}) =$ **24 W**

(d) $P = VI = (12.6\text{ V})(0.50\text{ A}) =$ **6.3 W**

15. To find the spring constant, find the slope of the line.

$$k = \text{slope} = \frac{\Delta y}{\Delta x} = \frac{75\text{ N}}{3.0\text{ m}} = \mathbf{25\ \frac{N}{m}}$$

16.
$$D = R \times T$$
$$3500\text{ m} = 360\ \frac{\text{m}}{\text{s}} \times T$$
$$T = 9.72\text{ s} \xrightarrow{\text{SD}} \mathbf{9.7\ s}$$

17. Begin by calculating the amount of heat needed to obtain liquid mercury at 357°C.

$$Q_1 = 0.750\ \cancel{\text{kg}} \times 11.8 \times 10^3\ \frac{\text{J}}{\cancel{\text{kg}}} = 8850\text{ J}$$

$$Q_2 = 0.750\ \cancel{\text{kg}} \times 140\ \frac{\text{J}}{\cancel{\text{kg}}\cdot\cancel{\text{C}^\circ}} \times 396\ \cancel{\text{C}^\circ} = 41{,}580\text{ J}$$

$$Q_T = Q_1 + Q_2 = 8850\text{ J} + 41{,}580\text{ J} = 50{,}430\text{ J}$$

Subtract Q_T from the total amount of heat needed to convert the solid mercury to gaseous mercury. This equals the heat needed to vaporize the liquid mercury.

$$Q_V = 254{,}430\text{ J} - 50{,}430\text{ J} = 204{,}000\text{ J}$$

Now solve for the heat of vaporization of mercury.

$$204{,}000\text{ J} = 0.750\text{ kg} \times H_V$$

$$H_V = \mathbf{2.72 \times 10^5\ \frac{J}{kg}}$$

18. (a)
$$m_1v_1 + m_2v_2 = (m_1 + m_2)v_3$$
$$(5.60 \times 10^{-3})(236) + (3.60)(0) = (3.6056)v_3$$
$$v_3 = +0.3665\ \frac{\text{m}}{\text{s}} \xrightarrow{\text{SD}} \mathbf{+0.367\ \frac{m}{s}}$$

(b)
$$KE = \frac{1}{2}mv_3^2 = \frac{1}{2}(3.6056)(0.3665)^2 = 0.2422\text{ J} \xrightarrow{\text{SD}} \mathbf{0.242\ J}$$

(c)
$$PE = mgh$$
$$0.2422 = (3.6056)(9.81)h$$
$$h = 6.847 \times 10^{-3}\text{ m} \xrightarrow{\text{SD}} \mathbf{6.85 \times 10^{-3}\ m}$$

19.
$$F = ma$$
$$560\text{ N} = 145\text{ kg} \times a$$
$$a = 3.86\ \frac{\text{m}}{\text{s}^2} \xrightarrow{\text{SD}} \mathbf{3.9\ \frac{m}{s^2}}$$

20.
$$287\ \frac{\cancel{\text{kg}}}{\cancel{\text{m}^3}} \times \frac{1000\text{ g}}{1\ \cancel{\text{kg}}} \times \frac{1\ \cancel{\text{m}^3}}{(100)^3\text{ cm}^3} = \mathbf{0.287\ \frac{g}{cm^3}}$$

PROBLEM SET 48

1. (a) Use the third equation for uniform acceleration to find the velocity.

$$2a\Delta x = v_t^2 - v_0^2$$
$$2(-9.81)(-26) = v_t^2 - (-17)^2$$
$$510.12 = v_t^2 - 289$$
$$v_t = -28.27\ \frac{\text{m}}{\text{s}} \xrightarrow{\text{SD}} \mathbf{28\ \frac{m}{s}\ downward}$$

(b)
$$KE = \frac{1}{2}mv_t^2 = \frac{1}{2}(1.2)(-28.27)^2 = 479.5\text{ J} \xrightarrow{\text{SD}} \mathbf{480\ J}$$

2.
$$W = FD\cos\theta = (29\text{ N})(6.0\cos 19^\circ\text{ m}) = 164.52\text{ J} \xrightarrow{\text{SD}} \mathbf{160\ J}$$

3. $I_2 = \frac{13.6\text{ V}}{50.0\ \Omega} = \mathbf{0.272\ A}$

$I_3 = \frac{13.6\text{ V}}{75.0\ \Omega} = 0.1813\text{ A} \xrightarrow{\text{SD}} \mathbf{0.181\ A}$

Use Kirchhoff's current law to find I_1.

$I_1 = I_2 + I_3 = 0.272\text{ A} + 0.1813\text{ A} = 0.4533\text{ A} \xrightarrow{\text{SD}} \mathbf{0.453\ A}$

4. Begin at the ground symbol, move clockwise, and sum the voltage changes to zero.

$-3.5\text{ V} + V_1 + 1.2\text{ V} - 2.0\text{ V} + 1.5\text{ V} = 0$

$V_1 = \mathbf{2.8\ V}$

5. Begin by finding the centripetal force, F_c, and the weight of the ball.

$F_c = \frac{mv^2}{r} = \frac{2.5(2.4)^2}{0.27} = 53.33\text{ N}$

$w = mg = (2.5)(9.81) = 24.525\text{ N}$

The tension, T, is equal to the vector sum of the horizontal force, F_c, and the vertical force, w.

$T = \sqrt{(53.33)^2 + (24.525)^2} = 58.699\text{ N} \xrightarrow{\text{SD}} \mathbf{59\ N}$

6. (a) $F_s = \mu_s F_N$

$F_s = \boldsymbol{\mu_s m_{bug} g}$

(b) $F_c = \frac{m_{bug} v^2}{r}$

$F_c = \frac{m_{bug}(\omega r)^2}{r}$

$F_c = \boldsymbol{m_{bug}\omega^2 r}$

(c) $F_s = F_c$

$\mu_s m_{bug} g = m_{bug}\omega^2 r$

$r = \boldsymbol{\frac{\mu_s g}{\omega^2}}$

7. Begin by finding the x and y components of the initial velocity.

$v_{x0} = 25 \cos 65° = 10.57\ \frac{\text{m}}{\text{s}}$

$v_{y0} = 25 \sin 65° = 22.66\ \frac{\text{m}}{\text{s}}$

(a) Use the y-displacement equation to find the time.

$\Delta y = v_{y0}t + \frac{1}{2}a_y t^2$

$(0) = 22.66t + \frac{1}{2}(-9.81)t^2$

$4.905t^2 = 22.66t$

$t = 4.62\text{ s} \xrightarrow{\text{SD}} \mathbf{4.6\ s}$

(b) Use this time in the x-position equation to find the distance.

$x = x_0 + v_{x0}t + \frac{1}{2}a_x t^2$

$= (0) + 10.57(4.62) + (0)$

$= 48.83\text{ m} \xrightarrow{\text{SD}} \mathbf{49\ m}$

(c) The ball is at its highest point when the time is half its total, or 2.31 s. Use this time in the y-displacement equation to find the height.

$\Delta y = v_{y0}t + \frac{1}{2}a_y t^2$

$= 22.66(2.31) + \frac{1}{2}(-9.81)(2.31)^2$

$= 26.17\text{ m} \xrightarrow{\text{SD}} \mathbf{26\ m}$

8. Decrease the mass per unit length of the string by a factor of one-half.

$v_1 = \sqrt{\frac{T}{M_L}} \rightarrow v_2 = \sqrt{\frac{T}{\frac{M_L}{2}}}$

Factor the 2 out from under the radical and get:

$v_2 = \sqrt{2}\sqrt{\frac{T}{M_L}}$

Now, note that $\sqrt{\frac{T}{M_L}}$ is equal to v_1. Substitute and get:

$v_2 = \boldsymbol{\sqrt{2}v_1}$

9. (a) $\Sigma F_y = 0$; $F_A + F_B - 240\text{ N} - 160\text{ N} = 0$
(b) $\Sigma M_B = 0$; $F_A(24\text{ m}) - 240\text{ N}(16\text{ m}) - 160\text{ N}(6\text{ m}) = 0$
Solve (b) for F_A and get:
(b) $F_A(24\text{ m}) - 3840\text{ N·m} - 960\text{ N·m} = 0$
$F_A(24\text{ m}) = 4800\text{ N·m}$
$F_A = \mathbf{200\ N}$

Substitute F_A into (a) to find F_B.
(a) $(200\text{ N}) + F_B - 240\text{ N} - 160\text{ N} = 0$
$F_B = \mathbf{200\ N}$

10. Begin by finding the components of the weight of the 6.50-kg block that are parallel and perpendicular to the plane.
$F_x = mg \sin 26° = (6.50)(9.81) \sin 26° = 27.95\text{ N}$
$F_N = mg \cos 26° = (6.50)(9.81) \cos 26° = 57.31\text{ N}$
Next, compute the weight of the 9.65-kg block.
$w = mg = (9.65)(9.81) = 94.67\text{ N}$
Since $w > F_x$, we choose the positive x direction to be up the plane. Now, write a $\Sigma F_x = ma_x$ equation for the 6.50-kg block.

$$\Sigma F_x = ma_x$$
$$T - F_x - \mu_k F_N = ma$$
$$T - 27.95 - (0.228)(57.31) = 6.50a$$
$$T = 41.02 + 6.50a \quad \text{(a)}$$

Now, write a $\Sigma F_y = ma_y$ equation for the 9.65-kg block.

$$\Sigma F_y = ma_y$$
$$mg - T = ma$$
$$(94.67) - T = 9.65a$$
$$T = 94.67 - 9.65a \quad \text{(b)}$$

Substitute (b) into (a) to find the acceleration.
(a) $(94.67 - 9.65a) = 41.02 + 6.50a$
$53.65 = 16.15a$
$a = 3.322\ \frac{\text{m}}{\text{s}^2} \xrightarrow{\text{SD}} \mathbf{3.32\ \frac{m}{s^2}}$ **up the plane**

Substitute the acceleration into (a) to find T.
(a) $T = 41.02 + 6.50(3.322) = 62.613\text{ N} \xrightarrow{\text{SD}} \mathbf{62.6\ N}$

11. (a) $I = \frac{V}{R} = \frac{15\text{ V}}{2220\ \Omega} = 6.76 \times 10^{-3}\text{ A} \xrightarrow{\text{SD}} \mathbf{6.8 \times 10^{-3}\ A}$
(b) $P = I^2R = (6.76 \times 10^{-3}\text{ A})^2(2220\ \Omega) = 0.101\text{ W} \xrightarrow{\text{SD}} \mathbf{0.10\ W}$
$P = VI = (15\text{ V})(6.76 \times 10^{-3}\text{ A}) = 0.101\text{ W} \xrightarrow{\text{SD}} \mathbf{0.10\ W}$
(c) $0.101\ \frac{\text{J}}{\not{\text{s}}} \times 6.0\not{\text{s}} = 0.606\text{ J} \xrightarrow{\text{SD}} \mathbf{0.61\ J}$

12. (a) $V_R = IR = (6\text{ A})(50\ \Omega) = \mathbf{300\ V}$
(b) $V_R = IR = (-2.0\text{ A})(10\ \Omega) = \mathbf{-20\ V}$
(c) $P = VI = (24.0\text{ V})(6.00\text{ A}) = \mathbf{144\ W}$
(d) $P = VI = (6.5\text{ V})(3.5\text{ A}) = 22.75\text{ W} \xrightarrow{\text{SD}} \mathbf{23\ W}$

13. (a) $F = kx$
$55(9.81) = k(1.6 \times 10^{-2})$
$k = 3.37 \times 10^4\ \frac{\text{N}}{\text{m}} \xrightarrow{\text{SD}} \mathbf{3.4 \times 10^4\ \frac{N}{m}}$
(b) $W = \frac{1}{2}kx^2$
$= \frac{1}{2}(3.37 \times 10^4)(1.6 \times 10^{-2})^2$
$= 4.314\text{ J} \xrightarrow{\text{SD}} \mathbf{4.3\ J}$

14. $D = R \times T$
$5000\text{ m} = 346\ \frac{\text{m}}{\text{s}} \times T$
$T = 14.45\text{ s} \xrightarrow{\text{SD}} \mathbf{14\ s}$

15. $Q_1 = 2.50(2050)(42.0) = 215{,}250\text{ J}$
$Q_2 = 2.50(3.34 \times 10^5) = 835{,}000\text{ J}$
$Q_3 = 2.50(4186)(100) = 1{,}046{,}500\text{ J}$
$Q_4 = 2.50(2.256 \times 10^6) = 5{,}640{,}000\text{ J}$
$Q_5 = 2.50(2009)(461) = 2{,}315{,}373\text{ J}$
$Q_T = 1.005 \times 10^7\text{ J} \xrightarrow{\text{SD}} \mathbf{1.01 \times 10^7\ J}$

16. Begin by finding the cross-sectional area of the bar.

$A = (0.0050 \text{ m})(0.020 \text{ m}) = 1.0 \times 10^{-4} \text{ m}^2$

Now find the electrical resistance.

$$R = \rho \frac{L}{A} = \frac{(1.7 \times 10^{-8}\,\Omega\cdot\text{m})(0.15 \text{ m})}{1.0 \times 10^{-4} \text{ m}^2}$$
$$= 2.55 \times 10^{-5}\,\Omega \xrightarrow{\text{SD}} \mathbf{2.6 \times 10^{-5}\,\Omega}$$

17. Begin by converting 1.78 g/cm^3 to kg/m^3.

$$1.78 \frac{\text{g}}{\text{cm}^3} \times \frac{1 \text{ kg}}{1000 \text{ g}} \times \frac{(100)^3 \text{cm}^3}{1 \text{ m}^3} = 1780 \frac{\text{kg}}{\text{m}^3}$$

Now find the pressure produced by the fluid.

$$P_F = 1780 \frac{\text{kg}}{\text{m}^{3\,2}} \times 9.81 \frac{\text{N}}{\text{kg}} \times 0.100 \text{ m} = 1746.18 \text{ Pa}$$

Now sum this pressure with the atmospheric pressure and find P.

$P = 1746.18 \text{ Pa} + 1.013 \times 10^5 \text{ Pa}$

$= 1.030 \times 10^5 \text{ Pa} \xrightarrow{\text{SD}} \mathbf{1.03 \times 10^5 \text{ Pa}}$

18. (a) $a = \frac{\Delta v}{\Delta t} = \frac{17 - 29 \text{ m/s}}{10 \text{ s}} = \mathbf{-1.2 \frac{m}{s^2}}$

(b) Use the x-displacement equation to find the distance.

$$\Delta x = v_0 t + \frac{1}{2}at^2$$
$$= 29(10) + \frac{1}{2}(-1.2)(10)^2$$
$$= \mathbf{230 \text{ m}}$$

19. $W = F \times D = 650 \text{ N} \times 12 \text{ m} = \mathbf{7800 \text{ J}}$

20. $$\rho = \frac{60 \text{ kg}}{0.051684 \text{ m}^3} \times \frac{1000 \text{ g}}{1 \text{ kg}} \times \frac{1 \text{ m}^3}{(100)^3 \text{cm}^3}$$
$$= 1.161 \frac{\text{g}}{\text{cm}^3} \xrightarrow{\text{SD}} \mathbf{1 \frac{g}{cm^3}}$$

PROBLEM SET 49

1. Begin by labeling the direction of the current and denoting the signs on the resistors.

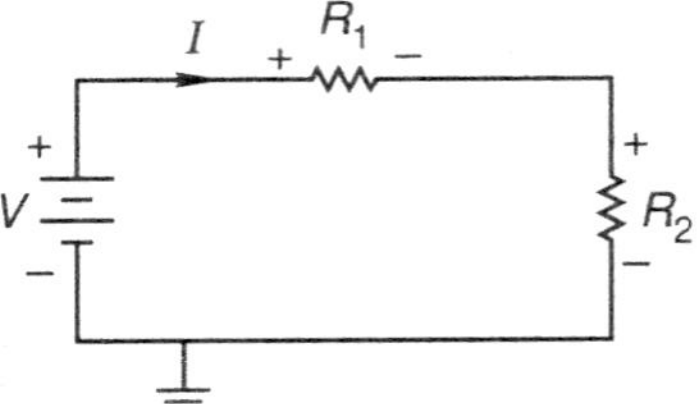

Start at the ground symbol, move clockwise, and sum the voltage changes to zero.

$$-V + IR_1 + IR_2 = 0$$
$$IR_1 + IR_2 = V$$
$$I(R_1 + R_2) = V$$
$$I = \mathbf{\frac{V}{R_1 + R_2}}$$

2. (a) $\Delta KE = KE_f - KE_i$

$$= \frac{1}{2}(0.250)(3.00)^2 - \frac{1}{2}(0.250)(0)^2$$
$$= 1.125 \text{ J} \xrightarrow{\text{SD}} \mathbf{1.13 \text{ J}}$$

(b) The total work done by Suzy on the ball equals the change in kinetic energy of the ball or **1.13 J.** Refer to section 48.C, if needed.

3. $I_2 = \frac{24 \text{ V}}{3.0\,\Omega} = \mathbf{8.0 \text{ A}}$

$I_3 = \frac{24 \text{ V}}{8.0\,\Omega} = \mathbf{3.0 \text{ A}}$

Use Kirchhoff's current law to find I_1.

$I_1 = I_2 + I_3 = 8.0 \text{ A} + 3.0 \text{ A} = \mathbf{11 \text{ A}}$

4. To find V_{CA}, begin at A and move counterclockwise to C.

$V_{CA} = -6\text{ V} + 4\text{ V} + 3\text{ V} = \mathbf{+1\ V}$

To find V_{BD}, begin at D and move counterclockwise to B.

$V_{BD} = +6\text{ V} - 6\text{ V} + 4\text{ V} = \mathbf{+4\ V}$

5. The tension in the string is equal to the centripetal force.

$$T = \frac{mv^2}{r} = \frac{1.05(4.00)^2}{0.593} = 28.33\text{ N} \xrightarrow{\text{SD}} \mathbf{28.3\ N}$$

6. To find the angular speed, set the tensile strength equal to the centripetal force.

$$T_s = mr\omega^2$$
$$36 = (1.3)(0.73)\omega^2$$
$$\omega = 6.159\ \frac{\text{rad}}{\text{s}}$$

Convert 6.159 rad/s to rev/min and get:

$$6.159\ \frac{\cancel{\text{rad}}}{\cancel{\text{s}}} \times \frac{1\text{ rev}}{2\pi\ \cancel{\text{rad}}} \times \frac{60\ \cancel{\text{s}}}{1\text{ min}} = 58.81\ \frac{\text{rev}}{\text{min}} \xrightarrow{\text{SD}} \mathbf{59\ \frac{rev}{min}}$$

7. Begin by finding the x and y components of the initial velocity.

$$v_{x0} = 42\cos 54° = 24.69\ \frac{\text{m}}{\text{s}}$$
$$v_{y0} = 42\sin 54° = 33.98\ \frac{\text{m}}{\text{s}}$$

(a) Use the y-displacement equation to find the time.

$$\Delta y = v_{y0}t + \frac{1}{2}a_y t^2$$
$$(0) = 33.98t + \frac{1}{2}(-9.81)t^2$$
$$4.905t^2 = 33.98t$$
$$t = 6.928\text{ s} \xrightarrow{\text{SD}} \mathbf{6.9\ s}$$

(b) Use this time in the x-position equation to find the distance.

$$x = x_0 + v_{x0}t + \frac{1}{2}a_x t^2$$
$$= (0) + 24.69(6.928) + (0)$$
$$= 171.1\text{ m} \xrightarrow{\text{SD}} \mathbf{170\ m}$$

(c) The ball is at its highest point when the time is half its total, or 3.464 s. Use this time in the y-displacement equation to find the height.

$$\Delta y = v_{y0}t + \frac{1}{2}a_y t^2$$
$$= 33.98(3.464) + \frac{1}{2}(-9.81)(3.464)^2$$
$$= 58.85\text{ m} \xrightarrow{\text{SD}} \mathbf{59\ m}$$

8. Increasing the mass by a factor of 2 increases the tension in the string by a factor of 2.

$$v_1 = \sqrt{\frac{T}{M_L}} \longrightarrow v_2 = \sqrt{\frac{2T}{M_L}}$$

Factor the 2 out from under the radical and get:

$$v_2 = \sqrt{2}\sqrt{\frac{T}{M_L}}$$

Now, note that $\sqrt{\frac{T}{M_L}}$ is equal to v_1. Substitute and get:

$$\mathbf{v_2 = \sqrt{2}v_1}$$

9. (a) Begin by finding the tension, mg, and the mass per unit length of the string.

$$T = mg = 3.22\ \cancel{\text{kg}} \times 9.81\ \frac{\text{N}}{\cancel{\text{kg}}} = 31.59\text{ N}$$
$$M_L = \frac{0.712\text{ kg}}{3.65\text{ m}} = 0.195\ \frac{\text{kg}}{\text{m}}$$

Insert these values into the formula below to find v.

$$v = \sqrt{\frac{T}{M_L}} = \sqrt{\frac{31.59\text{ N}}{0.195\ \frac{\text{kg}}{\text{m}}}} = 12.73\ \frac{\text{m}}{\text{s}} \xrightarrow{\text{SD}} \mathbf{12.7\ \frac{m}{s}}$$

(b)
$$v = f\lambda$$
$$12.73\ \frac{\text{m}}{\text{s}} = f(2.88\text{ m})$$
$$f = 4.4201\text{ Hz} \xrightarrow{\text{SD}} \mathbf{4.42\ Hz}$$

10. Begin by writing a $\sum F_x = ma_x$ equation for the 5.19-kg block. Choose to the right as the positive direction for motion.

$$\sum F_x = ma_x$$
$$T - \mu_k mg = ma$$
$$T - (0.395)(5.19)(9.81) = 5.19a$$
$$T = 20.11 + 5.19a \quad \text{(a)}$$

Next, write a $\sum F_y = ma_y$ equation for the 7.66-kg block.

$$\sum F_y = ma_y$$
$$mg - T = ma$$
$$(7.66)(9.81) - T = 7.66a$$
$$T = 75.14 - 7.66a \quad \text{(b)}$$

Substitute (b) into (a) to find the acceleration.

(a) $(75.14 - 7.66a) = 20.11 + 5.19a$

$$55.03 = 12.85a$$
$$a = 4.282 \frac{\text{m}}{\text{s}^2} \xrightarrow{\text{SD}} \mathbf{4.28 \frac{m}{s^2}} \textbf{ to the right}$$

Substitute the acceleration into (a) to find T.

(a) $T = 20.11 + 5.19(4.282) = 42.33 \text{ N} \xrightarrow{\text{SD}} \mathbf{42.3\ N}$

11. (a) $I = \frac{V}{R} = \frac{16.0 \text{ V}}{120\ \Omega} = 0.1333 \text{ A} \xrightarrow{\text{SD}} \mathbf{0.133\ A}$

(b) $P = I^2R = (0.1333 \text{ A})^2(120\ \Omega) = 2.132 \text{ W} \xrightarrow{\text{SD}} \mathbf{2.13\ W}$

(c) $P = VI = (16.0 \text{ V})(0.1333 \text{ A}) = 2.133 \text{ W} \xrightarrow{\text{SD}} \mathbf{2.13\ W}$

$2.133 \frac{\text{J}}{\cancel{\text{s}}} \times 3.50 \cancel{\text{s}} = 7.466 \text{ J} \xrightarrow{\text{SD}} \mathbf{7.47\ J}$

12. (a) $V_R = IR = (-3.6 \text{ A})(36\ \Omega) = -129.6 \text{ V} \xrightarrow{\text{SD}} \mathbf{-130\ V}$

(b) $V_R = IR = (2.5 \text{ A})(450\ \Omega) = 1125 \text{ V} \xrightarrow{\text{SD}} \mathbf{1100\ V}$

(c) $P = VI = (6.0 \text{ V})(2.0 \text{ A}) = \mathbf{12\ W}$

(d) $P = VI = (24 \text{ V})(1.5 \text{ A}) = \mathbf{36\ W}$

13. (a) $F = kx$

$$780 \text{ N} = k(0.0860 \text{ m})$$
$$k = 9.070 \times 10^3 \frac{\text{N}}{\text{m}} \xrightarrow{\text{SD}} \mathbf{9.07 \times 10^3 \frac{N}{m}}$$

(b) $W = \frac{1}{2}kx^2$

$$= \frac{1}{2}(9.070 \times 10^3)(0.0860)^2 = 33.54 \text{ J} \xrightarrow{\text{SD}} \mathbf{33.5\ J}$$

14. $D = R \times T$

$$6540 \text{ m} = 362 \frac{\text{m}}{\text{s}} \times T$$
$$T = 18.07 \text{ s} \xrightarrow{\text{SD}} \mathbf{18.1\ s}$$

15. Begin by finding the heat necessary to heat the lead to its melting point.

$$Q_1 = 900 \cancel{\text{kg}} \times 31.008 \frac{\text{cal}}{\cancel{\text{kg}} \cdot \cancel{\text{C}°}} \times 302.259 \cancel{\text{C}°} = 8.435 \times 10^6 \text{ cal}$$

Convert this to joules and get:

$$Q_1 = 8.435 \times 10^6 \cancel{\text{cal}} \times \frac{4.186 \text{ J}}{1 \cancel{\text{cal}}} = 3.531 \times 10^7 \text{ J}$$

Next, find the heat necessary to melt the lead.

$$Q_2 = 900 \cancel{\text{kg}} \times 24.58 \times 10^3 \frac{\text{J}}{\cancel{\text{kg}}} = 2.212 \times 10^7 \text{ J}$$

To find the total heat, sum Q_1 and Q_2.

$$Q_T = (3.531 \times 10^7 \text{ J}) + (2.212 \times 10^7 \text{ J})$$
$$= 5.743 \times 10^7 \text{ J} \xrightarrow{\text{SD}} \mathbf{6 \times 10^7\ J}$$

16. Begin by converting the temperature to kelvins.

$T_1 = 21.0 + 273 = 294 \text{ K}$

Now use the ideal gas law and get:

$$\frac{V_1}{T_1} = \frac{V_2}{T_2}$$
$$\frac{1.55 \text{ m}^3}{294 \text{ K}} = \frac{4.33 \text{ m}^3}{T_2}$$
$$T_2 = 821.30 \text{ K} \xrightarrow{\text{SD}} \mathbf{821\ K = 548°C}$$

17. $F = \frac{Gm_1m_2}{r^2} = \frac{(6.67 \times 10^{-11})(2.34 \times 10^4)(2.34 \times 10^4)}{(2.81 \times 10^5)^2}$

$= 4.625 \times 10^{-13}\text{ N} \xrightarrow{\text{SD}} \mathbf{4.63 \times 10^{-13}\ N}$

18. $Q = mc\Delta T$

$4.87 \times 10^6\text{ J} = 34\text{ kg} \times c \times 73\text{ C°}$

$c = 1.962 \times 10^3 \frac{\text{J}}{\text{kg·C°}} \xrightarrow{\text{SD}} \mathbf{2.0 \times 10^3\ \frac{J}{kg·C°}}$

19. Answers to this problem may vary due to differing data points. One possible solution is given here. Choose the points (2.5, 50) and (5, 30) and get:

$v_{\text{inst}} = \frac{\Delta x}{\Delta t} = \frac{30 - 50}{5 - 2.5}\frac{\text{m}}{\text{s}} = \mathbf{-8.0\ \frac{m}{s}}$

20. Begin by drawing a diagram and recording the data.

$D_W = 22.5$ mi
$T_W = 0.50$ hr
$D_N = 8.0$ mi
$T_N = 0.333$ hr

(a) $D_T = 8.0\text{ mi} + 22.5\text{ mi} = 30.5\text{ mi} \xrightarrow{\text{SD}} \mathbf{31\ mi}$

(b) $D = \sqrt{(8.0)^2 + (22.5)^2} = 23.88\text{ mi}$

$\theta = \tan^{-1}\frac{22.5}{8.0} = 70.43°$

Since θ is a 2nd-quadrant angle: $\alpha = 70.43° + 90° = 160.43°$

$\vec{D} = 23.88\underline{/160.43°}\text{ mi} \xrightarrow{\text{SD}} \mathbf{24\underline{/160.43°}\ mi}$

(c) $v = \frac{D_T}{T_T} = \frac{30.5\text{ mi}}{0.833\text{ hr}} = 36.61\frac{\text{mi}}{\text{hr}} \xrightarrow{\text{SD}} \mathbf{37\ \frac{mi}{hr}}$

$\vec{v} = \frac{\vec{D}}{T_T} = \frac{23.88\underline{/160.43°}\text{ mi}}{0.833\text{ hr}}$

$= 28.67\underline{/160.43°}\frac{\text{mi}}{\text{hr}} \xrightarrow{\text{SD}} \mathbf{29\underline{/160.43°}\ \frac{mi}{hr}}$

Problem Set 50

1. $PE = \frac{1}{2}kx^2 = \frac{1}{2}(980)(2.0)^2 = 1960\text{ J}$

$KE = \frac{1}{2}mv^2$

$1960 = \frac{1}{2}(20)v^2$

$v = \mathbf{14\ \frac{m}{s}}$

2. (a) $PE = \frac{1}{2}kx^2$

$250 = \frac{1}{2}(2540)x^2$

$x = 0.444\text{ m} \xrightarrow{\text{SD}} \mathbf{0.44\ m}$

(b) $PE = \frac{1}{2}kx^2 = \frac{1}{2}(2540)(0.36)^2 = 164.59\text{ J} \xrightarrow{\text{SD}} \mathbf{160\ J}$

(c) Total energy $= \frac{1}{2}kx^2 + \frac{1}{2}mv^2$

$250 = \frac{1}{2}(2540)(0.36)^2 + \frac{1}{2}(34)v^2$

$250 = 164.59 + 17v^2$

$v = 2.241\text{ m/s} \xrightarrow{\text{SD}} \mathbf{2.2\ m/s}$

3. Begin by labeling the direction of the current and denoting the signs on the resistors.

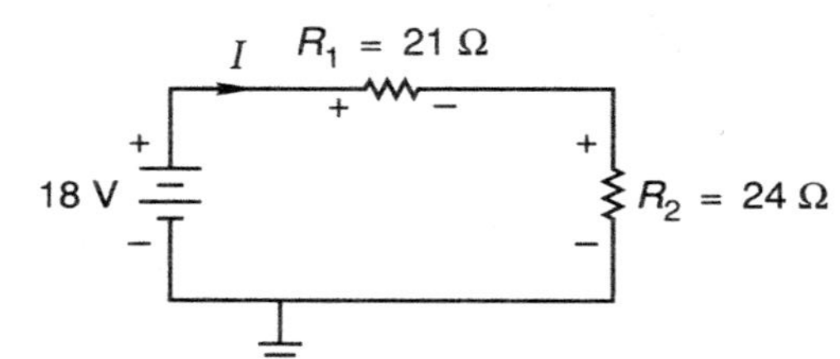

Start at the ground symbol, move clockwise, and sum the voltage changes to zero.

$-18\text{ V} + IR_1 + IR_2 = 0$

$-18\text{ V} + I(21\ \Omega) + I(24\ \Omega) = 0$

$I(45\ \Omega) = 18\text{ V}$

$I = \mathbf{0.40\ A}$

4. (a) $KE = \frac{1}{2}mv^2$

$= \frac{1}{2}(2000.0)(40)^2$

$= \mathbf{1.6 \times 10^6\ J}$

(b) $W = Fd$

$1.6 \times 10^6 = F(150.77)$

$F = 1.06 \times 10^4\ \text{N} \xrightarrow{\text{SD}} \mathbf{1.1 \times 10^4\ N}$

5. $I_2 = \frac{V_2}{R_2} = \frac{4\ \text{V}}{5\ \Omega} = \mathbf{0.8\ A}$

Use Kirchhoff's current law to find I_3.

$I_3 = 1\ \text{A} - I_2 = 1\ \text{A} - 0.8\ \text{A} = \mathbf{0.2\ A}$

6. To find V_{AD}, begin at D and move clockwise to A.

$V_{AD} = \mathbf{-3\ V}$

To find V_{DC}, begin at C and move clockwise to D.

$V_{DC} = -4\ \text{V} + 7\ \text{V} = \mathbf{+3\ V}$

7. To find the angular speed, set the tensile strength equal to the centripetal force.

$T_s = mr\omega^2$

$34 = (4.6)(0.540)\omega^2$

$\omega = 3.70\ \frac{\text{rad}}{\text{s}}$

Convert 3.70 rad/s to rev/min and get:

$3.70\ \frac{\cancel{\text{rad}}}{\cancel{\text{s}}} \times \frac{1\ \text{rev}}{2\pi\ \cancel{\text{rad}}} \times \frac{60\ \cancel{\text{s}}}{1\ \text{min}} = 35.33\ \frac{\text{rev}}{\text{min}} \xrightarrow{\text{SD}} \mathbf{35\ \frac{rev}{min}}$

8. Begin by finding the x and y components of the initial velocity.

$v_{x0} = 189 \cos 67° = 73.85\ \frac{\text{m}}{\text{s}}$

$v_{y0} = 189 \sin 67° = 173.98\ \frac{\text{m}}{\text{s}}$

(a) Use the y-displacement equation to find the time.

$\Delta y = v_{y0}t + \frac{1}{2}a_y t^2$

$(0) = 173.98t + \frac{1}{2}(-9.81)t^2$

$4.905t^2 = 173.98t$

$t = 35.47\ \text{s} \xrightarrow{\text{SD}} \mathbf{35.5\ s}$

(b) Use this time in the x-position equation to find the distance.

$x = x_0 + v_{x0}t + \frac{1}{2}a_x t^2$

$= (0) + 73.85(35.47) + (0)$

$= 2.619 \times 10^3\ \text{m} \xrightarrow{\text{SD}} \mathbf{2.62 \times 10^3\ m}$

(c) The cannonball is at its highest point when the time is half its total, or 17.74 s. Use this time in the y-displacement equation to find the height.

$\Delta y = v_{y0}t + \frac{1}{2}a_y t^2$

$= 173.98(17.74) + \frac{1}{2}(-9.81)(17.74)^2$

$= 1.543 \times 10^3\ \text{m} \xrightarrow{\text{SD}} \mathbf{1.54 \times 10^3\ m}$

9. (a) Begin by finding the tension, mg, and the mass per unit length of the string.

$T = mg = 16.2\ \cancel{\text{kg}} \times 9.81\ \frac{\text{N}}{\cancel{\text{kg}}} = 158.92\ \text{N}$

$M_L = \frac{0.564\ \text{kg}}{10.3\ \text{m}} = 0.0548\ \frac{\text{kg}}{\text{m}}$

Insert these values into the formula below to find v.

$v = \sqrt{\frac{T}{M_L}} = \sqrt{\frac{158.92\ \text{N}}{0.0548\ \frac{\text{kg}}{\text{m}}}} = 53.85\ \frac{\text{m}}{\text{s}} \xrightarrow{\text{SD}} \mathbf{53.9\ \frac{m}{s}}$

(b) $v = f\lambda$

$53.85 = f(3.45)$

$f = 15.61\ \text{Hz} \xrightarrow{\text{SD}} \mathbf{15.6\ Hz}$

10. Begin by writing a $\Sigma F_x = ma_x$ equation for the 34.9-kg block. Choose to the right as the positive direction for motion.

$$\Sigma F_x = ma_x$$
$$T - \mu_k mg = ma$$
$$T - (0.421)(34.9)(9.81) = 34.9a$$
$$T = 144.137 + 34.9a \qquad \text{(a)}$$

Next, write a $\Sigma F_y = ma_y$ equation for the 84.3-kg block.

$$\Sigma F_y = ma_y$$
$$mg - T = ma$$
$$(84.3)(9.81) - T = 84.3a$$
$$T = 826.98 - 84.3a \qquad \text{(b)}$$

Substitute (b) into (a) to find the acceleration.

$$\text{(a)}\ (826.98 - 84.3a) = 144.137 + 34.9a$$
$$682.84 = 119.2a$$
$$a = 5.729\ \frac{\text{m}}{\text{s}^2} \xrightarrow{\text{SD}} \mathbf{5.73\ \frac{m}{s^2}\ \text{to the right}}$$

Substitute the acceleration into (a) to find T.

$$\text{(a)}\ T = 144.137 + 34.9(5.729) = 344.079\ \text{N} \xrightarrow{\text{SD}} \mathbf{344\ N}$$

11. (a) $I = \frac{V}{R} = \frac{16\ \text{V}}{30{,}000\ \Omega} = 5.333 \times 10^{-4}\ \text{A} \xrightarrow{\text{SD}} \mathbf{5.3 \times 10^{-4}\ A}$

(b) $P = I^2R = (5.333 \times 10^{-4}\ \text{A})^2(30{,}000\ \Omega)$

$= 8.53 \times 10^{-3}\ \text{W} \xrightarrow{\text{SD}} \mathbf{8.5 \times 10^{-3}\ W}$

(c) $8.53 \times 10^{-3}\ \frac{\text{J}}{\cancel{\text{s}}} \times 15\ \cancel{\text{s}} = 0.128\ \text{J} \xrightarrow{\text{SD}} \mathbf{0.13\ J}$

12. (a) $V_R = IR = (-2.5\ \text{A})(15\ \Omega) = -37.5\ \text{V} \xrightarrow{\text{SD}} \mathbf{-38\ V}$

(b) $V_R = IR = (4.0\ \text{A})(8.0\ \Omega) = \mathbf{32\ V}$

(c) $P = VI = (12\ \text{V})(2.0\ \text{A}) = \mathbf{24\ W}$

(d) $P = VI = (6.0\ \text{V})(0.25\ \text{A}) = \mathbf{1.5\ W}$

13. (a)

$$F = kx$$
$$240\ \text{N} = k(1.90\ \text{m})$$
$$k = 126.32\ \frac{\text{N}}{\text{m}} \xrightarrow{\text{SD}} \mathbf{126\ \frac{N}{m}}$$

(b) $W = \frac{1}{2}kx^2 = \frac{1}{2}(126.32)(1.90)^2 = 228.01\ \text{J} \xrightarrow{\text{SD}} \mathbf{228\ J}$

14.

$$D = R \times T$$
$$2700\ \text{m} = 371\ \frac{\text{m}}{\text{s}} \times T$$
$$T = 7.278\ \text{s} \xrightarrow{\text{SD}} \mathbf{7.3\ s}$$

15. $Q_1 = 0.123\ \cancel{\text{kg}} \times 129\ \frac{\text{J}}{\cancel{\text{kg}}\cdot\cancel{\text{C°}}} \times 1038\ \cancel{\text{C°}} = 1.647 \times 10^4\ \text{J}$

$Q_2 = 0.123\ \cancel{\text{kg}} \times 64.5 \times 10^3\ \frac{\text{J}}{\cancel{\text{kg}}} = 7.934 \times 10^3\ \text{J}$

To find the total heat, sum Q_1 and Q_2.

$$Q_T = (1.647 \times 10^4\ \text{J}) + (7.934 \times 10^3\ \text{J})$$
$$= 2.4404 \times 10^4\ \text{J} \xrightarrow{\text{SD}} \mathbf{2.44 \times 10^4\ J}$$

16. (a) Begin by converting 915 rev/min to rad/s.

$$915\ \frac{\cancel{\text{rev}}}{\cancel{\text{min}}} \times \frac{2\pi\ \text{rad}}{1\ \cancel{\text{rev}}} \times \frac{1\ \cancel{\text{min}}}{60\ \text{s}} = 95.82\ \frac{\text{rad}}{\text{s}}$$

Now use the angular motion equation to find the angular speed after 1.90 s.

$$\omega(t) = \omega_0 + \alpha t$$
$$\omega(1.90) = 95.82 + 56.0(1.90) = 202.22\ \frac{\text{rad}}{\text{s}} \xrightarrow{\text{SD}} \mathbf{202\ \frac{rad}{s}}$$

(b) $\Delta\theta = \omega_0 t + \frac{1}{2}\alpha t^2$

$= 95.82(1.90) + \frac{1}{2}(56.0)(1.90)^2 = 283.1\ \text{rad} \xrightarrow{\text{SD}} \mathbf{283\ rad}$

17. $PE = mgh = 231(9.81)(13.4) = 3.037 \times 10^4$ J

$$KE = \frac{1}{2}mv^2$$

$$3.037 \times 10^4 = \frac{1}{2}(231)v^2$$

$$v = 16.22\ \frac{\text{m}}{\text{s}} \xrightarrow{\text{SD}} \mathbf{16.2\ \frac{m}{s}}$$

18. (a) Impulse $= F\Delta t = 4500$ N(10 s) $=$ **4.5 × 10⁴ N·s**

(b) $F\Delta t = m(v_2 - v_1)$

$$4.5 \times 10^4 = 983(v_2 - 0)$$

$$v_2 = 45.78\ \frac{\text{m}}{\text{s}} \xrightarrow{\text{SD}} \mathbf{46\ \frac{m}{s}}$$

19. Begin by finding the weight of the mass and drawing a free-body diagram of the forces acting on the junction of the ropes.

$w = mg$

$= 340\ \text{kg} \times 9.81\ \frac{\text{N}}{\text{kg}}$

$= 3335.4$ N

30° 40° T_1 T_2 3335.4 N

Now sum the horizontal and vertical forces to zero.

(a) $\Sigma F_x = 0;\ T_2 \cos 40° - T_1 \cos 30° = 0$

(b) $\Sigma F_y = 0;\ T_1 \sin 30° + T_2 \sin 40° - 3335.4\ \text{N} = 0$

Solve (a) for T_2 and get:

(a) $T_2 \cos 40° = T_1 \cos 30°$

$T_2 = 1.13T_1$ (a′)

Substitute (a′) into (b) and get:

(b) $T_1 \sin 30° + (1.13T_1) \sin 40° = 3335.4$ N

$1.2263T_1 = 3335.4$ N

$$T_1 = 2719.9\ \text{N} \xrightarrow{\text{SD}} \mathbf{2720\ N}$$

Substitute T_1 into (a′) and get:

(a′) $T_2 = 1.13(2719.9\ \text{N}) = 3073.5\ \text{N} \xrightarrow{\text{SD}} \mathbf{3070\ N}$

20. Convert 98.6°F to °C.

$$T_C = \frac{5}{9}(T_F - 32)$$

$$= \frac{5}{9}(98.6° - 32)$$

$$= 37°\text{C}$$

Convert 37°C to kelvins.

$$T_K = T_C + 273$$

$$= 37 + 273$$

$$= \mathbf{31\bar{0}\ K}$$

PROBLEM SET 51

1. Begin by converting 9.0 rev/s to rad/s.

$$9.0\ \frac{\text{rev}}{\text{s}} \times \frac{2\pi\ \text{rad}}{1\ \text{rev}} = 56.55\ \frac{\text{rad}}{\text{s}}$$

Now find the tension in the string when the ball is at the bottom of the circle.

$T = F_c + w = mr\omega^2 + mg$

$= 40(0.36)(56.55)^2 + (40)(9.81)$

$= 4.644 \times 10^4\ \text{N} \xrightarrow{\text{SD}} \mathbf{4.6 \times 10^4\ N}$

2. Note that the centripetal force must equal the weight of the car.

$$F_c = \frac{mv^2}{r}$$

$$mg = \frac{mv^2}{r}$$

$$9.81 = \frac{v^2}{20}$$

$$v = 14.01\ \frac{\text{m}}{\text{s}} \xrightarrow{\text{SD}} \mathbf{14\ \frac{m}{s}}$$

3. $PE = \frac{1}{2}kx^2 = \frac{1}{2}(7500)(1.3)^2 = 6337.5$ J

$$KE = \frac{1}{2}mv^2$$

$$6337.5 = \frac{1}{2}(39)v^2$$

$$v = 18.03\ \frac{\text{m}}{\text{s}} \xrightarrow{\text{SD}} \mathbf{18\ \frac{m}{s}}$$

4. (a) $\text{Total energy} = \frac{1}{2}kx^2 + \frac{1}{2}mv^2$

$$52 = \frac{1}{2}(640)(0.25)^2 + \frac{1}{2}(3.7)v^2$$

$$52 = 20 + 1.85v^2$$

$$v = 4.159\ \frac{\text{m}}{\text{s}} \xrightarrow{\text{SD}} \mathbf{4.2\ \frac{m}{s}}$$

(b) $PE = \frac{1}{2}kA^2$

$$52 = \frac{1}{2}(640)A^2$$

$$A = 0.403\text{ m} \xrightarrow{\text{SD}} \mathbf{0.40\ m}$$

5. Begin at the ground symbol, move clockwise, and sum the voltage changes to zero.

$$-28\text{ V} + IR_1 + IR_2 = 0$$

$$-28\text{ V} + I(6.0\ \Omega) + I(8.0\ \Omega) = 0$$

$$I(14\ \Omega) = 28\text{ V}$$

$$I = \mathbf{2.0\ A}$$

$$V_1 = IR_1 = (2.0\text{ A})(6.0\ \Omega) = \mathbf{12\ V}$$

$$V_2 = IR_2 = (2.0\text{ A})(8.0\ \Omega) = \mathbf{16\ V}$$

6. (a) Use the third equation for uniform acceleration to find the velocity.

$$2a\Delta x = v_t^2 - v_0^2$$

$$2(-9.81)(-25.0) = v_t^2 - (-6.30)^2$$

$$490.5 = v_t^2 - 39.69$$

$$v_t = -23.03\ \frac{\text{m}}{\text{s}} \xrightarrow{\text{SD}} \mathbf{-23.0\ \frac{m}{s}}$$

(b) $KE = \frac{1}{2}mv_t^2$

$$= \frac{1}{2}(2.20)(-23.03)^2$$

$$= 583.4\text{ J} \xrightarrow{\text{SD}} \mathbf{583\ J}$$

7. (a) $I_2 = \frac{V_2}{24\ \Omega} = \frac{0.60\text{ V}}{24\ \Omega} = \mathbf{2.5 \times 10^{-2}\ A}$

(b) $I_3 = 0.10\text{ A} - I_2 = 0.10\text{ A} - \left(2.5 \times 10^{-2}\text{ A}\right) = \mathbf{7.5 \times 10^{-2}\ A}$

8. Begin by finding the centripetal force, F_c, and the weight of the yo-yo.

$$F_c = \frac{mv^2}{r} = \frac{0.75(1.5)^2}{0.31} = 5.44\text{ N}$$

$$w = mg = (0.75)(9.81) = 7.36\text{ N}$$

The tension, T, is equal to the vector sum of the horizontal force, F_c, and the vertical force, w.

$$T = \sqrt{(5.44)^2 + (7.36)^2} = 9.15\text{ N} \xrightarrow{\text{SD}} \mathbf{9.2\ N}$$

9. Begin by finding the x and y components of the initial velocity.

$$v_{x0} = 175 \cos 34° = 145.08\ \frac{\text{m}}{\text{s}}$$

$$v_{y0} = 175 \sin 34° = 97.86\ \frac{\text{m}}{\text{s}}$$

(a) Use the y-displacement equation to find the time.

$$\Delta y = v_{y0}t + \frac{1}{2}a_y t^2$$

$$-15 = 97.86t + \frac{1}{2}(-9.81)t^2$$

$$0 = 4.905t^2 - 97.86t - 15$$

Use the quadratic formula to solve this equation for t.

$$t = \frac{-(-97.86) \pm \sqrt{(-97.86)^2 - 4(4.905)(-15)}}{2(4.905)} = 20.1\text{ s} \xrightarrow{\text{SD}} \mathbf{2\bar{0}\ s}$$

(b) *Use this time in the x-position equation to find the distance.*

$$x = x_0 + v_{x0}t + \frac{1}{2}a_x t^2$$

$$= (0) + 145.08(20.1) + (0)$$

$$= 2.92 \times 10^3\text{ m} \xrightarrow{\text{SD}} \mathbf{2.9 \times 10^3\ m}$$

(c) Use the motion equation to find the time when the vertical velocity is zero.

$$v(t) = v_{y0} + a_y t$$

$$0 = 97.86 + (-9.81)t$$

$$t = 9.976\text{ s}$$

Use this time in the y-position equation to find the height.

$$y = y_0 + v_{y0}t + \frac{1}{2}a_y t^2$$

$$= 15 + 97.86(9.976) + \frac{1}{2}(-9.81)(9.976)^2$$

$$= 503.1\text{ m} \xrightarrow{\text{SD}} \mathbf{5\bar{0}0\ m}$$

10. Increase the mass per unit length of the string by a factor of two.

$$v_1 = \sqrt{\frac{T}{M_L}} \longrightarrow v_2 = \sqrt{\frac{T}{2M_L}}$$

Factor the 2 out from under the radical and get:

$$v_2 = \frac{1}{\sqrt{2}}\sqrt{\frac{T}{M_L}}$$

Now, note that $\sqrt{\frac{T}{M_L}}$ is equal to v_1. Substitute and get:

$$v_2 = \mathbf{\frac{1}{\sqrt{2}} v_1}$$

11. Begin by finding the components of the weight of the 65-kg block that are parallel and perpendicular to the plane.

$F_x = mg \sin 29° = (65)(9.81) \sin 29° = 309.1 \text{ N}$

$F_N = mg \cos 29° = (65)(9.81) \cos 29° = 557.7 \text{ N}$

Next, compute the weight of the 53-kg block.

$w = mg = (53)(9.81) = 519.93 \text{ N}$

Since $w > F_x$, we choose the positive x direction to be up the plane. Now, write a $\Sigma F_x = ma_x$ equation for the 65-kg block.

$$\Sigma F_x = ma_x$$
$$T - F_x - \mu_k F_N = ma$$
$$T - 309.1 - (0.20)(557.7) = 65a$$
$$T = 420.64 + 65a \qquad \text{(a)}$$

Now, write a $\Sigma F_y = ma_y$ equation for the 53-kg block.

$$\Sigma F_y = ma_y$$
$$mg - T = ma$$
$$(519.93) - T = 53a$$
$$T = 519.93 - 53a \qquad \text{(b)}$$

Substitute (b) into (a) to find the acceleration.

(a) $(519.93 - 53a) = 420.64 + 65a$

$99.29 = 118a$

$$a = 0.841 \frac{\text{m}}{\text{s}^2} \xrightarrow{\text{SD}} \mathbf{0.84 \frac{m}{s^2}} \textbf{ up the plane}$$

Substitute the acceleration into (a) to find T.

(a) $T = 420.64 + 65(0.841) = 475.3 \text{ N} \xrightarrow{\text{SD}} \mathbf{480 \text{ N}}$

12. (a) $I = \frac{V}{R_1} = \frac{18 \text{ V}}{360 \ \Omega} = \mathbf{5.0 \times 10^{-2} \text{ A}}$

(b) $P = VI = (18 \text{ V})(5.0 \times 10^{-2} \text{ A}) = \mathbf{0.90 \text{ W}}$

(c) $P = I^2R = (5.0 \times 10^{-2} \text{ A})^2(360 \ \Omega) = \mathbf{0.90 \text{ W}}$

(d) $0.90 \frac{\text{J}}{\cancel{\text{s}}} \times 0.60 \cancel{\text{s}} = \mathbf{0.54 \text{ J}}$

13. (a) $F = kx = 486 \frac{\text{N}}{\cancel{\text{m}}} \times 0.650 \cancel{\text{m}} = 315.9 \text{ N} \xrightarrow{\text{SD}} \mathbf{316 \text{ N}}$

(b) $W = \frac{1}{2}kx^2 = \frac{1}{2}(486)(0.650)^2 = 102.7 \text{ J} \xrightarrow{\text{SD}} \mathbf{103 \text{ J}}$

14.

$$D = R \times T$$
$$4500 \text{ m} = 351 \frac{\text{m}}{\text{s}} \times T$$
$$T = 12.82 \text{ s} \xrightarrow{\text{SD}} \mathbf{12.8 \text{ s}}$$

15. $Q_1 = 2.40 \cancel{\text{kg}} \times 234 \frac{\text{J}}{\cancel{\text{kg}} \cdot \cancel{\text{C°}}} \times 973.1 \cancel{\text{C°}} = 5.465 \times 10^5 \text{ J}$

$Q_2 = 2.40 \cancel{\text{kg}} \times 88.3 \times 10^3 \frac{\text{J}}{\cancel{\text{kg}}} = 2.119 \times 10^5 \text{ J}$

To find the total heat, sum Q_1 and Q_2.

$Q_T = 5.465 \times 10^5 \text{ J} + 2.119 \times 10^5 \text{ J}$

$= 7.584 \times 10^5 \text{ J} \xrightarrow{\text{SD}} \mathbf{7.58 \times 10^5 \text{ J}}$

16. (a) Begin by finding the volume of the branch that is submerged.

$V_s = 2.50 \text{ m}^3 \times 0.71 = 1.775 \text{ m}^3$

Now find the mass of the water displaced.

$m_w = 1000 \frac{\text{kg}}{\cancel{\text{m}^3}} \times 1.775 \cancel{\text{m}^3} = 1.775 \times 10^3 \text{ kg} \xrightarrow{\text{SD}} \mathbf{1.8 \times 10^3 \text{ kg}}$

(b) $F_B = 1.775 \times 10^3 \cancel{kg} \times 9.81 \frac{N}{\cancel{kg}}$

$= 1.74 \times 10^4 \text{ N} \xrightarrow{SD} \mathbf{1.7 \times 10^4 \text{ N}}$

(c) The weight of the branch equals the buoyancy force of the water, and the mass of the branch equals the mass of the water displaced.

$w_b = F_B = \mathbf{1.7 \times 10^4 \text{ N}}$

$m_b = m_w = \mathbf{1.8 \times 10^3 \text{ kg}}$

17. (a) $m_1 v_1 + m_2 v_2 = (m_1 + m_2) v_3$

$(6.50 \times 10^{-3})(245) + (2.60)(0) = (2.6065) v_3$

$v_3 = +0.61097 \frac{m}{s} \xrightarrow{SD} \mathbf{+0.611 \frac{m}{s}}$

(b) $KE = \frac{1}{2} m v_3^2$

$= \frac{1}{2}(2.6065)(0.61097)^2$

$= 0.48648 \text{ J} \xrightarrow{SD} \mathbf{0.486 \text{ J}}$

(c) $PE = mgh$

$0.48648 = (2.6065)(9.81)h$

$h = 1.903 \times 10^{-2} \text{ m} \xrightarrow{SD} \mathbf{1.90 \times 10^{-2} \text{ m}}$

18. Use the motion equation to find the time when the vertical velocity is zero.

$v(t) = v_0 + at$

$0 = 23 + (-9.81)t$

$t = 2.34 \text{ s}$

Use this time in the y-displacement equation to find the height.

$\Delta y = v_0 t + \frac{1}{2}at^2$

$= 23(2.34) + \frac{1}{2}(-9.81)(2.34)^2$

$= 26.96 \text{ m} \xrightarrow{SD} \mathbf{27 \text{ m}}$

19. (a) $\Sigma F_y = 0;\ F_A + F_B - 25 \text{ N} - 18 \text{ N} - 36 \text{ N} = 0$

(b) $\Sigma M_B = 0;\ 36(3.0) - 18(13) + F_A(17) - 25(21) = 0$

Solve (b) for F_A and get:

(b) $108 - 234 + F_A(17) - 525 = 0$

$F_A(17) = 651$

$F_A = 38.29 \text{ N} \xrightarrow{SD} \mathbf{38 \text{ N}}$

Substitute F_A into (a) to find F_B.

(a) $(38.29 \text{ N}) + F_B - 25 \text{ N} - 18 \text{ N} - 36 \text{ N} = 0$

$F_B = 40.71 \text{ N} \xrightarrow{SD} \mathbf{41 \text{ N}}$

20. $a_{av} = \frac{v_2 - v_1}{t_2 - t_1} = \frac{9.3000 - 4.585}{20.048 - 10} \frac{m/s}{s} = +0.469 \frac{m}{s^2} \xrightarrow{SD} \mathbf{+0.5 \frac{m}{s^2}}$

Problem Set 52

1. The image is **approximately 4.3 cm in front of the mirror, it is inverted, and the height of the image is approximately 1.7 cm.**

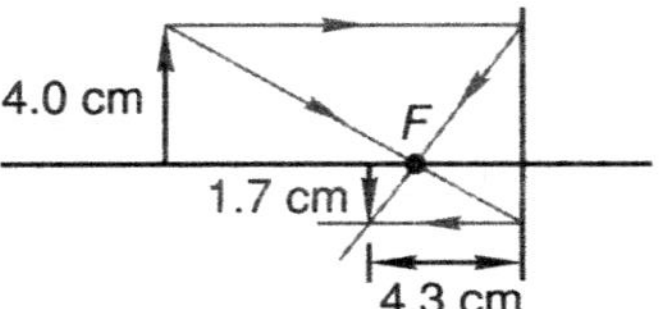

2. The image is **approximately 9.3 cm behind the mirror, it is upright, and the height of the image is approximately 7.0 cm.**

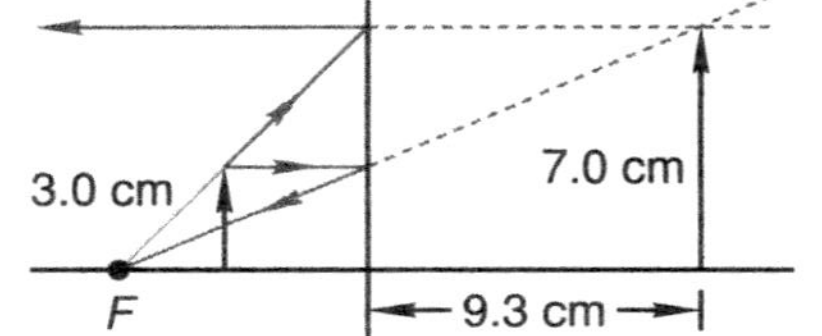

3. Begin by converting 13 rev/s to rad/s.

$$13\ \frac{\cancel{\text{rev}}}{\text{s}} \times \frac{2\pi\ \text{rad}}{1\ \cancel{\text{rev}}} = 81.68\ \frac{\text{rad}}{\text{s}}$$

Now find the tension in the string when the ball is at the top of the circle.

$$T = F_c - w = mr\omega^2 - mg$$
$$= 3.0(0.12)(81.68)^2 - (3.0)(9.81)$$
$$= 2.37 \times 10^3\ \text{N} \xrightarrow{\text{SD}} \mathbf{2.4 \times 10^3\ N}$$

4. Note that the centripetal force must equal the weight of the car.

$$F_c = \frac{mv^2}{r}$$
$$\cancel{m}g = \frac{\cancel{m}v^2}{r}$$
$$9.81 = \frac{v^2}{0.60}$$
$$v = 2.426\ \frac{\text{m}}{\text{s}} \xrightarrow{\text{SD}} \mathbf{2.4\ \frac{m}{s}}$$

5. $$PE = \frac{1}{2}kx^2 = \frac{1}{2}(2300)(3.1)^2 = 1.105 \times 10^4\ \text{J}$$
$$KE = \frac{1}{2}mv^2$$
$$1.105 \times 10^4 = \frac{1}{2}(17)v^2$$
$$v = 36.06\ \frac{\text{m}}{\text{s}} \xrightarrow{\text{SD}} \mathbf{36\ \frac{m}{s}}$$

6. (a) $$\text{Total energy} = \frac{1}{2}kx^2 + \frac{1}{2}mv^2$$
$$1600 = \frac{1}{2}(92.418)(0.08)^2 + \frac{1}{2}(142.056)v^2$$
$$1600 = 0.296 + 71.028v^2$$
$$v = 4.75\ \frac{\text{m}}{\text{s}} \xrightarrow{\text{SD}} \mathbf{5\ \frac{m}{s}}$$

(b) $$PE = \frac{1}{2}kA^2$$
$$1600 = \frac{1}{2}(92.418)A^2$$
$$A = 5.8843\ \text{m} \xrightarrow{\text{SD}} \mathbf{5.884\ m}$$

7. When working this problem, note that the current must always enter a resistor at a plus sign. Begin at the ground symbol, move clockwise, and sum the voltage changes to zero.

$$-21\ \text{V} + IR_1 + IR_2 = 0$$
$$-21\ \text{V} + I(12\ \Omega) + I(30\ \Omega) = 0$$
$$I(42\ \Omega) = 21\ \text{V}$$
$$I = \mathbf{0.50\ A}$$

$$V_1 = IR_1 = (0.50\ \text{A})(12\ \Omega) = \mathbf{6.0\ V}$$
$$V_2 = -(IR_2) = -(0.50\ \text{A})(30\ \Omega) = \mathbf{-15\ V}$$

8. $$W = FD\cos\theta = (38\ \text{N})(13.2\cos 21°\ \text{m}) = 468.28\ \text{J} \xrightarrow{\text{SD}} \mathbf{470\ J}$$

9. (a) $$I_1 = \frac{V}{R_1} = \frac{12\ \text{V}}{30\ \Omega} = \mathbf{0.40\ A}$$
$$I_2 = \frac{V}{R_2} = \frac{12\ \text{V}}{8.0\ \Omega} = \mathbf{1.5\ A}$$

Now use Kirchhoff's current law to find I_3.

$$I_3 = I_1 + I_2 = 0.40\ \text{A} + 1.5\ \text{A} = \mathbf{1.9\ A}$$

(b) $$P_1 = I_1^2R_1 = (0.40\ \text{A})^2(30\ \Omega) = \mathbf{4.8\ W}$$
$$P_2 = I_2^2R_2 = (1.5\ \text{A})^2(8.0\ \Omega) = \mathbf{18\ W}$$

(c) $$P = VI_3 = (12\ \text{V})(1.9\ \text{A}) = 22.8\ \text{W} \xrightarrow{\text{SD}} \mathbf{23\ W}$$

(d) $$E_1 = P_1\Delta t = 4.8\ \frac{\text{J}}{\cancel{\text{s}}} \times 10\ \cancel{\text{s}} = \mathbf{48\ J}$$

10. (a) Begin by finding the voltage drop across resistor R_1.

$$V_1 = I_1R_1 = (1.0\ \text{A})(16\ \Omega) = 16\ \text{V}$$

Thus, the voltage drop across each of the resistors R_2 and R_3 is 20 V − 16 V, or 4.0 V. Use this voltage to find I_3.

$$I_3 = \frac{V_3}{R_3} = \frac{4.0\ \text{V}}{12\ \Omega} = 0.333\ \text{A}$$

Now find the power used by R_3.

$$P_3 = V_3I_3 = (4.0\ \text{V})(0.333\ \text{A}) = 1.332\ \text{W} \xrightarrow{\text{SD}} \mathbf{1.3\ W}$$

(b) $$P = VI_1 = (20\ \text{V})(1.0\ \text{A}) = \mathbf{2\bar{0}\ W}$$

11. Begin by finding the x and y components of the initial velocity.

$$v_{x0} = 253 \cos 46° = 175.75 \ \frac{\text{m}}{\text{s}}$$

$$v_{y0} = 253 \sin 46° = 181.99 \ \frac{\text{m}}{\text{s}}$$

(a) Use the y-displacement equation to find the time.

$$\Delta y = v_{y0}t + \frac{1}{2}a_y t^2$$

$$-190 = 181.99t + \frac{1}{2}(-9.81)t^2$$

$$0 = 4.905t^2 - 181.99t - 190$$

Use the quadratic formula to solve this equation for t.

$$t = \frac{-(-181.99) \pm \sqrt{(-181.99)^2 - 4(4.905)(-190)}}{2(4.905)}$$

$$= 38.12 \text{ s} \xrightarrow{\text{SD}} \mathbf{38 \text{ s}}$$

(b) Use this time in the x-position equation to find the distance.

$$x = x_0 + v_{x0}t + \frac{1}{2}a_x t^2$$

$$= 0 + 175.75(38.12) + 0$$

$$= 6.6996 \times 10^3 \text{ m} \xrightarrow{\text{SD}} \mathbf{6.7 \times 10^3 \text{ m}}$$

(c) Use the motion equation to find the time when the vertical velocity is zero.

$$v(t) = v_{y0} + a_y t$$

$$0 = 181.99 + (-9.81)t$$

$$t = 18.55 \text{ s}$$

Use this time in the y-position equation to find the height.

$$y = y_0 + v_{y0}t + \frac{1}{2}a_y t^2$$

$$= 190 + 181.99(18.55) + \frac{1}{2}(-9.81)(18.55)^2$$

$$= 1.878 \times 10^3 \text{ m} \xrightarrow{\text{SD}} \mathbf{1.9 \times 10^3 \text{ m}}$$

12. Increasing the mass by a factor of 5 increases the tension in the string by a factor of 5.

$$v_1 = \sqrt{\frac{T}{M_L}} \rightarrow v_2 = \sqrt{\frac{5T}{M_L}}$$

Factor the 5 out from under the radical and get:

$$v_2 = \sqrt{5}\sqrt{\frac{T}{M_L}}$$

Now, note that $\sqrt{\frac{T}{M_L}}$ is equal to v_1. Substitute and get:

$$\mathbf{v_2 = \sqrt{5}v_1}$$

13. Begin by finding the components of the weight of the 31-kg block that are parallel and perpendicular to the plane.

$F_x = mg \sin 37° = (31)(9.81) \sin 37° = 183.02 \text{ N}$

$F_N = mg \cos 37° = (31)(9.81) \cos 37° = 242.87 \text{ N}$

Next, compute the weight of the 10-kg block.

$w = mg = (10)(9.81) = 98.1 \text{ N}$

Since $F_x > w$, we choose the positive x direction to be down the plane. Now, write a $\sum F_x = ma_x$ equation for the 31-kg block.

$$\sum F_x = ma_x$$

$$F_x - T - \mu_k F_N = ma$$

$$183.02 - T - (0.13)(242.87) = 31a$$

$$T = 151.45 - 31a \quad \text{(a)}$$

Now, write a $\sum F_y = ma_y$ equation for the 10-kg block.

$$\sum F_y = ma_y$$

$$T - mg = ma$$

$$T - (98.1) = 10a$$

$$T = 98.1 + 10a \quad \text{(b)}$$

Substitute (b) into (a) to find the acceleration.

(a) $(98.1 + 10a) = 151.45 - 31a$

$53.35 = 41a$

$$a = 1.301 \ \frac{\text{m}}{\text{s}^2} \xrightarrow{\text{SD}} \mathbf{1.3 \ \frac{m}{s^2} \text{ down the plane}}$$

Substitute the acceleration into (a) to find T.

(a) $T = 151.45 - 31(1.301) = 111.1 \text{ N} \xrightarrow{\text{SD}} \mathbf{110 \text{ N}}$

14. (a) $I = \frac{V}{R} = \frac{16 \text{ V}}{350 \, \Omega} = 4.57 \times 10^{-2} \text{ A} \xrightarrow{SD} \mathbf{4.6 \times 10^{-2} \text{ A}}$

(b) $P = I^2R = (4.57 \times 10^{-2} \text{ A})^2(350 \, \Omega) = 0.731 \text{ W} \xrightarrow{SD} \mathbf{0.73 \text{ W}}$

(c) $0.731 \frac{\text{J}}{\cancel{\text{s}}} \times 1.30 \cancel{\text{s}} = 0.9503 \text{ J} \xrightarrow{SD} \mathbf{0.95 \text{ J}}$

15. (a) $F = kx = 211 \frac{\text{N}}{\cancel{\text{m}}} \times 0.184 \cancel{\text{m}} = 38.82 \text{ N} \xrightarrow{SD} \mathbf{38.8 \text{ N}}$

(b) $W = \frac{1}{2}kx^2 = \frac{1}{2}(211)(0.184)^2 = 3.572 \text{ J} \xrightarrow{SD} \mathbf{3.57 \text{ J}}$

16. Begin by finding the cross-sectional area of the bar.

$A = (1.00 \times 10^{-3} \text{ m})(8.0 \times 10^{-2} \text{ m}) = 8.0 \times 10^{-5} \text{ m}^2$

Now find the electrical resistance.

$$R = \rho \frac{L}{A} = \frac{(3.5 \times 10^{-5} \, \Omega \cdot \text{m})(0.100 \text{ m})}{8.0 \times 10^{-5} \text{ m}^2}$$

$$= 4.375 \times 10^{-2} \, \Omega \xrightarrow{SD} \mathbf{4.4 \times 10^{-2} \, \Omega}$$

17.

$$n_1 \sin \theta_1 = n_2 \sin \theta_2$$
$$(1.723) \sin 27° = (1) \sin \theta_r$$
$$\theta_r = \mathbf{51.46°}$$

18. (a) $\omega(t) = \omega_0 + \alpha t$

$$\omega(4.2) = 19 + 2.6(4.2) = 29.92 \frac{\text{rad}}{\text{s}} \xrightarrow{SD} \mathbf{3\bar{0} \frac{rad}{s}}$$

(b) $\Delta\theta = \omega_0 t + \frac{1}{2}\alpha t^2$

$$= 19(4.2) + \frac{1}{2}(2.6)(4.2)^2 = 102.7 \text{ rad} \xrightarrow{SD} \mathbf{1\bar{0}0 \text{ rad}}$$

19. (a) Begin by finding the weight of the object.

$w = (415)(9.81) = 4071.15 \text{ N}$

Use this value for w to find F.

$$FR_1 = wR_2$$
$$F(95) = 4071.15(30)$$
$$F = 1.2856 \times 10^3 \text{ N} \xrightarrow{SD} \mathbf{1.3 \times 10^3 \text{ N}}$$

(b) Mechanical adv. $= \frac{F_{out}}{F_{in}} = \frac{4071.15 \text{ N}}{1.2856 \times 10^3 \text{ N}} = 3.167 \xrightarrow{SD} \mathbf{3.2}$

20. Begin by finding the combined weight of the man and the chair and drawing a free-body diagram of the forces at the point where the weight of the chair and man acts on the rope. Note that the tension everywhere in the rope equals 2468 newtons.

2468 N 2468 N θ 843.66 N

$w = (86.0)(9.81) = 843.66 \text{ N}$

Now sum the vertical forces to zero.

$$\Sigma F_y = 0$$
$$2468 \sin \theta + 2468 \sin \theta - 843.66 = 0$$
$$4936 \sin \theta = 843.66$$
$$\theta = \mathbf{9.84°}$$

PROBLEM SET 53

1. Begin by finding the equivalent resistance of the two parallel resistors.

$$\frac{1}{R_E} = \frac{1}{42} + \frac{1}{7}$$
$$\frac{1}{R_E} = 0.1667$$
$$R_E = 6 \, \Omega$$

Use this resistance to find I_1.

$$I_1 = \frac{V}{R_E} = \frac{12 \text{ V}}{6 \, \Omega} = \mathbf{2 \text{ A}}$$

2. Begin by finding the equivalent resistance of the four series resistors.

$R_E = 10 \, \Omega + 20 \, \Omega + 40 \, \Omega + 10 \, \Omega = 80 \, \Omega$

Use this resistance to find I_1.

$$I_1 = \frac{V}{R_E} = \frac{20 \text{ V}}{80 \, \Omega} = \mathbf{0.25 \text{ A}}$$

3. The image is **approximately 11 cm behind the mirror, it is upright, and the height of the image is approximately 4.5 cm**.

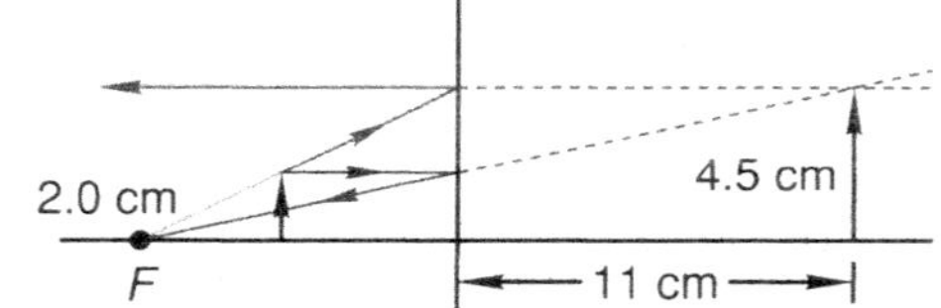

4. The image is **approximately 7.2 cm in front of the mirror, it is inverted, and the height of the image is approximately 2.4 cm.**

5. Begin by converting 4.1 rev/s to rad/s.

$$4.1 \frac{\cancel{rev}}{s} \times \frac{2\pi \text{ rad}}{1 \cancel{rev}} = 25.76 \frac{\text{rad}}{s}$$

Now find the tension in the string when the ball is at the top of the circle.

$$T = F_c - w = mr\omega^2 - mg$$
$$= 2.7(0.16)(25.76)^2 - (2.7)(9.81)$$
$$= 260.18 \text{ N} \xrightarrow{SD} \mathbf{260\ N}$$

6. Note that the centripetal force must equal the weight of the truck.

$$F_c = \frac{mv^2}{r}$$
$$\cancel{m}g = \frac{\cancel{m}v^2}{r}$$
$$9.81 = \frac{v^2}{0.31}$$
$$v = 1.744 \frac{m}{s} \xrightarrow{SD} \mathbf{1.7\ \frac{m}{s}}$$

7. $PE = \frac{1}{2}kx^2 = \frac{1}{2}(454)(4.0)^2 = 3632 \text{ J}$

$$KE = \frac{1}{2}mv^2$$
$$3632 = \frac{1}{2}(10)v^2$$
$$v = 26.95 \frac{m}{s} \xrightarrow{SD} \mathbf{27\ \frac{m}{s}}$$

8. Begin at the ground symbol, move clockwise, and sum the voltage changes to zero.

$$-12 \text{ V} + IR_1 + IR_2 = 0$$
$$-12 \text{ V} + I(120\ \Omega) + I(220\ \Omega) = 0$$
$$I(340\ \Omega) = 12 \text{ V}$$
$$I = 3.529 \times 10^{-2} \text{ A} \xrightarrow{SD} \mathbf{3.5 \times 10^{-2}\ A}$$

$$V_1 = IR_1 = (3.529 \times 10^{-2} \text{ A})(120\ \Omega) = 4.23 \text{ V} \xrightarrow{SD} \mathbf{4.2\ V}$$
$$V_2 = IR_2 = (3.529 \times 10^{-2} \text{ A})(220\ \Omega) = 7.76 \text{ V} \xrightarrow{SD} \mathbf{7.8\ V}$$

9. $W = FD \cos \theta$

$$= (1430.5 \text{ N})(20 \cos 41° \text{ m}) = 2.159 \times 10^4 \text{ J} \xrightarrow{SD} \mathbf{2 \times 10^4\ J}$$

10. Begin by finding the equivalent resistance of the two parallel resistors.

$$\frac{1}{R_E} = \frac{1}{150} + \frac{1}{75}$$
$$\frac{1}{R_E} = 0.02$$
$$R_E = 50\ \Omega$$

Now, combine this with the 100-Ω resistor to find the equivalent resistance of the circuit.

$$R_E = (50\ \Omega) + 100\ \Omega = 150\ \Omega$$

Use this resistance to find I_1.

$$I_1 = \frac{V}{R_E} = \frac{12 \text{ V}}{150\ \Omega} = \mathbf{0.08\ A}$$

11. To find the angular speed, set the tensile strength equal to the centripetal force.

$$T_s = mr\omega^2$$
$$20 = 30(0.50)\omega^2$$
$$\omega = 1.155 \frac{\text{rad}}{s}$$

Convert 1.155 rad/s to rev/min and get:

$$1.155 \frac{\cancel{rad}}{\cancel{s}} \times \frac{1 \text{ rev}}{2\pi \cancel{rad}} \times \frac{60 \cancel{s}}{1 \text{ min}} = 11.03 \frac{\text{rev}}{\text{min}} \xrightarrow{SD} \mathbf{11\ \frac{rev}{min}}$$

12. Begin by finding the x and y components of the initial velocity.

$$v_{x0} = 215 \cos 15° = 207.67 \ \frac{\text{m}}{\text{s}}$$

$$v_{y0} = 215 \sin 15° = 55.65 \ \frac{\text{m}}{\text{s}}$$

(a) Use the y-displacement equation to find the time.

$$\Delta y = v_{y0}t + \frac{1}{2}a_y t^2$$

$$-15.0 = 55.65t + \frac{1}{2}(-9.81)t^2$$

$$0 = 4.905t^2 - 55.65t - 15.0$$

Use the quadratic formula to solve this equation for t.

$$t = \frac{-(-55.65) \pm \sqrt{(-55.65)^2 - 4(4.905)(-15.0)}}{2(4.905)}$$

$$= 11.61 \text{ s} \xrightarrow{\text{SD}} \mathbf{11.6\ s}$$

(b) Use this time in the x-displacement equation to find the distance.

$$\Delta x = v_{x0}t + \frac{1}{2}a_x t^2$$

$$= 207.67(11.61) + (0)$$

$$= 2.411 \times 10^3 \text{ m} \xrightarrow{\text{SD}} \mathbf{2.41 \times 10^3\ m}$$

(c) Use the motion equation to find the time when the vertical velocity is zero.

$$v(t) = v_{y0} + a_y t$$

$$0 = 55.65 + (-9.81)t$$

$$t = 5.67 \text{ s}$$

Use this time in the y-position equation to find the height.

$$y = y_0 + v_{y0}t + \frac{1}{2}a_y t^2$$

$$= 15.0 + 55.65(5.67) + \frac{1}{2}(-9.81)(5.67)^2$$

$$= 172.85 \text{ m} \xrightarrow{\text{SD}} \mathbf{173\ m}$$

13. Begin by finding the components of the weight of the 2.0-kg block that are parallel and perpendicular to the plane.

$F_x = mg \sin 36° = (2.0)(9.81) \sin 36° = 11.53$ N

$F_N = mg \cos 36° = (2.0)(9.81) \cos 36° = 15.87$ N

Next, compute the weight of the 6.0-kg block.

$w = mg = (6.0)(9.81) = 58.86$ N

Since $w > F_x$, we choose the positive x direction to be up the plane. Now, write a $\sum F_x = ma_x$ equation for the 2.0-kg block.

$$\sum F_x = ma_x$$

$$T - F_x - \mu_k F_N = ma$$

$$T - 11.53 - (0.30)(15.87) = 2.0a$$

$$T = 16.29 + 2.0a \qquad \text{(a)}$$

Now, write a $\sum F_y = ma_y$ equation for the 6.0-kg block.

$$\sum F_y = ma_y$$

$$mg - T = ma$$

$$(58.86) - T = 6.0a$$

$$T = 58.86 - 6.0a \qquad \text{(b)}$$

Substitute (b) into (a) to find the acceleration.

(a) $(58.86 - 6.0a) = 16.29 + 2.0a$

$42.57 = 8.0a$

$$a = 5.32 \ \frac{\text{m}}{\text{s}^2} \xrightarrow{\text{SD}} \mathbf{5.3\ \frac{m}{s^2}\ up\ the\ plane}$$

Substitute the acceleration into (a) to find T.

(a) $T = 16.29 + 2.0(5.32) = 26.93 \text{ N} \xrightarrow{\text{SD}} \mathbf{27\ N}$

14. (a) $I_2 = \dfrac{9.00 \text{ V}}{4.00\ \Omega} = \mathbf{2.25\ A}$

(b) $I_3 = 3.00 \text{ A} - I_2 = 3.00 \text{ A} - 2.25 \text{ A} = \mathbf{0.750\ A}$

15. (a) $F = kx = 400 \ \dfrac{\text{N}}{\cancel{\text{m}}} \times 6.0 \ \cancel{\text{m}} = \mathbf{2400\ N}$

(b) $W = \dfrac{1}{2}kx^2 = \dfrac{1}{2}(400)(6.0)^2 = \mathbf{7200\ J}$

16.

$$v = f\lambda$$

$$2.9 \times 10^8 \ \frac{\text{m}}{\text{s}} = (6.4 \times 10^{14} \text{ s}^{-1})\lambda$$

$$\lambda = 4.53 \times 10^{-7} \text{ m} \xrightarrow{\text{SD}} \mathbf{4.5 \times 10^{-7}\ m}$$

17. Begin by converting the temperatures to kelvins.

$T_1 = 100 + 273 = 373\text{ K}$

$T_2 = 25 + 273 = 298\text{ K}$

Now use the ideal gas law and get:

$$\frac{P_1V_1}{T_1} = \frac{P_2V_2}{T_2}$$

$$\frac{(3.01 \times 10^5\text{ Pa})(0.55\text{ m}^3)}{373\text{ K}} = \frac{(2.20 \times 10^5\text{ Pa})V_2}{298\text{ K}}$$

$$V_2 = 0.601\text{ m}^3 \xrightarrow{\text{SD}} \mathbf{0.60\ m^3}$$

18. Begin by finding the pressure produced by the fluid.

$$P_F = 13{,}600\frac{\cancel{\text{kg}}}{\text{m}^{\cancel{3}2}} \times 9.81\frac{\text{N}}{\cancel{\text{kg}}} \times (0.450 - 0.140)\cancel{\text{m}} = 4.1359 \times 10^4\text{ Pa}$$

Now sum this pressure with the atmospheric pressure and find P.

$P = 4.1359 \times 10^4\text{ Pa} + 101{,}300\text{ Pa}$

$= 1.427 \times 10^5\text{ Pa} \xrightarrow{\text{SD}} \mathbf{1.43 \times 10^5\ Pa}$

19. (a) $P_M = 1320\text{ W} \times 0.33 = 435.6\text{ W} \xrightarrow{\text{SD}} \mathbf{440\ W}$

(b) $P_T = 435.6\text{ W} \times 0.67 = 291.9\text{ W} \xrightarrow{\text{SD}} \mathbf{290\ W}$

(c) $\text{Percent eff.} = \frac{P_{\text{out}}}{P_{\text{in}}} \times 100\%$

$$= \frac{291.9\text{ W}}{1320\text{ W}} \times 100\% = 22.11\% \xrightarrow{\text{SD}} \mathbf{22\%}$$

20. Answers to this problem may vary due to differing data points. One possible solution is given here. Choose the points (0, 30) and (4, 60) and get:

$$v_3 = \frac{\Delta x}{\Delta t} = \frac{60 - 30}{4 - 0}\frac{\text{m}}{\text{s}} = \mathbf{+7.5\ \frac{m}{s}}$$

Choose the points (2.5, 0) and (7, 140) and get:

$$v_7 = \frac{\Delta x}{\Delta t} = \frac{140 - 0}{7 - 2.5}\frac{\text{m}}{\text{s}} = +31.1\frac{\text{m}}{\text{s}} \xrightarrow{\text{SD}} \mathbf{+31\ \frac{m}{s}}$$

Problem Set 54

1. Begin by finding the moment of inertia of the system.

$I = m_1r_1^{\,2} + m_2r_2^{\,2} + m_3r_3^{\,2}$

$= (1.5)(0.03)^2 + (2.0)(0.04)^2 + (1.7)(0.03)^2 = 6.08 \times 10^{-3}\text{ kg·m}^2$

$$\tau = I\alpha = \left(6.08 \times 10^{-3}\text{ kg·m}^2\right) \times 3.5\frac{\text{rad}}{\text{s}^2}$$

$$= 2.128 \times 10^{-2}\text{ N·m} \xrightarrow{\text{SD}} \mathbf{2 \times 10^{-2}\ N{\cdot}m}$$

2. $\tau = \left(m_1r_1^{\,2}\right)\alpha + \left(m_2r_2^{\,2}\right)\alpha$

$250\text{ N·m} = (5.0\text{ kg})(5.0\text{ m})^2\alpha + (3.5\text{ kg})(5.0\text{ m})^2\alpha$

$250\text{ N·m} = \left(125\text{ kg·m}^2\right)\alpha + \left(87.5\text{ kg·m}^2\right)\alpha$

$$\alpha = 1.176\frac{\text{rad}}{\text{s}^2} \xrightarrow{\text{SD}} \mathbf{1.2\ \frac{rad}{s^2}}$$

3. Begin by finding the equivalent resistance of the two parallel resistors.

$$\frac{1}{R_E} = \frac{1}{12} + \frac{1}{36}$$

$R_E = 9.0\ \Omega$

Now, combine this with the 9.0-Ω resistor to find the equivalent resistance of the circuit.

$R_E = (9.0\ \Omega) + 9.0\ \Omega = 18\ \Omega$

Use this resistance to find I_1.

$$I_1 = \frac{V}{R_E} = \frac{18\text{ V}}{18\ \Omega} = \mathbf{1.0\ A}$$

4. Begin by finding the voltage drop across resistor R_1.

$V_1 = I_1R_1 = (5.0\text{ A})(4.0\ \Omega) = 20\text{ V}$

Thus, the voltage drop across each of the resistors R_2 and R_3 is 35 V − 20 V, or 15 V. Use this voltage to find I_2.

$$I_2 = \frac{V_2}{R_2} = \frac{15\text{ V}}{12\ \Omega} = 1.25\text{ A}$$

Now find the power used by the 12-ohm resistor.

$$P_2 = I_2^{\,2}R_2 = (1.25\text{ A})^2(12\ \Omega) = 18.75\text{ W} \xrightarrow{\text{SD}} \mathbf{19\ W}$$

5. The image is **approximately 3.0 cm behind the mirror, it is upright, and the height of the image is approximately 6.0 cm**.

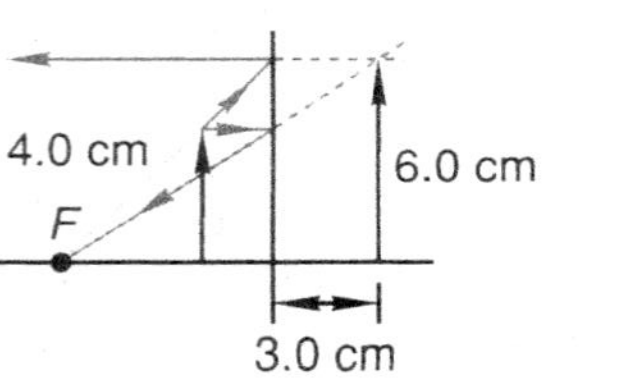

6. Begin by converting 21 rev/s to rad/s.

$$21\,\frac{\text{rev}}{\text{s}} \times \frac{2\pi\ \text{rad}}{1\ \text{rev}} = 131.95\,\frac{\text{rad}}{\text{s}}$$

Now find the tension in the string when the ball is at the bottom of the circle.

$$T = F_c + w = mr\omega^2 + mg$$
$$= (0.40)(0.30)(131.95)^2 + (0.40)(9.81)$$
$$= 2.093 \times 10^3\ \text{N} \xrightarrow{\text{SD}} \mathbf{2.1 \times 10^3\ N}$$

7. $PE = \frac{1}{2}kx^2 = \frac{1}{2}(320)(2.25)^2 = 810\ \text{J}$

$$KE = \frac{1}{2}mv^2$$
$$810 = \frac{1}{2}(3.0)v^2$$
$$v = 23.24\,\frac{\text{m}}{\text{s}} \xrightarrow{\text{SD}} \mathbf{23\,\frac{m}{s}}$$

8. Begin by finding the equivalent resistance of the two series resistors.

$R_E = 2.0\ \Omega + 4.0\ \Omega = 6.0\ \Omega$

Use this resistance to find I.

$$I = \frac{V}{R_E} = \frac{12\ \text{V}}{6.0\ \Omega} = 2.0\ \text{A}$$
$$P_2 = I^2R_2 = (2.0\ \text{A})^2(4.0\ \Omega) = \mathbf{16\ W}$$

9. $W = FD\cos\theta$

$$= (400\ \text{N})(22\cos 15^\circ\ \text{m})$$
$$= 8.5001 \times 10^3\ \text{J} \xrightarrow{\text{SD}} \mathbf{8.5 \times 10^3\ J}$$

10. The voltage drop across each of the resistors is 12 V. Use this voltage to find the current through the 2.0-Ω resistor.

$$I = \frac{V}{R} = \frac{12\ \text{V}}{2.0\ \Omega} = 6.0\ \text{A}$$
$$P_{2.0} = I^2R = (6.0\ \text{A})^2(2.0\ \Omega) = \mathbf{72\ W}$$

Now find the energy consumed in 10 s.

$$72\,\frac{\text{J}}{\cancel{\text{s}}} \times 10\,\cancel{\text{s}} = \mathbf{720\ J}$$

11. The tension in the string is equal to the centripetal force.

$$T = \frac{mv^2}{r} = \frac{(0.9841)(15.7770)^2}{0.5} = 489.9\ \text{N} \xrightarrow{\text{SD}} \mathbf{500\ N}$$

12. Begin by finding the x and y components of the initial velocity.

$$v_{x0} = 1.2\cos 24^\circ = 1.096\,\frac{\text{m}}{\text{s}}$$
$$v_{y0} = 1.2\sin 24^\circ = 0.488\,\frac{\text{m}}{\text{s}}$$

(a) Use the y-displacement equation to find the time.

$$\Delta y = v_{y0}t + \frac{1}{2}a_yt^2$$
$$-5 = 0.488t + \frac{1}{2}(-9.81)t^2$$
$$0 = 4.905t^2 - 0.488t - 5$$

Use the quadratic formula to solve this equation for t.

$$t = \frac{-(-0.488) \pm \sqrt{(-0.488)^2 - 4(4.905)(-5)}}{2(4.905)} = 1.06\ \text{s} \xrightarrow{\text{SD}} \mathbf{1\ s}$$

(b) Use this time in the x-displacement equation to find the distance.

$$\Delta x = v_{x0}t + \frac{1}{2}a_xt^2$$
$$= (1.096)(1.06) + 0$$
$$= 1.16\ \text{m} \xrightarrow{\text{SD}} \mathbf{1\ m}$$

(c) Use the motion equation to find the time when the vertical velocity is zero.

$$v(t) = v_{y0} + a_y t$$
$$0 = 0.488 + (-9.81)t$$
$$t = 0.0497 \text{ s}$$

Use this time in the *y*-position equation to find the height.

$$y = y_0 + v_{y0}t + \frac{1}{2}a_y t^2$$
$$= 5 + (0.488)(0.0497) + \frac{1}{2}(-9.81)(0.0497)^2$$
$$= 5.012 \text{ m} \xrightarrow{\text{SD}} \mathbf{5\ m}$$

13. Begin by finding the components of the weight of the 6-kg block that are parallel and perpendicular to the plane.

$F_x = mg \sin 29° = (6)(9.81) \sin 29° = 28.54$ N

$F_N = mg \cos 29° = (6)(9.81) \cos 29° = 51.48$ N

Next, compute the weight of the 9-kg block.

$w = mg = (9)(9.81) = 88.29$ N

Since $w > F_x$, we choose the positive *x* direction to be up the plane. Now, write a $\Sigma F_x = ma_x$ equation for the 6-kg block.

$$\Sigma F_x = ma_x$$
$$T - F_x - \mu_k F_N = ma$$
$$T - 28.54 - (0.28)(51.48) = 6a$$
$$T = 42.95 + 6a \quad \text{(a)}$$

Now, write a $\Sigma F_y = ma_y$ equation for the 9-kg block.

$$\Sigma F_y = ma_y$$
$$mg - T = ma$$
$$(88.29) - T = 9a$$
$$T = 88.29 - 9a \quad \text{(b)}$$

Substitute (b) into (a) to find the acceleration.

(a) $(88.29 - 9a) = 42.95 + 6a$

$45.34 = 15a$

$$a = 3.02 \frac{\text{m}}{\text{s}^2} \xrightarrow{\text{SD}} \mathbf{3\ \frac{m}{s^2}\ up\ the\ plane}$$

Substitute the acceleration into (a) to find *T*.

(a) $T = 42.95 + 6(3.02) = 61.07 \text{ N} \xrightarrow{\text{SD}} \mathbf{60\ N}$

14. To find V_{CA}, begin at *A* and move clockwise to *C*.

$V_{CA} = -6 \text{ V} + 2 \text{ V} = \mathbf{-4\ V}$

15. Note that distance is the product of rate and time and that the distance the sound travels in water, D_W, equals the distance the sound travels in air, D_A. Then write two equations given by the information in the problem statement.

(a) $R_W T_W = R_A T_A$

(b) $T_W = T_A - 4.0$

Substitute (b) into (a) to find T_A.

(a)
$$R_W T_W = R_A T_A$$
$$(1500)(T_A - 4.0) = (330)T_A$$
$$1500T_A - 6000 = 330T_A$$
$$1170T_A = 6000$$
$$T_A = 5.128 \text{ s}$$

$$D = R_A T_A = 330 \frac{\text{m}}{\cancel{\text{s}}} \times 5.128\cancel{\text{s}} = 1.69 \times 10^3 \text{ m} \xrightarrow{\text{SD}} \mathbf{1.7 \times 10^3\ m}$$

16. (a) $Q_1 = 2.1\cancel{\text{kg}} \times 580 \frac{\text{cal}}{\cancel{\text{kg}}\cdot\cancel{\text{C°}}} \times 93\cancel{\text{C°}}$

$= 1.133 \times 10^5 \text{ cal} \xrightarrow{\text{SD}} \mathbf{1.1 \times 10^5\ cal}$

Convert this to joules and get:

$1.133 \times 10^5 \cancel{\text{cal}} \times \frac{4.186 \text{ J}}{1 \cancel{\text{cal}}} = 4.743 \times 10^5 \text{ J} \xrightarrow{\text{SD}} \mathbf{4.7 \times 10^5\ J}$

(b) $Q_2 = 2.1\cancel{\text{kg}} \times 854 \times 10^3 \frac{\text{J}}{\cancel{\text{kg}}} = 1.793 \times 10^6 \text{ J} \xrightarrow{\text{SD}} \mathbf{1.8 \times 10^6\ J}$

17. $\frac{P_1V_1}{T_1} = \frac{P_2V_2}{T_2} \rightarrow \frac{P_1V_1}{T_1} = \frac{\left(\frac{P_1}{2}\right)V_2}{(3T_1)}$

$$\frac{\cancel{P_1}V_1}{\cancel{T_1}} \times \frac{\cancel{T_1}}{\cancel{P_1}} = \frac{\left(\frac{\cancel{P_1}}{2}\right)V_2}{(3\cancel{T_1})} \times \frac{\cancel{T_1}}{\cancel{P_1}}$$

$$\mathbf{6V_1 = V_2}$$

18. $F = \frac{Gm_1m_2}{r^2}$

$= \frac{(6.67 \times 10^{-11})(3.45 \times 10^7)(4.12 \times 10^7)}{(3.23 \times 10^6)^2}$

$= 9.087 \times 10^{-9}\text{ N} \xrightarrow{SD}$ **9.09×10^{-9} N**

19. (a) Begin by finding the force needed if no friction was present.

$F_{NF} = ma$

$= 245\text{ kg} \times 1.40\text{ m}\cdot\text{s}^{-2}$

$= 343\text{ N}$

The magnitude of the kinetic friction force equals the total force minus F_{NF}.

$F_k = 356\text{ N} - 343\text{ N} = 13.0\text{ N}$

The direction of the friction force is always opposite the direction of motion.

Thus, $\vec{F}_k$ = **13.0/210° N**

(b) $F_k = \mu_k F_N$

$13.0\text{ N} = \mu_k(245\text{ kg})\left(9.81 \frac{\text{N}}{\text{kg}}\right)$

$\mu_k = 5.409 \times 10^{-3} \xrightarrow{SD}$ **5.41×10^{-3}**

20. (a) $\Sigma F_x = ma_x;\ 752 \cos 22° - \mu_k F_N = ma_x$

(b) $\Sigma F_y = 0;\ 752 \sin 22° + F_N - w = 0$

Solve (b) for F_N and get:

(b) $F_N = mg - 752 \sin 22°$

Substitute F_N into (a) to find the mass.

(a) $752 \cos 22° - 0.347(m(9.81) - 752 \sin 22°) = m(1.23)$

$697.24 - 3.40m + 97.75 = 1.23m$

$794.99 = 4.63m$

$m = 171.7\text{ kg} \xrightarrow{SD}$ **172 kg**

Problem Set 55

1. Begin by finding the centripetal force and the static friction force.

$F_c = \frac{mv^2}{r} = \frac{650(25)^2}{75} = 5416.7\text{ N}$

$F_s = mg\mu_s = (650)(9.81)\mu_s = (6376.5\text{ N})\mu_s$

The required centripetal force must equal the static friction force.

$F_c = F_s$

$5416.7\text{ N} = (6376.5\text{ N})\mu_s$

$\mu_s = 0.849 \xrightarrow{SD}$ **0.85**

2. Begin by finding the centripetal force and the static friction force.

$F_c = \frac{mv^2}{r} = \frac{(740)v^2}{56} = 13.21v^2$

$F_s = mg\mu_s = (740)(9.81)(0.76) = 5517.14\text{ N}$

The required centripetal force must equal the static friction force.

$F_c = F_s$

$13.21v^2 = 5517.14$

$v = 20.44\ \frac{\text{m}}{\text{s}} \xrightarrow{SD}$ **$2\bar{0}\ \frac{\text{m}}{\text{s}}$**

3. Begin by finding the moment of inertia of the system.

$I = m_1r_1^2 + m_2r_2^2 + m_3r_3^2$

$= (4)(0.05)^2 + (2)(0.07)^2 + (3)(0.10)^2 = 4.98 \times 10^{-2}\text{ kg}\cdot\text{m}^2$

$\tau = I\alpha = (4.98 \times 10^{-2}\text{ kg}\cdot\text{m}^2) \times 9.5\ \frac{\text{rad}}{\text{s}^2}$

$= 0.4731\text{ N}\cdot\text{m} \xrightarrow{SD}$ **0.5 N·m**

4. $\tau = (m_1r_1^2)\alpha + (m_2r_2^2)\alpha$

$600\text{ N}\cdot\text{m} = (9.00\text{ kg})(0.180\text{ m})^2\alpha + (2.50\text{ kg})(0.180\text{ m})^2\alpha$

$600\text{ N}\cdot\text{m} = (0.2916\text{ kg}\cdot\text{m}^2)\alpha + (0.081\text{ kg}\cdot\text{m}^2)\alpha$

$\alpha = 1610.31\ \frac{\text{rad}}{\text{s}^2} \xrightarrow{SD}$ **$1610\ \frac{\text{rad}}{\text{s}^2}$**

5. Begin by finding the equivalent resistance of the two parallel resistors.

$$R_E = \frac{(420)(550)}{420 + 550} = 238.14\ \Omega$$

Now, combine this with the 360-Ω resistor to find the equivalent resistance of the circuit.

$$R_E = (238.14\ \Omega) + 360\ \Omega = 598.14\ \Omega$$

Use this resistance to find I_1.

$$I_1 = \frac{V}{R_E} = \frac{15\text{ V}}{598.14\ \Omega} = 2.508 \times 10^{-2}\text{ A} \xrightarrow{\text{SD}} \mathbf{2.5 \times 10^{-2}\ A}$$

6. Begin by finding the voltage drop across resistor R_1.

$$V_1 = I_1R_1 = (1.50\text{ A})(8.0\ \Omega) = 12\text{ V}$$

Thus, the voltage drop across each of the resistors R_2 and R_3 is 24 V − 12 V, or 12 V. Use this voltage to find I_3.

$$I_3 = \frac{V_3}{R_3} = \frac{12\text{ V}}{12\ \Omega} = \mathbf{1.0\ A}$$

7. The image is **approximately 8.0 cm in front of the mirror, it is inverted, and the height of the image is equal to the height of the object, or 5.0 cm.**

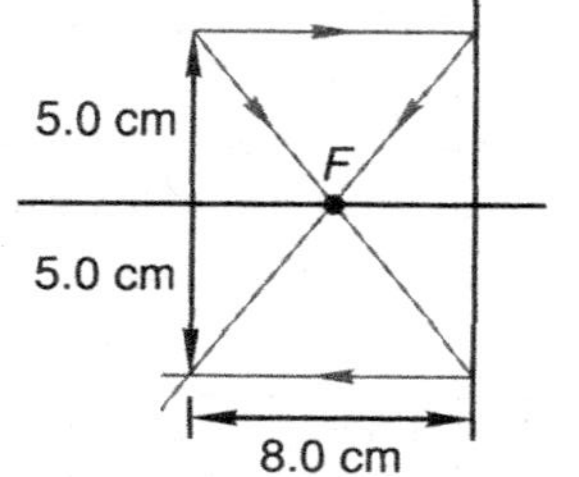

8. $T = F_c + w = mr\omega^2 + mg$

$$= 1.5(0.15)(16)^2 + (1.5)(9.81)$$

$$= 72.315\text{ N} \xrightarrow{\text{SD}} \mathbf{72\ N}$$

9. (a) $\text{Total energy} = \frac{1}{2}kx^2 + \frac{1}{2}mv^2$

$$95 = \frac{1}{2}(2500)(0.060)^2 + \frac{1}{2}(5.5)v^2$$

$$95 = 4.5 + 2.75v^2$$

$$v = 5.737\text{ m/s} \xrightarrow{\text{SD}} \mathbf{5.7\ m/s}$$

(b) $PE = \frac{1}{2}kA^2$

$$95 = \frac{1}{2}(2500)A^2$$

$$A = 0.2757\text{ m} \xrightarrow{\text{SD}} \mathbf{0.28\ m}$$

10. To find V_{BC}, begin at C and move clockwise to B.

$$V_{BC} = +18\text{ V} - 8\text{ V} - 13\text{ V} = \mathbf{-3\ V}$$

11. Begin at the ground symbol, move clockwise, and sum the voltage changes to zero.

$$+IR_2 - 10\text{ V} + IR_1 = 0$$

$$+I(120\ \Omega) - 10\text{ V} + I(40\ \Omega) = 0$$

$$I(160\ \Omega) = 10\text{ V}$$

$$I = 0.0625\text{ A}$$

The energy used by R_2 equals the power used by R_2 multiplied by the time.

$$E = P_2t$$

$$= (I^2R_2)t$$

$$= (0.0625)^2(120)(20)$$

$$= 9.375\text{ J} \xrightarrow{\text{SD}} \mathbf{9.4\ J}$$

12. Begin by finding the centripetal force, F_c, and the weight of the yo-yo.

$$F_c = \frac{mv^2}{r} = \frac{0.250(2.50)^2}{0.260} = 6.010\text{ N}$$

$$w = mg = (0.250)(9.81) = 2.453\text{ N}$$

The tension, T, is equal to the vector sum of the horizontal force, F_c, and the vertical force, w.

$$T = \sqrt{(6.010)^2 + (2.453)^2} = 6.491\text{ N} \xrightarrow{\text{SD}} \mathbf{6.49\ N}$$

13. Begin by finding the x and y components of the initial velocity.

$v_{x0} = 18 \cos 55° = 10.32$ m/s

$v_{y0} = 18 \sin 55° = 14.74$ m/s

(a) Use the y-position equation to find the time. Label the ground above the ravine as the vertical origin, or 0 m.

$$y = y_0 + v_{y0}t + \frac{1}{2}a_y t^2$$

$$0 = -6.0 + 14.74t + \frac{1}{2}(-9.81)t^2$$

$$0 = 4.905t^2 - 14.74t + 6.0$$

Use the quadratic formula to solve this equation for t.

$$t = \frac{-(-14.74) \pm \sqrt{(-14.74)^2 - 4(4.905)(6.0)}}{2(4.905)}$$

$$= 0.485 \text{ s or } 2.52 \text{ s} \xrightarrow{SD} \mathbf{2.5\ s}$$

Note, the smaller positive value of t from the above equation is the time at which the rock passes the top of the ravine on its upward journey, not the total time.

(b) Use this time in the x-displacement equation to find the distance.

$$\Delta x = v_{x0}t + \frac{1}{2}a_x t^2$$

$$= (10.32)(2.52) + 0$$

$$= 26.01 \text{ m} \xrightarrow{SD} \mathbf{26\ m}$$

(c) Use the motion equation to find the time when the vertical velocity is zero.

$$v(t) = v_{y0} + a_y t$$

$$0 = 14.74 + (-9.81)t$$

$$t = 1.50 \text{ s}$$

Use this time in the y-position equation to find the height.

$$y = y_0 + v_{y0}t + \frac{1}{2}a_y t^2$$

$$= -6.0 + 14.74(1.50) + \frac{1}{2}(-9.81)(1.50)^2$$

$$= 5.07 \text{ m} \xrightarrow{SD} \mathbf{5.1\ m}$$

14. Begin by finding the components of the weight of the 136-kg block that are parallel and perpendicular to the plane.

$F_x = mg \sin 47° = (136)(9.81) \sin 47° = 975.74$ N

$F_N = mg \cos 47° = (136)(9.81) \cos 47° = 909.89$ N

Next, compute the weight of the 251-kg object.

$w = mg = (251)(9.81) = 2462.31$ N

Since $w > F_x$, we choose the positive x direction to be up the plane. Now, write a $\Sigma F_x = ma_x$ equation for the 136-kg block.

$$\Sigma F_x = ma_x$$

$$T - F_x - \mu_k F_N = ma$$

$$T - 975.74 - (0.155)(909.89) = 136a$$

$$T = 1116.8 + 136a \qquad \text{(a)}$$

Now, write a $\Sigma F_y = ma_y$ equation for the 251-kg object.

$$\Sigma F_y = ma_y$$

$$mg - T = ma$$

$$(2462.31) - T = 251a$$

$$T = 2462.31 - 251a \qquad \text{(b)}$$

Substitute (b) into (a) to find the acceleration.

(a) $(2462.31 - 251a) = 1116.8 + 136a$

$1345.51 = 387a$

$$a = 3.4768 \frac{\text{m}}{\text{s}^2} \xrightarrow{SD} \mathbf{3.48\ \frac{m}{s^2}\ up\ the\ plane}$$

Substitute the acceleration into (a) to find T.

(a) $T = 1116.8 + 136(3.4768) = 1589.6 \text{ N} \xrightarrow{SD}$ **1590 N**

15. (a) Begin by finding the tension, mg, and the mass per unit length of the string.

$$T = mg = 13.0 \text{ kg} \times 9.81 \frac{\text{N}}{\text{kg}} = 127.53 \text{ N}$$

$$M_L = \frac{0.355 \text{ kg}}{2.67 \text{ m}} = 0.133 \frac{\text{kg}}{\text{m}}$$

Insert these values into the formula below to find v.

$$v = \sqrt{\frac{T}{M_L}} = \sqrt{\frac{127.53 \text{ N}}{0.133 \frac{\text{kg}}{\text{m}}}} = 30.97 \frac{\text{m}}{\text{s}} \xrightarrow{SD} \mathbf{31.0\ \frac{m}{s}}$$

(b) $v = f\lambda$

$30.97 = f(0.560)$

$f = 55.30 \text{ Hz} \xrightarrow{SD}$ **55.3 Hz**

16. Begin by converting 35 rev/min to rad/s.

$$35\ \frac{\text{rev}}{\text{min}} \times \frac{2\pi\ \text{rad}}{1\ \text{rev}} \times \frac{1\ \text{min}}{60\ \text{s}} = 3.665\ \frac{\text{rad}}{\text{s}}$$

(a) $\omega(t) = \omega_0 + \alpha t$

$$\omega(6.0) = 3.665 + (15)(6.0) = 93.665\ \frac{\text{rad}}{\text{s}} \xrightarrow{SD} \mathbf{94\ \frac{rad}{s}}$$

(b) $\Delta\theta = \omega_0 t + \frac{1}{2}\alpha t^2$

$$= 3.665(6.0) + \frac{1}{2}(15)(6.0)^2 = 291.99\ \text{rad} \xrightarrow{SD} \mathbf{290\ rad}$$

17. (a) $m_1v_1 + m_2v_2 = (m_1 + m_2)v_3$

$$(7.75 \times 10^{-3})(95.0) + (6.70)(0) = (6.70775)v_3$$

$$v_3 = +0.10976\ \frac{\text{m}}{\text{s}} \xrightarrow{SD} \mathbf{+0.110\ \frac{m}{s}}$$

(b) $KE = \frac{1}{2}mv_3^2 = \frac{1}{2}(6.70775)(0.10976)^2$

$$= 4.0405 \times 10^{-2}\ \text{J} \xrightarrow{SD} \mathbf{4.04 \times 10^{-2}\ J}$$

(c) $PE = mgh$

$$4.0405 \times 10^{-2} = (6.70775)(9.81)h$$

$$h = 6.1403 \times 10^{-4}\ \text{m} \xrightarrow{SD} \mathbf{6.14 \times 10^{-4}\ m}$$

18. (a) Impulse $= F\Delta t = 3400\ \text{N} \times 5.0\ \text{s} = \mathbf{1.7 \times 10^4\ N{\cdot}s}$

(b) $F\Delta t = m(v_2 - v_1)$

$$1.7 \times 10^4 = 850(v_2 - 0)$$

$$v_2 = \mathbf{2\bar{0}\ \frac{m}{s}}$$

19. (a) $a = \frac{\Delta v}{\Delta t} = \frac{13 - 31}{12}\ \frac{\text{m/s}}{\text{s}} = \mathbf{-1.5\ \frac{m}{s^2}}$

(b) Use the x-displacement equation to find the distance.

$$\Delta x = v_0t + \frac{1}{2}at^2 = 31(12) + \frac{1}{2}(-1.5)(12)^2 = 264\ \text{m} \xrightarrow{SD} \mathbf{260\ m}$$

20. (a) $W = Fd = 450\ \text{N} \times 12\ \text{m} = \mathbf{5.4 \times 10^3\ J}$

(b) $P_{av} = \frac{W}{\Delta t} = \frac{5.4 \times 10^3\ \text{J}}{15\ \text{s}} = \mathbf{360\ W}$

Problem Set 56

1. $v_1A_1 = v_2A_2$

$$5.641\ \frac{\text{m}}{\text{s}}(2000\ \text{m})(17.4\ \text{m}) = 11.111\ \frac{\text{m}}{\text{s}}(8\ \text{m})d$$

$$1.963 \times 10^5\ \frac{\text{m}^3}{\text{s}} = \left(88.888\ \frac{\text{m}^2}{\text{s}}\right)d$$

$$d = 2208\ \text{m} \xrightarrow{SD} \mathbf{2000\ m}$$

2. $v_1A_1 = v_2A_2$

$$36\ \frac{\text{cm}}{\text{s}}\left[\pi(3.5\ \text{cm})^2\right] = 53\ \frac{\text{cm}}{\text{s}}\left[\pi r^2\right]$$

$$1385.44\ \frac{\text{cm}^3}{\text{s}} = \left(166.50\ \frac{\text{cm}}{\text{s}}\right)r^2$$

$$r = 2.8846\ \text{cm} \xrightarrow{SD} \mathbf{2.9\ cm}$$

3. Begin by finding the centripetal force and the static friction force.

$$F_c = \frac{mv^2}{r} = \frac{750(15)^2}{36} = 4687.5\ \text{N}$$

$$F_s = mg\mu_s = (750)(9.81)\mu_s = (7357.5\ \text{N})\mu_s$$

The required centripetal force must equal the static friction force.

$$F_c = F_s$$

$$4687.5\ \text{N} = (7357.5\ \text{N})\mu_s$$

$$\mu_s = 0.6371 \xrightarrow{SD} \mathbf{0.64}$$

4. Begin by finding the centripetal force and the static friction force.

$$F_c = \frac{mv^2}{r} = \frac{(861)v^2}{86.0} = 10.01v^2$$

$$F_s = mg\mu_s = (861)(9.81)(0.633) = 5346.58\ \text{N}$$

The required centripetal force must equal the static friction force.

$$F_c = F_s$$

$$10.01v^2 = 5346.58$$

$$v = 23.11\ \frac{\text{m}}{\text{s}} \xrightarrow{SD} \mathbf{23.1\ \frac{m}{s}}$$

5. Begin by finding the moment of inertia of the system.

$$I = m_1r_1^2 + m_2r_2^2 + m_3r_3^2$$
$$= (6)(0.06)^2 + (2)(0.04)^2 + (8)(0.12)^2 = 0.14\ \text{kg·m}^2$$

$$\tau = I\alpha = \left(0.14\ \text{kg·m}^2\right) \times 5.4\ \frac{\text{rad}}{\text{s}^2}$$
$$= 0.756\ \text{N·m} \xrightarrow{\text{SD}} \mathbf{0.8\ N·m}$$

6.
$$\tau = \left(m_1r_1^2\right)\alpha + \left(m_2r_2^2\right)\alpha$$
$$350\ \text{N·m} = (6.0\ \text{kg})(0.25\ \text{m})^2\alpha + (6.5\ \text{kg})(0.25\ \text{m})^2\alpha$$
$$350\ \text{N·m} = \left(0.375\ \text{kg·m}^2\right)\alpha + \left(0.40625\ \text{kg·m}^2\right)\alpha$$
$$\alpha = 448\ \frac{\text{rad}}{\text{s}^2} \xrightarrow{\text{SD}} \mathbf{450\ \frac{rad}{s^2}}$$

7. Begin by finding the equivalent resistance of the two parallel resistors.

$$R_E = \frac{(100)(710)}{100 + 710} = 87.65\ \Omega$$

Now, combine this with the 850-Ω resistor to find the equivalent resistance of the circuit.

$$R_E = (87.65\ \Omega) + 850\ \Omega = 937.65\ \Omega$$

Use this resistance to find I_1.

$$I_1 = \frac{V}{R_E} = \frac{14\ \text{V}}{937.65\ \Omega} = 1.493 \times 10^{-2}\ \text{A} \xrightarrow{\text{SD}} \mathbf{1.5 \times 10^{-2}\ A}$$

8. Begin by finding the voltage drop across resistor R_2.

$$V_2 = I_2R_2 = (2.00\ \text{A})(9\ \Omega) = 18\ \text{V}$$

Thus, the voltage drop across resistor R_3 is equal to the voltage drop across resistor R_2, or 18 V. Use this voltage to find I_3.

$$I_3 = \frac{V_3}{R_3} = \frac{18\ \text{V}}{18\ \Omega} = \mathbf{1\ A}$$

9. The image is **approximately 15 cm in front of the mirror, it is inverted, and the height of the image is approximately 5.3 cm.**

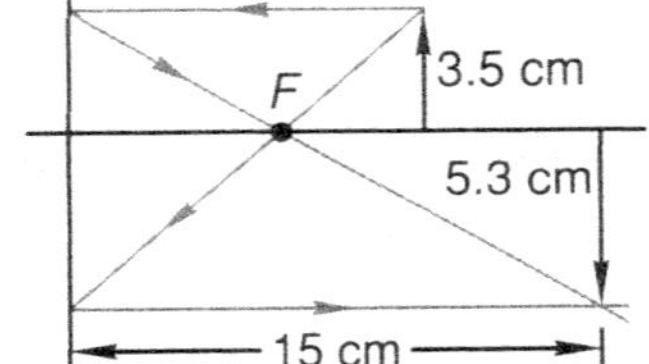

10. $$T = F_c + w = mr\omega^2 + mg$$
$$= 0.75(0.35)(32)^2 + (0.75)(9.81)$$
$$= 276.16\ \text{N} \xrightarrow{\text{SD}} \mathbf{280\ N}$$

11. (a) $$\text{Total energy} = \frac{1}{2}kx^2 + \frac{1}{2}mv^2$$
$$120.6 = \frac{1}{2}(3500)(0.1872)^2 + \frac{1}{2}(25.15)v^2$$
$$120.6 = 61.33 + 12.575v^2$$
$$v = 2.17102\ \frac{\text{m}}{\text{s}} \xrightarrow{\text{SD}} \mathbf{2.171\ \frac{m}{s}}$$

(b) $$PE = \frac{1}{2}kA^2$$
$$120.6 = \frac{1}{2}(3500)A^2$$
$$A = 0.26252\ \text{m} \xrightarrow{\text{SD}} \mathbf{0.2625\ m}$$

12. Begin at the ground symbol, move clockwise, and sum the voltage changes to zero.

$$-6.0\ \text{V} + 3.4\ \text{V} - 5.5\ \text{V} + V_1 + 2.6\ \text{V} = 0$$
$$V_1 = \mathbf{5.5\ V}$$

13. Begin at the ground symbol, move clockwise, and sum the voltage changes to zero.

$$-16\ \text{V} + I_1(60\ \Omega) + I_1(80\ \Omega) - 9\ \text{V} + I_1(110\ \Omega) = 0$$
$$I_1(250\ \Omega) = 25\ \text{V}$$
$$I_1 = \mathbf{0.1\ A}$$

14. Begin by finding the x and y components of the initial velocity.

$v_{x0} = 18 \cos 35° = 14.74$ m/s

$v_{y0} = 18 \sin 35° = 10.32$ m/s

(a) Use the y-displacement equation to find the time.

$$\Delta y = v_{y0}t + \frac{1}{2}a_y t^2$$

$$-15 = 10.32t + \frac{1}{2}(-9.81)t^2$$

$$0 = 4.905t^2 - 10.32t - 15$$

Use the quadratic formula to solve this equation for t.

$$t = \frac{-(-10.32) \pm \sqrt{(-10.32)^2 - 4(4.905)(-15)}}{2(4.905)}$$

$$= 3.093 \text{ s} \xrightarrow{\text{SD}} \mathbf{3.1\ s}$$

(b) Use this time in the x-displacement equation to find the distance.

$$\Delta x = v_{x0}t + \frac{1}{2}a_x t^2$$

$$= 14.74(3.093) + (0)$$

$$= 45.59 \text{ m} \xrightarrow{\text{SD}} \mathbf{46\ m}$$

(c) Use the motion equation to find the time when the vertical velocity is zero.

$$v(t) = v_{y0} + a_y t$$

$$0 = 10.32 + (-9.81)t$$

$$t = 1.052 \text{ s}$$

Use this time in the y-position equation to find the height.

$$y = y_0 + v_{y0}t + \frac{1}{2}a_y t^2$$

$$= 15 + 10.32(1.052) + \frac{1}{2}(-9.81)(1.052)^2$$

$$= 20.43 \text{ m} \xrightarrow{\text{SD}} \mathbf{2\bar{0}\ m}$$

15. (a)

$$F = kx$$

$$258 \text{ N} = k(36.0 \text{ cm})$$

$$k = 7.167 \frac{\text{N}}{\text{cm}} \xrightarrow{\text{SD}} \mathbf{7.17\ \frac{N}{cm}}$$

Convert 7.167 N/cm to N/m and get:

$$7.167 \frac{\text{N}}{\cancel{\text{cm}}} \times \frac{100 \cancel{\text{cm}}}{1 \text{ m}} = 716.7 \frac{\text{N}}{\text{m}} \xrightarrow{\text{SD}} \mathbf{717\ \frac{N}{m}}$$

(b) $W = \frac{1}{2}kx^2 = \frac{1}{2}(716.7)(0.360)^2 = 46.44 \text{ J} \xrightarrow{\text{SD}} \mathbf{46.4\ J}$

16. Begin by finding the weight and volume of the sphere that is submerged.

$w_s = mg = (35.1)(9.81) = 344.33$ N

$V_s = \frac{4}{3}\pi r^3 = \frac{4}{3}(\pi)(1.525)^3 = 14.856 \text{ m}^3$

Now find the weight of the water displaced, or the buoyancy force, F_B.

$$F_B = 14.856 \cancel{\text{m}^3} \times 1000 \frac{\cancel{\text{kg}}}{\cancel{\text{m}^3}} \times 9.81 \frac{\text{N}}{\cancel{\text{kg}}}$$

$$= 1.457 \times 10^5 \text{ N}$$

The tension in the cable equals the buoyancy force minus the weight of the sphere.

$$T = F_B - w_s$$

$$= 1.457 \times 10^5 \text{ N} - 344.33 \text{ N}$$

$$= 1.454 \times 10^5 \text{ N} \xrightarrow{\text{SD}} \mathbf{1.45 \times 10^5\ N}$$

17. (a) Find x by equating the potential energy of the ball before it was dropped and the kinetic energy of the ball just before it strikes the ground.

$$PE = KE$$

$$\cancel{m}gx = \frac{1}{2}\cancel{m}v^2$$

$$(9.81)x = \frac{1}{2}(-31)^2$$

$$x = 48.98 \text{ m} \xrightarrow{\text{SD}} \mathbf{49\ m}$$

(b) Find the maximum vertical velocity on the way up by equating the potential and kinetic energies after the ball strikes the ground.

$$\cancel{m}g(0.85x) = \frac{1}{2}\cancel{m}v^2$$

$$(9.81)[(0.85)(48.98)] = \frac{1}{2}v^2$$

$$v = +28.58 \frac{\text{m}}{\text{s}} \xrightarrow{\text{SD}} \mathbf{+29\ \frac{m}{s}}$$

(c) $270 = KE_i - KE_f$

$$270 = \frac{1}{2}m(-31)^2 - \frac{1}{2}m(+28.58)^2$$

$$270 = 480.5m - 408.4m$$

$$m = 3.745 \text{ kg} \xrightarrow{\text{SD}} \mathbf{3.7\ kg}$$

18. (a) $\Sigma F_y = 0$; $2568\text{ N} + 1842\text{ N} - w = 0$
(b) $\Sigma M = 0$; $-2568\text{ N}(3.0\text{ m}) - 1842\text{ N}(9.0\text{ m}) + w(x) = 0$

Solve (a) for w and get:
(a) $w = 2568\text{ N} + 1842\text{ N} = 4410\text{ N}$

Substitute w into (b) to find x.
(b) $-7704\text{ N·m} - 16{,}578\text{ N·m} + 4410\text{ N}(x) = 0$

$$4410\text{ N}(x) = 24{,}282\text{ N·m}$$
$$x = 5.506\text{ m} \xrightarrow{\text{SD}} \mathbf{5.5\ m}$$

19. Begin by finding the weight of the mass and drawing a free-body diagram of the forces acting on the junction of the ropes.

$$w = mg$$
$$= 560\text{ kg} \times 9.81\ \frac{\text{N}}{\text{kg}}$$
$$= 5493.6\text{ N}$$

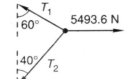

Now sum the horizontal and vertical forces to zero.
(a) $\Sigma F_x = 0$; $5493.6\text{ N} - T_1 \sin 60° - T_2 \sin 40° = 0$
(b) $\Sigma F_y = 0$; $T_1 \cos 60° - T_2 \cos 40° = 0$

Solve (b) for T_2 and get:
(b) $T_2 \cos 40° = T_1 \cos 60°$
$T_2 = 0.653T_1$ (b′)

Substitute (b′) into (a) and get:
(a) $5493.6\text{ N} = T_1 \sin 60° + (0.653T_1) \sin 40°$
$5493.6\text{ N} = 1.286T_1$
$T_1 = 4.272 \times 10^3\text{ N} \xrightarrow{\text{SD}} \mathbf{4.27 \times 10^3\ N}$

Substitute T_1 into (b′) and get:
(b′) $T_2 = 0.653(4.272 \times 10^3\text{ N})$
$= 2.7896 \times 10^3\text{ N} \xrightarrow{\text{SD}} \mathbf{2.79 \times 10^3\ N}$

20. Choose the points (3, –5) and (4, –5) to find a_3.

$$a_3 = \frac{\Delta v}{\Delta t} = \frac{-5 - (-5)}{4 - 3}\ \frac{\text{m/s}}{\text{s}} = \mathbf{0\ \frac{m}{s^2}}$$

Choose the points (4.5, –5) and (7, 10) to find a_6.

$$a_6 = \frac{\Delta v}{\Delta t} = \frac{10 - (-5)}{7 - 4.5}\ \frac{\text{m/s}}{\text{s}} = \mathbf{+6.0\ \frac{m}{s^2}}$$

Problem Set 57

1. The image is **approximately 2.9 cm behind the mirror, it is upright, and the height of the image is approximately 1.4 cm**.

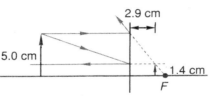

2. The image is **approximately 2.2 cm behind the mirror, it is upright, and the height of the image is approximately 2.6 cm**.

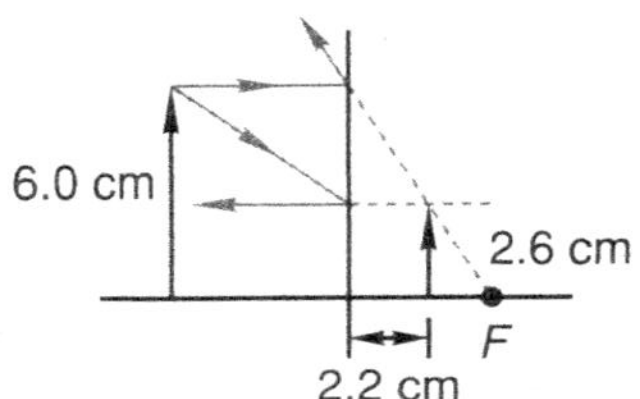

3.
$$v_1A_1 = v_2A_2$$
$$8.5\ \frac{\text{m}}{\text{s}}(3.5\text{ m})(35\text{ m}) = 12\ \frac{\text{m}}{\text{s}}(12\text{ m})d$$
$$1041.25\ \frac{\text{m}^3}{\text{s}} = \left(144\ \frac{\text{m}^2}{\text{s}}\right)d$$
$$d = 7.23\text{ m} \xrightarrow{\text{SD}} \mathbf{7.2\ m}$$

4.
$$v_1A_1 = v_2A_2$$
$$21\ \frac{\text{cm}}{\text{s}}[\pi(2.6\text{ cm})^2] = 12\ \frac{\text{cm}}{\text{s}}[\pi r^2]$$
$$445.98\ \frac{\text{cm}^3}{\text{s}} = \left(37.70\ \frac{\text{cm}}{\text{s}}\right)r^2$$
$$r = 3.44\text{ cm} \xrightarrow{\text{SD}} \mathbf{3.4\ cm}$$

5. Begin by finding the centripetal force and the static friction force.
$$F_c = \frac{mv^2}{r} = \frac{650(32)^2}{85} = 7830.59\text{ N}$$
$$F_s = mg\mu_s = (650)(9.81)\mu_s = (6376.5\text{ N})\mu_s$$
The required centripetal force must equal the static friction force.
$$F_c = F_s$$
$$7830.59\text{ N} = (6376.5\text{ N})\mu_s$$
$$\mu_s = 1.228 \xrightarrow{\text{SD}} \mathbf{1.2}$$

6. Begin by finding the centripetal force and the static friction force.
$$F_c = \frac{mv^2}{r} = \frac{(750)v^2}{95.0} = 7.895v^2$$
$$F_s = mg\mu_s = (750)(9.81)(0.865) = 6364.24\text{ N}$$
The required centripetal force must equal the static friction force.
$$F_c = F_s$$
$$7.895v^2 = 6364.24$$
$$v = 28.39\ \frac{\text{m}}{\text{s}} \xrightarrow{\text{SD}} \mathbf{28.4\ \frac{m}{s}}$$

7. Begin by finding the moment of inertia of the system.
$$I = m_1r_1^2 + m_2r_2^2 + m_3r_3^2$$
$$= (1)(0.06)^2 + (4)(0.07)^2 + (2)(0.08)^2 = 0.036\text{ kg·m}^2$$
$$\tau = I\alpha = \left(0.036\text{ kg·m}^2\right) \times 3.30\ \frac{\text{rad}}{\text{s}^2}$$
$$= 0.12\text{ N·m} \xrightarrow{\text{SD}} \mathbf{0.1\ N·m}$$

8.
$$\tau = \left(m_1r_1^2\right)\alpha + \left(m_2r_2^2\right)\alpha$$
$$348.740 = (12.2405)(0.30)^2\alpha + (5.1331)(0.30)^2\alpha$$
$$348.740 = 1.1016\alpha + 0.4620\alpha$$
$$\alpha = 223\ \frac{\text{rad}}{\text{s}^2} \xrightarrow{\text{SD}} \mathbf{200\ \frac{rad}{s^2}}$$

9. Begin by finding the equivalent resistance of the two parallel resistors.
$$R_E = \frac{(500)(50)}{500 + 50} = 45.45\ \Omega$$
Now, combine this with the 75-Ω resistor to find the equivalent resistance of the circuit.
$$R_E = (45.45\ \Omega) + 75\ \Omega = 120.45\ \Omega$$
Use this resistance to find I_1.
$$I_1 = \frac{V}{R_E} = \frac{10\text{ V}}{120.45\ \Omega} = 8.302 \times 10^{-2}\text{ A} \xrightarrow{\text{SD}} \mathbf{8.3 \times 10^{-2}\ A}$$

10. The image is **approximately 2.7 cm behind the mirror, it is upright, and the height of the image is approximately 4.0 cm**.

2.7 cm
3.0 cm
4.0 cm
F

11.
$$T = F_c - w = mr\omega^2 - mg$$
$$= 2.50(0.230)(26.0)^2 - (2.50)(9.81)$$
$$= 364.18\text{ N} \xrightarrow{\text{SD}} \mathbf{364\ N}$$

12. (a)
$$\text{Total energy} = \frac{1}{2}kx^2 + \frac{1}{2}mv^2$$
$$155 = \frac{1}{2}(2650)(0.250)^2 + \frac{1}{2}(12.5)v^2$$
$$155 = 82.81 + 6.25v^2$$
$$v = 3.399\ \frac{\text{m}}{\text{s}} \xrightarrow{\text{SD}} \mathbf{3.40\ \frac{m}{s}}$$

(b)
$$PE = \frac{1}{2}kA^2$$
$$155 = \frac{1}{2}(2650)A^2$$
$$A = 0.3420\text{ m} \xrightarrow{\text{SD}} \mathbf{0.342\ m}$$

13. Begin by finding the voltage drop across resistor R_3.

$V_3 = I_3R_3 = (0.20\text{ A})(15\ \Omega) = 3.0\text{ V}$

Thus, the voltage drop across resistor R_2 is equal to the voltage drop across resistor R_3, or 3.0 V. Use this voltage to find I_2.

$$I_2 = \frac{V_2}{R_2} = \frac{3.0\text{ V}}{30\ \Omega} = 0.1\text{ A}$$

Now use Kirchhoff's current law to find I_1.

$I_1 = I_2 + I_3 = 0.1\text{ A} + 0.20\text{ A} = \mathbf{0.3\ A}$

14. Begin at the ground symbol, move clockwise, and sum the voltage changes to zero.

$$-40.0\text{ V} + I_1(10.0\ \Omega) - 10.0\text{ V} + I_1(20.0\ \Omega) + I_1(10.0\ \Omega) = 0$$
$$I_1(40.0\ \Omega) = 50.0\text{ V}$$
$$I_1 = \mathbf{1.25\ A}$$

15. $Q_1 = 29.3\ \text{kg} \times 55.9\ \frac{\text{cal}}{\text{kg}\cdot\text{C}^\circ} \times 935.8\ \text{C}^\circ = 1.533 \times 10^6\text{ cal}$

Convert 1.533×10^6 cal to joules and get:

$$Q_1 = 1.533 \times 10^6\ \text{cal} \times \frac{4.186\text{ J}}{1\ \text{cal}} = 6.417 \times 10^6\text{ J}$$

$$Q_2 = 29.3\ \text{kg} \times 88.3 \times 10^3\ \frac{\text{J}}{\text{kg}} = 2.587 \times 10^6\text{ J}$$

To find the total heat, sum Q_1 and Q_2.

$$Q_T = 6.417 \times 10^6\text{ J} + 2.587 \times 10^6\text{ J}$$
$$= 9.004 \times 10^6\text{ J} \xrightarrow{\text{SD}} \mathbf{9.00 \times 10^6\ J}$$

16. Begin by finding the cross-sectional area of the wire.

$A = \pi r^2 = \pi(1.00 \times 10^{-3}\text{ m})^2 = 3.14 \times 10^{-6}\text{ m}^2$

Now find the electrical resistance.

$$R = \rho\frac{L}{A} = \frac{(1.59 \times 10^{-8}\ \Omega\cdot\text{m})(0.100\text{ m})}{3.14 \times 10^{-6}\text{ m}^2}$$
$$= 5.064 \times 10^{-4}\ \Omega \xrightarrow{\text{SD}} \mathbf{5.06 \times 10^{-4}\ \Omega}$$

17. Begin by finding the components of the weight of the 125.0-kg block that are parallel and perpendicular to the plane.

$F_x = mg \sin 36° = (125.0)(9.81) \sin 36° = 720.8\text{ N}$

$F_N = mg \cos 36° = (125.0)(9.81) \cos 36° = 992.1\text{ N}$

Next, compute the weight of the 50-kg object.

$w = mg = (50)(9.81) = 490.5\text{ N}$

Since $F_x > w$, we choose the positive x direction to be down the plane. Now, write a $\Sigma F_x = ma_x$ equation for the 125.0-kg block.

$$\Sigma F_x = ma_x$$
$$F_x - T - \mu_k F_N = ma$$
$$720.8 - T - (0.228)(992.1) = 125.0a$$
$$T = 494.6 - 125.0a \qquad \text{(a)}$$

Now, write a $\Sigma F_y = ma_y$ equation for the 50-kg object.

$$\Sigma F_y = ma_y$$
$$T - mg = ma$$
$$T - (490.5) = 50a$$
$$T = 490.5 + 50a \qquad \text{(b)}$$

Substitute (b) into (a) to find the acceleration.

(a) $(490.5 + 50a) = 494.6 - 125.0a$

$$4.1 = 175a$$
$$a = 0.02343\ \frac{\text{m}}{\text{s}^2} \xrightarrow{\text{SD}} \mathbf{0.023\ \frac{m}{s^2}\ down\ the\ plane}$$

Substitute the acceleration into (a) to find T.

(a) $T = 494.6 - 125.0(0.02343) = 491.7\text{ N} \xrightarrow{\text{SD}} \mathbf{490\ N}$

18. (a) $n_a \sin 56° = n_g \sin\theta_1$

$(1) \sin 56° = (1.560) \sin\theta_1$

$$\theta_1 = 32.102° \xrightarrow{\text{SD}} \mathbf{32.10°}$$

(b) $n_g \sin\theta_1 = n_w \sin\theta_2$

$(1.560) \sin 32.102° = (1.333) \sin\theta_2$

$$\theta_2 = 38.457° \xrightarrow{\text{SD}} \mathbf{38.46°}$$

19. Begin by drawing a diagram and recording the data.

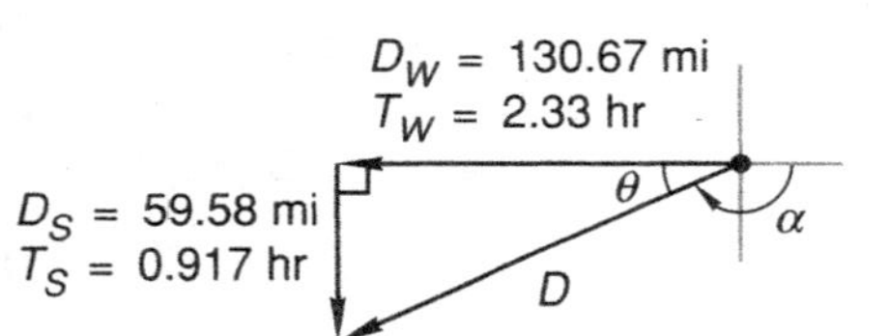

(a) $D_T = 130.67 \text{ mi} + 59.58 \text{ mi} = 190.25 \text{ mi} \xrightarrow{SD} \mathbf{190 \text{ mi}}$

(b) $D = \sqrt{(130.67)^2 + (59.58)^2} = 143.61 \text{ mi}$

$\theta = \tan^{-1} \frac{59.58}{130.67} = 24.51°$

Since θ is a 3rd-quadrant angle: $\alpha = -180° + 24.51° = -155.49°$

$\vec{D} = 143.61\angle{-155.49°} \text{ mi} \xrightarrow{SD} \mathbf{140\angle{-155.49°} \text{ mi}}$

(c) $v = \frac{D_T}{T_T} = \frac{190.25 \text{ mi}}{3.247 \text{ hr}} = 58.6 \frac{\text{mi}}{\text{hr}} \xrightarrow{SD} \mathbf{59 \frac{mi}{hr}}$

$\vec{v} = \frac{\vec{D}}{T_T} = \frac{143.61\angle{-155.49°} \text{ mi}}{3.247 \text{ hr}}$

$= 44.2\angle{-155.49°} \frac{\text{mi}}{\text{hr}} \xrightarrow{SD} \mathbf{44\angle{-155.49°} \frac{mi}{hr}}$

20. $\rho = \frac{m}{V} = \frac{812 \text{ kg}}{0.185 \text{ m}^3} \times \frac{1000 \text{ g}}{1 \text{ kg}} \times \frac{1 \text{ m}^3}{(100)^3 \text{ cm}^3}$

$= 4.389 \frac{\text{g}}{\text{cm}^3} \xrightarrow{SD} \mathbf{4.39 \frac{g}{cm^3}}$

Problem Set 58

1. $V_C(t) = 66e^{-t/RC}$

$= 66e^{-(3.0RC)/RC}$

$= 66e^{-3.0} = 3.286 \text{ V} \xrightarrow{SD} \mathbf{3.3 \text{ V}}$

2. (a) $I = m_1r_1^2 + m_2r_2^2 + m_3r_3^2$

$= (0.50)(0.75)^2 + (0.35)(0.75)^2 + (0.60)(0.75)^2$

$= 0.8156 \text{ kg·m}^2 \xrightarrow{SD} \mathbf{0.82 \text{ kg·m}^2}$

(b) $\tau = I\alpha$

$57 = (0.8156)\alpha$

$\alpha = 69.89 \frac{\text{rad}}{\text{s}^2} \xrightarrow{SD} \mathbf{7\bar{0} \frac{rad}{s^2}}$

3. $\tau = I\alpha = \left(\frac{2}{5}mr^2\right)\alpha$

$= \left(\frac{2}{5}(12.0081)(3.800)^2\right)(2)$

$= 138.7 \text{ N·m} \xrightarrow{SD} \mathbf{100 \text{ N·m}}$

4. The image is **approximately 2.4 cm behind the mirror, it is upright, and the height of the image is approximately 2.4 cm.**

5. The image is **approximately 3.3 cm behind the mirror, it is upright, and the height of the image is approximately 2.7 cm.**

6. $v_1A_1 = v_2A_2$

$14 \frac{\text{m}}{\text{s}}(0.7 \text{ m})(5 \text{ m}) = 6 \frac{\text{m}}{\text{s}}(16 \text{ m})d$

$49 \frac{\text{m}^3}{\text{s}} = \left(96 \frac{\text{m}^2}{\text{s}}\right)d$

$d = 0.5104 \text{ m} \xrightarrow{SD} \mathbf{0.5 \text{ m}}$

7.

$$v_1A_1 = v_2A_2$$

$$50\ \frac{\text{m}}{\text{s}}\left[\pi(0.50\ \text{m})^2\right] = 88\ \frac{\text{m}}{\text{s}}\left[\pi r^2\right]$$

$$39.27\ \frac{\text{m}^3}{\text{s}} = \left(276.46\ \frac{\text{m}}{\text{s}}\right)r^2$$

$$r = 0.377\ \text{m} \xrightarrow{\text{SD}} \mathbf{0.38\ m}$$

8. Begin by finding the centripetal force and the static friction force.

$$F_c = \frac{mv^2}{r} = \frac{540(27)^2}{120} = 3280.5\ \text{N}$$

$$F_s = mg\mu_s = (540)(9.81)\mu_s = (5297.4\ \text{N})\mu_s$$

The required centripetal force must equal the static friction force.

$$F_c = F_s$$

$$3280.5\ \text{N} = (5297.4\ \text{N})\mu_s$$

$$\mu_s = 0.6193 \xrightarrow{\text{SD}} \mathbf{0.62}$$

9. Begin by finding the centripetal force and the static friction force.

$$F_c = \frac{mv^2}{r} = \frac{(659)v^2}{114} = 5.781v^2$$

$$F_s = mg\mu_s = (659)(9.81)(1.09) = 7046.6\ \text{N}$$

The required centripetal force must equal the static friction force.

$$F_c = F_s$$

$$5.781v^2 = 7046.6$$

$$v = 34.91\ \frac{\text{m}}{\text{s}} \xrightarrow{\text{SD}} \mathbf{34.9\ \frac{m}{s}}$$

10.

$$\tau = \left(m_1r_1^{\,2}\right)\alpha + \left(m_2r_2^{\,2}\right)\alpha$$

$$77 = (33)(0.22)^2\alpha + (44)(0.22)^2\alpha$$

$$77 = 1.597\alpha + 2.130\alpha$$

$$\alpha = 20.66\ \frac{\text{rad}}{\text{s}^2} \xrightarrow{\text{SD}} \mathbf{21\ \frac{rad}{s^2}}$$

11. Begin by finding the equivalent resistance of the three parallel resistors.

$$\frac{1}{R_E} = \frac{1}{50} + \frac{1}{75} + \frac{1}{150}$$

$$R_E = 25\ \Omega$$

Now, combine this with the 500-Ω resistor to find the equivalent resistance of the circuit.

$$R_E = (25\ \Omega) + 500\ \Omega = 525\ \Omega$$

Use this resistance to find I_1.

$$I_1 = \frac{V}{R_E} = \frac{18\ \text{V}}{525\ \Omega} = 3.429 \times 10^{-2}\ \text{A} \xrightarrow{\text{SD}} \mathbf{3.4 \times 10^{-2}\ A}$$

12.

$$T = F_c + w = mr\omega^2 + mg = 1.1(0.41)(4.0)^2 + (1.1)(9.81)$$

$$= 18.007\ \text{N} \xrightarrow{\text{SD}} \mathbf{18\ N}$$

13. (a)

$$\text{Total energy} = \frac{1}{2}kx^2 + \frac{1}{2}mv^2$$

$$212 = \frac{1}{2}(1134)(0.140)^2 + \frac{1}{2}(21.0)v^2$$

$$212 = 11.11 + 10.5v^2$$

$$v = 4.374\ \frac{\text{m}}{\text{s}} \xrightarrow{\text{SD}} \mathbf{4.37\ \frac{m}{s}}$$

(b)

$$PE = \frac{1}{2}kA^2$$

$$212 = \frac{1}{2}(1134)A^2$$

$$A = 0.61147\ \text{m} \xrightarrow{\text{SD}} \mathbf{0.611\ m}$$

14. Begin at the ground symbol, move clockwise, and sum the voltage changes to zero.

$$-18\ \text{V} + 3\ \text{V} - 10\ \text{V} - V_1 + 15\ \text{V} = 0$$

$$V_1 = \mathbf{-10\ V}$$

15. Begin by finding the voltage drop across the 20.0-Ω resistor.

$$V_2 = (1.60\ \text{A})(20.0\ \Omega) = 32.0\ \text{V}$$

Thus, the voltage drop across the 60.0-Ω resistor is equal to the voltage drop across the 20.0-Ω resistor, or 32.0 V. Use this voltage to find I_3.

$$I_3 = \frac{32.0\ \text{V}}{60.0\ \Omega} = 0.533\ \text{A}$$

Now use Kirchhoff's current law to find I_1.

$I_1 = I_2 + I_3 = 1.60\text{ A} + 0.533\text{ A} = 2.133\text{ A}$

Use this current to find the voltage drop across the 9.00-Ω resistor.

$V_1 = (2.133\text{ A})(9.00\ \Omega) = 19.197\text{ V}$

The total voltage must equal V_1 plus V_2.

$$V = 19.197\text{ V} + 32.0\text{ V} = 51.197\text{ V} \xrightarrow{\text{SD}} \mathbf{51.2\ V}$$

16. (a) $a_c = \frac{v^2}{r} = \frac{(20)^2}{60} = 6.667\ \frac{\text{m}}{\text{s}^2} \xrightarrow{\text{SD}} \mathbf{6.7\ \frac{m}{s^2}}$

(b) $a_c = \frac{v^2}{r} = \frac{(20)^2}{130} = 3.077\ \frac{\text{m}}{\text{s}^2} \xrightarrow{\text{SD}} \mathbf{3.1\ \frac{m}{s^2}}$

17. Begin by finding the components of the weight of m_1 that are parallel and perpendicular to the plane.

$F_x = mg \sin 20° = m_1(9.81) \sin 20° = 3.355m_1$

$F_N = mg \cos 20° = m_1(9.81) \cos 20° = 9.218m_1$

Next, write a $\Sigma F_x = 0$ equation (constant velocity, so $a = 0$) for m_1. Choose up the plane as the positive x direction.

$$\Sigma F_x = 0$$
$$T - F_x - \mu_k F_N = 0$$
$$T - 3.355m_1 - (0.10)(9.218m_1) = 0$$
$$T = 4.277m_1 \qquad \text{(a)}$$

Now, write a $\Sigma F_y = 0$ equation for m_2.

$$\Sigma F_y = 0$$
$$m_2 g - T = 0$$
$$m_2(9.81) - T = 0$$
$$T = 9.81m_2 \qquad \text{(b)}$$

Substitute (b) into (a) to find the ratio of the masses m_1/m_2.

(a) $(9.81m_2) = 4.277m_1$

$$\frac{m_1}{m_2} = 2.294 \xrightarrow{\text{SD}} \mathbf{2.3}$$

18.
$$Q = mc\Delta T$$
$$3.65 \times 10^5\text{ J} = m \times 1500\ \frac{\text{J}}{\text{kg}\cdot\text{C}°} \times 45\text{ C}°$$
$$m = 5.407\text{ kg} \xrightarrow{\text{SD}} \mathbf{5.4\ kg}$$

19.
$$\Sigma F_y = ma_y$$
$$120\text{ N} - mg = ma$$
$$120\text{ N} - m\left(9.81\ \frac{\text{N}}{\text{kg}}\right) = m\left(5.0\ \frac{\text{m}}{\text{s}^2}\right)$$
$$120\text{ N} = m\left(14.81\ \frac{\text{m}}{\text{s}^2}\right)$$
$$m = 8.103\text{ kg} \xrightarrow{\text{SD}} \mathbf{8.1\ kg}$$

20. $a_{av} = \frac{v_2 - v_1}{t_2 - t_1} = \frac{45 - 5}{50 - 10}\ \frac{\text{km/hr}}{\text{s}} = \mathbf{1\ \frac{km}{hr\cdot s}}$

Convert to m·s^{-2} and get:

$$1\ \frac{\cancel{\text{km}}}{\cancel{\text{hr}}\cdot\text{s}} \times \frac{1000\text{ m}}{1\ \cancel{\text{km}}} \times \frac{1\ \cancel{\text{hr}}}{60\ \cancel{\text{min}}} \times \frac{1\ \cancel{\text{min}}}{60\text{ s}} = 0.278\ \frac{\text{m}}{\text{s}^2} \xrightarrow{\text{SD}} \mathbf{0.3\ \frac{m}{s^2}}$$

PROBLEM SET 59

1. $V = \frac{Q}{C} = \frac{2.5 \times 10^{-6}\text{ C}}{15.2 \times 10^{-6}\text{ F}} = 0.1645\text{ V} \xrightarrow{\text{SD}} \mathbf{0.16\ V}$

2. Begin by finding the time constant RC.

$RC = (1000\ \Omega)(18 \times 10^{-6}\text{ F}) = 1.8 \times 10^{-2}\text{ s}$

Sketch the voltage across the capacitor as a function of time.

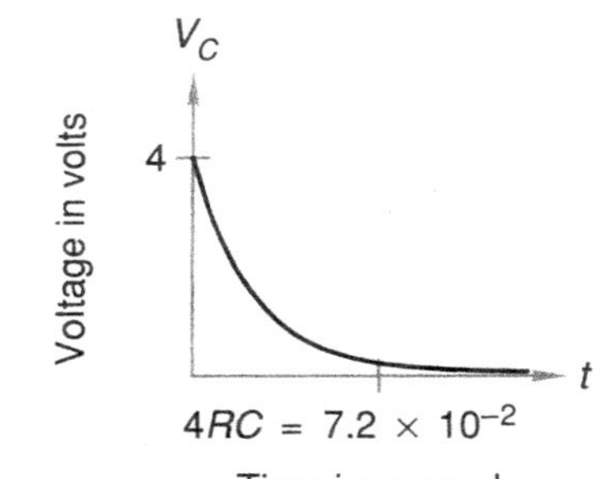

3. Sketch the current through the resistor as a function of time.

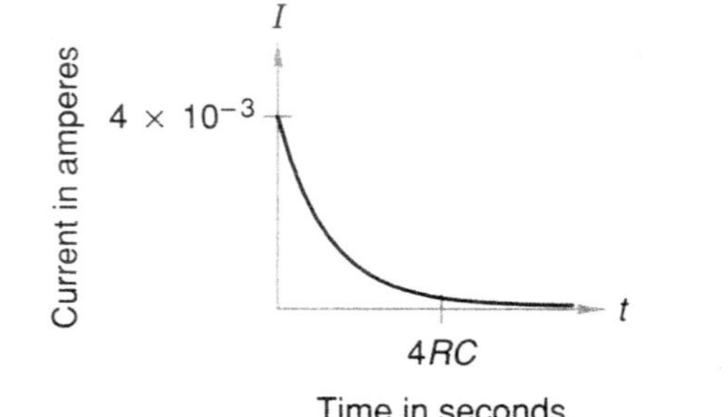

4. (a) $I = m_1r_1^2 + m_2r_2^2 + m_3r_3^2 + m_4r_4^2$

$= (1.0)(0.080)^2 + (1.5)(0.080)^2 + (1.3)(0.080)^2 + (1.8)(0.080)^2$

$= 3.584 \times 10^{-2}\ \text{kg·m}^2 \xrightarrow{\text{SD}}$ $\mathbf{3.6 \times 10^{-2}\ kg{\cdot}m^2}$

(b) $\tau = I\alpha$

$145\ \text{N·m} = (3.584 \times 10^{-2}\ \text{kg·m}^2)\alpha$

$\alpha = 4.046 \times 10^3\ \text{rad·s}^{-2} \xrightarrow{\text{SD}}$ $\mathbf{4.0 \times 10^3\ rad{\cdot}s^{-2}}$

5. $\tau = I\alpha = \left(\frac{1}{2}mr^2\right)\alpha = \left(\frac{1}{2}(10)(6.0)^2\right)(5.5) =$ **990 N·m**

6. The image is **approximately 4.0 cm behind the mirror, it is upright, and the height of the image is approximately 1.7 cm**.

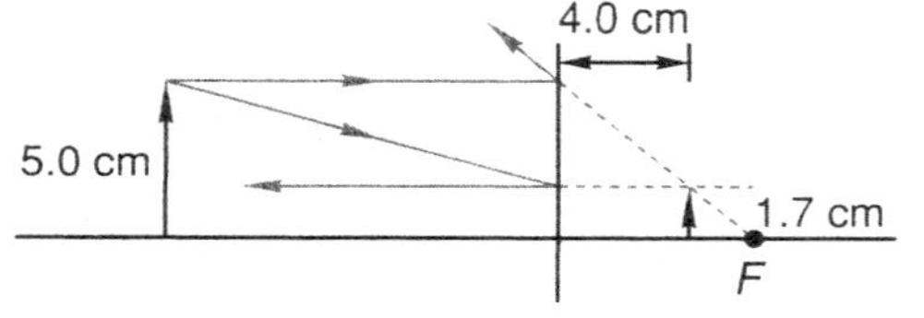

7. The image is **approximately 4.8 cm behind the mirror, it is upright, and the height of the image is approximately 4.2 cm**.

8.
$$v_1A_1 = v_2A_2$$
$$9.0\ \frac{\text{m}}{\text{s}}(2.2\ \text{m})(13\ \text{m}) = 22.0\ \frac{\text{m}}{\text{s}}(6.0\ \text{m})d$$
$$257.4\ \frac{\text{m}^3}{\text{s}} = \left(132\ \frac{\text{m}^2}{\text{s}}\right)d$$
$$d = 1.95\ \text{m} \xrightarrow{\text{SD}} \mathbf{2.0\ m}$$

9.
$$v_1A_1 = v_2A_2$$
$$90\ \frac{\text{m}}{\text{s}}\left[\pi(1.6\ \text{m})^2\right] = 20\ \frac{\text{m}}{\text{s}}\left[\pi r^2\right]$$
$$723.82\ \frac{\text{m}^3}{\text{s}} = \left(62.83\ \frac{\text{m}}{\text{s}}\right)r^2$$
$$r = 3.394\ \text{m} \xrightarrow{\text{SD}} \mathbf{3.4\ m}$$

10. Begin by finding the centripetal force and the static friction force.

$$F_c = \frac{mv^2}{r} = \frac{600(50)^2}{400} = 3750\ \text{N}$$
$$F_s = mg\mu_s = (600)(9.81)\mu_s = (5886\ \text{N})\mu_s$$

The required centripetal force must equal the static friction force.

$$F_c = F_s$$
$$3750\ \text{N} = (5886\ \text{N})\mu_s$$
$$\mu_s = 0.6371 \xrightarrow{\text{SD}} \mathbf{0.64}$$

11. Begin by finding the equivalent resistance of the two parallel resistors.

$$R_E = \frac{(50)(150)}{50 + 150} = 37.5\ \Omega$$

Now, combine this with the 75-Ω resistor to find the equivalent resistance of the circuit.

$$R_E = (37.5\ \Omega) + 75\ \Omega = 112.5\ \Omega$$

Use this resistance to find I_1.

$$I_1 = \frac{V}{R_E} = \frac{15\ \text{V}}{112.5\ \Omega} = 0.1333\ \text{A} \xrightarrow{\text{SD}} \mathbf{0.1\ A}$$

Use this current to find the voltage across the 75-Ω resistor.

$$V_1 = I_1R_1 = (0.1333\ \text{A})(75\ \Omega) = 9.998\ \text{V} \xrightarrow{\text{SD}} \mathbf{10\ V}$$

The voltage across R_2 must equal the total voltage minus V_1.

$V_2 = 15\text{ V} - 9.998\text{ V} = 5.002\text{ V} \xrightarrow{SD} \mathbf{5\text{ V}}$

Use this voltage to find I_2.

$$I_2 = \frac{V_2}{R_2} = \frac{5.002\text{ V}}{50\ \Omega} = 0.10004\text{ A} \xrightarrow{SD} \mathbf{0.1\text{ A}}$$

12. (a) $\text{Total energy} = \frac{1}{2}kx^2 + \frac{1}{2}mv^2$

$$943 = \frac{1}{2}(4345)(0.25)^2 + \frac{1}{2}(99)v^2$$

$$943 = 135.78 + 49.5v^2$$

$$v = 4.038\ \frac{\text{m}}{\text{s}} \xrightarrow{SD} \mathbf{4.0\ \frac{m}{s}}$$

(b) $PE = \frac{1}{2}kA^2$

$$943 = \frac{1}{2}(4345)A^2$$

$$A = 0.6588\text{ m} \xrightarrow{SD} \mathbf{0.659\text{ m}}$$

13. To find V_{BD}, begin at D and move clockwise to B.

$V_{BD} = -9.0\text{ V} - 16\text{ V} + 8.0\text{ V} = \mathbf{-17\text{ V}}$

14. Begin by finding the x and y components of the initial velocity.

$$v_{x0} = 350\cos 20° = 328.89\ \frac{\text{m}}{\text{s}}$$

$$v_{y0} = 350\sin 20° = 119.71\ \frac{\text{m}}{\text{s}}$$

(a) Use the y-displacement equation to find the time.

$$\Delta y = v_{y0}t + \frac{1}{2}a_y t^2$$

$$-12 = 119.71t + \frac{1}{2}(-9.81)t^2$$

$$0 = 4.905t^2 - 119.71t - 12$$

Use the quadratic formula to solve this equation for t.

$$t = \frac{-(-119.71) \pm \sqrt{(-119.71)^2 - 4(4.905)(-12)}}{2(4.905)}$$

$$= 24.5\text{ s} \xrightarrow{SD} \mathbf{25\text{ s}}$$

(b) Use this time in the x-displacement equation to find the distance.

$$\Delta x = v_{x0}t + \frac{1}{2}a_x t^2$$

$$= 328.89(24.5) + (0)$$

$$= 8.058 \times 10^3\text{ m} \xrightarrow{SD} \mathbf{8.1 \times 10^3\text{ m}}$$

15. (a) $F = kx$

$$50.0\text{ N} = k(2.4\text{ m})$$

$$k = 20.83\ \frac{\text{N}}{\text{m}} \xrightarrow{SD} \mathbf{21\ \frac{N}{m}}$$

(b) $W = \frac{1}{2}kx^2 = \frac{1}{2}(20.83)(2.4)^2 = 59.99\text{ J} \xrightarrow{SD} \mathbf{6\bar{0}\text{ J}}$

16. (a) $m_w = 2564\ \cancel{\text{cm}^3} \times \frac{1\ \cancel{\text{m}^3}}{(100)^3\ \cancel{\text{cm}^3}} \times 1000\ \frac{\text{kg}}{\cancel{\text{m}^3}}$

$$= 2.564\text{ kg} \xrightarrow{SD} \mathbf{2.56\text{ kg}}$$

(b) $F_B = 2.564\ \cancel{\text{kg}} \times 9.81\ \frac{\text{N}}{\cancel{\text{kg}}} = 25.15\text{ N} \xrightarrow{SD} \mathbf{25.2\text{ N}}$

(c) $F = w_b - F_B = 20.0\ \cancel{\text{kg}}\left(9.81\ \frac{\text{N}}{\cancel{\text{kg}}}\right) - 25.15\text{ N}$

$$= 171.05\text{ N} \xrightarrow{SD} \mathbf{171\text{ N}}$$

17. Begin by converting the temperature to kelvins.

$T_1 = 20.0 + 273 = 293\text{ K}$

Now use the ideal gas law and get:

$$\frac{V_1}{T_1} = \frac{V_2}{T_2}$$

$$\frac{14.3\text{ m}^3}{293\text{ K}} = \frac{45.0\text{ m}^3}{T_2}$$

$$T_2 = 922.03\text{ K}$$

Convert 922.03 K to degrees Celsius and get:

$T_2 = 922.03 - 273 = 649.03°\text{C} \xrightarrow{SD} \mathbf{649°C}$

18. Begin by finding the pressure produced by the fluid.

$$P_F = 12{,}510\,\frac{\text{kg}}{\text{m}^{3}} \times 9.81\,\frac{\text{N}}{\text{kg}} \times 0.100\,\text{m} = 1.227 \times 10^4\ \text{Pa}$$

Now sum this pressure with the atmospheric pressure and find P.

$$P = 1.227 \times 10^4\ \text{Pa} + 1.01 \times 10^5\ \text{Pa}$$
$$= 1.133 \times 10^5\ \text{Pa} \xrightarrow{\text{SD}} \mathbf{1.13 \times 10^5\ Pa}$$

19. (a) $\Sigma F_y = 0;\ 75.00 + F_2 - F_1 - 487.5 = 0$
(b) $\Sigma M_2 = 0;\ 75.00(13.6566) - 10.0046F_1 - 487.5(2.0046) = 0$

Solve (b) for F_1 and get:
(b) $1024.245 - 10.0046F_1 - 977.243 = 0$
$$10.0046F_1 = 47.002$$
$$F_1 = 4.698\ \text{N} \xrightarrow{\text{SD}} \mathbf{5\ N}$$

Substitute F_1 into (a) to find F_2.
(a) $75.00 + F_2 - (4.698) - 487.5 = 0$
$$F_2 = 417.198\ \text{N} \xrightarrow{\text{SD}} \mathbf{400\ N}$$

20.
$$\tau = F \times D$$
$$240\ \text{N·m} = F \times 0.08\ \text{m}$$
$$F = \mathbf{3000\ N}$$

PROBLEM SET 60

1. (a) $\Delta L = \alpha L_0 \Delta T$
$$= \frac{2.4 \times 10^{-5}}{\text{C}^\circ}(11\ \text{cm})(43\ \text{C}^\circ)$$
$$= 1.135 \times 10^{-2}\ \text{cm} \xrightarrow{\text{SD}} \mathbf{1.1 \times 10^{-2}\ cm}$$

(b) Begin by finding the initial volume of the block.
$$V_0 = L_O \times W_O \times H_O = (11\ \text{cm})(6.0\ \text{cm})(5.0\ \text{cm}) = 330\ \text{cm}^3$$

Now calculate the change in volume.
$$\Delta V = \beta V_0 \Delta T$$
$$= \frac{7.2 \times 10^{-5}}{\text{C}^\circ}(330\ \text{cm}^3)(43\ \text{C}^\circ)$$
$$= 1.02\ \text{cm}^3 \xrightarrow{\text{SD}} \mathbf{1.0\ cm^3}$$

2. $\Delta V = \beta V_0 \Delta T$
$$= \frac{4.85 \times 10^{-4}}{\text{C}^\circ}(424\ \text{L})(10\ \text{C}^\circ)$$
$$= 2.056\ \text{L} \xrightarrow{\text{SD}} \mathbf{2.1\ L}$$

3. $V = \dfrac{Q}{C} = \dfrac{5.10 \times 10^{-8}\ \text{C}}{125 \times 10^{-12}\ \text{F}} = \mathbf{408\ V}$

4. $RC = (422 \times 10^3\ \Omega)(42 \times 10^{-6}\ \text{F}) = 17.72\ \text{s} \xrightarrow{\text{SD}} \mathbf{18\ s}$

5. (a) Begin by finding the initial voltage across the capacitor, V_0.
$$V_0 = \frac{Q}{C} = \frac{7.35 \times 10^{-3}\ \text{C}}{98 \times 10^{-6}\ \text{F}} = 75\ \text{V}$$
Next, find the time constant RC.
$RC = (1530\ \Omega)(98 \times 10^{-6}\ \text{F}) = 0.15\ \text{s}$
Sketch V_C as a function of time.

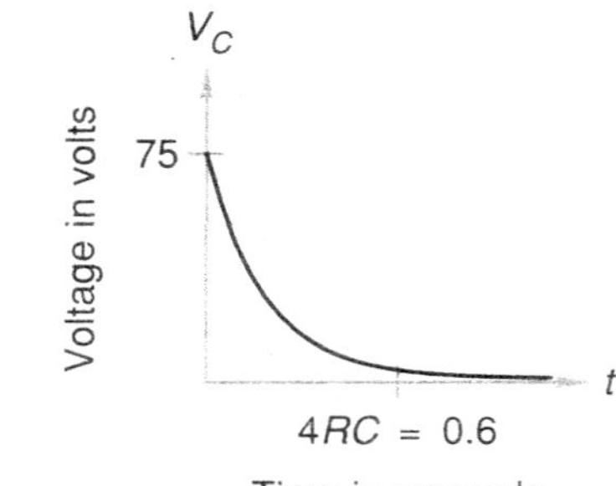

(b) $V_C(t) = V_0 e^{-t/RC}$
$$= 75e^{-2.0RC/RC}$$
$$= 75e^{-2.0} = 10.15\ \text{V} \xrightarrow{\text{SD}} \mathbf{1\bar{0}\ V}$$

$V_C(t) = V_0 e^{-t/RC}$
$$= 75e^{-4.0RC/RC}$$
$$= 75e^{-4.0} = 1.37\ \text{V} \xrightarrow{\text{SD}} \mathbf{1.4\ V}$$

6. $\tau = I\alpha = \left(\frac{1}{3}mL^2\right)\alpha = \left(\frac{1}{3}(4.6\text{ kg})(0.25\text{ m})^2\right)\left(5.5\ \frac{\text{rad}}{\text{s}^2}\right)$

$= 0.527\text{ N}\cdot\text{m} \xrightarrow{\text{SD}} \mathbf{0.53\ N\cdot m}$

7. The image is **approximately 4.5 cm behind the mirror, it is upright, and the height of the image is approximately 3.0 cm**.

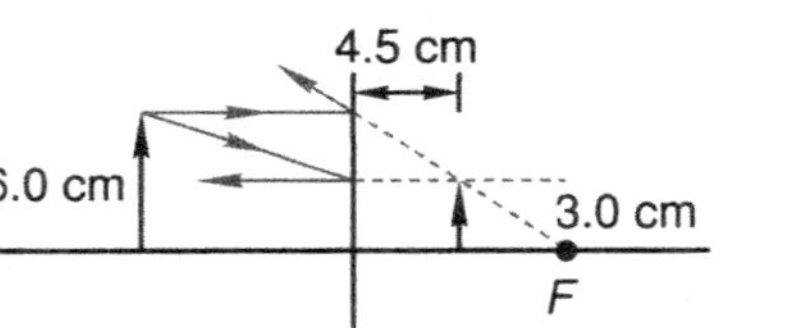

8.
$$v_1A_1 = v_2A_2$$
$$5.4\ \frac{\text{m}}{\text{s}}\left[\pi(0.34\text{ m})^2\right] = 15.3\ \frac{\text{m}}{\text{s}}\left[\pi r^2\right]$$
$$1.96\ \frac{\text{m}^3}{\text{s}} = \left(48.1\ \frac{\text{m}}{\text{s}}\right)r^2$$
$$r = 0.202\text{ m} \xrightarrow{\text{SD}} \mathbf{0.20\ m}$$

9. Begin by finding the centripetal force and the static friction force.

$F_c = \frac{mv^2}{r} = \frac{1000(97)^2}{1600} = 5881\text{ N}$

$F_s = mg\mu_s = (1000)(9.81)\mu_s = (9810\text{ N})\mu_s$

The required centripetal force must equal the static friction force.

$F_c = F_s$

$5881\text{ N} = (9810\text{ N})\mu_s$

$\mu_s = 0.5995 \xrightarrow{\text{SD}} \mathbf{0.60}$

10. Begin by finding the equivalent resistance of the two parallel resistors.

$R_E = \frac{(50)(75)}{50 + 75} = 30\ \Omega$

Now, combine this with the 100-Ω resistor to find the equivalent resistance of the circuit.

$R_E = (30\ \Omega) + 100\ \Omega = 130\ \Omega$

Use this resistance to find I_3.

$I_3 = \frac{V}{R_E} = \frac{10\text{ V}}{130\ \Omega} = 7.69 \times 10^{-2}\text{ A} \xrightarrow{\text{SD}} \mathbf{7.7 \times 10^{-2}\ A}$

11. The image is **approximately 6.0 cm behind the mirror, it is upright, and the height of the image is approximately 3.0 cm**.

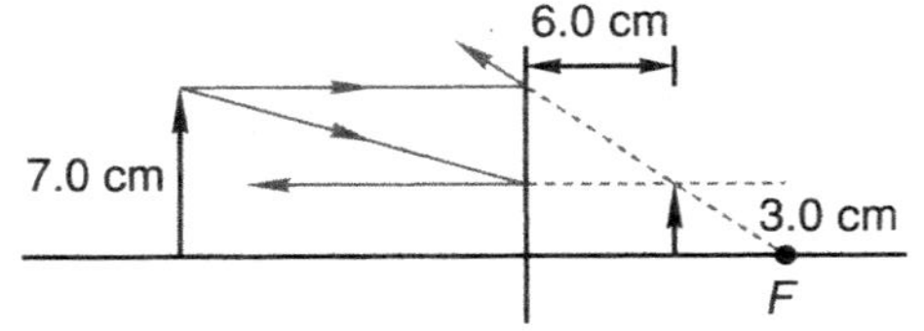

12. Note that the centripetal force must equal the weight of the car.

$F_c = \frac{mv^2}{r}$

$\not{m}g = \frac{\not{m}v^2}{r}$

$9.81 = \frac{v^2}{1.3}$

$v = 3.57\ \frac{\text{m}}{\text{s}} \xrightarrow{\text{SD}} \mathbf{3.6\ \frac{m}{s}}$

13. Begin by finding the equivalent resistance of the two parallel resistors.

$R_E = \frac{(60)(180)}{60 + 180} = 45\ \Omega$

Now, combine this with the 55-Ω resistor to find the equivalent resistance of the circuit.

$R_E = (45\ \Omega) + 55\ \Omega = 100\ \Omega$

Use this resistance to find I_1.

$I_1 = \frac{V}{R_E} = \frac{12\text{ V}}{100\ \Omega} = \mathbf{0.12\ A}$

Use this current to find the voltage across the 55-Ω resistor.

$V_1 = I_1R_1 = (0.12\text{ A})(55\ \Omega) = \mathbf{6.6\ V}$

The voltage across R_2 must equal the total voltage minus V_1.

$V_2 = 12\text{ V} - 6.6\text{ V} = \mathbf{5.4\ V}$

Use this voltage to find I_2.

$I_2 = \frac{V_2}{R_2} = \frac{5.4\text{ V}}{60\ \Omega} = \mathbf{0.090\ A}$

14. (a) $\text{Work} = FD\cos\theta$
$= 62.740\text{ N}(15.80\text{ m})\cos 20°$
$= 931.51\text{ J} \xrightarrow{SD} \mathbf{931.5\ J}$

(b) The amount of work done on the block must be equal to its final kinetic energy. Thus, the final kinetic energy also equals **931.5 J**.

$$KE_f = \frac{1}{2}mv_f^2$$
$$931.5\text{ J} = \frac{1}{2}(4\text{ kg})v_f^2$$
$$v_f = 21.58\ \frac{\text{m}}{\text{s}} \xrightarrow{SD} \mathbf{20\ \frac{m}{s}\ to\ the\ right}$$

15. (a) $I_1 = I_2 + I_3$
$3.00\text{ A} = 0.750\text{ A} + I_3$
$I_3 = \mathbf{2.25\ A}$

(b) $V_3 = I_3R = (2.25\text{ A})(40\ \Omega) = \mathbf{90\ V}$

16. (a) $I_3 = \frac{V_3}{R_3} = \frac{6.0\text{ V}}{3.0\ \Omega} = \mathbf{2.0\ A}$

(b) In the left-hand loop, begin at the ground symbol, move clockwise, and sum the voltage changes to zero.
$-10\text{ V} + I_1(8.0\ \Omega) + 6.0\text{ V} = 0$
$I_1(8.0\ \Omega) = 4.0\text{ V}$
$I_1 = \mathbf{0.50\ A}$

(c) Use Kirchhoff's current law to find I_2.
$I_1 + I_2 = I_3$
$0.50\text{ A} + I_2 = 2.0\text{ A}$
$I_2 = \mathbf{1.5\ A}$

17. $Q = mc\Delta T$
$5600\text{ J} = (107\text{ kg})c(59\text{ C°})$
$$c = 0.887\ \frac{\text{J}}{\text{kg}\cdot\text{C°}} \xrightarrow{SD} \mathbf{0.89\ \frac{J}{kg\cdot C°}}$$

18. (a) $m_1v_1 + m_2v_2 = (m_1 + m_2)v_3$
$(2.3 \times 10^{-3})(210) + (0.40)(0) = (0.4023)v_3$
$$v_3 = +1.2006\ \frac{\text{m}}{\text{s}} \xrightarrow{SD} \mathbf{+1.2\ \frac{m}{s}}$$

(b) $KE = \frac{1}{2}mv_3^2$
$= \frac{1}{2}(0.4023)(1.2006)^2$
$= 0.2899\text{ J} \xrightarrow{SD} \mathbf{0.29\ J}$

(c) $PE = mgh$
$0.2899 = (0.4023)(9.81)h$
$h = 7.346 \times 10^{-2}\text{ m} \xrightarrow{SD} \mathbf{7.3 \times 10^{-2}\ m}$

19. Begin by finding the weight of the crate.
$$w = mg = 225\ \cancel{\text{kg}} \times 9.81\ \frac{\text{N}}{\cancel{\text{kg}}} = 2207.25\text{ N}$$

There are 3 upward forces acting on the crate, so the force needed to lift the crate at a constant speed is equal to the weight divided by 3.
$$F = \frac{2207.25\text{ N}}{3} = 735.75\text{ N} \xrightarrow{SD} \mathbf{736\ N}$$
$$\text{Mechanical advantage} = \frac{F_{out}}{F_{in}} = \frac{2207.25\text{ N}}{735.75\text{ N}} = \mathbf{3.00}$$

20. $$v_{av} = \frac{x_2 - x_1}{t_2 - t_1} = \frac{25 - (-30)}{18 - 11}\ \frac{\text{m}}{\text{s}} = +7.86\ \frac{\text{m}}{\text{s}} \xrightarrow{SD} \mathbf{+7.9\ \frac{m}{s}}$$

Problem Set 61

1. (a) $v_1A_1 = v_2A_2$
$1.2\ \frac{\text{m}}{\text{s}}(4.0\text{ m}^2) = v_2(1.0\text{ m}^2)$
$v_2 = \mathbf{4.8\ \frac{m}{s}}$

(b) $P_1 + \frac{1}{2}\rho v_1^2 = P_2 + \frac{1}{2}\rho v_2^2$
$7.0 \times 10^5 + \frac{1}{2}(1000)(1.2)^2 = P_2 + \frac{1}{2}(1000)(4.8)^2$
$7.0 \times 10^5 + 720 = P_2 + 11{,}520$
$$P_2 = 6.89 \times 10^5\ \frac{\text{N}}{\text{m}^2} \xrightarrow{SD} \mathbf{6.9 \times 10^5\ \frac{N}{m^2}}$$

2. Begin by finding v_1 and v_2.

$$v_1 = \frac{Q_1}{A_1} = \frac{1.28}{1.05} = 1.22\ \frac{\text{m}}{\text{s}}$$

$$v_2 = \frac{Q_2}{A_2} = \frac{1.28}{4.63} = 0.276\ \frac{\text{m}}{\text{s}}$$

Now use Bernoulli's equation to find P_2. Note that h_1 is zero, so the $\rho g h_1$ term falls out of the equation.

$$P_1 + \frac{1}{2}\rho v_1^2 = P_2 + \frac{1}{2}\rho v_2^2 + \rho g h_2$$

$$84{,}278 + \frac{1}{2}(1025)(1.22)^2 = P_2 + \frac{1}{2}(1025)(0.276)^2 + (1025)(9.81)(4.27)$$

$$84{,}278 + 762.8 = P_2 + 39.04 + 42{,}936$$

$$P_2 = 4.207 \times 10^4 \text{ Pa} \xrightarrow{\text{SD}} \mathbf{4.21 \times 10^4\ Pa}$$

3. $\Delta L = \alpha L_0 \Delta T$

$$= \frac{2.0 \times 10^{-5}}{\text{C}^\circ}(453.7 \text{ m})(53 \text{ C}^\circ)$$

$$= 0.4809 \text{ m} \xrightarrow{\text{SD}} \mathbf{0.48\ m}$$

4. $\Delta V = \beta V_0 \Delta T$

$$= \frac{1.24 \times 10^{-4}}{\text{C}^\circ}(313 \text{ m}^3)(4.0 \text{ C}^\circ)$$

$$= 0.155 \text{ m}^3 \xrightarrow{\text{SD}} \mathbf{0.16\ m^3}$$

5. $Q = CV = (58 \times 10^{-6} \text{ F})(126 \text{ V}) = 7.31 \times 10^{-3} \text{ C} \xrightarrow{\text{SD}} \mathbf{7.3 \times 10^{-3}\ C}$

6. (a) $RC = (12{,}000\ \Omega)(54 \times 10^{-6} \text{ F}) = 0.648 \text{ s} \xrightarrow{\text{SD}} \mathbf{0.65\ s}$

(b) Begin by finding the initial voltage across the capacitor, V_C.

$$V_C = \frac{Q}{C} = \frac{6.48 \times 10^{-3} \text{ C}}{54 \times 10^{-6} \text{ F}} = 120 \text{ V}$$

Now find the initial value of the current.

$$I = \frac{V_C}{R} = \frac{120 \text{ V}}{12{,}000\ \Omega} = 0.010 \text{ A}$$

Sketch the current as a function of time.

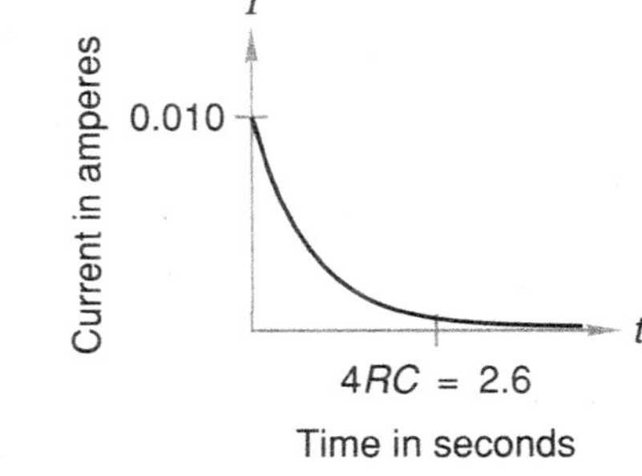

7. (a) $I = m_1 r_1^2 + m_2 r_2^2 + m_3 r_3^2$

$$= 1.2(0.23)^2 + 3.4(0.23)^2 + 1.2(0.23)^2$$

$$= 0.3068 \text{ kg}\cdot\text{m}^2 \xrightarrow{\text{SD}} \mathbf{0.31\ kg\cdot m^2}$$

(b) $\tau = I\alpha$

$$79 \text{ N}\cdot\text{m} = (0.3068 \text{ kg}\cdot\text{m}^2)\alpha$$

$$\alpha = 257.5\ \frac{\text{rad}}{\text{s}^2} \xrightarrow{\text{SD}} \mathbf{260\ \frac{rad}{s^2}}$$

8. $\tau = I\alpha = \left(\frac{1}{2}mr^2\right)\alpha$

$$= \left(\frac{1}{2}(12.5182 \text{ kg})(0.3604 \text{ m})^2\right)\left(3\ \frac{\text{rad}}{\text{s}^2}\right)$$

$$= 2.439 \text{ N}\cdot\text{m} \xrightarrow{\text{SD}} \mathbf{2\ N\cdot m}$$

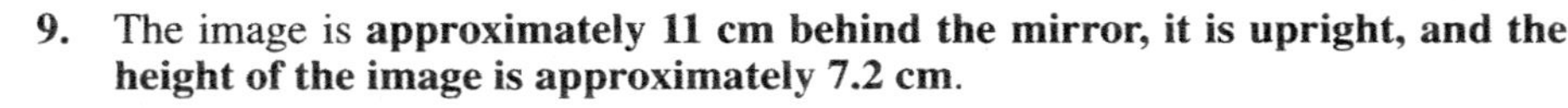

9. The image is **approximately 11 cm behind the mirror, it is upright, and the height of the image is approximately 7.2 cm.**

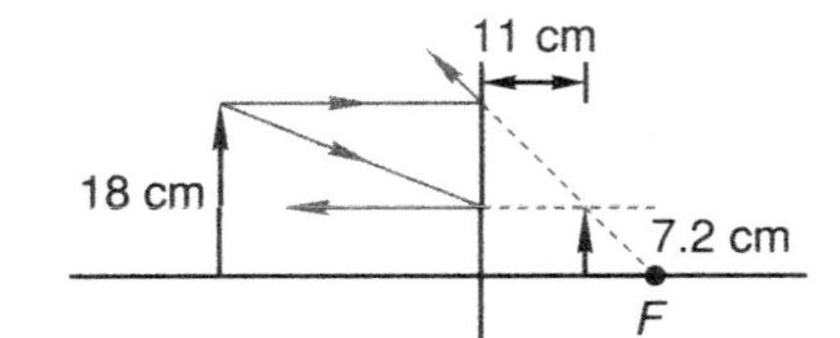

10.

$$v_1A_1 = v_2A_2$$
$$12.2\ \frac{\text{m}}{\text{s}}[\pi(1.83\text{ m})^2] = 7.7\ \frac{\text{m}}{\text{s}}[\pi r^2]$$
$$128.4\ \frac{\text{m}^3}{\text{s}} = \left(24.2\ \frac{\text{m}}{\text{s}}\right)r^2$$
$$r = 2.303\text{ m} \xrightarrow{\text{SD}} \mathbf{2.3\ m}$$

11. Begin by finding the centripetal force and the static friction force.

$$F_c = \frac{mv^2}{r} = \frac{720(33)^2}{190} = 4126.74\text{ N}$$
$$F_s = mg\mu_s = (720)(9.81)\mu_s = (7063.2\text{ N})\mu_s$$

The required centripetal force must equal the static friction force.

$$F_c = F_s$$
$$4126.74\text{ N} = (7063.2\text{ N})\mu_s$$
$$\mu_s = 0.584 \xrightarrow{\text{SD}} \mathbf{0.58}$$

12. (a) To find V_{AB}, begin at B and move counterclockwise to A.

$$V_{AB} = +(1.00\text{ A})(60.0\ \Omega) = \mathbf{+60.0\ V}$$

(b) $I_2 = \frac{V_2}{R_2} = \frac{60.0\text{ V}}{120\ \Omega} = \mathbf{0.500\ A}$

(c) Begin by finding the total current through the circuit.

$$I = I_1 + I_2 = 1.00\text{ A} + 0.500\text{ A} = 1.50\text{ A}$$

Begin at the ground symbol, move clockwise, and sum the voltage changes to zero.

$$-V_x + 60.0\text{ V} + 1.50\text{ A}(30.0\ \Omega) = 0$$
$$60.0\text{ V} + 45\text{ V} = V_x$$
$$V_x = \mathbf{105\ V}$$

13. Begin by finding the voltage drop across the 55-Ω resistor.

$$V_1 = I_1R_1 = (4.0\text{ A})(55\ \Omega) = 220\text{ V}$$

Thus, the voltage drop across the 54-Ω resistor is 400 V − 220 V, or 180 V. Use this voltage to find I_3.

$$I_3 = \frac{V_3}{R_3} = \frac{180\text{ V}}{54\ \Omega} = 3.33\text{ A}$$

Now find the energy consumed by the 54-Ω resistor.

$$\text{Energy} = I^2Rt$$
$$= (3.33\text{ A})^2(54\ \Omega)(30\text{ s})$$
$$= 1.796 \times 10^4\text{ J} \xrightarrow{\text{SD}} \mathbf{1.8 \times 10^4\ J}$$

14. Begin by finding the components of the weight of the 23-kg block that are parallel and perpendicular to the plane.

$$F_x = mg\sin 30° = (23)(9.81)\sin 30° = 112.815\text{ N}$$
$$F_N = mg\cos 30° = (23)(9.81)\cos 30° = 195.401\text{ N}$$

Next, compute the weight of the 19-kg block.

$$w = mg = (19)(9.81) = 186.39\text{ N}$$

Since $w > F_x$, we choose the positive x direction to be up the plane. Now, write a $\Sigma F_x = ma_x$ equation for the 23-kg block.

$$\Sigma F_x = ma_x$$
$$T - F_x - \mu_kF_N = ma$$
$$T - 112.815 - (0.19)(195.401) = 23a$$
$$T = 149.94 + 23a \qquad \text{(a)}$$

Now, write a $\Sigma F_y = ma_y$ equation for the 19-kg block.

$$\Sigma F_y = ma_y$$
$$mg - T = ma$$
$$(186.39) - T = 19a$$
$$T = 186.39 - 19a \qquad \text{(b)}$$

Substitute (b) into (a) to find the acceleration.

(a) $(186.39 - 19a) = 149.94 + 23a$

$$36.45 = 42a$$
$$a = 0.868\ \frac{\text{m}}{\text{s}^2} \xrightarrow{\text{SD}} \mathbf{0.87\ \frac{m}{s^2}\ up\ the\ plane}$$

Substitute the acceleration into (a) to find T.

(a) $T = 149.94 + 23(0.868)$

$$= 169.90\text{ N} \xrightarrow{\text{SD}} \mathbf{170\ N}$$

15. Begin by finding the x and y components of the initial velocity.

$$v_{x0} = 200 \cos 30° = 173.2 \ \frac{\text{m}}{\text{s}}$$

$$v_{y0} = 200 \sin 30° = 100.0 \ \frac{\text{m}}{\text{s}}$$

(a) Use the y-displacement equation to find the time.

$$\Delta y = v_{y0}t + \frac{1}{2}a_y t^2$$

$$-11 = 100.0t + \frac{1}{2}(-9.81)t^2$$

$$0 = 4.905t^2 - 100.0t - 11$$

Use the quadratic formula to solve this equation for t.

$$t = \frac{-(-100.0) \pm \sqrt{(-100.0)^2 - 4(4.905)(-11)}}{2(4.905)} = 20.5 \text{ s}$$

Use this time in the x-displacement equation to find the distance.

$$\Delta x = v_{x0}t + \frac{1}{2}a_x t^2$$

$$= 173.2(20.5) + (0)$$

$$= 3.5506 \times 10^3 \text{ m} \xrightarrow{\text{SD}} \mathbf{3.6 \times 10^3 \ m}$$

(b) Since the ship is now traveling forward, add 15.2 m/s to v_{x0} to find the new initial velocity.

$$v_x = 15.2 \text{ m/s} + 173.2 \text{ m/s} = 188.4 \text{ m/s}$$

Use this velocity in the x-displacement equation and again find the distance.

$$\Delta x = v_x t + \frac{1}{2}a_x t^2$$

$$= 188.4(20.5) + (0)$$

$$= 3.8622 \times 10^3 \text{ m} \xrightarrow{\text{SD}} \mathbf{3.9 \times 10^3 \ m}$$

Note that increasing the horizontal velocity does not increase the time the shell is in the air.

16. $D = R \times T$

$$= 350 \ \frac{\text{m}}{\text{s}} \times 7.53 \text{ s}$$

$$= 2.636 \times 10^3 \text{ m} \xrightarrow{\text{SD}} \mathbf{2.64 \times 10^3 \ m}$$

17. (a) Note that the centripetal force must equal the weight of the car.

$$F_c = \frac{mv^2}{r}$$

$$mg = \frac{mv^2}{r}$$

$$9.81 = \frac{v^2}{1.4}$$

$$v = 3.706 \ \frac{\text{m}}{\text{s}} \xrightarrow{\text{SD}} \mathbf{3.7 \ \frac{m}{s}}$$

(b) $KE_t = \frac{1}{2}mv^2$

$$= \frac{1}{2}(2.0)(3.706)^2$$

$$= 13.73 \text{ J} \xrightarrow{\text{SD}} \mathbf{14 \ J}$$

(c) $KE_b = KE_t + mgh$

$$= 13.73 + 2.0(9.81)(2.8)$$

$$= 68.67 \text{ J} \xrightarrow{\text{SD}} \mathbf{69 \ J}$$

(d) $KE_b = \frac{1}{2}mv_b^2$

$$68.67 = \frac{1}{2}(2.0)v_b^2$$

$$v_b = 8.29 \ \frac{\text{m}}{\text{s}} \xrightarrow{\text{SD}} \mathbf{8.3 \ \frac{m}{s}}$$

18. (a) $p = mv = 56 \text{ kg}\left(22 \ \frac{\text{m}}{\text{s}}\right)$

$$= 1232 \text{ kg}\cdot\text{m}\cdot\text{s}^{-1} \xrightarrow{\text{SD}} \mathbf{1.2 \times 10^3 \ kg \cdot m \cdot s^{-1}}$$

(b) $F\Delta t = m(v_2 - v_1)$

$$F(10 \text{ s}) = 56 \text{ kg}\left(22 \ \frac{\text{m}}{\text{s}} - 0 \ \frac{\text{m}}{\text{s}}\right)$$

$$F(10 \text{ s}) = 1232 \ \frac{\text{kg}\cdot\text{m}}{\text{s}}$$

$$F = 123.2 \text{ N} \xrightarrow{\text{SD}} \mathbf{1.2 \times 10^2 \ N}$$

19. Begin by finding the weight of the mass and drawing a free-body diagram of the forces acting on the junction of the ropes.

$$w = mg$$
$$= 63.7\ \text{kg} \times 9.81\ \frac{\text{N}}{\text{kg}}$$
$$= 624.9\ \text{N}$$

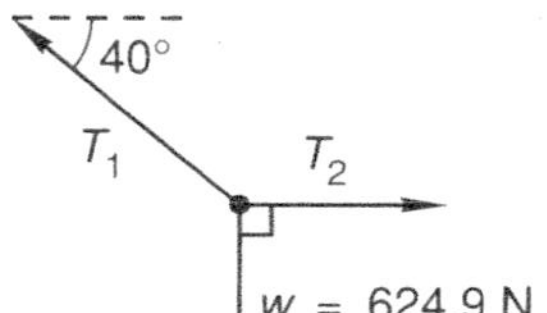

Now sum the horizontal and vertical forces to zero.

(a) $\Sigma F_x = 0;\ T_2 - T_1 \cos 40° = 0$

(b) $\Sigma F_y = 0;\ T_1 \sin 40° - 624.9\ \text{N} = 0$

Solve (b) for T_1 and get:

(b) $T_1 \sin 40° = 624.9\ \text{N}$

$$T_1 = 972.2\ \text{N} \xrightarrow{\text{SD}} \mathbf{972\ N}$$

Substitute T_1 into (a) to find T_2.

(a) $T_2 = T_1 \cos 40° = (972.2\ \text{N}) \cos 40° = 744.7\ \text{N} \xrightarrow{\text{SD}} \mathbf{745\ N}$

20.
$$\Sigma F_x = ma_x$$
$$F - \mu_k mg = ma_x$$
$$F - 0.5482(26.200)(9.81) = (26.200)(3.1418)$$
$$F = 223.2\ \text{N} \xrightarrow{\text{SD}} \mathbf{223\ N}$$

PROBLEM SET 62

1. Begin by finding the angular speed and the moment of inertia of the hoop.

$$\omega = \frac{v}{r} = \frac{4.0\ \text{m/s}}{1.0\ \text{m}} = 4.0\ \frac{\text{rad}}{\text{s}}$$

$I = mr^2 = (1.2\ \text{kg})(1.0\ \text{m})^2 = 1.2\ \text{kg}\cdot\text{m}^2$

Now find the total kinetic energy.

$$KE = \frac{1}{2}mv^2 + \frac{1}{2}I\omega^2$$
$$= \frac{1}{2}(1.2)(4.0)^2 + \frac{1}{2}(1.2)(4.0)^2$$
$$= 19.2\ \text{J} \xrightarrow{\text{SD}} \mathbf{19\ J}$$

2. (a)
$$\tau \Delta t = \Delta(I\omega)$$
$$(3.9 \times 10^{-2})(1.3) = \Delta(I\omega)$$
$$\Delta(I\omega) = 5.07 \times 10^{-2}\ \frac{\text{kg}\cdot\text{m}^2}{\text{s}}$$
$$\xrightarrow{\text{SD}} \mathbf{5.1 \times 10^{-2}\ \frac{kg\cdot m^2}{s}}$$

(b) Begin by finding the moment of inertia.

$$I = \frac{1}{2}mr^2 = \frac{1}{2}(0.20)(0.030)^2 = 9.0 \times 10^{-5}\ \text{kg}\cdot\text{m}^2$$

Now find the angular speed.

$$\tau \Delta t = I(\omega_2 - \omega_1)$$
$$5.07 \times 10^{-2} = (9.0 \times 10^{-5})(\omega_2 - 0)$$
$$\omega_2 = 563.3\ \frac{\text{rad}}{\text{s}} \xrightarrow{\text{SD}} \mathbf{560\ \frac{rad}{s}}$$

3. Begin by finding v_A and v_B.

$$v_A = \frac{Q}{A_A} = \frac{3.9418}{2.2006} = 1.7912\ \frac{\text{m}}{\text{s}}$$
$$v_B = \frac{Q}{A_B} = \frac{3.9418}{4} = 0.9855\ \frac{\text{m}}{\text{s}}$$

Now use Bernoulli's equation to find P_B.

$$P_A + \frac{1}{2}\rho {v_A}^2 = P_B + \frac{1}{2}\rho {v_B}^2$$
$$4480 + \frac{1}{2}(1010)(1.7912)^2 = P_B + \frac{1}{2}(1010)(0.9855)^2$$
$$4480 + 1620.24 = P_B + 490.46$$
$$P_B = 5609.78\ \text{Pa} \xrightarrow{\text{SD}} \mathbf{6000\ Pa}$$

4. Begin by finding v_1 and v_2.

$$v_1 = \frac{Q}{A_1} = \frac{0.25}{0.40} = 0.625\ \frac{\text{m}}{\text{s}}$$
$$v_2 = \frac{Q}{A_2} = \frac{0.25}{0.20} = 1.25\ \frac{\text{m}}{\text{s}}$$

Now use Bernoulli's equation to find P_2. Note that h_2 is zero, so the $\rho g h_2$ term falls out of the equation.

$$P_1 + \frac{1}{2}\rho v_1^2 + \rho g h_1 = P_2 + \frac{1}{2}\rho v_2^2$$

$$31{,}051 + \frac{1}{2}(670)(0.625)^2 + 670(9.81)(2.2) = P_2 + \frac{1}{2}(670)(1.25)^2$$

$$31{,}051 + 130.86 + 14{,}459.94 = P_2 + 523.44$$

$$P_2 = 4.512 \times 10^4 \text{ Pa} \xrightarrow{\text{SD}} \mathbf{4.5 \times 10^4 \text{ Pa}}$$

5. $\Delta L = \alpha L_0 \Delta T$

$$= \frac{1.7 \times 10^{-5}}{\text{C}^\circ}(91 \text{ m})(23 \text{ C}^\circ)$$

$$= 3.558 \times 10^{-2} \text{ m} \xrightarrow{\text{SD}} \mathbf{3.6 \times 10^{-2} \text{ m}}$$

6. $\Delta V = 3\alpha V_0 \Delta T$

$$= (3)\frac{0.09 \times 10^{-5}}{\text{C}^\circ}(3.4 \text{ m}^3)(43 \text{ C}^\circ)$$

$$= 3.95 \times 10^{-4} \text{ m}^3 \xrightarrow{\text{SD}} \mathbf{4 \times 10^{-4} \text{ m}^3}$$

7. $V = \dfrac{Q}{C} = \dfrac{4.5 \times 10^{-5} \text{ C}}{15 \times 10^{-6} \text{ F}} = \mathbf{3.0 \text{ V}}$

8. Sketch the voltage across the capacitor as a function of time.

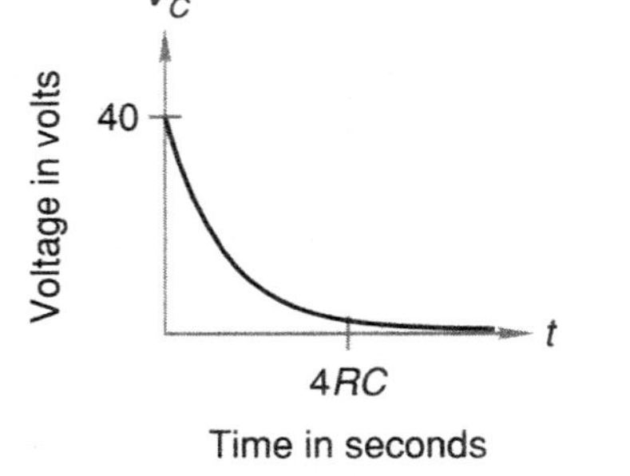

9. $\tau = I\alpha$

$$\tau = \left(\frac{1}{3}mL^2\right)\alpha$$

$$5.3 \text{ N}\cdot\text{m} = \left(\frac{1}{3}(3.5 \text{ kg})(1.7 \text{ m})^2\right)\alpha$$

$$\alpha = 1.57 \frac{\text{rad}}{\text{s}^2} \xrightarrow{\text{SD}} \mathbf{1.6 \frac{rad}{s^2}}$$

10. Begin by finding the centripetal force and the static friction force.

$$F_c = \frac{mv^2}{r} = \frac{547(28.5)^2}{114} = 3897.38 \text{ N}$$

$$F_s = mg\mu_s = (547)(9.81)\mu_s = (5366.07 \text{ N})\mu_s$$

The required centripetal force must equal the static friction force.

$$F_c = F_s$$

$$3897.38 \text{ N} = (5366.07 \text{ N})\mu_s$$

$$\mu_s = 0.726301 \xrightarrow{\text{SD}} \mathbf{0.726}$$

11. (a) $I_3 = \dfrac{18 \text{ V}}{9.0\ \Omega} = \mathbf{2.0 \text{ A}}$

(b) $-6.0 \text{ V} + I_1(4.0\ \Omega) + 18 \text{ V} = 0$

$$I_1(4.0\ \Omega) = -12 \text{ V}$$

$$I_1 = \mathbf{-3.0 \text{ A}}$$

(c) $P_{6.0 \text{ V}} = VI_1 = (6.0 \text{ V})(-3.0 \text{ A}) = \mathbf{-18 \text{ W}}$

To find $P_{18 \text{ V}}$, use Kirchhoff's current law to first find I_2.

$$I_2 = I_3 - I_1 = 2.0 \text{ A} - (-3.0 \text{ A}) = 5.0 \text{ A}$$

$$P_{18 \text{ V}} = VI_2 = (18 \text{ V})(5.0 \text{ A}) = \mathbf{9\overline{0} \text{ W}}$$

12. Note that the kinetic energy of the block once it impacts the spring equals the potential energy of the block at the top of the plane.

$$mgh = \frac{1}{2}kx^2$$

$$12(9.81)(4.2) = \frac{1}{2}(3340)x^2$$

$$x = 0.544 \text{ m} \xrightarrow{\text{SD}} \mathbf{0.54 \text{ m}}$$

13. (a) $PE = \frac{1}{2}kx^2$

$457 = \frac{1}{2}(1470)x^2$

$x = 0.7885\text{ m} \xrightarrow{SD} \mathbf{0.789\ m}$

(b) $PE = \frac{1}{2}kx^2$

$= \frac{1}{2}(1470)(0.217)^2$

$= 34.61\text{ J} \xrightarrow{SD} \mathbf{34.6\ J}$

(c) Total energy $= \frac{1}{2}kx^2 + \frac{1}{2}mv^2$

$457 = \frac{1}{2}(1470)(0.217)^2 + \frac{1}{2}(13.8)v^2$

$457 = 34.61 + 6.90v^2$

$v = 7.824\ \frac{\text{m}}{\text{s}} \xrightarrow{SD} \mathbf{7.82\ \frac{m}{s}}$

14. Begin by finding the equivalent resistance of the two parallel resistors.

$R_E = \frac{(12)(12)}{12 + 12} = 6\ \Omega$

Now, combine this with the 14-Ω resistor to find the equivalent resistance of the circuit.

$R_E = (6\ \Omega) + 14\ \Omega = 20\ \Omega$

(a) Use this resistance to find I_3.

$I_3 = \frac{V}{R_E} = \frac{30\text{ V}}{20\ \Omega} = \mathbf{1.5\ A}$

(b) The voltage across the 14-Ω resistor is $(1.5\text{ A})(14\ \Omega) = 21$ V. Therefore, the voltage across each of the parallel resistors is $30\text{ V} - 21\text{ V}$, or 9 V. Use this voltage to find I_1 and I_2.

$I_1 = \frac{V}{R_1} = \frac{9\text{ V}}{12\ \Omega} = \mathbf{0.75\ A}$

$I_2 = \frac{V}{R_2} = \frac{9\text{ V}}{12\ \Omega} = \mathbf{0.75\ A}$

(c) $P = I^2R = (0.75\text{ A})^2(12\ \Omega) = 6.75\text{ W} \xrightarrow{SD} \mathbf{6.8\ W}$

15. (a) Begin by finding the weight of the mass.

$w = mg = 6.4\ \cancel{\text{kg}} \times 9.81\ \frac{\text{N}}{\cancel{\text{kg}}} = 62.8\text{ N}$

Now calculate the distance the spring is stretched.

$F = kx$

$62.8\text{ N} = \left(246\ \frac{\text{N}}{\text{m}}\right)x$

$x = 0.255\text{ m} \xrightarrow{SD} \mathbf{0.26\ m}$

(b) $W = \frac{1}{2}kx^2 = \frac{1}{2}(246)(0.255)^2 = 7.998\text{ J} \xrightarrow{SD} \mathbf{8.0\ J}$

16. Begin by finding the cross-sectional area of the bar.

$A = (0.064\text{ m})(0.027\text{ m}) = 1.728 \times 10^{-3}\text{ m}^2$

Now find the electrical resistance.

$R = \rho\frac{L}{A} = \frac{(5.6 \times 10^{-8}\ \Omega\cdot\text{m})(1.12\text{ m})}{1.728 \times 10^{-3}\text{ m}^2}$

$= 3.630 \times 10^{-5}\ \Omega \xrightarrow{SD} \mathbf{3.6 \times 10^{-5}\ \Omega}$

17. (a) Begin by finding the volume of the boat that is submerged.

$V_s = 87\text{ m}^3 \times 0.81 = 70.47\text{ m}^3$

Now find the mass of the water displaced.

$m_w = 1000\ \frac{\text{kg}}{\cancel{\text{m}^3}} \times 70.47\ \cancel{\text{m}^3}$

$= 7.047 \times 10^4\text{ kg} \xrightarrow{SD} \mathbf{7.0 \times 10^4\ kg}$

(b) $F_B = 7.047 \times 10^4\ \cancel{\text{kg}} \times 9.81\ \frac{\text{N}}{\cancel{\text{kg}}}$

$= 6.91 \times 10^5\text{ N} \xrightarrow{SD} \mathbf{6.9 \times 10^5\ N}$

(c) The weight of the boat equals the buoyancy force of the water, and the mass of the boat equals the mass of the water displaced.

$w_b = F_B = \mathbf{6.9 \times 10^5\ N}$

$m_b = m_w = \mathbf{7.0 \times 10^4\ kg}$

18. $F = \frac{Gm_1m_2}{r^2} = \frac{(6.67 \times 10^{-11})(34{,}516)(48{,}919)}{(21)^2}$

$= 2.554 \times 10^{-4}\text{ N} \xrightarrow{SD} \mathbf{2.6 \times 10^{-4}\ N}$

19. Begin by finding the components of the weight of the 9.4-kg block that are parallel and perpendicular to the plane.

$F_x = mg \sin 27° = (9.4)(9.81) \sin 27° = 41.86 \text{ N}$

$F_N = mg \cos 27° = (9.4)(9.81) \cos 27° = 82.16 \text{ N}$

Next, compute the weight of the 3.6-kg block.

$w = mg = (3.6)(9.81) = 35.316 \text{ N}$

Since $F_x > w$, we choose the positive x direction to be down the plane. Now, write a $\Sigma F_x = ma_x$ equation for the 9.4-kg block.

$$\Sigma F_x = ma_x$$
$$F_x - T - \mu_s F_N = ma$$
$$41.86 - T - (0.34)(82.16) = 9.4a$$
$$T = 13.93 - 9.4a \quad \text{(a)}$$

Now write a $\Sigma F_x = ma_x$ equation for the 3.6-kg block.

$$\Sigma F_x = ma_x$$
$$T - \mu_s mg = ma$$
$$T - (0.34)(35.316) = 3.6a$$
$$T = 12.01 + 3.6a \quad \text{(b)}$$

Substitute (b) into (a) to find the acceleration.

(a) $(12.01 + 3.6a) = 13.93 - 9.4a$

$$1.92 = 13a$$
$$a = 0.148 \frac{\text{m}}{\text{s}^2}$$

The acceleration is positive. **Yes, the block will slide down the plane.**

20. $W = F \times D = 200 \text{ kg}\left(9.81 \frac{\text{N}}{\text{kg}}\right) \times 3.6 \text{ m}$

$$= 7.06 \times 10^3 \text{ J} \xrightarrow{\text{SD}} \mathbf{7 \times 10^3 \text{ J}}$$

$$P_{av} = \frac{W}{\Delta t} = \frac{7.06 \times 10^3 \text{ J}}{25 \text{ s}} = 282 \text{ W} \xrightarrow{\text{SD}} \mathbf{300 \text{ W}}$$

Problem Set 63

1. (a) $f = \frac{1}{2\pi}\sqrt{\frac{k}{m}} = \frac{1}{2\pi}\sqrt{\frac{1600}{60}} = 0.822 \text{ Hz} \xrightarrow{\text{SD}} \mathbf{0.82 \text{ Hz}}$

(b) $T = \frac{1}{f} = \frac{1}{0.822 \text{ Hz}} = 1.22 \text{ s} \xrightarrow{\text{SD}} \mathbf{1.2 \text{ s}}$

2. (a) $f = \frac{45 \text{ cycles}}{10 \text{ s}} = \mathbf{4.5 \text{ Hz}}$

(b)
$$f = \frac{1}{2\pi}\sqrt{\frac{k}{m}}$$
$$4.5 = \frac{1}{2\pi}\sqrt{\frac{k}{12}}$$
$$799.4 = \frac{k}{12}$$
$$k = 9.59 \times 10^3 \frac{\text{N}}{\text{m}} \xrightarrow{\text{SD}} \mathbf{9.6 \times 10^3 \frac{N}{m}}$$

3. (a) Note that the initial angular momentum of the clutch is zero. Then find the initial angular momentum of the flywheel.

$$L_{fly} = I\omega = \left(\frac{1}{2}mr^2\right)\omega$$
$$= \left(\frac{1}{2}(12 \text{ kg})(0.10 \text{ m})^2\right)\left(68 \frac{\text{rad}}{\text{s}}\right)$$
$$= (0.06 \text{ kg·m}^2)\left(68 \frac{\text{rad}}{\text{s}}\right) = 4.08 \frac{\text{kg·m}^2}{\text{s}}$$

The sum of the moments of inertia after the clutch latches onto the flywheel is 3.2×10^{-3} kg·m^2 for the clutch and 0.06 kg·m^2 for the flywheel. So the final angular momentum is

$$L_f = I\omega$$
$$= [(3.2 \times 10^{-3} + 0.06) \text{ kg·m}^2]\omega$$
$$= (6.32 \times 10^{-2} \text{ kg·m}^2)\omega$$

Angular momentum of the system is conserved, so

$$L_{fly} = L_f$$
$$4.08 \frac{\text{kg·m}^2}{\text{s}} = (6.32 \times 10^{-2} \text{ kg·m}^2)\omega$$
$$\omega = 64.56 \frac{\text{rad}}{\text{s}} \xrightarrow{\text{SD}} \mathbf{65 \frac{rad}{s}}$$

(b) $KE = \frac{1}{2}I\omega^2$

$$= \frac{1}{2}(6.32 \times 10^{-2} \text{ kg·m}^2)\left(64.56 \frac{\text{rad}}{\text{s}}\right)^2$$
$$= 131.7 \text{ J} \xrightarrow{\text{SD}} \mathbf{130 \text{ J}}$$

4. The kinetic energy at the bottom of the plane must equal the potential energy at the top.

$$PE = \frac{1}{2}mv^2 + \frac{1}{2}I\omega^2$$

$$mgh = \frac{1}{2}mv^2 + \frac{1}{2}\left(\frac{2}{5}mr^2\right)\left(\frac{v}{r}\right)^2$$

$$mgh = \frac{1}{2}mv^2 + \frac{1}{5}mv^2$$

$$(5.3)(9.81)(4.7) = \frac{1}{2}(5.3)v^2 + \frac{1}{5}(5.3)v^2$$

$$244.4 = 3.71v^2$$

$$v = 8.12\ \frac{\text{m}}{\text{s}} \xrightarrow{\text{SD}} \mathbf{8.1\ \frac{m}{s}}$$

5.

$$v_1A_1 = v_2A_2$$

$$5 \times 10^{-3}\ \frac{\text{m}}{\text{s}}(40\ \text{m}^2) = v_2(0.10\ \text{m}^2)$$

$$v_2 = \mathbf{2\ \frac{m}{s}}$$

6. (a) Begin by finding Q and v_2.

$$Q = v_1A_1 = (2.73)(1.08 \times 10^{-3}) = 2.95 \times 10^{-3}\ \frac{\text{m}^3}{\text{s}}$$

$$v_2 = \frac{Q}{A_2} = \frac{2.95 \times 10^{-3}}{6.29 \times 10^{-4}} = 4.69\ \frac{\text{m}}{\text{s}}$$

Now use Bernoulli's equation to find P_2.

$$P_1 + \frac{1}{2}\rho v_1^2 = P_2 + \frac{1}{2}\rho v_2^2$$

$$202{,}600 + \frac{1}{2}(1000)(2.73)^2 = P_2 + \frac{1}{2}(1000)(4.69)^2$$

$$202{,}600 + 3726.5 = P_2 + 10{,}998$$

$$P_2 = 1.9533 \times 10^5\ \text{Pa} \xrightarrow{\text{SD}} \mathbf{1.95 \times 10^5\ Pa}$$

(b)

$$\rho g l_1 + P_{atm} = P_1$$

$$(1000)(9.81)l_1 + 101{,}300 = 202{,}600$$

$$l_1 = 10.33\ \text{m} \xrightarrow{\text{SD}} \mathbf{10.3\ m}$$

$$\rho g l_2 + P_{atm} = P_2$$

$$(1000)(9.81)l_2 + 101{,}300 = 1.9533 \times 10^5$$

$$l_2 = 9.585\ \text{m} \xrightarrow{\text{SD}} \mathbf{9.59\ m}$$

7.

$$\Delta L = \alpha L_0 \Delta T$$

$$(4.9612 - 4.9664) = \alpha(4.9664)(35 - 112)$$

$$0.0052 = \alpha(382.41)$$

$$\alpha = 1.36 \times 10^{-5}\ (\text{C}°)^{-1} \xrightarrow{\text{SD}} \mathbf{1.4 \times 10^{-5}\ (C°)^{-1}}$$

8. Begin by finding the equivalent resistance of the two parallel resistors.

$$R_E = \frac{(40{,}000)(120{,}000)}{40{,}000 + 120{,}000} = \mathbf{3 \times 10^4\ \Omega}$$

Next, find the time constant RC.

$$RC = (3 \times 10^4\ \Omega)(400 \times 10^{-6}\ \text{F}) = 12\ \text{s}$$

Sketch the voltage across the capacitor as a function of time.

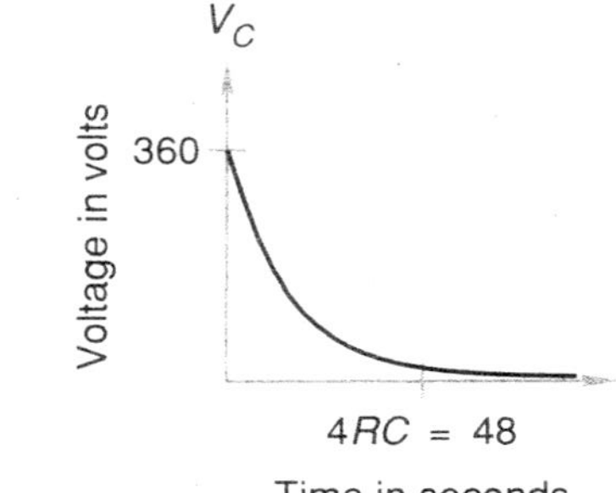

9.

$$\tau = I\alpha = \left(\frac{2}{5}mr^2\right)\alpha$$

$$= \left(\frac{2}{5}(22\ \text{kg})(1.1\ \text{m})^2\right)\left(1.6\ \frac{\text{rad}}{\text{s}^2}\right)$$

$$= 17.04\ \text{N·m} \xrightarrow{\text{SD}} \mathbf{17\ N·m}$$

10.

$$v_1A_1 = v_2A_2$$

$$3.9\ \frac{\text{m}}{\text{s}}(1.2\ \text{m}^2) = v_2(4.7\ \text{m}^2)$$

$$v_2 = 0.996\ \frac{\text{m}}{\text{s}} \xrightarrow{\text{SD}} \mathbf{1.0\ \frac{m}{s}}$$

11. Begin by finding the centripetal force and the static friction force.

$$F_c = \frac{mv^2}{r} = \frac{1100(70)^2}{1055} = 5109\text{ N}$$
$$F_s = mg\mu_s = (1100)(9.81)\mu_s = (10{,}791\text{ N})\mu_s$$

The required centripetal force must equal the static friction force.

$$F_c = F_s$$
$$5109\text{ N} = (10{,}791\text{ N})\mu_s$$
$$\mu_s = 0.4735 \xrightarrow{\text{SD}} \mathbf{0.5}$$

12. Begin by finding the equivalent resistance of the two parallel resistors.

$$R_E = \frac{(120)(60)}{120 + 60} = 40\ \Omega$$

Next, start at the ground symbol, move clockwise, and sum the voltage changes to zero.

$$-48 + I(110) + I(200) + I(40) + I(130) = 0$$
$$I(480) = 48$$
$$I = \mathbf{0.1\ A}$$

13. The image is **approximately 7.2 cm in front of the mirror, it is inverted, and the height of the image is approximately 2.4 cm.**

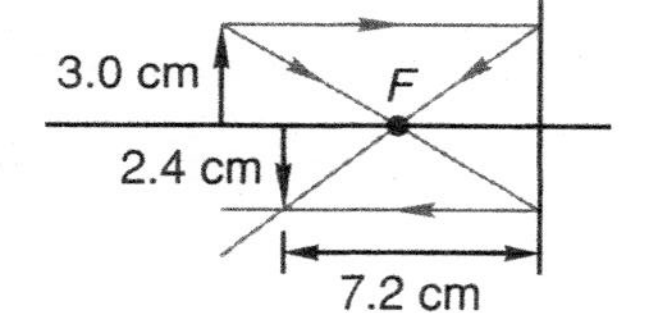

14. To find V_{DA}, begin at A and move clockwise to D.

$$V_{DA} = +40\text{ V} + 11\text{ V} + 12\text{ V} + 2.0\text{ V} = \mathbf{+65\ V}$$

15. (a) Begin by finding the tension, mg, and the mass per unit length of the string.

$$T = mg = 12\text{ kg} \times 9.81\ \frac{\text{N}}{\text{kg}} = 117.72\text{ N}$$
$$M_L = \frac{0.300\text{ kg}}{2.9\text{ m}} = 0.1034\ \frac{\text{kg}}{\text{m}}$$

Insert these values into the formula below to find v.

$$v = \sqrt{\frac{T}{M_L}} = \sqrt{\frac{117.72\text{ N}}{0.1034\ \frac{\text{kg}}{\text{m}}}} = 33.7\ \frac{\text{m}}{\text{s}} \xrightarrow{\text{SD}} \mathbf{34\ \frac{m}{s}}$$

(b)
$$v = f\lambda$$
$$33.7\text{ m/s} = f(0.90\text{ m})$$
$$f = 37.4\text{ Hz} \xrightarrow{\text{SD}} \mathbf{37\ Hz}$$

16. Begin by finding the equivalent resistance of the two series resistors.

$$R_E = 80\ \Omega + 40\ \Omega = 120\ \Omega$$

Use this resistance to find I.

$$I = \frac{V}{R_E} = \frac{12\text{ V}}{120\ \Omega} = 0.1\text{ A}$$

Now find the power dissipated by the 40-Ω resistor.

$$P = I^2R = (0.1\text{ A})^2(40\ \Omega) = \mathbf{0.4\ W}$$

17. (a) $\omega(t) = \omega_0 + \alpha t$

$$\omega(5.0) = 0.50 + 1.04(5.0) = \mathbf{5.7\ \frac{rad}{s}}$$

(b) $\Delta\theta = \omega_0 t + \frac{1}{2}\alpha t^2$

$$= 0.50(5.0) + \frac{1}{2}(1.04)(5.0)^2 = 15.5\text{ rad} \xrightarrow{\text{SD}} \mathbf{16\ rad}$$

18.
$$\frac{\sin\theta_1}{v_1} = \frac{\sin\theta_2}{v_2}$$
$$\frac{\sin 30°}{0.91c} = \frac{\sin\theta_r}{c}$$
$$\theta_r = \mathbf{33.33°}$$

19. (a) Begin by finding the final potential energy of the ball.

$$PE = mgh = (12)(9.81)(32) = 3767.04\text{ J}$$

This must equal the kinetic energy just after the ball left the ground.

$$KE = \frac{1}{2}mv^2$$
$$3767.04\text{ J} = \frac{1}{2}(12\text{ kg})v^2$$
$$v = +25.06\ \frac{\text{m}}{\text{s}} \xrightarrow{\text{SD}} \mathbf{+25\ \frac{m}{s}}$$

(b)
$$\Delta KE = KE_i - KE_f$$
$$= mgh_i - mgh_f$$
$$= (12)(9.81)(40) - 3767.04$$
$$= 941.76\text{ J} \xrightarrow{\text{SD}} \mathbf{940\ J}$$

20. Answers to this problem may vary due to differing data points. One possible solution is given here. To find a_3, choose the data points (3, 45) and (8.1, 0).

$$a_3 = \frac{0 - 45}{8.1 - 3}\frac{\text{m/s}}{\text{s}} = -8.824\ \frac{\text{m}}{\text{s}^2} \xrightarrow{\text{SD}} \mathbf{-8.8\ \frac{m}{s^2}}$$

To find a_8, choose the data points (5.0, 0) and (8.0, 39).

$$a_8 = \frac{39 - 0}{8.0 - 5.0}\frac{\text{m/s}}{\text{s}} = \mathbf{+13\ \frac{m}{s^2}}$$

PROBLEM SET 64

1. (a) Begin by finding the mass of the truck.

$$m = \frac{w}{g} = \frac{15{,}000\ \text{N}}{9.81\ \text{N/kg}} = 1529\ \text{kg}$$

Now find the centripetal force.

$$F_c = \frac{mv^2}{r} = \frac{1529(60)^2}{250} = 2.202 \times 10^4\ \text{N} \xrightarrow{\text{SD}} \mathbf{2.2 \times 10^4\ N}$$

(b) The weight of the truck is given by vector F_y. Use the Pythagorean theorem to find F_N.

$$F_N = \sqrt{(15{,}000)^2 + (2.202 \times 10^4)^2}$$
$$= 2.66 \times 10^4\ \text{N} \xrightarrow{\text{SD}} \mathbf{2.7 \times 10^4\ N}$$

(c) $\theta = \arctan \dfrac{F_c}{w} = \arctan \dfrac{2.202 \times 10^4}{15{,}000} = \mathbf{55.74°}$

2. (a)

$$r = 1.00 \sin\theta$$
$$\sin\theta = \frac{0.20\ \text{m}}{1.00\ \text{m}}$$
$$\theta = \mathbf{11.54°}$$

(b)

$$T\cos\theta = mg$$
$$T\cos 11.54° = 2.05(9.81)$$
$$T = 20.53\ \text{N} \xrightarrow{\text{SD}} \mathbf{21\ N}$$

(c) $F_c = T\sin\theta = (20.53)\sin 11.54° = 4.11\ \text{N} \xrightarrow{\text{SD}} \mathbf{4.1\ N}$

$$F_c = mr\omega^2$$
$$4.11 = (2.05)(0.20)\omega^2$$
$$\omega = 3.17\ \frac{\text{rad}}{\text{s}} \xrightarrow{\text{SD}} \mathbf{3.2\ \frac{rad}{s}}$$

3. (a) $f = \dfrac{1}{2\pi}\sqrt{\dfrac{k}{m}} = \dfrac{1}{2\pi}\sqrt{\dfrac{485}{22}} = 0.747\ \text{Hz} \xrightarrow{\text{SD}} \mathbf{0.75\ Hz}$

(b) $T = \dfrac{1}{f} = \dfrac{1}{0.747\ \text{Hz}} = 1.34\ \text{s} \xrightarrow{\text{SD}} \mathbf{1.3\ s}$

4. Begin by finding the angular speed and the moment of inertia of the cylinder.

$$\omega = \frac{v}{r} = \frac{12\ \text{m/s}}{0.75\ \text{m}} = 16\ \frac{\text{rad}}{\text{s}}$$
$$I = \frac{1}{2}mr^2 = \frac{1}{2}(3.5\ \text{kg})(0.75\ \text{m})^2 = 0.984\ \text{kg·m}^2$$

Now find the total kinetic energy.

$$KE = \frac{1}{2}mv^2 + \frac{1}{2}I\omega^2$$
$$= \frac{1}{2}(3.5)(12)^2 + \frac{1}{2}(0.984)(16)^2$$
$$= 378\ \text{J} \xrightarrow{\text{SD}} \mathbf{380\ J}$$

5. The kinetic energy at the bottom of the plane must equal the potential energy at the top.

$$PE = \frac{1}{2}mv^2 + \frac{1}{2}I\omega^2$$
$$mgh = \frac{1}{2}mv^2 + \frac{1}{2}\left(\frac{1}{2}mr^2\right)\left(\frac{v}{r}\right)^2$$
$$mgh = \frac{1}{2}mv^2 + \frac{1}{4}mv^2$$
$$(5.0)(9.81)(11) = \frac{1}{2}(5.0)v^2 + \frac{1}{4}(5.0)v^2$$
$$539.55 = 3.75v^2$$
$$v = 11.995\ \frac{\text{m}}{\text{s}} \xrightarrow{\text{SD}} \mathbf{12\ \frac{m}{s}}$$

6. Begin by finding v_1 and v_2.

$$v_1 = \frac{Q}{A_1} = \frac{2.4}{2.0} = 1.2\ \frac{\text{m}}{\text{s}}$$

$$v_2 = \frac{Q}{A_2} = \frac{2.4}{5.2} = 0.462\ \frac{\text{m}}{\text{s}}$$

Now use Bernoulli's equation to find P_2. Note that h_1 is zero, so the $\rho g h_1$ term falls out of the equation.

$$P_1 + \frac{1}{2}\rho v_1^2 = P_2 + \frac{1}{2}\rho v_2^2 + \rho g h_2$$

$$93{,}119 + \frac{1}{2}(1000)(1.2)^2 = P_2 + \frac{1}{2}(1000)(0.462)^2 + (1000)(9.81)(9.2)$$

$$93{,}119 + 720 = P_2 + 106.7 + 90{,}252$$

$$P_2 = 3.48 \times 10^3\ \text{Pa} \xrightarrow{\text{SD}} \mathbf{3.5 \times 10^3\ Pa}$$

7. (a) Begin by finding v_1 and v_2.

$$v_1 = \frac{Q_1}{A_1} = \frac{0.143}{0.0816} = 1.752\ \frac{\text{m}}{\text{s}}$$

$$v_2 = \frac{Q_2}{A_2} = \frac{0.143}{0.0136} = 10.51\ \frac{\text{m}}{\text{s}}$$

Now use Bernoulli's equation to find P_1.

$$P_1 + \frac{1}{2}\rho v_1^2 = P_2 + \frac{1}{2}\rho v_2^2$$

$$P_1 + \frac{1}{2}(1000)(1.752)^2 = 191{,}423 + \frac{1}{2}(1000)(10.51)^2$$

$$P_1 + 1534.75 = 191{,}423 + 55{,}230$$

$$P_1 = 2.451 \times 10^5\ \text{Pa} \xrightarrow{\text{SD}} \mathbf{2.45 \times 10^5\ Pa}$$

(b)

$$\rho g l_1 + P_{\text{atm}} = P_1$$

$$(1000)(9.81)l_1 + 101{,}300 = 2.451 \times 10^5$$

$$l_1 = 14.66\ \text{m} \xrightarrow{\text{SD}} \mathbf{14.7\ m}$$

$$\rho g l_2 + P_{\text{atm}} = P_2$$

$$(1000)(9.81)l_2 + 101{,}300 = 191{,}423$$

$$l_2 = 9.187\ \text{m} \xrightarrow{\text{SD}} \mathbf{9.19\ m}$$

8.

$$\Delta L = \alpha L_0 \Delta T$$

$$(527.5 - 527.3) = \left(1.7 \times 10^{-5}\right)(527.3)(T_2 - 11)$$

$$0.2 = \left(8.964 \times 10^{-3}\right)T_2 - 9.861 \times 10^{-2}$$

$$0.29861 = \left(8.964 \times 10^{-3}\right)T_2$$

$$T_2 = 33.31°\text{C} \xrightarrow{\text{SD}} \mathbf{33°C}$$

9. (a) Begin by finding the equivalent resistance of the two parallel resistors.

$$R_E = \frac{(400)(100)}{400 + 100} = 80\ \Omega$$

Next, calculate the time constant RC.

$$RC = (80\ \Omega)\left(126 \times 10^{-6}\ \text{F}\right)$$

$$= 1.008 \times 10^{-2}\ \text{s} \xrightarrow{\text{SD}} \mathbf{1.01 \times 10^{-2}\ s}$$

(b) Now find the initial voltage across the capacitor, V_0.

$$V_0 = \frac{Q}{C} = \frac{1.26 \times 10^{-2}\ \text{C}}{126 \times 10^{-6}\ \text{F}} = 100\ \text{V}$$

Use this voltage to find the initial current.

$$I = \frac{V_0}{R_E} = \frac{100\ \text{V}}{80\ \Omega} = 1.25\ \text{A}$$

Sketch the current as a function of time.

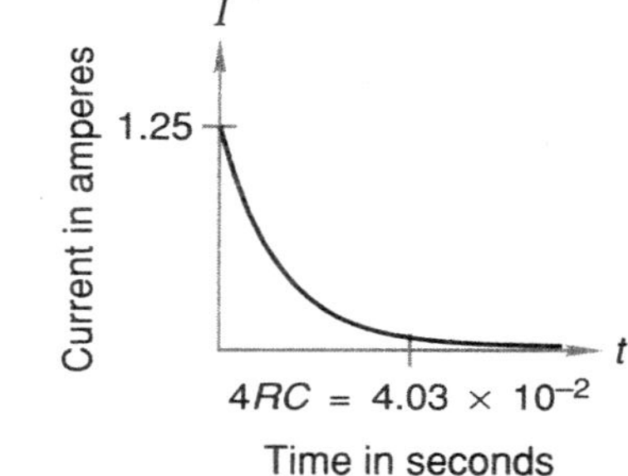

10.

$$\tau = I\alpha = \left(\frac{1}{2}mr^2\right)\alpha$$

$$= \left(\frac{1}{2}(55\ \text{kg})(3.0\ \text{m})^2\right)\left(0.40\ \frac{\text{rad}}{\text{s}^2}\right) = \mathbf{99\ N{\cdot}m}$$

11. $v_1A_1 = v_2A_2$

$12\ \frac{\text{m}}{\text{s}}(0.36\text{ m}^2) = v_2(8.9\text{ m}^2)$

$v_2 = 0.485\ \frac{\text{m}}{\text{s}} \xrightarrow{\text{SD}} \mathbf{0.49\ \frac{m}{s}}$

12. The image is **appproximately 1.2 cm behind the mirror, it is upright, and the height of the image is approximately 0.60 cm**.

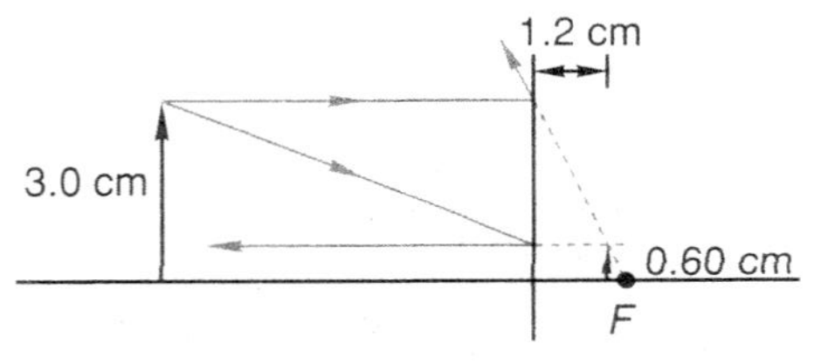

13. In the left-hand loop, move clockwise, and sum the voltage changes to zero.

$-40\text{ V} + (1.00\text{ A})(12\ \Omega) + I_2(108\ \Omega) + (1.00\text{ A})(10\ \Omega) = 0$

$I_2(108\ \Omega) = 18\text{ V}$

$I_2 = 0.167\text{ A}$

$P_{108} = I_2^2R = (0.167\text{ A})^2(108\ \Omega) = 3.012\text{ W} \xrightarrow{\text{SD}} \mathbf{3.0\ W}$

14. To find V_{CA}, begin at A and move counterclockwise to C.

$V_{CA} = -7.0\text{ V} + (0.10\text{ A})(18\ \Omega) = \mathbf{-5.2\ V}$

15. (a) $a_c = \frac{v^2}{r} = \frac{(25.3)^2}{53.6} = 11.94\ \frac{\text{m}}{\text{s}^2} \xrightarrow{\text{SD}} \mathbf{11.9\ \frac{m}{s^2}}$

(b) $\Sigma F_y = ma_y$

$F_N - mg = ma_c$

$F_N - (72.5)(9.81) = 72.5(11.94)$

$F_N = 1.577 \times 10^3\text{ N} \xrightarrow{\text{SD}} \mathbf{1.58 \times 10^3\ N}$

16. Note that the horizontal velocity component is 110 m/s.

$v_{x0} = 110\ \frac{\text{m}}{\text{s}}$

Use this in the x-displacement equation to find the time.

$\Delta x = v_{x0}t + \frac{1}{2}a_xt^2$

$200 = (110)t + 0$

$t = 1.8182\text{ s}$

Use this time in the y-displacement equation to find v_{y0}.

$\Delta y = v_{y0}t + \frac{1}{2}a_yt^2$

$0 = v_{y0}(1.8182) + \frac{1}{2}(-9.81)(1.8182)^2$

$v_{y0}(1.8182) = 16.215$

$v_{y0} = 8.9182\ \frac{\text{m}}{\text{s}}$

Now use trigonometry to solve for θ.

$\tan\theta = \frac{v_{y0}}{v_{x0}}$

$\tan\theta = \frac{8.9182}{110}$

$\theta = \mathbf{4.64°}$

17. Begin by writing a $\Sigma F_x = ma_x$ equation for the 20.0-kg block. Choose to the right as the positive direction for motion.

$\Sigma F_x = ma_x$

$T - \mu_k mg = ma$

$T - (0.200)(20.0)(9.81) = 20.0a$

$T = 39.24 + 20.0a$ (a)

Next, write a $\Sigma F_y = ma_y$ equation for the 30.0-kg mass.

$\Sigma F_y = ma_y$

$mg - T = ma$

$(30.0)(9.81) - T = 30.0a$

$T = 294.30 - 30.0a$ (b)

Substitute (b) into (a) to find the acceleration.

(a) $(294.30 - 30.0a) = 39.24 + 20.0a$

$255.06 = 50.0a$

$a = 5.1012\ \frac{\text{m}}{\text{s}^2}$

Substitute the acceleration into (a) to find T.

(a) $T = 39.24 + 20.0(5.1012) = 141.264\text{ N} \xrightarrow{\text{SD}} \mathbf{141\ N}$

18.

$$\begin{aligned} P_1V_1 &= P_2V_2 \\ (3.4 \times 10^5 \text{ Pa})(100 \text{ cm}^3) &= P_2(5.0 \text{ cm}^3) \\ P_2 &= \mathbf{6.8 \times 10^6 \text{ Pa}} \end{aligned}$$

19.

$$\begin{aligned} \Sigma M_J &= 0 \\ m_b g(0.36 \text{ m}) + m_f g(0.16 \text{ m}) - F_M(0.037 \text{ m}) &= 0 \\ (6.2)(9.81)(0.36) + (2.1)(9.81)(0.16) &= F_M(0.037) \\ 25.19 &= F_M(0.037) \\ F_M &= 680.8 \text{ N} \xrightarrow{\text{SD}} \mathbf{680 \text{ N}} \end{aligned}$$

20.

$$\begin{aligned} \Sigma F_y &= ma_y \\ F_N - w &= ma_y \\ F_N - (60)(9.81) &= 60(-4.0) \\ F_N &= 348.6 \text{ N} \xrightarrow{\text{SD}} \mathbf{350 \text{ N}} \end{aligned}$$

PROBLEM SET 65

1. Begin by writing a $\Sigma F = ma$ equation for the weight.

$$\begin{aligned} \Sigma F &= ma \\ mg - T &= ma \\ 4.0(9.81) - T &= 4.0a \\ T &= 39.24 - 4.0a \qquad \text{(a)} \end{aligned}$$

Next, write a $\Sigma\tau = I\alpha$ equation for the cylinder.

$$\begin{aligned} \tau &= I\alpha \\ (0.25)T &= \left(\frac{1}{2}mr^2\right)\alpha \\ (0.25)T &= \left(\frac{1}{2}(12)(0.25)^2\right)\alpha \\ T &= 1.5\alpha \qquad \text{(b)} \end{aligned}$$

Now note that α is equal to $\frac{a}{0.25}$. Substitute into (b) and get:

$$\text{(b)}\ T = 1.5\left(\frac{a}{0.25}\right) = 6.0a$$

Substitute this value for T into (a) to find the acceleration.

$$\begin{aligned} \text{(a)}\ (6.0a) &= 39.24 - 4.0a \\ 10a &= 39.24 \\ a &= 3.924 \frac{\text{m}}{\text{s}^2} \xrightarrow{\text{SD}} \mathbf{3.9 \frac{m}{s^2}} \end{aligned}$$

2. Begin by noting the moment of inertia of the pulley and the relationship between a and α.

$I = 0.010 \text{ kg·m}^2$

$a = r\alpha = 0.10\alpha \longrightarrow \alpha = \frac{a}{0.10}$

Next, write a $\Sigma F_x = ma_x$ equation for the 16-kg block. Choose to the right as the positive direction for motion.

$$\begin{aligned} \Sigma F_x &= ma_x \\ T_1 - \mu_k mg &= ma \\ T_1 - 0.26(16)(9.81) &= 16a \\ T_1 &= 40.81 + 16a \qquad \text{(a)} \end{aligned}$$

Now, write a $\Sigma F_y = ma_y$ equation for the 8.2-kg block.

$$\begin{aligned} \Sigma F_y &= ma_y \\ mg - T_2 &= ma \\ 8.2(9.81) - T_2 &= 8.2a \\ T_2 &= 80.44 - 8.2a \qquad \text{(b)} \end{aligned}$$

Next, write a $\Sigma\tau = I\alpha$ equation for the pulley.

$$\begin{aligned} \Sigma\tau &= I\alpha \\ 0.10T_2 - 0.10T_1 &= (0.010)\left(\frac{a}{0.10}\right) \\ 0.10T_2 - 0.10T_1 &= 0.10a \\ T_2 - T_1 &= a \qquad \text{(c)} \end{aligned}$$

Substitute (a) and (b) into (c) to find the acceleration.

$$\begin{aligned} \text{(c)}\ (80.44 - 8.2a) - (40.81 + 16a) &= a \\ 39.63 &= 25.2a \\ a &= 1.57 \frac{\text{m}}{\text{s}^2} \\ &\xrightarrow{\text{SD}} \mathbf{1.6 \frac{m}{s^2} \textbf{ to the right}} \end{aligned}$$

3. Begin by converting the angular speed to radians per second.

$$\omega = 1.12 \frac{\cancel{\text{rev}}}{\text{s}} \times \frac{2\pi\,\text{rad}}{1\,\cancel{\text{rev}}} = 7.037\ \frac{\text{rad}}{\text{s}}$$

$$T\sin\theta = mr\omega^2$$
$$T\cancel{\sin\theta} = (4.33)(0.229\ \cancel{\sin\theta})(7.037)^2$$
$$T = 49.102\ \text{N} \xrightarrow{\text{SD}} \mathbf{49.1\ N}$$

$$T\cos\theta = mg$$
$$49.102\cos\theta = 4.33(9.81)$$
$$\theta = \mathbf{30.11°}$$

4. (a) $\tan\theta = \dfrac{v^2}{rg}$

$$v^2 = (387\ \text{m})\left(9.81\ \frac{\text{m}}{\text{s}^2}\right)\tan 15°$$
$$v = 31.89\ \frac{\text{m}}{\text{s}} \xrightarrow{\text{SD}} \mathbf{31.9\ \frac{m}{s}}$$

(b) $a_c = \dfrac{v^2}{r}$

$$= \frac{(31.89)^2}{387}$$
$$= 2.628\ \frac{\text{m}}{\text{s}^2} \xrightarrow{\text{SD}} \mathbf{2.63\ \frac{m}{s^2}}$$

5. (a) $f = \dfrac{36\ \text{cycles}}{12\ \text{seconds}} = \mathbf{3.0\ Hz}$

(b)
$$f = \frac{1}{2\pi}\sqrt{\frac{k}{m}}$$
$$3.0 = \frac{1}{2\pi}\sqrt{\frac{k}{45}}$$
$$355.31 = \frac{k}{45}$$
$$k = 1.599 \times 10^4\ \frac{\text{N}}{\text{m}} \xrightarrow{\text{SD}} \mathbf{1.6 \times 10^4\ \frac{N}{m}}$$

6. Begin by finding the angular speed and the moment of inertia of the hoop.

$$\omega = \frac{v}{r} = \frac{12\ \text{m/s}}{1.5\ \text{m}} = 8.0\ \frac{\text{rad}}{\text{s}}$$
$$I = mr^2 = (4.2\ \text{kg})(1.5\ \text{m})^2 = 9.45\ \text{kg·m}^2$$

Now find the total kinetic energy.

$$KE = \frac{1}{2}mv^2 + \frac{1}{2}I\omega^2$$
$$= \frac{1}{2}(4.2)(12)^2 + \frac{1}{2}(9.45)(8.0)^2$$
$$= 604.8\ \text{J} \xrightarrow{\text{SD}} \mathbf{6\bar{0}0\ J}$$

7. (a) Note that the initial angular momentum of the clutch is zero. Then find the initial angular momentum of the flywheel.

$$L_{\text{fly}} = I\omega = \left(\frac{1}{2}mr^2\right)\omega$$
$$= \left(\frac{1}{2}(18\ \text{kg})(0.25\ \text{m})^2\right)\left(102\ \frac{\text{rad}}{\text{s}}\right)$$
$$= (0.5625\ \text{kg·m}^2)\left(102\ \frac{\text{rad}}{\text{s}}\right) = 57.375\ \frac{\text{kg·m}^2}{\text{s}}$$

The sum of the moments of inertia after the clutch latches onto the flywheel is 5.0×10^{-3} kg·m^2 for the clutch and 0.5625 kg·m^2 for the flywheel. So the final angular momentum is

$$L_f = I\omega$$
$$= [(5.0 \times 10^{-3} + 0.5625)\ \text{kg·m}^2]\omega$$
$$= (0.5675\ \text{kg·m}^2)\omega$$

Angular momentum of the system is conserved, so

$$L_{\text{fly}} = L_f$$
$$57.375\ \frac{\text{kg·m}^2}{\text{s}} = (0.5675\ \text{kg·m}^2)\omega$$
$$\omega = 101.10\ \frac{\text{rad}}{\text{s}} \xrightarrow{\text{SD}} \mathbf{1\bar{0}0\ \frac{rad}{s}}$$

(b) $KE = \dfrac{1}{2}I\omega^2$

$$= \frac{1}{2}(0.5675\ \text{kg·m}^2)\left(101.10\ \frac{\text{rad}}{\text{s}}\right)^2$$
$$= 2.9003 \times 10^3\ \text{J} \xrightarrow{\text{SD}} \mathbf{2.9 \times 10^3\ J}$$

8. Use Bernoulli's equation to find the speed of the water leaving the pipe. Note that the initial and final pressures are equal and that v_1 and h_2 are zero so all but the following terms fall out of the equation.

$$\rho g h_1 = \frac{1}{2}\rho v_2^2$$

$$(1000)(9.81)(20) = \frac{1}{2}(1000)v_2^2$$

$$v_2 = 19.81\ \frac{\text{m}}{\text{s}} \xrightarrow{\text{SD}} \mathbf{20\ \frac{m}{s}}$$

9. Begin by finding v_1 and v_2.

$$v_1 = \frac{Q}{A_1} = \frac{3.6}{1.25} = 2.88\ \frac{\text{m}}{\text{s}}$$

$$v_2 = \frac{Q}{A_2} = \frac{3.6}{0.575} = 6.26\ \frac{\text{m}}{\text{s}}$$

Now use Bernoulli's equation to find P_2. Note that h_2 is zero, so the $\rho g h_2$ term falls out of the equation.

$$P_1 + \frac{1}{2}\rho v_1^2 + \rho g h_1 = P_2 + \frac{1}{2}\rho v_2^2$$

$$98{,}400 + \frac{1}{2}(1000)(2.88)^2 + 1000(9.81)(12) = P_2 + \frac{1}{2}(1000)(6.26)^2$$

$$98{,}400 + 4147.2 + 117{,}720 = P_2 + 19{,}593.8$$

$$P_2 = 2.01 \times 10^5\ \text{Pa}$$

$$\xrightarrow{\text{SD}} \mathbf{2.0 \times 10^5\ Pa}$$

10. Begin by finding the initial volume of the block.

$$V_0 = V_{\text{block}} - V_{\text{hole}}$$
$$= lwh - \pi r^2 h$$
$$= (12\ \text{m})(6.2\ \text{m})(4.4\ \text{m}) - \pi(2.0\ \text{m})^2(4.4\ \text{m})$$
$$= 327.36\ \text{m}^3 - 55.29\ \text{m}^3 = 272.07\ \text{m}^3$$

Now calculate the change in volume.

$$\Delta V = 3\alpha V_0 \Delta T$$
$$= (3)\frac{1.65 \times 10^{-5}}{\text{C}^\circ}(272.07\ \text{m}^3)(85\ \text{C}^\circ)$$
$$= 1.14\ \text{m}^3 \xrightarrow{\text{SD}} \mathbf{1.1\ m^3}$$

11. (a) $RC = (5000\ \Omega)(14 \times 10^{-6}\ \text{F}) = \mathbf{7.0 \times 10^{-2}\ s}$

(b) $V_C = 400e^{-t/RC}$

$$= 400e^{-0.14/7.0 \times 10^{-2}}$$
$$= 400e^{-2}$$
$$= 54.134\ \text{V} \xrightarrow{\text{SD}} \mathbf{54\ V}$$

12. $$\tau = I\alpha = \left(\frac{1}{2}mr^2\right)\alpha$$

$$= \left(\frac{1}{2}(30.0\ \text{kg})(1.50\ \text{m})^2\right)\left(2.65\ \frac{\text{rad}}{\text{s}^2}\right)$$

$$= 89.44\ \text{N·m} \xrightarrow{\text{SD}} \mathbf{89.4\ N{\cdot}m}$$

13. Begin by finding the centripetal force and the static friction force.

$$F_c = \frac{mv^2}{r} = \frac{650(35)^2}{560} = 1421.88\ \text{N}$$

$$F_s = mg\mu_s = (650)(9.81)\mu_s = (6376.5\ \text{N})\mu_s$$

The required centripetal force must equal the static friction force.

$$F_c = F_s$$
$$1421.88\ \text{N} = (6376.5\ \text{N})\mu_s$$
$$\mu_s = 0.223 \xrightarrow{\text{SD}} \mathbf{0.22}$$

14. Begin by finding the voltage drop across the 30-Ω resistor.

$$V_1 = I_1 R_1 = (2\ \text{A})(30\ \Omega) = 60\ \text{V}$$

This must equal the voltage drop across the 60-Ω resistor. Use this voltage to find I.

$$I = \frac{60\ \text{V}}{60\ \Omega} = 1\ \text{A}$$

Now find the power consumed by the 60-Ω resistor.

$$P = VI = (60\ \text{V})(1\ \text{A}) = \mathbf{60\ W}$$

15. Note that the kinetic energy of the block once it impacts the spring equals the potential energy of the block at the top of the plane.

$$PE = \frac{1}{2}kx^2$$
$$mgh = \frac{1}{2}kx^2$$
$$15(9.81)(8.0) = \frac{1}{2}(7500)x^2$$
$$x = 0.5603 \text{ m} \xrightarrow{SD} \mathbf{0.56\ m}$$

16. Begin at the ground symbol, move clockwise, and sum the voltage changes to zero.

$$-13 \text{ V} + I(1200\ \Omega) + I(770\ \Omega) = 0$$
$$I(1970\ \Omega) = 13 \text{ V}$$
$$I = 6.60 \times 10^{-3} \text{ A}$$

$$V_1 = IR_1 = (6.60 \times 10^{-3} \text{ A})(1200\ \Omega) = 7.92 \text{ V} \xrightarrow{SD} \mathbf{7.9\ V}$$
$$V_2 = IR_2 = (6.60 \times 10^{-3} \text{ A})(770\ \Omega) = 5.08 \text{ V} \xrightarrow{SD} \mathbf{5.1\ V}$$

17. $F = kx = 9500 \frac{\text{N}}{\cancel{\text{m}}} \times 0.80 \cancel{\text{m}} = \mathbf{7600\ N}$

18. $\frac{P_1V_1}{T_1} = \frac{P_2V_2}{T_2} \rightarrow \frac{P_1V_1}{T_1} = \frac{P_2(3V_1)}{(2T_1)}$

$$\frac{P_1\cancel{V_1}}{\cancel{T_1}} \times \frac{\cancel{T_1}}{\cancel{V_1}} = \frac{P_2(3\cancel{V_1})}{(2\cancel{T_1})} \times \frac{\cancel{T_1}}{\cancel{V_1}}$$
$$\mathbf{\frac{2P_1}{3}} = P_2$$

19. Begin by finding the pressure produced by the fluid.

$$P_F = 1550 \frac{\cancel{\text{kg}}}{\text{m}^{\cancel{3}2}} \times 9.81 \frac{\text{N}}{\cancel{\text{kg}}} \times 1.5 \cancel{\text{m}} = 2.28 \times 10^4 \text{ Pa}$$

Now sum this pressure with the atmospheric pressure and find P.

$$P = 2.28 \times 10^4 \text{ Pa} + 1.005 \times 10^5 \text{ Pa}$$
$$= 1.233 \times 10^5 \text{ Pa} \xrightarrow{SD} \mathbf{1.2 \times 10^5\ Pa}$$

20. (a) $P_M = 10{,}486 \text{ W} \times 0.5517 = 5785.1 \text{ W} \xrightarrow{SD} \mathbf{5785\ W}$

(b) $P_T = 5785.1 \text{ W} \times 0.8 = 4628.1 \text{ W} \xrightarrow{SD} \mathbf{5000\ W}$

(c) $\text{Percent eff.} = \frac{P_{out}}{P_{in}} \times 100\%$

$$= \frac{4628.1 \text{ W}}{10{,}486 \text{ W}} \times 100\%$$
$$= 44.14\% \xrightarrow{SD} \mathbf{40\%}$$

PROBLEM SET 66

1. (a) $U_1 = \frac{3}{2}nRT_1$

$$= \frac{3}{2}(8.27 \text{ mol})\left(8.31 \frac{\text{J}}{\text{K}\cdot\text{mol}}\right)(210 \text{ K})$$
$$= 2.1648 \times 10^4 \text{ J} \xrightarrow{SD} \mathbf{2.16 \times 10^4\ J}$$

(b) $U_2 = \frac{3}{2}nRT_2$

$$= \frac{3}{2}(8.27 \text{ mol})\left(8.31 \frac{\text{J}}{\text{K}\cdot\text{mol}}\right)(340 \text{ K})$$
$$= 3.5049 \times 10^4 \text{ J} \xrightarrow{SD} \mathbf{3.50 \times 10^4\ J}$$

(c) $Q = \Delta U + W$

$$= (3.5049 \times 10^4 \text{ J} - 2.1648 \times 10^4 \text{ J}) + 0$$
$$= 1.3401 \times 10^4 \text{ J} \xrightarrow{SD} \mathbf{1.34 \times 10^4\ J}$$

2.
$$Q = \Delta U + W$$
$$0 = \Delta U + 10^3 \text{ J}$$
$$\Delta U = \mathbf{-10^3\ J}$$

3. Begin by writing a $\sum F = ma$ equation for the block.

$$\sum F = ma$$
$$mg - T = ma$$
$$5.0(9.81) - T = 5.0a$$
$$T = 49.05 - 5.0a \qquad \text{(a)}$$

Next, write a $\Sigma\tau = I\alpha$ equation for the cylinder.

$$\Sigma\tau = I\alpha$$
$$(0.020)T = \left(\frac{1}{2}mr^2\right)\alpha$$
$$(0.020)T = \left(\frac{1}{2}(25.0)(0.020)^2\right)\alpha$$
$$T = 0.25\alpha \qquad \text{(b)}$$

Now note that α is equal to $\frac{a}{0.020}$. Substitute into (b) and get:

$$\text{(b) } T = 0.25\left(\frac{a}{0.020}\right) = 12.5a$$

Substitute this value for T into (a) to find the acceleration.

$$\text{(a) } (12.5a) = 49.05 - 5.0a$$
$$17.5a = 49.05$$
$$a = 2.803\ \frac{\text{m}}{\text{s}^2} \xrightarrow{\text{SD}} \mathbf{2.8\ \frac{m}{s^2}}$$

4. Begin by finding the moment of inertia of the pulley and noting the relationship between a and α.

$$I = \frac{1}{2}mr^2 = \frac{1}{2}(6.0\text{ kg})(0.15\text{ m})^2 = 0.0675\text{ kg}\cdot\text{m}^2$$
$$a = r\alpha \longrightarrow \alpha = \frac{a}{0.15}$$

Next, write a $\Sigma F_x = ma_x$ equation for the 9.0-kg block. Choose to the right as the positive direction for motion.

$$\Sigma F_x = ma_x$$
$$T_1 = ma$$
$$T_1 = 9.0a \qquad \text{(a)}$$

Now, write a $\Sigma F_y = ma_y$ equation for the 16-kg block.

$$\Sigma F_y = ma_y$$
$$mg - T_2 = ma$$
$$16(9.81) - T_2 = 16a$$
$$T_2 = 156.96 - 16a \qquad \text{(b)}$$

Next, write a $\Sigma\tau = I\alpha$ equation for the pulley.

$$\Sigma\tau = I\alpha$$
$$0.15T_2 - 0.15T_1 = (0.0675)\left(\frac{a}{0.15}\right)$$
$$0.15T_2 - 0.15T_1 = 0.45a$$
$$T_2 - T_1 = 3a \qquad \text{(c)}$$

Substitute (a) and (b) into (c) to find the acceleration.

$$\text{(c) } (156.96 - 16a) - (9.0a) = 3a$$
$$156.96 = 28a$$
$$a = 5.606\ \frac{\text{m}}{\text{s}^2} \xrightarrow{\text{SD}} \mathbf{5.6\ \frac{m}{s^2}\ to\ the\ right}$$

5. (a) $a_c = \frac{v^2}{r} = \frac{(47.2)^2}{573} = 3.888\ \frac{\text{m}}{\text{s}^2} \xrightarrow{\text{SD}} \mathbf{3.89\ \frac{m}{s^2}}$

(b) $\theta = \arctan\frac{v^2}{rg} = \arctan\frac{(47.2)^2}{(573)(9.81)} = \mathbf{21.62°}$

(c) $a_N = \sqrt{a_c^{\,2} + a_y^{\,2}}$

$$= \sqrt{(3.888)^2 + (9.81)^2} = 10.55\ \frac{\text{m}}{\text{s}^2} \xrightarrow{\text{SD}} \mathbf{10.6\ \frac{m}{s^2}}$$

6. (a) Write equations for the horizontal and vertical components of the tension.

(a′) $T\sin\theta = mr\omega^2 = m(L\sin\theta)\omega^2$
(b′) $T\cos\theta = mg$

Divide (b′) by (a′) and solve for θ.

$$\frac{(b')}{(a')} = \frac{\cancel{T}\cos\theta}{\cancel{T}\cancel{\sin\theta}} = \frac{\cancel{m}g}{\cancel{m}(L\cancel{\sin\theta})\omega^2}$$
$$\cos\theta = \frac{g}{L\omega^2}$$
$$\cos\theta = \frac{(9.81)}{(0.884)(3.87)^2}$$
$$\theta = \mathbf{42.19°}$$

(b)
$$T\cos\theta = mg$$
$$T\cos 42.19° = 3.37(9.81)$$
$$T = 44.62\text{ N} \xrightarrow{\text{SD}} \mathbf{44.6\ N}$$

(c) $F_c = T\sin\theta = (44.62\text{ N})\sin 42.19° = 29.97\text{ N} \xrightarrow{\text{SD}} \mathbf{30.0\ N}$

7. (a) $f = \dfrac{24 \text{ cycles}}{4.8 \text{ seconds}} = \mathbf{5.0\ Hz}$

(b) $$f = \frac{1}{2\pi}\sqrt{\frac{k}{m}}$$

$$5.0 = \frac{1}{2\pi}\sqrt{\frac{k}{2.2}}$$

$$k = 2.171 \times 10^3\ \frac{\text{N}}{\text{m}} \xrightarrow{\text{SD}} \mathbf{2.2 \times 10^3\ \frac{N}{m}}$$

8. (a) $$KE_{disk} = \frac{1}{2}mv^2 + \frac{1}{2}I\omega^2$$

$$= \frac{1}{2}mv^2 + \frac{1}{2}\left(\frac{1}{2}mr^2\right)\left(\frac{v}{r}\right)^2$$

$$= \frac{1}{2}mv^2 + \frac{1}{4}mv^2$$

$$= \frac{1}{2}(4.5)(3.2)^2 + \frac{1}{4}(4.5)(3.2)^2$$

$$= 34.56\text{ J} \xrightarrow{\text{SD}} \mathbf{35\ J}$$

$$KE_{hoop} = \frac{1}{2}mv^2 + \frac{1}{2}I\omega^2$$

$$= \frac{1}{2}mv^2 + \frac{1}{2}\left(mr^2\right)\left(\frac{v}{r}\right)^2$$

$$= \frac{1}{2}mv^2 + \frac{1}{2}mv^2$$

$$= \frac{1}{2}(4.5)(3.2)^2 + \frac{1}{2}(4.5)(3.2)^2$$

$$= 46.08\text{ J} \xrightarrow{\text{SD}} \mathbf{46\ J}$$

(b) Note that these kinetic energies must equal the final potential energies.

$$KE_{disk} = mgh_{disk}$$

$$34.56 = 4.5(9.81)h_{disk}$$

$$h_{disk} = 0.783\text{ m} \xrightarrow{\text{SD}} \mathbf{0.78\ m}$$

$$KE_{hoop} = mgh_{hoop}$$

$$46.08 = 4.5(9.81)h_{hoop}$$

$$h_{hoop} = 1.04\text{ m} \xrightarrow{\text{SD}} \mathbf{1.0\ m}$$

9. (a) Begin by finding v_1 and v_2.

$$v_1 = \frac{Q_1}{A_1} = \frac{0.215}{0.0297} = 7.239\ \frac{\text{m}}{\text{s}}$$

$$v_2 = \frac{Q_2}{A_2} = \frac{0.215}{0.0324} = 6.636\ \frac{\text{m}}{\text{s}}$$

Now use Bernoulli's equation to find P_1.

$$P_1 + \frac{1}{2}\rho v_1^2 = P_2 + \frac{1}{2}\rho v_2^2$$

$$P_1 + \frac{1}{2}(13{,}600)(7.239)^2 = 242{,}000 + \frac{1}{2}(13{,}600)(6.636)^2$$

$$P_1 + 356{,}341.22 = 242{,}000 + 299{,}448.17$$

$$P_1 = 1.851 \times 10^5\text{ Pa} \xrightarrow{\text{SD}} \mathbf{1.85 \times 10^5\ Pa}$$

(b) $$\rho g l_1 + P_{atm} = P_1$$

$$(13{,}600)(9.81)l_1 + 101{,}300 = 1.851 \times 10^5$$

$$l_1 = 0.6281\text{ m} \xrightarrow{\text{SD}} \mathbf{0.628\ m}$$

$$\rho g l_2 + P_{atm} = P_2$$

$$(13{,}600)(9.81)l_2 + 101{,}300 = 242{,}000$$

$$l_2 = 1.0546\text{ m} \xrightarrow{\text{SD}} \mathbf{1.05\ m}$$

10. Use Bernoulli's equation to find the speed of the water leaving the pipe. Note that the initial and final pressures are equal and v_1 and h_2 are zero so all but the following terms fall out of the equation.

$$\rho g h_1 = \frac{1}{2}\rho v_2^2$$

$$(1000)(9.81)(15.2) = \frac{1}{2}(1000)v_2^2$$

$$v_2 = 17.27\ \frac{\text{m}}{\text{s}} \xrightarrow{\text{SD}} \mathbf{17.3\ \frac{m}{s}}$$

11. (a) $$\Delta V = \beta V_0 \Delta T$$

$$= \frac{9.6 \times 10^{-4}}{\text{C}^\circ}(245\text{ gal})(70.169\text{ C}^\circ)$$

$$= 16.5\text{ gallons} \xrightarrow{\text{SD}} \mathbf{20\ gallons}$$

(b) The volume of the tank is 260 gallons, but the change in volume of the gasoline causes its volume to reach 245 gal + 16.5 gal, or 261.5 gallons. **No,** the tank will not hold the warm gasoline.

12.

$$\tau = I\alpha$$

$$25.6 \text{ N·m} = I\left(0.567 \frac{\text{rad}}{\text{s}^2}\right)$$

$$I = 45.1499 \text{ kg·m}^2 \xrightarrow{\text{SD}} \mathbf{45.1\ kg{\cdot}m^2}$$

Replace the m term in the moment of inertia with $4m$.

$$I = (4m)r^2$$

$$45.1499 \text{ kg·m}^2 = (4m)(0.825 \text{ m})^2$$

$$m = 16.58 \text{ kg} \xrightarrow{\text{SD}} \mathbf{16.6\ kg}$$

13. The image is **approximately 15 cm in front of the mirror, it is inverted, and the height of the image is approximately 2.5 cm**.

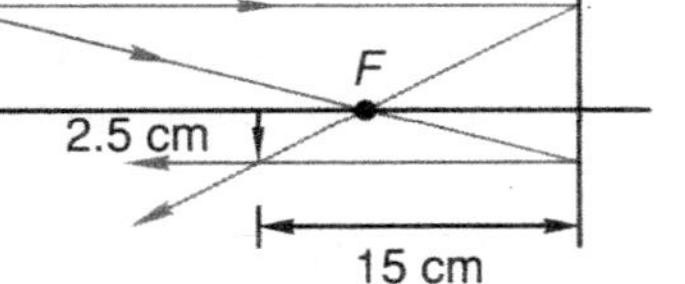

14.

$$F_c = F_N + w$$

$$\frac{mv^2}{r} = 1.50w + w$$

$$\frac{\cancel{m}v^2}{r} = 2.50\cancel{m}g$$

$$v^2 = 2.50(8.92)(9.81)$$

$$v = 14.79 \frac{\text{m}}{\text{s}} \xrightarrow{\text{SD}} \mathbf{14.8\ \frac{m}{s}}$$

15. Begin by converting horsepower to watts and finding the total energy.

$$14 \cancel{\text{hp}} \times \frac{746 \text{ W}}{1 \cancel{\text{hp}}} = 10{,}444 \text{ W}$$

$$KE = 10{,}444 \text{ W} \times 5.7 \text{ s} = 5.953 \times 10^4 \text{ J}$$

This must equal the final kinetic energy of the tractor.

$$5.953 \times 10^4 \text{ J} = \frac{1}{2}(590 \text{ kg})v^2$$

$$v = 14.206 \frac{\text{m}}{\text{s}} \xrightarrow{\text{SD}} \mathbf{14\ \frac{m}{s}}$$

16. Begin by redrawing the figure and finding the current labeled I_3.

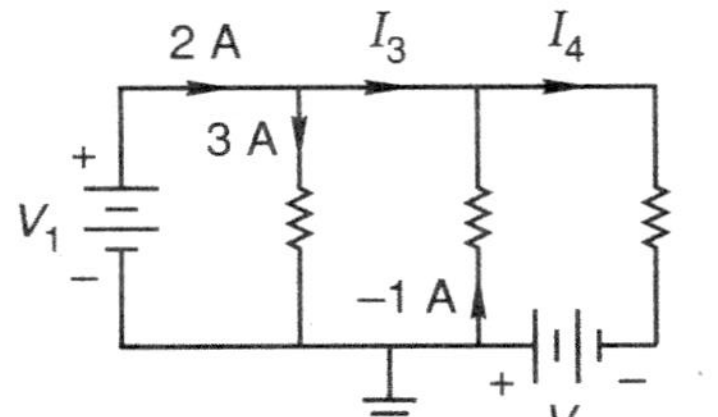

Use KCL to solve for I_3.

$$I_3 + 3 \text{ A} = 2 \text{ A}$$

$$I_3 = -1 \text{ A}$$

Use KCL again to solve for I_4.

$$I_3 + (-1 \text{ A}) = I_4$$

$$-1 \text{ A} + (-1 \text{ A}) = I_4$$

$$\mathbf{-2\ A} = I_4$$

17. Begin by finding the initial current in the circuit.

$$I_0 = \frac{400 \text{ V}}{50.0\ \Omega} = 8.00 \text{ A}$$

Now calculate the current when $t = 2.8$ s.

$$I = I_0 e^{-t/RC}$$

$$= 8.00e^{-2.8/1.2}$$

$$= 8.00e^{-2.33}$$

$$= 0.778 \text{ A} \xrightarrow{\text{SD}} \mathbf{0.78\ A}$$

18.

$$Q_1 = 0.112(2050)(10.0) = 2296 \text{ J}$$

$$Q_2 = 0.112(334 \times 10^3) = 37{,}408 \text{ J}$$

$$Q_3 = 0.112(4186)(100) = 46{,}883.2 \text{ J}$$

$$Q_4 = 0.112(2256 \times 10^3) = 252{,}672 \text{ J}$$

$$Q_5 = 0.112(2009)(10) = 2250.08 \text{ J}$$

$$Q_T = 3.415 \times 10^5 \text{ J} \xrightarrow{\text{SD}} \mathbf{3.42 \times 10^5\ J}$$

19.
$$m_1v_1 + m_2v_2 = (m_1 + m_2)v_3$$
$$0.40(32\angle 85^\circ) + 0.40v_2 = 0.80(30\angle 88^\circ)$$
$$12.8\angle 85^\circ + 0.40v_2 = 24\angle 88^\circ \qquad \text{(a)}$$

In order to add these values of momentum, first convert them to rectangular form.

$m_1v_1 = 12.8\angle 85^\circ = (1.116i + 12.75j)\text{ kg·m·s}^{-1}$

$(m_1 + m_2)v_3 = 24\angle 88^\circ = (0.8376i + 23.985j)\text{ kg·m·s}^{-1}$

Substitute these into (a) and get:

(a) $(1.116i + 12.75j) + 0.40v_2 = (0.8376i + 23.985j)$
$$0.40v_2 = (-0.278i + 11.235j)$$

Convert this to polar form and get:

$0.40v_2 = \sqrt{(-0.278)^2 + (11.235)^2} = 11.24\text{ kg·m·s}^{-1}$

$\theta = \tan^{-1}\dfrac{11.235}{-0.278} = -88.58^\circ$

Since θ is a 2nd-quadrant angle: $\theta = -88.58^\circ + 180^\circ = 91.42^\circ$

$0.40v_2 = 11.24\angle 91.42^\circ\text{ kg·m·s}^{-1} \xrightarrow{\text{SD}}$ **$11\angle 91.42^\circ$ kg·m·s^{-1}**

Therefore to find the velocity, we divide the momentum by the mass.

Momentum $= 0.40v_2 = 11.24\angle 91.42^\circ$

$v_2 = 28.10\angle 91.42^\circ\text{ m·s}^{-1} \xrightarrow{\text{SD}}$ **$28\angle 91.42^\circ$ m·s^{-1}**

20. $a_{av} = \dfrac{0 - 40}{8.0}\,\dfrac{\text{m/s}}{\text{s}} = \mathbf{-5.0\ \dfrac{m}{s^2}}$

Use the motion equation to find the time.

$v(t) = v_0 + at$

$0 = 16 + (-4.0)t$

$t =$ **4.0 s**

Use this time in the x-displacement equation to find the distance.

$\Delta x = v_0t + \dfrac{1}{2}at^2$

$= 16(4.0) + \dfrac{1}{2}(-4.0)(4.0)^2$

$=$ **32 m**

Problem Set 67

1.
$$n_1 \sin\theta_1 = n_2 \sin\theta_2$$
$$1.333 \sin\theta_c = (1.309) \sin 90^\circ$$
$$\theta_c = \mathbf{79.11^\circ}$$

2.
$$n_1 \sin\theta_1 = n_2 \sin\theta_2$$
$$2.417 \sin\theta_c = 1.000 \sin 90^\circ$$
$$\theta_c = 24.44^\circ$$

Yes, since the 26° angle is greater than θ_c, the light will be totally internally reflected.

3.
$$Q = \Delta U + W$$
$$1.3 \times 10^4\text{ J} = 0 + W$$
$$W = \mathbf{+1.3 \times 10^4\ J}$$

The system did work.

4. (a) $\Delta U = \dfrac{3}{2}nR\Delta T$

$= \dfrac{3}{2}(0.03)(8.31)(-246.77)$

$= -92.28\text{ J} \xrightarrow{\text{SD}}$ **−90 J**

(b) $Q = \Delta U + W$

$= (-92.28\text{ J}) + 0$

$= -92.28\text{ J} \xrightarrow{\text{SD}}$ **−90 J**

5. Begin by writing a $\sum F = ma$ equation for the block.

$$\sum F = ma$$
$$mg - T = ma$$
$$14(9.81) - T = 14a$$
$$T = 137.34 - 14a \quad \text{(a)}$$

Next, write a $\sum \tau = I\alpha$ equation for the cylinder.

$$\sum \tau = I\alpha$$
$$(1.2)T = \left(\frac{1}{2}mr^2\right)\alpha$$
$$(1.2)T = \left(\frac{1}{2}(12)(1.2)^2\right)\alpha$$
$$T = 7.2\alpha \quad \text{(b)}$$

Now note that α is equal to $\frac{a}{1.2}$. Substitute into (b) and get:

$$\text{(b)}\ T = 7.2\left(\frac{a}{1.2}\right) = 6.0a$$

Substitute this value for T into (a) to find the acceleration.

$$\text{(a)}\ (6.0a) = 137.34 - 14a$$
$$20a = 137.34$$
$$a = 6.867\ \frac{\text{m}}{\text{s}^2} \xrightarrow{\text{SD}} \mathbf{6.9\ \frac{m}{s^2}}$$

6. Begin by finding the moment of inertia of the pulley and noting the relationship between a and α.

$$I = \frac{1}{2}mr^2 = \frac{1}{2}(21\ \text{kg})(0.45\ \text{m})^2 = 2.126\ \text{kg·m}^2$$

$$a = r\alpha \longrightarrow \alpha = \frac{a}{0.45}$$

Next, write a $\sum F_x = ma_x$ equation for the 9.7-kg block. Choose to the right as the positive direction for motion.

$$\sum F_x = ma_x$$
$$T_1 = ma$$
$$T_1 = 9.7a \quad \text{(a)}$$

Now, write a $\sum F_y = ma_y$ equation for the 32-kg block.

$$\sum F_y = ma_y$$
$$mg - T_2 = ma$$
$$32(9.81) - T_2 = 32a$$
$$T_2 = 313.92 - 32a \quad \text{(b)}$$

Next, write a $\sum \tau = I\alpha$ equation for the pulley.

$$\sum \tau = I\alpha$$
$$0.45T_2 - 0.45T_1 = (2.126)\left(\frac{a}{0.45}\right)$$
$$0.45T_2 - 0.45T_1 = 4.724a$$
$$T_2 - T_1 = 10.498a \quad \text{(c)}$$

Substitute (a) and (b) into (c) to find the acceleration.

$$\text{(c)}\ (313.92 - 32a) - (9.7a) = 10.498a$$
$$313.92 = 52.198a$$
$$a = 6.014\ \frac{\text{m}}{\text{s}^2} \xrightarrow{\text{SD}} \mathbf{6.0\ \frac{m}{s^2}\ to\ the\ right}$$

7. (a) $\theta = \arctan \frac{v^2}{rg} = \arctan \frac{(29.7)^2}{(125)(9.81)} = \mathbf{35.73°}$

(b) $a_c = \frac{v^2}{r} = \frac{(29.7)^2}{125} = 7.057\ \frac{\text{m}}{\text{s}^2} \xrightarrow{\text{SD}} \mathbf{7.06\ \frac{m}{s^2}}$

8. (a) $f = \frac{1}{2\pi}\sqrt{\frac{k}{m}} = \frac{1}{2\pi}\sqrt{\frac{830}{43}} = 0.699\ \text{Hz} \xrightarrow{\text{SD}} \mathbf{0.70\ Hz}$

(b) $T = \frac{1}{f} = \frac{1}{0.699\ \text{Hz}} = 1.43\ \text{s} \xrightarrow{\text{SD}} \mathbf{1.4\ s}$

9. Begin by finding the angular speed and the moment of inertia of the bearing.

$$\omega = \frac{v}{r} = \frac{2.3\ \text{m/s}}{0.0052\ \text{m}} = 442.31\ \frac{\text{rad}}{\text{s}}$$
$$I = \frac{2}{5}mr^2 = \frac{2}{5}(0.057\ \text{kg})(0.0052\ \text{m})^2 = 6.165 \times 10^{-7}\ \text{kg·m}^2$$

Now find the total kinetic energy.

$$KE = \frac{1}{2}mv^2 + \frac{1}{2}I\omega^2$$
$$= \frac{1}{2}(0.057)(2.3)^2 + \frac{1}{2}(6.165 \times 10^{-7})(442.31)^2$$
$$= 0.211\ \text{J} \xrightarrow{\text{SD}} \mathbf{0.21\ J}$$

10. (a) Begin by finding v_1 and v_2.

$$v_1 = \frac{Q}{A_1} = \frac{0.52}{\pi(0.6)^2} = 0.460\ \frac{\text{m}}{\text{s}}$$

$$v_2 = \frac{Q}{A_2} = \frac{0.52}{0.38} = 1.368\ \frac{\text{m}}{\text{s}}$$

Now use Bernoulli's equation to find $P_2 - P_1$. Note that h_1 is zero, so the $\rho g h_1$ term falls out of the equation.

$$P_1 + \frac{1}{2}\rho v_1^2 = P_2 + \frac{1}{2}\rho v_2^2 + \rho g h_2$$

$$P_1 + \frac{1}{2}(1000)(0.460)^2 = P_2 + \frac{1}{2}(1000)(1.368)^2 + 1000(9.81)(3.5)$$

$$P_1 + 105.8 = P_2 + 935.71 + 34{,}335$$

$$P_2 - P_1 = -3.516 \times 10^4\ \text{Pa} \xrightarrow{\text{SD}} \mathbf{-3.5 \times 10^4\ Pa}$$

(b)

$$P_2 - P_1 = -3.516 \times 10^4$$

$$P_2 - 225{,}300 = -3.516 \times 10^4$$

$$P_2 = 1.9014 \times 10^5\ \text{Pa} \xrightarrow{\text{SD}} \mathbf{1.9 \times 10^5\ Pa}$$

11.

$$\Delta A = 2\alpha A_0 \Delta T$$

$$(7.429 - 7.432) = 2(7.5 \times 10^{-6})(7.432)(T_2 - 25)$$

$$-0.003 = (1.115 \times 10^{-4})T_2 - (2.787 \times 10^{-3})$$

$$T_2 = -1.91°\text{C} \xrightarrow{\text{SD}} \mathbf{-1.9°C}$$

12. (a) $I = (m_1 + m_2 + m_3 + m_4 + m_5)r^2$

$= (0.542 + 2.13 + 3.27 + 1.89 + 2.32)(0.525)^2$

$= 2.798\ \text{kg·m}^2 \xrightarrow{\text{SD}} \mathbf{2.80\ kg·m^2}$

(b) $\tau = I\alpha$

$= (2.798\ \text{kg·m}^2)(134\ \text{rad·s}^{-2})$

$= 374.93\ \text{N·m} \xrightarrow{\text{SD}} \mathbf{375\ N·m}$

13. Begin at the ground symbol, move clockwise, and sum the voltage changes to zero.

$$-40\ \text{V} - 11\ \text{V} - 12\ \text{V} - 2\ \text{V} + 14\ \text{V} + V_1 + 3\ \text{V} + 8\ \text{V} = 0$$

$$V_1 = \mathbf{40\ V}$$

14. $V_C = \dfrac{Q}{C} = \dfrac{4.5 \times 10^{-5}\ \text{C}}{20 \times 10^{-6}\ \text{F}} = 2.25\ \text{V} \xrightarrow{\text{SD}} \mathbf{2.3\ V}$

15.

$$v_1 A_1 = v_2 A_2$$

$$5.2\ \frac{\text{m}}{\text{s}}(4.9\ \text{m}^2) = v_2(2.1\ \text{m}^2)$$

$$v_2 = 12.13\ \frac{\text{m}}{\text{s}} \xrightarrow{\text{SD}} \mathbf{12\ \frac{m}{s}}$$

16. Begin at the ground symbol, move clockwise, and sum the voltage changes to zero.

$$-15\ \text{V} + I(800\ \Omega) + I(450\ \Omega) = 0$$

$$I(1250\ \Omega) = 15\ \text{V}$$

$$I = 0.012\ \text{A}$$

$$V_1 = IR_1 = (0.012\ \text{A})(800\ \Omega) = \mathbf{9.6\ V}$$

$$V_2 = IR_2 = (0.012\ \text{A})(450\ \Omega) = \mathbf{5.4\ V}$$

17. (a) Begin by finding the volume of the iceberg that is submerged.

$$V_s = 2.50 \times 10^5\ \text{m}^3 \times 0.852 = 2.13 \times 10^5\ \text{m}^3$$

Now find the mass of the water displaced.

$$m_w = 1025\ \frac{\text{kg}}{\cancel{\text{m}^3}} \times 2.13 \times 10^5\ \cancel{\text{m}^3}$$

$$= 2.183 \times 10^8\ \text{kg} \xrightarrow{\text{SD}} \mathbf{2.18 \times 10^8\ kg}$$

(b) The water's buoyancy force is equal to the weight of the water displaced.

$$F_B = 2.183 \times 10^8\ \cancel{\text{kg}} \times 9.81\ \frac{\text{N}}{\cancel{\text{kg}}}$$

$$= 2.142 \times 10^9\ \text{N} \xrightarrow{\text{SD}} \mathbf{2.14 \times 10^9\ N}$$

(c) The weight of the iceberg equals the buoyancy force of the water, and the mass of the iceberg equals the mass of the water displaced.

$$w_i = F_B = \mathbf{2.14 \times 10^9\ N}$$

$$m_i = m_w = \mathbf{2.18 \times 10^8\ kg}$$

18. (a) $n = \frac{c}{v}$

$1.52 = \frac{3.00 \times 10^8 \text{ m/s}}{v}$

$v = 1.974 \times 10^8 \frac{\text{m}}{\text{s}} \xrightarrow{\text{SD}} \mathbf{1.97 \times 10^8 \frac{m}{s}}$

(b) $v = f\lambda$

$1.974 \times 10^8 \frac{\text{m}}{\text{s}} = f(7.0 \times 10^{-7} \text{ m})$

$f = 2.82 \times 10^{14} \text{ Hz} \xrightarrow{\text{SD}} \mathbf{2.8 \times 10^{14}\ Hz}$

19. (a) $PE = mgh$

$= 175 \cancel{\text{kg}}\left(9.81 \frac{\text{N}}{\cancel{\text{kg}}}\right)(52.5 \text{ m})$

$= 9.013 \times 10^4 \text{ J} \xrightarrow{\text{SD}} \mathbf{9.01 \times 10^4\ J}$

(b) $KE = \frac{1}{2}mv^2$

$9.013 \times 10^4 \text{ J} = \frac{1}{2}(175 \text{ kg})v^2$

$v = -32.09 \frac{\text{m}}{\text{s}} \xrightarrow{\text{SD}} \mathbf{-32.1 \frac{m}{s}}$

20. (a) $\Sigma F_y = 0;\ F_A + F_B - 127 \text{ N} - 81.8 \text{ N} = 0$
(b) $\Sigma M_A = 0;\ 127 \text{ N}(3.25 \text{ m}) + 81.8 \text{ N}(8.40 \text{ m}) - F_B(6.55 \text{ m}) = 0$

Solve (b) for F_B and get:

(b) $412.75 \text{ N·m} + 687.12 \text{ N·m} - F_B(6.55 \text{ m}) = 0$

$F_B(6.55 \text{ m}) = 1099.87 \text{ N·m}$

$F_B = 167.92 \text{ N} \xrightarrow{\text{SD}} \mathbf{168\ N}$

Substitute F_B into (a) to find F_A.

(a) $F_A + (167.92 \text{ N}) - 127 \text{ N} - 81.8 \text{ N} = 0$

$F_A = 40.88 \text{ N} \xrightarrow{\text{SD}} \mathbf{40.9\ N}$

PROBLEM SET 68

1. Sketch the voltage V_C across the capacitor as a function of time.

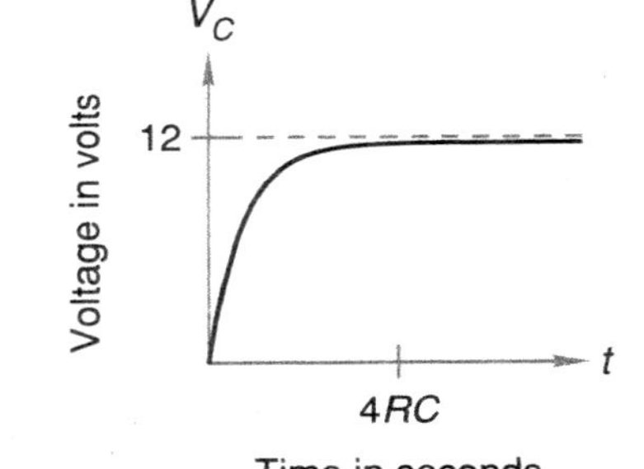

2. Energy $= \frac{1}{2}CV^2$

$= \frac{1}{2}(200 \times 10^{-6} \text{ F})(9.0 \text{ V})^2$

$= \mathbf{8.1 \times 10^{-3}\ J}$

3. $n_1 \sin \theta_1 = n_2 \sin \theta_2$

$1.49 \sin \theta_c = 1.329 \sin 90°$

$\theta_c = \mathbf{63.12°}$

4. $n_1 \sin \theta_1 = n_2 \sin \theta_2$

$1.923 \sin \theta_c = 1.544 \sin 90°$

$\theta_c = \mathbf{53.41°}$

5. $Q = \Delta U + W$

$0 = \Delta U + (4.0 \times 10^5 \text{ J})$

$\Delta U = \mathbf{-4.0 \times 10^5\ J}$

6. $Q = \Delta U + W$

$4.8 \times 10^6 \text{ J} = \Delta U + 0$

$\mathbf{4.8 \times 10^6\ J} = \Delta U$

7. Begin by writing a $\sum F = ma$ equation for the mass.

$$\sum F = ma$$
$$mg - T = ma$$
$$8.5(9.81) - T = 8.5a$$
$$T = 83.385 - 8.5a \qquad \text{(a)}$$

Next, write a $\sum \tau = I\alpha$ equation for the cylinder.

$$\sum \tau = I\alpha$$
$$(0.35)T = \left(\frac{1}{2}mr^2\right)\alpha$$
$$(0.35)T = \left(\frac{1}{2}(18)(0.35)^2\right)\alpha$$
$$T = 3.15\alpha \qquad \text{(b)}$$

Now note that α is equal to $\frac{a}{0.35}$. Substitute into (b) and get:

(b) $T = 3.15\left(\frac{a}{0.35}\right) = 9.0a$

Substitute this value for T into (a) to find the acceleration.

(a) $(9.0a) = 83.385 - 8.5a$

$$17.5a = 83.385$$
$$a = 4.7649\ \frac{\text{m}}{\text{s}^2} \xrightarrow{\text{SD}} \mathbf{4.8\ \frac{m}{s^2}}$$

8. Begin by finding the moment of inertia of the pulley and noting the relationship between a and α.

$$I = \frac{1}{2}mr^2 = \frac{1}{2}(5.0\text{ kg})(0.50\text{ m})^2 = 0.625\text{ kg}\cdot\text{m}^2$$

$$a = r\alpha \longrightarrow \alpha = \frac{a}{0.50}$$

Next, write a $\sum F_x = ma_x$ equation for the 12-kg block. Choose to the right as the positive direction for motion.

$$\sum F_x = ma_x$$
$$T_1 = ma$$
$$T_1 = 12a \qquad \text{(a)}$$

Now, write a $\sum F_y = ma_y$ equation for the 16-kg block.

$$\sum F_y = ma_y$$
$$mg - T_2 = ma$$
$$16(9.81) - T_2 = 16a$$
$$T_2 = 156.96 - 16a \qquad \text{(b)}$$

Next, write a $\sum \tau = I\alpha$ equation for the pulley.

$$\sum \tau = I\alpha$$
$$0.50T_2 - 0.50T_1 = (0.625)\left(\frac{a}{0.50}\right)$$
$$0.50T_2 - 0.50T_1 = 1.25a$$
$$T_2 - T_1 = 2.5a \qquad \text{(c)}$$

Substitute (a) and (b) into (c) to find the acceleration.

(c) $(156.96 - 16a) - (12a) = 2.5a$

$$30.5a = 156.96$$
$$a = 5.146\ \frac{\text{m}}{\text{s}^2} \xrightarrow{\text{SD}} \mathbf{5.1\ \frac{m}{s^2}}\ \textbf{to the right}$$

9. (a) $a_c = \frac{v^2}{r} = \frac{(43.3)^2}{158} = 11.87\ \frac{\text{m}}{\text{s}^2} \xrightarrow{\text{SD}} \mathbf{11.9\ \frac{m}{s^2}}$

(b) $\theta = \arctan\frac{v^2}{rg} = \arctan\frac{(43.3)^2}{(158)(9.81)} = \mathbf{50.42°}$

10. (a) $f = \frac{18\text{ cycles}}{7.5\text{ s}} = \mathbf{2.4\ Hz}$

(b)

$$f = \frac{1}{2\pi}\sqrt{\frac{k}{m}}$$
$$2.4 = \frac{1}{2\pi}\sqrt{\frac{k}{13}}$$
$$227.4 = \frac{k}{13}$$
$$k = 2.956 \times 10^3\ \frac{\text{N}}{\text{m}} \xrightarrow{\text{SD}} \mathbf{3.0 \times 10^3\ \frac{N}{m}}$$

11. Begin by finding the angular speed and the moment of inertia of the disk.

$$\omega = \frac{v}{r} = \frac{15 \text{ m/s}}{0.80 \text{ m}} = 18.75 \frac{\text{rad}}{\text{s}}$$

$$I = \frac{1}{2}mr^2 = \frac{1}{2}(12 \text{ kg})(0.80 \text{ m})^2 = 3.84 \text{ kg·m}^2$$

Now find the total kinetic energy.

$$KE = \frac{1}{2}mv^2 + \frac{1}{2}I\omega^2$$

$$= \frac{1}{2}(12)(15)^2 + \frac{1}{2}(3.84)(18.75)^2$$

$$= 2.025 \times 10^3 \text{ J} \xrightarrow{\text{SD}} \mathbf{2.0 \times 10^3 \text{ J}}$$

12. (a) $I = \frac{1}{3}mL^2$

$$= \frac{1}{3}(3.2186 \text{ kg})(2 \text{ m})^2$$

$$= 4.29 \text{ kg·m}^2 \xrightarrow{\text{SD}} \mathbf{4 \text{ kg·m}^2}$$

(b) $\tau = I\alpha$

$$= 4.29 \text{ kg·m}^2\left(4.222 \frac{\text{rad}}{\text{s}^2}\right)$$

$$= 18.11 \text{ N·m} \xrightarrow{\text{SD}} \mathbf{20 \text{ N·m}}$$

13. Begin by finding the centripetal force and the static friction force.

$$F_c = \frac{mv^2}{r} = \frac{907(32.5)^2}{257} = 3727.70 \text{ N}$$

$$F_s = mg\mu_s = (907)(9.81)\mu_s = (8897.67 \text{ N})\mu_s$$

The required centripetal force must equal the static friction force.

$$F_c = F_s$$

$$3727.70 \text{ N} = (8897.67 \text{ N})\mu_s$$

$$\mu_s = 0.41895 \xrightarrow{\text{SD}} \mathbf{0.419}$$

14. Begin by finding the voltage drop across the 300-Ω resistor.

$$V = I_1R = \left(2.50 \times 10^{-2} \text{ A}\right)(300 \ \Omega) = 7.5 \text{ V}$$

This must equal the voltage drop across the 200-Ω resistor. Use this voltage to find the current through the 200-Ω resistor.

$$I = \frac{7.5 \text{ V}}{200 \ \Omega} = 3.75 \times 10^{-2} \text{ A}$$

Use KCL to find the current through the 100-Ω resistor. Then find the voltage drop across the 100-Ω resistor.

$$I = \left(2.50 \times 10^{-2} \text{ A}\right) + \left(3.75 \times 10^{-2} \text{ A}\right) = 6.25 \times 10^{-2} \text{ A}$$

$$V = \left(6.25 \times 10^{-2} \text{ A}\right)(100 \ \Omega) = 6.25 \text{ V}$$

The total voltage, V_x, is equal to the sum of 7.5 V and 6.25 V.

$$V_x = 7.5 \text{ V} + 6.25 \text{ V} = 13.75 \text{ V} \xrightarrow{\text{SD}} \mathbf{13.8 \text{ V}}$$

15. Total energy $= \frac{1}{2}mv^2 + \frac{1}{2}kx^2$

$$2755 = \frac{1}{2}(15.2)(16.1)^2 + \frac{1}{2}(k)(0.100)^2$$

$$2755 = 1970 + (0.005)k$$

$$k = \mathbf{1.57 \times 10^5 \frac{N}{m}}$$

16. Begin by finding the voltage drop across the 125-Ω resistor.

$$V = (0.125 \text{ A})(125 \ \Omega) = 15.625 \text{ V}$$

Use this voltage to find the current through the 250-Ω resistor.

$$I = \frac{15.625 \text{ V}}{250 \ \Omega} = 6.25 \times 10^{-2} \text{ A}$$

Now find the energy consumed by the 250-Ω resistor.

$$E = VIt$$

$$= (15.625 \text{ V})\left(6.25 \times 10^{-2} \text{ A}\right)(27.5 \text{ s})$$

$$= 26.86 \text{ J} \xrightarrow{\text{SD}} \mathbf{26.9 \text{ J}}$$

17. Begin by finding the x and y components of the initial velocity.

$$v_{x0} = 38.7 \cos 15° = 37.38 \frac{\text{m}}{\text{s}}$$

$$v_{y0} = 38.7 \sin 15° = 10.02 \frac{\text{m}}{\text{s}}$$

Use the x-displacement equation to find the time.

$$\Delta x = v_{x0}t + \frac{1}{2}a_x t^2$$
$$32.5 = (37.38)t + 0$$
$$t = 0.869 \text{ s}$$

Use this time in the y-displacement equation to find the height.

$$\Delta y = v_{y0}t + \frac{1}{2}a_y t^2$$
$$= 10.02(0.869) + \frac{1}{2}(-9.81)(0.869)^2$$
$$= 5.0033 \text{ m} \xrightarrow{\text{SD}} \mathbf{5.00\ m}$$

18.

$$F = kx$$
$$8.25 \text{ N} = 31.4 \frac{\text{N}}{\text{m}} \times x$$
$$x = 0.2627 \text{ m} \xrightarrow{\text{SD}} \mathbf{0.263\ m}$$

$$W = \frac{1}{2}kx^2 = \frac{1}{2}\left(31.4 \frac{\text{N}}{\text{m}}\right)(0.2627 \text{ m})^2 = 1.083 \text{ J} \xrightarrow{\text{SD}} \mathbf{1.08\ J}$$

19.

$$n_A \sin \theta_A = n_1 \sin \theta_1$$
$$(1) \sin 48° = (1.5014) \sin \theta_1$$
$$\theta_1 = 29.6676°$$

$$n_1 \sin \theta_1 = n_2 \sin \theta_2$$
$$(1.5014) \sin 29.6676° = (1.434) \sin \theta_2$$
$$\theta_2 = 31.2137° \xrightarrow{\text{SD}} \mathbf{31.21°}$$

20. Begin by finding the weight of the mass and drawing a free-body diagram of the forces acting on the junction of the ropes.

$$w = mg$$
$$= 584 \text{ kg} \times 9.81 \frac{\text{N}}{\text{kg}}$$
$$= 5729.04 \text{ N}$$

Now sum the horizontal and vertical forces to zero.

(a) $\Sigma F_x = 0;\ T_2 \sin 64° - T_1 \cos 30° = 0$

(b) $\Sigma F_y = 0;\ T_1 \sin 30° + T_2 \cos 64° - 5729.04 \text{ N} = 0$

Solve (a) for T_2 and get:

(a) $T_2 \sin 64° = T_1 \cos 30°$

$T_2 = 0.9635T_1$ (a′)

Substitute (a′) into (b) and get:

(b) $T_1 \sin 30° + (0.9635T_1) \cos 64° = 5729.04 \text{ N}$

$0.9224T_1 = 5729.04 \text{ N}$

$T_1 = 6.211 \times 10^3 \text{ N} \xrightarrow{\text{SD}} \mathbf{6.21 \times 10^3\ N}$

Substitute T_1 into (a′) and get:

(a′) $T_2 = 0.9635(6.211 \times 10^3 \text{ N})$

$= 5.984 \times 10^3 \text{ N} \xrightarrow{\text{SD}} \mathbf{5.98 \times 10^3\ N}$

Note that T_3 is equal to the weight of the mass.

$T_3 = 5729.04 \text{ N} \xrightarrow{\text{SD}} \mathbf{5.73 \times 10^3\ N}$

Problem Set 69

1. (a) The image is **approximately 3.3 cm behind the lens, it is upright, and the height of the image is approximately 1.7 cm**.

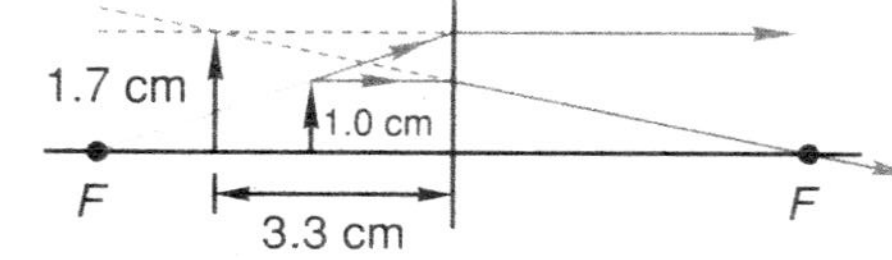

(b) $M = \frac{H_I}{H_O} = \frac{1.7 \text{ cm}}{1.0 \text{ cm}} = \mathbf{1.7}$

(c) The image is **virtual** because it is upright and behind the lens.

2. (a) The image is **approximately 2.2 cm behind the lens, it is upright, and the height of the image is approximately 1.1 cm.**

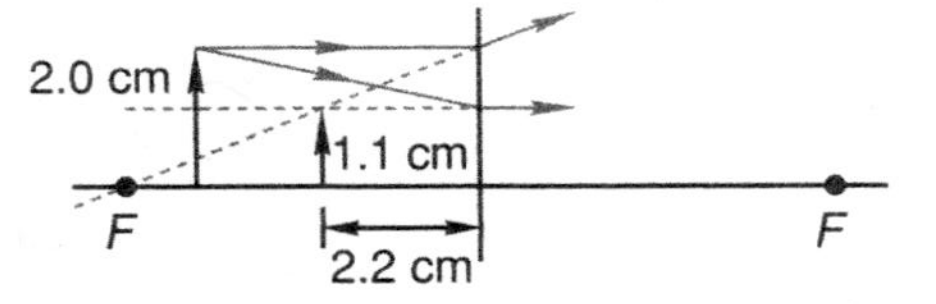

(b) $M = \frac{H_I}{H_O} = \frac{1.1\text{ cm}}{2.0\text{ cm}} = \mathbf{0.55}$

(c) The image is **virtual** because it is upright and behind the lens.

3. $E = \frac{1}{2}CV^2 = \frac{1}{2}(28 \times 10^{-6}\text{ F})(55\text{ V})^2 = \mathbf{4.2 \times 10^{-2}\text{ J}}$

4. Begin by finding the equivalent resistance of the two series resistors.

$R_E = 1000\ \Omega + 1000\ \Omega = 2000\ \Omega$

Next, find the time constant RC.

$RC = (2000\ \Omega)(150 \times 10^{-6}\text{ F}) = \mathbf{0.30\text{ s}}$

Now find the initial current in the circuit.

$I_0 = \frac{V}{R} = \frac{40\text{ V}}{2000\ \Omega} = 0.020\text{ A}$

Sketch the current as a function of time.

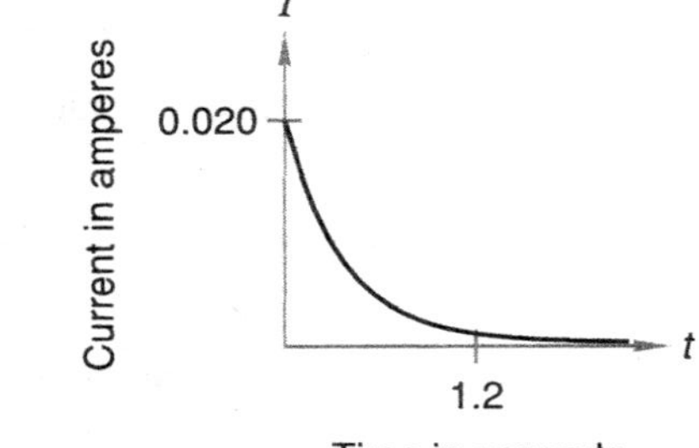

5. $n_1 \sin\theta_1 = n_2 \sin\theta_2$

$1.579 \sin\theta_c = 1.333 \sin 90°$

$\theta_c = \mathbf{57.59°}$

6. $n_1 \sin\theta_1 = n_2 \sin\theta_2$

$2.417 \sin\theta_c = (1) \sin 90°$

$\theta_c = \mathbf{24.44°}$

7. (a) $\Delta U = \frac{3}{2}nR\Delta T$

$= \frac{3}{2}(1.5)(8.31)(80) = 1.496 \times 10^3\text{ J} \xrightarrow{SD} \mathbf{1.5 \times 10^3\text{ J}}$

(b) $Q = \Delta U + W$

$= (1.496 \times 10^3\text{ J}) + 0$

$= 1.496 \times 10^3\text{ J} \xrightarrow{SD} \mathbf{1.5 \times 10^3\text{ J}}$

8. Begin by finding the moment of inertia of the pulley and noting the relationship between a and α.

$I = \frac{1}{2}mr^2 = \frac{1}{2}(8.0\text{ kg})(0.58\text{ m})^2 = 1.346\text{ kg·m}^2$

$a = r\alpha \rightarrow \alpha = \frac{a}{0.58}$

Next, write a $\sum F_x = ma_x$ equation for the 24-kg block. Choose up the plane as the positive direction for motion.

$\sum F_x = ma_x$

$T_1 - mg\sin\theta = ma$

$T_1 - 24(9.81)(\sin 25°) = 24a$

$T_1 = 99.5 + 24a$ (a)

Now, write a $\sum F_y = ma_y$ equation for the 29-kg block.

$\sum F_y = ma_y$

$mg - T_2 = ma$

$29(9.81) - T_2 = 29a$

$T_2 = 284.49 - 29a$ (b)

Next, write a $\sum\tau = I\alpha$ equation for the pulley.

$\sum\tau = I\alpha$

$0.58T_2 - 0.58T_1 = (1.346)\left(\frac{a}{0.58}\right)$

$0.58T_2 - 0.58T_1 = 2.321a$

$T_2 - T_1 = 4a$ (c)

Substitute (a) and (b) into (c) to find the acceleration.

(c) $(284.49 - 29a) - (99.5 + 24a) = 4a$

$184.99 = 57a$

$a = 3.245\text{ m/s}^2$

$\xrightarrow{SD}$ **3.2 m/s² up the plane**

9. (a) Begin by converting the angular speed to rad/s.

$$0.25\ \frac{\cancel{\text{rev}}}{\text{s}} \times \frac{2\pi\ \text{rad}}{1\ \cancel{\text{rev}}} = 1.5708\ \frac{\text{rad}}{\text{s}}$$

$$T\sin\theta = mr\omega^2$$
$$T\cancel{\sin\theta} = m(4.3\ \cancel{\sin\theta})\omega^2$$
$$T = 5.2(4.3)(1.5708)^2$$
$$= 55.17\ \text{N} \xrightarrow{\text{SD}} \mathbf{55\ N}$$

(b)
$$T\cos\theta = mg$$
$$(55.17)\cos\theta = 5.2(9.81)$$
$$\theta = \mathbf{22.39°}$$

10. $$f = \frac{1}{2\pi}\sqrt{\frac{k}{m}} = \frac{1}{2\pi}\sqrt{\frac{1200}{15}} = 1.42\ \text{Hz} \xrightarrow{\text{SD}} \mathbf{1.4\ Hz}$$

The period is the reciprocal of the frequency.

$$T = \frac{1}{f} = \frac{1}{1.42\ \text{Hz}} = 0.704\ \text{s} \xrightarrow{\text{SD}} \mathbf{0.70\ s}$$

11. The kinetic energy at the bottom of the plane must equal the potential energy at the top.

$$mgh = \frac{1}{2}mv^2 + \frac{1}{2}I\omega^2$$
$$mgh = \frac{1}{2}mv^2 + \frac{1}{2}\left(mr^2\right)\left(\frac{v}{r}\right)^2$$
$$mgh = \frac{1}{2}mv^2 + \frac{1}{2}mv^2$$
$$(5.5)(9.81)(6.9) = \frac{1}{2}(5.5)v^2 + \frac{1}{2}(5.5)v^2$$
$$372.29 = 5.5v^2$$
$$v = 8.227\ \frac{\text{m}}{\text{s}} \xrightarrow{\text{SD}} \mathbf{8.2\ \frac{m}{s}}$$

12. Begin by finding v_1 and v_2.

$$v_1 = \frac{Q_1}{A_1} = \frac{0.75}{0.070} = 10.71\ \frac{\text{m}}{\text{s}}$$
$$v_2 = \frac{Q_2}{A_2} = \frac{0.75}{0.25} = 3.00\ \frac{\text{m}}{\text{s}}$$

Now use Bernoulli's equation to find h_1. Note that h_2 is zero, so the $\rho g h_2$ term falls out of the equation.

$$P_1 + \frac{1}{2}\rho v_1^2 + \rho g h_1 = P_2 + \frac{1}{2}\rho v_2^2$$
$$229{,}750 + \frac{1}{2}(1035)(10.71)^2 + 1035(9.81)h_1 = 334{,}250 + \frac{1}{2}(1035)(3.00)^2$$
$$229{,}750 + 59{,}359.37 + (10{,}153.35)h_1 = 334{,}250 + 4657.5$$
$$(10{,}153.35)h_1 = 49{,}798.13$$
$$h_1 = 4.905\ \text{m} \xrightarrow{\text{SD}} \mathbf{4.9\ m}$$

13. Begin by finding the initial volume of the beam.

$V_0 = A_{\text{end}} \times L = 0.0140\ \text{m}^2 \times 2.54\ \text{m} = 0.03556\ \text{m}^3$

Now calculate the change in volume.

$$\Delta V = \beta V_0 \Delta T = \frac{3.6 \times 10^{-5}}{\text{C°}}\left(0.03556\ \text{m}^3\right)(-295\ \text{C°})$$
$$= -3.776 \times 10^{-4}\ \text{m}^3 \xrightarrow{\text{SD}} \mathbf{-3.8 \times 10^{-4}\ m^3}$$

14. Begin by finding the equivalent resistance of the two series resistors.

$R_E = 150\ \Omega + 30\ \Omega = 180\ \Omega$

Now, combine this with the 60-Ω resistor in parallel.

$$R_E = \frac{(180)(60)}{180 + 60} = 45\ \Omega$$

Next, combine this with the 5.0-Ω resistor to find the equivalent resistance of the circuit.

$R_E = (45\ \Omega) + 5.0\ \Omega = 50\ \Omega$

Use this resistance to find the time constant RC.

$RC = (50\ \Omega)\left(2500 \times 10^{-6}\ \text{F}\right) = 0.125\ \text{s} \xrightarrow{\text{SD}} \mathbf{0.13\ s}$

Sketch the capacitor voltage as a function of time.

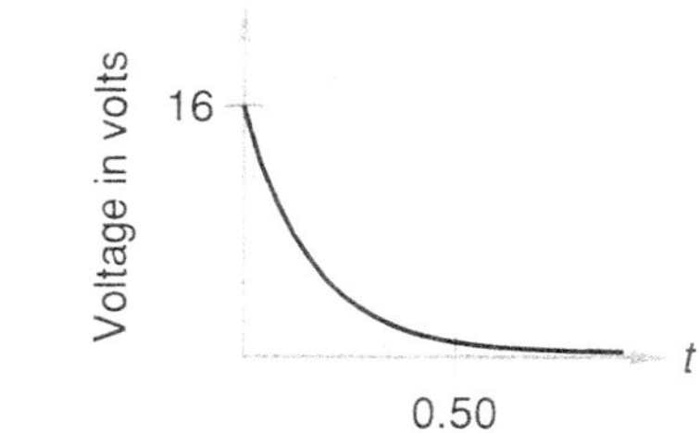

15. The image is **approximately 4.3 cm behind the mirror, it is upright, and the height of the image is approximately 4.3 cm**.

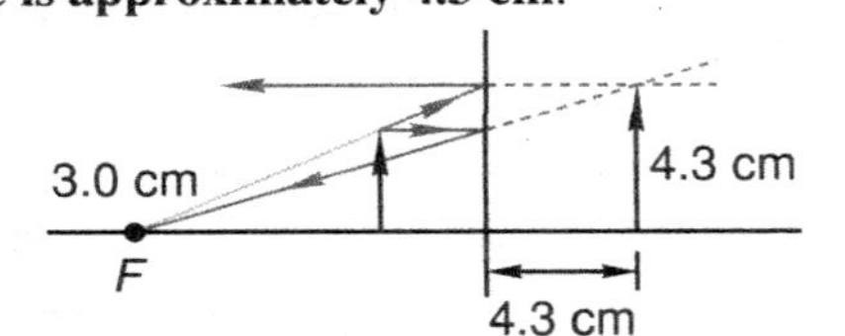

16. In the outside loop, begin at the ground symbol, move clockwise, and sum the voltage changes to zero.

$$+I_3(240\ \Omega) - 140\text{ V} + (1.40\text{ A})(40\ \Omega) = 0$$
$$I_3(240\ \Omega) = 84\text{ V}$$
$$I_3 = \mathbf{0.35\ A}$$

17. (a) $a_c = \frac{v^2}{r} = \frac{(5.210)^2}{4} = 6.786\ \frac{\text{m}}{\text{s}^2} \xrightarrow{\text{SD}} \mathbf{7\ \frac{m}{s^2}}$

(b) $F_c = ma_c = 15.875(6.786)$
$= 107.73\text{ N} \xrightarrow{\text{SD}} \mathbf{100\ N}$

18. Begin at the ground symbol, move clockwise, and sum the voltage changes to zero.

$$-20\text{ V} - 10\text{ V} - 8\text{ V} - 3\text{ V} - 12\text{ V} + V_x - 2\text{ V} = 0$$
$$V_x = 55\text{ V} \xrightarrow{\text{SD}} \mathbf{60\ V}$$

19. Begin by equating the resistances of each of the bars.

$$R_G = R_S$$
$$\frac{\rho_G L}{A_G} = \frac{\rho_S L}{A_S}$$
$$\frac{(2.44 \times 10^{-8}\ \Omega\cdot\text{m})(\cancel{L})}{7.21 \times 10^{-4}\text{ m}^2} = \frac{(1.59 \times 10^{-8}\ \Omega\cdot\text{m})(\cancel{L})}{\pi r^2}$$
$$\pi r^2 = 4.698 \times 10^{-4}\text{ m}^2$$
$$r = 1.223 \times 10^{-2}\text{ m}$$

The diameter is twice the radius, or $2r$.

$$d = 2r = 2(1.223 \times 10^{-2}\text{ m}) = 2.446 \times 10^{-2}\text{ m} \xrightarrow{\text{SD}} \mathbf{2.45 \times 10^{-2}\ m}$$

20.
$$Q = mc\Delta T$$
$$38{,}220 = 6.53(840)(T_2 - 20.0)$$
$$38{,}220 = 5485.2T_2 - 109{,}704$$
$$T_2 = 26.97°\text{C} \xrightarrow{\text{SD}} \mathbf{27°C}$$

Problem Set 70

1. The right conductor possesses a positive charge and the left conductor possesses a negative charge.

2. Refer to Section 70.C.

3. (a) The image is **approximately 6.0 cm in front of the lens, it is inverted, and the height of the image is approximately 2.0 cm**.

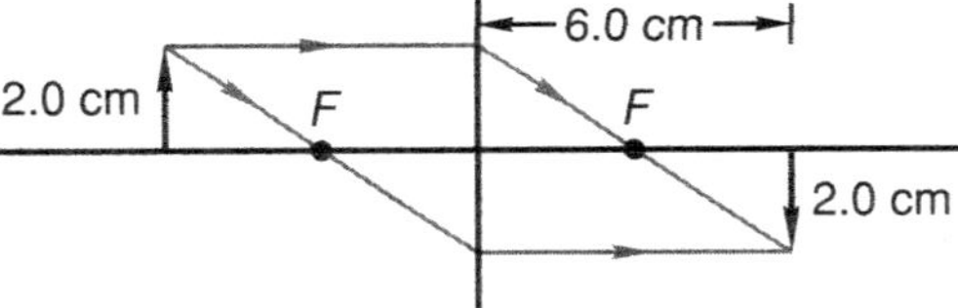

(b) $M = \frac{H_I}{H_O} = \frac{2.0\text{ cm}}{2.0\text{ cm}} = \mathbf{1.0}$

(c) The image is **real** because it is inverted and in front of the lens.

4. (a) The image is **approximately 1.7 cm behind the lens, it is upright, and the height of the image is approximately 0.33 cm**.

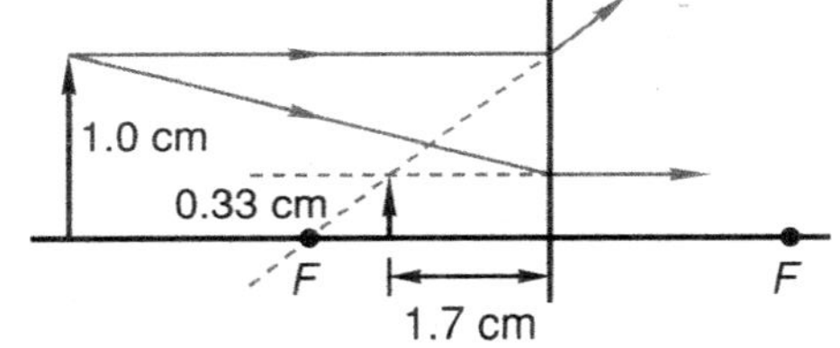

(b) $M = \frac{H_I}{H_O} = \frac{0.33\text{ cm}}{1.0\text{ cm}} = \mathbf{0.33}$

(c) The image is **virtual** because it is upright and behind the lens.

5. Begin by finding the time constant RC.

$RC = (5.0 \times 10^3\ \Omega)(75 \times 10^{-6}\ \text{F}) = 0.375\ \text{s}$

Sketch the voltage V_C versus the time.

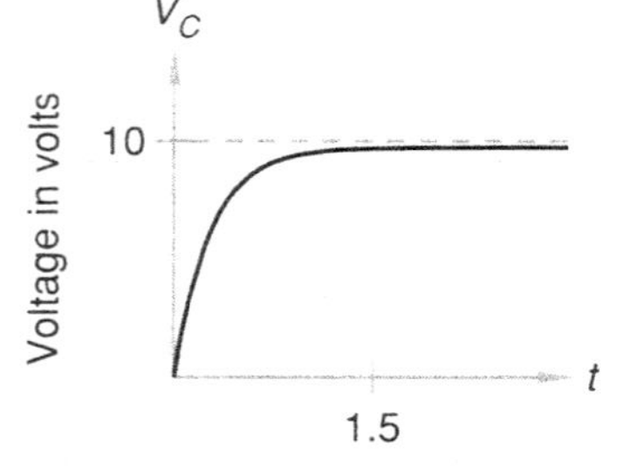

Now calculate the voltage when $t = 0.750$ s.

$$\begin{aligned} V_C &= V_0 - V_0 e^{-t/RC} \\ &= 10 - 10e^{-0.750/0.375} \\ &= 10 - 10e^{-2} \\ &= 8.647\ \text{V} \xrightarrow{\text{SD}} \mathbf{8.6\ V} \end{aligned}$$

6. Begin by finding the time constant RC.

$RC = (10.0 \times 10^3\ \Omega)(98.0 \times 10^{-6}\ \text{F}) = 0.98\ \text{s}$

Now calculate the voltage when $t = 2.94$ s.

$$\begin{aligned} V_C &= V_0 e^{-t/RC} \\ &= 40.0e^{-2.94/0.98} \\ &= 40.0e^{-3} \\ &= 1.9915\ \text{V} \xrightarrow{\text{SD}} \mathbf{1.99\ V} \end{aligned}$$

7.

$$\begin{aligned} n_1 \sin\theta_1 &= n_2 \sin\theta_2 \\ 1.362 \sin\theta_c &= 1.309 \sin 90° \\ \theta_c &= \mathbf{73.96°} \end{aligned}$$

8. $Q = \Delta U + W$

$= (0) + (-5.5 \times 10^6\ \text{J}) = \mathbf{-5.5 \times 10^6\ J}$

9. Begin by finding the moment of inertia of the pulley and noting the relationship between a and α.

$$I = \frac{1}{2}mr^2 = \frac{1}{2}(5.3\ \text{kg})(0.29\ \text{m})^2 = 0.2229\ \text{kg·m}^2$$

$$a = r\alpha \longrightarrow \alpha = \frac{a}{0.29}$$

Next, write a $\sum F_x = ma_x$ equation for the 15-kg block. Choose up the plane as the positive direction for motion.

$$\begin{aligned} \sum F_x &= ma_x \\ T_1 - mg\sin\theta &= ma \\ T_1 - 15(9.81)(\sin 25°) &= 15a \\ T_1 &= 62.19 + 15a \qquad \text{(a)} \end{aligned}$$

Now, write a $\sum F_y = ma_y$ equation for the 21-kg block.

$$\begin{aligned} \sum F_y &= ma_y \\ mg - T_2 &= ma \\ 21(9.81) - T_2 &= 21a \\ T_2 &= 206.01 - 21a \qquad \text{(b)} \end{aligned}$$

Next, write a $\sum\tau = I\alpha$ equation for the pulley.

$$\begin{aligned} \sum\tau &= I\alpha \\ 0.29T_2 - 0.29T_1 &= (0.2229)\left(\frac{a}{0.29}\right) \\ 0.29T_2 - 0.29T_1 &= 0.7686a \\ T_2 - T_1 &= 2.65a \qquad \text{(c)} \end{aligned}$$

Substitute (a) and (b) into (c) to find the acceleration.

$$\begin{aligned} \text{(c)}\ (206.01 - 21a) - (62.19 + 15a) &= 2.65a \\ 143.82 &= 38.65a \\ a &= 3.721\ \frac{\text{m}}{\text{s}^2} \end{aligned}$$

$$\xrightarrow{\text{SD}} \mathbf{3.7\ \frac{m}{s^2}\ up\ the\ plane}$$

10. (a) $F_c = \dfrac{mv^2}{r} = \dfrac{245(27.0)^2}{25.0} = 7.144 \times 10^3\ \text{N} \xrightarrow{\text{SD}} \mathbf{7.14 \times 10^3\ N}$

(b) $w = mg = (245)(9.81) = 2.403 \times 10^3\ \text{N} \xrightarrow{\text{SD}} \mathbf{2.40 \times 10^3\ N}$

(c) $\theta = \arctan\dfrac{F_c}{F_y} = \arctan\dfrac{7.144 \times 10^3\ \text{N}}{2.403 \times 10^3\ \text{N}} = \mathbf{71.41°}$

11. (a) $T = \frac{1}{f} = \frac{1}{3.2\text{ Hz}} = 0.3125\text{ s} \xrightarrow{\text{SD}}$ **0.31 s**

(b)
$$f = \frac{1}{2\pi}\sqrt{\frac{k}{m}}$$
$$3.2 = \frac{1}{2\pi}\sqrt{\frac{1500}{m}}$$
$$404.26 = \frac{1500}{m}$$
$$m = 3.71\text{ kg} \xrightarrow{\text{SD}} \mathbf{3.7\ kg}$$

12. (a) Begin by finding the moment of inertia of each disk.

$$I_1 = \frac{1}{2}m_1 r_1^2 = \frac{1}{2}(2.0\text{ kg})(0.15\text{ m})^2 = 0.0225\text{ kg}\cdot\text{m}^2$$
$$I_2 = \frac{1}{2}m_2 r_2^2 = \frac{1}{2}(1.5\text{ kg})(0.15\text{ m})^2 = 0.0169\text{ kg}\cdot\text{m}^2$$

Angular momentum is conserved, so the initial angular momentum of the first disk must equal the final angular momentum of both disks combined.

$$I_1\omega_1 = (I_1 + I_2)\omega_2$$
$$(0.0225)(15) = (0.0225 + 0.0169)\omega_2$$
$$0.3375 = (0.0394)\omega_2$$
$$\omega_2 = 8.566\ \frac{\text{rad}}{\text{s}} \xrightarrow{\text{SD}} \mathbf{8.6\ \frac{rad}{s}}$$

(b)
$$KE = \frac{1}{2}(I_1 + I_2)\omega_2^2$$
$$= \frac{1}{2}(0.0394\text{ kg}\cdot\text{m}^2)\left(8.566\ \frac{\text{rad}}{\text{s}}\right)^2$$
$$= 1.446\text{ J} \xrightarrow{\text{SD}} \mathbf{1.4\ J}$$

13.
$$\tau = I\alpha$$
$$\tau = \left(\frac{2}{5}mr^2\right)\alpha$$
$$275\text{ N}\cdot\text{m} = \left(\frac{2}{5}(22\text{ kg})(0.87\text{ m})^2\right)\alpha$$
$$\alpha = 41.287\ \frac{\text{rad}}{\text{s}^2} \xrightarrow{\text{SD}} \mathbf{41\ \frac{rad}{s^2}}$$

14. The image is **approximately 3.5 cm behind the mirror, it is upright, and the height of the image is approximately 1.5 cm**.

3.0 cm
1.5 cm
3.5 cm
F

15.
$$v_1A_1 = v_2A_2$$
$$8\ \frac{\text{m}}{\text{s}}(1.2784\text{ m}^2) = \left(16.150\ \frac{\text{m}}{\text{s}}\right)A_2$$
$$A_2 = 0.633\text{ m}^2 \xrightarrow{\text{SD}} \mathbf{0.6\ m^2}$$

16. Begin by finding the voltage drop across the 75-Ω resistor.
$V = I_3R = (-0.080\text{ A})(75\ \Omega) = -6.0\text{ V}$

This must equal the voltage drop across the 300-Ω resistor. Use this voltage to find I_2.

$$I_2 = \frac{V}{R_2} = \frac{-6.0\text{ V}}{300\ \Omega} = -0.02\text{ A}$$

Use KCL to find I_1.

$I_1 = I_2 + I_3 = -0.02\text{ A} + (-0.080\text{ A}) = \mathbf{-0.1\ A}$

17. Begin by finding the tension, mg, and the mass per unit length of the string.
$T = mg = (52)(9.81) = 510.12\text{ N}$

$$M_L = \frac{m_s}{L} = \frac{0.800}{L}$$

Insert these values into the formula below to find L.

$$v = \sqrt{\frac{T}{M_L}}$$
$$71.38 = \sqrt{\frac{510.12}{\frac{0.800}{L}}}$$
$$5095.1 = \frac{(510.12)L}{0.800}$$
$$L = 7.99\text{ m} \xrightarrow{\text{SD}} \mathbf{8.0\ m}$$

18. $D = R \times T = 350\ \frac{\text{m}}{\not{\text{s}}} \times 2.24\not{\text{s}} = \mathbf{784\ m}$

19.
$$\frac{P_1V_1}{T_1} = \frac{P_2V_2}{T_2}$$
$$\frac{(2.50 \times 10^3 \text{ Pa})V_1}{623 \text{ K}} = \frac{(7.00 \times 10^3 \text{ Pa})V_2}{873 \text{ K}}$$
$$\frac{V_1}{V_2} = 1.998 \xrightarrow{\text{SD}} \mathbf{2.00}$$

20. Use the y-displacement equation to find the time.
$$\Delta y = v_0t + \frac{1}{2}at^2$$
$$-52.3 = 5.27t + \frac{1}{2}(-9.81)t^2$$
$$0 = 4.905t^2 - 5.27t - 52.3$$
Use the quadratic formula to solve this equation for t.
$$t = \frac{-(-5.27) \pm \sqrt{(-5.27)^2 - 4(4.905)(-52.3)}}{2(4.905)} = 3.846 \text{ s} \xrightarrow{\text{SD}} \mathbf{3.85 \text{ s}}$$

PROBLEM SET 71

1. $$T = 2\pi\frac{\sqrt{L}}{\sqrt{g}} = 2\pi\frac{\sqrt{2.45}}{\sqrt{9.81}} = 3.13999 \text{ s} \xrightarrow{\text{SD}} \mathbf{3.14 \text{ s}}$$
$$f = \frac{1}{T} = \frac{1}{3.13999 \text{ s}} = 0.31847 \text{ Hz} \xrightarrow{\text{SD}} \mathbf{0.318 \text{ Hz}}$$

2. Begin by finding the initial period.
$$T = 2\pi\frac{\sqrt{L}}{\sqrt{g}} = 2\pi\frac{\sqrt{0.90}}{\sqrt{g}} = \frac{5.96}{\sqrt{g}}$$
Since T_2 equals $0.85T$, we substitute and get:
$$T_2 = 0.85T = 0.85\left(\frac{5.96}{\sqrt{g}}\right) = \frac{5.07}{\sqrt{g}}$$
Set this value equal to the period T_2 and solve for L.
$$T_2 = 2\pi\frac{\sqrt{L}}{\sqrt{g}}$$
$$\frac{5.07}{\sqrt{g}} = 2\pi\frac{\sqrt{L}}{\sqrt{g}}$$
$$L = 0.6511 \text{ m} \xrightarrow{\text{SD}} \mathbf{0.65 \text{ m}}$$

3. When the negatively charged piece of foil touches the neutral piece of foil, negative charge is distributed over both pieces. Since like charges repel each other, the two pieces of foil repel each other.

4. (a) The image is **approximately 1.4 cm behind the lens, it is upright, and the height of the image is approximately 0.29 cm**.

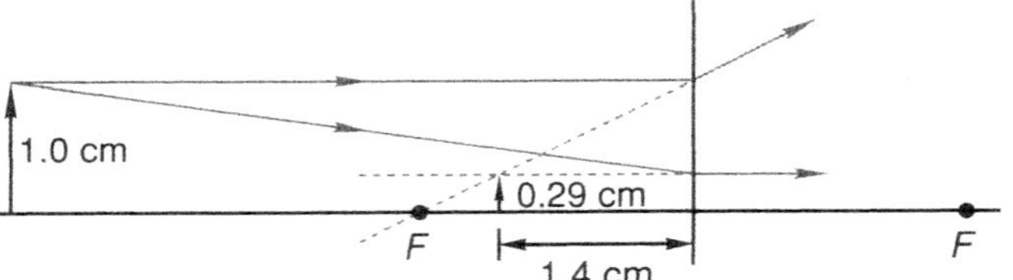

(b) $$M = \frac{H_I}{H_O} = \frac{0.29 \text{ cm}}{1.0 \text{ cm}} = \mathbf{0.29}$$

(c) The image is **virtual** because it is upright and behind the lens.

5. Begin by finding the time constant RC.
$$RC = (31{,}500 \ \Omega)(3.0 \times 10^{-4} \text{ F}) = 9.45 \text{ s}$$
Now calculate the voltage when $t = 23$ s.
$$V_C = V_0 - V_0e^{-t/RC}$$
$$= 25 - 25e^{-23/9.45}$$
$$= 25 - 25e^{-2.43}$$
$$= 22.799 \text{ V} \xrightarrow{\text{SD}} \mathbf{23 \text{ V}}$$

6. $$\text{Energy} = \frac{1}{2}CV^2$$
$$= \frac{1}{2}(425 \times 10^{-6} \text{ F})(42 \text{ V})^2$$
$$= 0.3749 \text{ J} \xrightarrow{\text{SD}} \mathbf{0.37 \text{ J}}$$

7. $$n_1 \sin\theta_1 = n_2 \sin\theta_2$$
$$2.417 \sin\theta_c = 1.517 \sin 90°$$
$$\theta_c = \mathbf{38.88°}$$

8. $$Q = \Delta U + W$$
$$9.8 \times 10^6 \text{ J} = \Delta U + 0$$
$$\Delta U = \mathbf{9.8 \times 10^6 \text{ J}}$$

9. Begin by finding the moment of inertia of the pulley and noting the relationship between a and α.

$$I = \frac{1}{2}mr^2$$
$$= \frac{1}{2}(3\text{ kg})(0.20\text{ m})^2 = 0.06\text{ kg}\cdot\text{m}^2$$
$$a = r\alpha \longrightarrow \alpha = \frac{a}{0.20}$$

Next, write a $\sum F_x = ma_x$ equation for the 27.150-kg block. Choose up the plane as the positive direction for motion.

$$\sum F_x = ma_x$$
$$T_1 - mg\sin\theta = ma$$
$$T_1 - 27.150(9.81)\sin 25° = 27.150a$$
$$T_1 = 112.56 + 27.150a \quad \text{(a)}$$

Now, write a $\sum F_y = ma_y$ equation for the 39.455-kg block.

$$\sum F_y = ma_y$$
$$mg - T_2 = ma$$
$$39.455(9.81) - T_2 = 39.455a$$
$$T_2 = 387.05 - 39.455a \quad \text{(b)}$$

Next, write a $\sum \tau = I\alpha$ equation for the pulley.

$$\sum \tau = I\alpha$$
$$0.20T_2 - 0.20T_1 = (0.06)\left(\frac{a}{0.20}\right)$$
$$0.20T_2 - 0.20T_1 = 0.3a$$
$$T_2 - T_1 = 1.5a \quad \text{(c)}$$

Substitute (a) and (b) into (c) to find the acceleration.

(c) $(387.05 - 39.455a) - (112.56 + 27.150a) = 1.5a$
$$274.49 = 68.11a$$
$$a = 4.03\ \frac{\text{m}}{\text{s}^2} \xrightarrow{\text{SD}} \mathbf{4\ \frac{m}{s^2}\ up\ the\ plane}$$

10. (a) Begin by converting the angular speed to rad/s.

$$0.333\ \frac{\cancel{\text{rev}}}{\text{s}} \times \frac{2\pi\text{ rad}}{1\ \cancel{\text{rev}}} = 2.0923\ \frac{\text{rad}}{\text{s}}$$

Next, equate the horizontal forces to find T.

$$T\sin\theta = mr\omega^2$$
$$T\cancel{\sin\theta} = m(4.21\ \cancel{\sin\theta})\omega^2$$
$$T = 17.5(4.21)(2.0923)^2$$
$$= 322.53\text{ N} \xrightarrow{\text{SD}} \mathbf{323\ N}$$

(b)
$$T\cos\theta = mg$$
$$(322.53)\cos\theta = 17.5(9.81)$$
$$\theta = \mathbf{57.84°}$$

11. Begin by converting the temperatures to kelvins.

$$T_1 = 20.0 + 273$$
$$= 293\text{ K}$$

$$T_2 = 37 + 273$$
$$= 310\text{ K}$$

Now use the ideal gas law and get:

$$\frac{V_1}{T_1} = \frac{V_2}{T_2}$$
$$\frac{6.0\text{ L}}{293\text{ K}} = \frac{V_2}{310\text{ K}}$$
$$V_2 = 6.348\text{ L} \xrightarrow{\text{SD}} \mathbf{6.3\ L}$$

12. The centripetal force equals the static friction force.

$$F_c = F_s$$
$$\frac{\cancel{m}v^2}{r} = \cancel{m}g\mu_s$$
$$\frac{(25)^2}{r} = (9.81)(0.77)$$
$$r = 82.74\text{ m} \xrightarrow{\text{SD}} \mathbf{83\ m}$$

13. Begin by finding the equivalent resistance of the two parallel resistors.

$$R_E = \frac{(180)(120)}{180 + 120} = 72\ \Omega$$

Now, combine this with the 78-Ω resistor to find the equivalent resistance of the circuit.

$$R_E = (72\ \Omega) + 78\ \Omega = 150\ \Omega$$

Use this resistance to find I_1.

$$I_1 = \frac{V}{R_E} = \frac{19\text{ V}}{150\ \Omega} = 0.127\text{ A} \xrightarrow{\text{SD}} \mathbf{0.13\ A}$$

Use this current to find the voltage across the 78-Ω resistor.

$$V_1 = I_1R_1 = (0.127\text{ A})(78\ \Omega) = 9.91\text{ V} \xrightarrow{\text{SD}} \mathbf{9.9\ V}$$

The voltage across R_3 must equal the total voltage minus V_1.

$$V_3 = 19\text{ V} - 9.91\text{ V} = 9.09\text{ V} \xrightarrow{\text{SD}} \mathbf{9.1\ V}$$

Use this voltage to find I_3.

$$I_3 = \frac{V_3}{R_3} = \frac{9.09\text{ V}}{180\ \Omega} = 0.0505\text{ A} \xrightarrow{\text{SD}} \mathbf{0.051\ A}$$

14. $PE = \frac{1}{2}kx^2 = \frac{1}{2}(1250)(3.35)^2 = 7014.06\text{ J}$

$$KE = \frac{1}{2}mv^2$$

$$7014.06 = \frac{1}{2}(32)v^2$$

$$v = 20.94\ \frac{\text{m}}{\text{s}} \xrightarrow{\text{SD}} \mathbf{21\ \frac{m}{s}}$$

15. Begin at the ground symbol, move clockwise, and sum the voltage changes to zero.

$$0 = -10.5 + 23.2I_1 - 12.3 + 34.8I_1 + 77.6I_1 + 56.4I_1$$

$$22.8 = 192I_1$$

$$I_1 = 0.11875\text{ A} \xrightarrow{\text{SD}} \mathbf{0.119\ A}$$

To find V_{BA}, begin at A and move clockwise to B.

$$V_{BA} = +10.5\text{ V} - (0.11875\text{ A})(23.2\ \Omega) = +7.745\text{ V} \xrightarrow{\text{SD}} \mathbf{+7.75\ V}$$

16. (a) Use the y-displacement equation to find the time.

$$\Delta y = v_{y0}t + \frac{1}{2}a_yt^2$$

$$-31.5 = (0) + \frac{1}{2}(-9.81)t^2$$

$$31.5 = 4.905t^2$$

$$t = 2.534\text{ s} \xrightarrow{\text{SD}} \mathbf{2.53\ s}$$

(b) Use this time in the x-displacement equation to find the distance.

$$\Delta x = v_{x0}t + \frac{1}{2}a_xt^2$$

$$= (52.0)(2.534) + (0)$$

$$= 131.77\text{ m} \xrightarrow{\text{SD}} \mathbf{132\ m}$$

(c) Use the motion equation to find the vertical velocity before impact.

$$v_y = v_{y0} + a_yt$$

$$= (0) + (-9.81)(2.534)$$

$$= -24.86\ \frac{\text{m}}{\text{s}} \xrightarrow{\text{SD}} \mathbf{-24.9\ \frac{m}{s}}$$

17. To find the spring constant, find the slope of the line.

$$k = \text{slope} = \frac{\Delta y}{\Delta x} = \frac{20\text{ N}}{0.100\text{ m}} = \mathbf{200\ \frac{N}{m}}$$

18. Begin by converting 1000 revolutions to radians.

$$1000\ \cancel{\text{rev}} \times \frac{2\pi\text{ rad}}{1\ \cancel{\text{rev}}} = 6283.19\text{ rad}$$

Use the angular displacement equation to find the angular acceleration.

$$\Delta\theta = \omega_0t + \frac{1}{2}\alpha t^2$$

$$6283.19 = (6.44)(500) + \frac{1}{2}(\alpha)(500)^2$$

$$\alpha = 2.451 \times 10^{-2}\ \frac{\text{rad}}{\text{s}^2} \xrightarrow{\text{SD}} \mathbf{2.45 \times 10^{-2}\ \frac{rad}{s^2}}$$

19. $F = \frac{Gm_1m_2}{r^2} = \frac{(6.67 \times 10^{-11})(5.98 \times 10^{24})(1850)}{(3.00 \times 10^7)^2}$

$$= 819.89\text{ N} \xrightarrow{\text{SD}} \mathbf{82\bar{0}\ N}$$

20. $P = \frac{F_1}{A_1} = \frac{235 \text{ N}}{7.85 \times 10^{-3} \text{ m}^2}$

$= 2.994 \times 10^4 \frac{\text{N}}{\text{m}^2} \xrightarrow{\text{SD}} \mathbf{2.99 \times 10^4 \frac{N}{m^2}}$

$\frac{F_1}{A_1} = \frac{F_2}{A_2} \rightarrow F_2 = \frac{F_1 A_2}{A_1}$

$= \left(2.994 \times 10^4 \frac{\text{N}}{\text{m}^2}\right)(0.01234 \text{ m}^2)$

$= 369.46 \text{ N} \xrightarrow{\text{SD}} \mathbf{369 \text{ N}}$

PROBLEM SET 72

1. (a) The amplitude is the maximum value of the function.
Amplitude = **10 m**
(b) The coefficient of t is ω, which equals $2\pi f$.
$2\pi f = 2\pi(0.25)$
$f = \mathbf{0.25 \text{ Hz}}$
(c) The period is the reciprocal of the frequency.
$T = \frac{1}{f} = \frac{1}{0.25 \text{ Hz}} = \mathbf{4 \text{ s}}$

2. $f = \frac{1}{T} = \frac{1}{1.45 \text{ s}} = 0.690 \text{ Hz}$
The maximum displacement is 0.32 m, and the frequency is 0.690 Hz.
$x = A \cos 2\pi f t$
$x = \mathbf{0.32 \cos 2\pi(0.690)t}$ **meters**

3. $T = \frac{3.6 \text{ s}}{\text{cycle}} = 3.6 \text{ s}$

Substitute the value for T and get:

$T = \frac{2\pi\sqrt{L}}{\sqrt{g}} = 3.6$

$\sqrt{L} = \frac{3.6\sqrt{9.81}}{2\pi}$

$L = 3.22 \text{ m} \xrightarrow{\text{SD}} \mathbf{3.2 \text{ m}}$

4. Increase the length of the pendulum to $1.86L$.

$T = \frac{2\pi\sqrt{L}}{\sqrt{g}} \rightarrow T_2 = \frac{2\pi\sqrt{1.86L}}{\sqrt{g}}$

Factor the 1.86 out from under the radical and get:

$T_2 = (\sqrt{1.86})\frac{2\pi\sqrt{L}}{\sqrt{g}}$

Now, note that $\frac{2\pi\sqrt{L}}{\sqrt{g}}$ is equal to T, which is 3.00 s. Substitute and get:

$T_2 = (\sqrt{1.86})(3.00 \text{ s}) = 4.091 \text{ s} \xrightarrow{\text{SD}} \mathbf{4.09 \text{ s}}$

5. When the negatively charged particle touches the ball, negative charge is distributed to each of the leaves. Since like charges repel each other, the leaves move apart.

6. (a) The image is **approximately 7.5 cm in front of the lens, it is inverted, and the height of the image is approximately 2.5 cm**.

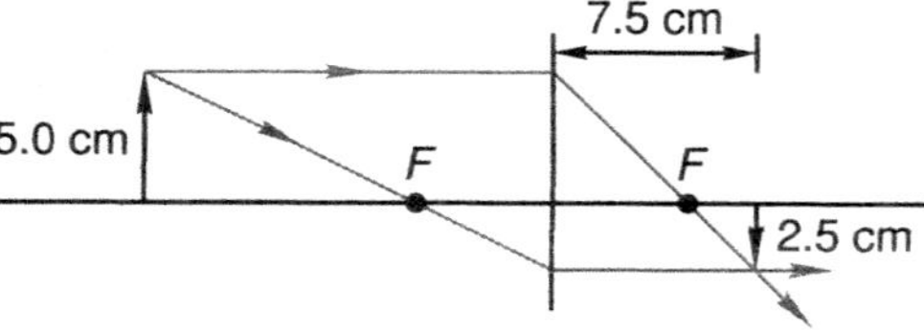

(b) The image is **real** because it is inverted and in front of the lens.

7. (a) $RC = 16 \text{ s}$
$R(8.0 \times 10^{-4} \text{ F}) = 16 \text{ s}$
$R = \mathbf{2.0 \times 10^4 \ \Omega}$
(b) $V_C = V_0 - V_0 e^{-t/RC}$
$= 75 - 75e^{-32/16}$
$= 75 - 75e^{-2}$
$= 64.85 \text{ V} \xrightarrow{\text{SD}} \mathbf{65 \text{ V}}$

8. $n_1 \sin \theta_1 = n_2 \sin \theta_2$
$1.333 \sin \theta_{max} = (1) \sin 90°$
$\theta_{max} = \mathbf{48.61°}$

9. $\Delta U = \frac{3}{2}nR\Delta T$

$= \frac{3}{2}(2.0)(8.31)(150 - 250)$

$= -2.493 \times 10^3 \text{ J} \xrightarrow{SD} \mathbf{-2.5 \times 10^3\ J}$

10. (a) Begin by writing a $\sum F = ma$ equation for the block.

$$\sum F = ma$$
$$mg - T = ma$$
$$51.2(9.81) - T = 51.2a$$
$$T = 502.27 - 51.2a \qquad \text{(a)}$$

Next, write a $\sum \tau = I\alpha$ equation for the cylinder.

$$\sum \tau = I\alpha$$
$$(0.724)T = \left(\frac{1}{2}mr^2\right)\alpha$$
$$(0.724)T = \left(\frac{1}{2}(7.25)(0.724)^2\right)\alpha$$
$$T = 2.62\alpha \qquad \text{(b)}$$

Now note that α is equal to $\frac{a}{0.724}$. Substitute into (b) and get:

(b) $T = 2.62\left(\frac{a}{0.724}\right) = 3.62a$

Substitute this value for T into (a) to find the acceleration.

(a) $(3.62a) = 502.27 - 51.2a$

$54.82a = 502.27$

$a = 9.162 \frac{\text{m}}{\text{s}^2} \xrightarrow{SD} \mathbf{9.16\ \frac{m}{s^2}}$

(b) $\alpha = \frac{a}{0.724} = \frac{9.162}{0.724} = 12.65 \frac{\text{rad}}{\text{s}^2} \xrightarrow{SD} \mathbf{12.7\ \frac{rad}{s^2}}$

11. (a) $a_c = \frac{v^2}{r} = \frac{(23.7)^2}{227} = 2.474 \frac{\text{m}}{\text{s}^2} \xrightarrow{SD} \mathbf{2.47\ \frac{m}{s^2}}$

(b) $\theta = \arctan \frac{v^2}{rg} = \arctan \frac{(23.7)^2}{(227)(9.81)} = \mathbf{14.16°}$

12. Begin by finding the moment of inertia.

$I = mr^2 = (2.5)(8.0)^2 = 160 \text{ kg}\cdot\text{m}^2$

Next, compute the required torque.

$\tau = I\left(\frac{\omega_2 - \omega_1}{\Delta t}\right)$

$= 160\left(\frac{10.2 - 3.2}{6.0}\right)$

$= 186.67 \text{ N}\cdot\text{m} \xrightarrow{SD} \mathbf{190\ N\cdot m}$

13. Begin by finding v_1 and v_2.

$v_1 = \frac{Q_1}{A_1} = \frac{1.04}{1.24} = 0.84 \frac{\text{m}}{\text{s}}$

$v_2 = \frac{Q_2}{A_2} = \frac{1.04}{0.24} = 4.33 \frac{\text{m}}{\text{s}}$

Now use Bernoulli's equation to solve for P_2. Note that h_1 is zero, so the $\rho g h_1$ term falls out of the equation.

$$P_1 + \frac{1}{2}\rho {v_1}^2 = P_2 + \frac{1}{2}\rho {v_2}^2 + \rho g h_2$$
$$225{,}000 + \frac{1}{2}(680)(0.84)^2 = P_2 + \frac{1}{2}(680)(4.33)^2 + (680)(9.81)(10.0)$$
$$225{,}000 + 239.90 = P_2 + 6374.63 + 66{,}708$$
$$P_2 = 1.52 \times 10^5 \text{ Pa} \xrightarrow{SD} \mathbf{1.5 \times 10^5\ Pa}$$

14. $4.6 \frac{\text{coulombs}}{\text{s}} \times \frac{1 \text{ electron}}{1.60 \times 10^{-19} \text{ coulomb}}$

$= 2.875 \times 10^{19} \text{ electrons} \xrightarrow{SD} \mathbf{2.9 \times 10^{19}\ electrons}$

15. The image is **approximately 9.3 cm in front of the mirror, it is inverted, and the height of the image is approximately 2.7 cm.**

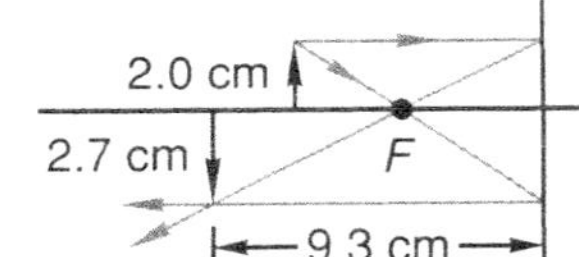

16. Begin by converting horsepower to watts.

$$5.0\,\text{hp} \times \frac{746\text{ W}}{1\text{ hp}} = 3730\text{ W}$$

Now find the work done.
$W = P\Delta t = 3730\text{ W} \times 7.0\text{ s} = 26{,}110\text{ J}$

This must equal the final kinetic energy of the mower.

$$W = \frac{1}{2}mv^2$$
$$26{,}110\text{ J} = \frac{1}{2}(226\text{ kg})v^2$$
$$v = 15.20\ \frac{\text{m}}{\text{s}} \xrightarrow{\text{SD}} \mathbf{15\ \frac{m}{s}}$$

17. Begin by finding the voltage drop across the 6.25-Ω resistor.
$V_1 = I_1R = (6.25\text{ A})(6.25\ \Omega) = 39.063\text{ V}$
This must equal the voltage drop across the 12.8-Ω resistor. Use this voltage to find the current through the 12.8-Ω resistor.

$$I_2 = \frac{V_2}{R} = \frac{39.063\text{ V}}{12.8\ \Omega} = 3.052\text{ A}$$

Use KCL to find the current I_3 through the 21.7-Ω resistor.
$I_3 = I_2 + I_1 = 3.052\text{ A} + 6.25\text{ A} = 9.302\text{ A}$
Use this current to find the voltage drop across the 21.7-Ω resistor.
$V_3 = I_3R = (9.302\text{ A})(21.7\ \Omega) = 201.853\text{ V}$
The total voltage V_x is equal to the sum of the voltage drop across the 21.7-Ω resistor and the voltage drop across the 6.25-Ω resistor.
$V_x = V_3 + V_1 = 201.853\text{ V} + 39.063\text{ V} = 240.916\text{ V} \xrightarrow{\text{SD}} \mathbf{241\ V}$

18.
$$\frac{P_1V_1}{T_1} = \frac{P_2V_2}{T_2} \longrightarrow \frac{P_1V_1}{T_1} = \frac{(3P_1)V_2}{\left(\frac{T_1}{2}\right)}$$
$$\frac{\cancel{P_1}V_1}{\cancel{T_1}} \times \frac{\cancel{T_1}}{\cancel{P_1}} = \frac{(3\cancel{P_1})V_2}{\left(\frac{\cancel{T_1}}{2}\right)} \times \frac{\cancel{T_1}}{\cancel{P_1}}$$
$$V_2 = \mathbf{\frac{V_1}{6}}$$

19.
$$m_Bv_B = -(m_Rv_R)$$
$$(0.15\text{ kg})\left(+420\ \frac{\text{m}}{\text{s}}\right) = -5.2\text{ kg}(v_R)$$
$$v_R = -12.12\ \frac{\text{m}}{\text{s}} \xrightarrow{\text{SD}} \mathbf{-12\ \frac{m}{s}}$$

20. (a) $\Sigma F_y = 0;\ 525.40 - w + 113.2 + 405.164 = 0$
(b) $\Sigma M = 0;\ -525.40(1) + w(x) - 113.2(4.554) - 405.164(8.108) = 0$

Solve (a) for w and get:
(a) $w = 525.40 + 113.2 + 405.164 = 1043.76\text{ N} \xrightarrow{\text{SD}} \mathbf{1044\ N}$

Substitute w into (b) to find x.
(b) $0 = -525.40 + 1043.76(x) - 515.51 - 3285.07$
$1043.76(x) = 4325.98$
$x = 4.14\text{ m} \xrightarrow{\text{SD}}$ **4 m from the left end**

Problem Set 73

1. (a) Determine the parameters of the sound wave if the car is not moving.

$$v_{SND} = f_s\lambda$$
$$345 = (750)\lambda$$
$$\lambda = 0.46\text{ m}$$

As the car approaches the boy, v_s is positive. Now, compute the observed wavelength λ'.

$$\lambda' = \left(\lambda - \frac{v_s}{f_s}\right)$$
$$= \left(0.46 - \frac{23.3}{750}\right)$$
$$= 0.4289\text{ m} \xrightarrow{\text{SD}} \mathbf{0.429\ m}$$

(b) Use λ' to compute the observed frequency f'.

$$v_{SND} = f'\left(\lambda - \frac{v_s}{f_s}\right)$$
$$v_{SND} = f'\lambda'$$
$$345 = f'(0.4289)$$
$$f' = 804.38\text{ Hz} \xrightarrow{\text{SD}} \mathbf{804\ Hz}$$

2. (a) Determine the parameters of the sound wave if the siren is not moving.

$$v_{SND} = f_s\lambda$$
$$345 = (552)\lambda$$
$$\lambda = 0.625 \text{ m}$$

As the fire engine and car approach each other, v_s and v_{OB} are positive. Therefore, the speed of the siren's sound relative to the car is

$$v_{SND} + v_{OB} = 345 + 21.5 = 366.5 \text{ m/s}$$

Now, compute the observed frequency f'''.

$$v_{SND} + v_{OB} = f'''\left(\lambda - \frac{v_s}{f_s}\right)$$

$$366.5 = f'''\left(0.625 - \frac{32.5}{552}\right)$$

$$f''' = 647.39 \text{ Hz} \xrightarrow{SD} \mathbf{647\ Hz}$$

(b) As the fire engine and car move away from each other, v_s and v_{OB} are negative. Therefore, the speed of the siren's sound relative to the car is

$$v_{SND} + v_{OB} = 345 - 21.5 = 323.5 \text{ m/s}$$

Now, compute the observed frequency f'''.

$$v_{SND} + v_{OB} = f'''\left(\lambda - \frac{v_s}{f_s}\right)$$

$$323.5 = f'''\left(0.625 - \frac{(-32.5)}{552}\right)$$

$$f''' = 473.04 \text{ Hz} \xrightarrow{SD} \mathbf{473\ Hz}$$

3. (a) The amplitude is the maximum value of the function.
Amplitude = **2 m**

(b) The coefficient of t is ω, which equals $2\pi f$.

$$2\pi f = \frac{3\pi}{4}$$

$$f = \mathbf{\frac{3}{8}\ Hz}$$

(c) The period is the reciprocal of the frequency.

$$T = \frac{1}{f} = \frac{1}{\frac{3}{8}\text{ Hz}} = \mathbf{\frac{8}{3}\ s}$$

4. (a) The maximum displacement is 2.5 m, and the frequency is 2.1 Hz.

$$x = A\cos 2\pi ft$$
$$x = \mathbf{2.5\cos 2\pi(2.1)}\boldsymbol{t}\ \mathbf{meters}$$

(b) $v = f\lambda$

$$= (2.1 \text{ Hz})(2.0 \text{ m})$$
$$= \mathbf{4.2\ \frac{m}{s}}$$

5. $$T = 2\pi\frac{\sqrt{L}}{\sqrt{g}} = 2\pi\frac{\sqrt{6.10}}{\sqrt{9.81}} = 4.9546 \text{ s} \xrightarrow{SD} \mathbf{4.95\ s}$$

The frequency is the reciprocal of the period.

$$f = \frac{1}{T} = \frac{1}{4.9546 \text{ s}} = 0.2018 \text{ Hz} \xrightarrow{SD} \mathbf{0.202\ Hz}$$

6. $$T = 2\pi\frac{\sqrt{L}}{\sqrt{g}}$$

$$1.63 = 2\pi\frac{\sqrt{(0.650 + 0.03)}}{\sqrt{g}}$$

$$\sqrt{g} = 3.1787$$

$$g = 10.10\ \frac{\text{m}}{\text{s}^2} \xrightarrow{SD} \mathbf{10\ \frac{m}{s^2}}$$

7. The section nearest the negatively charged object possesses a net positive charge; the other section possesses a net negative charge.

8. (a) The image is **approximately 3.4 cm behind the lens, it is upright, and the height of the image is approximately 1.7 cm.**

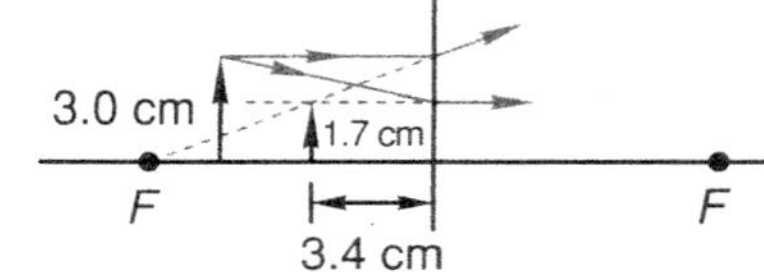

(b) $$M = \frac{H_I}{H_O} = \frac{1.7}{3.0} = \mathbf{0.57}$$

(c) The image is **virtual** because it is upright and behind the lens.

9. Begin by finding the time constant RC.

$$RC = (2250\ \Omega)(25.5 \times 10^{-6}\ \text{F}) = 5.738 \times 10^{-2}\ \text{s}$$

Now calculate the voltage when $t = 0.15$ s.

$$V_C = V_0 e^{-t/RC}$$
$$= 51.5e^{-0.15/5.738\times10^{-2}}$$
$$= 51.5e^{-2.614}$$
$$= 3.772\ \text{V} \xrightarrow{\text{SD}} \mathbf{3.8\ V}$$

10.
$$Q = \Delta U + W$$
$$420\ \text{J} = \Delta U + 230\ \text{J}$$
$$\Delta U = \mathbf{190\ J}$$

11. Begin by noting the moment of inertia of the pulley and the relationship between a and α.

$$I = 2.97 \times 10^{-2}\ \text{kg}\cdot\text{m}^2$$

$$a = r\alpha \rightarrow \alpha = \frac{a}{12.5} = \frac{1.12}{12.5} = 0.0896$$

Next, write a $\Sigma F_x = ma_x$ equation for the boy. Choose to the right as the positive direction for motion.

$$\Sigma F_x = ma_x$$
$$T_1 - \mu_k mg = ma$$
$$T_1 - (0.512)m(9.81) = m(1.12)$$
$$T_1 = 6.143m \qquad \text{(a)}$$

Now, write a $\Sigma F_y = ma_y$ equation for the 48.7-kg crate.

$$\Sigma F_y = ma_y$$
$$mg - T_2 = ma$$
$$(48.7)(9.81) - T_2 = 48.7(1.12)$$
$$T_2 = 423.20 \qquad \text{(b)}$$

Next, write a $\Sigma\tau = I\alpha$ equation for the pulley.

$$\Sigma\tau = I\alpha$$
$$12.5T_2 - 12.5T_1 = (2.97 \times 10^{-2})(0.0896)$$
$$12.5T_2 - 12.5T_1 = 2.66 \times 10^{-3}$$
$$T_2 - T_1 = 2.13 \times 10^{-4} \qquad \text{(c)}$$

Substitute (a) and (b) into (c) to find the mass of the boy.

(c) $(423.20) - (6.143m) = 2.13 \times 10^{-4}$
$$6.143m = 4.23 \times 10^2$$
$$m = 68.86\ \text{kg} \xrightarrow{\text{SD}} \mathbf{68.9\ kg}$$

12. $PE = \frac{1}{2}kx^2 = \frac{1}{2}(2575)(2.23)^2 = 6402.61\ \text{J}$

$$KE = \frac{1}{2}mv_{max}^2$$
$$6402.61 = \frac{1}{2}(15.3)v_{max}^2$$
$$v_{max} = 28.93\ \frac{\text{m}}{\text{s}} \xrightarrow{\text{SD}} \mathbf{28.9\ \frac{m}{s}}$$

13. $\Delta V = \beta V_0 \Delta T$

$$= \frac{1.12 \times 10^{-4}}{\text{C}^\circ}(350\ \text{L})(40\ \text{C}^\circ)$$
$$= 1.568\ \text{L} \xrightarrow{\text{SD}} \mathbf{1.6\ L}$$

14. The image is **approximately 29 mm behind the mirror, it is upright, and the height of the image is approximately 14 mm.**

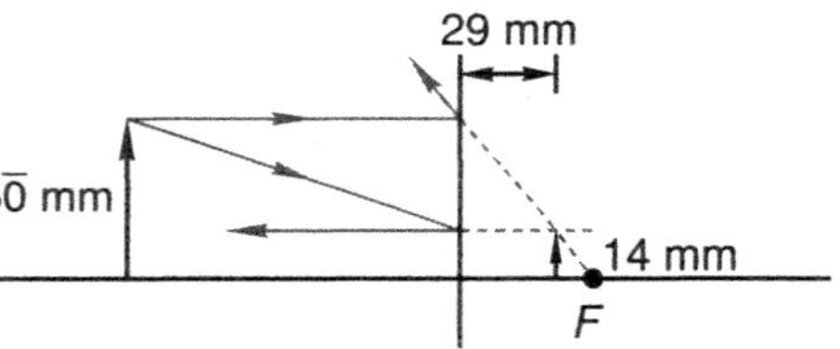

15.
$$v_1A_1 = v_2A_2$$
$$12.5\ \frac{\text{cm}}{\text{s}}[\pi(1.75\ \text{cm})^2] = v_2[\pi(2.16\ \text{cm})^2]$$
$$120.264\ \frac{\text{cm}^3}{\text{s}} = v_2(14.657\ \text{cm}^2)$$
$$v_2 = 8.205\ \frac{\text{cm}}{\text{s}} \xrightarrow{\text{SD}} \mathbf{8.21\ \frac{cm}{s}}$$

16. (a) Begin by converting rev/s to rad/s.

$$2.430\,\frac{\text{rev}}{\text{s}} \times \frac{2\pi\text{ rad}}{1\text{ rev}} = 15.268\,\frac{\text{rad}}{\text{s}}$$

Next, equate the horizontal forces to find T.

$$T = F_c = mr\omega^2$$
$$= (0.2)(0.5178)(15.268)^2$$
$$= 24.141\text{ N} \xrightarrow{\text{SD}} \mathbf{20\ N}$$

(b) $v = r\omega$

$$= (0.5178)(15.268)$$
$$= 7.9058\,\frac{\text{m}}{\text{s}} \xrightarrow{\text{SD}} \mathbf{7.906\,\frac{m}{s}}$$

17. Begin at G, move clockwise, and sum the voltage changes to zero.

$$-5.0\text{ V} + 2.0\text{ V} + 6.0\text{ V} + V_1 - 30\text{ V} + 4.0\text{ V} = 0$$
$$V_1 = \mathbf{23\ V}$$

To find V_{AF}, begin at F and move clockwise to A.

$$V_{AF} = +30\text{ V} - 4.0\text{ V} + 5.0\text{ V} = \mathbf{+31\ V}$$

18.

$$Q_1 = 0.352(2050)(12.0) = 8659.2\text{ J}$$
$$Q_2 = 0.352(334 \times 10^3) = 117{,}568\text{ J}$$
$$Q_3 = 0.352(4186)(100) = 147{,}347.2\text{ J}$$
$$Q_4 = 0.352(2256 \times 10^3) = 794{,}112\text{ J}$$
$$Q_5 = 0.352(2009)(207) = 146{,}383.78\text{ J}$$
$$Q_T = 1.214 \times 10^6\text{ J} \xrightarrow{\text{SD}} \mathbf{1.21 \times 10^6\ J}$$

19. Use the y-displacement equation to find the time.

$$\Delta y = v_0 t + \frac{1}{2}at^2$$
$$-10 = (0) + \frac{1}{2}(-9.81)t^2$$
$$10 = 4.905t^2$$
$$t = 1.428\text{ s}$$

Use this time in the motion equation to find the velocity.

$$v(t) = v_0 + at$$
$$= (0) + (-9.81)(1.428)$$
$$= -14.009\,\frac{\text{m}}{\text{s}} \xrightarrow{\text{SD}} \mathbf{-14\,\frac{m}{s}}$$

20.

$$\vec{F} = m\vec{a}$$
$$21.5\angle 22.5 = (115)\vec{a}$$
$$\vec{a} = 0.187\angle 22.5^\circ\,\frac{\text{m}}{\text{s}^2}$$

Use this in the motion equation to find the maximum velocity.

$$v = v_0 + at$$
$$= 3.16\angle 22.5^\circ + (0.187\angle 22.5^\circ)(30.5)$$
$$= 8.864\angle 22.5^\circ\,\frac{\text{m}}{\text{s}} \xrightarrow{\text{SD}} \mathbf{8.86\angle 22.5^\circ\,\frac{m}{s}}$$

PROBLEM SET 74

1. Begin by converting the temperatures to kelvins.

$$T_H = 2000°\text{C} + 273 = 2273\text{ K}$$
$$T_C = 800°\text{C} + 273 = 1073\text{ K}$$

Thus, the maximum possible efficiency is

$$\text{eff}_{\text{max}} = 1 - \frac{T_C}{T_H}$$
$$= 1 - \frac{1073}{2273}$$
$$= 0.5279$$

Multiply this by 100% and get:

$$\text{eff}_{\text{max}} = 0.5279 \times 100\% = 52.79\% \xrightarrow{\text{SD}} \mathbf{52.8\%}$$

2. Begin by converting the temperature to kelvins.

$$T_H = 427°\text{C} + 273 = 700\text{ K}$$

Thus, the cold temperature is

$$\text{eff}_{\text{max}} = 1 - \frac{T_C}{T_H}$$
$$0.8838 = 1 - \frac{T_C}{700}$$
$$T_C = 81.34\text{ K} \xrightarrow{\text{SD}} \mathbf{81.3\ K = -192°C}$$

3. (a) Begin by converting the temperature to kelvins.

$T_H = 2200°\text{C} + 273 = 2473 \text{ K}$

Thus, the cold temperature is

$$Q = mc\Delta T$$

$$2.080 \times 10^7 = (5.115)(2009)(2473 - T_C)$$

$$T_C = 448.87 \text{ K} \xrightarrow{\text{SD}} \mathbf{448.9\ K = 175.9°C}$$

(b) $$\text{eff}_{max} = 1 - \frac{T_C}{T_H}$$

$$= 1 - \frac{448.87}{2473}$$

$$= 0.81849$$

$$\text{eff}_{max} = 0.81849 \times 100\% = 81.849\% \xrightarrow{\text{SD}} \mathbf{81.85\%}$$

4. Determine the parameters of the sound wave if the car is not moving.

$$v_{SND} = f_s\lambda$$

$$337.158 = (2000)\lambda$$

$$\lambda = 0.1686 \text{ m}$$

As the car approaches the observer, v_s is positive. Now, compute the observed wavelength λ'.

$$\lambda' = \left(\lambda - \frac{v_s}{f_s}\right)$$

$$= \left(0.1686 - \frac{22.10}{2000}\right)$$

$$= 0.1576 \text{ m} \xrightarrow{\text{SD}} \mathbf{0.2\ m}$$

5. (a) Determine the whistle's wavelength.

$$v_{SND} = f_s\lambda$$

$$345 = (2415)\lambda$$

$$\lambda = 0.1429 \text{ m}$$

As Curt approaches the whistle, v_{OB} is positive. Therefore, the speed of the whistle's sound relative to Curt is

$$v_{SND} + v_{OB} = 345 + 8.73 = 353.73 \text{ m/s}$$

Now, compute the observed frequency f''.

$$v_{SND} + v_{OB} = f''\lambda$$

$$353.73 = f''(0.1429)$$

$$f'' = 2475.37 \text{ Hz} \xrightarrow{\text{SD}} \mathbf{2480\ Hz}$$

(b) As Curt moves away from the whistle, v_{OB} is negative. Therefore, the speed of the whistle's sound relative to Curt is

$$v_{SND} + v_{OB} = 345 - 8.73 = 336.27 \text{ m/s}$$

Now, compute the observed frequency f''.

$$v_{SND} + v_{OB} = f''\lambda$$

$$336.27 = f''(0.1429)$$

$$f'' = 2353.18 \text{ Hz} \xrightarrow{\text{SD}} \mathbf{2350\ Hz}$$

6. (a) $f = \frac{1}{T} = \frac{1}{0.35 \text{ s}} = 2.857143 \text{ Hz} \xrightarrow{\text{SD}} 2.9 \text{ Hz}$

The maximum displacement is 2.0 m, and the frequency is 2.9 Hz.

$x = A\cos 2\pi ft$

$\mathbf{x = 2.0\cos 2\pi(2.9)t}$ **meters**

(b) $x = 2.0\cos 2\pi ft$

$x = 2.0\cos 2\pi(2.857143)(1.5)$

To evaluate this equation, make sure your calculator is in the radian (RAD) mode.

$$x = -0.445 \text{ m} \xrightarrow{\text{SD}} \mathbf{-0.45\ m}$$

7. The coefficient of t is ω, which is $2\pi f$.

$$2\pi f = \frac{\pi}{2}$$

$$f = \frac{1}{4} \text{ Hz}$$

Now find the wavelength.

$$v = f\lambda$$

$$45 = \left(\frac{1}{4}\right)\lambda$$

$$\lambda = \mathbf{180\ m}$$

8. $$f = \frac{1}{2\pi}\frac{\sqrt{g}}{\sqrt{L}}$$

$$0.75 = \frac{1}{2\pi}\frac{\sqrt{9.81}}{\sqrt{L}}$$

$$\sqrt{L} = 0.6647$$

$$L = 0.4418 \text{ m} \xrightarrow{\text{SD}} \mathbf{0.44\ m}$$

9. Refer to Section 70.C.

10. (a) The image is **approximately 9.3 cm behind the lens, it is upright, and the height of the image is approximately 6.2 cm**.

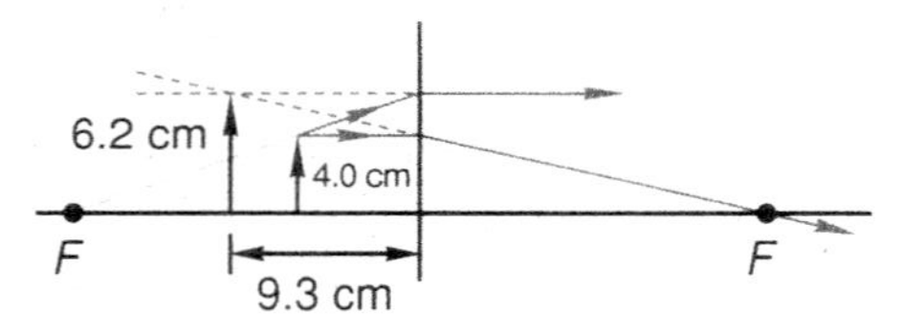

(b) $M = \frac{H_I}{H_O} = \frac{6.2 \text{ cm}}{4.0 \text{ cm}} = \mathbf{1.6}$

11. Begin by finding the time constant RC.
$RC = (5500\ \Omega)(3.5 \times 10^{-3}\text{ F}) = 19.25\text{ s}$

Now calculate the voltage when $t = 12$ s.

$$V_C = V_0 - V_0 e^{-t/RC}$$
$$= 12 - 12e^{-12/19.25}$$
$$= 12 - 12e^{-0.623}$$
$$= 5.564\text{ V}$$

Thus, the charge on the capacitor is

$$Q = CV = (3.5 \times 10^{-3}\text{ F})(5.564\text{ V})$$
$$= 1.947 \times 10^{-2}\text{ C} \xrightarrow{\text{SD}} \mathbf{1.9 \times 10^{-2}\ C}$$

12. (a) $PE_d = mgh = (1.4)(9.81)(12) = 164.808\text{ J}$
$PE_u = mgh = (1.4)(9.81)(9.0) = 123.606\text{ J}$

$$\Delta PE = PE_d - PE_u = 164.808\text{ J} - 123.606\text{ J}$$
$$= 41.202\text{ J} \xrightarrow{\text{SD}} \mathbf{41\ J}$$

(b) $KE = PE_u$

$$\frac{1}{2}mv_u^2 = 123.606$$
$$\frac{1}{2}(1.4)v_u^2 = 123.606$$
$$v_u = 13.29\ \frac{\text{m}}{\text{s}} \xrightarrow{\text{SD}} \mathbf{13\ \frac{m}{s}}$$

13. Begin by writing a $\sum F = ma$ equation for the block.

$$\sum F = ma$$
$$mg - T = ma$$
$$m(9.81) - T = m(2.94)$$
$$T = 6.87m \qquad \text{(a)}$$

Next, write a $\sum \tau = I\alpha$ equation for the cylinder.

$$\sum \tau = I\alpha$$
$$0.250T = \left(\frac{1}{2}mr^2\right)\alpha$$
$$0.250T = \left(\frac{1}{2}(3.20)(0.250)^2\right)\alpha$$
$$T = 0.4\alpha \qquad \text{(b)}$$

Now note that α is equal to $\frac{a}{0.250}$. Substitute into (b) and get:

(b) $T = 0.4\left(\frac{a}{0.250}\right) = 0.4\left(\frac{2.94}{0.250}\right) = 4.704$

Substitute this value for T into (a) to find the mass.
(a) $(4.704) = 6.87m$

$$m = 0.6847\text{ kg} \xrightarrow{\text{SD}} \mathbf{0.685\ kg}$$

14. Begin by converting rev/s to rad/s.

$$0.75\ \frac{\cancel{\text{rev}}}{\text{s}} \times \frac{2\pi\text{ rad}}{1\ \cancel{\text{rev}}} = 4.712\ \frac{\text{rad}}{\text{s}}$$

Next, equate the horizontal forces to find T.

$$T \sin\theta = mr\omega^2$$
$$T \cancel{\sin\theta} = m(1.27 \cancel{\sin\theta})\omega^2$$
$$T = (1.5)(1.27)(4.712)^2$$
$$T = 42.30\text{ N}$$

Now equate the vertical forces to find θ.

$$T\cos\theta = mg$$
$$(42.30)\cos\theta = (1.5)(9.81)$$
$$\theta = \mathbf{69.64°}$$

15. Begin by finding the equivalent resistance of the two 5-Ω series resistors.

$R_E = 5\ \Omega + 5\ \Omega = 10\ \Omega$

Use this resistance to find the voltage drop across the 10-Ω resistor.

$V_2 = I_2R = (2\text{ A})(10\ \Omega) = 20\text{ V}$

Next, find the voltage drop across the 5-Ω resistor.

$V_1 = I_1R = (6\text{ A})(5\ \Omega) = 30\text{ V}$

The total voltage V_x is equal to the sum of the voltage drop across the 5-Ω resistor and the voltage drop across the 10-Ω resistor.

$V_x = V_1 + V_2 = 30\text{ V} + 20\text{ V} = \mathbf{50\text{ V}}$

16. Begin by finding the current I_2 through the 12-Ω resistor.

$$I_2 = \frac{V}{R_2} = \frac{25\text{ V}}{12\ \Omega} = 2.083\text{ A}$$

Next, find the current I_3 through the 3.4-Ω resistor.

$$I_3 = \frac{V}{R_3} = \frac{25\text{ V}}{3.4\ \Omega} = 7.353\text{ A}$$

Use KCL to find I_1.

$$\begin{aligned} I_1 &= I_2 + I_3 \\ &= 2.083\text{ A} + 7.353\text{ A} \\ &= 9.436\text{ A} \xrightarrow{\text{SD}} \mathbf{9.4\text{ A}} \end{aligned}$$

17. Use the y-displacement equation to find the time.

$$\begin{aligned} \Delta y &= v_{y0}t + \frac{1}{2}a_yt^2 \\ -525 &= (0) + \frac{1}{2}(-9.81)t^2 \\ 525 &= 4.905t^2 \\ t &= 10.346\text{ s} \end{aligned}$$

Use this time in the x-position equation to find the distance.

$$\begin{aligned} x &= x_0 + v_{x0}t + \frac{1}{2}a_xt^2 \\ &= (0) + (225)(10.346) + (0) \\ &= 2327.85\text{ m} \xrightarrow{\text{SD}} \mathbf{2.33 \times 10^3\text{ m}} \end{aligned}$$

18. Begin by finding the current I_1 through the 12-Ω resistor.

$$\begin{aligned} P &= I_1^2R \\ 48 &= I_1^2(12) \\ I_1 &= 2\text{ A} \end{aligned}$$

Use this current to find the voltage drop across the 12-Ω resistor.

$V_1 = I_1R = (2\text{ A})(12\ \Omega) = 24\text{ V}$

Use this voltage to find the current I_2 through the 24-Ω resistor.

$$I_2 = \frac{V}{R} = \frac{24\text{ V}}{24\ \Omega} = 1\text{ A}$$

Use KCL to find the current I_3 through the 10-Ω resistor.

$I_3 = I_2 + I_1 = 1\text{ A} + 2\text{ A} = 3\text{ A}$

Use this current to find the voltage drop across the 10-Ω resistor.

$V_3 = I_3R = (3\text{ A})(10\ \Omega) = 30\text{ V}$

The total voltage V_x is equal to the sum of the voltage drop across the 12-Ω resistor and the voltage drop across the 10-Ω resistor.

$V_x = V_1 + V_3 = 24\text{ V} + 30\text{ V} = \mathbf{54\text{ V}}$

19. (a) Find the mass of the water displaced.

$$m_w = 1025\ \frac{\text{kg}}{\cancel{\text{m}^3}} \times 0.515\ \cancel{\text{m}^3} = 527.875\text{ kg}$$

Now find the buoyancy force.

$$F_B = m_wg = 527.875\ \cancel{\text{kg}} \times 9.81\ \frac{\text{N}}{\cancel{\text{kg}}} = 5178.45\text{ N}$$

Thus the force needed to lift the chest is

$$\begin{aligned} F_{\text{Needed}} &= mg - F_B \\ &= (685.0)(9.81) - 5178.45 \\ &= 1541.40\text{ N} \xrightarrow{\text{SD}} \mathbf{1540\text{ N}} \end{aligned}$$

(b) **No,** because the weight mg is $(685.0)(9.81) = 6720$ N, which is greater than 3000 N, the maximum lift force of Jacques.

20. $n = \dfrac{c}{v} = \dfrac{c}{0.83c} = 1.205 \xrightarrow{\text{SD}} \mathbf{1.2}$

Problem Set 75

1.
$$\frac{1}{f} = \frac{1}{D_O} + \frac{1}{D_I}$$
$$\frac{1}{-3.0} = \frac{1}{5.0} + \frac{1}{D_I}$$
$$D_I = -1.875 \text{ cm} \xrightarrow{\text{SD}} \mathbf{-1.9\ cm}$$

$$\frac{H_I}{H_O} = \frac{-D_I}{D_O}$$
$$\frac{H_I}{1.0} = \frac{-(-1.875)}{5.0}$$
$$H_I = 0.375 \text{ cm} \xrightarrow{\text{SD}} \mathbf{0.38\ cm}$$

$$M = \frac{H_I}{H_O} = \frac{0.375}{1.0} = 0.375 \xrightarrow{\text{SD}} \mathbf{0.38}$$

2. Begin by converting 2.4 cm to millimeters.

$$2.4 \cancel{\text{cm}} \times \frac{10 \text{ mm}}{1 \cancel{\text{cm}}} = 24 \text{ mm}$$

Now use the mirror-thin lens equation to find the image distance and image height.

$$\frac{1}{f} = \frac{1}{D_O} + \frac{1}{D_I}$$
$$\frac{1}{12} = \frac{1}{24} + \frac{1}{D_I}$$
$$D_I = \mathbf{24\ mm}$$

$$\frac{H_I}{H_O} = \frac{-D_I}{D_O}$$
$$\frac{H_I}{60} = \frac{-24}{24}$$
$$H_I = \mathbf{-60\ mm}$$

3. Begin by converting the temperatures to kelvins.
$T_H = 1280°\text{C} + 273 = 1553 \text{ K}$
$T_C = 154°\text{C} + 273 = 427 \text{ K}$

Thus, the maximum possible efficiency is

$$\text{eff}_{\text{max}} = 1 - \frac{T_C}{T_H}$$
$$= 1 - \frac{427}{1553}$$
$$= 0.7250$$

Multiply this by 100% and get:

$$\text{eff}_{\text{max}} = 0.7250 \times 100\% = 72.50\% \xrightarrow{\text{SD}} \mathbf{72.5\%}$$

4. Begin by converting the temperature to kelvins.
$T_C = 232°\text{C} + 273 = 505 \text{ K}$

Thus, the temperature of the steam is

$$\text{eff}_{\text{max}} = 1 - \frac{T_C}{T_H}$$
$$0.823 = 1 - \frac{505}{T_H}$$
$$T_H = 2853.11 \text{ K} \xrightarrow{\text{SD}} \mathbf{2850\ K = 2580°C}$$

5. Determine the parameters of the sound wave if the speedboat is not moving.

$$v_{\text{SND}} = f_s\lambda$$
$$345 = (1440)\lambda$$
$$\lambda = 0.2396 \text{ m}$$

As the speedboat moves away from the observer, v_s is negative. Now, compute the observed wavelength λ'.

$$\lambda' = \left(\lambda - \frac{v_s}{f_s}\right)$$
$$= \left(0.2396 - \frac{(-36.2)}{1440}\right)$$
$$= 0.2647 \text{ m} \xrightarrow{\text{SD}} \mathbf{0.265\ m}$$

6. Begin by converting km/hr to m/s.

$$80.3\ \frac{\text{km}}{\text{hr}} \times \frac{1000\ \text{m}}{1\ \text{km}} \times \frac{1\ \text{hr}}{3600\ \text{s}} = 22.31\ \frac{\text{m}}{\text{s}}$$

Determine the parameters of the sound wave if the ambulance is not moving.

$$v_{SND} = f_s\lambda$$
$$355 = (2520)\lambda$$
$$\lambda = 0.1409\ \text{m}$$

As the ambulance approaches Jonathan, v_s is positive. Now, compute the observed frequency f'.

$$v_{SND} = f'\left(\lambda - \frac{v_s}{f_s}\right)$$
$$355 = f'\left(0.1409 - \frac{22.31}{2520}\right)$$
$$f' = 2.68844 \times 10^3\ \text{Hz} \xrightarrow{\text{SD}} \mathbf{2.69 \times 10^3\ Hz}$$

7. $f = \frac{3.06\ \text{cycles}}{\text{second}} = 3.06\ \text{Hz}$

The maximum displacement is 0.60 m, and the frequency is 3.06 Hz.

$x = A \cos 2\pi ft$

$x = \mathbf{0.60 \cos 2\pi(3.06)t}$ **meters**

8. $T = 2\pi\frac{\sqrt{L}}{\sqrt{g}} = 2\pi\frac{\sqrt{0.54}}{\sqrt{9.81}} = 1.474\ \text{s} \xrightarrow{\text{SD}} \mathbf{1.5\ s}$

9. The section nearest to the positively charged object possesses a net negative charge; the other section possesses a net positive charge.

10. (a) The image is **approximately 3.4 cm behind the lens, it is upright, and the height of the image is approximately 1.7 cm.**

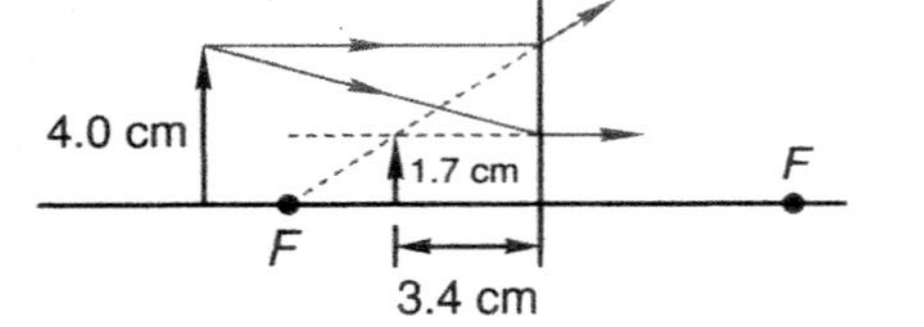

(b) $M = \frac{H_I}{H_O} = \frac{1.7}{4.0} = \mathbf{0.43}$

(c) The image is **virtual** because it is upright and behind the lens.

11. $Q = \Delta U + W$

$= 0 + (-3.4 \times 10^4\ \text{J})$

$= \mathbf{-3.4 \times 10^4\ J}$

12. Begin by finding the moment of inertia of the pulley and noting the relationship between a and α.

$$I = \frac{1}{2}mr^2 = \frac{1}{2}(5.4\ \text{kg})(0.57\ \text{m})^2 = 0.877\ \text{kg}\cdot\text{m}^2$$

$$a = r\alpha \longrightarrow \alpha = \frac{a}{0.57}$$

Next, write a $\Sigma F_x = ma_x$ equation for the 17.3-kg block. Choose up the plane as the positive direction for motion.

$$\Sigma F_x = ma_x$$
$$T_1 - mg \sin\theta = ma$$
$$T_1 - (17.3)(9.81) \sin 20° = 17.3a$$
$$T_1 = 58.045 + 17.3a \qquad \text{(a)}$$

Now, write a $\Sigma F_y = ma_y$ equation for the 24.7-kg block.

$$\Sigma F_y = ma_y$$
$$mg - T_2 = ma$$
$$(24.7)(9.81) - T_2 = 24.7a$$
$$T_2 = 242.307 - 24.7a \qquad \text{(b)}$$

Next, write a $\Sigma\tau = I\alpha$ equation for the pulley.

$$\Sigma\tau = I\alpha$$
$$0.57T_2 - 0.57T_1 = (0.877)\left(\frac{a}{0.57}\right)$$
$$0.57T_2 - 0.57T_1 = 1.539a$$
$$T_2 - T_1 = 2.7a \qquad \text{(c)}$$

Substitute (a) and (b) into (c) to find the acceleration.

(c) $(242.307 - 24.7a) - (58.045 + 17.3a) = 2.7a$

$$184.26 = 44.7a$$
$$a = 4.122\ \frac{\text{m}}{\text{s}^2}$$
$$\xrightarrow{\text{SD}} \mathbf{4.1\ \frac{m}{s^2}}\ \textbf{up the plane}$$

13.

$$n_1 \sin\theta_1 = n_2 \sin\theta_2$$
$$2.42 \sin\theta_c = 1.33 \sin 90°$$
$$\theta_c = \mathbf{33.34°}$$

14.

$$KE = \frac{1}{2}I\omega^2$$
$$= \frac{1}{2}\left(\frac{1}{2}mr^2\right)\omega^2$$
$$= \frac{1}{2}\left(\frac{1}{2}(20.405)(0.2521)^2\right)(30)^2$$
$$= 291.79 \text{ J} \xrightarrow{\text{SD}} \mathbf{300 \ J}$$

15. Begin by finding v_A and P_B.

$v_A = 2v_B;\ P_B = 3P_A$

Now use Bernoulli's equation to find P_A.

$$P_A + \frac{1}{2}\rho v_A^2 = P_B + \frac{1}{2}\rho v_B^2$$
$$P_A + \frac{1}{2}\rho(2v_B)^2 = (3P_A) + \frac{1}{2}\rho v_B^2$$
$$P_A + \frac{1}{2}\rho(4v_B^2) = 3P_A + \frac{1}{2}\rho v_B^2$$
$$P_A + 2\rho v_B^2 = 3P_A + \frac{1}{2}\rho v_B^2$$
$$2\rho v_B^2 - \frac{1}{2}\rho v_B^2 = 3P_A - P_A$$
$$\frac{3}{2}\rho v_B^2 = 2P_A$$
$$P_A = \mathbf{\frac{3}{4}\rho v_B^2}$$

16.

$$Q = CV$$
$$(5.37 \times 10^{-12}\text{ C}) = (20.4 \times 10^{-6}\text{ F})V$$
$$V = 2.632 \times 10^{-7}\text{ V} \xrightarrow{\text{SD}} \mathbf{2.63 \times 10^{-7}\ V}$$

17. The image is **approximately 12 cm in front of the mirror, it is inverted, and the height of the image is approximately 3 cm**.

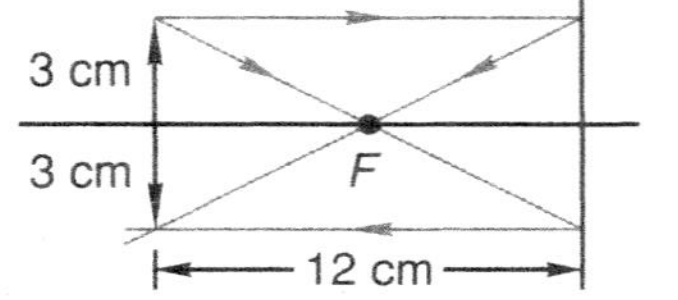

18. Begin by finding the equivalent resistance of the two parallel resistors.

$$R_E = \frac{(750)(150)}{750 + 150} = 125\ \Omega$$

Now, combine this with the 875-Ω resistor to find the equivalent resistance of the circuit.

$$R_E = (125\ \Omega) + 875\ \Omega = 1000\ \Omega$$

Next, find the time constant RC.

$$RC = (1000\ \Omega)(3000 \times 10^{-6}\text{ F}) = \mathbf{3\ s}$$

Sketch the voltage across the capacitor as a function of time.

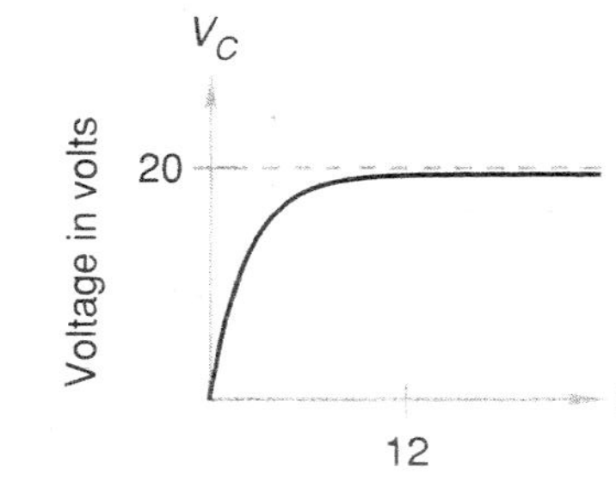

19. (a) $\Sigma F_y = 0;\ 300\text{ N} + 600\text{ N} - F_A = 0$

(b) $\Sigma M = 0;\ F_A(x) - 600\text{ N}(12\text{ m}) = 0$

Solve (a) for F_A and get:

(a) $F_A = 300\text{ N} + 600\text{ N} = \mathbf{900\ N}$

Substitute F_A into (b) to find x.

(b) $(900\text{ N})(x) - 7200\text{ N·m} = 0$

$$x = \mathbf{8\ m}$$

20. (a) Begin by finding the frequency.

$$f = \frac{1}{T} = \frac{1}{556 \times 10^{-9}\ \text{s}} = 1.7986 \times 10^{6}\ \text{Hz}$$

Now find the wavelength.

$$v = f\lambda$$
$$(0.95)(3.00 \times 10^{8}) = (1.7986 \times 10^{6})\lambda$$
$$\lambda = 1.585 \times 10^{2}\ \text{m} \xrightarrow{\text{SD}} \mathbf{1.6 \times 10^{2}\ m}$$

(b) $$n = \frac{c}{v} = \frac{c}{0.95c} = 1.053 \xrightarrow{\text{SD}} \mathbf{1.1}$$

Problem Set 76

1. (a) $$q_A = 1.275 \times 10^{8}\ \cancel{\text{electrons}} \times \frac{1.60 \times 10^{-19}\ \text{C}}{1\ \cancel{\text{electron}}} = \mathbf{2.04 \times 10^{-11}\ C}$$

$$q_B = 5.85 \times 10^{7}\ \cancel{\text{electrons}} \times \frac{1.60 \times 10^{-19}\ \text{C}}{1\ \cancel{\text{electron}}} = \mathbf{9.36 \times 10^{-12}\ C}$$

(b) $$F = \frac{kq_1q_2}{r^2}$$
$$= \frac{(9.0 \times 10^{9})(2.04 \times 10^{-11})(9.36 \times 10^{-12})}{(5.25 \times 10^{-3})^2}$$
$$= 6.235 \times 10^{-8}\ \text{N} \xrightarrow{\text{SD}} \mathbf{6.2 \times 10^{-8}\ N}$$

2. Begin by finding the weight of the sphere and drawing a free-body diagram of the sphere on the left.

$$w = mg$$
$$= 0.256\ \cancel{\text{kg}} \times 9.81\ \frac{\text{N}}{\cancel{\text{kg}}}$$
$$= 2.511\ \text{N}$$

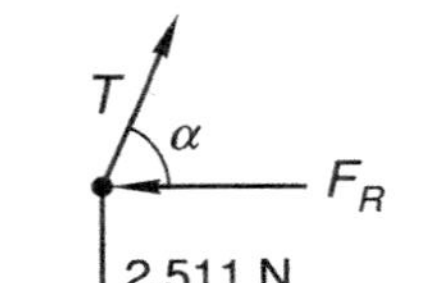

In this case, $\alpha = 90° - \theta/2$. The weight of the sphere equals the vertical component of the tension.

$$w = T\sin\alpha$$
$$2.511 = T\sin\alpha$$
$$T = \frac{2.511}{\sin\alpha}$$

The horizontal component of the tension equals the force of repulsion F_R.

$$F_R = T\cos\alpha$$
$$= \left(\frac{2.511}{\sin\alpha}\right)\cos\alpha$$
$$= \frac{2.511}{\tan\alpha}$$

Now, we can use Coulomb's law to find α.

$$F_R = \frac{kq_1q_2}{r^2}$$
$$\frac{2.511}{\tan\alpha} = \frac{(9.0 \times 10^{9})(1.57 \times 10^{-7})(1.57 \times 10^{-7})}{(0.0327)^2}$$
$$\frac{2.511}{\tan\alpha} = 0.20747$$
$$\alpha = 85.2767°$$

Since $\alpha = 90° - \theta/2$ we get: $85.2767° = 90° - \frac{\theta}{2}$

$$\theta = \mathbf{9.45°}$$

3. $$\frac{1}{f} = \frac{1}{D_O} + \frac{1}{D_I}$$
$$\frac{1}{45} = \frac{1}{15} + \frac{1}{D_I}$$
$$D_I = -22.5\ \text{mm} \xrightarrow{\text{SD}} \mathbf{-23\ mm}$$

$$\frac{H_I}{H_O} = \frac{-D_I}{D_O}$$
$$\frac{H_I}{110} = \frac{-(-22.5)}{15}$$
$$H_I = 165\ \text{mm} \xrightarrow{\text{SD}} \mathbf{170\ mm}$$

$$M = \frac{H_I}{H_O} = \frac{165}{110} = \mathbf{1.5}$$

4.
$$\frac{1}{f} = \frac{1}{D_O} + \frac{1}{D_I}$$
$$\frac{1}{-2.0} = \frac{1}{3.7} + \frac{1}{D_I}$$
$$D_I = -1.298 \text{ cm} \xrightarrow{\text{SD}} \mathbf{-1.3\ cm}$$

$$\frac{H_I}{H_O} = \frac{-D_I}{D_O}$$
$$\frac{H_I}{4.0} = \frac{-(-1.298)}{3.7}$$
$$H_I = 1.403 \text{ cm} \xrightarrow{\text{SD}} \mathbf{1.4\ cm}$$

5. Begin by converting the temperature to kelvins.

$T_H = 2700°\text{C} + 273 = 2973 \text{ K}$

Thus, the cold temperature is
$$\text{eff}_{max} = 1 - \frac{T_C}{T_H}$$
$$0.78 = 1 - \frac{T_C}{2973}$$
$$0.22 = \frac{T_C}{2973}$$
$$T_C = 654.06 \text{ K} \xrightarrow{\text{SD}} \mathbf{650\ K = 380°C}$$

6. Begin by converting the temperatures to kelvins.

$T_H = 3600°\text{C} + 273 = 3873 \text{ K}$

$T_C = 410°\text{C} + 273 = 683 \text{ K}$

Thus, the maximum possible efficiency is
$$\text{eff}_{max} = 1 - \frac{T_C}{T_H}$$
$$= 1 - \frac{683}{3873}$$
$$= 0.8237$$

Multiply this by 100% and get:
$$\text{eff}_{max} = 0.8237 \times 100\% = 82.37\% \xrightarrow{\text{SD}} \mathbf{82\%}$$

7. Determine the parameters of the sound wave if the train is not moving.
$$v_{\text{SND}} = f_s\lambda$$
$$345 = (650)\lambda$$
$$\lambda = 0.5308 \text{ m}$$

As the train moves toward the observer, v_s is positive. Now, compute the observed wavelength λ'.
$$\lambda' = \left(\lambda - \frac{v_s}{f_s}\right)$$
$$= \left(0.5308 - \frac{20.8}{650}\right)$$
$$= 0.4988 \text{ m} \xrightarrow{\text{SD}} \mathbf{0.50\ m}$$

8. Determine the fire alarm's wavelength.
$$v_{\text{SND}} = f_s\lambda$$
$$331 = (1175)\lambda$$
$$\lambda = 0.2817 \text{ m}$$

As the student runs away from the fire alarm, v_{OB} is negative. Therefore, the speed of the fire alarm's sound relative to the student is
$$v_{\text{SND}} + v_{\text{OB}} = 331 - 5.10 = 325.9 \text{ m/s}$$

Now, compute the observed frequency f''.
$$v_{\text{SND}} + v_{\text{OB}} = f''\lambda$$
$$325.9 = f''(0.2817)$$
$$f'' = 1156.9 \text{ Hz} \xrightarrow{\text{SD}} \mathbf{1160\ Hz}$$

9. (a) The amplitude is the maximum value of the function.

Amplitude = **10.75 m**

(b) The coefficient of t is ω, which equals $2\pi f$. The frequency is $1/T$ so ω also equals $2\pi/T$.
$$\frac{2\pi}{T} = \frac{2\pi}{3}$$
$$T = \mathbf{3\ s}$$

(c) The frequency is the reciprocal of the period.
$$f = \frac{1}{T} = \frac{1}{3 \text{ s}} = \mathbf{\frac{1}{3}\ Hz}$$

10. $T = 2\pi \frac{\sqrt{L}}{\sqrt{g}}$

$7.2 = 2\pi \frac{\sqrt{L}}{\sqrt{9.81}}$

$3.589 = \sqrt{L}$

$L = 12.88 \text{ m} \xrightarrow{SD} \mathbf{13\ m}$

11. (a) The image is **approximately 4.3 cm in front of the lens, it is inverted, and the height of the image is approximately 1.3 cm.**

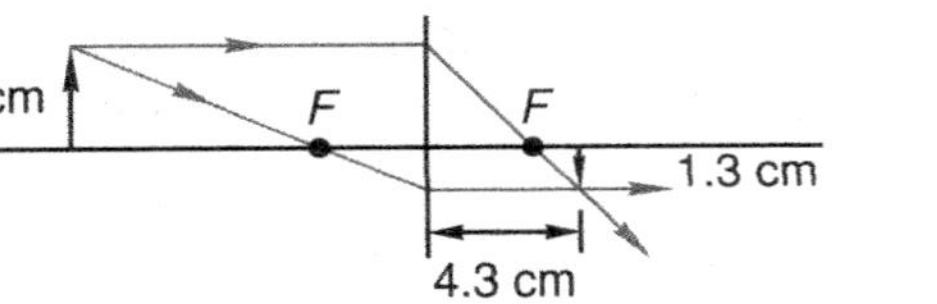

(b) $M = \frac{H_I}{H_O} = \frac{1.3}{3.0} = \mathbf{0.43}$

12. $Q = \Delta U + W$

$1270 \text{ J} = \Delta U + 630 \text{ J}$

$\Delta U = \mathbf{640\ J}$

13. Begin by writing a $\sum F = ma$ equation for the mass.

$\sum F = ma$

$mg - T = ma$

$(12.009)(9.81) - T = 12.009a$

$T = 117.8 - 12.009a$ (a)

Next, write a $\sum \tau = I\alpha$ equation for the cylinder.

$\sum \tau = I\alpha$

$0.70T = \left(\frac{1}{2} mr^2\right)\alpha$

$0.70T = \left(\frac{1}{2}(2.560)(0.70)^2\right)\alpha$

$T = 0.896\alpha$ (b)

Now note that α is equal to $\frac{a}{0.70}$. Substitute into (b) and get:

(b) $T = 0.896\left(\frac{a}{0.70}\right) = 1.28a$

Substitute this value for T into (a) to find the acceleration.

(a) $(1.28a) = 117.8 - 12.009a$

$13.289a = 117.8$

$a = 8.864 \frac{\text{m}}{\text{s}^2} \xrightarrow{SD} \mathbf{9\ \frac{m}{s^2}}$

14. Begin by finding the time constant RC.

$RC = (15{,}200\ \Omega)(5.25 \times 10^{-6}\text{ F}) = 7.98 \times 10^{-2}\text{ s}$

Now calculate the voltage when $t = 0.399$ s.

$V_C = V_0 - V_0 e^{-t/RC}$

$= 12.5 - 12.5e^{-0.399/7.98 \times 10^{-2}}$

$= 12.5 - 12.5e^{-5}$

$= 12.42 \text{ V} \xrightarrow{SD} \mathbf{12.4\ V}$

15. (a) $T = \frac{33.0 \text{ s}}{8.25 \text{ oscillations}} = \mathbf{4.00\ s}$

(b) Begin by finding the spring constant.

$T = 2\pi \frac{\sqrt{m}}{\sqrt{k}}$

$4.00 = 2\pi \frac{\sqrt{125}}{\sqrt{k}}$

$\sqrt{k} = 17.562$

$k = 308.42 \frac{\text{N}}{\text{m}}$

Now compute the potential energy.

$PE = \frac{1}{2}kx^2$

$= \frac{1}{2}(308.42)(0.795)^2$

$= 97.46 \text{ J} \xrightarrow{SD} \mathbf{97.5\ J}$

16. $\Delta A = (2\alpha)A_0\Delta T$

$= (2)(2.4 \times 10^{-5})[\pi(0.094)^2](150 - 27)$

$= 1.639 \times 10^{-4} \text{ m}^2 \xrightarrow{SD} \mathbf{1.6 \times 10^{-4}\ m^2 = 1.6\ cm^2}$

17. The image is **approximately 12.0 cm behind the mirror, it is upright, and the height of the image is approximately 6.00 cm.**

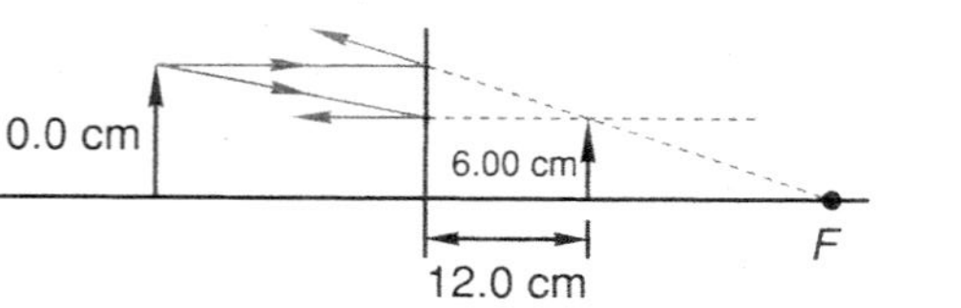

18. Begin by finding the equivalent resistance of the 43-Ω and 32-Ω resistors.
$R_E = 43\ \Omega + 32\ \Omega = 75\ \Omega$
Next, compute the voltage drop across this resistance.
$V_1 = I_1 R = (0.20\ \text{A})(75\ \Omega) = 15\ \text{V}$
This must equal the voltage drop across the 25-Ω and R_1 resistors. Use this voltage to find R_1.
$15 = I_2(R_{25,R_1})$

$15 = (0.18)(25 + R_1)$

$R_1 = 58.33\ \Omega \xrightarrow{\text{SD}}$ **58 Ω**

19. Begin by solving for the mass m_1.

$$v_1 = \frac{\sqrt{T}}{\sqrt{M_L}} = \frac{\sqrt{m_1 g}}{\sqrt{M_L}} \rightarrow m_1 = \frac{M_L v_1^2}{g}$$

Increasing the speed by a factor of 5 increases the mass by a factor of 25.

$$m_1 = \frac{M_L v_1^2}{g} \rightarrow 25m_1 = \frac{M_L(5v_1)^2}{g}$$

Therefore, $m_2 = \mathbf{25m_1}$.

20. Begin by converting the temperatures to kelvins.
$T_1 = 130 + 273 = 403\ \text{K}$
$T_2 = 13 + 273 = 286\ \text{K}$
Now use the ideal gas law and get:

$$\frac{P_1}{T_1} = \frac{P_2}{T_2}$$

$$\frac{3.6 \times 10^6\ \text{N/m}^2}{403\ \text{K}} = \frac{P_2}{286\ \text{K}}$$

$$P_2 = 2.55 \times 10^6\ \frac{\text{N}}{\text{m}^2} \xrightarrow{\text{SD}} \mathbf{2.6 \times 10^6\ \frac{N}{m^2}}$$

Problem Set 77

1. Begin by finding the equivalent capacitance of the two parallel capacitors.
$C_E = 20\ \mu\text{F} + 65\ \mu\text{F} = 85\ \mu\text{F}$

Next, find the time constant RC.
$RC = (5000\ \Omega)(85 \times 10^{-6}\ \text{F}) = 0.425\ \text{s}$

Now calculate the voltage when $t = 0.85$ s.

$$V_C = V_0 - V_0 e^{-t/RC}$$
$$= 40 - 40e^{-0.85/0.425}$$
$$= 40 - 40e^{-2}$$
$$= 34.59\ \text{V} \xrightarrow{\text{SD}} \mathbf{35\ V}$$

2. Begin by finding the equivalent capacitance of the two series capacitors.

$$C_E = \frac{(12)(24)}{12 + 24} = 8\ \mu\text{F}$$

Next, find the time constant RC.
$RC = (8000\ \Omega)(8 \times 10^{-6}\ \text{F}) = \mathbf{6.4 \times 10^{-2}\ s}$

Now find the initial current.

$$I_0 = \frac{V}{R} = \frac{14\ \text{V}}{8000\ \Omega} = 1.8 \times 10^{-3}\ \text{A}$$

Sketch the current as a function of time.

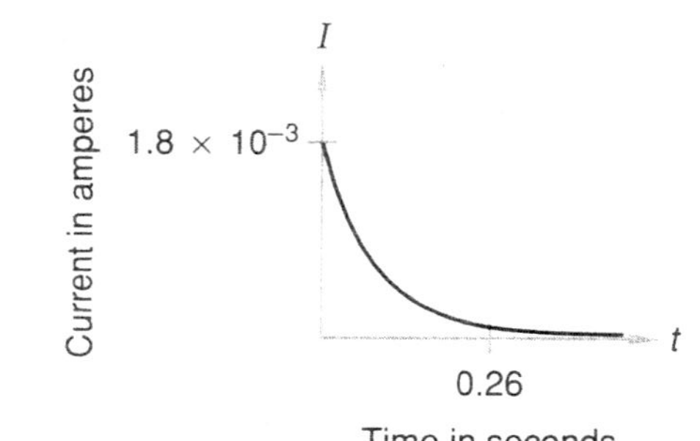

3. $F = \frac{kq_1q_2}{r^2}$

$= \frac{(9.0 \times 10^9)(1.60 \times 10^{-19})(1.60 \times 10^{-19})}{(0.50 \times 10^{-6})^2}$

$= 9.216 \times 10^{-16}\text{ N} \xrightarrow{\text{SD}}$ $\mathbf{9.2 \times 10^{-16}}$ **N**

The charges are like charges so the force is **repulsive.**

4. We need to find the forces at A caused by charge B and charge C and then add them vectorially.

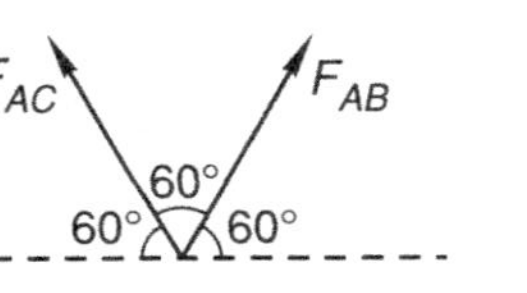

Use Coulomb's law to find the magnitude of the force exerted on A by charge B.

$F_{AB} = \frac{kq_Aq_B}{r^2}$

$= \frac{(9.0 \times 10^9)(4.6 \times 10^{-14})(4.6 \times 10^{-14})}{(0.018)^2}$

$= 5.878 \times 10^{-14}\text{ N}$

Use Coulomb's law to find the magnitude of the force exerted on A by charge C.

$F_{AC} = \frac{kq_Aq_C}{r^2}$

$= \frac{(9.0 \times 10^9)(4.6 \times 10^{-14})(4.6 \times 10^{-14})}{(0.018)^2}$

$= 5.878 \times 10^{-14}\text{ N}$

The vector components of F_{AB} are:

$F_{AB}\sin\theta$, F_{AB}, 60°, $F_{AB}\cos\theta$

$F_{AB}\cos\theta = (5.878 \times 10^{-14})\cos 60°$

$= 2.94 \times 10^{-14}\text{ N}$

$F_{AB}\sin\theta = (5.878 \times 10^{-14})\sin 60°$

$= 5.09 \times 10^{-14}\text{ N}$

The vector components of F_{AC} are:

F_{AC}, $F_{AC}\sin\theta$, 60°, $F_{AC}\cos\theta$

$F_{AC}\cos\theta = (5.878 \times 10^{-14})\cos 60°$

$= 2.94 \times 10^{-14}\text{ N}$

$F_{AC}\sin\theta = (5.878 \times 10^{-14})\sin 60°$

$= 5.09 \times 10^{-14}\text{ N}$

Thus, the sum of the horizontal and vertical components are:

$F_x = 2.94 \times 10^{-14}\text{ N} - 2.94 \times 10^{-14}\text{ N} = 0\text{ N}$

$F_y = 5.09 \times 10^{-14}\text{ N} + 5.09 \times 10^{-14}\text{ N} = 1.02 \times 10^{-13}\text{ N}$

So, now we have the horizontal and vertical components of F_A as

$1.02 \times 10^{-13}\text{ N}$ $\quad F_A = 1.02 \times 10^{-13}\angle 90°\text{ N} \xrightarrow{\text{SD}}$ $\mathbf{1.0 \times 10^{-13}\angle 90°}$ **N**

5. $\frac{1}{f} = \frac{1}{D_O} + \frac{1}{D_I}$

$\frac{1}{1.5} = \frac{1}{4.0} + \frac{1}{D_I}$

$D_I =$ **2.4 cm**

$\frac{H_I}{H_O} = \frac{-D_I}{D_O}$

$\frac{H_I}{10} = \frac{-2.4}{4.0}$

$H_I =$ **−6.0 cm**

6. $\frac{1}{f} = \frac{1}{D_O} + \frac{1}{D_I}$

$\frac{1}{-45.054} = \frac{1}{100} + \frac{1}{D_I}$

$D_I = -31.06\text{ mm} \xrightarrow{\text{SD}}$ **−30 mm**

$\frac{H_I}{H_O} = \frac{-D_I}{D_O}$

$\frac{H_I}{56.110} = \frac{-(-31.06)}{100}$

$H_I = 17.43\text{ mm} \xrightarrow{\text{SD}}$ **20 mm**

$M = \frac{H_I}{H_O} = \frac{17.43}{56.110} = 0.311 \xrightarrow{\text{SD}}$ **0.3**

7. $$\text{eff}_{max} = 1 - \frac{T_C}{T_H}$$
$$0.64 = 1 - \frac{T_C}{T_H}$$
$$\frac{T_H}{T_C} = 2.78 \xrightarrow{SD} \mathbf{2.8}$$

8. Begin by converting the temperatures to kelvins.
$T_H = 248°C + 273 = 521$ K
$T_C = 87°C + 273 = 360$ K
Thus, the maximum possible efficiency is
$$\text{eff}_{max} = 1 - \frac{T_C}{T_H} = 1 - \frac{360}{521} = 0.3090$$
$$\text{eff}_{max} = 0.3090 \times 100\% = 30.90\% \xrightarrow{SD} \mathbf{31\%}$$

9. (a) Determine the jackhammer's wavelength.
$$v_{SND} = f_s\lambda$$
$$331 = (2150)\lambda$$
$$\lambda = 0.1540 \text{ m}$$
As Kelly drives toward the jackhammer, v_{OB} is positive. Therefore, the speed of the jackhammer's sound relative to Kelly is
$$v_{SND} + v_{OB} = 331 + 25 = 356 \text{ m/s}$$
Now, compute the observed frequency f''.
$$v_{SND} + v_{OB} = f''\lambda$$
$$356 = f''(0.1540)$$
$$f'' = 2312 \text{ Hz} \xrightarrow{SD} \mathbf{2300 \text{ Hz}}$$
(b) As Kelly drives away from the jackhammer, v_{OB} is negative. Therefore, the speed of the jackhammer's sound relative to Kelly is
$$v_{SND} + v_{OB} = 331 - 25 = 306 \text{ m/s}$$
Now, compute the observed frequency f''.
$$v_{SND} + v_{OB} = f''\lambda$$
$$306 = f''(0.1540)$$
$$f'' = 1987 \text{ Hz} \xrightarrow{SD} \mathbf{2\bar{0}00 \text{ Hz}}$$

10. (a) The maximum displacement is 5.5 m, and the frequency is 1.91 Hz.
$$x = A\cos 2\pi ft$$
$$x = \mathbf{5.5 \cos 2\pi(1.91)t \text{ meters}}$$
(b) $$v = f\lambda = (1.91)(0.75) = 1.43 \frac{\text{m}}{\text{s}} \xrightarrow{SD} \mathbf{1.4 \frac{m}{s}}$$

11. $$T = 2\pi\frac{\sqrt{L}}{\sqrt{g}}$$
$$1.00 = 2\pi\frac{\sqrt{L}}{\sqrt{9.81}}$$
$$\sqrt{L} = 0.49849$$
$$L = 0.24849 \text{ m} \xrightarrow{SD} \mathbf{0.248 \text{ m}}$$

12. (a) The image is **approximately 2.9 cm behind the lens, it is upright, and the height of the image is approximately 2.3 cm**.

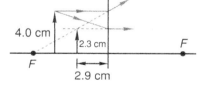

4.0 cm
2.3 cm
F
F
2.9 cm

(b) $$M = \frac{H_I}{H_O} = \frac{2.3}{4.0} = \mathbf{0.58}$$

13. Begin by finding the moment of inertia of the pulley and noting the relationship between a and α.
$$I = \frac{1}{2}mr^2 = \frac{1}{2}(4.5 \text{ kg})(0.518 \text{ m})^2 = 0.604 \text{ kg}\cdot\text{m}^2$$
$$a = r\alpha \rightarrow \alpha = \frac{a}{0.518}$$
Next, write a $\sum F_x = ma_x$ equation for the 25.3-kg block. Choose to the right as the positive direction for motion.
$$\sum F_x = ma_x$$
$$T_1 = ma$$
$$T_1 = 25.3a \qquad \text{(a)}$$

Now, write a $\sum F_y = ma_y$ equation for the 34.1-kg block.

$$\begin{aligned} \sum F_y &= ma_y \\ mg - T_2 &= ma \\ (34.1)(9.81) - T_2 &= 34.1a \\ T_2 &= 334.52 - 34.1a \qquad \text{(b)} \end{aligned}$$

Next, write a $\sum \tau = I\alpha$ equation for the pulley.

$$\begin{aligned} \sum \tau &= I\alpha \\ 0.518T_2 - 0.518T_1 &= (0.604)\left(\frac{a}{0.518}\right) \\ 0.518T_2 - 0.518T_1 &= 1.17 \\ T_2 - T_1 &= 2.26a \qquad \text{(c)} \end{aligned}$$

Substitute (a) and (b) into (c) to find the acceleration.

$$\begin{aligned} \text{(c)}\ (334.52 - 34.1a) - (25.3a) &= 2.26a \\ 61.66a &= 334.52 \\ a &= 5.43\ \frac{\text{m}}{\text{s}^2} \xrightarrow{\text{SD}} \mathbf{5.4\ \frac{m}{s^2}\ to\ the\ right} \end{aligned}$$

14. For the object to be in equilibrium, the buoyancy force must equal the weight of the object.

$$\begin{aligned} F_B &= w \\ (1000)(0.35)(9.81) &= mg \\ 3433.5 &= (\rho V)g \\ 3433.5 &= \rho(0.45)(9.81) \\ \rho &= 777.78\ \frac{\text{kg}}{\text{m}^3} \xrightarrow{\text{SD}} \mathbf{780\ \frac{kg}{m^3}} \end{aligned}$$

15. $\sum \tau = I\alpha$

$$\begin{aligned} 525 &= \left(\frac{1}{2}mr^2\right)\alpha \\ 525 &= \left(\frac{1}{2}(37.4)(0.985)^2\right)\alpha \\ \alpha &= 28.94\ \frac{\text{rad}}{\text{s}^2} \xrightarrow{\text{SD}} \mathbf{28.9\ \frac{rad}{s^2}} \end{aligned}$$

16. Begin by finding the centripetal force and the static friction force.

$$F_c = \frac{mv^2}{r} = \frac{(2300)v^2}{110} = 20.91v^2$$

$$F_s = mg\mu_s = (2300)(9.81)(0.73) = 16{,}470.99\ \text{N}$$

The required centripetal force must equal the static friction force.

$$\begin{aligned} F_c &= F_s \\ 20.91v^2 &= 16{,}470.99 \\ v &= 28.07\ \frac{\text{m}}{\text{s}} \xrightarrow{\text{SD}} \mathbf{28\ \frac{m}{s}} \end{aligned}$$

17. Begin by finding the equivalent resistance of the 40-Ω and 200-Ω resistors.

$R_E = 40\ \Omega + 200\ \Omega = 240\ \Omega$

Next, compute the voltage drop across this resistance.

$V_2 = I_2R = (0.50\ \text{A})(240\ \Omega) = 120\ \text{V}$

This must equal the voltage drop across the 80-Ω resistor. Use this voltage to find I_3.

$$I_3 = \frac{V}{R} = \frac{120\ \text{V}}{80\ \Omega} = 1.5\ \text{A}$$

Use KCL to find I_1.

$I_1 = I_2 + I_3 = 0.50\ \text{A} + 1.5\ \text{A} = 2.0\ \text{A}$

Use this current to find the voltage drop across the 120-Ω resistor.

$V_1 = I_1R = (2.0\ \text{A})(120\ \Omega) = 240\ \text{V}$

The total voltage V_x is equal to the sum of the voltage drop across the 240-Ω resistor and the voltage drop across the 120-Ω resistor.

$V_x = V_2 + V_1 = 120\ \text{V} + 240\ \text{V} = \mathbf{360\ V}$

18. (a) Total energy $= \frac{1}{2}kx^2 + \frac{1}{2}mv^2$

$$\begin{aligned} 785 &= \frac{1}{2}(4.25 \times 10^4)(0.187)^2 + \frac{1}{2}(4.05)v^2 \\ 785 &= 743.09 + 2.025v^2 \\ v &= 4.549\ \frac{\text{m}}{\text{s}} \xrightarrow{\text{SD}} \mathbf{4.55\ \frac{m}{s}} \end{aligned}$$

(b)

$$\begin{aligned} PE &= \frac{1}{2}kA^2 \\ 785 &= \frac{1}{2}(4.25 \times 10^4)A^2 \\ A &= 0.1922\ \text{m} \xrightarrow{\text{SD}} \mathbf{0.192\ m} \end{aligned}$$

19. Begin at the ground symbol, move clockwise, and sum the voltage changes to zero.

$$+20I_1 - 5.0 + 80I_1 - 12 + 40I_1 - 3.0 + 60I_1 - 10 = 0$$
$$200I_1 = 30$$
$$I_1 = \mathbf{0.15\ A}$$

20.

$$F = kx$$
$$(172)(9.81) = (227 \times 10^6)x$$
$$x = 7.433 \times 10^{-6}\text{ m} \xrightarrow{\text{SD}} \mathbf{7.43 \times 10^{-6}\ m}$$

$$W = \frac{1}{2}kx^2 = \frac{1}{2}(227 \times 10^6)(7.433 \times 10^{-6})^2$$
$$= 6.271 \times 10^{-3}\text{ J} \xrightarrow{\text{SD}} \mathbf{6.27 \times 10^{-3}\ J}$$

Problem Set 78

1.
$$v = f(2L)$$
$$= (633)(2)(0.473)$$
$$= 598.82\ \frac{\text{m}}{\text{s}} \xrightarrow{\text{SD}} \mathbf{599\ \frac{m}{s}}$$

2.
$$v = f(2L)$$
$$945 = (636)(2)L$$
$$L = 0.7429\text{ m} \xrightarrow{\text{SD}} \mathbf{0.743\ m}$$

3. (a) $V_1 + V_2 = 28.0$

(b) $C_1V_1 = C_2V_2$

Solve (b) for V_2 and substitute into (a) and get:

(a)
$$V_1 + \frac{C_1V_1}{C_2} = 28.0$$
$$V_1 + \frac{(12.0 \times 10^{-6})V_1}{(8.00 \times 10^{-6})} = 28.0$$
$$2.5V_1 = 28.0$$
$$V_1 = \mathbf{11.2\ V}$$

Substitute V_1 into (a) and solve for V_2.

(a) $(11.2) + V_2 = 28.0$
$$V_2 = \mathbf{16.8\ V}$$

4. Begin by finding the equivalent capacitance of the circuit.

$C_E = 43\ \mu\text{F} + 14\ \mu\text{F} + 15\ \mu\text{F} = 72\ \mu\text{F}$

Next, find the time constant RC.

$RC = (750\ \Omega)(72 \times 10^{-6}\text{ F}) = \mathbf{5.4 \times 10^{-2}\ s}$

Sketch the voltage across the capacitor as a function of time.

V_C

Voltage in volts

15

t

0.22

Time in seconds

5.
$$F = \frac{kq_1q_2}{r^2}$$
$$6.3 = \frac{(9.0 \times 10^9)(3.8 \times 10^{-14})(5.3 \times 10^{-14})}{r^2}$$
$$r = 1.696 \times 10^{-9}\text{ m} \xrightarrow{\text{SD}} \mathbf{1.7 \times 10^{-9}\ m}$$

6.
$$F = \frac{kq_1q_2}{r^2}$$
$$6.4 \times 10^{-8} = \frac{(9.0 \times 10^9)q^2}{(5.3 \times 10^{-4})^2}$$
$$q = 1.413 \times 10^{-12}\text{ C} \xrightarrow{\text{SD}} \mathbf{1.4 \times 10^{-12}\ C}$$

7.
$$\frac{1}{f} = \frac{1}{D_O} + \frac{1}{D_I}$$
$$\frac{1}{-4.0} = \frac{1}{10} + \frac{1}{D_I}$$
$$D_I = -2.857\text{ mm} \xrightarrow{\text{SD}} \mathbf{-2.9\ mm}$$

$$\frac{H_I}{H_O} = \frac{-D_I}{D_O}$$

$$\frac{H_I}{18} = \frac{-(-2.857)}{10}$$

$$H_I = 5.143 \text{ mm} \xrightarrow{\text{SD}} \mathbf{5.1\ mm}$$

8. Begin by converting the temperature to kelvins.
$T_H = 4177°\text{C} + 273 = 4450 \text{ K}$

Thus, the cold temperature is

$$\text{eff}_{max} = 1 - \frac{T_C}{T_H}$$

$$0.77 = 1 - \frac{T_C}{4450}$$

$$T_C = 1023.5 \text{ K} \xrightarrow{\text{SD}} \mathbf{1\bar{0}00\ K = 750°C}$$

9. (a) Determine the parameters of the sound wave if the airplane is not moving.

$$v_{SND} = f_s\lambda$$

$$345 = (1270)\lambda$$

$$\lambda = 0.2717 \text{ m}$$

As the airplane approaches, v_s is positive. Now, compute the observed wavelength λ'.

$$\lambda' = \left(\lambda - \frac{v_s}{f_s}\right)$$

$$= \left(0.2717 - \frac{135}{1270}\right)$$

$$= 0.1654 \text{ m} \xrightarrow{\text{SD}} \mathbf{0.165\ m}$$

(b) As the airplane moves away, v_s is negative. Now, compute the observed wavelength λ'.

$$\lambda' = \left(\lambda - \frac{v_s}{f_s}\right)$$

$$= \left(0.2717 - \frac{(-135)}{1270}\right)$$

$$= 0.3780 \text{ m} \xrightarrow{\text{SD}} \mathbf{0.378\ m}$$

10. The coefficient of t is ω, which is $2\pi f$.

$$2\pi f = \frac{3\pi}{4}$$

$$f = \frac{3}{8} \text{ Hz}$$

Now find the wavelength.

$$v = f\lambda$$

$$36 = \left(\frac{3}{8}\right)\lambda$$

$$\lambda = \mathbf{96\ m}$$

11. $T = 2\pi\frac{\sqrt{L}}{\sqrt{g}} = 2\pi\frac{\sqrt{2}}{\sqrt{9.81}} = 2.84 \text{ s} \xrightarrow{\text{SD}} \mathbf{3\ s}$

The frequency is the reciprocal of the period.

$$f = \frac{1}{T} = \frac{1}{2.84 \text{ s}} = 0.352 \text{ Hz} \xrightarrow{\text{SD}} \mathbf{0.4\ Hz}$$

12.

$$n_1 \sin\theta_1 = n_2 \sin\theta_2$$

$$1.58 \sin\theta_c = 1.54 \sin 90°$$

$$\theta_c = \mathbf{77.08°}$$

13. (a) Begin by finding v_1 and v_2.

$$v_1 = \frac{Q}{A_1} = \frac{0.347}{1.09 \times 10^{-1}} = 3.1835 \frac{\text{m}}{\text{s}}$$

$$v_2 = \frac{Q}{A_2} = \frac{0.347}{7.29 \times 10^{-2}} = 4.76 \frac{\text{m}}{\text{s}}$$

Next, compute how much greater v_2 is than v_1.

$$v_2 - v_1 = 4.76 \frac{\text{m}}{\text{s}} - 3.1835 \frac{\text{m}}{\text{s}} = 1.5765 \frac{\text{m}}{\text{s}} \xrightarrow{\text{SD}} \mathbf{1.58\ \frac{m}{s}}$$

(b)

$$P_1 + \frac{1}{2}\rho v_1^2 = P_2 + \frac{1}{2}\rho v_2^2$$

$$1.04 \times 10^5 + \frac{1}{2}(3250)(3.1835)^2 = P_2 + \frac{1}{2}(3250)(4.76)^2$$

$$1.04 \times 10^5 + 16{,}468.84 = P_2 + 36{,}818.60$$

$$P_2 = 8.365 \times 10^4 \text{ Pa}$$

$$\xrightarrow{\text{SD}} \mathbf{8.37 \times 10^4\ Pa}$$

14.
$$Q = CV$$
$$8.0 \times 10^{-4} = (27.4 \times 10^{-6})V$$
$$V = 29.197 \text{ V} \xrightarrow{\text{SD}} \mathbf{29\ V}$$

15. The image is **approximately 6.3 cm in front of the mirror, it is inverted, and the height of the image is approximately 2.9 cm**.

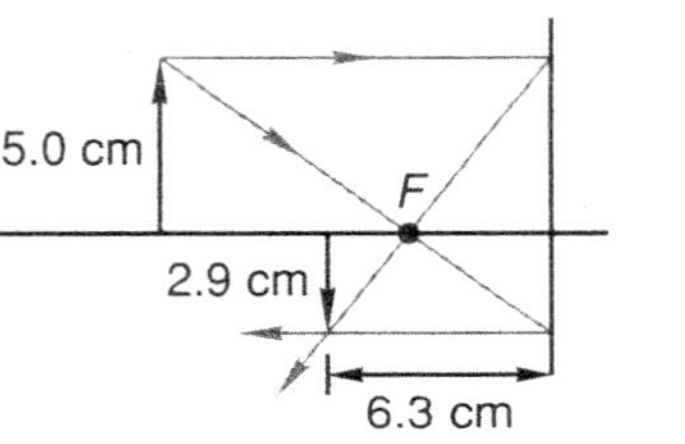

The image is **real** because it is inverted and in front of the mirror.

16.
$$W = FD\cos\theta$$
$$= (82 \text{ N})(9.8 \cos 56° \text{ m})$$
$$= 449.37 \text{ J} \xrightarrow{\text{SD}} \mathbf{450\ J}$$

17. Begin by denoting the signs on the resistors.

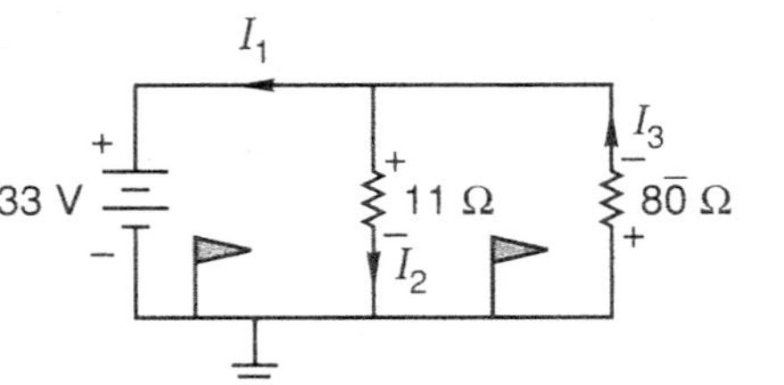

In the left-hand loop, begin at the starting flag, move clockwise, and sum the voltage changes to zero.

(a) $-33 + 11I_2 = 0$

In the right-hand loop, begin at the starting flag, move clockwise, and sum the voltage changes to zero.

(b) $-11I_2 - 80I_3 = 0$

Solve (a) for I_2 and get:

(a) $11I_2 = 33$

$I_2 = \mathbf{3.0\ A}$

Substitute I_2 into (b) and solve for I_3.

(b) $-11(3.0) - 80I_3 = 0$

$80I_3 = -33$

$$I_3 = -0.413 \text{ A} \xrightarrow{\text{SD}} \mathbf{-0.41\ A}$$

Use KCL to find I_1.

$$I_3 = I_1 + I_2$$
$$-0.413 = I_1 + 3.0$$
$$I_1 = -3.413 \text{ A} \xrightarrow{\text{SD}} \mathbf{-3.4\ A}$$

18. Begin by finding the x and y components of the initial velocity.

$$v_{x0} = 26.8 \cos 53.5° = 15.94 \frac{\text{m}}{\text{s}}$$
$$v_{y0} = 26.8 \sin 53.5° = 21.54 \frac{\text{m}}{\text{s}}$$

Use the y-displacement equation to find the time.

$$\Delta y = v_{y0}t + \frac{1}{2}a_y t^2$$
$$0 = 21.54t + \frac{1}{2}(-9.81)t^2$$
$$4.905t^2 = 21.54t$$
$$t = 4.391 \text{ s}$$

Use this time in the x-position equation to find the distance.

$$x = x_0 + v_{x0}t + \frac{1}{2}a_x t^2$$
$$= (0) + 15.94(4.391) + (0)$$
$$= 69.993 \text{ m} \xrightarrow{\text{SD}} \mathbf{70.0\ m}$$

19.
$$R = \frac{\rho L}{A} \rightarrow R_2 = \frac{\rho(3L)}{(2A)} = \frac{3}{2}\frac{\rho L}{A}$$

Now, note that $\frac{\rho L}{A}$ equals 88.0 Ω. Substitute and get:

$$R_2 = \frac{3}{2}\frac{\rho L}{A} = \frac{3}{2}(88.0\ \Omega) = \mathbf{132\ \Omega}$$

20. Begin by writing a momentum equation.

$$m_1v_1 + m_2v_2 = (m_1 + m_2)v_3$$
$$13{,}607(20.5\angle 90^\circ) + 1975(26.8\angle 0^\circ) = (13{,}607 + 1975)v_3$$
$$278{,}943.5\angle 90^\circ + 52{,}930\angle 0^\circ = (15{,}582)v_3 \quad \text{(a)}$$

Now find the sum of the x and y components of the initial momenta.

$\Sigma mv_x = 278{,}943.5 \cos 90^\circ + 52{,}930 \cos 0^\circ = 52{,}930 \text{ kg·m·s}^{-1}$

$\Sigma mv_y = 278{,}943.5 \sin 90^\circ + 52{,}930 \sin 0^\circ = 278{,}943.5 \text{ kg·m·s}^{-1}$

$\Sigma mv_R = (52{,}930i + 278{,}943.5j) \text{ kg·m·s}^{-1}$

Convert this resultant to polar form and get:

$\Sigma mv_R = \sqrt{(52{,}930)^2 + (278{,}943.5)^2} = 2.839 \times 10^5 \text{ kg·m·s}^{-1}$

$\theta = \tan^{-1} \dfrac{278{,}943.5}{52{,}930} = 79.26^\circ$

$\Sigma mv_R = 2.839 \times 10^5\angle 79.26^\circ \text{ kg·m·s}^{-1}$

Use this momentum in (a) to find v_3.

(a) $2.839 \times 10^5\angle 79.26^\circ = (15{,}582)v_3$

$$v_3 = 18.22\angle 79.26^\circ \frac{\text{m}}{\text{s}} \xrightarrow{\text{SD}} \mathbf{18.2\angle 79.26^\circ \frac{m}{s}}$$

PROBLEM SET 79

1. $\Delta U = W = PA\Delta x$

$= (15{,}400)(0.340)(0.05)$

$= 261.8 \text{ J} \xrightarrow{\text{SD}} \mathbf{300\ J}$

2.

$$\Sigma F_x = ma_x$$
$$405 - \mu_k F_N = ma$$
$$405 - (0.24)m(9.81) = m(4.0)$$
$$405 - 2.35m = 4.0m$$
$$m = 63.78 \text{ kg} \xrightarrow{\text{SD}} \mathbf{64\ kg}$$

3. $v = f(2L)$

$= (386)(2)(1)$

$= 772 \dfrac{\text{m}}{\text{s}} \xrightarrow{\text{SD}} \mathbf{800 \dfrac{m}{s}}$

4. (a) All vibrations will be integral multiples of the fundamental frequency.

$f_1 = 7\bar{5}0 \text{ Hz}$

$f_2 = 2 \times 750 = 15\bar{0}0 \text{ Hz}$

$f_3 = 3 \times 750 = 2250 \text{ Hz}$

$f_4 = 4 \times 750 = 30\bar{0}0 \text{ Hz}$

Thus the string will vibrate at **$7\bar{5}0$ Hz, $15\bar{0}0$ Hz, 2250 Hz, ...**

(b) $v_1 = f(2L) = 750(2)(2) = $ **3000 m/s**

$v_2 = f(2L) = 1500(2)(2) = $ **6000 m/s**

$v_3 = f(2L) = 2250(2)(2) = $ **9000 m/s**

$v_4 = f(2L) = 3000(2)(2) = 12{,}000 \text{ m/s} \xrightarrow{\text{SD}}$ **10,000 m/s**

5. Begin by finding the equivalent capacitance of the two parallel capacitors.

$C_E = 15\ \mu\text{F} + 25\ \mu\text{F} = 40\ \mu\text{F}$

Next, find the time constant RC.

$RC = (1500\ \Omega)(40 \times 10^{-6}\text{ F}) = 6 \times 10^{-2}\text{ s}$

Now calculate the voltage when $t = 0.12$ s.

$V_C = V_0 - V_0 e^{-t/RC}$

$= 15 - 15e^{-0.12/6\times 10^{-2}}$

$= 15 - 15e^{-2}$

$= 12.97 \text{ V} \xrightarrow{\text{SD}} \mathbf{13\ V}$

6. $\dfrac{1}{C_E} = \dfrac{1}{50} + \dfrac{1}{40} + \dfrac{1}{20}$

$C_E = 10.53\ \mu\text{F} \xrightarrow{\text{SD}} \mathbf{10\ \mu F}$

7. (a) $q_1 = 72{,}000 \cancel{\text{electrons}} \times \frac{1.60 \times 10^{-19}\text{ C}}{1 \cancel{\text{electron}}}$

$= 1.15 \times 10^{-14}\text{ C} \xrightarrow{\text{SD}} \mathbf{1.2 \times 10^{-14}\text{ C}}$

$q_2 = 180{,}000 \cancel{\text{electrons}} \times \frac{1.60 \times 10^{-19}\text{ C}}{1 \cancel{\text{electron}}}$

$= 2.88 \times 10^{-14}\text{ C} \xrightarrow{\text{SD}} \mathbf{2.9 \times 10^{-14}\text{ C}}$

(b) $F = \frac{kq_1q_2}{r^2}$

$= \frac{(9.0 \times 10^9)(1.15 \times 10^{-14})(2.88 \times 10^{-14})}{(0.12)^2}$

$= 2.07 \times 10^{-16}\text{ N} \xrightarrow{\text{SD}} \mathbf{2.1 \times 10^{-16}\text{ N}}$

8. $\frac{1}{f} = \frac{1}{D_O} + \frac{1}{D_I}$

$\frac{1}{-12.0} = \frac{1}{6.0} + \frac{1}{D_I}$

$D_I = \mathbf{-4.0\text{ cm}}$

$\frac{H_I}{H_O} = \frac{-D_I}{D_O}$

$\frac{H_I}{3.0} = \frac{-(-4.0)}{6.0}$

$H_I = \mathbf{2.0\text{ cm}}$

$M = \frac{H_I}{H_O} = \frac{2.0}{3.0} = 0.667 \xrightarrow{\text{SD}} \mathbf{0.67}$

9. Begin by converting the temperature to kelvins.
$T_H = 4400°\text{C} + 273 = 4673\text{ K}$

Thus, the cold temperature is

$\text{eff}_{\text{max}} = 1 - \frac{T_C}{T_H}$

$0.82 = 1 - \frac{T_C}{4673}$

$T_C = 841.14\text{ K} \xrightarrow{\text{SD}} \mathbf{840\text{ K} = 570°\text{C}}$

10. (a) Determine the parameters of the sound wave if the siren is not moving.

$v_{\text{SND}} = f_s\lambda$

$345 = (825)\lambda$

$\lambda = 0.4182\text{ m}$

As the siren moves toward the observer, v_s is positive. Now, compute the observed wavelength λ'.

$\lambda' = \left(\lambda - \frac{v_s}{f_s}\right)$

$= \left(0.4182 - \frac{35.0}{825}\right)$

$= 0.3758\text{ m} \xrightarrow{\text{SD}} \mathbf{0.376\text{ m}}$

(b) As the siren moves away from the observer, v_s is negative. Now, compute the observed frequency f'.

$v_{\text{SND}} = f'\left(\lambda - \frac{v_s}{f_s}\right)$

$345 = f'\left(0.4182 - \frac{(-35.0)}{825}\right)$

$f' = 748.98\text{ Hz} \xrightarrow{\text{SD}} \mathbf{749\text{ Hz}}$

11. (a) The maximum displacement is 2.35 m, and the frequency is 0.8276 Hz.

$x = A\cos 2\pi ft$

$x = \mathbf{2.35\cos 2\pi(0.8276)}\boldsymbol{t}\ \mathbf{meters}$

(b) $v = f\lambda$

$= (0.8276)(2.05)$

$= 1.697\ \frac{\text{m}}{\text{s}} \xrightarrow{\text{SD}} \mathbf{1.70\ \frac{m}{s}}$

12. Begin by finding the time constant RC.
$RC = (5500\ \Omega)(2.4 \times 10^{-4}\text{ F}) = 1.32\text{ s}$

Now calculate the voltage when $t = 5.0$ s.

$V_C = V_0 - V_0e^{-t/RC}$

$= 75 - 75e^{-5.0/1.32}$

$= 75 - 75e^{-3.79}$

$= 73.3\text{ V} \xrightarrow{\text{SD}} \mathbf{73\text{ V}}$

13.
$$Q = \Delta U + W$$
$$\left(-1.5 \times 10^6 \text{ J}\right) = \Delta U + \left(5.0 \times 10^4 \text{ J}\right)$$
$$\Delta U = -1.55 \times 10^6 \text{ J} \xrightarrow{\text{SD}} \mathbf{-1.6 \times 10^6 \ J}$$

14. $\tan\theta = \dfrac{v^2}{rg}$
$$v^2 = (49.8)(9.81)\tan 48°$$
$$v = 23.29 \ \frac{\text{m}}{\text{s}} \xrightarrow{\text{SD}} \mathbf{23.3 \ \frac{m}{s}}$$

15. Begin by finding the angular speed and the moment of inertia of the ball.
$$\omega = \frac{v}{r} = \frac{6.12 \text{ m/s}}{0.1375 \text{ m}} = 44.51 \ \frac{\text{rad}}{\text{s}}$$
$$I = \frac{2}{5}mr^2 = \frac{2}{5}(32.3 \text{ kg})(0.1375 \text{ m})^2 = 0.244 \text{ kg·m}^2$$
Now find the total kinetic energy.
$$KE = \frac{1}{2}mv^2 + \frac{1}{2}I\omega^2$$
$$= \frac{1}{2}(32.3)(6.12)^2 + \frac{1}{2}(0.244)(44.51)^2$$
$$= 846.59 \text{ J} \xrightarrow{\text{SD}} \mathbf{847 \ J}$$

16. The image is **approximately 2.8 mm behind the mirror, it is upright, and the height of the image is approximately 4.0 mm.**

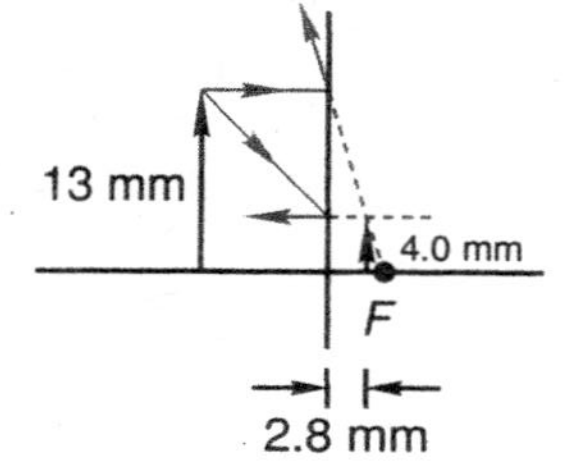

17. Note that the centripetal force must equal the weight of the marble.
$$\not{m}g = \frac{\not{m}v^2}{r}$$
$$9.81 = \frac{v^2}{0.5}$$
$$v = 2.21 \ \frac{\text{m}}{\text{s}} \xrightarrow{\text{SD}} \mathbf{2 \ \frac{m}{s}}$$

18. Begin by denoting the signs on the resistors.

In the left-hand loop, begin at the starting flag, move clockwise, and sum the voltage changes to zero.

(a) $-32 + 11I_1 + 4.0I_3 = 0$

In the right-hand loop, begin at the starting flag, move clockwise, and sum the voltage changes to zero.

(b) $-4.0I_3 + 8.0I_2 + V_Q = 0$

Substitute $I_1 = 2.0$ A into (a) and solve for I_3.

(a) $-32 + 11(2.0) + 4.0I_3 = 0$
$$4.0I_3 = 10$$
$$I_3 = 2.5 \text{ A}$$

Use KCL to find I_2.
$$I_1 = I_2 + I_3$$
$$2.0 = I_2 + 2.5$$
$$I_2 = -0.5 \text{ A}$$

Substitute I_2 and I_3 into (b) and solve for V_Q.

(b) $-4.0(2.5) + 8.0(-0.5) + V_Q = 0$
$$V_Q = \mathbf{14 \ V}$$

Since the mysterious object produced power, it must be an active circuit element. The sign convention for an active element which produces power is shown below.

In our problem, the current -0.5 A is entering the positive terminal of the object. Thus, for the current to obey the sign convention, it must be $-(-0.5 \text{ A})$ or 0.5 A. Therefore, the power produced is VI.

$P = VI = (14 \text{ V})(0.5 \text{ A}) = \mathbf{7.0 \ W}$

19. (a) Since $t = D/R$, calculate the times.

$$t_A = \frac{150 \text{ m}}{331 \text{ m/s}} = 0.453 \text{ s}$$

$$t_W = \frac{150 \text{ m}}{1530 \text{ m/s}} = 0.098 \text{ s}$$

Thus, his **right ear or the ear in the water** will hear the ignition first because the sound traveled faster in the water.

(b) $\Delta t = t_A - t_W$

$= 0.453 \text{ s} - 0.098 \text{ s}$

$= 0.355 \text{ s} \xrightarrow{\text{SD}}$ **0.36 s**

20. $Q_5 = 5.21(2009)(403) = 4.218 \times 10^6 \text{ J}$

$Q_4 = 5.21(2256 \times 10^3) = 1.175 \times 10^7 \text{ J}$

$Q_3 = 5.21(4186)(100) = 2.181 \times 10^6 \text{ J}$

$Q_2 = 5.21(334 \times 10^3) = 1.740 \times 10^6 \text{ J}$

$Q_1 = 5.21(2050)(82.5) = 8.811 \times 10^5 \text{ J}$

$Q_T = 2.077 \times 10^7 \text{ J} \xrightarrow{\text{SD}}$ $\mathbf{2.08 \times 10^7}$ **J**

Problem Set 80

1. We need to find the electric field component at P caused by the charge at B and add the two field components vectorially.

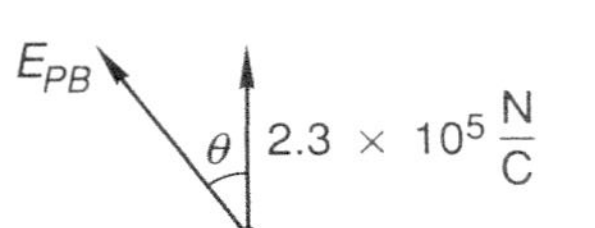

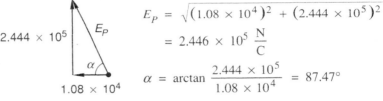

The electric component of P caused by q_B is away from q_B (because q_B is positive) and has a value of

$$E_{PB} = \frac{kq_B}{r^2} = \frac{(9.0 \times 10^9)(2.0 \times 10^{-6})}{(1.0)^2} = 1.8 \times 10^4 \text{ N/C}$$

From the diagram of the position of the charges, we see that

$$\sin\theta = \frac{0.6}{1.0} = 0.6 \quad \text{and} \quad \cos\theta = \frac{0.8}{1.0} = 0.8$$

The vector components of E_{PB} are

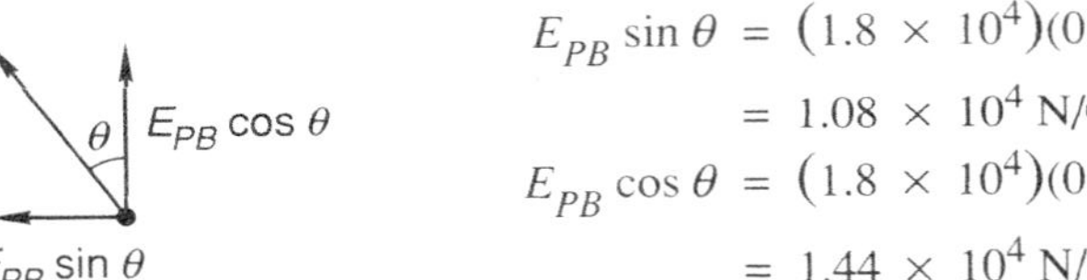

$$E_{PB} \sin\theta = (1.8 \times 10^4)(0.6) = 1.08 \times 10^4 \text{ N/C}$$

$$E_{PB} \cos\theta = (1.8 \times 10^4)(0.8) = 1.44 \times 10^4 \text{ N/C}$$

The sum of the horizontal and vertical components is

$E_x = (0) - 1.08 \times 10^4 = -1.08 \times 10^4 \text{ N/C}$

$E_y = 2.3 \times 10^5 + 1.44 \times 10^4 = 2.444 \times 10^5 \text{ N/C}$

So now we have the horizontal and vertical components of E_P as

2.444 × 10^5; E_P; α; 1.08 × 10^4

$$E_P = \sqrt{(1.08 \times 10^4)^2 + (2.444 \times 10^5)^2} = 2.446 \times 10^5 \frac{\text{N}}{\text{C}}$$

$$\alpha = \arctan\frac{2.444 \times 10^5}{1.08 \times 10^4} = 87.47°$$

Since α is a 2nd-quadrant angle: $\alpha = 180° - 87.47° = 92.53°$

$E_P = 2.446 \times 10^5 \underline{/92.53°} \frac{\text{N}}{\text{C}} \xrightarrow{\text{SD}}$ $\mathbf{2 \times 10^5 \underline{/92.53°} \frac{N}{C}}$

2. Since the electric field points toward negative charges and away from positive charges, the electric field for these charges is illustrated in the following diagram.

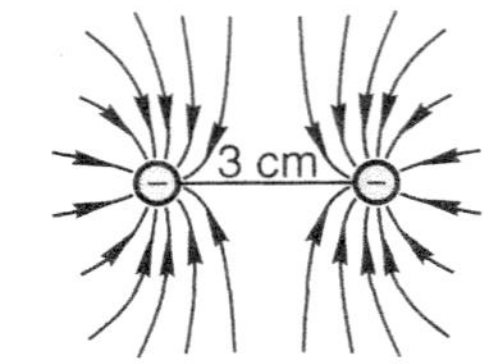

3. Begin by finding the power output of the second machine.

$$P_2 = \frac{W}{\Delta t} = \frac{4689 \text{ J}}{9.0 \text{ s}} = 521 \text{ W}$$

Therefore, the efficiency of the second machine is equal to the power output divided by the power input.

$$\text{Efficiency} = \frac{521 \text{ W}}{862 \text{ W}} = 0.6044$$

Thus, the overall efficiency is

Efficiency $= 0.86 \times 0.6044 = 0.5198$

Multiply this by 100% and get:

Percent efficiency $= 0.5198 \times 100\% = 51.98\% \xrightarrow{\text{SD}}$ **52%**

4. $$\text{eff}_{max} = 1 - \frac{T_C}{T_H}$$
$$= 1 - \frac{949}{1560}$$
$$= 0.3917$$

Multiply this by 100% and get:

$$\text{eff}_{max} = 0.3917 \times 100\% = 39.17\% \xrightarrow{SD} \mathbf{39.2\%}$$

5. $$v = f(2L)$$
$$= (880)(2)(0.53)$$
$$= 932.8\ \frac{\text{m}}{\text{s}} \xrightarrow{SD} \mathbf{930\ \frac{m}{s}}$$

6. Begin by finding the equivalent capacitance of the two parallel capacitors.
$C_E = 35\ \mu\text{F} + 120\ \mu\text{F} = 155\ \mu\text{F}$
Now, combine this with the 25-μF capacitor to find the equivalent capacitance of the circuit.
$$C_E = \frac{(155)(25)}{155 + 25} = 21.53\ \mu\text{F} \xrightarrow{SD} \mathbf{22\ \mu F}$$

7. Begin by finding the weight of the ball and drawing a free-body diagram of the ball on the left.
$$w = mg$$
$$= 5.4 \times 10^{-2}\ \cancel{\text{kg}} \times 9.81\ \frac{\text{N}}{\cancel{\text{kg}}}$$
$$= 0.5297\ \text{N}$$

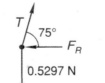

The weight of the ball equals the vertical component of the tension.
$$w = T \sin 75°$$
$$0.5297 = T \sin 75°$$
$$T = 0.548\ \text{N}$$
The horizontal component of the tension equals the force of repulsion F_R.
$$F_R = T \cos 75°$$
$$= (0.548) \cos 75°$$
$$= 0.142\ \text{N}$$

Now, we can use Coulomb's law to find the charge on each ball.
$$F_R = \frac{kq_1q_2}{r^2}$$
$$0.142 = \frac{(9.0 \times 10^9)q^2}{(0.16)^2}$$
$$q = 6.36 \times 10^{-7}\ \text{C} \xrightarrow{SD} \mathbf{6.4 \times 10^{-7}\ C}$$

8. $$\frac{1}{f} = \frac{1}{D_O} + \frac{1}{D_I}$$
$$\frac{1}{25} = \frac{1}{52} + \frac{1}{D_I}$$
$$D_I = 48.1\ \text{m} \xrightarrow{SD} \mathbf{48\ m}$$

$$\frac{H_I}{H_O} = \frac{-D_I}{D_O}$$
$$\frac{H_I}{5.0} = \frac{-48.1}{52}$$
$$H_I = -4.625\ \text{m} \xrightarrow{SD} \mathbf{-4.6\ m}$$

9. Begin by converting the temperature to kelvins.
$T_C = 123°\text{C} + 273 = 396\ \text{K}$

Thus, the hot temperature is
$$\text{eff}_{max} = 1 - \frac{T_C}{T_H}$$
$$0.870 = 1 - \frac{396}{T_H}$$
$$0.13 = \frac{396}{T_H}$$
$$T_H = 3046.15\ \text{K} \xrightarrow{SD} \mathbf{3050\ K = 2770°C}$$

10. Determine the parameters of the sound wave if the siren is not moving.

$$v_{SND} = f_s\lambda$$
$$335 = (620)\lambda$$
$$\lambda = 0.5403 \text{ m}$$

As the police car and the passenger approach each other, v_s and v_{OB} are positive. Therefore, the speed of the siren's sound relative to the passenger is

$$v_{SND} + v_{OB} = 335 + 15 = 350 \text{ m/s}$$

Now, compute the observed frequency f'''.

$$v_{SND} + v_{OB} = f'''\left(\lambda - \frac{v_s}{f_s}\right)$$

$$350 = f'''\left(0.5403 - \frac{25}{620}\right)$$

$$f''' = 700.03 \text{ Hz} \xrightarrow{SD} \mathbf{7\bar{0}0\ Hz}$$

11. (a) $f = \dfrac{7.5 \text{ cycles}}{\text{second}} = 7.5 \text{ Hz}$

The maximum displacement is 5 m, and the frequency is 7.5 Hz.

$x = A\cos 2\pi ft$

$x =$ **5 cos 2π(7.5)t meters**

(b) $v = f\lambda$

$= (7.5)(0.0010)$

$= \mathbf{7.5 \times 10^{-3}\ \frac{m}{s}}$

12. Since opposite charges attract, negative charges will accumulate on the left side of the ball causing it to move toward the rod.

13. **The image is approximately 4.8 cm behind the lens, it is upright, and the height of the image is approximately 3.2 cm.**

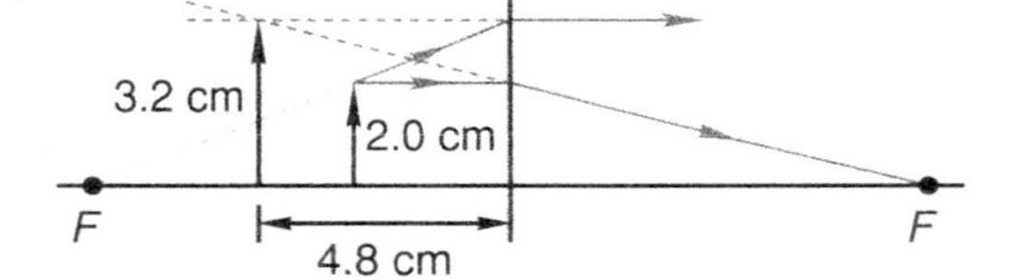

14. Begin by finding the moment of inertia of the pulley and noting the relationship between a and α.

$$I = \frac{1}{2}mr^2 = \frac{1}{2}(9.6 \text{ kg})(0.39 \text{ m})^2 = 0.73 \text{ kg·m}^2$$

$$a = r\alpha \longrightarrow \alpha = \frac{a}{0.39}$$

Next, find the component of the weight of the 42-kg block that is parallel to the plane.

$F_x = mg\sin 23° = (42)(9.81)\sin 23° = 161 \text{ N}$

Next, compute the weight of the 59-kg block.

$w = mg = (59)(9.81) = 578.79 \text{ N}$

Since $w > F_x$, we choose the positive x direction to be up the plane. Now, write a $\sum F_x = ma_x$ equation for the 42-kg block.

$$\sum F_x = ma_x$$
$$T_1 - F_x - \mu_k mg\cos\theta = ma$$
$$T_1 - 161 - (0.21)(42)(9.81)\cos 23° = 42a$$
$$T_1 = 240.65 + 42a \qquad \text{(a)}$$

Next, write a $\sum F_y = ma_y$ equation for the 59-kg block.

$$\sum F_y = ma_y$$
$$mg - T_2 = ma$$
$$(578.79) - T_2 = 59a$$
$$T_2 = 578.79 - 59a \qquad \text{(b)}$$

Now, write a $\sum\tau = I\alpha$ equation for the pulley.

$$\sum\tau = I\alpha$$
$$0.39T_2 - 0.39T_1 = (0.73)\left(\frac{a}{0.39}\right)$$
$$0.39T_2 - 0.39T_1 = 1.87a$$
$$T_2 - T_1 = 4.79a \qquad \text{(c)}$$

Substitute (a) and (b) into (c) to find the acceleration.

(c) $(578.79 - 59a) - (240.65 + 42a) = 4.79a$

$$338.14 = 105.79a$$
$$a = 3.196 \frac{\text{m}}{\text{s}^2}$$
$$\xrightarrow{SD} \mathbf{3.2\ \frac{m}{s^2}\ up\ the\ plane}$$

15. Begin by finding the radius r_1.

$$r_1 = \frac{\text{diameter}}{2} = \frac{5.478 \text{ cm}}{2} = 2.739 \text{ cm} = 0.02739 \text{ m}$$

Now find the speed v_2.

$$v_1A_1 = v_2A_2$$
$$v_1[\pi r_1^2] = v_2[\pi r_2^2]$$
$$3\ \frac{\text{m}}{\text{s}}[\pi(0.02739 \text{ m})^2] = v_2[\pi(0.050 \text{ m})^2]$$
$$0.00707\ \frac{\text{m}^3}{\text{s}} = v_2(0.00785 \text{ m}^2)$$
$$v_2 = 0.9006\ \frac{\text{m}}{\text{s}} \xrightarrow{\text{SD}} \mathbf{0.9\ \frac{m}{s}}$$

16. Begin at the ground symbol, move clockwise, and sum the voltage changes to zero.

$$+V + 12 \text{ V} - 20 \text{ V} - 14 \text{ V} + 10 \text{ V} - 4 \text{ V} + 14 \text{ V} = 0$$
$$V = \mathbf{2\ V}$$

17. Begin by finding the voltage drop across the 60-Ω resistor.

$V_1 = I_1R = (0.20 \text{ A})(60\ \Omega) = 12 \text{ V}$

This must equal the voltage drop across the 10-Ω resistor. Use this voltage to find the current I_2 through the 10-Ω resistor in parallel.

$$I_2 = \frac{V}{R} = \frac{12 \text{ V}}{10\ \Omega} = 1.2 \text{ A}$$

Use KCL to find the current I_3 through the 10-Ω resistor.

$I_3 = I_1 + I_2 = 0.20 \text{ A} + 1.2 \text{ A} = 1.4 \text{ A}$

Use this current to find the voltage drop across the 10-Ω resistor.

$V_3 = I_3R = (1.4 \text{ A})(10\ \Omega) = 14 \text{ V}$

The total voltage V_x is equal to the sum of the voltage drop across the 60-Ω resistor and the voltage drop across the 10-Ω resistor.

$V_x = V_1 + V_3 = 12 \text{ V} + 14 \text{ V} = \mathbf{26\ V}$

18. Begin by finding the volume of the sphere that is submerged.

$$V_s = \frac{4}{3}\pi r^3 = \frac{4}{3}\pi(0.87)^3 = 2.76 \text{ m}^3$$

Now find the mass of the water displaced.

$$m_w = 1025\ \frac{\text{kg}}{\cancel{\text{m}^3}} \times 2.76\ \cancel{\text{m}^3} = 2829 \text{ kg}$$
$$F_B = 2829\ \cancel{\text{kg}} \times 9.81\ \frac{\text{N}}{\cancel{\text{kg}}} = 27{,}752.49 \text{ N}$$
$$T = F_B - mg = 27{,}752.49 \text{ N} - (12\ \cancel{\text{kg}})\left(9.81\ \frac{\text{N}}{\cancel{\text{kg}}}\right)$$
$$= 2.76 \times 10^4 \text{ N} \xrightarrow{\text{SD}} \mathbf{2.8 \times 10^4\ N}$$

19. Begin by converting 1800 rad/min to rad/s.

$$1800\ \frac{\text{rad}}{\cancel{\text{min}}} \times \frac{1\ \cancel{\text{min}}}{60 \text{ s}} = 30\ \frac{\text{rad}}{\text{s}}$$

Now find the angular acceleration.

$$\alpha = \frac{\omega_2 - \omega_1}{\Delta t} = \frac{30 - 3.0}{10.0}\ \frac{\text{rad/s}}{\text{s}} = \mathbf{2.7\ \frac{rad}{s^2}}$$

20. $$F = \frac{Gm_1m_2}{r^2} = \frac{(6.67 \times 10^{-11})(5.98 \times 10^{24})(527)}{(252{,}000 + 6.37 \times 10^6)^2}$$
$$= 4.794 \times 10^3 \text{ N} \xrightarrow{\text{SD}} \mathbf{4.79 \times 10^3\ N}$$

Problem Set 81

1. The PV diagram for the Otto cycle is shown below.

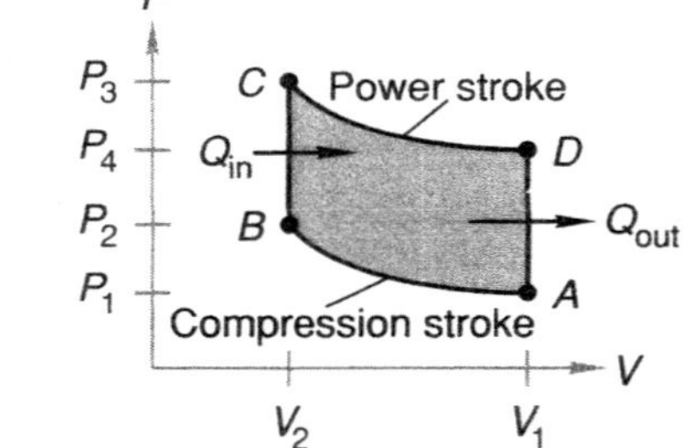

2. The compression stroke for the Otto cycle is shown below.

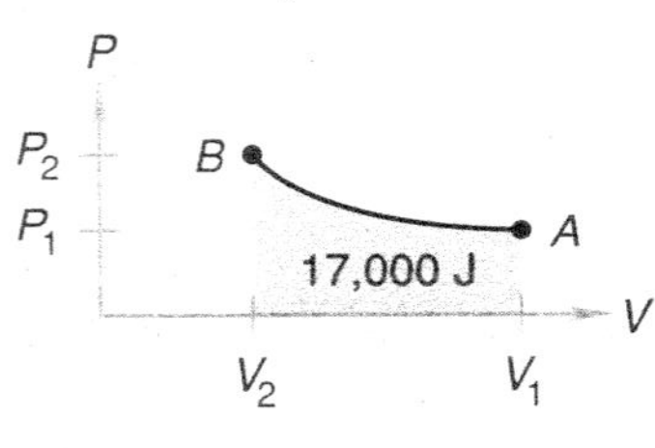

3. $E_{AB} = \frac{kq_B}{r^2}$

$= \frac{(9.0 \times 10^9)(4.3 \times 10^{-4})}{(0.95)^2}$

$= 4.288 \times 10^6 \frac{\text{N}}{\text{C}} \xrightarrow{\text{SD}}$ $\mathbf{4.3 \times 10^6 \frac{N}{C}}$

4. $PE = Q\,\Delta V$

$= (1.60 \times 10^{-19}\text{ C})(10{,}000\text{ V})$

$= 1.6 \times 10^{-15}\text{ J}$

The potential energy will be converted to kinetic energy.

$$KE = \frac{1}{2}mv^2$$

$$1.6 \times 10^{-15}\text{ J} = \frac{1}{2}(9.11 \times 10^{-31}\text{ kg})v^2$$

$$v = 5.927 \times 10^7 \frac{\text{m}}{\text{s}} \xrightarrow{\text{SD}} \mathbf{6 \times 10^7 \frac{m}{s}}$$

5. Begin by converting the temperature to kelvins.
$T_C = 148°\text{C} + 273 = 421\text{ K}$

Thus, the high temperature is

$$\text{eff}_{\text{max}} = 1 - \frac{T_C}{T_H}$$

$$0.47 = 1 - \frac{421}{T_H}$$

$$T_H = 794.34\text{ K} \xrightarrow{\text{SD}} \mathbf{790\text{ K} = 520°C}$$

6. $W = P\Delta V$

$88{,}000\text{ J} = (6.4 \times 10^5\text{ Pa})\Delta V$

$\Delta V = 0.1375\text{ m}^3 \xrightarrow{\text{SD}}$ $\mathbf{0.14\text{ m}^3}$

7. $v = f(2L)$

$= (370)(2)(0.35)$

$= 259 \frac{\text{m}}{\text{s}} \xrightarrow{\text{SD}}$ $\mathbf{260 \frac{m}{s}}$

8. Begin by finding the equivalent capacitance of the two parallel capacitors.
$C_E = 42\ \mu\text{F} + 18\ \mu\text{F} = 60\ \mu\text{F}$
Next, find the time constant RC.
$RC = (4000\ \Omega)(60 \times 10^{-6}\text{ F}) = 0.24\text{ s}$

Now calculate the voltage when $t = 0.24$ s.

$V_C = V_0 - V_0e^{-t/RC}$

$= 30 - 30e^{-0.24/0.24}$

$= 30 - 30e^{-1}$

$= 18.964\text{ V} \xrightarrow{\text{SD}}$ $\mathbf{19\text{ V}}$

9. Begin by finding the weight of the sphere and drawing a free-body diagram of the sphere on the left.

$w = mg$

$= 0.397\text{ kg} \times 9.81 \frac{\text{N}}{\text{kg}}$

$= 3.8946\text{ N}$

T
α
F_R
3.8946 N

In this case, $\alpha = 90° - \theta/2$. The weight of the sphere equals the vertical component of the tension.

$w = T\sin\alpha$

$3.8946 = T\sin\alpha$

$T = \frac{3.8946}{\sin\alpha}$

The horizontal component of the tension equals the force of repulsion F_R.

$$F_R = T\cos\alpha$$
$$= \left(\frac{3.8946}{\sin\alpha}\right)\cos\alpha$$
$$= \frac{3.8946}{\tan\alpha}$$

Now, we can use Coulomb's law to find α.

$$F_R = \frac{kq_1q_2}{r^2}$$
$$F_R = \frac{(9.0\times10^9)(2.52\times10^{-7})(2.52\times10^{-7})}{(0.0526)^2}$$
$$\frac{3.8946}{\tan\alpha} = 0.2065723$$
$$\alpha = 86.9638°$$

Since $\alpha = 90° - \theta/2$, we get: $86.9638° = 90° - \frac{\theta}{2}$

$$\theta = \mathbf{6.07°}$$

10. $\frac{1}{f} = \frac{1}{D_O} + \frac{1}{D_I}$

$$\frac{1}{5.0} = \frac{1}{7.0} + \frac{1}{D_I}$$
$$D_I = 17.5 \text{ cm} \xrightarrow{\text{SD}} \mathbf{18\ cm}$$
$$\frac{H_I}{H_O} = \frac{-D_I}{D_O}$$
$$\frac{H_I}{3.0} = \frac{-17.5}{7.0}$$
$$H_I = \mathbf{-7.5\ cm}$$
$$M = \frac{H_I}{H_O} = \frac{-7.5}{3.0} = \mathbf{-2.5}$$

11. $\text{eff}_{max} = 1 - \frac{T_C}{T_H}$

$$0.645 = 1 - \frac{T_C}{T_H}$$
$$\frac{T_C}{T_H} = \mathbf{0.355}$$

12. Determine the parameters of the sound wave if the jet is not moving.

$$v_{SND} = f_s\lambda$$
$$331 = (325)\lambda$$
$$\lambda = 1.0185 \text{ m}$$

As the jet airplane dives toward the observer, v_s is positive. Now, compute the observed frequency f'.

$$v_{SND} = f'\left(\lambda - \frac{v_s}{f_s}\right)$$
$$331 = f'\left(1.0185 - \frac{157}{325}\right)$$
$$f' = 618.20 \text{ Hz} \xrightarrow{\text{SD}} \mathbf{618\ Hz}$$

13. $n_1 \sin\theta_1 = n_2 \sin\theta_2$

$$1.33 \sin\theta_c = (1)\sin 90°$$
$$\theta_c = 48.75°$$

This is the angle between the ray and the vertical. To get the complimentary angle, we subtract it from 90° and get $90° - 48.75° = \mathbf{41.25°}$.

14. Begin by finding v_1 and v_2.

$$v_1 = \frac{Q}{A_1} = \frac{0.95}{1.29} = 0.74\ \frac{\text{m}}{\text{s}}$$
$$v_2 = \frac{Q}{A_2} = \frac{0.95}{0.55} = 1.73\ \frac{\text{m}}{\text{s}}$$

Now use Bernoulli's equation to find P_2. Note that h_1 is zero, so the $\rho g h_1$ term falls out of the equation.

$$P_1 + \frac{1}{2}\rho v_1^2 = P_2 + \frac{1}{2}\rho v_2^2 + \rho g h_2$$
$$75{,}200 + \frac{1}{2}(680)(0.74)^2 = P_2 + \frac{1}{2}(680)(1.73)^2 + (680)(9.81)(5.50)$$
$$75{,}200 + 186.184 = P_2 + 1017.586 + 36{,}689.4$$
$$P_2 = 3.768\times10^4 \text{ Pa} \xrightarrow{\text{SD}} \mathbf{3.8\times10^4\ Pa}$$

15. Energy $= \frac{1}{2}CV^2$

$= \frac{1}{2}(12 \times 10^{-6}\text{ F})(27\text{ V})^2$

$= 4.374 \times 10^{-3}\text{ J} \xrightarrow{\text{SD}} \mathbf{4.4 \times 10^{-3}\text{ J}}$

16. The image is **approximately 2.8 cm behind the mirror, it is upright, and the height of the image is approximately 4.2 cm.**

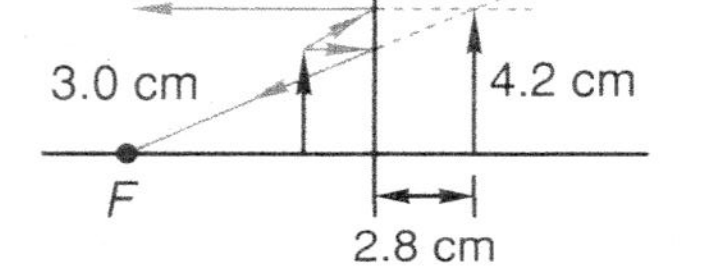

The image is **virtual** because it is upright and behind the mirror.

17. Begin by finding the equivalent resistance of the 20-Ω and 40-Ω resistors.

$R_E = 20\ \Omega + 40\ \Omega = 60\ \Omega$

Use this resistance to find the voltage V_1.

$V_1 = I_1R_E = (0.40\text{ A})(60\ \Omega) = 24\text{ V}$

This must equal the voltage drop across the 10-Ω and R_1 resistors. Use this voltage to find R_1.

$V_1 = I_2(10 + R_1)$

$24 = (0.15)(10 + R_1)$

$24 = 1.5 + 0.15R_1$

$R_1 = \mathbf{150\ \Omega}$

18. (a) Begin by finding the x and y components of the initial velocity.

$v_{x0} = 15.7 \cos 30° = 13.60\ \frac{\text{m}}{\text{s}}$

$v_{y0} = 15.7 \sin 30° = 7.85\ \frac{\text{m}}{\text{s}}$

Use the y-displacement equation to find the time.

$\Delta y = v_{y0}t + \frac{1}{2}a_yt^2$

$-255 = 7.85t + \frac{1}{2}(-9.81)t^2$

$0 = 4.905t^2 - 7.85t - 255$

Use the quadratic formula to solve this equation for t.

$$t = \frac{-(-7.85) \pm \sqrt{(-7.85)^2 - 4(4.905)(-255)}}{2(4.905)} = 8.055\text{ s}$$

Use the motion equation to find the vertical velocity.

$v(t) = v_{y0} + a_yt$

$= (7.85) + (-9.81)(8.055)$

$= -71.17\text{ m/s}$

Therefore, the velocity (horizontal and vertical components) of the stone just before it strikes the ground is:

$\vec{v} = (13.60i - 71.17j)\text{ m/s} \xrightarrow{\text{SD}} (13.6i - 71.2j)\text{ m/s}$

Convert this to polar form and get:

13.60
θ
R
71.17

$R = \sqrt{(13.60)^2 + (-71.17)^2} = 72.46\text{ m/s}$

$\theta = \tan^{-1}\frac{-71.17}{13.60} = -79.18°$

$\vec{v} = 72.46\underline{/-79.18°}\text{ m/s} \xrightarrow{\text{SD}} 72.5\underline{/-79.18°}\text{ m/s}$

Thus, the velocity is

$\vec{v} = \mathbf{(13.6i - 71.2j)\ \frac{m}{s} = 72.5\underline{/-79.18°}\ \frac{m}{s}}$

(b) Use the x-displacement equation to find the distance.

$\Delta x = v_{x0}t + \frac{1}{2}a_xt^2$

$= (13.60)(8.055) + (0)$

$= 109.55\text{ m} \xrightarrow{\text{SD}} \mathbf{11\bar{0}\text{ m}}$

19. In the circuit, when the capacitors are fully charged, the sum of the voltages V_1 and V_2 is 42 V.

(a) $V_1 + V_2 = 42$

Since the capacitors are in series, the charge on each capacitor is the same, $Q = CV$.

(b) $C_1V_1 = C_2V_2$

Solve (b) for V_2 and substitute into (a).

$$\text{(a)} \qquad V_1 + \frac{C_1V_1}{C_2} = 42$$

$$V_1 + \frac{(8.0 \times 10^{-6})V_1}{(16 \times 10^{-6})} = 42$$

$$1.5V_1 = 42$$

$$V_1 = \mathbf{28\ V}$$

Substitute V_1 into (a) and solve for V_2.

$$\text{(a)}\ (28) + V_2 = 42$$

$$V_2 = \mathbf{14\ V}$$

20. $$\frac{P_1V_1}{T_1} = \frac{P_2V_2}{T_2} \rightarrow \frac{P_1V_1}{T_1} = \frac{P_2\left(\frac{V_1}{2}\right)}{(3T_1)}$$

$$\frac{P_1\cancel{V_1}}{\cancel{T_1}} \times \frac{\cancel{T_1}}{\cancel{V_1}} = \frac{P_2\left(\frac{\cancel{V_1}}{2}\right)}{(3\cancel{T_1})} \times \frac{\cancel{T_1}}{\cancel{V_1}}$$

$$P_2 = \mathbf{6P_1}$$

PROBLEM SET 82

1. $$F = qvB$$
$$= (1.60 \times 10^{-19})(177)(56)$$
$$= 1.586 \times 10^{-15}\text{ N} \xrightarrow{\text{SD}} \mathbf{1.6 \times 10^{-15}\ N}$$

To find which path the particle follows, place your right hand flat so that your fingers point in the original direction of the particle and bend your fingers to point in the direction of the magnetic field. Since the particle has a positive charge, the direction of the force on the particle is in the direction of your thumb. Therefore, the particle follows **path** ***A***.

2. **No force** is exerted on an electron moving parallel to a magnetic field.

3. The PV diagram for the Otto cycle is shown below.

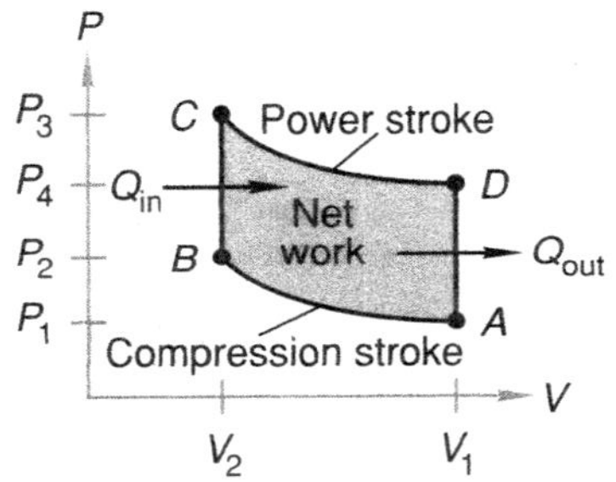

4. The net work done equals the work done on the power stroke minus the work done on the compression stroke.
Net work = 76 kJ − 32 kJ = **44 kJ**

5. $$PE = Q\,\Delta V$$
$$= (1.60 \times 10^{-19}\text{ C})(30{,}000\text{ V})$$
$$= 4.8 \times 10^{-15}\text{ J}$$

The potential energy will be converted to kinetic energy.

$$KE = \frac{1}{2}mv^2$$

$$4.8 \times 10^{-15}\text{ J} = \frac{1}{2}(9.11 \times 10^{-31}\text{ kg})v^2$$

$$v = 1.03 \times 10^8\ \frac{\text{m}}{\text{s}} \xrightarrow{\text{SD}} \mathbf{1 \times 10^8\ \frac{m}{s}}$$

6. $$F = \frac{kq_1q_2}{r^2}$$

$$0.25 = \frac{(9.0 \times 10^9)q^2}{(0.075)^2}$$

$$q = 3.95 \times 10^{-7}\text{ C} \xrightarrow{\text{SD}} \mathbf{4.0 \times 10^{-7}\ C}$$

7. $$W = P\Delta V$$
$$= (8.74 \times 10^6)(0.842 - 0.564)$$
$$= 2.4297 \times 10^6\text{ J} \xrightarrow{\text{SD}} \mathbf{2.43 \times 10^6\ J}$$

$$Q = \Delta U + W$$
$$= (0) + 2.4297 \times 10^6\text{ J}$$
$$= 2.4297 \times 10^6\text{ J} \xrightarrow{\text{SD}} \mathbf{2.43 \times 10^6\ J}$$

8. Begin by finding the equivalent capacitance of the two series capacitors.

$$C_E = \frac{(6.0)(12)}{6.0 + 12} = 4.0\ \mu\text{F}$$

Next, find the time constant RC.

$$RC = (2000\ \Omega)(4.0 \times 10^{-6}\ \text{F}) = 8 \times 10^{-3}\ \text{s}$$

Now find the initial current.

$$I_0 = \frac{V}{R} = \frac{14\ \text{V}}{2000\ \Omega} = 0.007\ \text{A}$$

Now calculate the current when $t = 0.016$ s.

$$I = I_0 e^{-t/RC}$$
$$= 0.007e^{-0.016/8 \times 10^{-3}}$$
$$= 0.007e^{-2}$$
$$= 9.473 \times 10^{-4}\ \text{A} \xrightarrow{\text{SD}} \mathbf{9.5 \times 10^{-4}\ A}$$

9.

$$F = \frac{kq_1q_2}{r^2}$$
$$9.2 \times 10^{-8} = \frac{(9.0 \times 10^9)q^2}{(5.3 \times 10^{-4})^2}$$
$$q = 1.69 \times 10^{-12}\ \text{C} \xrightarrow{\text{SD}} \mathbf{1.7 \times 10^{-12}\ C}$$

10. Begin by converting the temperature to kelvins.

$$T_C = 95°\text{C} + 273 = 368\ \text{K}$$

Thus, the hot temperature is

$$\text{eff}_{\text{max}} = 1 - \frac{T_C}{T_H}$$
$$0.97 = 1 - \frac{368}{T_H}$$
$$T_H = 12{,}267\ \text{K} \xrightarrow{\text{SD}} \mathbf{12{,}000\ K = 12{,}000°C}$$

11.

$$T = \frac{2\pi\sqrt{L}}{\sqrt{g}} = \frac{2\pi\sqrt{3.2}}{\sqrt{9.81}} = 3.59\ \text{s} \xrightarrow{\text{SD}} \mathbf{3.6\ s}$$

The frequency is the reciprocal of the period.

$$f = \frac{1}{T} = \frac{1}{3.59\ \text{s}} = 0.279\ \text{Hz} \xrightarrow{\text{SD}} \mathbf{0.28\ Hz}$$

12. Begin by finding the equivalent resistance of the 6.0-Ω and 3.0-Ω resistors.

$$R_E = \frac{(6.0)(3.0)}{6.0 + 3.0} = 2.0\ \Omega$$

Next, find the equivalent resistance of the 18-Ω and 9.0-Ω resistors.

$$R_E = \frac{(18)(9.0)}{18 + 9.0} = 6.0\ \Omega$$

Now, combine the 2.0-Ω, 6.0-Ω, and 5.0-Ω resistors to find the equivalent resistance of the circuit.

$$R_E = (2.0\ \Omega) + (6.0\ \Omega) + 5.0\ \Omega = 13\ \Omega$$

Use this resistance to find the current I through the 5.0-Ω resistor.

$$I = \frac{V}{R_E} = \frac{24\ \text{V}}{13\ \Omega} = 1.85\ \text{A}$$

Now find the energy used by the 5.0-Ω resistor.

$$E = I^2Rt = (1.85\ \text{A})^2(5.0\ \Omega)(10\ \text{s}) = 171.13\ \text{J} \xrightarrow{\text{SD}} \mathbf{170\ J}$$

13.

$$Q = \Delta U + W$$
$$3.5 \times 10^6\ \text{J} = \Delta U + 1.6 \times 10^6\ \text{J}$$
$$\Delta U = \mathbf{1.9 \times 10^6\ J}$$

14. (a) $f = \dfrac{35\ \text{cycles}}{15\ \text{seconds}} = 2.333\ \text{Hz} \xrightarrow{\text{SD}} \mathbf{2.3\ Hz}$

(b)

$$f = \frac{1}{2\pi}\frac{\sqrt{k}}{\sqrt{m}}$$
$$2.333 = \frac{1}{2\pi}\frac{\sqrt{k}}{\sqrt{24}}$$
$$k = 5.157 \times 10^3\ \frac{\text{N}}{\text{m}} \xrightarrow{\text{SD}} \mathbf{5.2 \times 10^3\ \frac{N}{m}}$$

15.

$$\Delta L = \alpha L_0 \Delta T$$
$$= (2.0 \times 10^{-5})(27)(720 - 25)$$
$$= 0.375\ \text{m} \xrightarrow{\text{SD}} \mathbf{0.38\ m}$$

16.

$$\tau = I\alpha = \left(\frac{1}{3}mL^2\right)\alpha$$
$$= \left(\frac{1}{3}(5.00)(0.750)^2\right)(3.50)$$
$$= 3.281\ \text{N}\cdot\text{m} \xrightarrow{\text{SD}} \mathbf{3.28\ N \cdot m}$$

17. Begin by finding the equivalent resistance of the three parallel resistors.

$$\frac{1}{R_E} = \frac{1}{36} + \frac{1}{18} + \frac{1}{6}$$

$$R_E = 4\ \Omega$$

Now, combine this with the 6-Ω resistor to find the equivalent resistance of the circuit.

$$R_E = (4\ \Omega) + 6\ \Omega = 10\ \Omega$$

Use this resistance to find V_x.

$$V_x = I_1 R_E = (3\text{ A})(10\ \Omega) = \mathbf{30\ V}$$

18. Begin by finding the centripetal force, F_c, and the weight of the yo-yo.

$$F_c = \frac{mv^2}{r} = \frac{0.75(2.5)^2}{1.75} = 2.679\text{ N}$$

$$w = mg = (0.75)(9.81) = 7.358\text{ N}$$

The tension, T, is equal to the vector sum of the horizontal force, F_c, and the vertical force, w.

$$T = \sqrt{(2.679)^2 + (7.358)^2} = 7.831\text{ N} \xrightarrow{\text{SD}} \mathbf{7.8\ N}$$

19. Begin by finding the tension, mg, and the mass per unit length of the string.

$$T = mg = 15.0\cancel{\text{kg}} \times 9.81\,\frac{\text{N}}{\cancel{\text{kg}}} = 147.15\text{ N}$$

$$M_L = \frac{0.0230\text{ kg}}{1.75\text{ m}} = 0.0131\,\frac{\text{kg}}{\text{m}}$$

Insert these values into the formula below to find v.

$$v = \sqrt{\frac{T}{M_L}} = \sqrt{\frac{147.15\text{ N}}{0.0131\,\frac{\text{kg}}{\text{m}}}} = 105.985\,\frac{\text{m}}{\text{s}} \xrightarrow{\text{SD}} \mathbf{106\ \frac{m}{s}}$$

20. Begin by converting the temperatures to kelvins.

$$T_1 = 25 + 273 = 298\text{ K}$$

$$T_2 = 103 + 273 = 376\text{ K}$$

Now use the ideal gas law and get:

$$\frac{V_1}{T_1} = \frac{V_2}{T_2}$$

$$\frac{52.0\text{ m}^3}{298\text{ K}} = \frac{V_2}{376\text{ K}}$$

$$V_2 = 65.61\text{ m}^3 \xrightarrow{\text{SD}} \mathbf{66\ m^3}$$

PROBLEM SET 83

1. (a) $Q = (0.425\cancel{\text{kg}})\left(3.34 \times 10^5\,\frac{\text{J}}{\cancel{\text{kg}}}\right)$

$$= 1.4195 \times 10^5\text{ J} \xrightarrow{\text{SD}} \mathbf{1.42 \times 10^5\ J}$$

(b) $\Delta S = \frac{\Delta Q}{T} = \frac{+1.4195 \times 10^5\text{ J}}{273\text{ K}} = +519.96\,\frac{\text{J}}{\text{K}} \xrightarrow{\text{SD}} \mathbf{+52\bar{0}\ \frac{J}{K}}$

2. Begin by computing the amount of heat required to melt 0.0250 kg of ice.

$$Q = (0.0250\cancel{\text{kg}})\left(3.34 \times 10^5\,\frac{\text{J}}{\cancel{\text{kg}}}\right) = 8.35 \times 10^3\text{ J}$$

Next, compute the change in entropies.

(a) $\Delta S_{\text{ice}} = \frac{\Delta Q}{T}$

$$= \frac{+8.35 \times 10^3\text{ J}}{273\text{ K}}$$

$$= +30.59\text{ J/K} \xrightarrow{\text{SD}} \mathbf{+30.6\ J/K}$$

(b) $\Delta S_{\text{ground}} = \frac{\Delta Q}{T}$

$$= \frac{-8.35 \times 10^3\text{ J}}{(25.0° + 273)\text{ K}}$$

$$= -28.02\text{ J/K} \xrightarrow{\text{SD}} \mathbf{-28.0\ J/K}$$

(c) $\Delta S_{total} = \Delta S_{ice} + \Delta S_{ground}$

$$= (+30.59\text{ J/K}) + (-28.02\text{ J/K})$$

$$= \mathbf{+2.57\ J/K}$$

3. $\Phi = AB\cos\theta$

$$= \left[\pi(0.50)^2\right](2.3)\cos 0°$$

$$= 1.806\text{ Wb} \xrightarrow{\text{SD}} \mathbf{1.8\ Wb}$$

4. $F = qvB$

$$= \left(1.60 \times 10^{-19}\right)\left(4.1 \times 10^4\right)(5.5)$$

$$= 3.608 \times 10^{-14}\text{ N} \xrightarrow{\text{SD}} \mathbf{3.6 \times 10^{-14}\ N}$$

To find which path the electron follows, place your right hand flat so that your fingers point in the original direction of the electron and bend your fingers to point in the direction of the magnetic field. Since the electron has a negative charge, the direction of force on the electron is opposite the direction of your thumb. Therefore, the electron follows **path *B***.

5. The compression stroke of the Otto cycle is shown below.

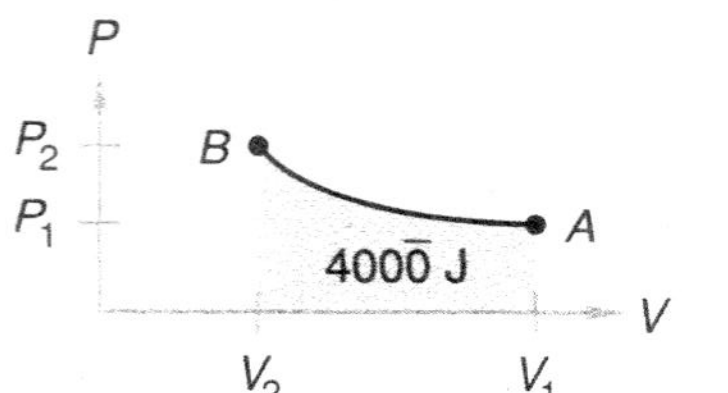

6. $F = \frac{kq_1q_2}{r^2}$

$0.35 = \frac{(9.0 \times 10^9)(1.3 \times 10^{-7})q_2}{(0.14)^2}$

$q_2 = 5.863 \times 10^{-6}\text{ C} \xrightarrow{SD} \mathbf{5.9 \times 10^{-6}\text{ C}}$

This charge must be **negative** because unlike charges attract.

7. $KE = \frac{1}{2}mv^2$

$= \frac{1}{2}(9.11 \times 10^{-31})(9.35 \times 10^6)^2$

$= 3.982 \times 10^{-17}\text{ J}$

This energy equals the potential energy.

$PE = Q\,\Delta V$

$3.982 \times 10^{-17} = (1.60 \times 10^{-19})V$

$V = 248.88\text{ V} \xrightarrow{SD} \mathbf{249\text{ V}}$

8. (a) $\text{eff}_{max} = 1 - \frac{T_C}{T_H}$

$= 1 - \frac{312}{1642}$

$= 0.80999$

Multiply this by 100% and get:

$\text{eff}_{max} = 0.80999 \times 100\% = 80.999\% \xrightarrow{SD} \mathbf{81.0\%}$

(b) $W = 0.80999 \times 4864 = 3.9398 \times 10^3\text{ J} \xrightarrow{SD} \mathbf{3.94 \times 10^3\text{ J}}$

9. In the circuit, when the capacitors are fully charged, the sum of the voltages V_1 and V_2 is 18.0 volts.

(a) $V_1 + V_2 = 18.0$

Since the capacitors are in series, the charge on each capacitor is the same, $Q = CV$.

(b) $C_1V_1 = C_2V_2$

Solve (b) for V_2 and substitute into (a) and get:

(a) $V_1 + \frac{C_1V_1}{C_2} = 18.0$

$V_1 + \frac{(6.00 \times 10^{-6})V_1}{14.0 \times 10^{-6}} = 18.0$

$1.429V_1 = 18.0$

$V_1 = 12.596\text{ V} \xrightarrow{SD} \mathbf{12.6\text{ V}}$

Substitute V_1 into (a) and solve for V_2.

(a) $(12.596) + V_2 = 18.0$

$V_2 = 5.404\text{ V} \xrightarrow{SD} \mathbf{5.40\text{ V}}$

10. $v = f(2L)$

$= (659)(2)(0.331)$

$= 436.3\ \frac{\text{m}}{\text{s}} \xrightarrow{SD} \mathbf{436\ \frac{m}{s}}$

11. $\frac{1}{f} = \frac{1}{D_O} + \frac{1}{D_I}$

$\frac{1}{7.0} = \frac{1}{14} + \frac{1}{D_I}$

$D_I = \mathbf{14\text{ cm}}$

$\frac{H_I}{H_O} = \frac{-D_I}{D_O}$

$\frac{H_I}{5.0} = \frac{-14}{14}$

$H_I = \mathbf{-5.0\text{ cm}}$

$M = \frac{H_I}{H_O} = \frac{-5.0}{5.0} = \mathbf{-1.0}$

12. The maximum displacement is 0.32 meters, and the frequency is 2.5 Hz.

$x = A \cos 2\pi ft$

$x =$ **$0.32 \cos 2\pi(2.5)t$ meters**

13. Begin by finding the moment of inertia of the pulley and noting the relationship between a and α.

$$I = \frac{1}{2}mr^2 = \frac{1}{2}(2.8\text{ kg})(0.45\text{ m})^2 = 0.284\text{ kg}\cdot\text{m}^2$$

$$a = r\alpha \longrightarrow \alpha = \frac{a}{0.45}$$

Next, write a $\sum F_x = ma_x$ equation for the 15-kg block. Choose up the plane as the positive direction for motion.

$$\sum F_x = ma_x$$
$$T_1 - mg\sin\theta = ma$$
$$T_1 - (15)(9.81)\sin 22° = 15a$$
$$T_1 = 55.12 + 15a \qquad \text{(a)}$$

Now, write a $\sum F_y = ma_y$ equation for the 29-kg block.

$$\sum F_y = ma_y$$
$$mg - T_2 = ma$$
$$(29)(9.81) - T_2 = 29a$$
$$T_2 = 284.49 - 29a \qquad \text{(b)}$$

Next, write a $\sum\tau = I\alpha$ equation for the pulley.

$$\sum\tau = I\alpha$$
$$0.45T_2 - 0.45T_1 = (0.284)\left(\frac{a}{0.45}\right)$$
$$0.45T_2 - 0.45T_1 = 0.631a$$
$$T_2 - T_1 = 1.402 \qquad \text{(c)}$$

Substitute (a) and (b) into (c) to find the acceleration.

(c) $(284.49 - 29a) - (55.12 + 15a) = 1.402a$

$$229.37 = 45.402a$$
$$a = 5.052\ \frac{\text{m}}{\text{s}^2} \xrightarrow{\text{SD}} \mathbf{5.1\ \frac{m}{s^2}\ \text{up the plane}}$$

14. The image is **approximately 10.5 cm behind the mirror, it is upright, and the height of the image is approximately 4.5 cm.**

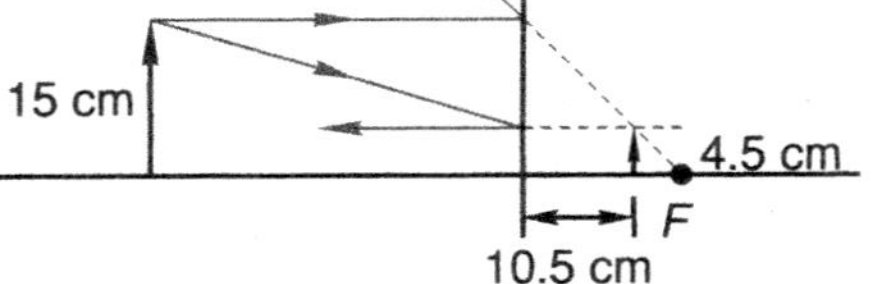

$$M = \frac{H_I}{H_O} = \frac{4.5}{15} = \mathbf{0.30}$$

15. Begin by finding the centripetal force and the static friction force.

$$F_c = \frac{mv^2}{r} = \frac{(500)(20)^2}{70.148} = 2851.11\text{ N}$$
$$F_s = mg\mu_s = (500)(9.81)\mu_s = (4905\text{ N})\mu_s$$

The required centripetal force must equal the static friction force.

$$F_c = F_s$$
$$2851.11\text{ N} = (4905\text{ N})\mu_s$$
$$\mu_s = 0.581 \xrightarrow{\text{SD}} \mathbf{0.6}$$

16. Begin by finding the equivalent resistance of the two parallel resistors.

$$R_E = \frac{(48)(36)}{48 + 36} = 20.57\ \Omega$$

Now, combine this with the 24-Ω resistor to find the equivalent resistance of the circuit.

$$R_E = (20.57\ \Omega) + 24\ \Omega = 44.57\ \Omega$$

Use this resistance to find I_1.

$$I_1 = \frac{V}{R} = \frac{15\text{ V}}{44.57\ \Omega} = 0.337\text{ A} \xrightarrow{\text{SD}} \mathbf{0.34\ A}$$

17. $PE = \frac{1}{2}kx^2 = \frac{1}{2}(720)(3.0)^2 = 3240\text{ J}$

$$KE = \frac{1}{2}mv^2$$
$$3240 = \frac{1}{2}(12)v^2$$
$$v = 23.24\ \frac{\text{m}}{\text{s}} \xrightarrow{\text{SD}} \mathbf{23\ \frac{m}{s}}$$

18. Begin by finding the equivalent resistance of the three series resistors.

$R_E = 46\ \Omega + 20\ \Omega + 10\ \Omega = 76\ \Omega$

Use this resistance to find the current I through the circuit.

$$I = \frac{V}{R} = \frac{38\text{ V}}{76\ \Omega} = 0.5\text{ A}$$

Now find the energy consumed by the 20-Ω resistor.

$E = I^2Rt = (0.5\text{ A})^2(20\ \Omega)(40\text{ s}) = \mathbf{2\bar{0}0\ J}$

19.

$$F = kx$$
$$58 = k(0.052)$$
$$k = 1.115 \times 10^3\ \frac{\text{N}}{\text{m}} \xrightarrow{\text{SD}} \mathbf{1.1 \times 10^3\ \frac{N}{m}}$$

20. (a) $\Sigma F_y = 0;\ 300\text{ N} - 150\text{ N} - F_B + F_A = 0$

(b) $\Sigma M_A = 0;\ 300\text{ N}(11\text{ m}) - 150\text{ N}(8.65\text{ m}) - F_B(5.20\text{ m}) = 0$

Solve (b) for F_B and get:

(b) $3300\text{ N·m} - 1297.5\text{ N·m} - F_B(5.20\text{ m}) = 0$

$$F_B(5.20\text{ m}) = 2002.5\text{ N·m}$$
$$F_B = 385.1\text{ N} \xrightarrow{\text{SD}} \mathbf{385\ N}$$

Substitute F_B into (a) to find F_A.

(a) $300\text{ N} - 150\text{ N} - (385.1\text{ N}) + F_A = 0$

$$F_A = 235.1\text{ N} \xrightarrow{\text{SD}} \mathbf{235\ N}$$

PROBLEM SET 84

1.

$$C = \frac{K\varepsilon_0 A}{d} = \frac{(1)\left(8.85 \times 10^{-12}\ \frac{\text{F}}{\text{m}}\right)(0.15\text{ m}^2)}{(1.0 \times 10^{-3}\text{ m})}$$
$$= 1.328 \times 10^{-9}\text{ F} \xrightarrow{\text{SD}} \mathbf{1.3 \times 10^{-9}\ F}$$

2.

$$C = \frac{K\varepsilon_0 A}{d} = \frac{(3.40)\left(8.85 \times 10^{-12}\ \frac{\text{F}}{\text{m}}\right)(0.15\text{ m}^2)}{(1.0 \times 10^{-3}\text{ m})}$$
$$= 4.514 \times 10^{-9}\text{ F} \xrightarrow{\text{SD}} \mathbf{4.5 \times 10^{-9}\ F}$$

3.

$$\Delta S = \frac{\Delta Q}{T} = \frac{+3320\text{ J}}{(97.8° + 273)\text{ K}}$$
$$= +8.954\text{ J/K} \xrightarrow{\text{SD}} \mathbf{+8.95\ J/K}$$

4.

$$\Delta S = \frac{\Delta Q}{T}$$
$$+5.06\text{ kJ/K} = \frac{2302\text{ kJ}}{T}$$
$$T = 454.94\text{ K} \xrightarrow{\text{SD}} \mathbf{455\ K = 182°C}$$

5. To find the sign of the charge on the particle, place your right hand flat so that your fingers point in the original direction (north) of the particle and bend your fingers to point in the direction of the magnetic field (upward). Since the force on the particle is in the direction of your thumb (east), the particle has a **positive charge.**

6.

$$F = qvB = (3.2 \times 10^{-8})(8.3 \times 10^4)(6.2)$$
$$= 1.647 \times 10^{-2}\text{ N} \xrightarrow{\text{SD}} \mathbf{1.6 \times 10^{-2}\ N}$$

To find which path the particle follows, place your right hand flat so that your fingers point in the original direction of the particle and bend your fingers to point in the direction of the magnetic field. Since the particle has a positive charge, the direction of the force on the particle is in the direction of your thumb. Therefore, the particle follows **path *B***.

7. During the ignition portion of the Otto cycle, the volume of the gas stays constant. Since the pressure of the gas rises 800 Pa, the diagram is as follows.

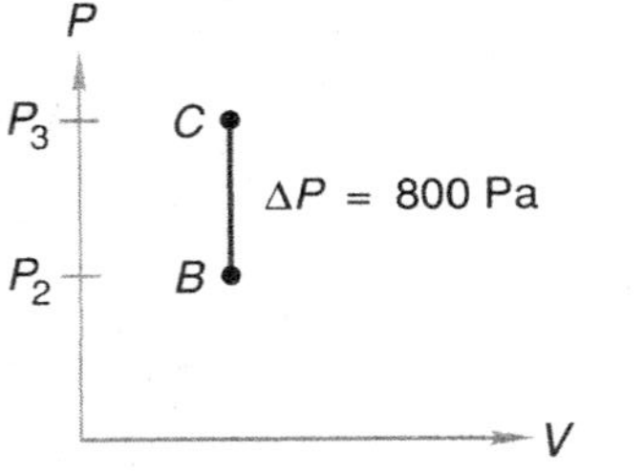

8. We need to find the electric field component at P caused by the charge at B and add the two field components vectorially.

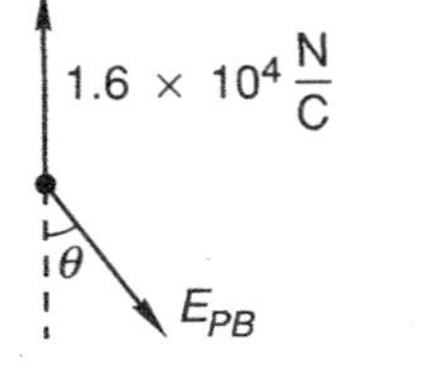

The electric component of P caused by q_B is toward q_B (because q_B is negative) and has a value of

$$E_{PB} = \frac{kq_B}{r^2} = \frac{(9.0 \times 10^9)(4.3 \times 10^{-7})}{(0.50)^2} = 15{,}480 \text{ N/C}$$

From the diagram of the position of the charges, we see that

$$\sin\theta = \frac{0.30}{0.50} = 0.6 \quad \text{and} \quad \cos\theta = \frac{0.40}{0.50} = 0.8$$

The vector components of E_{PB} are

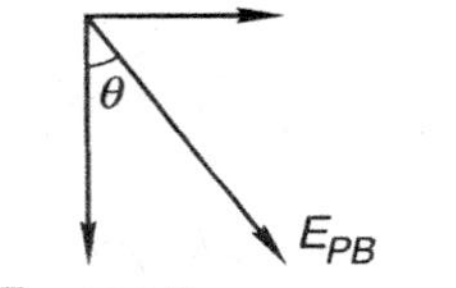

$$E_{PB}\sin\theta = (15{,}480)(0.6) = 9288 \text{ N/C}$$
$$E_{PB}\cos\theta = (15{,}480)(0.8) = 12{,}384 \text{ N/C}$$

The sum of the horizontal and vertical components is

$E_x = (0) + 9288 = 9288$ N/C

$E_y = 1.6 \times 10^4 - 12{,}384 = 3616$ N/C

So now we have the horizontal and vertical components of E_P as

$$E_P = \sqrt{(9288)^2 + (3616)^2}$$
$$= 9.967 \times 10^3 \frac{\text{N}}{\text{C}}$$
$$\alpha = \arctan\frac{3616}{9288} = 21.27°$$

E_P / α / 9288 / 3616

$$E_P = 9.967 \times 10^3 \underline{/21.27°} \frac{\text{N}}{\text{C}} \xrightarrow{\text{SD}} \mathbf{1.0 \times 10^4 \underline{/21.27°} \frac{N}{C}}$$

9.
$$\text{eff}_{max} = \frac{W}{Q_H} = \frac{4.8 \text{ kJ}}{8.7 \text{ kJ}} = 0.5517$$

Multiply this by 100% and get:

$$\text{eff}_{max} = 0.5517 \times 100\% = 55.17\% \xrightarrow{\text{SD}} \mathbf{55\%}$$

10. Begin by converting the temperature to kelvins.

$T_H = 1700°\text{C} + 273 = 1973$ K

Thus, the cold temperature is

$$\text{eff}_{max} = 1 - \frac{T_C}{T_H}$$
$$0.49 = 1 - \frac{T_C}{1973}$$
$$0.51 = \frac{T_C}{1973}$$
$$T_C = 1006.2 \text{ K} \xrightarrow{\text{SD}} \mathbf{1\bar{0}00 \text{ K} = 730°C}$$

11. Determine the parameters of the sound wave if the train is not moving.

$$v_{SND} = f_s \lambda$$
$$330 = (1684)\lambda$$
$$\lambda = 0.19596 \text{ m}$$

As the train approaches Angela, v_s is positive. Now, compute the observed frequency f'.

$$v_{SND} = f'\left(\lambda - \frac{v_s}{f_s}\right)$$
$$330 = f'\left(0.19596 - \frac{38}{1684}\right)$$
$$f' = 1903.2 \text{ Hz} \xrightarrow{SD} \mathbf{1900\ Hz}$$

12. Positive charge will be on the right-hand conductor and negative charge will be on the left-hand conductor.

13. (a) Begin by calculating the maximum vertical velocity of the ball on the way down.

$$PE = mgh = 0.950 \cancel{\text{kg}} \times 9.81 \frac{\text{N}}{\cancel{\text{kg}}} \times 12.5 \text{ m} = 116.494 \text{ J}$$
$$KE = \frac{1}{2}mv^2$$
$$116.494 \text{ J} = \frac{1}{2}(0.950 \text{ kg})v^2$$
$$v = -15.66 \frac{\text{m}}{\text{s}} \xrightarrow{SD} \mathbf{-15.7 \frac{m}{s}}$$

Now calculate the maximum vertical velocity of the ball on the way up.

$$PE = mgh = 0.950 \cancel{\text{kg}} \times 9.81 \frac{\text{N}}{\cancel{\text{kg}}} \times 12.0 \text{ m} = 111.834 \text{ J}$$
$$KE = \frac{1}{2}mv^2$$
$$111.834 \text{ J} = \frac{1}{2}(0.950 \text{ kg})v^2$$
$$v = +15.34 \frac{\text{m}}{\text{s}} \xrightarrow{SD} \mathbf{+15.3 \frac{m}{s}}$$

(b) $\Delta KE = 116.494 \text{ J} - 111.834 \text{ J} = \mathbf{4.66\ J}$

14. Begin by converting 0.792 revolution per second to radians per second.

$$0.792 \frac{\cancel{\text{rev}}}{\text{s}} \times \frac{2\pi \text{ rad}}{1 \cancel{\text{rev}}} = 4.976 \frac{\text{rad}}{\text{s}}$$

Now calculate the tension in the string.

$$T \sin\theta = mr\omega^2$$
$$T \cancel{\sin\theta} = m(0.542 \cancel{\sin\theta})\omega^2$$
$$T = 12.2(0.542)(4.976)^2$$
$$= 163.7 \text{ N} \xrightarrow{SD} \mathbf{164\ N}$$

15. Begin by finding v_A and P_B.

$v_A = 4v_B$; $P_B = 2P_A$

Now use Bernoulli's equation to find P_A.

$$P_A + \frac{1}{2}\rho v_A^2 = P_B + \frac{1}{2}\rho v_B^2$$
$$P_A + \frac{1}{2}\rho(4v_B)^2 = (2P_A) + \frac{1}{2}\rho v_B^2$$
$$P_A + \frac{1}{2}\rho\left(16v_B^2\right) = 2P_A + \frac{1}{2}\rho v_B^2$$
$$P_A + 8\rho v_B^2 = 2P_A + \frac{1}{2}\rho v_B^2$$
$$8\rho v_B^2 - \frac{1}{2}\rho v_B^2 = 2P_A - P_A$$
$$\frac{15}{2}\rho v_B^2 = P_A$$
$$P_A = \mathbf{\frac{15}{2}\rho v_B^2}$$

16. Begin by finding the equivalent capacitance of the two parallel capacitors.

$C_E = 8.0 + 8.0 = 16\ \mu\text{F}$

Next, find the time constant RC.

$RC = (3000\ \Omega)\left(16 \times 10^{-6} \text{ F}\right) = 0.048 \text{ s}$

Now find the initial current.

$$I_0 = \frac{V}{R} = \frac{32 \text{ V}}{3000\ \Omega} = 0.01067 \text{ A}$$

Now calculate the current when $t = 0.096$ s.

$$I = I_0 e^{-t/RC}$$
$$= 0.01067 e^{-0.096/0.048}$$
$$= 0.01067 e^{-2}$$
$$= 1.444 \times 10^{-3} \text{ A} \xrightarrow{SD} \mathbf{1.4 \times 10^{-3}\ A}$$

17. Begin by finding the angular speed and the moment of inertia of the sphere.

$$\omega = \frac{v}{r} = \frac{9.0145\text{ m/s}}{0.1845\text{ m}} = 48.9\ \frac{\text{rad}}{\text{s}}$$

$$I = \frac{2}{5}mr^2 = \frac{2}{5}(5\text{ kg})(0.1845\text{ m})^2 = 0.06808\text{ kg}\cdot\text{m}^2$$

Now find the total kinetic energy.

$$KE = \frac{1}{2}mv^2 + \frac{1}{2}I\omega^2$$
$$= \frac{1}{2}(5)(9.0145)^2 + \frac{1}{2}(0.06808)(48.9)^2$$
$$= 284.5\text{ J} \xrightarrow{SD} \mathbf{300\ J}$$

18. Begin by finding the equivalent resistance of the two 10-Ω parallel resistors.

$$R_E = \frac{(10)(10)}{10 + 10} = 5\ \Omega$$

Next, find the equivalent resistance of the other two 10-Ω parallel resistors.

$$R_E = \frac{(10)(10)}{10 + 10} = 5\ \Omega$$

Now, combine these with the 10-Ω resistor to find the equivalent resistance of the circuit.

$$R_E = (5\ \Omega) + (5\ \Omega) + 10\ \Omega = 20\ \Omega$$

Use this resistance to find I.

$$I = \frac{V}{R} = \frac{50\text{ V}}{20\ \Omega} = \mathbf{2.5\ A}$$

19. Begin by finding the x and y components of the initial velocity.

$$v_{x0} = 42.5\cos 50° = 27.32\ \frac{\text{m}}{\text{s}}$$

$$v_{y0} = 42.5\sin 50° = 32.56\ \frac{\text{m}}{\text{s}}$$

(a) Use the y-displacement equation to find the time.

$$\Delta y = v_{y0}t + \frac{1}{2}a_y t^2$$
$$(0) = 32.56t + \frac{1}{2}(-9.81)t^2$$
$$4.905t^2 = 32.56t$$
$$t = 6.6381\text{ s} \xrightarrow{SD} \mathbf{6.64\ s}$$

(b) Use the x-displacement equation to find the distance.

$$\Delta x = v_{x0}t + \frac{1}{2}a_x t^2$$
$$= (27.32)(6.6381) + (0)$$
$$= 181.35\text{ m} \xrightarrow{SD} \mathbf{181\ m}$$

20. Begin by finding the initial momentum of each mass.

$$m_A v_A = 2.63 \times 10^5(472\angle{-30°}) = 1.241 \times 10^8\angle{-30°}\text{ kg}\cdot\text{m}\cdot\text{s}^{-1}$$

$$m_B v_B = 3.81 \times 10^5(434\angle 45°) = 1.654 \times 10^8\angle 45°\text{ kg}\cdot\text{m}\cdot\text{s}^{-1}$$

$$m_s v_s = 3.25 \times 10^6(306\angle 0°) = 9.945 \times 10^8\angle 0°\text{ kg}\cdot\text{m}\cdot\text{s}^{-1}$$

Now find the final momentum of the combined masses.

$$(m_A + m_B + m_s)v = (2.63 \times 10^5 + 3.81 \times 10^5 + 3.25 \times 10^6)v$$
$$= (3.894 \times 10^6)v$$

Next write a momentum equation equating the initial momenta to the final momentum.

$$m_A v_A + m_B v_B + m_s v_s = (m_A + m_B + m_s)v \qquad \text{(a)}$$

Now find the sum of the x and y components of the initial momenta.

$$\Sigma mv_x = 1.241 \times 10^8\cos -30° + 1.654 \times 10^8\cos 45°$$
$$+ 9.945 \times 10^8\cos 0° = 1.219 \times 10^9\text{ kg}\cdot\text{m}\cdot\text{s}^{-1}$$

$$\Sigma mv_y = 1.241 \times 10^8\sin -30° + 1.654 \times 10^8\sin 45°$$
$$+ 9.945 \times 10^8\sin 0° = 5.491 \times 10^7\text{ kg}\cdot\text{m}\cdot\text{s}^{-1}$$

$$\Sigma mv_R = (1.219 \times 10^9 i + 5.491 \times 10^7 j)\text{ kg}\cdot\text{m}\cdot\text{s}^{-1}$$

Convert this resultant to polar form and get:

$$\Sigma mv_R = \sqrt{(1.219 \times 10^9)^2 + (5.491 \times 10^7)^2} = 1.220 \times 10^9\text{ kg}\cdot\text{m}\cdot\text{s}^{-1}$$

$$\theta = \tan^{-1}\frac{5.491 \times 10^7}{1.219 \times 10^9} = 2.58°$$

$$\Sigma mv_R = 1.220 \times 10^9\angle 2.58°\text{ kg}\cdot\text{m}\cdot\text{s}^{-1}$$

Use this momentum in (a) to find v.

(a) $1.220 \times 10^9\angle 2.58° = (3.894 \times 10^6)v$

$$v = 313.30\angle 2.58°\ \frac{\text{m}}{\text{s}} \xrightarrow{SD} \mathbf{313\angle 2.58°\ \frac{m}{s}}$$

PROBLEM SET 85

1. $\text{emf} = N\frac{\Delta\Phi}{\Delta t} = (4)\left(\frac{608\text{ Wb} - 250\text{ Wb}}{10.0\text{ s}}\right) = 143.2\text{ V} \xrightarrow{\text{SD}} \mathbf{100\text{ V}}$

2. The induced current in the coil will try to produce magnetic flux to oppose the change in magnetic flux. The magnetic flux is decreasing so the current would try to keep it from decreasing by making magnetic flux in the same direction. The induced current would try to make magnetic flux that goes into the plane of the paper. To find the direction of the induced current, bend your right-hand fingers around the wire so that your fingers point in the direction of the magnetic flux produced by the induced current. Your thumb will point in the direction of the flow of the induced current which is clockwise. Since electrons move in the opposite direction of the conventional current, the free electrons would move **counterclockwise** if the switch were closed.

3. $$C = \frac{K\varepsilon_0 A}{d} = \frac{(3.1)\left(8.85\times10^{-12}\ \frac{\text{F}}{\text{m}}\right)(1.5\times10^{-5}\text{ m}^2)}{2.5\times10^{-3}\text{ m}}$$
$$= 1.6461\times10^{-13}\text{ F} \xrightarrow{\text{SD}} \mathbf{1.6\times10^{-13}\text{ F}}$$

4. For each capacitor, solve for $\varepsilon_0 A/d$. Since the dielectric is air, $K = 1$.

$$C_{42} = \frac{K\varepsilon_0 A}{d} \qquad C_{88} = \frac{K\varepsilon_0 A}{d}$$
$$42 = \frac{(1)\varepsilon_0 A}{d} \qquad 88 = \frac{(1)\varepsilon_0 A}{d}$$
$$\frac{\varepsilon_0 A}{d} = 42\ \mu\text{F} \qquad \frac{\varepsilon_0 A}{d} = 88\ \mu\text{F}$$

Now, calculate the new capacitance of each capacitor with Mylar as a dielectric, $K = 3.1$.

$$C = \frac{K\varepsilon_0 A}{d} = (3.1)(42\ \mu\text{F}) = 130.2\ \mu\text{F} \xrightarrow{\text{SD}} \mathbf{130\ \mu F}$$
$$C = \frac{K\varepsilon_0 A}{d} = (3.1)(88\ \mu\text{F}) = 272.8\ \mu\text{F} \xrightarrow{\text{SD}} \mathbf{270\ \mu F}$$

Now, calculate the equivalent capacitance of the two capacitors in series.

$$C_E = \frac{(130.2)(272.8)}{130.2 + 272.8} = 88.135\ \mu\text{F} \xrightarrow{\text{SD}} \mathbf{88\ \mu F}$$

5. $$\Delta S = \frac{\Delta Q}{T} = \frac{+3520\text{ J}}{(45.0^\circ + 273)\text{ K}} = +11.07\ \frac{\text{J}}{\text{K}} \xrightarrow{\text{SD}} \mathbf{+11.1\ \frac{J}{K}}$$

6. $$\Delta L = \alpha L_0 \Delta T = \frac{2.0\times10^{-5}}{\text{C}^\circ}(460\text{ m})(27\text{ C}^\circ) = 0.2484\text{ m} \xrightarrow{\text{SD}} \mathbf{0.25\text{ m}}$$

7. $$F = qvB = (2.5\times10^{-19})(22{,}468)(1950) = 1.095\times10^{-11}\text{ N} \xrightarrow{\text{SD}} \mathbf{1.1\times10^{-11}\text{ N}}$$

To find the path which the particle follows, place your right hand flat so that your fingers point in the original direction of the particle and bend your fingers to point in the direction of the magnetic field. Since the particle has a positive charge, the direction of the force on the particle is in the direction of your thumb. Therefore, the particle follows **path *B*.**

8. $$F = qvB$$
$$2\times10^{-15} = (1.60\times10^{-19})(985.105)B$$
$$B = 12.69\text{ T} \xrightarrow{\text{SD}} \mathbf{10\text{ T}}$$

To find the path which the electron follows, place your right hand flat so that your fingers point in the original direction of the electron and bend your fingers to point in the direction of the magnetic field. Since the electron has a negative charge, the direction of the force on the electron is opposite the direction of your thumb. Therefore, the electron follows **path *B*.**

9. $$\text{Net work} = W_{\text{by gas}} - W_{\text{on gas}} = 1200\text{ J} - 450\text{ J} = \mathbf{750\text{ J}}$$

10. We need to find the electric field component at P caused by the charge at B and add the two field components vectorially.

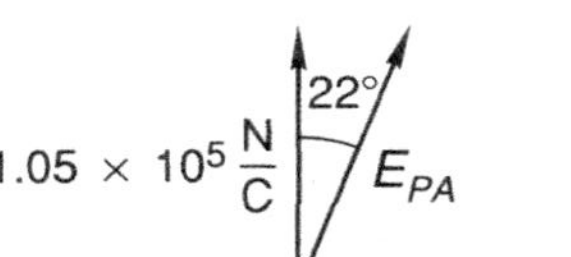

The electric component of P caused by q_A is away from q_A (because q_A is positive) and has a value of

$$E_{PA} = \frac{kq_A}{r^2} = \frac{(9.0 \times 10^9)(6.92 \times 10^{-6})}{\left(\frac{1.01}{\sin 22^\circ}\right)^2} = 8567.6 \text{ N/C}$$

The vector components of E_{PA} are

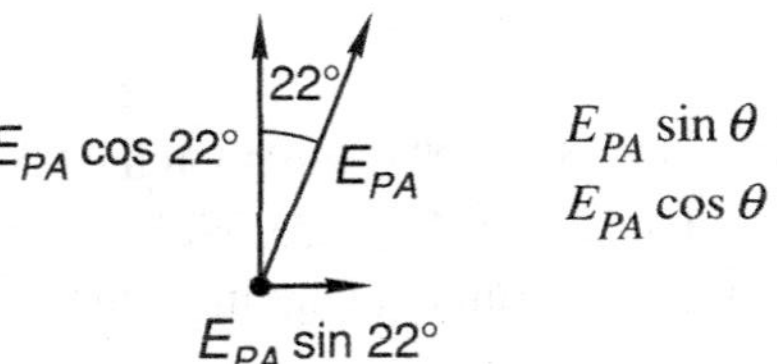

$$E_{PA} \sin\theta = 8567.6 \sin 22^\circ = 3209.5 \text{ N/C}$$
$$E_{PA} \cos\theta = 8567.6 \cos 22^\circ = 7943.7 \text{ N/C}$$

The sum of the horizontal and vertical components is

$$E_x = (0) + 3209.5 = 3209.5 \text{ N/C}$$
$$E_y = 1.05 \times 10^5 + 7943.7 = 1.129 \times 10^5 \text{ N/C}$$

So now we have the horizontal and vertical components of E_P as

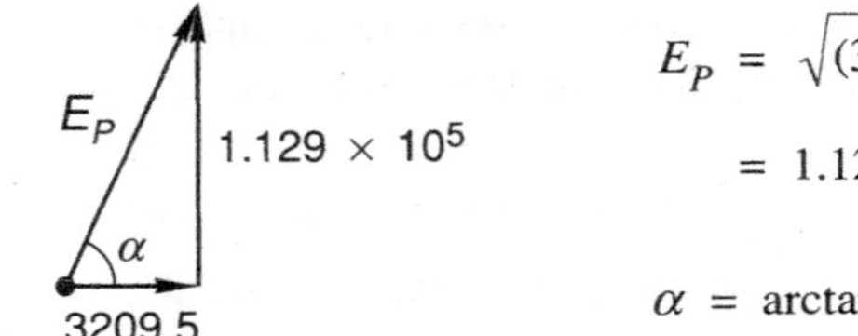

$$E_P = \sqrt{(3209.5)^2 + (1.129 \times 10^5)^2}$$
$$= 1.129 \times 10^5 \ \frac{\text{N}}{\text{C}}$$
$$\alpha = \arctan \frac{1.129 \times 10^5}{3209.5} = 88.37^\circ$$

$$E_P = 1.129 \times 10^5 \underline{/88.37^\circ} \ \frac{\text{N}}{\text{C}} \xrightarrow{\text{SD}} \mathbf{1.13 \times 10^5 \underline{/88.37^\circ}} \ \frac{\text{N}}{\text{C}}$$

11.
$$Q = \Delta U + W$$
$$0 = \Delta U + (-500 \text{ J})$$
$$\Delta U = \mathbf{500 \ J}$$

12.
$$v = f(2L)$$
$$740 = (440)(2L)$$
$$L = 0.8409 \text{ m} \xrightarrow{\text{SD}} \mathbf{0.84 \ m}$$

13. Begin by finding the weight of the sphere and drawing a free-body diagram of the sphere on the left.

$$w = mg$$
$$= 2.04 \times 10^{-1} \text{ kg} \times 9.81 \ \frac{\text{N}}{\text{kg}}$$
$$= 2.001 \text{ N}$$

In this case, $\alpha = 90^\circ - \theta/2$. The weight of the sphere equals the vertical component of the tension.

$$w = T \sin\alpha$$
$$2.001 = T \sin\alpha$$
$$T = \frac{2.001}{\sin\alpha}$$

The horizontal component of the tension equals the force of repulsion F_R.

$$F_R = T\cos\alpha$$
$$= \left(\frac{2.001}{\sin\alpha}\right)\cos\alpha$$
$$= \frac{2.001}{\tan\alpha}$$

Now, we can use Coulomb's law to find α.

$$F_R = \frac{kq_1q_2}{r^2}$$
$$F_R = \frac{(9.0 \times 10^9)(1.97 \times 10^{-7})(2.43 \times 10^{-7})}{(0.0504)^2}$$
$$\frac{2.001}{\tan\alpha} = 0.16961$$
$$\alpha = 85.155^\circ$$

Since $\alpha = 90^\circ - \theta/2$, we get: $85.155^\circ = 90^\circ - \dfrac{\theta}{2}$

$$\theta = \mathbf{9.69^\circ}$$

14. The original period of the pendulum was

$$T = \frac{2\pi\sqrt{L}}{\sqrt{g}} = \frac{2\pi\sqrt{1.0}}{\sqrt{9.81}} = 2.006 \text{ s}$$

The new period of the pendulum is

$$T = \frac{2\pi\sqrt{L}}{\sqrt{g}} = \frac{2\pi\sqrt{16}}{\sqrt{9.81}} = 8.024 \text{ s}$$

So the period of the pendulum was increased by:

$$8.024 \text{ s} - 2.006 \text{ s} = 6.018 \text{ s} \xrightarrow{\text{SD}} \mathbf{6.0\ s}$$

15. (a) The image is **approximately 1.3 cm behind the lens, it is upright, and the height of the image is approximately 1.3 cm.**

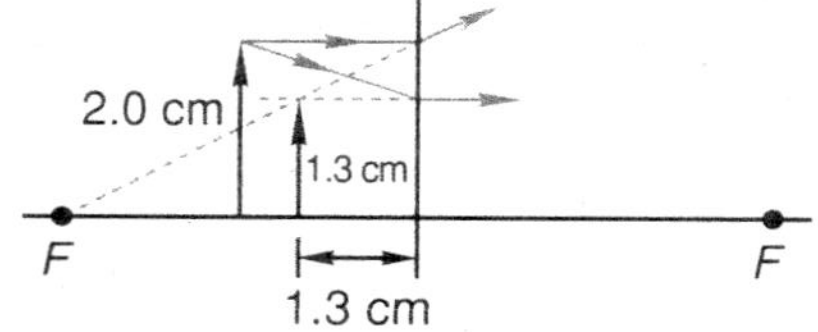

(b) The image is **virtual** because it is upright and behind the lens.

16. Begin by finding the time constant RC.

$$RC = (2500\ \Omega)(8.0 \times 10^{-6}\text{ F}) = 0.020 \text{ s}$$

Sketch the voltage across the capacitor as a function of time.

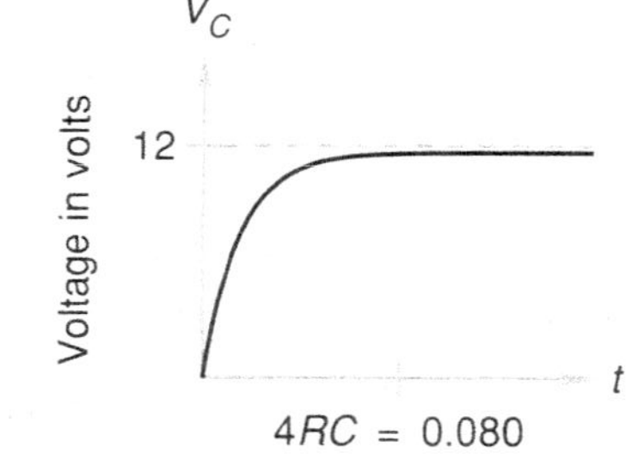

Now calculate the voltage when $t = 0.050$ s.

$$V_C = V_0 - V_0 e^{-t/RC}$$
$$= 12 - 12e^{-0.050/0.020}$$
$$= 12 - 12e^{-2.5}$$
$$= 11.01 \text{ V} \xrightarrow{\text{SD}} \mathbf{11\ V}$$

17. (a) $\Delta U = \frac{3}{2}nR\Delta T$

$$= \frac{3}{2}(5.2)(8.31)(298 - 25)$$
$$= 1.7695 \times 10^4 \text{ J} \xrightarrow{\text{SD}} \mathbf{1.8 \times 10^4\ J}$$

(b) $Q = \Delta U + W$

$$= (1.7695 \times 10^4 \text{ J}) + 0$$
$$= 1.7695 \times 10^4 \text{ J} \xrightarrow{\text{SD}} \mathbf{1.8 \times 10^4\ J}$$

18. Begin by finding the angular speed and the moment of inertia of the hoop.

$$\omega = \frac{v}{r} = \frac{7.23 \text{ m/s}}{2.75 \text{ m}} = 2.629 \frac{\text{rad}}{\text{s}}$$
$$I = mr^2 = (2.26 \text{ kg})(2.75 \text{ m})^2 = 17.09 \text{ kg}\cdot\text{m}^2$$

Now find the total kinetic energy.

$$KE = \frac{1}{2}mv^2 + \frac{1}{2}I\omega^2$$
$$= \frac{1}{2}(2.26)(7.23)^2 + \frac{1}{2}(17.09)(2.629)^2$$
$$= 118.13 \text{ J} \xrightarrow{\text{SD}} \mathbf{118\ J}$$

19. Begin by finding the equivalent resistance of the two parallel resistors.

$$R_E = \frac{(24)(12)}{24 + 12} = 8\ \Omega$$

Now, combine this with the 10-Ω resistor to find the equivalent resistance of the circuit.

$$R_E = (8\ \Omega) + 10\ \Omega = 18\ \Omega$$

Next, calculate the current I through the 10-Ω resistor.

$$I = \frac{V}{R} = \frac{36 \text{ V}}{18\ \Omega} = 2.0 \text{ A}$$

Now find the power consumed by the 10-Ω resistor.

$$P = I^2R = (2.0 \text{ A})^2(10\ \Omega) = \mathbf{4\bar{0}\ W}$$

20.

$$Q_1 = 0.50(2050)(25) = 25{,}625 \text{ J}$$
$$Q_2 = 0.50(334 \times 10^3) = 167{,}000 \text{ J}$$
$$Q_3 = 0.50(4186)(100) = 209{,}300 \text{ J}$$
$$Q_4 = 0.50(2256 \times 10^3) = 1{,}128{,}000 \text{ J}$$
$$Q_T = 1.5299 \times 10^6 \text{ J} \xrightarrow{\text{SD}} \mathbf{1.5 \times 10^6\ J}$$

Problem Set 86

1. Begin by finding the time constant L/R.

$$\frac{L}{R} = \frac{64\text{ H}}{2000\ \Omega} = 0.032\text{ s}$$

Sketch the voltage across the inductor as a function of time.

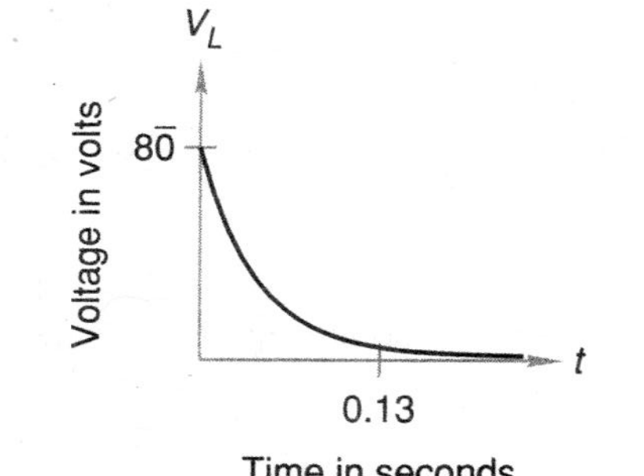

Now calculate the voltage when $t = 46 \times 10^{-3}$ second.

$$V_L = V_0 e^{-\left(\frac{t}{L/R}\right)}$$

$$= 80e^{-46\times10^{-3}/0.032}$$

$$= 80e^{-1.4375}$$

$$= 19.002\text{ V} \xrightarrow{\text{SD}} \mathbf{19\ V}$$

2. Begin by finding the time constant L/R.

$$\frac{L}{R} = \frac{64\text{ H}}{2000\ \Omega} = 0.032\text{ s}$$

Now find the final current.

$$I_F = \frac{V}{R} = \frac{80\text{ V}}{2000\ \Omega} = 0.040\text{ A}$$

Sketch the current in the circuit as a function of time.

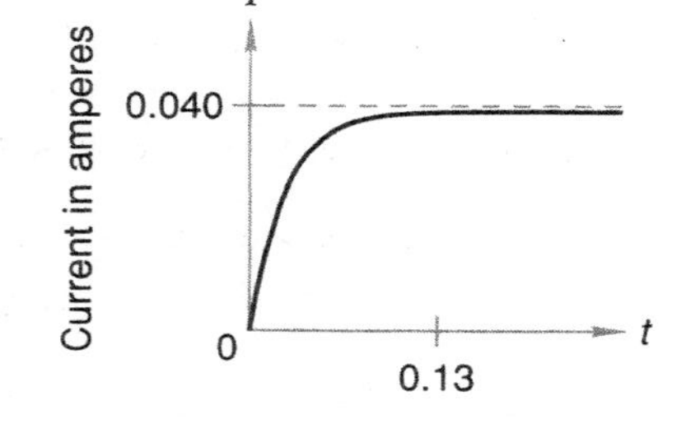

Now calculate the current when $t = 46 \times 10^{-3}$ second.

$$I = I_F - I_F e^{-\left(\frac{t}{L/R}\right)}$$

$$= 0.040 - 0.040e^{-46\times10^{-3}/0.032}$$

$$= 0.040 - 0.040e^{-1.4375}$$

$$= 0.030499\text{ A} \xrightarrow{\text{SD}} \mathbf{0.030\ A}$$

3. $$V_{AB} = N\frac{\Delta\Phi}{\Delta t}$$

$$= (6)\left(\frac{0\text{ Wb} - 360\text{ Wb}}{0.5\text{ s}}\right)$$

$$= -4.32 \times 10^3\text{ V} \xrightarrow{\text{SD}} \mathbf{-4 \times 10^3\ V}$$

4. $$C = \frac{K\varepsilon_0 A}{d} \longrightarrow K = \frac{Cd}{\varepsilon_0 A}$$

$$= \frac{(0.350 \times 10^{-6}\text{ F})(3.5 \times 10^{-4}\text{ m})}{\left(8.85 \times 10^{-12}\ \frac{\text{F}}{\text{m}}\right)(4.1\text{ m}^2)}$$

$$= 3.376 \xrightarrow{\text{SD}} \mathbf{3.4}$$

5. Begin by writing a momentum equation.

$$\Sigma mv_R = m_1v_1 + m_2v_2$$

$$= 4.0(2.0\underline{/0^\circ}) + 0.002(308\underline{/45^\circ})$$

$$= 8.0\underline{/0^\circ} + 0.616\underline{/45^\circ}$$

Now find the sum of the x and y components of the momenta.

$$\Sigma mv_x = 8.0\cos 0^\circ + 0.616\cos 45^\circ = 8.436\text{ kg}\cdot\text{m}\cdot\text{s}^{-1}$$

$$\Sigma mv_y = 8.0\sin 0^\circ + 0.616\sin 45^\circ = 0.436\text{ kg}\cdot\text{m}\cdot\text{s}^{-1}$$

$$\Sigma mv_R = (8.436i + 0.436j)\text{ kg}\cdot\text{m}\cdot\text{s}^{-1}$$

Convert this resultant to polar form and get:

$$\Sigma mv_R = \sqrt{(8.436)^2 + (0.436)^2} = 8.447\text{ kg}\cdot\text{m}\cdot\text{s}^{-1}$$

$$\theta = \tan^{-1}\frac{0.436}{8.436} = 2.96^\circ$$

$$\Sigma mv_R = 8.447\underline{/2.96^\circ}\ \frac{\text{kg}\cdot\text{m}}{\text{s}} \xrightarrow{\text{SD}} \mathbf{8.4\underline{/2.96^\circ}\ \frac{kg\cdot m}{s}}$$

6.
$$\Delta S = \frac{\Delta Q}{T}$$
$$+15.5 \text{ kJ/K} = \frac{\Delta Q}{45.0 \text{ K}}$$
$$\Delta Q = 697.5 \text{ kJ} \xrightarrow{\text{SD}} \mathbf{698\ kJ}$$

7. Begin by calculating the weight of the electron.
$$\begin{aligned} w &= mg \\ &= (9.11 \times 10^{-31})(9.81) \\ &= 8.937 \times 10^{-30} \text{ N} \end{aligned}$$

Now find the velocity of the electron.
$$F = qvB$$
$$8.937 \times 10^{-30} \text{ N} = (1.60 \times 10^{-19} \text{ C})(v)(3.5 \times 10^{-5} \text{ T})$$
$$v = 1.596 \times 10^{-6} \frac{\text{m}}{\text{s}} \xrightarrow{\text{SD}} \mathbf{1.6 \times 10^{-6}\ \frac{m}{s}}$$

To find which path the electron follows, place your right hand flat so that your fingers point in the original direction of the electron and bend your fingers to point in the direction of the magnetic field. Since the electron has a negative charge, the direction of the force on the electron is opposite the direction of your thumb. Therefore, the electron follows **path *A***.

8.
$$W_{\text{net}} = W_{\text{power stroke}} - W_{\text{compression stroke}}$$
$$4.59 \text{ kJ} = 6.13 \text{ kJ} - W_{\text{compression stroke}}$$
$$W_{\text{compression stroke}} = \mathbf{1.54\ kJ}$$

9. Begin by finding the weight of each balloon and drawing a free-body diagram of the balloon on the left.
$$\begin{aligned} w &= mg \\ &= 2.5 \times 10^{-3} \text{ kg} \times 9.81 \frac{\text{N}}{\text{kg}} \\ &= 0.02453 \text{ N} \end{aligned}$$

T
70°
F_R
0.02453 N

The weight of the balloon equals the vertical component of the tension.
$$w = T \sin 70°$$
$$0.02453 = T \sin 70°$$
$$T = 0.02610 \text{ N}$$

The horizontal component of the tension equals the force of repulsion F_R.
$$\begin{aligned} F_R &= T \cos 70° \\ &= (0.02610) \cos 70° \\ &= 8.927 \times 10^{-3} \text{ N} \end{aligned}$$

Now, we can use Coulomb's law to find the charge on each balloon.
$$F_R = \frac{kq_1q_2}{r^2}$$
$$8.927 \times 10^{-3} = \frac{(9.0 \times 10^9)q^2}{(0.75)^2}$$
$$q = 7.47 \times 10^{-7} \text{ C} \xrightarrow{\text{SD}} \mathbf{7.5 \times 10^{-7}\ C}$$

10. Begin by computing the change in entropy of each reservoir.
$$\begin{aligned} \Delta S_{\text{hot}} &= \frac{\Delta Q}{T} \\ &= \frac{-5000 \text{ J}}{700 \text{ K}} \\ &= -7.14 \text{ J/K} \xrightarrow{\text{SD}} \mathbf{-7\ J/K} \end{aligned}$$

$$\begin{aligned} \Delta S_{\text{cold}} &= \frac{\Delta Q}{T} \\ &= \frac{+6654.5 \text{ J}}{355 \text{ K}} \\ &= +18.745 \text{ J/K} \xrightarrow{\text{SD}} \mathbf{+18.7\ J/K} \end{aligned}$$

Next, compute the change in entropy of the system.
$$\begin{aligned} \Delta S_{\text{system}} &= \Delta S_{\text{hot}} + \Delta S_{\text{cold}} \\ &= (-7.14 \text{ J/K}) + (18.745 \text{ J/K}) \\ &= +11.605 \text{ J/K} \xrightarrow{\text{SD}} \mathbf{+10\ J/K} \end{aligned}$$

11.
$$\begin{aligned} C_E &= C_1 + C_2 + C_3 + C_4 \\ &= 12\ \mu\text{F} + 28\ \mu\text{F} + 128\ \mu\text{F} + 72\ \mu\text{F} \\ &= \mathbf{240\ \mu F} \end{aligned}$$

12. $$\frac{1}{f} = \frac{1}{D_O} + \frac{1}{D_I}$$

$$\frac{1}{-5.0} = \frac{1}{12} + \frac{1}{D_I}$$

$$D_I = -3.529 \text{ cm} \xrightarrow{SD} \mathbf{-3.5\ cm}$$

$$\frac{H_I}{H_O} = \frac{-D_I}{D_O}$$

$$\frac{H_I}{4.0} = \frac{-(-3.529)}{12}$$

$$H_I = 1.176 \text{ cm} \xrightarrow{SD} \mathbf{1.2\ cm}$$

$$M = \frac{H_I}{H_O} = \frac{1.176}{4.0} = 0.294 \xrightarrow{SD} \mathbf{0.29}$$

13. Determine the storm siren's wavelength.

$$v_{SND} = f_s\lambda$$
$$335 = (3300)\lambda$$
$$\lambda = 0.1015 \text{ m}$$

As Sam moves away from the siren, v_{OB} is negative. Therefore, the speed of the siren's sound relative to Sam is

$$v_{SND} + v_{OB} = 335 - 12 = 323 \text{ m/s}$$

Now, compute the observed frequency f''.

$$v_{SND} + v_{OB} = f''\lambda$$
$$323 = f''(0.1015)$$
$$f'' = 3182.3 \text{ Hz} \xrightarrow{SD} \mathbf{3200\ Hz}$$

14. (a) The maximum displacement is 1.3 cm, and the frequency is 0.667 Hz.

$x = A \cos 2\pi ft$

$x =$ **1.3 cos 2π(0.667)t centimeters**

(b) $v = f\lambda$

$= (0.667 \text{ Hz})(0.52 \text{ m})$

$= 0.3468 \frac{\text{m}}{\text{s}} \xrightarrow{SD} \mathbf{0.35\ \frac{m}{s}}$

15. Begin by writing a $\sum F = ma$ equation for the suspended mass.

$$\sum F = ma$$
$$mg - T = 11a$$
$$11(9.81) - T = 11a$$
$$T = 107.91 - 11a \qquad \text{(a)}$$

Next, write a $\sum \tau = I\alpha$ equation for the flywheel.

$$\sum \tau = I\alpha$$
$$(0.20)T = \left(\frac{1}{2}mr^2\right)\alpha$$
$$(0.20)T = \left(\frac{1}{2}(3.0)(0.20)^2\right)\alpha$$
$$T = 0.3\alpha \qquad \text{(b)}$$

Now note that α is equal to $\frac{a}{0.20}$. Substitute into (b) and get:

(b) $T = 0.3\left(\frac{a}{0.20}\right) = 1.5a$

Substitute this value for T into (a) to find the acceleration.

(a) $(1.5a) = 107.91 - 11a$

$12.5a = 107.91$

$$a = 8.633 \frac{\text{m}}{\text{s}^2} \xrightarrow{SD} \mathbf{8.6\ \frac{m}{s^2}}$$

16. $$v_1A_1 = v_2A_2$$

$$5.0 \frac{\text{m}}{\text{s}}(310 \text{ m})(92 \text{ m}) = v_2(110 \text{ m})(52 \text{ m})$$

$$v_2 = 24.93 \frac{\text{m}}{\text{s}} \xrightarrow{SD} \mathbf{25\ \frac{m}{s}}$$

17. Begin by finding the equivalent resistance of the 100-Ω and 260-Ω series resistors.

$R_E = 100\ \Omega + 260\ \Omega = 360\ \Omega$

Next, find the voltage across the 72-Ω resistor.

$V_2 = I_2R = (0.0833 \text{ A})(72\ \Omega) = 5.998 \text{ V}$

This must equal the voltage drop across the 100-Ω and 260-Ω resistors. Use this voltage to find I_3.

$$I_3 = \frac{V_2}{R} = \frac{5.998 \text{ V}}{360\ \Omega} = 0.0167 \text{ A} \xrightarrow{SD} \mathbf{0.017\ A}$$

Use KCL to find I_1.

$I_1 = I_2 + I_3 = 0.0833 \text{ A} + 0.0167 \text{ A} =$ **0.10 A**

18. Begin by converting 3.5 rev/s to rad/s.

$$3.5\,\frac{\text{rev}}{\text{s}} \times \frac{2\pi\text{ rad}}{1\text{ rev}} = 21.99\,\frac{\text{rad}}{\text{s}}$$

Now find the tension in the string when the ball is at the top of the circle.

$$T = F_c - w = mr\omega^2 - mg$$
$$= (1.5)(0.25)(21.99)^2 - (1.5)(9.81)$$
$$= 166.62\text{ N} \xrightarrow{\text{SD}} \mathbf{170\ N}$$

19. Begin at the ground symbol, move clockwise, and sum the voltage changes to zero.

$$+6\text{ V} + 2\text{ V} + 1\text{ V} - 24\text{ V} + 3\text{ V} + 2\text{ V} + 4\text{ V} + V_1 = 0$$
$$V_1 = \mathbf{6\ V}$$

Since all the circuit elements are connected in series, the current through any resistor is the same throughout the circuit.

$$I = \frac{3\text{ V}}{30\ \Omega} = 0.1\text{ A}$$

We can now use Ohm's law to find R_1.

$$V_1 = IR_1$$
$$6\text{ V} = (0.1\text{ A})R_1$$
$$R_1 = \mathbf{60\ \Omega}$$

20. (a) Begin by finding the volume of the boat that is submerged.

$$V_s = 57\text{ m}^3 \times 0.72 = 41.04\text{ m}^3$$

Now find the mass of the water displaced.

$$m_w = 1000\,\frac{\text{kg}}{\text{m}^3} \times 41.04\text{ m}^3 = 4.104 \times 10^4\text{ kg} \xrightarrow{\text{SD}} \mathbf{4.1 \times 10^4\ kg}$$

(b) $F_B = 4.104 \times 10^4\text{ kg} \times 9.81\,\frac{\text{N}}{\text{kg}}$

$$= 4.026 \times 10^5\text{ N} \xrightarrow{\text{SD}} \mathbf{4.0 \times 10^5\ N}$$

Problem Set 87

1. $$\text{eff}_{max} = 1 - \frac{T_C}{T_H} = 1 - \frac{480\text{ K}}{1200\text{ K}} = 0.60$$

The net work of the Carnot engine is equal to the amount of heat energy extracted from the hot reservoir multiplied by the maximum possible efficiency.

$$\text{Net work} = (100\text{ J})(0.60) = 60\text{ J}$$

The heat energy expelled to the cold reservoir is equal to the amount of heat energy extracted from the hot reservoir minus the net work.

$$Q_C = 100\text{ J} - 60\text{ J} = 40\text{ J}$$

The energy flow diagram is shown below.

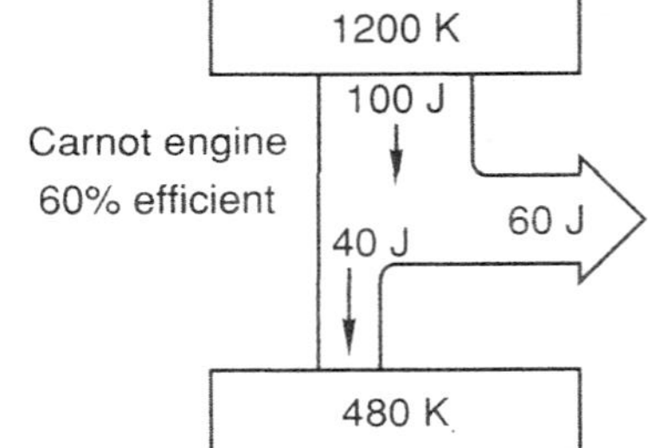

2. Begin by finding the time constant L/R.

$$\frac{L}{R} = \frac{52\text{ H}}{100\ \Omega} = 0.52\text{ s}$$

Sketch the voltage across the inductor as a function of time.

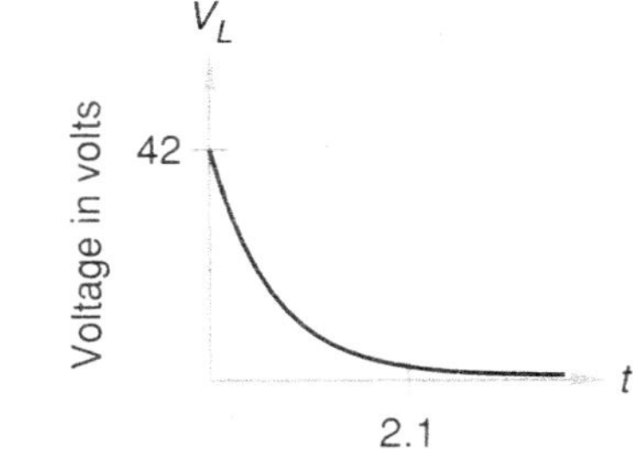

$$V_L = V_0 e^{-\left(\frac{t}{L/R}\right)}$$
$$= 42e^{-1.04/0.52}$$
$$= 42e^{-2} = 5.684\text{ V} \xrightarrow{\text{SD}} \mathbf{5.7\ V}$$

3. The induced voltage V_2 is directly proportional to the ratio of N_2 to N_1. Since the number of turns N_2 is greater than N_1, the ratio N_2/N_1 is larger than 1. Therefore, the induced voltage V_2 will be greater than V_1, $\mathbf{V_2 > V_1}$.

4. $$\text{emf} = N\frac{\Delta\Phi}{\Delta t} = (10)\left(\frac{75.004\text{ Wb} - 150.5\text{ Wb}}{5.141\text{ s}}\right) = -146.85\text{ V} \xrightarrow{SD} \mathbf{-100\ V}$$

5. First, solve for $\varepsilon_0 A/d$ using $K = 3.1$.

$$C_1 = \frac{K_1\varepsilon_0 A}{d}$$

$$150 \times 10^{-6} = \frac{(3.1)\varepsilon_0 A}{d}$$

$$\frac{\varepsilon_0 A}{d} = 4.84 \times 10^{-5}$$

Substitute $(\varepsilon_0 A/d)$ into the following and solve for K_2.

$$C_2 = \frac{K_2\varepsilon_0 A}{d}$$

$$130 \times 10^{-6} = K_2(4.84 \times 10^{-5})$$

$$K_2 = 2.69 \xrightarrow{SD} \mathbf{2.7}$$

6. (a) $$C = \frac{K\varepsilon_0 A}{d} = \frac{(1)\left(8.85 \times 10^{-12}\ \frac{\text{F}}{\text{m}}\right)(0.15\text{ m}^2)}{0.0075\text{ m}} = 1.77 \times 10^{-10}\text{ F} \xrightarrow{SD} \mathbf{1.8 \times 10^{-10}\ F}$$

(b) $$Q = CV = (1.77 \times 10^{-10}\text{ F})(550\text{ V}) = 9.735 \times 10^{-8}\text{ C} \xrightarrow{SD} \mathbf{9.7 \times 10^{-8}\ C}$$

7. Begin by computing the change in entropy of each reservoir.

$$\Delta S_{hot} = \frac{\Delta Q}{T} = \frac{+5400\text{ J}}{270\text{ K}} = +20.0\text{ J/K}$$

$$\Delta S_{cold} = \frac{\Delta Q}{T} = \frac{-5400\text{ J}}{70\text{ K}} = -77.14\text{ J/K}$$

Next, compute the change in entropy of the system.

$$\Delta S_{system} = \Delta S_{hot} + \Delta S_{cold} = (+20.0\text{ J/K}) + (-77.14\text{ J/K}) = -57.14\text{ J/K} \xrightarrow{SD} \mathbf{-57\ J/K}$$

8. Begin by finding the velocity of the proton in meters per second.

$$v = 0.34c = (0.34)(3.00 \times 10^8) = 1.02 \times 10^8\text{ m/s}$$

Now find the strength of the magnetic field.

$$F = qvB$$

$$3.48 \times 10^{-8}\text{ N} = (1.60 \times 10^{-19}\text{ C})\left(1.02 \times 10^8\ \frac{\text{m}}{\text{s}}\right)B$$

$$B = 2.132 \times 10^3\text{ T} \xrightarrow{SD} \mathbf{2.1 \times 10^3\ T}$$

To find which path the proton follows, place your right hand flat so that your fingers point in the original direction of the proton and bend your fingers to point in the direction of the magnetic field. Since the proton has a positive charge, the direction of the force on the proton is in the direction of your thumb. Therefore, the proton follows **path A.**

9. $$W_{net} = W_{power\ stroke} - W_{compression\ stroke}$$

$$18{,}000\text{ J} = 29{,}000\text{ J} - W_{compression\ stroke}$$

$$W_{compression\ stroke} = \mathbf{11{,}000\ J}$$

10. The net work done is equal to the work done by the gas while it was expanding at T_H minus the work done on the gas while it was being compressed at T_C.

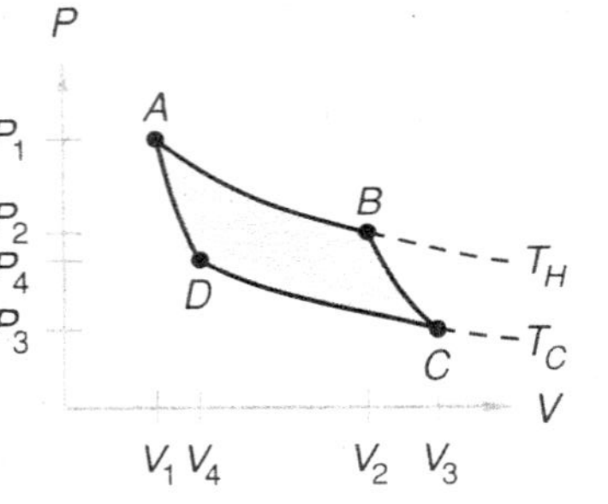

11. $v = f(2L) = (880)(2)(0.33) = 580.8 \frac{\text{m}}{\text{s}} \xrightarrow{\text{SD}} \mathbf{580 \frac{m}{s}}$

12. $$\text{eff}_{\text{max}} = 1 - \frac{T_C}{T_H}$$

$$0.42 = 1 - \frac{T_C}{T_H}$$

$$\frac{T_H}{T_C} = 1.724 \xrightarrow{\text{SD}} \mathbf{1.7}$$

13. Begin by finding v_1 and v_2.

$$v_1 = \frac{Q}{A_1} = \frac{0.55}{0.15} = 3.67 \frac{\text{m}}{\text{s}}$$

$$v_2 = \frac{Q}{A_2} = \frac{0.55}{0.50} = 1.10 \frac{\text{m}}{\text{s}}$$

Now use Bernoulli's equation to solve for h_2, the increased height of the elevation of the pipe. Note that the $\rho g h_1$ term falls out of the equation.

$$P_1 + \frac{1}{2}\rho v_1^2 = P_2 + \frac{1}{2}\rho v_2^2 + \rho g h_2$$

$$114{,}500 + \frac{1}{2}(1025)(3.67)^2 = 117{,}200 + \frac{1}{2}(1025)(1.10)^2 + (1025)(9.81)h_2$$

$$114{,}500 + 6902.8 = 117{,}200 + 620.1 + (10{,}055.3)h_2$$

$$(10{,}055.3)h_2 = 3582.7$$

$$h_2 = 0.3563 \text{ m} \xrightarrow{\text{SD}} \mathbf{0.36\ m}$$

14. In the circuit, when the capacitors are fully charged, the sum of the voltages V_1 and V_2 is 8 volts.

(a) $V_1 + V_2 = 8$

Since the capacitors are in series, the charge on each capacitor is the same, $Q = CV$.

(b) $C_1V_1 = C_2V_2$

Solve (b) for V_2 and substitute into (a) and get:

(a) $$V_1 + \frac{C_1V_1}{C_2} = 8$$

$$V_1 + \frac{(8 \times 10^{-6})V_1}{(22 \times 10^{-6})} = 8$$

$$1.364V_1 = 8$$

$$V_1 = 5.87 \text{ V} \xrightarrow{\text{SD}} \mathbf{6\ V}$$

Substitute V_1 into (a) and solve for V_2.

(a) $(5.87) + V_2 = 8$

$$V_2 = 2.13 \text{ V} \xrightarrow{\text{SD}} \mathbf{2\ V}$$

15. The image is **approximately $1\bar{0}$ cm in front of the mirror, it is inverted, and the height of the image is approximately 2.0 cm.**

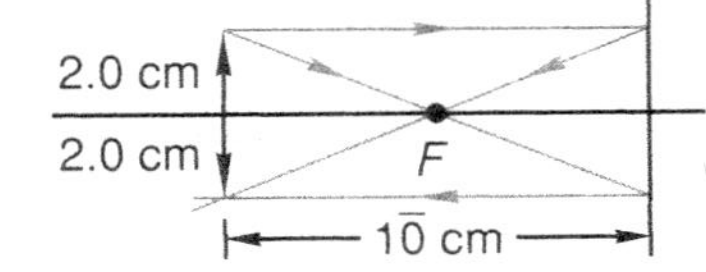

16. Begin by finding the equivalent resistance of the two parallel resistors.

$$R_E = \frac{(60)(30)}{60 + 30} = 20\ \Omega$$

Now, combine this with the 8-Ω resistor to find the equivalent resistance of the circuit.

$$R_E = (20\ \Omega) + 8\ \Omega = 28\ \Omega$$

Use this resistance to find the current I through the 8-Ω resistor.

$$I = \frac{V}{R} = \frac{56 \text{ V}}{28\ \Omega} = 2.0 \text{ A}$$

Now find the energy used by the 8-Ω resistor.

$E = I^2Rt = (2.0 \text{ A})^2(8\ \Omega)(25 \text{ s}) = \mathbf{800\ J}$

17. Begin by finding the centripetal force, F_c, and the weight of the ball.

$$F_c = \frac{mv^2}{r} = \frac{1.5(2.3)^2}{0.35} = 22.67 \text{ N}$$
$$w = mg = (1.5)(9.81) = 14.72 \text{ N}$$

The tension, T, is equal to the vector sum of the horizontal force, F_c, and the vertical force, w.

$$T = \sqrt{(22.67)^2 + (14.72)^2} = 27.03 \text{ N} \xrightarrow{\text{SD}} \mathbf{27\ N}$$

18. Begin by finding the x and y components of the initial velocity.

$$v_{x0} = 20.2 \cos 50° = 12.98 \frac{\text{m}}{\text{s}}$$
$$v_{y0} = 20.2 \sin 50° = 15.47 \frac{\text{m}}{\text{s}}$$

(a) Use the y-displacement equation to find the time.

$$\Delta y = v_{y0}t + \frac{1}{2}a_y t^2$$
$$-1.6 = 15.47t + \frac{1}{2}(-9.81)t^2$$
$$0 = 4.905t^2 - 15.47t - 1.6$$

Use the quadratic formula to solve this equation for t.

$$t = \frac{-(-15.47) \pm \sqrt{(-15.47)^2 - 4(4.905)(-1.6)}}{2(4.905)} = 3.254 \text{ s} \xrightarrow{\text{SD}} \mathbf{3.3\ s}$$

(b) Use the motion equation to find the time when the vertical velocity is zero.

$$v(t) = v_{y0} + a_y t$$
$$0 = 15.47 + (-9.81)t$$
$$t = 1.577 \text{ s}$$

Use this time in the y-position equation to find the height.

$$y = y_0 + v_{y0}t + \frac{1}{2}a_y t^2$$
$$= 1.6 + 15.47(1.577) + \frac{1}{2}(-9.81)(1.577)^2$$
$$= 13.80 \text{ m} \xrightarrow{\text{SD}} \mathbf{14\ m}$$

19. Begin by calculating the current I_1 that passes through the battery.

$$I_1 = \frac{P}{V} = \frac{1.50 \text{ W}}{15 \text{ V}} = \mathbf{0.10\ A}$$

Use this current to find the voltage drop across the 40-Ω resistor.

$$V_1 = I_1 R = (0.10 \text{ A})(40\ \Omega) = 4 \text{ V}$$

Thus, the voltage drop across the 132-Ω, 60-Ω, and 600-Ω resistors is 15 V − 4 V, or 11 V. Use this voltage to find I_2 and I_3.

$$I_2 = \frac{V}{R} = \frac{11 \text{ V}}{(600 + 60)\ \Omega} = 0.01667 \text{ A} \xrightarrow{\text{SD}} \mathbf{0.017\ A}$$
$$I_3 = \frac{V}{R} = \frac{11 \text{ V}}{132\ \Omega} = 0.08333 \text{ A} \xrightarrow{\text{SD}} \mathbf{0.083\ A}$$

20. Begin by finding the cross-sectional area of the rod.

$$A = \pi r^2 = \pi(2.6 \times 10^{-2} \text{ m})^2 = 2.124 \times 10^{-3} \text{ m}^2$$

Now find the electrical resistance.

$$R = \rho \frac{L}{A} = \frac{(1.59 \times 10^{-8}\ \Omega\cdot\text{m})(4.25 \text{ m})}{2.124 \times 10^{-3} \text{ m}^2}$$
$$= 3.181 \times 10^{-5}\ \Omega \xrightarrow{\text{SD}} \mathbf{3.2 \times 10^{-5}\ \Omega}$$

PROBLEM SET 88

1. At each instantaneous voltage, the current through the resistor is equal to the voltage divided by the resistance. The current peaks at 1.1 A and −1.1 A.

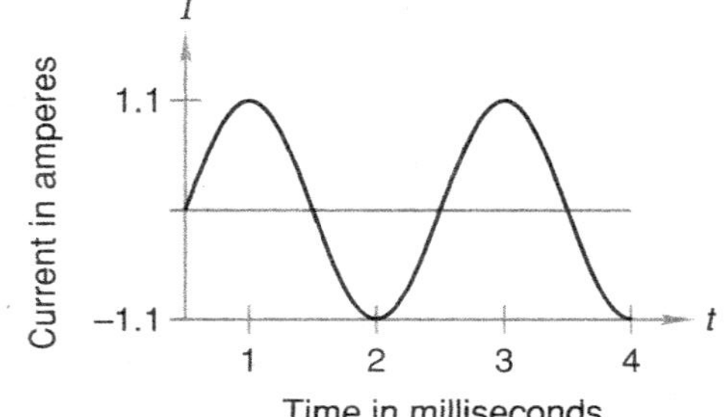

2. We know that $V_1I_1 = V_2I_2$. Since the current is inversely proportional to the number of coils through which it flows ($I_1N_1 = I_2N_2$), the original equation can be written as $V_1N_2 = V_2N_1$. So V_2 can be found by the following:

$$V_2 = \frac{N_2V_1}{N_1} = \frac{(400)(15 \sin \omega t)}{20} = \mathbf{300 \sin \omega t\ volts}$$

3. Begin by finding the time constant L/R.

$$\frac{L}{R} = \frac{75}{25} = 3\text{ s}$$

Sketch the current through the resistor as a function of time.

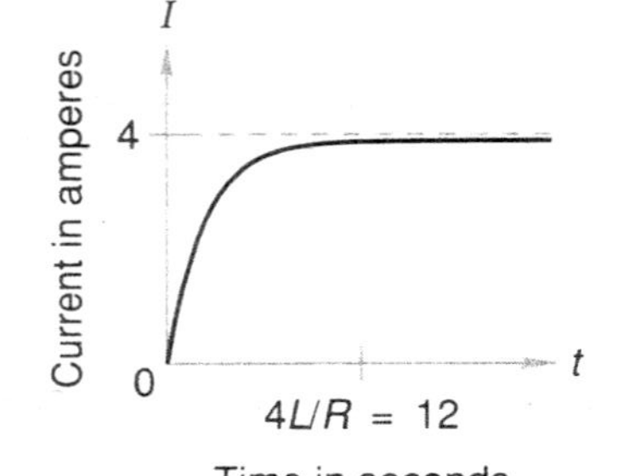

Now calculate the current when $t = 6$ seconds.

$$I = 4 - 4e^{-t/(L/R)}$$
$$= 4 - 4e^{-6/3}$$
$$= 4 - 4e^{-2}$$
$$= 3.46\text{ A} \xrightarrow{\text{SD}} \mathbf{3\ A}$$

4. Begin by finding the time constant RC.

$RC = (10{,}000\ \Omega)(25 \times 10^{-6}\text{ F}) = 0.25\text{ s}$

Sketch the voltage across the capacitor as a function of time.

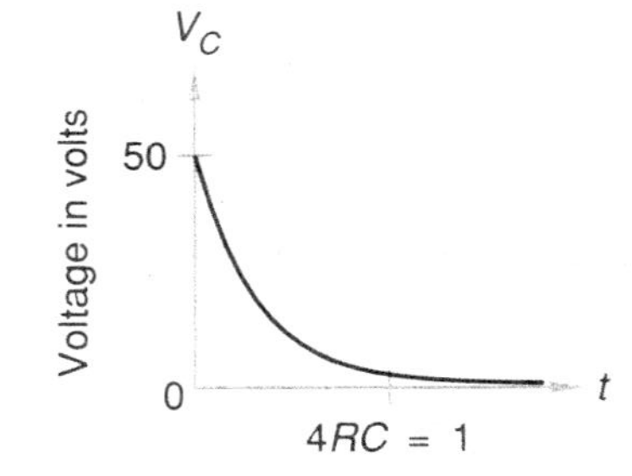

Now calculate the voltage when $t = 0.05$ second.

$$V_C = V_0 e^{-t/RC}$$
$$= 50e^{-0.05/0.25}$$
$$= 50e^{-0.2}$$
$$= 40.94\text{ V} \xrightarrow{\text{SD}} \mathbf{40\ V}$$

5. Begin by finding the time constant RC.

$RC = (10{,}000\ \Omega)(25 \times 10^{-6}\text{ F}) = 0.25\text{ s}$

Sketch the voltage across the capacitor as a function of time.

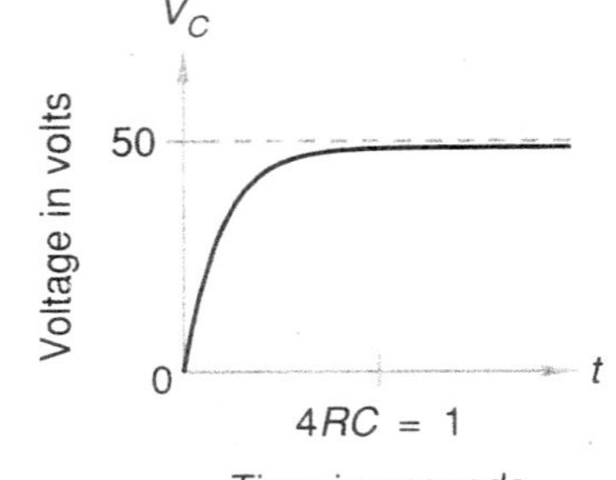

Now calculate the voltage when $t = 0.05$ second.

$$V_C = V_0 - V_0 e^{-t/RC}$$
$$= 50 - 50e^{-0.05/0.25}$$
$$= 50 - 50e^{-0.2}$$
$$= 9.06\text{ V} \xrightarrow{\text{SD}} \mathbf{9\ V}$$

6.

$$C = \frac{K\varepsilon_0 A}{d} \longrightarrow K = \frac{Cd}{\varepsilon_0 A}$$
$$= \frac{(0.350 \times 10^{-6}\text{ F})(7.0 \times 10^{-4}\text{ m})}{\left(8.85 \times 10^{-12}\ \frac{\text{F}}{\text{m}}\right)(4.1\text{ m}^2)}$$
$$= 6.752 \xrightarrow{\text{SD}} \mathbf{6.8}$$

7. For each section of the loop of wire, place your right hand flat so that your fingers point in the direction of the current and then bend your fingers to point in the direction of the magnetic field. Your thumb will then point in the direction of the force on the wire. Therefore, the torque on the loop of wire is in the **counterclockwise** direction.

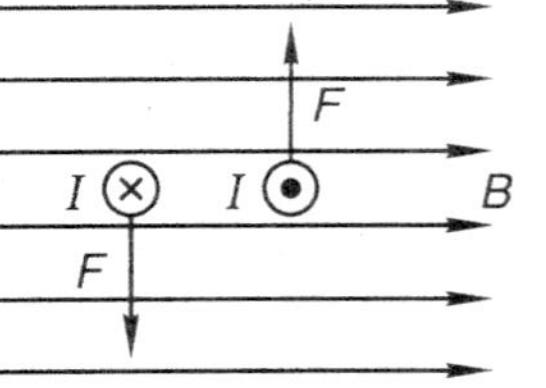

8. Refer to Section 86.A.

9. $$\text{emf} = N\frac{\Delta\Phi}{\Delta t}$$
$$= (195)\left(\frac{175\text{ Wb} - 650\text{ Wb}}{12\text{ s}}\right)$$
$$= -7.719 \times 10^3\text{ V} \xrightarrow{\text{SD}} \mathbf{-7.7 \times 10^3\ V}$$

10. $$C = \frac{K\varepsilon_0 A}{d}$$
$$= \frac{(2.75)\left(8.85 \times 10^{-12}\ \frac{\text{F}}{\text{m}}\right)(0.124\text{ m}^2)}{0.000520\text{ m}}$$
$$= 5.804 \times 10^{-9}\text{ F} \xrightarrow{\text{SD}} \mathbf{5.80 \times 10^{-9}\ F}$$

11. Begin by computing the amount of heat required to melt 113 grams of pentachloronitrobenzene.

$$Q = (113\,\cancel{\text{g}})\left(62.34\ \frac{\text{J}}{\cancel{\text{g}}}\right) = 7044.42\text{ J}$$

Next, compute the change in entropies.

$$\Delta S_{\text{PCNB}} = \frac{\Delta Q}{T}$$
$$= \frac{+7044.42\text{ J}}{(144.8° + 273)\text{ K}}$$
$$= +16.861\text{ J/K} \xrightarrow{\text{SD}} \mathbf{+16.9\ J/K}$$
$$\Delta S_{\text{oven}} = \frac{\Delta Q}{T}$$
$$= \frac{-7044.42\text{ J}}{(200° + 273)\text{ K}}$$
$$= -14.893\text{ J/K} \xrightarrow{\text{SD}} \mathbf{-14.9\ J/K}$$
$$\Delta S_{\text{comb}} = \Delta S_{\text{PCNB}} + \Delta S_{\text{oven}}$$
$$= (+16.861\text{ J/K}) + (-14.893\text{ J/K})$$
$$= +1.968\text{ J/K} \xrightarrow{\text{SD}} \mathbf{+1.97\ J/K}$$

12. In order to find the charge of the particle, the right-hand rule must be used. Place your right hand flat so that your fingers point in the original direction of the particle and bend your fingers to point in the direction of the magnetic field. Since your thumb points in the direction of the deflection of the particle, the charge on the particle is **positive.**

13. Begin by finding the charge at each point.

$$q_1 = 2.0 \times 10^6\,\cancel{\text{electrons}} \times \frac{1.60 \times 10^{-19}\text{ C}}{1\,\cancel{\text{electron}}} = 3.2 \times 10^{-13}\text{ C}$$
$$q_2 = 2.5 \times 10^8\,\cancel{\text{electrons}} \times \frac{1.60 \times 10^{-19}\text{ C}}{1\,\cancel{\text{electron}}} = 4.0 \times 10^{-11}\text{ C}$$

Compute the magnitude of the force.

$$F = \frac{kq_1q_2}{r^2}$$
$$= \frac{(9.0 \times 10^9)(3.2 \times 10^{-13})(4.0 \times 10^{-11})}{(3.0 \times 10^{-3})^2}$$
$$= 1.28 \times 10^{-8}\text{ N} \xrightarrow{\text{SD}} \mathbf{1.3 \times 10^{-8}\ N}$$

14. Increase the length of the pendulum to $3L$.

$$T = 2\pi\sqrt{\frac{L}{g}} \rightarrow T_2 = 2\pi\sqrt{\frac{3L}{g}}$$

Factor the 3 out from under the radical and get:

$$T_2 = (\sqrt{3})\,2\pi\sqrt{\frac{L}{g}}$$

Now note that $2\pi\sqrt{\frac{L}{g}}$ is equal to T. Substitute and get:

$$T_2 = \sqrt{3}T$$

Since $f = 1/T_2$, we get:

$$f = \frac{1}{T_2} = \mathbf{\frac{1}{\sqrt{3}T}}$$

15. $$Q = \Delta U + W$$
$$0 = \Delta U + (2.1 \times 10^5\text{ J})$$
$$\Delta U = \mathbf{-2.1 \times 10^5\ J}$$

16. (a) $f = \frac{1}{2\pi}\sqrt{\frac{k}{m}} = \frac{1}{2\pi}\sqrt{\frac{820}{23}} = 0.9503\text{ Hz} \xrightarrow{\text{SD}} \mathbf{0.95\ Hz}$

(b) $T = \frac{1}{f} = \frac{1}{0.9503\text{ Hz}} = 1.052\text{ s} \xrightarrow{\text{SD}} \mathbf{1.1\ s}$

17.
$$\Delta L = \alpha L_0 \Delta T$$
$$(53.9 - 52.9) = (2.0 \times 10^{-5})(52.9)(T_2 - 25)$$
$$1.0 = (1.058 \times 10^{-3})(T_2 - 25)$$
$$945.18 = T_2 - 25$$
$$T_2 = 970.18°\text{C} \xrightarrow{\text{SD}} \mathbf{970°C}$$

18. Begin by denoting the signs on the resistor.

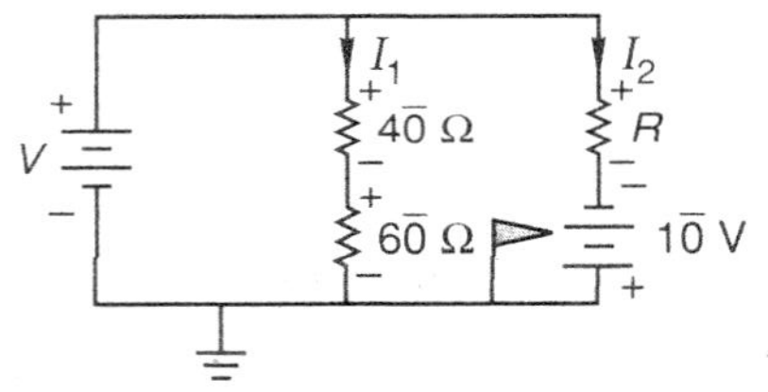

In the right-hand loop, begin at the starting flag, move clockwise, and sum the voltage changes to zero.
$$-60I_1 - 40I_1 + I_2R - 10 = 0$$
$$-60(0.40) - 40(0.40) + (0.20)R - 10 = 0$$
$$R(0.20) = 50$$
$$R = \mathbf{250\ \Omega}$$

19. $D = R \times T = (350)(1.6) = \mathbf{560\ m}$

20. Begin by converting 64.150 milliliters to cubic meters.
$$64.150\ \cancel{\text{ml}} \times \frac{1\ \cancel{\text{cm}^3}}{1\ \cancel{\text{ml}}} \times \frac{1\ \text{m}^3}{(100)^3\ \cancel{\text{cm}^3}} = 6.415 \times 10^{-5}\ \text{m}^3$$

Now use the ideal gas law and get:
$$\frac{P_1V_1}{T_1} = \frac{P_2V_2}{T_2}$$
$$\frac{(3.245 \times 10^6\ \text{Pa})(6.415 \times 10^{-5}\ \text{m}^3)}{(138° + 273)\ \text{K}} = \frac{P_2(10\ \text{m}^3)}{148.559\ \text{K}}$$
$$P = 7.524\ \text{Pa} \xrightarrow{\text{SD}} \mathbf{8\ Pa}$$

Problem Set 89

1. Begin by raising 10 to the Richter scale readings 6.5 and 4.7.
$$10^{x_1} = 10^{6.5} = 3{,}162{,}278$$
$$10^{x_2} = 10^{4.7} = 50{,}119$$
Next, divide the intensities.
$$\frac{3{,}162{,}278}{50{,}119} = 63.095 \xrightarrow{\text{SD}} \mathbf{63}$$

2. (a) Begin by converting decibels to intensities for $B_1 = 15$ and $B_2 = 125$.
$$I_1 = I_0 10^{B_1/10} = (1 \times 10^{-12})10^{1.5} = 3.162 \times 10^{-11}\ \text{W/m}^2$$
$$I_2 = I_0 10^{B_2/10} = (1 \times 10^{-12})10^{12.5} = 3.162\ \text{W/m}^2$$
Next, divide I_2 by I_1.
$$\frac{I_2}{I_1} = \frac{3.162\ \text{W/m}^2}{3.162 \times 10^{-11}\ \text{W/m}^2} = \mathbf{1.0 \times 10^{11}}$$
(b) Begin by finding the difference in decibel levels.
125 dB − 15 dB = 110 dB
Divide this 110-dB increase by 10 and use it as an exponent of 2.
$$2^{110/10} = 2^{11} = 2.048 \times 10^3 \xrightarrow{\text{SD}} \mathbf{2.0 \times 10^3}$$

3. (a) Power loss $= I^2R_T$
$$= (1000\ \text{A})^2(1500\ \Omega)$$
$$= 1.5 \times 10^9\ \text{W} \xrightarrow{\text{SD}} \mathbf{2 \times 10^9\ W}$$
(b) Power loss $= I^2R_T$
$$= (5\ \text{A})^2(1500\ \Omega)$$
$$= 3.75 \times 10^4\ \text{W} \xrightarrow{\text{SD}} \mathbf{4 \times 10^4\ W}$$

4. We know that $V_1I_1 = V_2I_2$. Since the current is inversely proportional to the number of coils through which it flows, $I_1N_1 = I_2N_2$, this equation becomes $V_1N_2 = V_2N_1$. So the ratio of V_1 to V_2 is
$$\frac{V_1}{V_2} = \frac{N_1}{N_2} = \frac{1000}{20} = \mathbf{50}$$

5. Begin by computing the amount of heat required to melt 0.042 kg of ice.

$$Q = (0.042\ \cancel{kg})\left(3.34 \times 10^5\ \frac{J}{\cancel{kg}}\right) = 14{,}028\ J$$

Next, compute the change in entropies.

(a) $$\Delta S_{ice} = \frac{\Delta Q}{T} = \frac{+14{,}028\ J}{273\ K} = +51.38\ J/K \xrightarrow{SD} \mathbf{+51\ J/K}$$

(b) $$\Delta S_{ground} = \frac{\Delta Q}{T} = \frac{-14{,}028\ J}{(25.0° + 273)\ K} = -47.07\ J/K \xrightarrow{SD} \mathbf{-47\ J/K}$$

(c) $$\Delta S_{total} = \Delta S_{ice} + \Delta S_{ground} = (+51.38\ J/K) + (-47.07\ J/K) = +4.31\ J/K \xrightarrow{SD} \mathbf{+4.3\ J/K}$$

6. The current produces a magnetic field around the wire. This magnetic field is present at the location of the stationary electron, but a magnetic field will not exert a force on a charge that does not have a velocity component perpendicular to the direction of the magnetic field. Since the electron is stationary, **the force has zero magnitude.**

7. The induced current in the closed loop will produce magnetic flux to oppose the change in magnetic flux. The magnetic flux is increasing, so the current would try to keep it from increasing by making magnetic flux in the opposite direction. The induced current would make magnetic flux that goes into the plane of the paper. To find the direction of the induced current, bend your right-hand fingers around the wire so that your fingers point in the direction of the magnetic flux produced by the induced current. Your thumb will point in the direction of flow of the induced current which is clockwise. Therefore, the induced current would flow in a **clockwise** direction.

8. $$C = \frac{K\varepsilon_0 A}{d} = \frac{(3.35)\left(8.85 \times 10^{-12}\ \frac{F}{m}\right)(0.025\ m^2)}{0.00025\ m} = 2.965 \times 10^{-9}\ F \xrightarrow{SD} \mathbf{3.0 \times 10^{-9}\ F}$$

9. Begin by computing the amount of heat that should be removed in order to freeze 130 grams of ethylene glycol.

$$Q = (130\ \cancel{g})\left(181\ \frac{J}{\cancel{g}}\right) = 23{,}530\ J$$

Next, compute the change in entropy.

$$\Delta S = \frac{\Delta Q}{T} = \frac{-23{,}530\ J}{(-11.5° + 273)\ K} = -89.98\ J/K \xrightarrow{SD} \mathbf{-9\bar{0}\ J/K}$$

10. $PE = Q\,\Delta V = (1.60 \times 10^{-19}\ C)(13{,}500\ V) = 2.16 \times 10^{-15}\ J$

This potential energy will be converted to kinetic energy.

$$KE = \frac{1}{2}mv^2$$

$$2.16 \times 10^{-15}\ J = \frac{1}{2}(9.11 \times 10^{-31}\ kg)v^2$$

$$v = 6.886 \times 10^7\ \frac{m}{s} \xrightarrow{SD} \mathbf{6.89 \times 10^7\ \frac{m}{s}}$$

11. $$\frac{1}{f} = \frac{1}{D_O} + \frac{1}{D_I}$$

$$\frac{1}{6.00} = \frac{1}{11.0} + \frac{1}{D_I}$$

$$D_I = \mathbf{13.2\ cm}$$

$$\frac{H_I}{H_O} = \frac{-D_I}{D_O}$$

$$\frac{H_I}{10.0} = \frac{-13.2}{11.0}$$

$$H_I = \mathbf{-12.0\ cm}$$

12. Determine the parameters of the sound wave if the ship is not moving.

$$v_{SND} = f_s\lambda$$
$$337 = (720)\lambda$$
$$\lambda = 0.4681 \text{ m}$$

As the ship approaches the dock, v_s is positive. Now, compute the observed wavelength λ'.

$$\lambda' = \left(\lambda - \frac{v_s}{f_s}\right)$$
$$= \left(0.4681 - \frac{15}{720}\right)$$
$$= 0.4473 \text{ m} \xrightarrow{SD} \mathbf{0.45\ m}$$

13. In the circuit, when the capacitors are fully charged, the sum of the voltages V_1 and V_2 is 15 volts.

(a) $V_1 + V_2 = 15$

Since the capacitors are in series, the charge on each capacitor is the same, $Q = CV$.

(b) $C_1V_1 = C_2V_2$

Solve (b) for V_2 and substitute into (a) and get:

(a) $$V_1 + \frac{C_1V_1}{C_2} = 15$$
$$V_1 + \frac{(8.0 \times 10^{-6})V_1}{(14 \times 10^{-6})} = 15$$
$$1.571V_1 = 15$$
$$V_1 = 9.548 \text{ V} \xrightarrow{SD} \mathbf{9.5\ V}$$

Substitute V_1 into (a) and solve for V_2.

(a) $(9.548) + V_2 = 15$
$$V_2 = 5.452 \text{ V} \xrightarrow{SD} \mathbf{5.5\ V}$$

14. Begin by finding the moment of inertia of the pulley and noting the relationship between a and α.

$$I = \frac{1}{2}mr^2 = \frac{1}{2}(3.7 \text{ kg})(0.27 \text{ m})^2 = 0.1349 \text{ kg}\cdot\text{m}^2$$

$$a = r\alpha \longrightarrow \alpha = \frac{a}{0.27}$$

Next, write a $\sum F_x = ma_x$ equation for the 34-kg block. Choose to the right as the positive direction for motion.

$$\sum F_x = ma_x$$
$$T_1 = ma$$
$$T_1 = 34a \qquad \text{(a)}$$

Now, write a $\sum F_y = ma_y$ equation for the 42-kg block.

$$\sum F_y = ma_y$$
$$mg - T_2 = ma$$
$$42(9.81) - T_2 = 42a$$
$$T_2 = 412.02 - 42a \qquad \text{(b)}$$

Next, write a $\sum \tau = I\alpha$ equation for the pulley.

$$\sum \tau = I\alpha$$
$$0.27T_2 - 0.27T_1 = (0.1349)\left(\frac{a}{0.27}\right)$$
$$0.27T_2 - 0.27T_1 = 0.4996a$$
$$T_2 - T_1 = 1.85a \qquad \text{(c)}$$

Substitute (a) and (b) into (c) to find the acceleration.

(c) $(412.02 - 42a) - (34a) = 1.85a$
$$412.02 = 77.85a$$
$$a = 5.29 \frac{\text{m}}{\text{s}^2} \xrightarrow{SD} \mathbf{5.3\ \frac{m}{s^2}\ to\ the\ right}$$

15. (a) $I = m_1r_1^2 + m_2r_2^2 + m_3r_3^2 + m_4r_4^2$
$$= 3.4(0.4)^2 + 2.0(0.4)^2 + 0.90(0.4)^2 + 2.4(0.4)^2$$
$$= 1.392 \text{ kg}\cdot\text{m}^2 \xrightarrow{SD} \mathbf{1\ kg\cdot m^2}$$

(b) $\tau = I\alpha$
$$= (1.392)(110)$$
$$= 153.12 \text{ N}\cdot\text{m} \xrightarrow{SD} \mathbf{200\ N\cdot m}$$

16. The image **is approximately 6.0 cm behind the mirror, it is upright, and the height of the image is approximately 1.2 cm.**

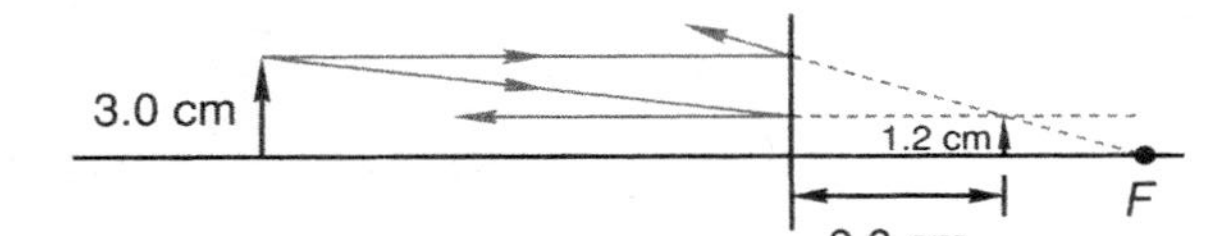

17. Begin by finding the centripetal force and the static friction force.

$$F_c = \frac{mv^2}{r} = \frac{(942)v^2}{86} = 10.95v^2$$
$$F_s = mg\mu_s = (942)(9.81)(0.76) = 7023.18 \text{ N}$$

The required centripetal force must equal the static friction force.

$$F_c = F_s$$
$$10.95v^2 = 7023.18$$
$$v = 25.33 \frac{\text{m}}{\text{s}} \xrightarrow{\text{SD}} \mathbf{25 \frac{m}{s}}$$

18. $PE = \frac{1}{2}kx^2 = \frac{1}{2}(300)(1.789)^2 = 480.1 \text{ J}$

$$KE = \frac{1}{2}mv^2$$
$$480.1 \text{ J} = \frac{1}{2}(35.406 \text{ kg})v^2$$
$$v = 5.208 \frac{\text{m}}{\text{s}} \xrightarrow{\text{SD}} \mathbf{5 \frac{m}{s}}$$

19. Begin by finding the weight of the mass.

$$w = mg = 12 \cancel{\text{kg}} \times 9.81 \frac{\text{N}}{\cancel{\text{kg}}} = 117.72 \text{ N}$$

Now calculate the distance the spring is stretched.

$$F = kx$$
$$117.72 \text{ N} = 220 \frac{\text{N}}{\text{m}} \times x$$
$$x = 0.5351 \text{ m} \xrightarrow{\text{SD}} \mathbf{0.54 \text{ m}}$$

20. Begin by converting 2300 rev/min to radians per second.

$$2300 \frac{\cancel{\text{rev}}}{\cancel{\text{min}}} \times \frac{2\pi \text{ rad}}{1 \cancel{\text{rev}}} \times \frac{1 \cancel{\text{min}}}{60 \text{ s}} = 240.86 \frac{\text{rad}}{\text{s}}$$

Now calculate the average angular acceleration. Be sure to convert 0.25 min to 15 s.

$$\alpha_{av} = \frac{\omega_2 - \omega_1}{t_2 - t_1} = \frac{180 - 240.86}{15} \frac{\text{rad/s}}{\text{s}}$$
$$= -4.057 \frac{\text{rad}}{\text{s}^2} \xrightarrow{\text{SD}} \mathbf{-4.1 \frac{rad}{s^2}}$$

Problem Set 90

1. $v = f\lambda$

$$3.00 \times 10^8 \frac{\text{m}}{\text{s}} = f(5.5 \times 10^{-4} \text{ m})$$
$$f = 5.455 \times 10^{11} \text{ Hz} \xrightarrow{\text{SD}} \mathbf{5.5 \times 10^{11} \text{ Hz}}$$

2. $v = f\lambda$

$$3.00 \times 10^8 \frac{\text{m}}{\text{s}} = f(2 \times 2.9 \text{ m})$$
$$f = 5.172 \times 10^7 \text{ Hz} \xrightarrow{\text{SD}} \mathbf{5.2 \times 10^7 \text{ Hz}}$$

3. Begin by converting decibels to intensities for $B_1 = 90$ and $B_2 = 40$.

$$I_1 = I_0 10^{B_1/10} = (1 \times 10^{-12})10^9 = 1 \times 10^{-3} \text{ W/m}^2$$
$$I_2 = I_0 10^{B_2/10} = (1 \times 10^{-12})10^4 = 1 \times 10^{-8} \text{ W/m}^2$$

Next, calculate the decrease as

$$I_1 - I_2 = (1 \times 10^{-3} \text{ W/m}^2) - (1 \times 10^{-8} \text{ W/m}^2)$$
$$= 10 \times 10^{-4} \frac{\text{W}}{\text{m}^2} \xrightarrow{\text{SD}} \mathbf{1 \times 10^{-3} \frac{W}{m^2}}$$

4. Begin by raising 10 to the Richter scale readings 4.7 and 2.2.

$$10^{x_1} = 10^{4.7} = 50{,}119$$
$$10^{x_2} = 10^{2.2} = 158$$

Next, divide the intensities.

$$\frac{50{,}119}{158} = 317.2 \xrightarrow{\text{SD}} \mathbf{320}$$

5. $V_I I_I = V_O I_O \longrightarrow \dfrac{I_I}{I_O} = \dfrac{V_O}{V_I}$

$$\frac{1000}{1} = \frac{V_O}{V_I}$$

$$\frac{V_I}{V_O} = \mathbf{\frac{1}{1000}}$$

6. Begin by finding the time constant L/R.

$$\frac{L}{R} = \frac{24\text{ H}}{4000\ \Omega} = 0.006\text{ s}$$

Next, find the final current.

$$I_F = \frac{V}{R} = \frac{145\text{ V}}{4000\ \Omega} = 0.03625\text{ A}$$

Now calculate the current when $t = 9.0 \times 10^{-3}$ s.

$$I = I_F - I_F e^{-\left(\frac{t}{L/R}\right)}$$

$$= 0.03625 - 0.03625e^{-9.0\times10^{-3}/0.006}$$

$$= 0.03625 - 0.03625e^{-1.5}$$

$$= 0.0282\text{ A} \xrightarrow{\text{SD}} \mathbf{0.028\ A}$$

7. Begin by converting the temperature to kelvins.

$T_H = 482°\text{C} + 273 = 755\text{ K}$

Thus, the cold temperature is

$$\text{eff}_{max} = 1 - \frac{T_C}{T_H}$$

$$0.755 = 1 - \frac{T_C}{755}$$

$$T_C = 184.98\text{ K} \xrightarrow{\text{SD}} \mathbf{185\ K}$$

8. $Q = CV = (4 \times 10^{-6}\text{ F})(1000\text{ V}) = \mathbf{4 \times 10^{-3}\ C}$

9. Place your right hand flat so that your fingers point in the direction of the current and then bend your fingers to point in the direction of the magnetic field. Your thumb will then point in the direction of the force on the wire.

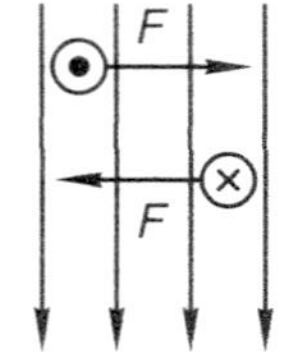

10. $C = \dfrac{K\varepsilon_0 A}{d} \longrightarrow K = \dfrac{Cd}{\varepsilon_0 A}$

$$= \frac{(1.215 \times 10^{-9}\text{ F})(3.654 \times 10^{-3}\text{ m})}{\left(8.85 \times 10^{-12}\ \frac{\text{F}}{\text{m}}\right)(0.1\text{ m}^2)}$$

$$= 5.017 \xrightarrow{\text{SD}} \mathbf{5}$$

11. Begin by computing the amount of heat required to melt 0.462 kg of mercury.

$$Q = (0.462\text{ kg})\left(11.8 \times 10^3\ \frac{\text{J}}{\text{kg}}\right) = 5.45 \times 10^3\text{ J}$$

Next, compute the change in entropies.

(a) $\Delta S_{\text{mercury}} = \dfrac{\Delta Q}{T}$

$$= \frac{+5.45 \times 10^3\text{ J}}{(-39° + 273)\text{ K}}$$

$$= +23.29\text{ J/K} \xrightarrow{\text{SD}} \mathbf{+23\ J/K}$$

(b) $\Delta S_{\text{ground}} = \dfrac{\Delta Q}{T}$

$$= \frac{-5.45 \times 10^3\text{ J}}{(14° + 273)\text{ K}}$$

$$= -18.99\text{ J/K} \xrightarrow{\text{SD}} \mathbf{-19\ J/K}$$

(c) $\Delta S_{\text{total}} = \Delta S_{\text{mercury}} + \Delta S_{\text{ground}}$

$$= (+23.29\text{ J/K}) + (-18.99\text{ J/K})$$

$$= \mathbf{+4.3\ J/K}$$

12. $v = f(2L)$

$896 = (440)(2L)$

$L = 1.018 \text{ m} \xrightarrow{SD} \mathbf{1.02\ m}$

13. Begin by finding the time constant RC.

$RC = (8000\ \Omega)(6.0 \times 10^{-6}\ \text{F}) = 4.8 \times 10^{-2}\ \text{s}$

Now calculate the voltage when $t = 0.144$ s.

$$V_C = V_0 - V_0 e^{-t/RC}$$
$$= 28 - 28e^{-0.144/4.8\times10^{-2}}$$
$$= 28 - 28e^{-3.0}$$
$$= 26.606 \text{ V} \xrightarrow{SD} \mathbf{27\ V}$$

14. Begin by finding the equivalent resistance of the two series resistors.

$R_E = 100\ \Omega + R_2 = 100\ \Omega + (100\ \Omega) = 200\ \Omega$

Use this resistance to find the current I through the circuit.

$$I = \frac{V}{R_E} = \frac{40\text{ V}}{200\ \Omega} = 0.20\text{ A}$$

Now find the power.

$P = I^2R = (0.20\text{ A})^2(100\ \Omega) = \mathbf{4.0\ W}$

Use this power to find the energy.

$E = Pt = (4.0\text{ W})(60\text{ s}) = 240\text{ J} \xrightarrow{SD} \mathbf{200\ J}$

15. $n_1 \sin\theta_1 = n_2 \sin\theta_2$

$(1) \sin 40° = 1.333 \sin\theta_2$

$\theta_2 = \mathbf{28.83°}$

16. $$\tan\theta = \frac{v^2}{rg} \rightarrow a_c = \frac{v^2}{r} = g\tan\theta$$
$$= (9.81)\tan 20°$$
$$= 3.571\ \frac{\text{m}}{\text{s}^2} \xrightarrow{SD} \mathbf{3.6\ \frac{m}{s^2}}$$

$$\tan\theta = \frac{v^2}{rg} \rightarrow v = \sqrt{rg\tan\theta}$$
$$= \sqrt{(38)(9.81)\tan 20°}$$
$$= 11.648\ \frac{\text{m}}{\text{s}} \xrightarrow{SD} \mathbf{12\ \frac{m}{s}}$$

17. Begin by finding v_1 and v_2.

$$v_1 = \frac{Q}{A_1} = \frac{4.9}{0.95} = 5.158\ \frac{\text{m}}{\text{s}}$$
$$v_2 = \frac{Q}{A_2} = \frac{4.9}{0.52} = 9.423\ \frac{\text{m}}{\text{s}}$$

Now use Bernoulli's equation to find P_2. Note that h_1 is zero, so the $\rho g h_1$ term falls out of the equation.

$$P_1 + \frac{1}{2}\rho v_1^2 = P_2 + \frac{1}{2}\rho v_2^2 + \rho g h_2$$
$$120{,}000 + \frac{1}{2}(1000)(5.158)^2 = P_2 + \frac{1}{2}(1000)(9.423)^2 + (1000)(9.81)(-22)$$
$$120{,}000 + 13{,}302.48 = P_2 + 44{,}396.46 - 215{,}820$$
$$P_2 = 3.047 \times 10^5\text{ Pa} \xrightarrow{SD} \mathbf{3.0 \times 10^5\ Pa}$$

18. Begin by converting horsepower to watts.

$$112\text{ hp} \times \frac{746\text{ W}}{1\text{ hp}} = 83{,}552\text{ W}$$

Now find the work done.

$W = (83{,}552\text{ W})(2.57\text{ s}) = 214{,}728.64\text{ J}$

The work must equal the final kinetic energy of the tractor.

$$W = \frac{1}{2}mv^2$$
$$214{,}728.64 = \frac{1}{2}(1810)v^2$$
$$v = 15.404\ \frac{\text{m}}{\text{s}} \xrightarrow{SD} \mathbf{15.4\ \frac{m}{s}}$$

19. Begin by denoting the signs on the resistors.

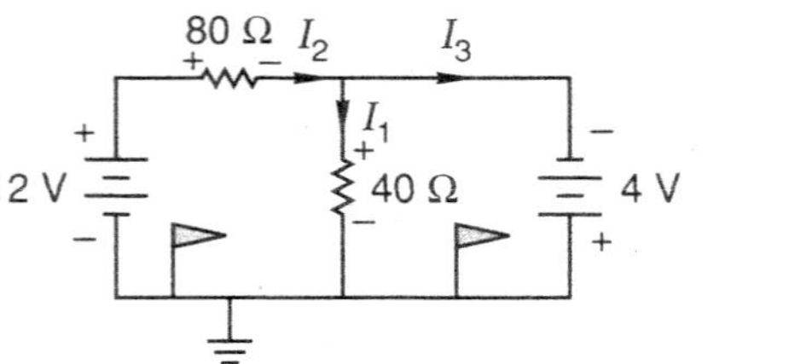

In the left-hand loop, begin at the starting flag, move clockwise, and sum the voltage changes to zero.

(a) $-12 + 80I_2 + 40I_1 = 0$

In the right-hand loop, begin at the starting flag, move clockwise, and sum the voltage changes to zero.

(b) $-40I_1 - 4 = 0$

Solve (b) for I_1 and get:

(b) $-40I_1 = 4$

$$I_1 = \mathbf{-0.1\ A}$$

Substitute I_1 into (a) and solve for I_2.

(a) $-12 + 80I_2 + 40(-0.1) = 0$

$$80I_2 = 16$$
$$I_2 = \mathbf{0.2\ A}$$

Use KCL to find I_3.

$$I_2 = I_1 + I_3$$
$$0.2 = -0.1 + I_3$$
$$I_3 = \mathbf{0.3\ A}$$

20. $$\frac{P_1V_1}{T_1} = \frac{P_2V_2}{T_2} \longrightarrow \frac{P_1V_1}{T_1} = \frac{(3P_1)V_2}{\left(\frac{T_1}{2}\right)}$$

$$\frac{\cancel{P_1}V_1}{\cancel{T_1}} \times \frac{\cancel{T_1}}{\cancel{P_1}} = \frac{(3\cancel{P_1})V_2}{\left(\frac{\cancel{T_1}}{2}\right)} \times \frac{\cancel{T_1}}{\cancel{P_1}}$$

$$V_2 = \mathbf{\frac{V_1}{6}}$$

Problem Set 91

1. The time for a round trip is the time for 1/120 of a revolution.

$$\frac{1}{120}\cancel{\text{rev}} \times \frac{1\text{ s}}{150\cancel{\text{rev}}} = 5.56 \times 10^{-5}\text{ s} \xrightarrow{\text{SD}} \mathbf{6 \times 10^{-5}\ s}$$

2. Distance $= 2 \times 72$ km $= 144$ km $= 144{,}000$ m

$$\text{Distance} = \text{speed} \times \text{time}$$
$$144{,}000\text{ m} = c(45 \times 10^{-4}\text{ s})$$
$$c = \mathbf{3.2 \times 10^7\ \frac{m}{s}}$$

3. Refer to Section 91.D.

4. $$v = f\lambda$$
$$3.00 \times 10^8\ \frac{\text{m}}{\text{s}} = f(850 \times 10^{-9}\text{ m})$$
$$f = 3.529 \times 10^{14}\text{ Hz} \xrightarrow{\text{SD}} \mathbf{3.5 \times 10^{14}\ Hz}$$

5. $$v = f\lambda$$
$$3.00 \times 10^8\ \frac{\text{m}}{\text{s}} = f(2 \times 2.8\text{ m})$$
$$f = 5.357 \times 10^7\text{ Hz} \xrightarrow{\text{SD}} \mathbf{5.4 \times 10^7\ Hz}$$

6. (a) Sixteen times as loud can be written as 2^4. To get this in decibels, we multiply the power of 2 by 10 and get $\mathbf{4\bar{0}\ dB}$.

(b) $$I = I_0 10^{B/10}$$
$$= (1 \times 10^{-12})10^{40/10}$$
$$= (1 \times 10^{-12})10^4$$
$$= \mathbf{1 \times 10^{-8}\ \frac{W}{m^2}}$$

7. $$10^x = 143{,}000$$
$$x = \log 143{,}000$$
$$x = 5.155 \xrightarrow{\text{SD}} \mathbf{5.16}$$

8. $V_I I_I = V_O I_O \rightarrow I_O = \dfrac{V_I I_I}{V_O}$

$$= \frac{(332.5 \text{ V})(10 \text{ A})}{643.498 \text{ V}}$$

$$= 5.167 \text{ A} \xrightarrow{\text{SD}} \mathbf{5\ A}$$

9. $\text{eff}_{max} = \dfrac{\text{Work out}}{\text{Energy in}} \times 100\% = \dfrac{150 \text{ J}}{280 \text{ J}} \times 100\% = 53.6\% \xrightarrow{\text{SD}} \mathbf{54\%}$

10. To determine the net magnetic field at point C, we must algebraically add the magnetic fields at point C caused by wire A and by wire B. Using the right-hand rule, place your thumb in the direction of current A and curl your fingers. The result is the magnetic field due to wire A will be going into the paper at C. Likewise, place your thumb in the direction of current B and curl your fingers. The result is the magnetic field due to wire B will be coming out of the paper at C. Therefore, 93.75 T is coming out of the paper at C and 22.86 T is going into the paper at C. So the net result is 93.75 T − 22.86 T = **70.89 T out of the paper.**

11. (a) $\text{emf} = N \dfrac{\Delta\Phi}{\Delta t}$

$$= (50)\left(\frac{75 \text{ Wb} - 350 \text{ Wb}}{12 \text{ s}}\right)$$

$$= -1145.8 \text{ V} \xrightarrow{\text{SD}} \mathbf{-1100\ V}$$

(b) A useful method for determining if terminal A has a higher or lower potential than terminal B is to connect a resistor between them and observe which direction the induced current flows.

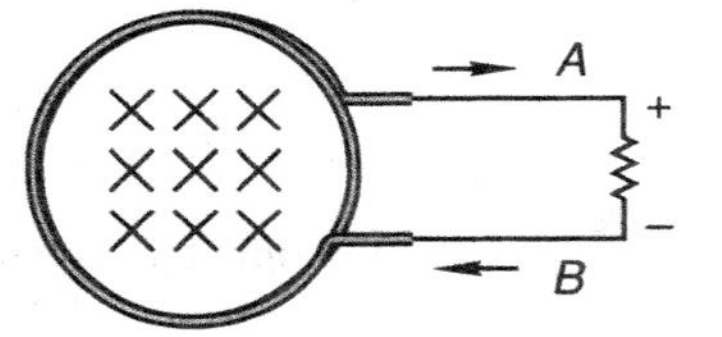

Using the right-hand rule and knowing that the flux is reducing, the induced current will oppose this change in flux by flowing in a clockwise direction. Therefore, the induced current will flow from A to B. Since the induced current flows from A to B through the resistor, terminal A is at a **higher** potential than terminal B.

12. $F = qvB$

$$= (1.60 \times 10^{-19})(7.5 \times 10^{7})(5.5 \times 10^{-3})$$

$$= \mathbf{6.6 \times 10^{-14}\ N}$$

To find the direction of the force, place your right hand flat so that your fingers point in the original direction of the electron and bend your fingers to point in the direction of the magnetic field. Since the electron has a negative charge, the direction of the force on the electron is opposite the direction of your thumb. Therefore, the direction of the force on the electron is **north.**

13. *Adiabatic* means that no heat is added or subtracted in a thermodynamic system.

14. *Isothermal* means that a process occurs at constant temperature.

15. $T = \dfrac{2\pi\sqrt{L}}{\sqrt{g}} = \dfrac{2\pi\sqrt{15.0}}{\sqrt{9.81}} = 7.7695 \text{ s} \xrightarrow{\text{SD}} \mathbf{7.77\ s}$

The frequency is the reciprocal of the period.

$$f = \frac{1}{T} = \frac{1}{7.7695 \text{ s}} = 0.1287 \text{ Hz} \xrightarrow{\text{SD}} \mathbf{0.129\ Hz}$$

16. (a) The image is **approximately 3.3 cm behind the lens, it is upright, and the height of the image is approximately 2.0 cm.**

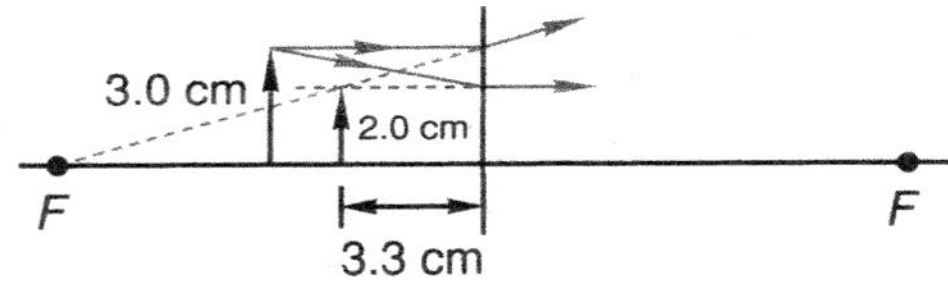

(b) The image is **virtual** because it is upright and behind the lens.

17. Begin by finding the moment of inertia.

$$I = mr^2 = (0.650 \text{ kg})(1.25 \text{ m})^2 = 1.016 \text{ kg}\cdot\text{m}^2$$

Now calculate the torque.

$$\tau = \frac{I(\omega_2 - \omega_1)}{\Delta t} = \frac{(1.016)(26.0 - 11.0)}{1.20} = \mathbf{12.7\ N\cdot m}$$

18. Begin by finding the tension, mg, and the mass per unit length of the string.

$$T = mg = 5.21\,\cancel{\text{kg}} \times 9.81\,\frac{\text{N}}{\cancel{\text{kg}}} = 51.11\text{ N}$$

$$M_L = \frac{0.105\text{ kg}}{2.05\text{ m}} = 0.0512\,\frac{\text{kg}}{\text{m}}$$

Insert these values into the formula below to find v.

$$v = \sqrt{\frac{T}{M_L}} = \sqrt{\frac{51.11\text{ N}}{0.0512\,\frac{\text{kg}}{\text{m}}}} = 31.59\,\frac{\text{m}}{\text{s}} \xrightarrow{\text{SD}} \mathbf{31.6\,\frac{m}{s}}$$

19.

$$Q_1 = 0.0046(2050)(98) = 924.14\text{ J}$$
$$Q_2 = 0.0046(334 \times 10^3) = 1536.4\text{ J}$$
$$Q_3 = 0.0046(4186)(100) = 1925.56\text{ J}$$
$$Q_4 = 0.0046(2256 \times 10^3) = 10{,}377.6\text{ J}$$
$$Q_5 = 0.0046(2009)(316) = 2920.28\text{ J}$$
$$Q_T = 17.684\text{ kJ} \xrightarrow{\text{SD}} \mathbf{17.7\ kJ}$$

20.

$$\Sigma M_A = 0$$
$$134\text{ N}(13\text{ m}) - 200\text{ N}(8.85\text{ m}) + F_B(2.5\text{ m}) = 0$$
$$1742\text{ N}\cdot\text{m} - 1770\text{ N}\cdot\text{m} + F_B(2.5\text{ m}) = 0$$
$$F_B(2.5\text{ m}) = 28\text{ N}\cdot\text{m}$$
$$F_B = \mathbf{11.2\ N}$$

$$\Sigma F_y = 0$$
$$134\text{ N} - 200\text{ N} + F_B - F_A = 0$$
$$134\text{ N} - 200\text{ N} + (11.2\text{ N}) - F_A = 0$$
$$F_A = \mathbf{-54.8\ N}$$

Problem Set 92

1. Use Poiseuille's equation and Q_0 to represent the original flow rate and r to represent the original radius.

(a) $Q_0 = kr^4(P_1 - P_2)$

Now replace r with the new radius, $0.62r$, and use Q_2 to represent the new flow rate.

$$Q_2 = k(0.62r)^4(P_1 - P_2)$$

(b) $Q_2 = (0.148)kr^4(P_1 - P_2)$

The flow rate in (b) is equal to the flow rate in (a) multiplied by 0.148, so

$$Q_2 = 0.148Q_0$$
$$= 0.148(2.57)$$
$$= 0.3804\text{ m}^3\cdot\text{s}^{-1} \xrightarrow{\text{SD}} \mathbf{0.38\ m^3\cdot s^{-1}}$$

2. $$\text{Stress} = \frac{F}{A} = \frac{400\text{ N}}{\pi(0.002\text{ m})^2} = 3.183 \times 10^7\text{ Pa} \xrightarrow{\text{SD}} \mathbf{3.2 \times 10^7\ Pa}$$

3. $$Y = \frac{\text{stress}}{\text{strain}} \rightarrow \text{Strain} = \frac{\text{stress}}{Y}$$
$$= \frac{40 \times 10^6\text{ N/m}^2}{11 \times 10^{10}\text{ N/m}^2}$$
$$= 3.636 \times 10^{-4} \xrightarrow{\text{SD}} \mathbf{3.6 \times 10^{-4}}$$

$$\text{Strain} = \frac{\Delta L}{L} \rightarrow \Delta L = (\text{strain})(L)$$
$$= (3.636 \times 10^{-4})(100\text{ m})$$
$$= 3.636 \times 10^{-2}\text{ m} \xrightarrow{\text{SD}} \mathbf{3.6 \times 10^{-2}\ m}$$

4. $$\text{Shear stress} = \frac{F}{A} = \frac{123\text{ N}}{\pi(2.15 \times 10^{-3}\text{ m})^2}$$
$$= 8.4699 \times 10^6\text{ Pa} \xrightarrow{\text{SD}} \mathbf{8.47 \times 10^6\ Pa}$$

5.

$$v = f\lambda$$
$$3.00 \times 10^8\text{ m}\cdot\text{s}^{-1} = (1.5 \times 10^9\text{ Hz})\lambda$$
$$\lambda = 0.20\text{ m}$$

To build a half-wavelength dipole antenna, divide the wavelength of 0.20 m by 2 and get **0.10 m**, which is the total length of the antenna.

6. Begin by finding the total charge at each point.

$$q_1, q_2 = 75 \cancel{\text{electrons}} \times \frac{1.60 \times 10^{-19}\text{ C}}{1 \cancel{\text{electron}}} = 1.2 \times 10^{-17}\text{ C}$$

Now find the magnitude of the force.

$$F = \frac{kq_1q_2}{r^2}$$
$$= \frac{(9.0 \times 10^9)(1.2 \times 10^{-17})(1.2 \times 10^{-17})}{(1.0 \times 10^{-3})^2}$$
$$= 1.296 \times 10^{-18}\text{ N} \xrightarrow{\text{SD}} \mathbf{1.3 \times 10^{-18}\text{ N}}$$

7. Begin by raising 10 to the Richter scale readings 6.9 and 3.2.

$$10^{x_1} = 10^{6.9} = 7{,}943{,}282$$
$$10^{x_2} = 10^{3.2} = 1585$$

Next, divide the intensities.

$$\frac{7{,}943{,}282}{1585} = 5012 \xrightarrow{\text{SD}} \mathbf{5.0 \times 10^3}\textbf{ times as intense}$$

8. (a) Convert 8000 times to a decibel reading.

$$10^x = 8000$$
$$x = \log 8000$$
$$x = 3.90$$

Multiply x by 10 to get an increase of 39.0 dB. Thus, the new noise is 22 dB + 39.0 dB = **61 dB**

(b) Divide this 39.0-dB increase by 10 and use it as an exponent of 2.

$$2^{39.0/10} = 2^{3.90} = 14.93 \xrightarrow{\text{SD}} \textbf{15 times as loud}$$

9.
$$B = \frac{\mu_0 I}{2\pi r}$$
$$= \frac{(4\pi \times 10^{-7})(2.0)}{2\pi(0.03)}$$
$$= 1.333 \times 10^{-5}\text{ tesla} \xrightarrow{\text{SD}} \mathbf{1.3 \times 10^{-5}}\textbf{ tesla}$$

10. Begin by computing the amount of heat required to melt 0.025 kg of ice.

$$Q = (0.025 \cancel{\text{kg}})\left(334 \times 10^3 \frac{\text{J}}{\cancel{\text{kg}}}\right) = 8.35 \times 10^3\text{ J}$$

Next, compute the change in entropy.

$$\Delta S = \frac{\Delta Q}{T} = \frac{+8.35 \times 10^3\text{ J}}{273\text{ K}} = +30.59\text{ J/K} \xrightarrow{\text{SD}} \mathbf{+31\text{ J/K}}$$

11.
$$V_{AB} = N\frac{\Delta\Phi}{\Delta t}$$
$$= (1)\left(\frac{130\text{ Wb} - 850\text{ Wb}}{14\text{ s}}\right)$$
$$= -51.43\text{ V} \xrightarrow{\text{SD}} \mathbf{-51\text{ V}}$$

A useful method for determining if V_{AB} is positive or negative is to connect a resistor between A and B and observe which direction the induced current flows.

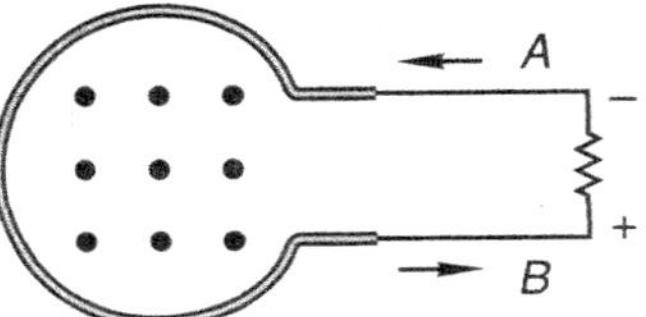

Using the right-hand rule and knowing that the flux is reducing, the induced current will oppose this change in flux by flowing in a counterclockwise direction. Therefore, the induced current will flow from B to A so V_{AB} is **negative.**

12. Since the acceleration is constant, the slope of the speed-versus-time curve must be a straight slanted line. Since the speed increases with time, the distance traveled must increase more rapidly as time progresses. The only pair of graphs which satisfies these conditions is **(d).**

13. The ball will begin its descent at the peak of its motion upward, which corresponds to the point where its velocity is zero. Use the motion equation and set the final velocity equal to zero and solve for the time.

$$v(t) = v_0 + at$$
$$0 = 70.7 + (-9.81)t$$
$$70.7 = 9.81t$$
$$t = 7.2069\text{ s} \xrightarrow{\text{SD}} \mathbf{7.21\text{ s}}$$

14. Begin by finding the x and y components of the initial velocity.

$$v_{x0} = 100\cos 45° = 70.71\ \frac{\text{m}}{\text{s}}$$

$$v_{y0} = 100\sin 45° = 70.71\ \frac{\text{m}}{\text{s}}$$

(a) Use the y-displacement equation to find the time.

$$\Delta y = v_{y0}t + \frac{1}{2}a_y t^2$$

$$0 = 70.71t + \frac{1}{2}(-9.81)t^2$$

$$4.905t^2 = 70.71t$$

$$t = 14.416\text{ s} \xrightarrow{\text{SD}} \mathbf{14.4\ s}$$

(b) Use this time in the x-position equation to find the distance.

$$x = x_0 + v_{x0}t + \frac{1}{2}a_x t^2$$

$$= 0 + 70.71(14.416) + 0$$

$$= 1.0194 \times 10^3\text{ m} \xrightarrow{\text{SD}} \mathbf{1.02 \times 10^3\ m}$$

15. Remember that long wavelengths correspond to low frequencies and energies, whereas short wavelengths correspond to high frequencies and energies. Therefore, according to ROY G BIV, red is the longest wavelength and violet is the shortest. Thus **(d) violet** has the highest energy.

16. (a) Increase the tension in the string by a factor of 2.

$$v = \sqrt{\frac{T}{M_L}} \rightarrow v_2 = \sqrt{\frac{2T}{M_L}}$$

Factor the 2 out from under the radical and get:

$$v_2 = \sqrt{2}\sqrt{\frac{T}{M_L}}$$

Now, note that $\sqrt{\frac{T}{M_L}}$ is equal to v. Substitute and get:

$$v_2 = \sqrt{2}v$$

Thus, v **increases by a factor of $\sqrt{2}$.**

(b) Since $v = f\lambda$, f is directly proportional to v. Thus, the new frequency will increase by the same factor as v, and the result is $\mathbf{\sqrt{2}f}$.

17. First, write the first law of thermodynamics.

$$Q = \Delta U + W$$

ΔU is positive, so we get

$$Q - W = +\Delta U$$

From the graph, P is constant and V_2 is greater than V_1; therefore,

$$W = P\Delta V = P(V_2 - V_1)$$

which means the work must also be positive ($W > 0$). Since ΔU and W are positive, Q must be positive ($Q > 0$) so that the law holds. Thus, the only statement which is true is **(e) $Q > 0$; $W > 0$.**

18. Since the block is moving down the plane, the frictional force must oppose the motion and thus be acting up the plane. The normal force acts perpendicular to the plane of motion and the weight acts vertically downward from the mass. The only diagram which illustrates these concepts is **(e).**

19. The total kinetic energy of the ball is transferred to potential energy as it rolls up the inclined plane.

$$mgh = \frac{1}{2}mv^2 + \frac{1}{2}I\left(\frac{v}{r}\right)^2$$

$$mgh = \frac{1}{2}mv^2 + \frac{1}{2}\left(\frac{2}{5}mr^2\right)\left(\frac{v}{r}\right)^2$$

$$mgh = \frac{1}{2}mv^2 + \frac{2}{10}mv^2$$

$$mgh = \frac{7}{10}mv^2$$

$$h = \mathbf{\frac{7}{10}\frac{v^2}{g}}$$

20. Begin by finding the volume of the sphere that is submerged.

$$V_s = \frac{4}{3}\pi r^3 = \frac{4}{3}\pi(1.2568\text{ m})^3 = 8.3155\text{ m}^3$$

Now find the mass of the water displaced.

$$m_w = 1025\ \frac{\text{kg}}{\text{m}^3} \times 8.3155\text{ m}^3 = 8523.39\text{ kg}$$

$$F_B = 8523.39\text{ kg} \times 9.81\ \frac{\text{N}}{\text{kg}} = 83{,}614.46\text{ N}$$

$$T = F_B - mg = 83{,}614.46\text{ N} - 20\text{ kg}\left(9.81\ \frac{\text{N}}{\text{kg}}\right)$$

$$= 8.342 \times 10^4\text{ N} \xrightarrow{\text{SD}} \mathbf{8 \times 10^4\ N}$$

Problem Set 93

1. He observes the speed to be **3.00 × 10⁸ m/s** because according to the second postulate, the observed speed of all frequencies of light is the same to every observer.

2. (a) Observer A sees the mass moving away from him at $4.0\ \text{m}\cdot\text{s}^{-1}$.

$$KE_A = \frac{1}{2}mv^2 = \frac{1}{2}(2.0\ \text{kg})(4.0\ \text{m}\cdot\text{s}^{-1})^2 = \mathbf{16\ J}$$

(b) Observer B sees the mass moving toward him at $(4.0 + 5.0)\ \text{m}\cdot\text{s}^{-1}$ or $9.0\ \text{m}\cdot\text{s}^{-1}$.

$$KE_B = \frac{1}{2}mv^2 = \frac{1}{2}(2.0\ \text{kg})(9.0\ \text{m}\cdot\text{s}^{-1})^2 = \mathbf{81\ J}$$

(c) **Both of the calculations are correct and neither is preferred** because the observed velocities are different in each observer's inertial reference frame.

3. See Lesson 93.

4. (a) $\text{Stress} = \frac{F}{A} = \frac{2.45 \times 10^3\ \text{N}}{\pi(0.080\ \text{m})^2} = 1.219 \times 10^5\ \text{Pa} \xrightarrow{\text{SD}} \mathbf{1.2 \times 10^5\ Pa}$

(b) $Y = \frac{\text{stress}}{\text{strain}} \rightarrow \text{Strain} = \frac{\text{stress}}{Y} = \frac{1.219 \times 10^5\ \text{Pa}}{9.1 \times 10^{10}\ \text{Pa}} = 1.3396 \times 10^{-6} \xrightarrow{\text{SD}} \mathbf{1.3 \times 10^{-6}}$

(c) $\text{Strain} = \frac{\Delta L}{L} \rightarrow \Delta L = (\text{strain})(L) = (1.3396 \times 10^{-6})(2.0\ \text{m}) = 2.679 \times 10^{-6}\ \text{m} \xrightarrow{\text{SD}} \mathbf{2.7 \times 10^{-6}\ m}$

5. $Y = \frac{\text{stress}}{\text{strain}} = \frac{F/A}{\Delta L/L} = \frac{FL}{A\Delta L} = \frac{(5.5489\ \text{N})(2.0\ \text{m})}{(1 \times 10^{-6}\ \text{m}^2)(19.547 \times 10^{-6}\ \text{m})}$

$Y = 5.677 \times 10^{11}\ \text{Pa} \xrightarrow{\text{SD}} \mathbf{6 \times 10^{11}\ Pa}$

6. Begin by raising 10 to the Richter scale readings 5.23 and 3.56.

$10^{x_1} = 10^{5.23} = 169{,}824$

$10^{x_2} = 10^{3.56} = 3631$

Next, divide the intensities.

$\frac{169{,}824}{3631} = 46.77 \xrightarrow{\text{SD}}$ **46.8 times as intense**

7. Begin by finding the difference in decibel levels.

54 dB − 25 dB = 29 dB

Divide this 29-dB increase by 10 and use it as an exponent of 10.

$10^{29/10} = 10^{2.9} = 794.3 \xrightarrow{\text{SD}}$ **790 times as intense**

8. Begin by finding the difference in decibel levels.

44 dB − 14 dB = 30 dB

Divide this 30-dB increase by 10 and use it as an exponent of 2.

$2^{30/10} = 2^3 =$ **8.0 times as loud**

9. $\text{eff}_{\text{max}} = 1 - \frac{Q_C}{Q_H} = 1 - \frac{2020\ \text{J}}{4050\ \text{J}} = 0.5012$

Multiply this by 100% and get:

$\text{eff}_{\text{max}} = 0.5012 \times 100\% = 50.12\% \xrightarrow{\text{SD}}$ **50.1%**

10. Determine the note's wavelength.

$$v_{\text{SND}} = f_s\lambda$$
$$352 = (1100)\lambda$$
$$\lambda = 0.32\ \text{m}$$

As Marla moves toward the purple martin, v_{OB} is positive. Therefore, the sound relative to Marla is

$$v_{\text{SND}} + v_{\text{OB}} = 352 + 6.70 = 358.7\ \text{m/s}$$

Now, compute the observed frequency f''.

$$v_{\text{SND}} + v_{\text{OB}} = f''\lambda$$
$$358.7 = f''(0.32)$$
$f'' = 1.1209 \times 10^3\ \text{Hz} \xrightarrow{\text{SD}} \mathbf{1.12 \times 10^3\ Hz}$

11. $$\frac{1}{f} = \frac{1}{D_O} + \frac{1}{D_I}$$

$$\frac{1}{10.0} = \frac{1}{7.0} + \frac{1}{D_I}$$

$$D_I = -23.33 \text{ cm} \xrightarrow{\text{SD}} \mathbf{-23\ cm}$$

$$\frac{H_I}{H_O} = \frac{-D_I}{D_O}$$

$$\frac{H_I}{4.0} = \frac{-(-23.33)}{7.0}$$

$$H_I = 13.33 \text{ cm} \xrightarrow{\text{SD}} \mathbf{13\ cm}$$

12. Begin by finding the equivalent resistance of the 2-Ω and 3-Ω series resistors.
$R_E = 2\ \Omega + 3\ \Omega = 5\ \Omega$
Use this resistance to find the current I through the 3-Ω resistor.

$$I = \frac{V}{R_E} = \frac{10 \text{ V}}{5\ \Omega} = 2 \text{ A}$$

Use this current to find the voltage across the 3-Ω resistor.
$V = IR = (2 \text{ A})(3\ \Omega) = 6 \text{ V}$
Use this voltage to find Q.

$$Q = CV$$
$$= (42 \times 10^{-6} \text{ F})(6 \text{ V})$$
$$= 2.52 \times 10^{-4} \text{ C} \xrightarrow{\text{SD}} \mathbf{3 \times 10^{-4}\ C}$$

13. $$F_c = T + mg$$
$$= 2mg + mg$$
$$= \mathbf{3mg}$$

14. $$T - mg = F_c$$

$$2mg - mg = \frac{mv^2}{L}$$

$$mg = \frac{mv^2}{L}$$

$$\mathbf{\sqrt{gL}} = v$$

15. First, sum the forces on the 1-kg block.

$$\Sigma F = m_1 a$$
$$T = (1)a \qquad \text{(a)}$$

Second, sum the forces on the 2-kg block.

$$\Sigma F = m_2 a$$
$$F - T = (2)a \qquad \text{(b)}$$

Substitute (a) into (b) and solve for T.

$$\text{(b)}\ F - T = 2(T)$$
$$F = 3T$$
$$T = \mathbf{\frac{F}{3}}$$

16. Use the displacement equation to find the time.

$$\Delta y = v_0 t + \frac{1}{2}at^2$$

$$-40 = -2t + \frac{1}{2}(-9.81)t^2$$

$$0 = 4.905t^2 + 2t - 40$$

Use the quadratic formula to solve this equation for t.

$$t = \frac{-2 \pm \sqrt{(2)^2 - 4(4.905)(-40)}}{2(4.905)} = 2.659 \text{ s} \xrightarrow{\text{SD}} \mathbf{3\ s}$$

17. Begin by drawing a free-body diagram of the plank.

2.5 m
w_p w_m
E
x
0.5 m

Compute the weight of the plank and the weight of the man.

$$w_p = m_p g = (100)(9.81) = 981 \text{ N}$$
$$w_m = m_m g = (70)(9.81) = 686.7 \text{ N}$$

Next, sum the moments about the edge point E and solve for x.

$$\Sigma M_E = 0$$
$$-w_p(0.5\text{ m}) + w_m(x) = 0$$
$$-981\text{ N}(0.5\text{ m}) + 686.7\text{ N}(x) = 0$$
$$686.7\text{ N}(x) = 490.5\text{ N}\cdot\text{m}$$
$$x = 0.714\text{ m} \xrightarrow{\text{SD}} \mathbf{0.7\ m}$$

18. Calculate the displacements for the following time intervals:

$$\Delta x_{0,1} = \frac{-1\frac{\text{m}}{\cancel{\text{s}}} \times 1\cancel{\text{s}}}{2} = -0.5\text{ m} \qquad \Delta x_{1,2} = \frac{2\frac{\text{m}}{\cancel{\text{s}}} \times 1\cancel{\text{s}}}{2} = +1\text{ m}$$

$$\Delta x_{2,3} = 2\frac{\text{m}}{\cancel{\text{s}}} \times 1\cancel{\text{s}} = +2\text{ m} \qquad \Delta x_{3,4} = \frac{2\frac{\text{m}}{\cancel{\text{s}}} \times 1\cancel{\text{s}}}{2} = +1\text{ m}$$

Sum these displacements with the initial position and get:
$x_{4.0} = 0\text{ m} - 0.5\text{ m} + 1\text{ m} + 2\text{ m} + 1\text{ m} = \mathbf{3.5\ m}$

19. Increase the mass by a factor of 2.

$$T = 2\pi\sqrt{\frac{m}{k}} \rightarrow T_2 = 2\pi\sqrt{\frac{2m}{k}}$$

Factor the 2 out from under the radical and get:

$$T_2 = (\sqrt{2})2\pi\sqrt{\frac{m}{k}}$$

Now, note that $2\pi\sqrt{\frac{m}{k}}$ is equal to 2.0 s. Substitute and get:

$$T_2 = (\sqrt{2})(2.0\text{ s})$$
$$= 2.828\text{ s} \xrightarrow{\text{SD}} \mathbf{2.8\ s}$$

20. (a) $PE = mgh$

$$= (2.39\,\cancel{\text{kg}})\left(9.81\,\frac{\text{N}}{\cancel{\text{kg}}}\right)(112\text{ m})$$
$$= 2.6259 \times 10^3\text{ J} \xrightarrow{\text{SD}} \mathbf{2.63 \times 10^3\ J}$$

(b) Decrease this energy by a factor of one-half and get: $PE = 1.313 \times 10^3$ J. Use this energy in the following equation to solve for ΔT.

$$Q = mc\Delta T$$
$$1.313 \times 10^3 = (2.39)(100)\Delta T$$
$$\Delta T = 5.494\text{ K} \xrightarrow{\text{SD}} \mathbf{5.49\ K}$$

Problem Set 94

1.
$$\Delta t = \frac{2L}{B\left(1 - \frac{W^2}{B^2}\right)} - \frac{2L}{B\sqrt{1 - \frac{W^2}{B^2}}}$$
$$= \frac{2(200)}{11\left(1 - \frac{(1.5)^2}{(11)^2}\right)} - \frac{2(200)}{11\sqrt{1 - \frac{(1.5)^2}{(11)^2}}}$$
$$= 37.05 - 36.71$$
$$= 0.34\text{ s} \xrightarrow{\text{SD}} \mathbf{0.3\ s}$$

2. Since the amount of work equals the kinetic energy, Bob must do **73.5 J** of work on the mass to bring it to rest in his reference frame.

3.
$$B = \frac{F/A}{\Delta V/V} \rightarrow \frac{\Delta V}{V} = \frac{F/A}{B}$$
$$= \frac{100\text{ Pa}}{2.0 \times 10^9\text{ Pa}}$$
$$= \mathbf{5.0 \times 10^{-8}}$$

$$\frac{\Delta V}{V} = 5.0 \times 10^{-8}$$
$$\Delta V = (5.0 \times 10^{-8})(206\text{ m}^3)$$
$$= 1.03 \times 10^{-5}\text{ m}^3 \xrightarrow{\text{SD}} \mathbf{1.0 \times 10^{-5}\ m^3}$$

4.
$$S = \frac{\text{shear stress}}{\text{shear strain}} \rightarrow \text{Shear strain} = \frac{\text{shear stress}}{S}$$
$$= \frac{12{,}000\text{ N}\cdot\text{m}^{-2}}{8.4 \times 10^{10}\text{ N}\cdot\text{m}^{-2}}$$
$$= 1.429 \times 10^{-7} \xrightarrow{\text{SD}} \mathbf{1.4 \times 10^{-7}}$$

5. $D = R \times T = (3.00 \times 10^8\text{ m}\cdot\text{s}^{-1})(2.15 \times 10^{-2}\text{ s}) = 6.45 \times 10^6\text{ m}$

This is the total distance, both to the target and back to Joe Bob. Therefore, we need to divide this in half to determine the distance Joe Bob was from the target.

$$\frac{6.45 \times 10^6\text{ m}}{2} = 3.225 \times 10^6\text{ m} \xrightarrow{\text{SD}} \mathbf{3.23 \times 10^6\ m}$$

6. Begin by finding the time constant RC.

$$RC = (2000\ \Omega)(25.178 \times 10^{-6}\ \text{F}) = 5.04 \times 10^{-2}\ \text{s}$$

Now calculate the voltage when $t = 0.12$ s.

$$V_C = V_0 - V_0 e^{-t/RC}$$
$$= 42.009 - 42.009e^{-0.12/5.04\times 10^{-2}}$$
$$= 42.009 - 42.009e^{-2.38}$$
$$= 38.12\ \text{V} \xrightarrow{\text{SD}} \mathbf{40\ V}$$

7. Divide the intensity of the second sound by the intensity of the first sound.

$$\frac{I_2}{I_1} = \frac{9.64 \times 10^{-2}\ \text{W/m}^2}{4.37 \times 10^{-6}\ \text{W/m}^2} = 2.206 \times 10^4$$

But 2.206×10^4 can be written as 10 to the 4.344.

$2.206 \times 10^4 = 10^{4.344}$

Multiply the exponent by 10 and find that the difference is **43.4 dB.**

8. (a) Begin by computing the amount of heat required to melt 597 grams of stearic acid.

$$Q = (597\ \text{g})\left(198.91\ \frac{\text{J}}{\text{g}}\right) = 1.18749 \times 10^5\ \text{J} \xrightarrow{\text{SD}} \mathbf{1.19 \times 10^5\ J}$$

(b) Next, compute the change in entropy.

$$\Delta S = \frac{\Delta Q}{T}$$
$$= \frac{+1.18749 \times 10^5\ \text{J}}{(68.82° + 273)\ \text{K}}$$
$$= +347.4\ \frac{\text{J}}{\text{K}} \xrightarrow{\text{SD}} \mathbf{+347\ \frac{J}{K}}$$

9. Increase the area by a factor of 2 and decrease the length by a factor of one-half.

$$H = \frac{kA\Delta T}{L} \longrightarrow H_2 = \frac{k(2A)\Delta T}{\left(\frac{L}{2}\right)} = \frac{4kA\Delta T}{L}$$

Now note that $\frac{kA\Delta T}{L}$ is equal to H, which is 2082 J/s. Substitute and get:

$$H_2 = 4\left(2082\ \frac{\text{J}}{\text{s}}\right) = \mathbf{8328\ \frac{J}{s}}$$

10. (a) $f = \dfrac{128\ \text{cycles}}{14.3\ \text{s}} = 8.951\ \text{Hz} \xrightarrow{\text{SD}} \mathbf{8.95\ Hz}$

(b)
$$f = \frac{1}{2\pi}\sqrt{\frac{k}{m}}$$
$$8.951 = \frac{1}{2\pi}\sqrt{\frac{k}{28.3}}$$
$$3163 = \frac{k}{28.3}$$
$$k = 8.9513 \times 10^4\ \frac{\text{N}}{\text{m}} \xrightarrow{\text{SD}} \mathbf{8.95 \times 10^4\ \frac{N}{m}}$$

11.
$$\Delta V = \beta V_0 \Delta T$$
$$= \frac{1.12 \times 10^{-4}}{\text{C}°}(755\ \text{L})(35.0\ \text{C}°)$$
$$= 2.9596\ \text{liters} \xrightarrow{\text{SD}} \mathbf{2.96\ liters}$$

12. The diameter is 3.76 cm, so the radius is 1.88 cm.

$$Q = Av$$
$$127 = \left[\pi(1.88)^2\right]v$$
$$v = 11.438\ \frac{\text{cm}}{\text{s}} \xrightarrow{\text{SD}} \mathbf{11.4\ \frac{cm}{s}}$$

13. First, use KCL at X to find the current through the branch XY. Assume the current flows from X to Y.

$2\ \text{A} = 1\ \text{A} + I_{XY}$

$I_{XY} = 1\ \text{A}$

To find V_{XY}, begin at Y and move upward to X.

$V_{XY} = +(1\ \text{A})(10\ \Omega) - 10\ \text{V} = \mathbf{0\ V}$

14.
$$F_c = T + mg$$
$$F_c = 0 + mg$$
$$\frac{mv^2}{L} = mg$$
$$v = \mathbf{\sqrt{gL}}$$

15. (a) Begin by finding the time constant L/R.

$$\frac{L}{R} = \frac{56\text{ H}}{8000\ \Omega} = 0.007\text{ s}$$

Sketch the voltage across the inductor as a function of time.

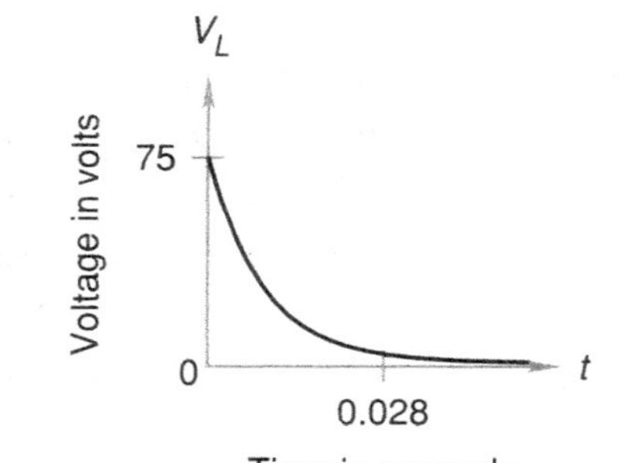

(b) $I_F = \frac{V}{R} = \frac{75\text{ V}}{8000\ \Omega} = 0.0094\text{ A}$

Sketch the current through the resistor as a function of time.

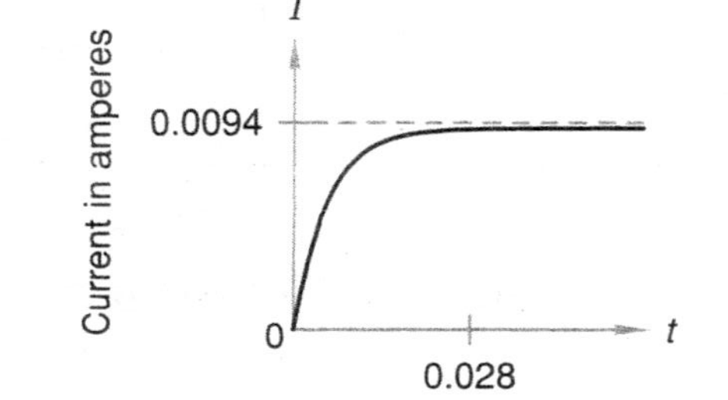

(c) This graph has the same shape as the current through the resistor.

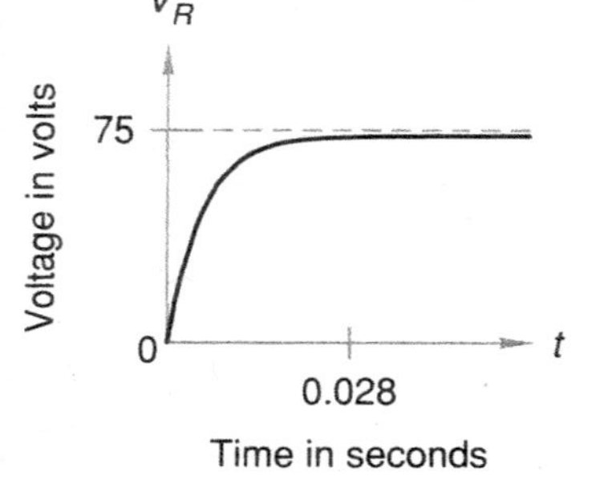

16. Begin by finding the time constant L/R.

$$\frac{L}{R} = \frac{56\text{ H}}{8000\ \Omega} = 0.007\text{ s}$$

Now calculate the voltage when $t = 14 \times 10^{-3}$ s.

$$V_L = V_0 e^{-\left(\frac{t}{L/R}\right)}$$
$$= 75e^{-14\times10^{-3}/0.007}$$
$$= 75e^{-2}$$
$$= 10.15\text{ V} \xrightarrow{\text{SD}} \mathbf{1\bar{0}\ V}$$

17. $\frac{P_1V_1}{T_1} = \frac{P_2V_2}{T_2} \rightarrow \frac{P_1V_1}{T_1} = \frac{P_2(4V_1)}{(2T_1)}$

$$\frac{P_1\cancel{V_1}}{\cancel{T_1}} \times \frac{\cancel{T_1}}{\cancel{V_1}} = \frac{P_2(4\cancel{V_1})}{(2\cancel{T_1})} \times \frac{\cancel{T_1}}{\cancel{V_1}}$$

$$P_2 = \mathbf{\frac{P_1}{2}}$$

18. Begin by finding the equivalent resistance of the two parallel resistors.

$$R_E = \frac{(204)(180)}{204 + 180} = 95.63\ \Omega$$

Now, combine this with the 78-Ω resistor to find the equivalent resistance of the circuit.

$$R_E = (95.63\ \Omega) + 78\ \Omega = 173.63\ \Omega$$

Use this resistance to find I_1.

$$I_1 = \frac{V}{R_E} = \frac{22\text{ V}}{173.63\ \Omega} = 0.127\text{ A} \xrightarrow{\text{SD}} \mathbf{0.13\ A}$$

The voltage across R_1 must equal I_1R_1.

$$V_1 = I_1R_1 = (0.127\text{ A})(78\ \Omega) = 9.906\text{ V} \xrightarrow{\text{SD}} \mathbf{9.9\ V}$$

The voltage across R_3 must equal the total voltage minus V_1.

$$V_3 = 22\text{ V} - 9.906\text{ V} = 12.094\text{ V} \xrightarrow{\text{SD}} \mathbf{12\ V}$$

Use this voltage to find I_3.

$$I_3 = \frac{V_3}{R_3} = \frac{12.094\text{ V}}{180\ \Omega} = 0.0672\text{ A} \xrightarrow{\text{SD}} \mathbf{0.067\ A}$$

19. $x(t) = x_0 + v_0 t + \frac{1}{2}at^2$

$$= 0 + 18(5) + \frac{1}{2}(-4)(5)^2$$

$$= \mathbf{40\ m}$$

20. $W = F \times D = (40\ \cancel{kg})\left(9.81\ \frac{N}{\cancel{kg}}\right)(0.25) \times 7.5\ m = 735.75\ J$

$$D = R \times T$$
$$7.5\ m = 0.50\ m/s \times T$$
$$T = 15\ s$$

$$P = \frac{W}{\Delta t} = \frac{735.75\ J}{15\ s} = 49.05\ W \xrightarrow{SD} \mathbf{49\ W}$$

Problem Set 95

1. $RF = \sqrt{1 - \frac{v^2}{c^2}} = \sqrt{1 - \frac{(0.9c)^2}{c^2}} = \sqrt{1 - 0.81} = 0.436 \xrightarrow{SD} \mathbf{0.4}$

2. First, calculate the relativity factor.

$$RF = \sqrt{1 - \frac{v^2}{c^2}} = \sqrt{1 - \frac{(0.85c)^2}{c^2}} = \sqrt{1 - 0.7225} = 0.527$$

Next, compute the observed time.

$$\Delta t = \frac{\Delta t_0}{\sqrt{1 - \frac{v^2}{c^2}}} = \frac{62\ hr}{0.527} = 117.6\ hr \xrightarrow{SD} \mathbf{120\ hr}$$

3. See Lesson 93.

4. Begin by writing equations for v and v_2.

$$Q = A_1 v_1 \qquad Q = A_2 v_2$$
$$16 = (\pi r^2)v \qquad 16 = [\pi(0.4r)^2]v_2$$

(a) $v = \frac{16}{\pi r^2}$ (b) $v_2 = \frac{16}{\pi(0.16)r^2}$

Since $v = 16/\pi r^2$, we can substitute this into (b) and solve for v_2.

(b) $v_2 = \frac{16}{\pi(0.16)r^2} = \frac{v}{0.16} = 6.25v \xrightarrow{SD} \mathbf{6v}$

5.
$$v = f\lambda$$
$$3.00 \times 10^8\ m \cdot s^{-1} = (180 \times 10^6\ Hz)\lambda$$
$$\lambda = 1.667\ m$$

To build a half-wavelength dipole antenna, divide the wavelength of 1.667 m by 2 and get **0.83 m,** which is the total length of the antenna.

6. (a) $F = qvB$

$$= (1.60 \times 10^{-19})(275)(57)$$
$$= 2.508 \times 10^{-15}\ N \xrightarrow{SD} \mathbf{2.5 \times 10^{-15}\ N}$$

(b) To find the direction of the force, place your right hand flat so that your fingers point in the original direction of the electron and bend your fingers to point in the direction of the magnetic field. Since the electron has a negative charge, the direction of the force on the electron is opposite the direction of your thumb. Therefore, the direction of the force on the electron is **west.**

7. We need to find the electric field component at P caused by the charge at B and add the two field components vectorially.

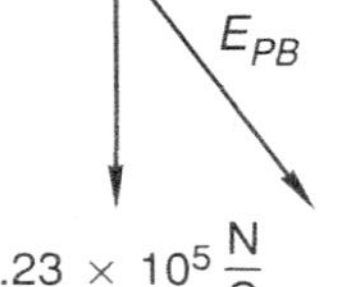

The electric component of P caused by q_B is toward q_B (because q_B is negative) and has a value of

$$E_{PB} = \frac{kq_B}{r^2} = \frac{(9.0 \times 10^9)(3.27 \times 10^{-6})}{(0.50)^2} = 1.177 \times 10^5\ N/C$$

From the diagram of the positions of the charges, we see that

$$\sin\theta = \frac{0.30}{0.50} = 0.60 \quad \text{and} \quad \cos\theta = \frac{0.40}{0.50} = 0.80$$

The vector components of E_{PB} are

$E_{PB}\sin\theta$
$E_{PB}\cos\theta$
θ
E_{PB}

$$E_{PB}\sin\theta = (1.177 \times 10^5)(0.60)$$
$$= 7.062 \times 10^4\ N/C$$
$$E_{PB}\cos\theta = (1.177 \times 10^5)(0.80)$$
$$= 9.416 \times 10^4\ N/C$$

The sum of the horizontal and vertical components is

$$E_x = (0) + 7.062 \times 10^4 = 7.062 \times 10^4\ N/C$$
$$E_y = -4.23 \times 10^5 - 9.416 \times 10^4 = -5.172 \times 10^5\ N/C$$

So now we have the horizontal and vertical components of E_P as

7.062×10^4, -5.172×10^5, α, E_P

$$E_P = \sqrt{(7.062 \times 10^4)^2 + (-5.172 \times 10^5)^2}$$
$$= 5.220 \times 10^5 \frac{N}{C}$$
$$\alpha = \arctan \frac{-5.172 \times 10^5}{7.062 \times 10^4} = -82.22°$$

$$E_P = 5.220 \times 10^5 \underline{/-82.22°} \frac{N}{C} \xrightarrow{SD} \mathbf{5.2 \times 10^5 \underline{/-82.22°} \frac{N}{C}}$$

8. Begin by finding the equivalent capacitance of the two parallel capacitors.
$C_E = 58\ \mu F + 84\ \mu F = 142\ \mu F$
Next, find the time constant RC.
$RC = (2000\ \Omega)(142 \times 10^{-6}\ F) = 0.284\ s$

Now calculate the voltage when $t = 1.15$ s.
$$V_C = V_0 - V_0 e^{-t/RC}$$
$$= 15 - 15e^{-1.15/0.284}$$
$$= 15 - 15e^{-4.05}$$
$$= 14.74\ V \xrightarrow{SD} \mathbf{15\ V}$$

9. $$\frac{1}{f} = \frac{1}{D_O} + \frac{1}{D_I}$$
$$\frac{1}{7.0} = \frac{1}{14} + \frac{1}{D_I}$$
$$D_I = \mathbf{14\ cm}$$

$$\frac{H_I}{H_O} = \frac{-D_I}{D_O}$$
$$\frac{H_I}{7.5} = \frac{-14}{14}$$
$$H_I = \mathbf{-7.5\ cm}$$

The image is **real** because it is inverted and in front of the mirror.

10. Begin by finding the centripetal force and the static friction force.
$$F_c = \frac{mv^2}{r} = \frac{(1810)v^2}{112} = 16.161v^2$$
$$F_s = mg\mu_s = (1810)(9.81)(0.793) = 14{,}080.59\ N$$

The required centripetal force must equal the static friction force.
$$F_c = F_s$$
$$16.161v^2 = 14{,}080.59$$
$$v = 29.517 \frac{m}{s} \xrightarrow{SD} \mathbf{29.5 \frac{m}{s}}$$

11. (a) $F = kx = 2500 \frac{N}{\cancel{m}} \times 1.32\ \cancel{m} = \mathbf{3300\ N}$

(b) $W = \frac{1}{2}kx^2 = \frac{1}{2}(2500)(1.32)^2 = 2178\ J \xrightarrow{SD} \mathbf{2200\ J}$

12. $$PE = \frac{1}{2}kx^2 = \frac{1}{2}(555)(0.62)^2 = 106.67\ J$$
$$KE = \frac{1}{2}mv^2$$
$$106.67 = \frac{1}{2}(8.6)v^2$$
$$v = 4.98 \frac{m}{s} \xrightarrow{SD} \mathbf{5.0 \frac{m}{s}}$$

13. Begin by finding the kinetic friction force.
$$F_k = \mu_k mg = (0.82)(26\ \cancel{kg})\left(9.81 \frac{N}{\cancel{kg}}\right) = 209.15\ N$$
Next, sum the horizontal forces to find the acceleration.
$$\Sigma F = ma_x$$
$$476\ N - 209.15\ N = (26\ kg)a$$
$$a = 10.26\ m{\cdot}s^{-2}$$

Determine the distance.
$$D = \frac{1}{2}at^2 = \frac{1}{2}(10.26\ m{\cdot}s^{-2})(8.0\ s)^2 = 328.32\ m \xrightarrow{SD} \mathbf{330\ m}$$

14. Begin by finding the weight of the block. Then find w_x and w_y.

$$w = mg = 22\,\text{kg} \times 9.81\,\frac{\text{N}}{\text{kg}} = 215.82\text{ N}$$
$$w_x = (215.82\text{ N})\sin 42° = 144.41\text{ N}$$
$$w_y = (215.82\text{ N})\cos 42° = 160.39\text{ N}$$

Next, compute the frictional force.

$$F_k = \mu_k F_N = (0.4)(160.39\text{ N}) = 64.16\text{ N}$$

Now sum the forces parallel to the plane and get:

$$-w_x + F_k = ma_x$$
$$-144.41\text{ N} + 64.16\text{ N} = (22\text{ kg})a_x$$
$$a_x = -3.65\,\frac{\text{m}}{\text{s}^2} \xrightarrow{\text{SD}} \mathbf{4\,\frac{m}{s^2}\ \text{down the plane}}$$

15.
$$\Delta(mv)_x = mv_2 - mv_1$$
$$= |-mv\cos\theta - mv\cos\theta|$$
$$= |-2mv\cos\theta|$$
$$= \mathbf{2mv\cos\theta}$$

16. (a)
$$T_{\text{Top}} = w_{\text{box}} + w_{\text{rope}}$$
$$= (143)(9.81) + 48.2$$
$$= 1451.03\text{ N} \xrightarrow{\text{SD}} \mathbf{1450\ N}$$

(b)
$$T_{\text{Bottom}} = w_{\text{box}}$$
$$= (143)(9.81)$$
$$= 1402.83\text{ N} \xrightarrow{\text{SD}} \mathbf{14\bar{0}0\ N}$$

17. Begin by finding the equivalent resistance of the two parallel 8-Ω resistors.

$$R_E = \frac{(8)(8)}{8 + 8} = 4\,\Omega$$

Combine this with the 4-Ω resistor in series.

$$R_E = (4\,\Omega) + 4\,\Omega = 8\,\Omega$$

Combine this with the 8-Ω resistor in parallel.

$$R_E = \frac{(8)(8)}{8 + 8} = 4\,\Omega$$

Now, combine this with the 4-Ω and 2-Ω resistors in series to find the equivalent resistance of the circuit.

$$R_E = (4\,\Omega) + 4\,\Omega + 2\,\Omega = \mathbf{10\,\Omega}$$

18. Begin by finding the weight of the mass and drawing a free-body diagram of the forces acting on the junction of the ropes.

$$w = mg$$

Now sum the horizontal and vertical forces to zero.

(a) $\Sigma F_x = 0;\ T\cos\theta - T\cos\theta = 0$

(b) $\Sigma F_y = 0;\ T\sin\theta + T\sin\theta - mg = 0$

Solve (b) for T and get:

(b)
$$T\sin\theta + T\sin\theta = mg$$
$$2T\sin\theta = mg$$
$$T = \frac{\mathbf{mg}}{\mathbf{2\sin\theta}}$$

19. Use the y-displacement equation to find the time.

$$\Delta y = v_0 t + \frac{1}{2}at^2$$
$$-9.8 = (0) + \frac{1}{2}(-9.81)t^2$$
$$4.905t^2 = 9.8$$
$$t = 1.41\text{ s} \xrightarrow{\text{SD}} \mathbf{1.4\ s}$$

20. Write the x-displacement equation where $v_{x0} = v$ and $\Delta x = d$.

$$\Delta x = v_{x0}t + \frac{1}{2}a_x t^2$$
$$d = vt + 0$$
$$d = vt \qquad \text{(a)}$$

Write the x-displacement equation where $v_{x0} = 2v$.

$$\Delta x = v_{x0}t + \frac{1}{2}a_x t^2$$
$$= 2vt + 0$$
$$= 2vt \qquad \text{(b)}$$

Substitute (a) into (b) and solve for Δx.

(b)
$$\Delta x = 2vt$$
$$= 2(d)$$
$$= \mathbf{2d}$$

PROBLEM SET 96

1. $RF = \sqrt{1 - \frac{v^2}{c^2}} = \sqrt{1 - \frac{(0.7c)^2}{c^2}} = \sqrt{1 - 0.49} = 0.714 \xrightarrow{\text{SD}} \mathbf{0.7}$

2. $RF = \sqrt{1 - \frac{v^2}{c^2}} = \sqrt{1 - \frac{(0.5c)^2}{c^2}} = \sqrt{1 - 0.25} = 0.866 \xrightarrow{\text{SD}} \mathbf{0.9}$

Compute the observed time.

$$\Delta t = \frac{\Delta t_0}{\sqrt{1 - \frac{v^2}{c^2}}} = \frac{329.172 \text{ s}}{0.866} = 380.11 \text{ s} \xrightarrow{\text{SD}} \mathbf{400\ s}$$

Compute the observed mass.

$$m = \frac{m_0}{\sqrt{1 - \frac{v^2}{c^2}}} = \frac{4440.19 \text{ g}}{0.866} = 5127.24 \text{ g} \xrightarrow{\text{SD}} \mathbf{5000\ g}$$

3. $RF = \sqrt{1 - \frac{v^2}{c^2}} = \sqrt{1 - \frac{(0.92c)^2}{c^2}} = \sqrt{1 - 0.8464} = 0.392$

Compute the observed length.

$$L = L_0\sqrt{1 - \frac{v^2}{c^2}} = (466 \text{ m})(0.392) = 182.67 \text{ m} \xrightarrow{\text{SD}} \mathbf{180\ m}$$

4. See Lesson 93.

5. $RF = \sqrt{1 - \frac{v^2}{c^2}} = \sqrt{1 - \frac{(0.990c)^2}{c^2}} = \sqrt{1 - 0.9801} = 0.141$

Compute the observed mass.

$$m = \frac{m_0}{\sqrt{1 - \frac{v^2}{c^2}}} = \frac{9.11 \times 10^{-31} \text{ kg}}{0.141} = 6.461 \times 10^{-30} \text{ kg}$$

Therefore, Sally Sue thinks the mass increased as

$$\frac{m}{m_0} = \frac{6.461 \times 10^{-30} \text{ kg}}{9.11 \times 10^{-31} \text{ kg}} = 7.092 \xrightarrow{\text{SD}} \mathbf{7.09}$$

6. Refer to Section 95.B.

7. Refer to Section 95.C; Refer to Section 96.A.

8.
$$\begin{aligned} \Phi &= AB \cos \theta \\ &= (0.35)(20.4 \times 10^{-3}) \cos 0° \\ &= 7.14 \times 10^{-3} \text{ Wb} \xrightarrow{\text{SD}} \mathbf{7.1 \times 10^{-3}\ Wb} \end{aligned}$$

$$\begin{aligned} \text{emf} &= N\frac{\Delta\Phi}{\Delta t} \\ &= (1)\left(\frac{0 \text{ Wb} - 7.14 \times 10^{-3} \text{ Wb}}{0.050 \text{ s}}\right) \\ &= -0.1428 \text{ V} \xrightarrow{\text{SD}} \mathbf{-0.14\ V} \end{aligned}$$

9. Since both horizontal components of each magnetic field at P point in the same direction, we must **add** the components and the result points to the **right.**

10.
$$\begin{aligned} T &= 2\pi\sqrt{\frac{L}{g}} \\ 1.0 &= 2\pi\sqrt{\frac{L}{9.81}} \\ 0.0253 &= \frac{L}{9.81} \\ L &= 0.248 \text{ m} \xrightarrow{\text{SD}} \mathbf{0.25\ m} \end{aligned}$$

11. $E = \frac{\text{force}}{\text{charge}} = \frac{1.25 \times 10^{-6} \text{ N}}{1.60 \times 10^{-19} \text{ C}} = 7.813 \times 10^{12} \frac{\text{N}}{\text{C}}$

Since $1\,\frac{\text{N}}{\text{C}} = 1\,\frac{\text{V}}{\text{m}}$, we get $\mathbf{7.81 \times 10^{12}\ \frac{V}{m}}$

12. First, solve for $\varepsilon_0 A/d$ using $K = 3.40$.

$$C_1 = \frac{K_1 \varepsilon_0 A}{d}$$

$$357 \times 10^{-6} = (3.40)\frac{\varepsilon_0 A}{d}$$

$$\frac{\varepsilon_0 A}{d} = 1.05 \times 10^{-4}$$

Substitute this into the following equation and solve for K_2.

$$C_2 = \frac{K_2 \varepsilon_0 A}{d}$$

$$542 \times 10^{-6} = K_2(1.05 \times 10^{-4})$$

$$K_2 = 5.162 \xrightarrow{\text{SD}} \mathbf{5.16}$$

13. $v = f(2L)$

$= (440)(2)(0.563)$

$= 495.44 \frac{\text{m}}{\text{s}} \xrightarrow{\text{SD}} \mathbf{5\bar{0}0 \frac{m}{s}}$

14. Begin by computing the amount of heat required to melt 0.0423 kg of ice.

$$Q = (0.0423 \cancel{\text{kg}})\left(334 \times 10^3 \frac{\text{J}}{\cancel{\text{kg}}}\right) = 1.413 \times 10^4 \text{ J}$$

Next, compute the change in entropies.

(a) $\Delta S_{\text{ice}} = \frac{\Delta Q}{T}$

$= \frac{+1.413 \times 10^4 \text{ J}}{273 \text{ K}}$

$= +51.758 \text{ J/K} \xrightarrow{\text{SD}} \mathbf{+51.8 \text{ J/K}}$

(b) $\Delta S_{\text{ground}} = \frac{\Delta Q}{T}$

$= \frac{-1.413 \times 10^4 \text{ J}}{(37° + 273) \text{ K}}$

$= -45.581 \text{ J/K} \xrightarrow{\text{SD}} \mathbf{-46 \text{ J/K}}$

(c) $\Delta S_{\text{total}} = \Delta S_{\text{ice}} + \Delta S_{\text{ground}}$

$= (+51.758 \text{ J/K}) + (-45.581 \text{ J/K})$

$= +6.177 \text{ J/K} \xrightarrow{\text{SD}} \mathbf{+6.2 \text{ J/K}}$

15. Write the equation for the force per mass on the earth.

$$\frac{F}{m} = G\frac{M}{r^2}$$

$$9.81 = G\frac{M}{r^2}$$

Next, write the equation for the force per mass on the other planet.

$$\frac{F}{m} = G\frac{(2M)}{(2r)^2}$$

$$\frac{F}{m} = G\frac{M}{2r^2}$$

Now, note that $G\frac{M}{r^2}$ is equal to 9.81. Substitute and get:

$$\frac{F}{m} = G\frac{M}{2r^2}$$

$= \frac{1}{2}(9.81)$

$= 4.905 \frac{\text{N}}{\text{kg}} \xrightarrow{\text{SD}} \mathbf{4.91 \frac{N}{kg}}$

16. $n_1 \sin \theta_1 = n_2 \sin \theta_2$

$2.417 \sin \theta_c = 1.517 \sin 90°$

$\theta_c = \mathbf{38.88°}$

17. $W = FD \cos \theta$

$= (64 \text{ N})(7.2 \cos 32° \text{ m}) = 390.78 \text{ J} \xrightarrow{\text{SD}} \mathbf{390 \text{ J}}$

18. To find the linear speed, set the tensile strength equal to the centripetal force.

$$T_s = \frac{mv^2}{r}$$

$$57.2 = \frac{(6.2)v^2}{2.37}$$

$v = 4.676 \frac{\text{m}}{\text{s}} \xrightarrow{\text{SD}} \mathbf{4.7 \frac{m}{s}}$

19. $14 \frac{\cancel{\text{coulombs}}}{\text{s}} \times \frac{1 \text{ electron}}{1.60 \times 10^{-19} \cancel{\text{coulomb}}}$

$= 8.75 \times 10^{19} \text{ electrons} \xrightarrow{\text{SD}} \mathbf{8.8 \times 10^{19} \text{ electrons}}$

20. $T \sin\theta = mr\omega^2$

$T \cancel{\sin\theta} = m(0.481 \cancel{\sin\theta})\omega^2$

$T = (0.526)(0.481)(2.3\pi)^2$

$= 13.21 \text{ N} \xrightarrow{SD}$ **13 N**

Problem Set 97

1. $E_p = hf$

$14.6 \text{ eV} = (4.136 \times 10^{-15} \text{ eV}\cdot\text{s})f$

$f = 3.530 \times 10^{15} \text{ Hz} \xrightarrow{SD}$ $\mathbf{3.53 \times 10^{15}}$ **Hz**

$v = f\lambda$

$3.00 \times 10^8 \frac{\text{m}}{\text{s}} = (3.530 \times 10^{15} \text{ Hz})\lambda$

$\lambda = 8.499 \times 10^{-8} \text{ m} \xrightarrow{SD}$ $\mathbf{8.50 \times 10^{-8}}$ **m**

2. $E_p = hf$

$= (6.626 \times 10^{-34} \text{ J}\cdot\text{s})(0.459 \times 10^{15} \text{ Hz})$

$= 3.0413 \times 10^{-19} \text{ J} \xrightarrow{SD}$ $\mathbf{3.04 \times 10^{-19}}$ **J**

3. The energy difference between the two energy levels is
$-0.85 \text{ eV} - (-13.6 \text{ eV}) = 12.75 \text{ eV}$

Use this energy difference to calculate the frequency of the photon of light.

$E_p = hf$

$12.75 \text{ eV} = (4.136 \times 10^{-15} \text{ eV}\cdot\text{s})f$

$f = 3.083 \times 10^{15} \text{ Hz} \xrightarrow{SD}$ $\mathbf{3.1 \times 10^{15}}$ **Hz**

4. $RF = \sqrt{1 - \frac{v^2}{c^2}} = \sqrt{1 - \frac{(0.94c)^2}{c^2}} = \sqrt{1 - 0.8836} = \mathbf{0.34}$

5. See Lesson 93.

6. $RF = \sqrt{1 - \frac{v^2}{c^2}} = \sqrt{1 - \frac{(0.92c)^2}{c^2}} = \sqrt{1 - 0.8464} = 0.392$

Compute the observed time.

$\Delta t = \frac{\Delta t_0}{\sqrt{1 - \frac{v^2}{c^2}}} = \frac{42 \text{ hr}}{0.392} = 107.14 \text{ hr} \xrightarrow{SD}$ **110 hr**

Compute the observed mass.

$m = \frac{m_0}{\sqrt{1 - \frac{v^2}{c^2}}} = \frac{5.0 \text{ kg}}{0.392} = 12.755 \text{ kg} \xrightarrow{SD}$ **13 kg**

Compute the observed length.

$L = L_0\sqrt{1 - \frac{v^2}{c^2}} = (105 \text{ cm})(0.392) = 41.16 \text{ cm} \xrightarrow{SD}$ **41 cm**

7. (a) $f = \frac{1}{T} = \frac{1}{2\pi\sqrt{\frac{L}{g}}} = \boldsymbol{\frac{1}{2\pi}\sqrt{\frac{g}{L}}}$

(b) $f = \frac{1}{2\pi}\sqrt{\frac{g}{L}}$

$4.0 = \frac{1}{2\pi}\sqrt{\frac{9.83}{L}}$

$631.65 = \frac{9.83}{L}$

$L = 0.0156 \text{ m} \xrightarrow{SD}$ **0.016 m = 1.6 cm**

8. (a) First, draw a diagram of the pendulum.

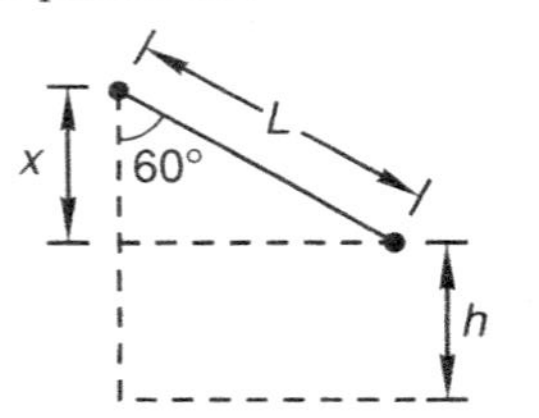

Then determine x using the cosine property.

$$\cos 60° = \frac{x}{L} \quad \longrightarrow \quad x = L\cos 60°$$

Since $x + h = L$, we get

$$x + h = L$$
$$(L\cos 60°) + h = L$$
$$h = \mathbf{L - L\cos 60°}$$

(b)

$$mgh = \frac{1}{2}mv^2$$
$$\frac{2\cancel{m}gh}{\cancel{m}} = v^2$$
$$v = \mathbf{\sqrt{2gh}}$$

9.

$$\frac{1}{f} = \frac{1}{D_O} + \frac{1}{D_I}$$
$$\frac{1}{20} = \frac{1}{10} + \frac{1}{D_I}$$
$$D_I = \mathbf{-20\ cm}$$

10. The original value of A is 7.

$$7 = \frac{B^2\sqrt{C}}{D^3}$$

Doubling B, C, and D, we get:

$$A = \frac{(2B)^2\sqrt{(2C)}}{(2D)^3} = \frac{4B^2\sqrt{2C}}{8D^3} = \frac{\sqrt{2}B^2\sqrt{C}}{2D^3}$$

Now, note that $\frac{B^2\sqrt{C}}{D^3} = 7$, the original value of A. Substitute and compute the new A.

$$A = \frac{\sqrt{2}}{2}\frac{B^2\sqrt{C}}{D^3} = \frac{\sqrt{2}}{2}(7) = \mathbf{\frac{7\sqrt{2}}{2}}$$

11. Using the right-hand rule, point your thumb in the direction of the current (into the paper), and then curl your fingers. Your fingers will point in the direction of the magnetic field. Note that the vertical components of the magnetic fields cancel each other and the horizontal components add. The resultant magnetic field points to the **left**.

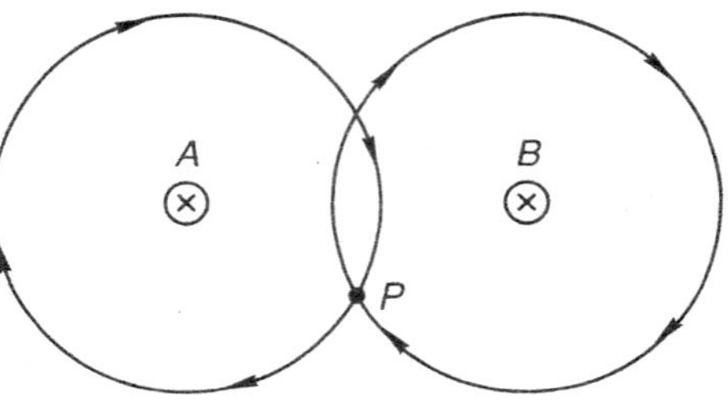

12. Begin by finding the equivalent resistance of the two parallel resistors.

$$R_E = \frac{(R)(R)}{R + R} = \frac{R^2}{2R} = \frac{R}{2}$$

Now find the power consumed by both resistors.

$$P = \frac{V^2}{R_E} = \frac{V^2}{\frac{R}{2}} = \mathbf{\frac{2V^2}{R}}$$

13. Begin by finding the equivalent resistance of the two series resistors.

$$R_E = R + R = 2R$$

Now find the power consumed by both resistors.

$$P = \frac{V^2}{R_E} = \mathbf{\frac{V^2}{2R}}$$

14. (a)

$$v = f\lambda$$
$$340\ \text{m}\cdot\text{s}^{-1} = (1450\ \text{Hz})\lambda$$
$$\lambda = 0.234\ \text{m} \xrightarrow{\text{SD}} \mathbf{0.23\ m}$$

(b) The distance a wave crest travels in one vibration is the wavelength, which is **0.23 m.**

15.
$$\tau = I\alpha$$
$$\tau = \left(\frac{1}{2}mr^2\right)\alpha$$
$$372.41 = \left(\frac{1}{2}(50)(0.24397)^2\right)\alpha$$
$$\alpha = 250.27\ \frac{\text{rad}}{\text{s}^2} \xrightarrow{\text{SD}} \mathbf{300\ \frac{rad}{s^2}}$$

16. Since the voltmeter is connected in parallel across all the circuit elements (voltage source and resistors), the reading will **stay the same.**

Since the resistors are connected in parallel, the equivalent resistance is $\frac{1}{2}R$. The current is equal to the voltage divided by the resistance; therefore, the current is $2V/R$, or twice as much as when the switch was open. Thus the ammeter reading will **increase.**

17. $P = I^2R = \frac{W}{t}$
$$W = \boldsymbol{I^2Rt}\ \textbf{joules}$$

18. Since $V = IR$, we get:
$W = I^2Rt = VIt =$ **30*At* joules**

19. The centrifugal force (reactive force of the centripetal force) acts outwardly from the center of the merry-go-round and causes the person to move outwardly or towards *A*. Since the friction force acts in opposition to the motion, the friction force must act towards ***C***.

20. The centripetal force must equal the static friction force.
$$F_c = mr\omega^2$$
$$mg\mu_s = mD\omega^2$$
$$D = \boldsymbol{\frac{\mu_s g}{\omega^2}}$$

Problem Set 98

1. Using the periodic table, the element which has 75 protons is **Rhenium;** $\mathbf{^{190}_{75}Re}$.

2. Radium isotope $^{226}_{88}\text{Ra}$ has 88 protons. If it loses 2 protons and 2 neutrons, it will then have 86 protons and 222 nucleons. Thus the element is **Radon.**

3. Using the periodic table, the element with 85 protons is **Astatine.**

4.
$$E_p = hf$$
$$(6.63 \times 10^{-14}\text{ J}) = (6.626 \times 10^{-34}\text{ J}\cdot\text{s})f$$
$$f = 1.0006 \times 10^{20}\text{ Hz} \xrightarrow{\text{SD}} \mathbf{1.00 \times 10^{20}\ Hz}$$

5.
$$E_p = hf$$
$$(15 \times 10^3\text{ eV}) = (4.136 \times 10^{-15}\text{ eV}\cdot\text{s})f$$
$$f = 3.627 \times 10^{18}\text{ Hz} \xrightarrow{\text{SD}} \mathbf{3.6 \times 10^{18}\ Hz}$$

6. The half-life is 24.1 days, so the number of half-lives in 143 days is
$$n = \frac{143}{24.1} = 5.9336$$
Thus the amount present after 143 days is
$$A_t = \frac{1}{2^n}A_0$$
$$A_{143} = \frac{1}{2^{5.9336}}(14.5)$$
$$= (0.01636)(14.5)$$
$$= 0.23722\text{ kg} \xrightarrow{\text{SD}} \mathbf{0.237\ kg}$$

7. The half-life is 69.4 days, so the number of half-lives in 722 days is
$$n = \frac{722}{69.4} = 10.40$$
Thus the amount present after 722 days is
$$A_t = \frac{1}{2^n}A_0$$
$$A_{722} = \frac{1}{2^{10.40}}(14)$$
$$= (7.40 \times 10^{-4})(14)$$
$$= 0.01036\text{ kg} \xrightarrow{\text{SD}} \mathbf{0.010\ kg = 1\bar{0}\ g}$$

8.
$$E_p = hf$$
$$8.92 \times 10^{-9}\text{ J} = (6.626 \times 10^{-34}\text{ J}\cdot\text{s})f$$
$$f = 1.346 \times 10^{25}\text{ Hz} \xrightarrow{\text{SD}} \mathbf{1.35 \times 10^{25}\ Hz}$$

9. See Lesson 93.

10. $RF = \sqrt{1 - \frac{v^2}{c^2}} = \sqrt{1 - \frac{(0.98c)^2}{c^2}} = \sqrt{1 - 0.9604} = 0.199$

Compute the observed time.

$$\Delta t = \frac{\Delta t_0}{\sqrt{1 - \frac{v^2}{c^2}}} = \frac{4 \text{ hr}}{0.199} = 20.1 \text{ hr} \xrightarrow{\text{SD}} \mathbf{20\ hr}$$

Compute the observed mass.

$$m = \frac{m_0}{\sqrt{1 - \frac{v^2}{c^2}}} = \frac{4 \text{ kg}}{0.199} = 20.1 \text{ kg} \xrightarrow{\text{SD}} \mathbf{20\ kg}$$

Compute the observed length.

$$L = L_0\sqrt{1 - \frac{v^2}{c^2}} = (4 \text{ m})(0.199) = 0.796 \text{ m} \xrightarrow{\text{SD}} \mathbf{0.8\ m}$$

11. (a) $Q = (400 \cancel{g})\left(21.460 \frac{\text{J}}{\cancel{g}}\right) = 8584 \text{ J} \xrightarrow{\text{SD}} \mathbf{9000\ J}$

(b) $\Delta S = \frac{\Delta Q}{T}$

$= \frac{+8584 \text{ J}}{(14.83° + 273) \text{ K}}$

$= +29.82 \frac{\text{J}}{\text{K}} \xrightarrow{\text{SD}} \mathbf{+30\ \frac{J}{K}}$

12. (a) $B = \frac{\mu_0 I}{2\pi r}$

$= \frac{(1.26 \times 10^{-6})(4.25)}{2\pi(0.0250)}$

$= 3.409 \times 10^{-5} \text{ T} \xrightarrow{\text{SD}} \mathbf{3.41 \times 10^{-5}\ T}$

(b) $\frac{F}{l} = BI$

$\frac{F}{(1)} = (3.409 \times 10^{-5})(4.25)$

$F = 1.4488 \times 10^{-4} \text{ N} \xrightarrow{\text{SD}} \mathbf{1 \times 10^{-4}\ N}$

13. (a) The amplitude is the maximum value of the function.
Amplitude = **35 m**

(b) $T = \frac{1}{f} = \frac{1}{0.375 \text{ Hz}} = 2.667 \text{ s} \xrightarrow{\text{SD}} \mathbf{2.67\ s}$

(c) The coefficient of t is ω, which is $2\pi f$.
Therefore, frequency = **0.375 Hz.**

14. Begin by finding the equivalent resistance of the three resistors in series.

$R_E = 125\ \Omega + 75\ \Omega + 25\ \Omega$

$= 225\ \Omega$

Combine this with the 35-Ω resistor in parallel.

$R_E = \frac{(35)(225)}{35 + 225} = 30.29\ \Omega$

Combine this with the 57-Ω resistor in series.

$R_E = (30.29\ \Omega) + 57\ \Omega$

$= 87.29\ \Omega$

Use this resistance to find I_1.

$I_1 = \frac{V}{R_E} = \frac{12 \text{ V}}{87.29\ \Omega} = 0.137 \text{ A} \xrightarrow{\text{SD}} \mathbf{0.14\ A}$

15. To find V_{AD}, begin at D and move clockwise to A.

$V_{AD} = +14 \text{ V} - 16.7 \text{ V} - 4.3 \text{ V} - 11 \text{ V} = \mathbf{-18\ V}$

16. When the solid substance is heated, it undergoes phase changes. Since the phase changes occur at a constant temperature and the heat required to melt the substance lasts over a period of time, T_1 signifies the **melting point of the substance.**

17. Use the ideal gas law to find the temperature at B.

$\frac{\cancel{P_A} V_A}{T_A} = \frac{\cancel{P_B} V_B}{T_B}$

$\frac{V_A}{T_A} = \frac{V_B}{T_B}$

$\frac{V_0}{200} = \frac{3V_0}{T_B}$

$T_B = \mathbf{600\ K}$

Use the ideal gas law to find the temperature at C.

$$\frac{P_D V_D}{T_D} = \frac{P_C V_C}{T_C}$$

$$\frac{V_D}{T_D} = \frac{V_C}{T_C}$$

$$\frac{V_0}{100} = \frac{3V_0}{T_C}$$

$$T_C = \mathbf{300\ K}$$

18. $$\frac{P_A V_A}{T_A} = \frac{P_B V_B}{T_B}$$

$$\frac{P_0 V_0}{30} = \frac{3P_0(3V_0)}{T_B}$$

$$T_B = \mathbf{270\ K}$$

19. The electric field component of A caused by q_B is away from q_B (because q_B is positive) and has a value of

$$E_{AB} = (9.0 \times 10^9)\frac{q_B}{r^2} = (9.0 \times 10^9)\frac{(1.0 \times 10^{-6})}{(1.0)^2} = 9.0 \times 10^3 \text{ N/C}$$

The electric field component of A caused by q_C is toward q_C (because q_C is negative) and has a value of

$$E_{AC} = (9.0 \times 10^9)\frac{q_C}{r^2} = (9.0 \times 10^9)\frac{(4.0 \times 10^{-6})}{(2.0)^2} = 9.0 \times 10^3 \text{ N/C}$$

Therefore, vectorially add E_{AB} and E_{AC} to find E_A.

E_{AB} E_{AC}

A B C

$$E_A = E_{AC} - E_{AB} = \left(9.0 \times 10^3 \ \frac{\text{N}}{\text{C}}\right) - \left(9.0 \times 10^3 \ \frac{\text{N}}{\text{C}}\right) = \mathbf{0 \ \frac{N}{C}}$$

20. The free-body diagram is shown as

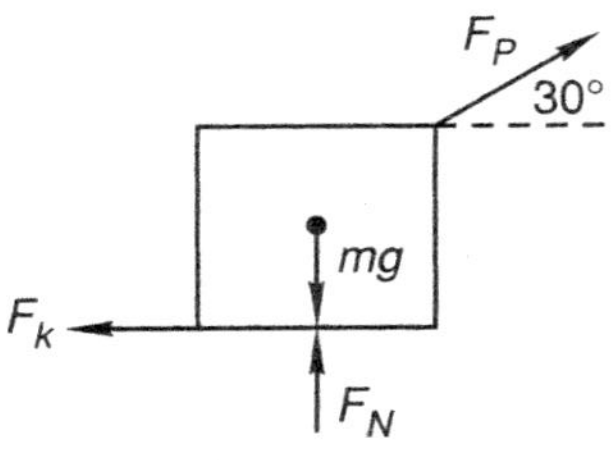

Problem Set 99

1. $WF = hf$

$= (4.136 \times 10^{-15} \text{ eV·s})(7.5 \times 10^{14} \text{ Hz})$

$= 3.102 \text{ eV} \xrightarrow{\text{SD}}$ **3.1 eV**

2. $E_p = WF + KE$

$= 3.3 \text{ eV} + 1.7 \text{ eV}$

$= 5 \text{ eV}$

$E_p = hf$

$5 \text{ eV} = (4.136 \times 10^{-15} \text{ eV·s})f$

$f = 1.209 \times 10^{15} \text{ Hz} \xrightarrow{\text{SD}}$ $\mathbf{1.2 \times 10^{15}\ Hz}$

3. (a) In alpha decay, **two protons and two neutrons** are emitted.

(b) Radon 222 has 86 protons. If it loses 2 protons and 2 neutrons, it will then have 84 protons and 218 nucleons. Thus the element becomes **Polonium;** $\mathbf{^{218}_{84}Po}$.

4. (a) In beta-minus decay, **a neutron transforms into a proton, an electron, and an antineutrino.**

(b) Lead 214 has 82 protons. If it gains one more proton, it will then have 83 protons. Thus the element becomes **Bismuth**.

5. $E_p = hf$

$= (6.626 \times 10^{-34}\ \text{J·s})(5 \times 10^{22}\ \text{Hz})$

$= 3.313 \times 10^{-11}\ \text{J} \xrightarrow{\text{SD}} \mathbf{3 \times 10^{-11}\ J}$

6. $E_p = hf$

$= (4.136 \times 10^{-15}\ \text{eV·s})(2 \times 10^{8}\ \text{Hz})$

$= 8.272 \times 10^{-7}\ \text{eV} \xrightarrow{\text{SD}} \mathbf{8 \times 10^{-7}\ eV}$

7. The half-life is 9.3 days, so the number of half-lives in 42 days is

$$n = \frac{42}{9.3} = 4.516$$

Thus the amount present after 42 days is

$$A_t = \frac{1}{2^n}A_0$$

$$A_{42} = \frac{1}{2^{4.516}}(9.0)$$

$= (0.04371)(9.0)$

$= 0.3934\ \text{g} \xrightarrow{\text{SD}} \mathbf{0.39\ g}$

8. $C = \dfrac{K\varepsilon_0 A}{d} \longrightarrow K = \dfrac{Cd}{\varepsilon_0 A}$

$$= \frac{(2.57 \times 10^{-8}\ \text{F})(5.23 \times 10^{-3}\ \text{m})}{\left(8.85 \times 10^{-12}\ \frac{\text{F}}{\text{m}}\right)(1.97\ \text{m}^2)}$$

$= 7.709 \xrightarrow{\text{SD}} \mathbf{7.71}$

9. $v = f(2L)$

$= (822)(2)(1.07)$

$= 1.759 \times 10^3\ \frac{\text{m}}{\text{s}} \xrightarrow{\text{SD}} \mathbf{1.76 \times 10^3\ \frac{m}{s}}$

10. In the circuit, when the capacitors are fully charged, the sum of the voltages V_1 and V_2 is 15 V.

(a) $V_1 + V_2 = 15$

Since the capacitors are in series, the charge on each capacitor is the same, $Q = CV$.

(b) $C_1V_1 = C_2V_2$

Solve (b) for V_2 and substitute into (a) and get:

(a) $V_1 + \dfrac{C_1V_1}{C_2} = 15$

$$V_1 + \frac{(2.5 \times 10^{-6})V_1}{(12 \times 10^{-6})} = 15$$

$1.208V_1 = 15$

$V_1 = 12.417\ \text{V} \xrightarrow{\text{SD}} \mathbf{12\ V}$

Substitute V_1 into (a) and solve for V_2.

(a) $(12.417) + V_2 = 15$

$V_2 = 2.583\ \text{V} \xrightarrow{\text{SD}} \mathbf{2.6\ V}$

11. $\text{eff}_{max} = 1 - \dfrac{T_C}{T_H}$

$= 1 - \dfrac{320\ \text{K}}{2750\ \text{K}}$

$= 0.8836$

Multiply this by 100% and get:

$\text{eff}_{max} = 0.8836 \times 100\% = 88.36\% \xrightarrow{\text{SD}} \mathbf{88\%}$

12. Begin by finding the initial period.

$$T = 2\pi\frac{\sqrt{L}}{\sqrt{g}} = 2\pi\frac{\sqrt{0.59}}{\sqrt{9.81}} = 1.54\ \text{s}$$

Since T_2 equals $1.50T$, we substitute and get:

$T_2 = 1.50T = 1.50(1.54) = 2.31\ \text{s}$

Set this value equal to the period T_2 and solve for L.

$$T_2 = 2\pi\frac{\sqrt{L}}{\sqrt{g}}$$

$$2.31 = 2\pi\frac{\sqrt{L}}{\sqrt{9.81}}$$

$1.1515 = \sqrt{L}$

$L = 1.326\ \text{m} \xrightarrow{\text{SD}} \mathbf{1.3\ m}$

13. $E = \frac{1}{2}CV^2$

$= \frac{1}{2}(5.35 \times 10^{-6}\text{ F})(273\text{ V})^2$

$= 0.1994\text{ J} \xrightarrow{\text{SD}}$ **0.199 J**

14. (a) Begin by finding Q and v_2.

$$Q = A_1v_1 = (4.28 \times 10^{-4})(3.43) = 1.468 \times 10^{-3}\ \frac{\text{m}^3}{\text{s}}$$

$$v_2 = \frac{Q}{A_2} = \frac{1.468 \times 10^{-3}}{1.98 \times 10^{-4}} = 7.414\ \frac{\text{m}}{\text{s}}$$

Now use Bernoulli's equation to find P_2.

$$P_1 + \frac{1}{2}\rho v_1^2 = P_2 + \frac{1}{2}\rho v_2^2$$

$$205{,}400 + \frac{1}{2}(1000)(3.43)^2 = P_2 + \frac{1}{2}(1000)(7.414)^2$$

$$205{,}400 + 5882.45 = P_2 + 27{,}483.70$$

$$P_2 = 1.838 \times 10^5\text{ Pa} \xrightarrow{\text{SD}} \mathbf{1.84 \times 10^5\ Pa}$$

(b)

$$\rho g l_1 + P_{\text{atm}} = P_1$$

$$(1000)(9.81)l_1 + 1.013 \times 10^5 = 205{,}400$$

$$l_1 = 10.612\text{ m} \xrightarrow{\text{SD}} \mathbf{10.6\ m}$$

$$\rho g l_2 + P_{\text{atm}} = P_2$$

$$(1000)(9.81)l_2 + 1.013 \times 10^5 = 1.838 \times 10^5$$

$$l_2 = 8.4098\text{ m} \xrightarrow{\text{SD}} \mathbf{8.41\ m}$$

15. $\frac{1}{f} = \frac{1}{D_O} + \frac{1}{D_I}$

$\frac{1}{7.0} = \frac{1}{3.0} + \frac{1}{D_I}$

$D_I = -5.25\text{ cm} \xrightarrow{\text{SD}}$ **−5.3 cm**

$\frac{H_I}{H_O} = \frac{-D_I}{D_O}$

$\frac{H_I}{5.0} = \frac{-(-5.25)}{3.0}$

$H_I = 8.75\text{ cm} \xrightarrow{\text{SD}}$ **8.8 cm**

The image is **virtual** because it is upright and behind the mirror.

16. Use the y-displacement equation to find the time.

$\Delta y = v_{y0}t + \frac{1}{2}a_yt^2$

$-37.5 = (0) + \frac{1}{2}(-9.81)t^2$

$37.5 = 4.905t^2$

$t = 2.765\text{ s}$

Use this time in the x-position equation to find the distance.

$x = x_0 + v_{x0}t + \frac{1}{2}a_xt^2$

$x = (0) + 25.2(2.765) + (0)$

$x = 69.678\text{ m} \xrightarrow{\text{SD}}$ **69.7 m**

17. Sum the horizontal forces to find F.

$\Sigma F_x = ma_x$

$F - 25\text{ N} = 0$

$F = 25\text{ N}$

Determine the distance, D.

$D = R \times T = (2.3\text{ m·s}^{-1}) \times (30\text{ s}) = 69\text{ m}$

Now, find the work.

$W = F \times D$

$= (25\text{ N}) \times (69\text{ m})$

$= 1.725 \times 10^3\text{ J} \xrightarrow{\text{SD}}$ $\mathbf{1.7 \times 10^3\ J}$

18. First, we must find the perpendicular distance, x, from the point of rotation to the line of action of the force, 40 N.

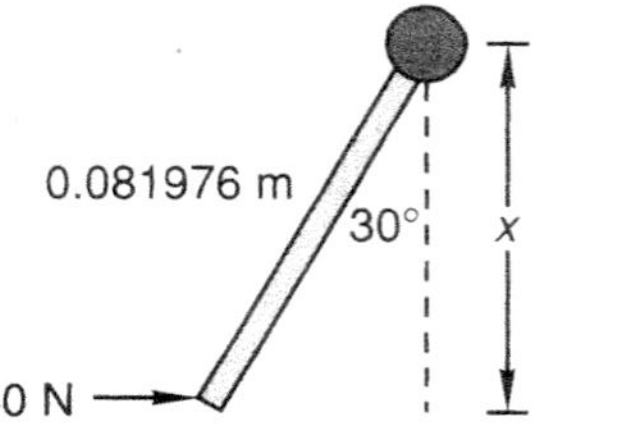

$$\cos 30° = \frac{x}{0.081976 \text{ m}}$$
$$x = 0.071 \text{ m}$$

Now, sum the torques to equal zero.

$$\Sigma\tau = 0$$
$$-40 \text{ N}(0.071 \text{ m}) + F(0.1984 \text{ m}) = 0$$
$$F(0.1984 \text{ m}) = 2.84 \text{ N·m}$$
$$F = 14.31 \text{ N} \xrightarrow{\text{SD}} \mathbf{10\ N}$$

19. Begin by finding the weight of the mass and drawing a free-body diagram of the forces acting on the junction of the ropes.

$$w = mg$$
$$= 96.0 \text{ kg} \times 9.81 \frac{\text{N}}{\text{kg}}$$
$$= 941.76 \text{ N}$$

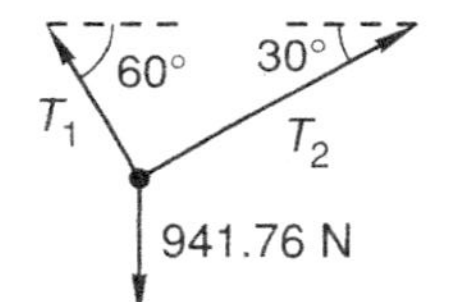

Now sum the horizontal and vertical forces to zero.

(a) $\Sigma F_x = 0;\ T_2 \cos 30° - T_1 \cos 60° = 0$

(b) $\Sigma F_y = 0;\ T_1 \sin 60° + T_2 \sin 30° - 941.76 \text{ N} = 0$

Solve (a) for T_2 and get:

(a) $T_2 \cos 30° = T_1 \cos 60°$

$T_2 = 0.5774T_1$ (a′)

Substitute (a′) into (b) and get:

(b) $T_1 \sin 60° + (0.5774T_1) \sin 30° = 941.76 \text{ N}$

$1.1547T_1 = 941.76 \text{ N}$

$T_1 = 815.59 \text{ N} \xrightarrow{\text{SD}} \mathbf{816\ N}$

Substitute T_1 into (a′) and get:

(a′) $T_2 = 0.5774(815.59 \text{ N}) = 470.92 \text{ N} \xrightarrow{\text{SD}} \mathbf{471\ N}$

20. (a) $\Sigma F_x = 0;\ F \cos 20° - \mu_k F_N = 0$

(b) $\Sigma F_y = 0;\ F_N - w - F \sin 20° = 0$

Solve (a) for F_N and get:

(a) $\mu_k F_N = F \cos 20°$

$(0.65)F_N = F \cos 20°$

$F_N = 1.446F$

Substitute F_N into (b) and get:

(b) $(1.446F) - (0.40)(9.81) - F \sin 20° = 0$

$1.104F = 3.924$

$F = 3.554 \text{ N} \xrightarrow{\text{SD}} \mathbf{3.6\ N}$

PROBLEM SET 100

1. $E = m_0c^2$

$= (0.001 \text{ kg})(3.00 \times 10^8 \text{ m·s}^{-1})^2$

$= \mathbf{9 \times 10^{13}\ J}$

$$\frac{9 \times 10^{13} \text{ J}}{2.6 \times 10^{13} \text{ J}} = 3.46 \xrightarrow{\text{SD}} \mathbf{3}$$

2. Since it gave up 1.5% or 0.015, this means that 98.5% or 0.985 of the original energy remains.

$1 - 0.015 = 0.985$

Therefore,

$$E_{\text{original}} = \frac{1292}{0.985} = 1.3117 \times 10^3 \text{ eV} \xrightarrow{\text{SD}} \mathbf{1.3 \times 10^3\ eV}$$

The frequency is equal to

$$E_{\text{original}} = hf$$
$$1.3117 \times 10^3 \text{ eV} = (4.136 \times 10^{-15} \text{ eV·s})f$$
$$f = 3.171 \times 10^{17} \text{ Hz} \xrightarrow{\text{SD}} \mathbf{3.2 \times 10^{17}\ Hz}$$

3. $mv = \frac{h}{\lambda} \quad \longrightarrow \quad \lambda = \frac{h}{mv}$

$$= \frac{(6.626 \times 10^{-34})}{(1.6749 \times 10^{-27})(4 \times 10^{6})}$$

$$= 9.89 \times 10^{-14}\text{ m} \xrightarrow{\text{SD}} \mathbf{1 \times 10^{-13}\ m}$$

4. $WF = hf$

$$= (4.136 \times 10^{-15}\text{ eV·s})(32 \times 10^{14}\text{ Hz})$$

$$= 13.24\text{ eV} \xrightarrow{\text{SD}} \mathbf{13\ eV}$$

5. $$hf = WF + \frac{1}{2}mv^2_{max}$$

$$(4.136 \times 10^{-15}\text{ eV·s})f = 3.0\text{ eV} + 2.0\text{ eV}$$

$$f = 1.21 \times 10^{15}\text{ Hz} \xrightarrow{\text{SD}} \mathbf{1.2 \times 10^{15}\ Hz}$$

6. In alpha decay, two protons and two neutrons are emitted. Therefore, bismuth 210, which has 83 protons, now becomes an element which has 81 protons. Using the periodic table, find the element with 81 protons. This element is

Thallium; $\mathbf{^{206}_{81}Tl}$.

7. In alpha decay, two protons and two neutrons are emitted. Therefore, thorium 234, which has 90 protons, now becomes an element which has 88 protons. Using the periodic table, find the element with 88 protons. This element is

Radium; $\mathbf{^{230}_{88}Ra}$.

8. $E_p = hf$

$$= (4.136 \times 10^{-15}\text{ eV·s})(8.5 \times 10^{21}\text{ Hz})$$

$$= 3.5156 \times 10^{7}\text{ eV} \xrightarrow{\text{SD}} \mathbf{3.5 \times 10^{7}\ eV}$$

9. $E_p = hf$

$$= (4.136 \times 10^{-15}\text{ eV·s})(4.0 \times 10^{18}\text{ Hz})$$

$$= 1.6544 \times 10^{4}\text{ eV} \xrightarrow{\text{SD}} \mathbf{1.7 \times 10^{4}\ eV}$$

10. The half-life is 8.0 days, so the number of half-lives in 36 days is

$$n = \frac{36}{8.0} = 4.5$$

Thus the amount present after 36 days is

$$A_t = \frac{1}{2^n}A_0$$

$$A_{36} = \frac{1}{2^{4.5}}(476)$$

$$= (0.044)(476)$$

$$= 20.944\text{ g} \xrightarrow{\text{SD}} \mathbf{21\ g}$$

11. $$\Sigma F_x = ma_x$$

$$F - \mu_k F_N = ma$$

$$1000 - (0.392)m(9.81) = m(8.340)$$

$$12.2m = 1000$$

$$m = 81.97\text{ kg} \xrightarrow{\text{SD}} \mathbf{80\ kg}$$

12. (a) $Q = (5.42\text{ kg})\left(3.34 \times 10^{5}\ \frac{\text{J}}{\text{kg}}\right)$

$$= 1.8103 \times 10^{6}\text{ J} \xrightarrow{\text{SD}} \mathbf{1.81 \times 10^{6}\ J}$$

(b) $\Delta S_{ice} = \frac{\Delta Q}{T}$

$$= \frac{+1.8103 \times 10^{6}\text{ J}}{273\text{ K}}$$

$$= +6.6311 \times 10^{3}\ \frac{\text{J}}{\text{K}} \xrightarrow{\text{SD}} \mathbf{+6.63 \times 10^{3}\ \frac{J}{K}}$$

13. (a) $f = \frac{1}{2\pi}\sqrt{\frac{k}{m}} = \frac{1}{2\pi}\sqrt{\frac{1250}{49}} = 0.804\text{ Hz} \xrightarrow{\text{SD}} \mathbf{0.80\ Hz}$

(b) $T = \frac{1}{f} = \frac{1}{0.804\text{ Hz}} = 1.244\text{ s} \xrightarrow{\text{SD}} \mathbf{1.2\ s}$

14. Begin by finding the weight of the sphere and drawing a free-body diagram of the sphere on the left.

$$w = mg$$
$$= 0.321\,\text{kg} \times 9.81\,\frac{\text{N}}{\text{kg}}$$
$$= 3.149\ \text{N}$$

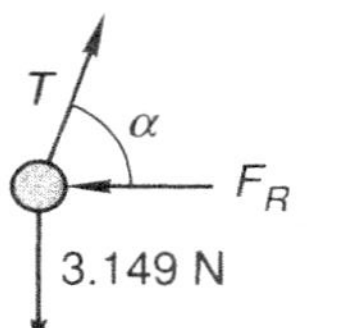

In this case, $\alpha = 90° - \theta/2$. The weight of the sphere equals the vertical component of the tension.

$$w = T \sin \alpha$$
$$3.149 = T \sin \alpha$$
$$T = \frac{3.149}{\sin \alpha}$$

The horizontal component of the tension equals the force of repulsion F_R.

$$F_R = T \cos \alpha$$
$$= \left(\frac{3.149}{\sin \alpha}\right) \cos \alpha$$
$$= \frac{3.149}{\tan \alpha}$$

Now, we can use Coulomb's law to find α.

$$F_R = \frac{kq_1q_2}{r^2}$$
$$\frac{3.149}{\tan \alpha} = \frac{(9.0 \times 10^9)(2.52 \times 10^{-7})(2.52 \times 10^{-7})}{(0.0282)^2}$$
$$\frac{3.149}{\tan \alpha} = 0.718696$$
$$\alpha = 77.144°$$

Since $\alpha = 90° - \theta/2$, we get: $77.144° = 90° - \frac{\theta}{2}$

$$\theta = \mathbf{25.71°}$$

15. Begin by finding the weight of the mass and drawing a free-body diagram of the forces acting on the junction of the ropes.

$$w = mg$$
$$= 942\,\text{kg} \times 9.81\,\frac{\text{N}}{\text{kg}}$$
$$= 9241\ \text{N}$$

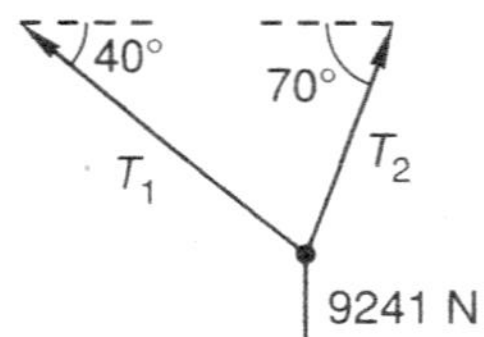

Now sum the horizontal and vertical forces to zero.

(a) $\sum F_x = 0;\ T_2 \cos 70° - T_1 \cos 40° = 0$

(b) $\sum F_y = 0;\ T_1 \sin 40° + T_2 \sin 70° - 9241\ \text{N} = 0$

Solve (a) for T_2 and get:

(a) $T_2 \cos 70° = T_1 \cos 40°$

$T_2 = 2.240T_1$ (a′)

Substitute (a′) into (b) and get:

(b) $T_1 \sin 40° + (2.240T_1) \sin 70° = 9241\ \text{N}$

$2.748T_1 = 9241\ \text{N}$

$T_1 = 3362.8\ \text{N} \xrightarrow{\text{SD}}$ **3360 N**

Substitute T_1 into (a′) and get:

(a′) $T_2 = 2.240(3362.8\ \text{N}) = 7532.7\ \text{N} \xrightarrow{\text{SD}}$ **7530 N**

16. Begin by writing a momentum equation.

$$m_1v_1 + m_2v_2 = (m_1 + m_2)v_3$$
$$4.0(8.4\angle 0°) + 2.2(6.4\angle 60°) = (4.0 + 2.2)v_3$$
$$33.6\angle 0° + 14.08\angle 60° = (6.2)v_3 \quad \text{(a)}$$

Now find the sum of the x and y components of the initial momenta.

$\sum mv_x = 33.6 \cos 0° + 14.08 \cos 60° = 40.64\ \text{kg·m·s}^{-1}$

$\sum mv_y = 33.6 \sin 0° + 14.08 \sin 60° = 12.19\ \text{kg·m·s}^{-1}$

$\sum mv_R = (40.64i + 12.19j)\ \text{kg·m·s}^{-1}$

Convert this resultant to polar form and get:

$$\Sigma mv_R = \sqrt{(40.64)^2 + (12.19)^2} = 42.43 \text{ kg·m·s}^{-1}$$

$$\theta = \tan^{-1}\frac{12.19}{40.64} = 16.70°$$

$$\Sigma mv_R = 42.43\angle 16.70° \text{ kg·m·s}^{-1}$$

Use this momentum in (a) to find v_3.

(a) $42.43\angle 16.70° = (6.2)v_3$

$$v_3 = 6.84\angle 16.70° \ \frac{\text{m}}{\text{s}} \xrightarrow{\text{SD}} \mathbf{6.8\angle 16.70° \ \frac{m}{s}}$$

17. First, we treat the two blocks as a system.

$F = ma$

$41 = 41a$

$a = 1\,\frac{\text{m}}{\text{s}}$

Now we treat the 37 kg block separately.

$F = ma$

$F = 37(1)$

$F = \mathbf{37\ N}$

18. $\Delta KE = Fd - mgh$

$= 32(6.0) - 2.2(9.81)(6.0)$

$= 62.508\text{ J} \xrightarrow{\text{SD}} \mathbf{63\ J}$

19. (a) $PE = mgh = 0.85\,\cancel{\text{kg}} \times 9.81\,\frac{\text{N}}{\cancel{\text{kg}}} \times 42\text{ m} = 350.217\text{ J}$

$$KE = \frac{1}{2}mv_d^{\,2}$$

$$350.217\text{ J} = \frac{1}{2}(0.85\text{ kg})v_d^{\,2}$$

$$v_d = -28.706\ \frac{\text{m}}{\text{s}} \xrightarrow{\text{SD}} \mathbf{-29\ \frac{m}{s}}$$

$PE = mgh = 0.85\,\cancel{\text{kg}} \times 9.81\,\frac{\text{N}}{\cancel{\text{kg}}} \times 14\text{ m} = 116.739\text{ J}$

$$KE = \frac{1}{2}mv_u^{\,2}$$

$$116.739\text{ J} = \frac{1}{2}(0.85\text{ kg})v_u^{\,2}$$

$$v_u = +16.573\ \frac{\text{m}}{\text{s}} \xrightarrow{\text{SD}} \mathbf{+17\ \frac{m}{s}}$$

(b) $\Delta KE = 350.217\text{ J} - 116.739\text{ J} = 233.478\text{ J} \xrightarrow{\text{SD}} \mathbf{230\ J}$

20. Begin by finding the equivalent resistance of the two parallel resistors.

$$R_E = \frac{(2R)(2R)}{2R + 2R} = \frac{4R^2}{4R} = R$$

Now, combine this with the 10-Ω resistor to find the equivalent resistance of the circuit.

$R_E = (R) + 10\,\Omega = (R + 10)\,\Omega$

Use this resistance to find R.

$$R_E = \frac{V}{I}$$

$$(R + 10)\,\Omega = \frac{9.0\text{ V}}{0.1\text{ A}}$$

$$R = \mathbf{80\ \Omega}$$